SOCIOLOGY AND SANITATION: THEMES AND PERSPECTIVES

"SOCIOLOGY OF SANITATION
TEXT BOOK SERIES"

under the aegis of

Sulabh International Centre for Action Sociology

in close collaboration with

Sulabh International Social Service Organisation

Dedicated to

Mahatma Gandhi
Father of the Nation

Shri. Narendra Damodardas Modi
Hon'ble Prime Minister of India

Dr. Bindeshwar Pathak
Sociologist and Social Reformer

Contents

Foreword

Sanitation is a basic condition for development. It is not only the problem of keeping clean; it is also an economic and social problem of raising production and promoting a good life. A lack of proper sanitation contributes to the death of millions of children below the age of five every year; and about 50 diseases are associated with poor sanitation. Sanitation related diseases are among the major causes of death in India and in most other low-income countries.

The sanitation situation in India has been dismal both in urban and rural areas and only few towns have provision of sewage system. A small number of people use septic tanks and only two systems are prevalent on large scale, that is, defecation in the open and manual cleaning of human excreta by the class of people called 'human scavengers'. The technology of two-pit, pour-flush toilet (popularly known as 'Sulabh' toilet) that is scientifically appropriate, economically affordable, and culturally acceptable is developed by me for the safe disposal of human waste from households. For the safe reuse of human waste from public toilets, housing colonies, high rise buildings, hostels, hospitals etc, I also developed the technology for complete recycling and reuse of excreta through biogas generation and on-site treatment of effluent through a simple and convenient technology for its safe reuse without health or environmental risk. Earlier, there was a social stigma and psychological taboo for handling of human excreta. It could also be due to the fact that only people of the lowest economic strata, 'scavengers', who were treated as untouchables, were associated with this dehumanizing job. Due to the technologies and efforts of Sulabh, over a million scavengers have been brought into the mainstream of society. Also, due to financial viability, people from higher social status are now competing to do the job without any psychological taboo. The initiatives taken by the Sulabh International Social Service Organization and the technology of low-cost sanitation advanced by it have been hailed as an outstanding innovation in combating the menace of environmental pollution in developing countries.

Sociologically speaking, a caste based and hereditary profession, which is handed down, as a legacy from one generation to the next; "manual scavenging" has been an age-old routine for few communities, which is untouched by technological advancement in sanitary practices. Not only does the prevalence of this culture seem antediluvian, but what is worse is the fact that those born in this community are considered agents of pollution due to their background of social hierarchy, based on birth. They are the most oppressed and suppressed class of Indian society - hated, ostracized, vilified and avoided by all other castes and classes. The appalling hardship, humiliation and exploitation they face, have no parallel in human history. The practice started in the Puranic period continued in the Buddhist, Mauryan, Mughal and British periods.

The problems arising from casteism and untouchability are complicated, old and deep-rooted. Even the scavengers, considered unclean and untouchable by society, accept their lowly position in society. It is observed that scavengers come in direct contact with human excreta and his/her hands are completely soiled. It is a common sight to see scavengers, mostly women, moving with excreta on the head, stored in bamboo-baskets, or in leaking drums, with the muck trickling down over face and body. Passers-by avoid such persons. If a scavenger comes in close proximity, he or she is showered with a hail of abuse. No human degradation could be more cruel and inhuman than the one suffered by scavengers. The problem of Balmikis is as much economic as it is socio-cultural. In fact, it is woven into the fabric of India's culture. Traditions take time to change and require the will and support from all sections of society. Sulabh has evolved the concept of 'social adoption' with this end in view. It is purely voluntary. All it costs is the willingness to shed social prejudice and show some compassion for fellow humans

It is my firm belief that it is high time when 'sanitation' should be included as a discipline in sociology because the core problem areas embodying sanitation like social deprivation, hygiene, ecology, water, public health, gender equality etc. require sociological intervention also being intertwined with spiritual and philosophical knowledge. My propounded theory on sociology of sanitation is as follows: 'Sociology of sanitation is a scientific study to solve the problem of society in relation to sanitation, social deprivation, water, public health, hygiene, ecology, environment, poverty, gender equality, welfare of children and empowering people for sustainable development and attainment of philosophical and spiritual knowledge to lead a happy life and to make a difference in the lives of others."

Sanitation includes water supply, safe disposal of human waste, waste water and solid waste management, control of vectors of diseases, domestic and personal hygiene, food, sanitation, housing etc. The US National Sanitation Foundation defines sanitation thus: "It is the quality of living expressed in clean homes, clean farms, clean neighbourhoods and clean community. Being a way of life, it must come from people, nourished as it is by knowledge and it grows as obligation and ideal in human relations". Environmental sanitation is vital for protecting the environment, improving health, alleviating poverty, enhancing quality of life and raising productivity – all of which are essential for sustainable development. It is to be emphasized that joint efforts are required for performance and management of the mission of holistic sanitation.

Shedding light on this splendidly compiled academic elucidation I will not hesitate in stating that in continuance of the diversified mission of the two days national conference on 'Sociology of Sanitation', held on January 28 and 29, 2013, by Sulabh International, the present book is a humble reflection of enthusiasm and commitment of the academicians towards the inclusion of the subject as one of the discipline in the study of sociology. It will not only enlarge the scope of sociology but will also be helpful in solving the problems of society in relation to sanitation, social deprivation, water, public, health, hygiene, poverty, gender equality, welfare of children and empowering knowledge for sustainable development. This academic initiative will definitely strengthen my mission and vision of 'Sulabh' toilet as a tool of social change.

Applauding this intellectually rich endeavor, I appreciate Dr. *Ashish Saxena,* a promising and committed sociologist, who very aptly synchronize our mission and broadens the horizon of sanitation beyond physical and environmental cleanliness and hygiene. He is of the opinion that sanitation encompasses overall transformation of the society in a desired direction which is pleasant to many (especially subaltern masses) and not all. His essence of the definition of 'Sociology of Sanitation' is to construct inclusiveness and progressive understanding of sanitation with contradictions as facilitators to sustainability of the well-being of individual and society. This volume no doubt, brings together an impressive array of discourse on sociology of sanitation to inquire into some of the most pressing problems of our times in this naïve field. Very meticulously, the book is divided into eleven highly enlightening chapters traversing various facets of sanitation. Chapter one highlights the nature, scope and subject matter of sanitation with due emphasis on the meaning and definition of sanitation in a global framework. Chapter two discusses on the evolution of sanitation discourse in the global framework. It presents the historiography of prominent nations and developing nations. Chapter three and four of the book very sophistically deliberates upon the theoretical and methodological issues involved in 'sociology of sanitation. Chapter five narrates the various facets of sanitation in a global framework. Another interesting segment of the book is Chapter six, which provides the array of terms having bearing on sanitation. It includes the concept such as justice, inequality, discrimination, exclusion, empowerment, hygiene, stigma etc. The other chapters covers the issues such as interrelation of sanitation concern with other domains, backdrop of social movement with emphasis on prominent social reformers contributing to sanitation of Indian nation, ramifications of the caste on sanitation in rural, industrial and urban India, statistics and policy measures in relation to sanitation and allied issues etc. The last Chapter lucidly expresses my tireless efforts on 'Sulabh' movement and nicely documented towards praxis of toilet in social life. Needless to mention, several of these chapters are manifestation of exemplary scholarly work. As such, the book can be invaluable not just to sociologists interested in the discourse of sanitation, but to numerous social scientists and policymakers actually trying to design policy and interventions in the field of sanitation.

As with all major issues on sanitation, we will never have final answers. Yet, by giving this pressing problem our best effort, we can make large gains in our understanding and, through that, craft policy to hopefully bring such pertaining problem to an end. The present book is a commendable start towards such a social action based agenda and I hope that this will draw more Indian social scientists into this lively field of 'sociology of sanitation.'

BINDESHWAR PATHAK,
Sociologist & Social Reformer
Founder, Sulabh Sanitation Movement
NEW DELHI

Preface and Acknowledgements

This work aptly titled *'Sociology of Sanitation: Themes and Perspectives'* is an anthology of discourse on sanitation in postmodern era. The novel theme of the work have emerged as momentous deliberations which evolved in th e National Conference on 'Sociology of Sanitation', organized by Sulabh International Social Service Organization on January 28-29th, 2013, New Delhi and subsequently followed by meaningful engagement on 'Text book on sociology of sanitation' under the rubric of workshop organized by Sulabh International Social Service Organization on June 13-14th, 2013, New Delhi. Keeping in view the imminent and novice area of research in social sciences in general and in sociology in particular, it involved experimentation and innovations of entirely new way of presenting the idea of 'sanitation' in an academic discourse, especially in sociology proper. Present attempt required a fascinating interplay of science, management, law and social sciences in spawning entirely new premise on the 'inclusive sanitation'. The challenging was the issue of unification of ideas cutting across disciplinary boundaries and its relevance in cross-cultural framework. In the present work sanitation is dealt in a holistic framework as a concept, phenomena, process, tool and theme in its own right. It stimulates conceptually, theoretically and methodologically the broader territory where issue of sanitation can be a pathway and discourse in a cross-disciplinary perspective. It may lead to an inquest as to how in the domain of 'Sociology of knowledge' new constituent can be fashioned and debated as seen from the point of view of sanitation.

Comprehending the closer association of sanitation with weakers sections of the society, the work theoretically provides subaltern lens to the phenomenon of sanitation and as an action sociology discovering the gaps in theory versus practice. Apprehending the multiplicity and vitality of the very question of sanitation in the global atlas as multi-fold, the methodological and operational tools to reach out to the problems and prospects require diverse perspectives, is also explored here. The work also narrates successful experiments and experiences with a logic to imitate and replicate across heterogeneous culture. The larger mission of the work is to address the concern of how sanitation principles and practices are accommodating and challenging the intricate cultural diversity at regional, national and global level. Keeping in view the supposed assignment, the constraint of the work lies in aligning the issue of sanitation with sociology mainly. The significance of the work however, lies in approaching the issue of sanitation through interdisciplinary and cross-cultural standpoint. It gives deeper insights to the exploration of the theme with other disciplines and also in converging and universalizing the theoretical model of sanitation.

Being located at the epicenter of sanitation i.e. holy *'Prayag'* and my enterprise at University of Allahabad played significant role in bridging teaching and research in desired direction. It provided plenteous prospects for shaping this work in phased manner. At the outset, I should pay my sincere indebtedness to *Padma Bhushan* awardee *Prof. Bindeshwar Pathak,* a true social practitioner and founder of the Sulabh Sanitation Movement, for accommodating me in his noble mission of 'Sulabh revolution'. His humbleness and zeal for social reform in contemporary India swayed me to contribute academically to his idea of sanitation.

I am equally thankful to the distinguished scholars encouraging my efforts in mapping diverse forms of academic sanitation. The interaction with *Prof. Partha Nath Mukherji, Prof. Nandu Ram, Prof. William Sax, Prof. Ishwar Modi, Prof. Anand Kumar, Prof. J.J.Kattakayam, Prof. Hetukar Jha, Prof. Vinay K. Srivastava, Prof. Richard Pais* and others reinforced my ideas on the theme.

As shared earlier, the present academic destination provided enough platforms to materialize my continuous academic efforts into a concrete outcome. At the outset, I am thankful to honorary Vice Chancellor of University of Allahabad and esteemed authorities for sustaining congenial academic environment for sincere faculties. I am equally grateful to Head, Department of Sociology, in trusting my humble academic efforts and in encouraging me for searching new directions of research, thus making the department a centre of excellence.

My respectable parents *Shri V.C. Saxena* and *Mrs. Pravesh Saxena*, deserves special attention for always encouraging me for academic excellence. A special name always behind my achievements is none other then *'Dr. Vijaylaxmi Saxena'*, my empathetic wife-cum-friend who always pursues me for reaching new heights of success. My smart tender kids *'Vasu'* and *'Shreya'*, needs special reference as they always patiently watching me working and feeling deprived of leisure time, owing to official and academic overshadows.

I should also like to express my special gratitude to Chairman, Sulabh International Centre for Action Sociology, Sulabh International Social Service Organization and the honorable Publisher of work and their respective team for promptly accepting the ideas and publishing it of international standards. Last but not the least, my deep sense of gratitude goes to all those who directly or indirectly supported my humble academic efforts.

Allahabad

Ashish Saxena

Sociology and Sanitation: Introducing the Endeavour

At the start of the 21st century the violation of the human rights in the context clean water and sanitation is destroying human potential, on an epic-scale. IUt is ironical that in today's increasingly prosperous and interconnected world more children die for want of clean water and a toilet than from any other reasons. Exclusion from clean water and basic sanitation destroys more lives than any war or terrorist act. It also reinforces the deep inequalities in life. It divides countries and people within countries on the basis of wealth, gender and other markers for deprivation.

Beyond the human waste and suffering, the global deficit in water and sanitation is undermining prosperity and retarding economic growth. Productivity losses linked to that deficit are blunting the efforts of millions of the world's poorest people to work their way out of poverty and holding back whole countries. Whether viewed from the perspective of human rights, social justice or economic common sense, the damage inflicted by deprivation in water and sanitation is indefensible. Overcoming that deprivation is not just a moral imperative and the right thing to do. It is also the sensible thing to do because the waste of human potential associated with unsafe water and poor sanitation ultimately hurts everybody.

Surprisingly, it might be argued that the trauma of toilet training is a particularly western phenomena, it is also true that many cultures tend to regard the act of "using the toilet," "going to the bathroom," "taking care of necessities"—or more correctly, defecating and urinating—as an essentially private experience that is only spoken about openly and in public when absolutely necessary. This attitude is further reinforced by the fact that much of the activity associated with digestion and excretion is conveniently relegated to the realm of the instinctive and mechanical, where we have very little voluntary control. But unlike eating, sleeping and sexual reproduction, all of which are somehow associated with pleasurable sensations, our sense of smell, in particular, tends to be offended by the aroma of faeces and urine —particularly that which is not our own. The important question is - why is it important to talk about toilets? The probable answering is that dialogue is an important way to raise awareness regarding limitations and serious risks to the environment, human health and the survival of human societies. It is also a way to share ideas on workable alternatives to conventional practices. It is a key mechanism for stimulating attitude changes among members of a peer group. Conversation provides a context for testing new concepts and positions— as a kind of rehearsal to initiating change itself.[1]

It is to be emphasised that the concept of sanitation is a buzz word for various development policies and planning. Contextually, absolute poverty was defined as a condition characterised by severe deprivation of basic human needs, including food, safe drinking water, sanitation facilities, health, shelter, education and information.... It depends not only on income but also on access to services (United Nations 1995).[2] The proportion living in slums is measured by a proxy, represented by the urban population living in households with at least one of the four characteristics: (a) lack of access to improved water supply; (b) lack of access to improved sanitation; (c) overcrowding (three or more persons per room); and (d) dwellings made of non-durable material (United Nations Statistics Division[3] 2008) Given that there are very large numbers of adults and children who suffer from water, sanitation and housing deprivation, it is surprising that the issues of water, sanitation and shelter are limited to two sub-sections of a single Millennium Development Goal (MDG). The lessons of history and the work of reformers like Chadwick[4] demonstrate a clear link between the unsanitary conditions of poverty and illness. Diarrheal diseases result in millions of child deaths in developing countries and an improvement of sanitation facilities is key to preventing them (Esrey and Habicht 1986;[5] UNICEF 1995; Lee, Rosenzweig and Pitt 1997).[6] In 2004, the GWSSA estimated that around 2.6 billion people lacked basic sanitation (WHO and UNICEF Joint Monitoring Programme 2004)[7] and the situation in rural areas was particularly bad, with around 60 per cent of households not served compared to 20 per cent of urban households. As with water deprivation, there are many reasons why large numbers of children still lack basic sanitation around the world. Existing infrastructure in many cities is limited, having lacked effective investment over past decades. With rapid increases in population driven by rural-to-urban migration, many cities and towns are struggling to cope with growing demand. Ventilated, improved pit latrines provide a means to dispose of excrement in a safe and hygienic manner, and public pressure in many countries has begun to provide basic water and sanitation facilities for those who cannot afford them (UNCHS and UNEP 2002)[8]. Unimproved sanitation facilities include public or shared latrines, open pit latrines and bucket latrines. Thus the various developmental plans give major thrust to sanitation. Here it is emphasised that sanitation should be treated as a core value for eradicating poor health, education, gender disparity etc.

Focusing on the significance of sanitation for overall development, the emphasis is that high population density, meager financial resources, poor nutrition and ignorance of basic hygiene combine in many rural and urban areas of the world to produce a very high incidence of debilitating or fatal gastro-intestinal and parasitic infection. The extremes of human degradation are found in disaster situations and refugee camps where such infections result from the non-containment of human excreta and consequent contamination of the food and water supply. The containment of excreta would greatly reduce the populations of pathogenic organisms in the environment and thus attack the endemic foci of disease by breaking the cycle of infection, excretion and re-infection. The desperate need for cheap and efficient sanitation has frustrated the civil engineering and public health professions for the following reasons. Septic tanks take weeks to construct, need skilled labour and costly materials such as cement, steel and bricks. Latrine trenches and boreholes are easily flooded and result in contamination of the water supply, which is usually unprotected. Furthermore, the latter cannot cope with large numbers of people.

It is to be emphasised that the core element of sanitation reform is to ensure community participation through the involvement and mobilisation of the communities in the selection of public stand posts, location of sites for latrines, organisation of hygiene education programmes and beneficiary meetings at the ward level (local level). To improve the conditions of life of people and implement activities effectively at the local level some sort of a set up or organisational net work or social group based at the local level is imperative. Community participation is regarded as the main spring of social development, yet this is more often rhetoric than reality. One way by which practical community participation in water supply and sanitation scheme can be encouraged is by the involvement of *'mohalla'* and ward committees. There are representative groups from each ward who determine the patterns by which water supply and sanitation programmes can be implemented in their locality. These committees are involved in site selection for public taps and latrines, distance criteria discussions, survey of existing water points, identifying and resolving problems of water, providing training and information regarding operation and maintenance of public taps and latrines and establishing links between users and relevant institutions.

Effective hygiene education requires a combined use of various approaches like interpersonal communication, group discussion and mass approach. There is no inherent contradiction between these approaches; each has its own advantages and limitations. The main consideration should be the right selection of approaches or combination of approaches appropriate to local situation and the ability on the part of the workers to select and use them effectively. It is easy to make changes in technological and other hardware aspects, but making changes in attitudinal and behavioural practices appropriate and sustainable approaches have to be developed[9].

Conditions for children need special consideration, since certain types of toilets can be quite dangerous to use (e.g., hanging latrines over lakes or rivers). In cases where toilets are shared, adults often get first preference and children end up having to wait or use any space they can—which often means defecating in the open, in fields, bushes or along railway tracks. Unfortunately, the statistics on access to improved sanitation are not broken down by either gender or age group so it is difficult to know how many children suffer from sanitation deprivation. There are 190 million households with children that suffer from severe shelter deprivation and a similar number that suffer from severe sanitation deprivation (Gordon et al. 2003).[10] Yet this is entirely unnecessary. Toilets were invented in pre-history and archaeologists have found remains of toilets which are over 4,000 years old. The Romans built public toilets throughout their empire 2,000 years ago and there is no state in the twenty-first century that has such a lack of knowledge and insufficient resources that it could not provide its child population with some sanitation facilities. The international community could easily match the sanitation accomplishments of the Roman Empire! Similarly, no scientific or technical breakthroughs are needed to end severe housing deprivation. All countries have building regulations and laws that should prevent overcrowding and dangerous and inadequate construction.[11]

Coming down to Indian development, one identifies that the diversity of India demands experiences of Indians from remote parts of the North-East be heard along with those in the crowded streets of old Delhi, and those of Adivasi and Dalit labourers be heard side by side with those of the upwardly mobile middle class. A search for a human face for the nation demands that individuals not be reduced to growth rates or poverty rates but that, instead, their lives be seen in holistic terms with special emphasis on sanitary reforms. This compilation attempts to balance competing goals of painting a broad panorama of sanitation, without ignoring the sociological details of sanitation. A holistic perspective on peoples' lives incorporates different dimensions of human development—livelihood, education, sanitation and health—play important roles in shaping personal well-being. However, these markers of individual well being are embedded in wider networks of family and kin groups, castes, tribes, and religious identities, the political economy of villages and towns, and the direct and indirect actions of the state and civic society.

Protecting and improving the sanitary health and well being of people, communities and the nation is at the heart of public health. Today, the challenges of our increasingly complex and interdependent world require new approaches to generating and disseminating the knowledge and innovations needed to promote well-being, improve health and sanitation. Developing methods to measure and compare the health status of various population groups and the relative burdens of specific diseases, injuries, and other adverse health conditions can facilitate appropriate implementation of health protection interventions. The sanitation conditions and environments in which people live, work, learn, and play influence our health in many ways—from the air we breathe to the communities we design. Although sanitation and environmental impacts (e.g., global climate change) can have far reaching health consequences, much still must be learned about how these sanitary and environmental changes will influence disease processes and patterns. How we use our land and design our communities (e.g., workplaces and schools) influences rates of obesity, injury, heart disease, diabetes, and many other acute and chronic diseases and conditions. Social determinants of health are those factors beyond individual behaviour and genetic endowment that impact individual, community, and societal health. These factors include prevalence of sanitary neighbourhood conditions and resources (e.g., food supply; economic and social relationships; housing; employment; air and water quality; and the availability of transportation, education, and health-care) for which distribution across populations effectively determines length and quality of life. Many of the social determinants of health exist outside of the formal health sector (sanitary conditions), even though they exert profound impacts on health status. Population and geographic distributions of the social determinants of health are not random. Structures, policies, practices, norms, and values on sanitary aspect can result in the differential allocation of resources and risks by race/ethnicity, social class, geography, sex, and other attributes of population disparity.

Issues of Sanitation and Purity in the Indian Social Reality

In Durkheimenian framework, one can observe 'sociology of sanitation' as a shift from profane to sacred elements. Locating the issue of sanitation L. Dumount rightly states that the Indian society is homo-hierarchicus resting on the religion with caste system having an element of 'pure' and 'impure'. Even M.N. Srinivas too speaks about 'purity and pollution', having bearing on caste interactions. His concept of *'sanskritisation'* has an inherent notion of sanitation for lower caste members. If one goes philosophically on the issue of sanitation of soul, one finds that 'secularisation' reflects decline in the religious intolerance and accommodation of diverse religious practices for healthy society. The doctrine of Hindu religion also focuses on sanitation with the purification of ones *'paap'* in the lifetime. Thus sanitation of body and soul as a precondition for attaining moksh after death and for once re-birth. Even, performing once duties in the holy pilgrimage is deeply embedded in religio-philosophical matrix of Indian psyche (2014),[12] the latrine used to be extremely small, just enough to accommodate one person, dingy, almost like a dungeon, and poorly-lit and ventilated, without any facility of water inside. When one returned from the latrine, a family member was entreated to pour water on his hands that were washed with ash (*râkh*) from the hearth, or soap, in case the family could afford it... After coming out of the latrine, one was more 'unclean', for one's fingers and palm (of the left hand) had come in touch with the faecal material and anus, and if one touched the tank or the vessels kept near it, they would all be consigned to 'uncleanliness', and thus the help of an 'assistant' was needed for washing one's hands. The 'assistant' was usually a younger member of the family, a boy in most cases, and in affluent families, one of the domestic servants. Anal cleaning was always done with left hand. One of the reasons of why the left hand was regarded as impure because of its association with faecal impurity; so left hand was not used for eating, writing, or for any ritual performance. Interestingly, although it had been washed, sometimes repeatedly, it harboured a kind of 'permanent impurity', therefore to be avoided forever for certain activities regarded as 'pure' (like ritual) or bearing semblance to purity (like eating)..... One of the verses commonly recited in this connection was: *'nâk mein unglî kân mein tinkâ mat kar mat kar mat kar; ankh mein anjan dânt mein manjan nit kar nit kar nit kar'* ['Don't put finger in (your) nose, don't poke a straw in (your) ears; apply kohl in [your] eyes everyday, brush (your) teeth everyday']. This indicates that personal hygiene was given the utmost importance.

The family entrusted with the task of cleaning latrines and the lanes used to arrive around seven in the morning. After their arrival to the neighbourhood, the first task the men of the scavenging caste did was to collect garbage from each house, which they did in a couple of baskets they carried from one house to the other. One of the men would go to a house, call out to the people in the household to bring their 'waste' (*kûrâ*) and deposit it in the basket he carried. The process of removing the garbage from each of these houses continued for an hour and a half; in some cases the men had to visit a particular house again since on an earlier visit the family just ignored the call for bringing their garbage out for disposal. Once over, then began the task of removing the night-soil from each house and cleaning the slab with water on which it laid. Interestingly, the term used for 'removing the night-soil' was *kamânâ,* which also meant 'to earn (one's livelihood)'.

The above instance depicts the everyday sanitary and ritual practices of members of Indian society. Indian caste system is based on hierarchy in accordance with the rules of purity and pollution. Occupations, food, materials and even persons were ranged on a scale from purest to most impure. For instance, occupations that involved contact with bodily or other waste—scavenging, leather-work and the like were considered deeply polluting. Meat was eaten only by the lower castes. The structural distance between castes was defined in terms of purity and impurity. A higher caste was pure and would therefore avoid certain forms of contact with the lower castes in terms of eating food cooked by them or marrying or having sexual relations. Sometimes, there could even be a ban on touching. This formed the basis for the notorious practice of untouchability, whereby the touch or even the shadow of certain castes was considered polluting for the higher castes. Castes considered untouchable would have to maintain a certain physical distance from the high castes. Inadvertent touch would entail a ritual cleansing process for the higher caste person. A person was born into a caste, practiced the caste occupation, married and died in the caste and could rarely hope for change or a better or different life.

Fortunately, avenues of mobility and flexibility were available within the structure of caste. Channels of mobility in the ancient period included religious conversion, migration and the renunciation of the world. An important path of mobility in both traditional and more contemporary periods has been what M N Srinivas calls as *sanskritisation. Sanskritisation* is a process where a low Hindu caste changes its customs, rites, rituals, ideology and way of life in the direction of a high and frequently twice-born caste. The twice-born castes are those belonging to the Brahmin, Kshatriya or Vaishya groups. Another path of mobility from the colonial period onwards has been that of westernisation. M.N. Srinivas defined westernisation as the changes brought about in Indian society and culture as a consequence of the over 150 years of British rule. It is a term that covers changes in technology, institutions, ideology and values.

Modern India is changing very rapidly and society today presents some fascinating as well as contradictory trends. One of the most important changes in India is economic change. Already during the colonial period the new means of transportation and communication and the development of cities had brought in a degree of economic and social change. People began to migrate to the cities in search of work and modern education. The barriers of caste began to slowly break down or become more flexible. The ideas of liberty, equality, democracy and the like began to have a slow but sure impact on the colonised people. Secularisation entailed a process of differentiation whereby the various aspects of society—economic, political, legal, moral, familial and religious—become *discrete* in relation with each other. This has occurred to some degree. For instance, the rules of purity and impurity that applied to castes have declined to a considerable extent. Urban life has its own pressures and does not permit rigid rules to remain in place.

Even some critical pieces of social legislation in modern India include the abolition of untouchability, equality for all, secularism and practice of positive discrimination in favour of former *avarna* communities. There has also been social legislation that radically alters the rights of women. In particular, Hindu marriage, inheritance and succession laws have been changed in order to achieve greater gender parity. It was during British times that schedules of lower-caste communities and isolated tribal groups came to be drawn up in order to implement certain practices of reservation in their favour. These schedules came to be included in the Indian Constitution: the list of Scheduled Castes and the list of Scheduled Tribes. Reservations in education, political representation and employment have been implemented for these groups. In general, there is the spread of modernity, particularly in the area of capitalist, consumerist and materialist values. There are also increasing spaces available for the struggle for rights—whether those of women, of marginalised castes or other social groups. Progressive legislation as well as the belief in the ideas of democracy and judicial justice permits the questioning of the denial of rights and justice to different sections of the population. The media does not only promote religious and traditional values. The media also provides scope for the expression of new ideas of masculinity and womanhood, for speaking about issues that remained otherwise hidden, such as: domestic violence, homosexuality or gender discrimination in the workplace.

Inevitability of Sanitation

The benefits of the sanitation movement had a very limited impact on the population as a whole in nineteenth century India. Whilst the colonial government did implement some of these ideas when attempting to control cholera epidemics, most of the expenditure went on military sanitation and protecting the health of government personnel. That is, "...the colonial régime built the unequal treatment of the native and colonial areas into the sanitation system itself: spatial domination was the everyday metaphor for colonial domination." Due to fiscal conservatism, municipalities were unable to provide the funds for a new sanitation system based on the construction of sewers and labour saving technologies. Instead, the colonial government intensified the use of labour in the manual scavenging of night soil and refuse removal, despite calls for the abolition of such practices. When the obvious inefficiencies of such a system were highlighted, colonial officials blamed the work practices of the scavengers.[14] Such unequal treatment in the provision of sanitation has continued in independent India. However, after independence there were collaborations between governments and non-government organisations, and the role of international organisations such as the World Bank and the World Health Organisation in the design and implementation of sanitation and public health programmes.

Keeping in view the idea of World Health Organisation, this work focuses on inevitability of sanitation on the following broader interrogations:[15]

(a) What do we mean by "sanitation"?

The first challenge for countries seeking to solve the problem of access to sanitation is to define what "sanitation" really means. The second challenge is to decide what aspects are the most important.

In other words, what aspect of the problem is going to be dealt with as a priority. With respect to defining sanitation most professionals would agree that "sanitation" as a whole is a "big idea" which covers inter alia:

- safe collection, storage, treatment and disposal/re-use/recycling of human excreta (faeces and urine);
- management/re-use/recycling of solid wastes (trash or rubbish);
- drainage and disposal/re-use/recycling of household wastewater (often referred to as sullage or grey water);
- drainage of storm water;
- treatment and disposal/re-use/recycling of sewage effluents;
- collection and management of industrial waste products; and
- management of hazardous wastes (including hospital wastes, and chemical/ radioactive and other dangerous substances).

(b) Why focus on sanitation?

Wherever humans gather, their waste also accumulates. Progress in sanitation and improved hygiene has greatly improved health, but many people still have no adequate means of disposing of their waste. This is a growing nuisance for heavily populated areas, carrying the risk of infectious disease, particularly to vulnerable groups such as the very young, the elderly and people suffering from diseases that lower their resistance. Poorly controlled waste also means daily exposure to an unpleasant environment. The build up of faecal contamination in rivers and other waters is not just a human risk: other species are affected, threatening the ecological balance of the environment. The discharge of untreated wastewater and excreta into the environment affects human health by several routes:

- By polluting drinking water;
- Entry into the food chain, for example via fruits, vegetables or fish and shellfish;
- Bathing, recreational and other contact with contaminated waters;
- By providing breeding sites for flies and insects that spread diseases;

(c) What diseases are associated with poor sanitation?

Human excreta have been implicated in the transmission of many infectious diseases including cholera, typhoid, infectious hepatitis, polio, cryptosporidiosis, and ascariasis. WHO (2004) estimates that about 1.8 million people die annually from diarrhoeal diseases where

90 per cent are children under five, mostly in developing countries. Poor sanitation gives many infections the ideal opportunity to spread: plenty of waste and excreta for the flies to breed on, and unsafe water to drink, wash with or swim in. Among human parasitic diseases, schistosomiasis (sometimes called bilharziasis) ranks second behind malaria in terms of socio-economic and public health importance in tropical and subtropical areas. The disease is endemic in 74 developing countries, infecting more than 200 million people. Of these, 20 million suffer severe consequences from the disease.

(d) How does sanitation prevent disease?

For a sanitation system to provide the greatest health protection to the individual, the community, and society at large it must:

- Isolate the user from their own excreta;
- Prevent nuisance organisms (e.g. flies) from contacting the excreta and subsequently transmitting disease to humans; and
- Inactivate the pathogens before they enter the environment or prevent the excreta from entering the environment.
- It is important to understand that sanitation can act at different levels, protecting the household, the community and 'society'.

In the case of latrines it is easy to see that this sanitation system acts at a household level. However, poor design or inappropriate location may lead to migration of waste matter and contamination of local water supplies putting the community at risk. In terms of waterborne sewage the containment may be effective for the individual and possibly also the community, but health effects and environmental damage may be seen far downstream of the original source, hence affecting 'society'.

(e) What are the economic costs of sanitation?

The health impact of inadequate sanitation leads to a number of financial and economic costs including direct medical costs associated with treating sanitation-related illnesses and lost income through reduced or lost productivity and the government costs of providing health services. Additionally, sanitation also leads to time and effort losses due to distant or inadequate sanitation facilities, lower product quality resulting from poor water quality, reduced income from tourism (due to high risk of contamination and disease) and clean up costs. Increases in female literacy (due to increased school attendance where proper sanitation facilities exist) contribute to economic growth.

(f) How does sanitation affect the environment?

In regions where a large proportion of the population is not served with adequate water supply and sanitation, sewage flows directly into streams, rivers, lakes and wetlands, affecting coastal and marine ecosystems, fouling the environment and exposing millions of children to disease. Particularly in the context of urbanisation, domestic wastewater, sewage and solid waste improperly discharged presents a variety of concerns from providing breeding grounds for communicable disease vectors to contributing air, water and soil pollution. The results of poor waste management also contribute to a loss of valuable biodiversity.

(g) How can we achieve sanitation targets?

To achieve the targets, action must start now. Now is the time to act. Households, communities, local and national governments, civil society, and private companies all need to work together. Media and public opinion around the world can influence political leaders to act now. For the principal target audience of politicians and government officials (particularly aid administrators), the strategy for this year's World Water Day is designed to increase substantive awareness, ideally leading to decisive actions in support of improved sanitation. Related communication also considers the media, in developed but especially in developing regions, since the media have excellent capacities to inform the population and guide their opinions. Key areas of action that could create impact are as follows: making political commitments; creating legislation and regulations to support improvement in access and quality of sanitation and hygiene services; bringing together more resources, having stronger institutions and better trained people; culturally sensitive and appropriate hygiene education; right choice of technology that are cost-effective and environment-friendly; giving attention to gender and equity; supporting small-scale entrepreneurs; monitoring progress; and making information flow.

State, Citizenship and Social Change: Overall Sanitarian Development

It is to be emphasised that the Constitution of India, for overall sanitarian reform, envisages an active role for the state in securing for Indian citizens entitlements and rights set out in the Constitution and in protecting the natural resources and other assets of the country. Directive Principles of State Policy as the Constitution enjoins upon the state to promote the welfare of the people, strive to minimise inequalities in different forms not only among individuals but also amongst groups of people, secure for its citizens the right of an adequate means of livelihood, consider the raising of the level of nutrition ... and the improvement of public health as among its primary duty, promote with special care the educational and economic interests of the weaker sections of the people, and ensure that the ownership and control of the material resources of the community are so distributed as to sub serve the common good.

A reliable indication of what affects the lives of the people are the issues raised by civil society organisations, people's movements, independent experts, public intellectuals and concerned citizens. Over the past few decades, they have relentlessly asserted people's right to life and personal liberty around issues of violence by state, non-state and private actors; conflict over common and natural resources; continuing deprivation of access to quality education for the vast majority of the poor and marginalised; lack of access to quality health care for the poor; impoverished and insecure communities from forestlands and cityscapes; and extreme threat to the safety and security of women.

Unfortunately, the lop-sided process of privatisation of social services has resulted in the continuing decay and dismantling of existing public institutions in health, education and scientific research without their being replaced in any significant way by new institutions built by the private sector or under public private partnership. The expectation that the withdrawal of the government from the process of production and distribution and the delivery of goods and services would remove a major cause of corruption has been belied. Instead, outsourcing and award of contracts to private operators and companies have spawned corruption on a scale infinitely larger than could have been imagined a few years ago. Social public goods and services are now being increasingly demanded by the people as their legal right. Yielding to the public pressure, the central government has enacted a number of legislations for putting its flagship programmes for social development on the legal basis and launching new rights-based programmes. These include Right to Information Act (2005), the Mahatma Gandhi National Rural Employment Guarantee Act (MGNREGA, 2005), Scheduled Tribes and other Traditional Forest Dwellers (Recognition of Rights) Act (2006), the Unorganised Workers Social Security Act (2008), and most recently, the Food Security Act and the Right to Fair Compensation and Transparency in Land Acquisition, Rehabilitation and Resettlement Act, (2013).[16]

These sanitarian reforms may directly or indirectly address the following agendas:

- *Opt for people-oriented growth:* The current corporate-driven growth strategy should be replaced by a people-oriented development strategy. The new development strategy should be based on the creation of demand within the country, the production of local mass consumption goods and generation of universal employment, as its principal objectives.
- *Protect the poor and marginalised:* In the new strategy, the highest priority should be accorded to meeting the essential needs of the poor, marginalised and underprivileged. The essential needs of these sections include but are not restricted to, school education, community health care, provision of productive assets and credit, sustainable livelihood support including unhindered access to land and forest-based livelihoods, including full access to the commons, public distribution system, food security, drinking water and sanitation.
- *Empower the disabled:* Persons with disability, who continue to be seen as dependent on state charity and denied fundamental rights to freedom and non-discrimination, should have in equal measures with others, the right to access all these essential needs, including barrier-free access to institutions and services.
- *Urgent steps to be taken to curb violence against women:* The civil society groups and government agencies have considered and taken many measures to protect women's rights. Concrete steps should be taken in the institutions of education, media and various other workplaces to create an environment to protect women's dignity and life.

Definition of Sanitation: A Herculean Task

Keeping in view the diversity of issues involved regarding the sanitation concerns in global framework there is an urgent need to tap the diversity in a holistic framework. The present compilation tries to broaden the horizon of sanitation beyond physical and environmental cleanliness and hygiene. I am of the opinion that sanitation encompasses overall transformation of the society in a desired direction which is pleasant to many (especially subaltern masses) and not all. I am therefore putting the major issues of sanitation in a jacketed format as follows:

"In a broader sense sanitation implies management, operation and maintenance of human/social ecology involving 'greater hygiene' and referring to scientifically derived people's capability to achieve their primal physical, biological, psychological, philosophical, social and economic needs and entitlements. It involves the well-being of individuals through exclusion or

neutralisation of elements (social or physical) dysfunctional to them and their community. Good sanitation is a 'way of life' and an effective tool for progress of one's mind, body and surroundings in terms of health, scientific temper, secular behaviour in an acceptable, affordable and sustainable way".

The essence of the above definition is to construct inclusiveness and progressive understanding of sanitation with contradictions as facilitators to sustainability of the well-being of individual and society. Needless to mention, that it is a humble attempt to converge my ideas on the issue on 'Sociology of Sanitation'.

Keeping in view the holistic management of the theme as well as harmonising the constituent of sociology in it, the broader outline of the book is divided into eleven chapters covering various themes, perspectives and aspects of sanitation. Chapter one explores the meaning and definition of sanitation in a global framework. It also highlights the nature, scope and subject matter of sanitation. It also deliberates upon the relevance of sanitation and finally expresses on the idea of 'Sociology of Sanitation'.

Chapter two discusses on the evolution of sanitation discourse in the global framework. It presents the historiography of prominent nations including Egypt, England, United States, Japan and developing nations. Indepth exploration of sanitation concerns in India has been dealt with in detailed manner. Chapter three provides the strong theoretical perspectives in social sciences with special emphasis on sociology as a discipline. It also provides detailed account of pioneer Indian sociologists contributed in understanding of society and culture of Indian society. It also deals with the sociological analysis of urban world with emphasis on sanitarian issues.

Chapter four expresses the methodological issues involved in the social science research. Needless to mention that sociology of sanitation borrows its methods from sociology proper. They will be helpful in understanding the phenomenon of sanitation in a scientific and systematic manner. Chapter five narrates the various facets of sanitation in a global framework. The chapter also brings the integration of religion and sanitation in Indian pilgrimages.

Chapter six provides the array of terms having bearing on sanitation. It includes the concept such as justice, inequality, discrimination, exclusion, empowerment, hygiene, stigma etc. The focus of the chapter is to strengthen the idea of sanitation in a more academic and theoretical structure. Chapter seven focuses upon the interrelation of sanitation concern with other domains such as health, disease, ecology, education, gender etc.

Chapter eight provides the backdrop of social movement with emphasis on prominent social reformers contributing to sanitation of Indian nation. It also gives the exemplifications of social reform movements in different parts of the country. The chapter also brings the implications of movement of globalisation towards dalits.

Chapter nine deliberates upon the issues of caste, practice of untouchability, cultural beliefs, scavenging and social mobility in an Indian society. It discusses the ramifications of the caste on sanitation in rural, industrial and urban India. Chapter ten provides indices, statistics and policy measures in relation to sanitation and allied issues. It narrates the governmental and non-governmental interventions towards sanitation. The chapter specifically emphasises the policies meant for women and children's and its implication on them.

The last chapter is more towards the praxis of toilet in social life. The discussion advocates toilet as a tool for change. It highlights various forms of toilets with its merits and demerits. It emphasises on the Community led toilet schemes in India and abroad. This chapter also provides a detailed account of Sulabh International Social Service Organisation' as an exemplification of toilet as a tool for empowerment and development. The chapter also narrates few successful case studies in India for its imitation in other parts of the country too.

Notes

1. See Ron Sawyer, 2003. Sanitation as if it really matters: Taking toilets out of the (water) closet and into the loop, Sarar Transformación SC, México.
2. United Nations (1995). The Copenhagen Declaration and Programme of Action: World Summit for Social Development. March 6-12. New York: United Nations.
3. United Nations Statistics Division (2008). "Official List of MDG Indicators." Available from: http://mdgs.un.org/unsd/mdg/Resources/Attach/Indicators/OfficialList2008.pdf
4. Chadwick, E. (1842). *Report on the Sanitary Conditions of the Labouring Population of Great Britain*. London.
5. Esrey, S.A. and J.P. Habicht (1986). "Epidemiological Evidence for Health Benefits from Improved Water and Sanitation in Developing Countries." *Epidemiologic Reviews* 8: 117-128.
6. Lee, L.F., M.R. Rosenzweig, and M.M. Pitt (1997). "The Effects of Improved Nutrition, Sanitation, and Water Quality on Child Health in High-Mortality Populations." *Journal of Econometrics* 77(1): 209-235.

7. WHO and UNICEF Joint Monitoring Programme (2004). *MDG Mid-Term Assessment Report* (2004). Geneva: World Health Organisation and UNICEF.
8. UNCHS and UNEP (2002). "Sulabh Sanitation Movement Restoring Dignity to 'Scavengers'." *Water for Cities Newsletter* 10.
9. See See K. Balachandra Kurup, Community Based Approaches in Water Supply and Sanitation Programme: An Indian Experience, Social Indicators Research, Vol. 24, No. 4 (Jun., 1991), pp. 403-414.
10. Gordon, D., S. Nandy, C. Pantazis, S. Pemberton, and P. Townsend (2003). *Child Poverty in the Developing World*. Bristol: The Policy Press.
11. See Shailen Nandy and David Gordon, 2009, Children, Youth and Environments, Vol. 19, No. 2, The Everyday Environments of Children's Poverty, pp. 202-228.
12. See Ashish Saxena (2013). 'Movement Towards The Green Pilgrimage: Mapping Environmental Sanitation Issues In *Kumbh Mela* At Prayag', Proceedings of Sociology of Sanitation, Sulabh International, New Delhi.
13. Vinay Kumar Srivastava, On Sanitation: A Memory Ethnography, *Social Change* 2014 44: 275.
14. Prashad, Vijay. (2000). *Untouchable freedom: A social history of a dalit community*. Oxford: Oxford University Press.
15. See 10 Things You Need to Know About Sanitation, *WHO in cooperation with UNICEF and WSSCC.*
16. For details see A Citizens' Agenda for Change, Council for Social Development, *Social Change* 2014 44: 301.

1

Meaning, Definition and Scope of Sanitation

Introduction

Multiple factors, most notably poverty, inequality and unequal power relationships, places like developing regions—sub-Saharan Africa and Southern and Eastern Asia are in a struggle for survival. Furthermore, social and environmental challenges like rapid urbanisation, climate change, increasing agriculture water consumption, rising pollution levels, and the depletion of water, exacerbate the problem and intensify the competition for available water. In addition to the lack of safe and potable water, inadequate access to improved sanitation facilities combined with poor hygienic practices contributes to impoverishment and spawns devastating health effects, especially in rural areas and urban slums in developing countries. Without effective sanitation systems, untreated human waste contaminates ground water and other water supplies that allows infections and diseases to spread.

The Human Development Report (2006) highlights that lack of sanitation kills 3900 children on average daily in Africa and Asia—2.6 billion people mostly from the developing world do not have access to toilets so they are forced to defecate in the open. Various programmes costing billions of dollars have been deployed to solve the developing world's sanitation problems, often with little success. This failure is frequently due to an inadequate understanding of people's approach to sanitation and their lack of education to motivate them to have toilets. The ongoing crisis in the lack of sanitation further frustrates developing nations to achieve the Millennium Development Goals' to help end the appalling state of sanitation in half by 2015 (WHO 2004). The health implications associated with unhygienic sanitary conditions such as increased risk of water-related diseases are well documented.

The main cause of the crisis in social relations is the privatisation of the public sphere, which is part of neo-liberal restructuring linked to the individualism which is central to neo-liberal ideology. Writing of this as a global trend Bauman has argued that the failure of the state means that individuals have to seek private remedies for socially produced problems. It implies that 'the meaning of citizenship has been emptied of much of its past contents' (Bauman, 2004:45)[1]. This is particularly serious for us in our struggle to create a shared, national sense of rights and responsibilities as citizens in an aspirant democracy. The consolidation of that democracy depends very largely on the capacity of the state to deliver 'social citizenship'.

It is to be emphasized that people want to have sanitation, and this is arguably the most important reason for promoting sanitation. However, people do not necessarily want it primarily for health reasons– they have other motives. A survey of people from rural areas of the Philippines who were asked why they liked to have latrines provided the following answers in the following way (Cairncross 1992):[2]

(i) A lack of smell and flies

(ii) Cleaner surroundings

(iii) Privacy

(iv) Less embarrassment when there were visitors

(v) Less disease

Thus, sanitation education be made part of the National Sanitation Policy and should embrace proper health practices, such as personal hygiene, the need for all family members (including the children) to use the toilet and the necessity of keeping the toilet building clean. Education should also include the proper operation of the system, such as what may and may not be disposed of in the toilet, the amount of water to add if necessary, and what chemicals should or should not be added to the system. The user must also be made aware of what needs to be done if the system fails or what options are available when the pit or vault fills up with sludge.

Meaning and Definition of Sanitation

"Great cities, when badly administered, cannot be sold or abolished; they simply become dirty, unhealthy, unsafe, disgraceful, and expensive."[3] No doubt, Sanitation is a very important index of socio-economic development in any society. The term implies a good water supply, safe disposal of human waste and waste water, solid waste management, control of vectors of diseases, domestic and personal hygiene, hygienically prepared food, clean housing, etc. UNDP (1998) defines sanitation as 'safe disposal of solid and liquid waste and maintaining a clean environment, which promotes the health and hygiene of the community'.

Sanitation is an integral part of human ecology and it is defined as safe handling of excreta in the human environment. It can also be simply labeled as people's approach to take care of their primal needs. Achieving and maintaining a healthful community environment, however, requires, among other things, control of activities which may adversely affect that environment. Such control is achieved by laws, municipal ordinances, or regulations which inevitably run afoul of private interests. The extent to which these private interests may be required to yield to the needs of the community is determined by the constitutional scope of the governmental power, called the "police power," exercised by the State and by the community as authorised by the State.

According to Reynold, the dictionary defines sanitation as the practical application of sanitary science through the removal or neutralisation of elements injurious to health. Strictly speaking, the sanitary engineer is concerned with construction of works for promoting the health of the community. However, his field has been widening to include the abatement of nuisances as well as dangers to health. Community attractiveness from the standpoint of comfort and enjoyment is intermingled with community safety from the standpoint of health.[4]

Sanitation as it relates to excreta disposal, which is 'the means of collecting and disposal of excreta and community liquid wastes in a hygienic manner' (World Health Organisation, 1987).[5] The more comprehensive term 'environmental sanitation' is concerned also with a healthy environment (UNICEF, 1997)[6] and includes drainage, solid waste management, vector control and hygiene promotion in addition to excreta disposal and treatment.

Tilly Elizabeth's compendium[7] defines sanitation as a 'multi-step process in which wastes are managed from the point of generation to the point of use or ultimate disposal. A sanitation system is comprised of Products (wastes) which travel through Functional Groups which contain Technologies which can be selected according to the context. A sanitation system also includes the management, operation and maintenance (O&M) required ensuring that the system functions safely and sustainably'.

According to UNICEF, the term *sanitation* refers to a process whereby 'people demand, effect, and sustain a hygienic and healthy environment for themselves by erecting barriers to prevent the transmission of disease agents.[8] Such an approach is needed not only to prevent disease and promote health, but also to lay the foundation for sustainable development'. Improved sanitation and hygiene behaviour involve change, which, to be meaningful, usually takes time—a fact that will affect a programme's planning, implementation, and resource allocation. In the past, hardware components have seized the lion's share of the budget—to the neglect or outright dropping of "software" components (meaning community education and participation, training, hygiene education, and other non-technology aspects). This mistake must be avoided throughout any programming exercise you will undertake. Hygiene behaviour programmes are not solely about improving people's knowledge of hygiene and health. Building latrines to improve sanitation cannot solve the entire problem. Indeed, much more will be required of either.

Definition of sanitation in the White Paper on Basic Household Sanitation of 2001 is the following: ' "Sanitation refers to the principles and practices relating to the collection, removal or disposal of human excreta, household wastewater and refuse as they impact upon people and the environment.[9] Good sanitation includes appropriate health and hygiene awareness and behaviour, and acceptable, affordable and sustainable sanitation services'.

The latest development in defining sanitation is by Kvarnström *et al.* (2011)[10] who proposed that access to sanitation be function-based (health functions and environmental functions), rather than, as done by JMP[11] (WHO/UNICEF Joint Monitoring Programme for Water Supply and Sanitation).

According to Prof. Bindeshwar Pathak (2013),[12] sanitation should be included as a discipline in sociology because the core problem areas embodying sanitation like social deprivation, hygiene, ecology, water, public health, poverty, gender equality, welfare of children etc., requires sociological intervention also being intertwined with spiritual and philosophical knowledge. To him, Sociology of Sanitation can be defined as "Sociology of sanitation is a scientific study to solve the problem of society in relation to sanitation, social deprivation, water, public health, hygiene, ecology, environment, poverty, gender equality, welfare of children and empowering people for sustainable development and attainment of philosophical and spiritual knowledge to lead a happy life and to make a difference in the lives of others."

UN-Habitat (2003)[13] introduced the term 'adequate' sanitation which went beyond mere access to a particular type of sanitation system. 'Adequate sanitation was defined as 'access to sanitation that is convenient for all household members, affordable, and that eliminates contact with human excreta and other wastewater in the home and neighbourhood'. In urban areas alone UN-Habitat estimated that around 850—1,130 million people lacked adequate sanitation *vs* 394 million lacking improved sanitation.

D. Joshi (2006) rightly points out that technically, sanitation implies greater hygiene, both personal and domestic, but the reasons for practicing locally perceived notions of sanitation 'are not always related to cleanliness and may often be deeply influenced by reasons completely unrelated to either cleanliness or hygiene.'[14]

Observing the complexity of the issue and also keeping in view the broader understanding of sanitation, I am inclined to define sanitation in following ways:

"In a broader sense sanitation implies management, operation and maintenance of human/social ecology involving 'greater hygiene' and referring to scientifically derived people's capability to achieve their primal physical, biological, psychological, philosophical, social and economic needs and entitlements. It involves the well-being of individuals through exclusion or neutralisation of elements (social or physical) dysfunctional to them and their community. Good sanitation is a 'way of life' and an effective tool for progress of one's mind, body and surroundings in terms of health, scientific temper, secular behaviour in an acceptable, affordable and sustainable way".

It is UNICEF policy that its water and sanitation (WATSAN) staff should focus on being "catalysts" of better programmes and policy, rather than to engage in project implementation for its own sake. Although the programming process is a straightforward cycle, the way you go about developing the programme and appropriate policies is critical. As a catalyst, rather than the owner of the programme, you will find many opportunities to set the stage for larger-scale collaborative action by engaging others in the process as "owners and partners" right from the start. In most cases, a good strategy will be to form a core group of sector professionals at the national level to help guide learning, programming, and policy development process. Such a group will start with identifying the current state of the sector, noting what is currently going on and what needs to be learned. Next, it will analyse available options, and, based on a deliberate process grounded in field experience and consultation with many levels and partners, ultimately seek to define better sanitation programmes and help evolve national policy. Activities for such joint programming and policy development will start by building trust and rapport with key counterparts in the "institutional community." Once formed, a core group of sector professionals should expand activities to other levels, including top policy makers, local governments, local nongovernmental organisations (NGOs), and communities.

Nature of Sanitation

Nature of sanitation is concerned with the scientific status of the discipline. Being a specialised area of sociology, its nature too had a bearing closer to sociology proper. In other words, we have to discuss whether sanitation is a science or not. This sort of inquiry of truth is based on certain fundamental assumptions which are often called as essential elements of science. These are as follows:-

1. Objectivity: Any body of knowledge, to be regarded as science must have objectivity. When any particular investigation is carried out without being influenced by the researcher's personal feelings, bias or attitude, that investigation becomes objective. This objectivity helps different researchers to reach at the same conclusion. So the primary duty of a researcher is to strive at self eliminatory in his judgments and provide an argument which is true for each individual mind as his own. This is attended under two conditions. The repeated investigation of one phenomenon by the same observer yield constant data; and the repeated observation of constant phenomena by different observers yield constant data.

2. Generality: The scientific theories or laws always try to discover under the surface level of diversity the thread of uniformity. Science is not interested in individual objects or individual groups of objects as such. Its primary aim is to trace order in nature, to this end; science seeks to as certain the common characteristics of types of objects and general laws or conditions of events. The conclusions arrived at a scientific method have general applicability.

3. Verifiability: The scientific findings are based on the empirical evidence. The speculation and imaginations have no place in science. The scientist believes that the rule source of knowledge is experience (i.e., data of senses) and that there are no universal and necessary truths from which valid existential inferences can be drawn. This sort of reliance on reality makes the scientific generalisations verifiable. Any knowledge or information which cannot be verified or tested cannot be science, they can at best be belief or philosophies.

4. Rationality: Science is not only based on empirical evidences, but also on rational arguments only the help of data collected from reality will yield no knowledge. They should be properly organised and rational thinking be applied to arrive at general truth.

The scientist does not accept uncritically whatever sense-datum offers itself before him. To this sense-datum, he applies the screws of reason so as to comprehend its true character. In other words the man of science regards rational ideas as the guiding principle on making prediction that are then to be tested by observation.

5. Predictability: By logical reasoning and inferences science establishes the cause and effect relationship among different phenomena. It also believes on the principles of law of uniformity of nature. Which states that the nature will be similar under similar conditions? Given the similar situation the same cause must produce the same effect. On the basis of these two principles i.e., (law of concession and law of uniformity of nature). Since predicts about future state of things with certain degree of accuracy.

6. System: Science deals with empirical truths. But the most important thing is that while analysing the true nature of these empirical objects, it follows a formal or rigorous method. This systematic method of analysis and generalisation enables the scientists to varify the findings again and again in different occasions. Generally two prevalent methods are found in realm of science i.e., deductive and inductive. In deductive methods the conclusion is drawn from a set of self-evident propositions. On the other hand in inductive method, the particular truths in empirical situation are gathered continually and gradually till the most general truth is established. Thus deduction proceeds from general to particular were as induction proceeds from particular to general often a scientist is confused as to which method is scientific. A valid scientific generation combines both induction and deduction. It borrows the element of formal truth from deduction and material truth from induction and established its own truth by application of logical reasoning. Though, it is difficult to establish any uniform law applicable to all the individuals and societies in variably.

One finds that sanitation employ these strategies to retain objectivity in analysis—(1) Use of scientific methods, (2) Factual study, (3) Discovery of cause and effect, relationship, (4) Universal laws, (5) Predictions.

Sanitation as a discipline incorporates these issues in order to make its claim more meaningfully and effectively. It adopts the scientific tools and statistical analysis for accuracy in generalisation and prediction.

Objective, Subject Matter and Scope of Sanitation

The health, social, and environmental benefits of improved sanitation are maximised when sanitation is planned for and provided in an integrated way with water supply and other municipal services.

The broader aims of the sanitation directly or indirectly deals with the following issues:

- Sanitation is about environment and health—Sanitation improvement is more than just the provision of toilets; it is a process of sustained environment and health improvement. Sanitation improvement must be accompanied by environmental, health and hygiene promotional activities.
- Basic sanitation is a human right—Government has an obligation to create an enabling environment through which all societies can gain access to basic sanitation services.
- The provision of access to sanitation services is a national and local government responsibility—All national and local government should have the constitutional responsibility to provide sanitation services.
- "Health for all" rather than "all for some"—The use of scarce public funds must be prioritised, in order to assist those who are faced with the greatest risk to health due to inadequate sanitation services.
- Equitable regional allocation of development resources—The limited national resources available to support the incremental improvement of sanitation services should be equitably distributed throughout the country, according to population, level of development, and the risk to health of not supporting sanitation improvement.
- Water has an economic value—The way in which sanitation services are provided must
- Take into account the growing scarcity of good quality water
- The "polluter pays" principle—Polluters must pay the cost of cleaning up the impact of their pollution on the environment.
- Sanitation services must be financially sustainable - Sanitation services must be sustainable, in terms of both capital and recurrent costs.

- Environmental integrity—The environment must be protected from the potentially negative impacts of sanitation systems.

Sanitation is to be understood as interplay between man, society and environment in private as well as public sphere. Some areas which may constitute the subject matter of sanitation are as discussed ahead. Firstly, the major concern of sanitation is creation of healthy society. It seeks to analyse the factors and forces promoting health and well-being of the individuals in any society. Secondly, sanitation gives sufficient attention to the study of primary units of social and environmental life. It is concerned with the social acts and social relationship, varied groups and institutions, organisations and association as well as ecological milieu in a cultural framework. Thirdly, it deals with various social processes such as co-operation, competition and conflicts in the sustainability of environment as well as holistic development of man in society. Fourthly, it involves the study of research methods and theorisation of the issues of health and well-being of man in a society. Fifthly, it deals with the remedial measures for eradication various social evils in a society.

Sanitation is an applied discipline. The scope of sanitation is basically the study of social, physical and physiological pathology with all its complexities. The prime scope of sanitation may be to make a scientific systematic and comprehensive study of the health and hygiene in relation to the social organisation and its associated structure-function. Sanitation being an interdisciplinary entity incorporates the broader areas under its framework, thus widening the scope from science to social sciences.

It may incorporate the following issues in a national and global framework:

- Evaluation of Health Outcomes
- Aerobic and Anaerobic Treatment
- Climate Change
- Corporate Social Responsibility
- Ecological Sanitation
- Equity Issues in Society
- Household Treatment and Safe Storage
- Hygiene and Behavioral Change
- ICT and Health, environment, Social Problems
- Industrial Hygiene
- Innovations in Water Supply and Waste Water

- Low Tech Treatment Systems
- Measurement and Risk Management
- Operation and Maintenance of Water Supply Systems
- Prevention and Treatment of Waterborne Illnesses
- Public Health Education
- River Restoration
- Sanitation and Health
- Sanitation: Urban and Rural
- School Sanitation
- Soil Quality
- Sustainable Development
- The Millennium Development Goals
- Waste Management
- Waste Water Reclamation and Reuse
- Water and Sanitation Services
- Water Economics
- Water Policy and Governance
- Water Quality
- Water Source Protection

The concept of sanitation was earlier limited to disposal of human excreta pools, open ditches, pit latrines, bucket system etc. Today it connotes a comprehensive concept, which includes liquid and solid waste disposal, food hygiene, personal, domestic as well as environmental hygiene. Proper sanitation is important not only from the general health point of view but it has a vital role to play in our individual and social life too. Sanitation is one of the basic determinants of quality of life and human development index. Good sanitary practices prevent contamination of water and soil and thereby prevent diseases. The concept of sanitation was, therefore, expanded to include personal hygiene, home sanitation, safe water, garbage disposal, excreta disposal and waste water disposal.[15]

Sanitation is the hygienic means of promoting health through prevention of human contact with the hazards of wastes as well as the treatment and proper disposal of sewage wastewater. Hazards can be physical, microbiological, biological or chemical agents of disease. Wastes that can cause health problems include human and animal feces, solid wastes, domestic wastewater (sewage, sullage, and grey water), industrial wastes and agricultural wastes. Hygienic means of prevention can be by using engineering solutions (e.g., sewerage and wastewater treatment), simple technologies (e.g., latrines, septic tanks), or even by personal hygiene practices (e.g., simple hand washing with soap).

The World Health Organisation states that: "Sanitation generally refers to the provision of facilities and services for the safe disposal of human urine and feces. Inadequate sanitation is a major cause of disease world-wide and improving sanitation is known to have a significant beneficial impact on health both in households and across communities. The word 'sanitation' also refers to the maintenance of hygienic conditions, through services such as garbage collection and wastewater disposal.

In context of the scope of application, the term "sanitation" is applied to a wide range of subjects such as:

- Improved sanitation - refers to the management of human faeces at the household level. This terminology is the indicator used to describe the target of the Millennium Development Goal on sanitation, by the WHO/UNICEF Joint Monitoring Programme for Water Supply and Sanitation.
- On-site sanitation - the collection and treatment of waste is done where it is deposited. Examples are the use of pit latrines, septic tanks, and Imhoff tanks.
- Food sanitation - refers to the hygienic measures for ensuring food safety.
- Environmental sanitation - the control of environmental factors that form links in disease transmission. Subsets of this category are solid waste management, water and wastewater treatment, industrial waste treatment and noise and pollution control.
- Ecological sanitation - an approach that tries to emulate nature through the recycling of nutrients and water from human and animal wastes in a hygienically safe manner.

Need and Importance of Sanitation

In developing countries, many urban water supply systems perform poorly. A significant number of people living in towns and cities do not have access to improved water sources at all. Developing countries face enormous challenges in providing reliable water supply and sanitation services. Public utilities are the world's main model of urban water service. Many developing countries have insufficient funding for maintenance and expansion of their network of utilities. This means the utilities are not functioning properly or reaching enough people.

There are not enough incentives for public utilities to improve their performance and sometimes politicians get involved directly in their management, making the delivery of services more difficult.

The reasons why many sanitation affairs are in a poor state include:

- Under-investment due to the lack of stable, predictable and sufficient volume of finance
- High population growth in urban areas without proportionate expansion in the services of utilities
- Public utilities have been treated as social services
- Insufficient operational and managerial autonomy from government
- Poor management—no regulatory mechanisms to monitor public utilities or make them accountable for performance
- Inefficiency—government is often forced to financially 'prop up' failing and bankrupt utilities.

Access to improved water and sanitation facilities does not, on its own, necessarily lead to improved health. There is now very clear evidence showing the importance of hygienic behaviour, in particular hand-washing with soap at critical times: after defecating and before eating or preparing food. Hand-washing with soap can significantly reduce the incidence of diarrhoea, which is the second leading cause of death amongst children under five years old. In fact, recent studies suggest that regular hand-washing with soap at critical times can reduce the number of diarrhoea bouts by almost 50 per cent.

Good hand-washing practices have also been shown to reduce the incidence of other diseases, notably pneumonia, trachoma, scabies, skin and eye infections and diarrhoea-related diseases like cholera and dysentery. The promotion of hand-washing with soap is also a key strategy for controlling the spread of Avian Influenza (bird flu).

The key to increasing the practice of hand-washing with soap is to promote behavioural change through motivation, information and education. There are a variety of ways to do this including high-profile national media campaign, peer-to-peer education techniques, hygiene lessons for children in schools and the encouragement of children to demonstrate good hygiene to their families and communities. It is also true that without water there is no hygiene. Research shows that the less readily available water is, the less likely that good hygiene will be practiced in households.

It is to be emphasised that the importance of sanitation in any country especially the developing and under-developed countries are prime owing to the following relevance[16]

(i) As an important intervention - Inadequate sanitation management is often seen as an outcome of poverty. It is not viewed as something that can reduce poverty. Evidence shows that providing people with sanitation and water services and promoting hygiene brings about greater improvements in public health than any other single intervention.

(ii) Sanitation can drive local economic development - Improving sanitation can drive local economic development. Making basic sanitation and hygiene services part of policies and programmes for urban development or improving slums can create jobs and generate economic activity while improving people's daily lives.

(iii) Sanitation is not a right enjoyed by everyone - Nearly 40 per cent of the world's populations are "sanitation-stressed". They might use plastic bags to go to the toilet in, defecate behind a bush or use a dirty and dark latrine.

(iv) Millennium Development Goal (MDG) - The sanitation MDG seeks to halve the proportion of people without access to basic sanitation between 1990 and 2015. To achieve the target an additional 285,000 people around the world need to gain access to basic sanitation every day from now until 2015—a 90 per cent increase in progress over the last 15 years.

ISSUES AND STRATEGIES IN SANITATION

The section explores different aspects of programming in depth, providing one with major questions, considerations, and possible options for strategies in a number of topical areas[17]*community identification; community participation; technology options; financing, institutional arrangements; and political will.*

Following are brief summaries of a few key issues and options.

(i) Identifying Communities

The enterprise begins with identifying communities, so that all other programming starts with and includes the communities who will be key players. To strategically identify communities, the programmatic challenge is to develop processes for selection and criteria—rather than to select specific communities, which is usually a project function. The central issue is how to allocate, or reallocate, available resources to eventually achieve the widest possible impact. In certain instances, this may mean starting on a narrow basis, if by so doing strategic gains can be greatest and better sustained in the long term; in other situations it might be more important to tackle a few behaviours over larger populations.

Options might include responding to those communities with expressed demand; to communities in areas where there is likely to be adequate software and hardware capacity to support community efforts; to communities from which there can be the most widespread effect; to communities that can be clustered, thus lowering costs; to communities that are poor; and/or communities having few facilities and lacking hygienic behaviours. To choose appropriate options you will have to *know* the communities you would identify.

(ii) Community Participation

In the community participation chapter, you will find a review of issues such as who to involve; types of interventions; specific options for education and communication approaches, and their uses; and building related skills capacity to sustain change at personal, household, and environmental levels. We may often underestimate what it takes to bring about sustained change at the community level, whilst at the same time underestimating people's capacity for change if a genuine effort is made. To evoke community participation, we need to yield control over key decisions—and we need ways to engage communities and their members in assessment, planning, action, and monitoring of their own progress. Problems rarely arise mainly out of a lack of "knowledge about hygiene and sanitation"; villagers and peri-urban dwellers have in many cases heard lectures about disease transmission. The issue tends to be whether they feel able and willing to challenge the problem and whether they have the internal resources and capacity to do so—individually and as part of a larger group.

(iii) Technology Options

The technology options explores the factors involved in selecting a range of technical options and discusses ways to establish processes for consumer choice. It is important to strike a balance between technology aspects and other project components: sanitation is not simply latrines, but rather an awareness and capacity for managing waste controls, domestic wastewater, solid waste, and human and animal wastes. No single technology option should be prescribed; for the effort to work, people need to have choices, and options should continue to evolve with the communities' growth over time. For technologies to be appropriate, they should generally evolve out of the local context and build on local innovations. Rather than provisioning, the role at the programme level is to stimulate and build upon such innovation, creating incentives and standards that ensure the chosen technologies are healthful, safe, technically adequate, environmentally sound, and sustainable. Another key role is to help forge and sustain the linkages between designers, producers, wholesalers, retailers, and consumers—creating an environment in which the private sector can thrive.

iv) Financing

The financing focuses on alternative arrangements for arranging programme costs consistent with goals of sustainability and cost-effectiveness, e.g., self-financing strategies. Who is the programme planning to assist? What is their willingness to pay or contribute? What strategies will best respond to community demand, ensure accountability, prioritise the use of local resources, promote greater equity, and not sacrifice long terms gains for shorter ones? In terms of options, programmers would prioritise financing from within communities, and then where needed, through the use ofcredit facilities. You may decide to explore options for private-sector financing, and for policies that encourage production and employment in the local market. There may even be possibilities for cross-subsidies, although this option is often difficult to arrange. Sometimes it is possible to demonstrate demand through whole communities, and thus compensate internally; such arrangements often need the help of an NGO or similar group to bring them about. Subsidies and grants are a last resort and should be avoided, as they can be counterproductive except in rare cases. Whatever financing strategy is chosen, it should be consistent.

(v) Institutional Arrangements

As institutions adjust themselves to play more useful roles in support of new approaches to sanitation, the issues of sector allocation of responsibilities arises. What roles will central and local governments, NGOs, the private sector, various donors, and others play? Who will take the lead, and in what institutional framework will sanitation programmes be designed and managed? In general, those at higher institutional levels need to find ways to stimulate and support local supply and demand systems—not to arrange provisioning or delivery of services themselves. For example, how can they make best use of local NGOs, the private sector, grassroots organisations, and communities themselves rather than relying upon large, centralised, and often ineffective departments? At the same time, how will they become protectors and nurturers of sector development: ensuring standards, environmental protection, human resource development, and careful monitoring? In this sensitive behavioural area, programmers need to ensure that above all they have made clear and adequate provisions for the building and strengthening of local and community-level institutions that are able to make decisions and manage the desired change in their communities. Who will do this and how will it be supported? How can resources and decision making shift to local levels in line with decentralisation? There are a range of options; from among them you will need to determine local solutions that are viable and realistic, yet proceed towards change.

(vi) Building Political Will

Finally, building political will explores ways that joint learning and programming can, over time, lead to policy change. It also examines how to build a foundation of support for the programme. Political will and sound policies need to be built upon a foundation of what communities want—as determined through programming work and study over time. To bring this about, a process starting with your core group and expanding both to local partners and to national policy makers can make an impact. As an effective catalyst, you can help to ensure that policy discussions are driven, not by whim, bias, or favouritism, but by learning on how to solve national sanitation problems. By adding rigour and solid evidence to back up your programming work, you can contribute to establishing better policies. And by including other levels and sectors—such as local communities, NGOs, and local and regional governments—you can build ownership and practice of the new policies at many levels.

Some of the basic concepts reflected here:

- Build trust and rapport, involving people from the start and working with various levels and groups to move through the programming cycle.
- Challenge assumptions. Stay aware of major questions and considerations, so you will develop a strategy that can make a difference.
- Get as much information as possible in the time available.
- Be realistic and systematic. Prepare a programme strategy that focuses on measurable results.

The UN-WHO Joint Monitoring Programme for Drinking Water

Supply and Sanitation (JMPDWSS, 2008, 2010) defines an "improved" sanitation facility as one that *hygienically separates human excreta from human contact*. These include facilities that flush or pour-flush into a piped sewer system, septic tanks, or pit latrines, as well as ventilated improved pit latrines (also known as VIP latrines) and pit latrines with slab or composting toilets.

According to ESI, Sanitation is broadly defined to include management of human excreta, solid waste, and drainage.[18] The ESI India study focused exclusively on the *safe management of human excreta and associated hygiene behaviour*.

"Unimproved" sanitation facilities include defecation in the open, bucket or hanging latrines, open pit latrines or those without a slab, and facilities flushing or pour-flushing into open drains or open areas (that is, not into a piped sewer system, septic tank, or pit latrine). Shared toilets are also considered unimproved facilities. It is not only a deficit of sanitary toilets that constitutes inadequate sanitation, but also the unsafe disposal of human excreta and, most important, the whole range of unhygienic practices that break down the separation of human excreta from human contact and thus expose people to fecal-oral pathogens.

Genesis of Sociology of Sanitation

Sociology of Sanitation is a sub branch of medical sociology that emerged in the United States during 1940s. The discipline that investigates the social causes and consequences of health and illness was inspired by the health and sanitary reforms that took place in western society. It was well recognised that the relations between sociology and sanitation are extremely intimate. The individual is the essential element of the society, his social values depends largely upon his health. Good health is a pre-requisite for the adequate functioning of an individual or society. If our health is sound, we can engage in numerous types of activities. But if we are ill, distressed or injured, we may face the curtailment of our usual round of daily life and we may also become so pre-occupied with our state of health that other pursuits are secondary importance or quite meaningless. Therefore as Rene Du Bos (1981) explains "health can be defined as the ability to function". While in turn his health is partly determined by the conditions which society imposes. Social factors play a critically important role in health. Social conditions and situations not only promote the possibility of illness and disability but they also enhance prospects for disease prevention and health maintenance. The disheartening status of mankind today is undoubtedly the result of the sanitary and social conditions of past ages and former generations. Clean food, adequate clean supply of water, sanitary schools, public baths, adequate housing are sanitary measures which are most effective in both sanitary and social results. Hence sanitation and sociology must go hand in hand in their effort to improve the race and now their relations are consciously and openly recognised.[19]

(a) Interlinkage Between Sanitation and Sociology

In Durkheimenian framework, one can observe 'sociology of sanitation' as a shift from profane to sacred elements. Locating the issue of sanitation L. Dumount rightly states that the Indian society is homo-hierarchicus resting on the religion with caste system having an element of 'pure' and 'impure'. Even M.N. Srinivas too speaks about 'purity and pollution', having bearing on caste interactions. His concept of *'sanskritisation'* has an inherent notion of sanitation for lower caste members. If one goes philosophically on the issue of sanitation of soul, one finds that 'secularisation' reflects decline in the religious intolerance and accommodation of diverse religious practices for healthy society. The doctrine of Hindu religion also focuses on sanitation with the purification of ones *'paap'* in the lifetime. Thus sanitation of body and soul as a precondition for attaining *moksh* after death and for once re-birth. Even, performing once duties in the holy pilgrimage is deeply embedded in religio-philosophical matrix of Indian psyche. At this juncture the pilgrimage of *'Prayag Kumbh'* becomes crucial. The paper locates issues of 'sanitation' in the pilgrimage of *'Prayag Kumbh'*. Here emphasis is on 'power of sanitation' as an ideology and an instrument of maintaining sanctity and religious purity.[20]

According to Talbot (1896), the duty of the sanitation is therefore acknowledged to be of greater scope as the years pass and the meaning of sanitary reform is proved not to be restricted to the physical life of man, but to affect all his activities as a human being. The interest of the sanitation is now said to be in "whatever can cause or help to cause discomfort, pain, sickness, death, vice or crime and whatever has a tendency to avert, destroy, or diminish such causes." We are told that preventable evils, such as loss of life, impairment of health, and physical disability, impose upon the people unnumbered and immeasurable calamities, pecuniary, social, physical, and moral, which ought to be avoided.

E.A. Parkes in the introduction to his work on Practical Hygiene says, "Taking the word hygiene in the largest sense, it signifies rules for perfect culture of mind and body. It is impossible to dissociate the two. The body is affected by every mental and moral action; the mind is profoundly influenced by bodily conditions. For a perfect system of hygiene we must train the body, the intellect and the moral faculties in a perfect and balanced order, looking only to the part of hygiene which concerns the physician, a perfect system of rules of health would consider the human being:

1. In relation to the natural conditions which surround him,
2. In his social and corporate relations,
3. In his capacity as an independent being, having within himself sources of action in thoughts, feelings, desires, personal habits, all of which affect health and which require self-regulation and control."

In the words of Sir John Simon, "When sanitary reformers appeal to the conscience of modern civilisation against the merely quantitative waste of human life, their deeper protest is against the heedless extinction of those high and beautiful possibilities of being, against the wanton interception of such powers for good, against the cruel smothering of such capacities for happiness.

If general assent is given to the proposition that the sanitarian has a part to play in promoting all the highest and best activities of mankind, the converse equally must be true that, if the sociologist is to study the facts of associated human activities with a view to social amelioration, he is but a partial and, in so far, a worthless observer, if he ignores the data which the sanitarian can furnish."

This relationship between physical and social conditions is shown in another form by the following statements in Giddings 'The Theory of Sociology': "Social aggregates are formed at first by external conditions, such as food supply, temperature, etc......that the resources and other circumstances of the physical environment must be regarded as the true cause of social aggregation is plainly shown." "Society like the individual must adjust itself to a physical environment." "What is the fact of progress? In what does it consist? The answer of sociology will be that progress includes an increase of material well-being, etc."

This, then, is the relationship between sanitation and sociology: The individual is the essential element of society; his social value depends largely upon his health, while in turn his health is partly determined by the conditions which society imposes. This conclusion leads to another which is of sheer to those who may perchance be discouraged and falter by the way. The disheartening status of mankind today is undoubtedly the result of the sanitary and social conditions of past ages and former generations, but the influences under which men of the present generation place themselves are more of less within their control and may be made to work for both present and future good.

Sanitation then will show what steps should be taken by society, individually and collectively, to secure the health of the race. Clean air, sunlight, wide streets, good pavements, public parks, nourishing food, sanitary schools, public baths, adequate housing, are sanitary measures which are most effective in both sanitary and social results if carried out at times when there seems no special cause for anxiety. Sanitation and sociology must go hand in hand in their effort to improve the race. The value of the relation which exists between them will be great in proportion as its importance is consciously and openly recognised.[21]

Notes

1. Bauman, Z. 2004. *Identity. Conversations with Benedetto Vecchi.* London: Polity.
2. Cairncross, S. (1992) Sanitation and Water Supply; Practical Lessons from the Decade. Water and Sanitation Discussion Paper Series Number 9. Washington DC: The World Bank.
3. See Werner, R.: Tammany Hall. Doubleday, Doran, New York, 1928, p. xx.
4. Leon B. Reynolds. 1930. State Sanitation in California, American Water Works Association, Vol. 22, No. 4 (April, 1930), pp. 531-536.
5. World Health Organisation. 1987. The community health worker: guidelines for training. WHO: Geneva.
6. UNICEF/USAID-EHP. 1997. Towards Better Programming: A Sanitation Handbook. Water, Environment and Sanitation Technical Guidelines Series No. 3, UNICEF, USA.
7. Tilley, Elizabeth et al, 2008. Compendium of Sanitation Systems and Technologies. Swiss Federal Institute of Aquatic Science and Technology (Eawag). Dübendorf, Switzerland.
8. Towards Better Programming - A Sanitation Handbook, 1997, Water, Environment and Sanitation Technical Guidelines Series-No. 3, United Nations Children's Fund, New York.
9. DWAF (2001). *White Paper on Basic Household Sanitation*. Department of Water Affairs and Forestry, September. South Africa
10. See Kvarnström, E.; McConville, J.; Bracken, P.; Johansson, M. and Fogde, M. (2011) 'The Sanitation Ladder: A Need for a Revamp?', Journal of Water, Sanitation and Hygiene for Development 1.1: 3–12.

11. See JMP (2011) *Types of Drinking-Water Sources and Sanitation,* New York: WHO/UNICEF Joint Monitoring Programme for Water Supply and Sanitation, www.wssinfo.org/definitionsmethods/watsan-categories/

12. See Bindeshwar Pathak (2013). *'Sociology of Sanitation', Proceedings of Sociology of Sanitation,* Sulabh International, New Delhi.

13. UN-Habitat (2003) Water and Sanitation in the World's Cities: Local Action for Global Goals, London: Earthscan.

14. Joshi, D. (2006). *Sanitation for the urban poor: Whose choice, theirs or ours*? Department of Engineering for Development, University of Southampton, UK.

15. Department of Drinking Water Supply Ministry of Rural Development Government of India, January, 2004.

16. See guidance manual on our water, our waste, our town - Supporting civil society to engage in urban water and sanitation reforms, WaterAid, 47-49 Durham Street, London.

17. Towards Better Programming - A Sanitation Handbook, 1997, Water, Environment and Sanitation Technical Guidelines Series - No. 3, United Nations Children's Fund, New York.

18. Economic Impacts of Inadequate Sanitation in India, 2010, Water and Sanitation Programme, www.wsp.org

19. See Shakuntala C. Shettar, Sociology of Sanitation: Incorporating Gender Issues in Sanitation, http://www.sociologyofsanitation.com/?page_id=694#sthash. qWhnjXTL.dpuf

20. See Ashish Saxena (2013). 'Movement Towards the Green Pilgrimage: Mapping Environmental Sanitation Issues In *Kuṃbh Mela* at Prayag', Proceedings of Sociology of Sanitation, Sulabh International, New Delhi.

21. See Marion Talbot, Sanitation and Sociology, American Journal of Sociology, Vol. 2, No. 1 (Jul., 1896), pp. 74-81.

2

Genesis of Sanitation: A Cross-cultural Framework

(I) Evolution of Sanitation in Global World: A Background

History presents little or no authentic information regarding the means employed in very early times for the protection of the public health, and it is doubtless that the measures enforced in dealing with outbreaks of infectious disease and sanitary conditions, depended chiefly upon the various theories of those in charge of this branch of the public service. The term plague constantly occurs in connection with the literature of these outbreaks, although cholera and typhus fever, particularly the former, were unquestionably frequently involved as well as plague. The loss of life reported to have been caused by these out breaks seems almost incredible, although it is verified by reliable statistics. During the fourteenth century plague brought from the East invaded Western Europe, and under the name of the "Black Death ", swept away within a few years one-quarter of the population of that section of the world, probably about twenty-five million inhabitants.[1]

Even as late as the last century typhus fever appeared in Ireland, and the rapidity of its extension and destruction of life almost equaled the outbreaks of earlier times. It is a significant fact that this outbreak occurred during the well known Irish famine, which was associated with great destitution, overcrowding and filth and did not disappear until the return of a plentiful harvest.

Belief still exists throughout the world that the East is the permanent home of cholera and plague and for some reason they cannot be exterminated. Nothing is further from the truth. The various religious beliefs, ignorance, and, more particularly, political conditions, have made it impossible, or rather impracticable, to carry out the necessary means to destroy these infected centres.

During the centuries which have passed there have been many students and indefatigable workers along the lines of public health protection who have added largely to the general knowledge of this subject. For instance, during the fourteenth century quarantine was first instituted. This occurred in Venice. The term quarantine is of Italian derivation and literally means a detention of forty days. No satisfactory information exists as to why this period should have been selected for the detention of vessels arriving from presumably infected ports; and although the earlier quarantine regulations were for various reasons defective, still it was an advanced step in public sanitation and particularly emphasised the value of preventive measures.

Further illustration of this may be cited; this is in connection with the work of Cardinal Gastaldi which occurred during the outbreak of plague in Rome in the seventeenth century. He not only assumed general management of this emergency, but looked after the details as well. His intense interest in the subject, his study of the course of the disease and the means of combating it, led him to insist upon cleanliness and so far as possible the careful isolation of the cases. Today, these two factors are regarded as among the most potent in preventing the extension of infection. As a result of Cardinal's effort, there were but fourteen thousand deaths in Rome, while at the same period three hundred thousand deaths occurred in Naples. While it cannot properly be said that this remarkable difference in mortality was due wholly to the precaution taken by Cardinal Gastaldi, it is entirely fair and logical to assume that the methods he employed were the chief causes of the more favourable result in Rome.

Although the effectiveness of sanitary methods continuously increased, it was not until about 1880 that public sanitation was placed on a scientific basis and a new era in the protection of the public health began. The public know but little of this important event and how far-reaching and successful it has been in defining, the means to be employed to secure this end. It may properly be said to mark one of the great discoveries in the history of the world, for at that time were made known the researches of Pasteur and Koch respectively, a French and a German bacteriologist who had been working independently of each other. The evidence they presented as to the germ origin of infectious diseases was absolute and conclusive. The announcement of their discoveries gave instant and enormous stimulus to further bacteriological investigation, and in comparatively quick succession followed the identification of the specific organism or germ of many of the infectious diseases. The list now includes tuberculosis, cholera, plague, typhoid fever, diphtheria, and others. It must be obvious to all that the value of this knowledge cannot be overestimated. It means we now know the enemy we deal with in the prevention of infectious diseases, its character and the means by which it can be attacked and destroyed; while before this discovery ignorance prevailed on this special subject.

Exhaustive investigation as to the means by which infectious germs are transmitted from one person to another has also been carried out. This has been rewarded by the most satisfactory results, and, among other things, has presented indisputable evidence of the falseness of some of the former theories relating to this subject. Clothing, baggage, money, cargoes of vessels, etc., are ordinary or common means of infection. This is now known as the Fomites theory. Proof that it was generally accepted as early as the fourteenth century, is shown by the fact that while vessels at that period were held in quarantine, certain portions of their cargo, clothing, etc., were placed on deck in order that they might be purified by the sun and air. Those who still accept this theory believe that various articles, particularly textile fabrics, are able to transmit the organisms of at least some of the infectious diseases in their active state from one person to another.

In the past vessels have been sunk by official order simply to prevent what was believed to be danger from the transmission of disease through the medium of the cargo. Even within a few years iron rails were disinfected to prevent the transmission of yellow fever, and it has been seriously stated that a coat worn by a well person who had been in the vicinity where yellow fever existed was responsible for an outbreak of this disease. However, it is now known that yellow fever is not only never transmitted by clothing, baggage, etc., but only by a variety of the mosquito known as the "Stegomyia." The credit of this important discovery belongs to a commission appointed by the President of the United States in 1900, and sent to Cuba for the purpose of investigating this subject.[2]

Historically, we have, first, disposal on the land, next, construction of sewers and disposal in the streams, and the various methods of purification as the streams were unable to carry the load of sewage from large cities. Sewage farms, one of the first methods of sewage disposal, were used by Berlin, Paris and other large cities. In Berlin, when the farms were first established, the city attempted to sell the vegetables grown on these farms. Sewage farm vegetables could not be sold. The city then leased the farms to peasants, and peasant-grown vegetables readily sold in Berlin markets. There is a limit to the amount of sewage that can be handled on land, and a limit to the amount of land available near large cities. Therefore, various methods requiring less space for disposal have been developed. Sand beds require less area. Still less is required by filters of various types in which the sewage is sprayed over beds of stone or cinders in such a manner that air is carried into the interstices of the stones or cinders, to destroy the organic matter by aerobic bacteria. Settling tanks and the so-called septic tanks are used alone or supplementing other methods. In the septic tanks decomposition takes place without air. Various methods of aeration have been developed, including slate beds, through which sewage passes, and into which air is blown. This scheme led to the activated sludge process of Ardern and Lockett. By blowing air into sewage sludge rich in aerobic bacteria is developed. The sludge, when mixed with incoming raw sewage and stirred with air, accomplishes the purification very rapidly. The process has been so successful that many large cities, including Indianapolis, Milwaukee and Chicago, have adopted it.[3]

An injunction against the Sanitary District of Chicago and the Corn Products Refining Company was threatened by the Illinois Rivers and Lakes Com-mission. The waste from the factory was proven equivalent to the sewage from a city of 380,000 people. The wastes could not be economically treated as sewage, but it was possible to use the waste within the plant in such a way that the load was reduced from the equivalent of 380,000 to 10,000 people. This was done with profit to the company. Today practically all corn products factories in the country are "bottled up."

Cities located on sea-coasts might dispose of sewage by dilution in the ocean without injury to drinking water supplies. Where the outlets are near seaside resorts, the wastes pollute the beaches, and these cities are being compelled to treat their sewage. Cities on large streams like the Ohio, Missouri and Mississippi Rivers have so much dilution that the oxygen dissolved in the water serves to destroy the organic matter and bacteria of the sewage, and there is less need for treatment. Minneapolis and St. Paul have a Sanitary District to treat the sewage which will have its organic matter so reduced that the upper Mississippi will be able to oxidize it and eliminate any nuisance to the cities downstream.[4]

It is been highlighted that the effectual progress depends upon positive ideas, and would we have our social theories pregnant for good, we must find for them a basis in positive ideas. It is, therefore, important that the social reformer and philosopher turn his eyes to the field of sanitation, where neither the specialist, the philosopher, nor the public has forsaken hopes, denied possibilities, nor abandoned positives. Of the achievements in this field the historian Lecky, writing his 'Map of Life' at the very close of the nineteenth century, was able to state: "The triumphs of sanitary reform are perhaps the brightest page in the history of our century.

Smallpox has been stamped out of every land where fanaticism or criminal neglect has not stayed the rescuing hand, plague has been put under control, typhoid abolished, diphtheria mastered, consumption explained and controlled, yellow fever driven even from the tropics. Whereas the savage dies at the rate of 60 to 100 in every 1,000, and suffers ravaging epidemics which periodically threaten the very existence of whole races, backward nations, such as Spain and Italy, lose but 30, while city rates in Germany and the United States are reduced to less than 20 in 1,000. The average age has advanced fifteen years in two generations. But not only has life's tenure lengthened, but life has been made more worth living. Sickness has decreased, air is purer, and water cleaner, large classes of men have for the first time known the pleasures of health.

New York has practically stamped out smallpox; Mississippi can do it by applying vaccine. Vienna University can hardly find enough typhoid patients to teach medical students the symptoms of the disease. Why has Philadelphia thousands of cases to spare? Pennsylvania will shortly rescue itself from polluted streams and typhoid havoc, as it has shown England how to stamp out tuberculosis among cattle. Consumption among men can be detected and checked more easily than diphtheria, and state sanatoria dare to point to the time when it will be difficult for medical colleges to find bacilli of tuberculosis for analysis. The limits to sanitary progress are not to be sought in sanitary science, but in social theories; not in the paucity of remedies, but in the unwillingness to justify them theoretically and to pay for their application.

It is certain that the thesis on public sanitation must put in the foreground diagrams showing the various differential and marginal advantages possessed by different factors in production. This is because sanitary science is a phase of social science rather than a branch of chemistry, medicine, or biology.

It is of such sanitary science that the historian speaks when he finds the high-water mark of the past century's achievements in the triumphs of sanitary reform. In England, Ireland, and Scotland sanitation implies statesmanship. It is state medicine, not laboratory medicine, which has re-housed Britain's poor; it is the application of vaccine lymph and the governmental utilisation of antitoxin that have robbed smallpox and diphtheria of their terrors. It is the use, the compulsory use, of tuberculin, and not its discovery, that has purified a meat supply. Lecky had in mind the sanitarian that used his art for the accomplishment of needed structural changes in society-science as handmade to statecraft.

No American historian would have paid such a tribute to the sanitarian. We are not yet in the habit of connecting sanitation and sociology. Discussion and responsibility are delegated to the physician, who, himself primarily a student of pathology and disease tends to emphasise pills rather than public welfare. We laymen, on the other side, think, because the physician is the best possible agent, he makes a safe exclusive guardian of society's health.

Chronologically there have been seven clearly marked stages in the evolution of what we now call public-health administration. Each state and each city, if left to itself, passes through the same stages in its administration, even where a complete code is legislated, not evolved.

The civilisational understanding of the world history reveals that the great cities have grown and passed out of existence. The enormous increase in urban population in very recent years has produced even greater cities, which may also in time cease to be. Where a complete sanitary code is accepted by a newborn town as a condition to its incorporation, we still have the seven distinct motives represented:

The first period is that of racial tutelage, of pain economy, when the primary lessons of personal hygiene are learned. Through the distribution of plant and animal life, of heat and moisture, primitive man was forced to a nomadic life, and per- force enjoyed pure air, pure water, and pure soil. In his conflict with nature he learned to shun certain plants as poisonous, and to reject discoloured and offensive water or meats. But when gregarious man settled in confined limits for definite and prolonged periods, nature could no longer perform the work of scavenger; sanitation must become conscious, and receive the sanction of law.

The second stage is that of the introduction of sanitary appliances for the health and comfort of the tribute-taking classes. Carthage has her paved streets. Greece worships Hygeia and idolizes her devotees.

Rome has paved streets, public sewers, extensive water-works, gem-bedecked public baths, and furnishes water more freely than any city of modern times, while the superintendency of water-works is allotted only to senators and honored officials. In the twelfth century Paris paves her streets, for the same reason that four centuries later London introduces water to serve wealth and power. In Rome, Paris, London, as in Boston, Chicago, and Seattle, these first steps are due to another motive than desire to protect either public or private health. These public works, so far as they are due to other than property considerations, are primarily evidences of advancing standards of comfort, or perhaps concessions to a growing aesthetic sensitiveness. Constructed by the few to gratify their taste for cleanliness, ease, or show, the benefits accrue to society without reference to social standing, except that the poor may be permitted only a partial exploitation.

The third period is that of commercial sanitation. This should have followed directly upon the second, but historically there was a period of two centuries "when Teutonic Europe was sleeping off its great debauch," when civilisation was without the fundamental motives to sanitary improvement. The barbarian glutton found more primitive means of comparing his success with that of his neighbors than the promenade, and obtained greater satisfaction from wine and the sword than from oriental finery and clean garments. The ideals of Christian and pagan became direct obstacles to sanitary advancement. In fact, Holy Hieronymus, the monastic corporation, and the feudal lord combined to undo the sanitary progress of centuries of slow adaptation. The ascetic violated all the laws of personal hygiene, the monastery's ideal was inconsistent with public hygiene, and both glorified God by teaching submission to the pestilence.

It is observed that in developed countries, the standard solution for the sanitary disposal of human waste is through sewerage systems. Due to severe financial constraints and exorbitant maintenance and operational costs, sewerage is not viewed as the answer to solve the problem of human waste management in India. Modern sewerage was first introduced in the world in London in 1850, followed by New York in 1860. Calcutta in India was the next city in the world to have this privilege in 1870, yet only 232 towns and cities out of 4,700 have partial sewerage systems.[5]

In developing countries neither the government, local authorities nor beneficiaries can afford the capital expenditure or maintenance costs of a sewerage system. Moreover, a sewerage system requires skilled people and good management for operation and maintenance. Natural resources also have to be taken into account, as to clear away human excreta with each flush sends more than 10l of clean water down the drain. This is particularly true as large dams and irrigation systems are constructed to move huge quantities of water only for it to be flushed down into an expensive sewerage system, all of which ends up polluting rivers and ponds. Most of the rivers in India today are highly polluted because of the domestic sewage load from cities, resulting in health hazards and the destruction of aquatic flora and fauna.

Sewerage systems are built to protect public health but badly managed sewers can become a serious health hazard, leading to potentially serious outbreaks of waterborne diseases. Due to high operational and maintenance costs, a sewerage system is not really affordable in developing countries like India. Septic tank systems are also expensive and require large volumes of water for flushing. However, as there is shortage of drinking water in most urban areas of the country, water has to be conserved. Other problems are associated with septic tanks, such as the need for periodic cleaning and disposal of sludge. Effluent disposal is also a potential source of foul smells, mosquito breeding and health hazards if not properly dealt with. Although the design of septic tank latrines was developed nearly 400 years ago and introduced in India about 150 years ago, less than 20 per cent of the houses have septic tank toilets even in urban areas.[6]

Goddess of the Sewers-cloacina

According to Schladweiler, mankind has routinely sought, through the ages, strength and guidance from the spirit world.[7] The Romans, during the course of their Empire (650 BCE—400 AD), worshipped many deities ... one of them being the Goddess Cloacina—in whom they placed their faith/trust for the wellbeing of Rome's sewers (and workers); a facet of Rome's public works infrastructure that was considered vital to their desired way of life - good health through sanitation.

Cloacina was the patron goddess of the Cloaca Maxima (the *main* drain of the City) and the city's overall sewer system. Over time, the Romans came to also think of her in a multitude of other ways including; as the goddess of purity, the goddess of filth and the protector of sexual intercourse in marriage. As such, over the ages, she came to be affiliated with Venus; and, gradually became known to many as the Venus Cloacina.

The first "sewer" segments (as opposed to Rome's initial surfaced and open topped drainage ditches) of the Cloaca Maxima were started in the late 500s BCE; the craftsmen were Etruscan—Rome's neighbours to the North. Soon thereafter, it is told that a statue of a woman was found in the sewer. She became known as the Goddess Cloacina; a deity that likely had its origin in the mythology of the Etruscans. Cloacina's name is possibly derived from either the Latin verb *"cloare* or cluere" (to wash, to purify or to clean) or, from the Latin word cloaca, meaning *"sewer"*. The need for the Goddess of the Sewers soon became recognised as an important aspect of the Romans' lifestyle/ beliefs during the next 600 or more years - as Rome grew and its sewer system was completed. One can only hope that the spirit of Cloacina has remained with us through the ages; and, is still available to help with the well being of our sewers and of the people who work so hard to plan, design, construct, administer, operate and maintain them today.[8]

(II) Historiography of Sanitation in Prominent Nations

(a) Egyptian Sanitation

The first annual report of the Director-General of the Sanitary Department of Egypt in 1893 is a document which demands more than a passing notice. Egypt is not only an important stage on the highway of commerce between East and West, but is also a stage on the highway of epidemic disease; and the sanitary state of the country is, therefore, a matter of vital interest to the whole of Europe as well as to the inhabitants, native and foreign, of the country itself. This report is admirably drawn up by Director-General J.G. Rogers. It is concise, exhaustive, clear, and trenchant, and furnishes an excellent sketch of the sanitary shortcomings and needs of Egypt, the efforts which have been made to cope with these, their partial success, and the urgent necessity of better organisation and stronger effort, if any real advance is to be made on the road to sanitary reform.

The catalogue of sanitary defects which exist in Egypt is long and formidable. They are in brief these : Polluted water; a polluted soil; overcrowded and insanitary dwellings; no building regulations; stagnant ponds in every village; cesspools, too often leaky, everywhere; cemeteries within a few feet of human habitations; imperfect burial; no proper scavenging arrangements; no drainage; water logging of soil in places; no slaughter houses; bad hospital buildings; defective lunatic asylum; no homes for paupers and lepers; overcrowded and unhealthy prisons; no hospitals for infectious-diseases; an underpaid staff over burdened with petty duties; complicated and ineffective registration laws; defective vital statistics; an inaccurate and unreliable census; no local organisation for sanitary work; insufficient funds; local revenues devoted to other than sanitary purposes. These sentences, gleaned from this report, constitute a terrible indictment, and it is not a subject of wonder that the death-rate of the country is 40 per 1,000, a rate which in all probability falls short of the reality.

Sanitary department has been organised, which, to quote from the report, is "charged with many and multifarious duties, dealing with the civil hospitals of the country, the annual outbreaks of typhus and small-pox, vaccination, the registration of births and deaths "(the actual work of which is entrusted to certain peripatetic officials belonging to the finance department), "the issue of permits for burial, the examination of medico-legal cases - grave and trivial - the examination as to the fitness for government service of all candidates, and the in validing and granting of sick leave to all Government employees."

The system of government is essentially bureaucratic, and sanitation to be of any real effect must be an affair of local rather than central energy. An attempt was made in the year under report to create municipalities, and provide for the satisfaction of local sanitary wants by local taxation, but the scheme, "owing to the refusal of certain powers," fell through. No doubt sanitary problems in Egypt are, for many reasons, hedged round with peculiar difficulties. At present the Nile is at once the source of the water supply and the main sewer of the country. This is an impossible combination, and full of peril to health

A scheme of drainage has been adopted for Cairo. Mosques have been prohibited by law from throwing their drainage into the Nile and its canals, and compelled to construct watertight cesspits for holding their sewage. The digging of brick pits which give rise to foul ponds (birkets) has been prohibited within one kilometer of dwellings. A law has been passed prescribing the enclosure of waste lands, thus preventing their pollution. The question of filling up filthy ponds (birkets) is under active consideration. A new ordinance for the registration of births and deaths has been enacted, but it is described as complicated, and practically unworkable. A decree for the removal of cemeteries from the neighbourhood of houses is under consideration. The towns of Assiout, Suez, and Ismailia have been partially supplied with filtered water. An intelligent interest in sanitation is being developed in the country.[9]

(b) Sanitation in England

The experience of rapid industrialisation, urbanisation, economic growth and environmental degradation in nineteenth century Great Britain was replicated in varying degrees in Europe, North America and other countries such as Australia. Rapid economic growth, Simon Szreter has argued, brings about a disruption in a society's structures of authority, social relations and ideologies. The result, in the second and third quarters of the nineteenth century in Britain, was, first, a period of political and administrative inaction in dealing with urban deterioration. Such inactivity was precipitated by the flight of the middle and upper-classes to the suburbs on the edge of cities. This residential segregation meant that "...the educated, literate élites no longer dared or cared to know their cities first hand", with the result that the inner suburbs became places of "deprivation, disease and death.[10]"

It is against this background of political and administrative inactivity in dealing with environmental degradation that the sanitary idea was brought to the attention of the middle and upper-classes by Edwin Chadwick and other sanitary reformers. In 1842, Chadwick published his famous *Report on the Sanitary Condition of the Labouring Population of Great Britain,* in which he argued that it was insanitation and poverty, rather than defects of character that inflicted the damage on the morals and habits of the working-class.[11] Hence, the guiding principle underlying the argument for sanitation reform was that the prevention of further environmental degradation was cheaper and more effective for society than continuing with expenditure on poor relief. Thus, sanitation reform became a political issue because it required state intervention to be implemented.

This inability of municipal governments to tackle environmental problems largely resulted from the rise of a middle-class electorate following the 1835 Municipal Reform Act which created representative local government based on property ownership. The elected councillors, in these reformed municipalities, generally represented the populations living in the crowded and polluted industrial and commercial areas of cities because, even though their wealth had increased, they were not able to afford housing in the new outer suburbs. Obstruction by the middle-class was evident in the rebellion against the 1848 Public Health Act. Even though the Act did not contain a system for a comprehensive national sewage plan or public health commissions, it did have local public health boards and established the Central Board of Health with Chadwick as its salaried commissioner. As such, boards were only compulsory in localities where the death rate exceeded 25 per 1,000 and could only be established elsewhere on petition by one-tenth of the ratepayers; it could at best only be a partial system. The outcome, then, was that this first attempt by the state in Britain to intervene in public health decision-making was, at best, tentative and easily opposed by local political interests.[12]

It was only from the late 1860s onwards that the public health/ sanitation movement became genuinely effective. This was marked by the Sanitation Act 1866 which made available to all localities the sanitary powers that had previously been restricted to the local boards of health under the 1848 Act. As a result of the technological and civil engineering advances made during the preceding decades, most parts of London had covered sewers by the 1870s and cesspools had been abolished. Between 1880 and 1891, urban authorities borrowed UK £ 7,738,522 for sewage works and UK£ 3,225,500 for waterworks and in the process, they transformed sewage and water supply services from being private concerns into public enterprises. The outcome was that the provision of such services became a true public good and so was extended to all citizens. As these new sanitary arrangements were so effective and successful, they soon became uncontroversial and just a part of everyday life.[13] The second consequence of rapid economic growth in nineteenth century Britain was the emergence of the "threat from below". These were the threats of the spread of disease and of social revolution. Whilst diseases such as typhoid, typhus and diarrhoea, for instance, were more devastating to the health of the working-class, it was cholera (especially during the four epidemics in 1831-2, 1848-9, 1853-4 and 1866), and its unpredictable nature which sometimes saw it spread to middleclass suburbs, which was so terribly feared. The spectre of cholera "...brought together in one grand obsession the preoccupations with the predicament and comportment of the poor, with the sanitary dangers these implied for the established citizens and with the need for urban sanitary and administrative reform.

The threat of social revolution was initially demonstrated by the 1848 revolutions which showed that the possibility existed of an uprising by the working-classes. The short lived Paris Commune of 1871 was perhaps more powerful as a symbol of what might come, rather than for what it achieved, and "...if it did not threaten the bourgeois order seriously, it frightened the wits out of it by its mere existence." In Britain, the growing public awareness of poverty, and the increasing middle-class concern that "...the masses would march onto the stage of politics, whether rulers liked it or not", eventually helped to force the state to include the working-class in the democratic process. The result was the enfranchisement of urban and rural workers which, along with the growing influence of the trade union movement, forced the state to mediate in the process of how the benefits of such rapid economic growth were being distributed within British society.

Sanitary reform in Britain was therefore the outcome of a change in the nature of the relationship between the state and society brought about by rapid economic development. The dominance of the middle-class, based on the exclusion of the working-class from political participation and a belief in the distributive justice of the market place - *laissez-faire* economics—was gradually replaced by the beginnings of the welfare state and the inclusion of the working-class. Against this background was advocacy for sanitary reform, conducted by medical practitioners and concerned citizens, the enlightened self-interest of the middle and upper-classes that recognised the interdependence of all groups within society, and the demands by trade unions for better working and living conditions. The success of the sanitation movement also brought about a "disciplining of human behaviour" as government intervention in daily lives introduced the restraints and controls that have become necessary to allow people to live in densely populated areas and, more generally, to keep a modern industrialised society functioning. Such values were predominantly middle-class, and so the "disciplining" of the working-class further lessened the perceived "threat from below" and brought about their inclusion in the political process.[14]

(c) United States Sanitation

Speaking about the urbanisation of the United States, it is observed that in 1790, 3.3 per cent of the population of the United States was urban. It was 33.1 per cent in 1900. The problems of the state and county become closely interwoven with those of the city. The city will no longer be merely an accumulation of human beings in a particular locality, with its local problems and influencing the state mainly in a financial way, but the city will have become the state. The individual needs fresh air, pure water, good food, safe shelter, and should have a clean body and something beautiful to look at. When he associates himself into a city his needs are not lessened, but emphasised. The growth of a city causes it to assume, willingly or no, corresponding obligations. The inhabitants must breathe, they must be fed and watered, its wastes must be got rid of, facilities for the safe coming and going of its people at all times must be provided, as well as protection from fire or other adventitious circumstances which concern the welfare of the citizens. The consideration of the air of cities involves not only the principles of ventilation, which will not be considered here, but the construction of the streets, means of transportation, the disposition of wastes, and the handling of the more unusual contaminants, which vary with conditions[15].

Even, the airport is believed to be the only one in the United States with a sanitarian on duty full time. Sanitation services were considered early in the planning of the airport by the Dade County Port Authority, established in 1945. Even before the opening of the airport, in December 1958, Donovan spent half of his time on the installation and operation of the aircraft catering kitchens and the facilities for storing, preparing, and serving food for employees and other patrons.[16]

Tracing the trajectory of evolution concern for sanitation, Americans living in the nineteenth century boasted of many aspects of their growing urban mosaic, hardly any talked in glowing terms about the cleanliness of their streets. The streets remained befouled with filth for the next several decades, despite New York's establishment in 1866 of the first metropolitan board of health in the country. When comprehensive reform attempts finally did come near the turn of the century, New York's street sanitation system served as a model for many other cities to follow and improve upon. However, one finds that street sanitation and related problems of garbage collection and sewerage systems seldom loomed large on nineteenth-century urban services priority lists. Since a majority of urban dwellers tended to take dirt, slime, and foul odor for granted, officials seldom found themselves under serious pressure to undertake corrective measures. Instead, they concentrated their activities and resources on areas that seemed of greater community concern-fire and police protection, school systems, water works, and gas lines. Moreover, the germ theory of disease was not generally accepted in the United States until relatively late in the century.

In the decades after the Civil War the continued rapid population growth of the American urban network, the appearance of a series of large metropolitan areas, and the conditions created by the rise of heavy industry helped to emphasise the need for more systematic corporate and technological responses in the street cleaning field. Moreover, the contributions of European scientists and sanitary engineers furthered acceptance in the United States of the germ theory of disease and of the need generally for better urban sanitation. Against a backdrop of increased public concern over recurring epidemics such as the serious yellow fever outbreaks in Memphis in the 1870s-reformers involved in the initial stages of the "Public Health movement" argued convincingly that municipalities must allot more money than previously in order to obtain pure water supplies, comprehensive systems of sewerage, and cleaner thoroughfares.[17] Consequently, when knowledgable and respected men with impressive medical credentials diagnosed cholera, yellow fever, typhoid, and smallpox as "Scourges of God" intended to punish the wicked, or as products of "swamp vapours" and "vitiated atmosphere," or as a consequence of earthquakes and comets, or as natural results of the odors given off by Irish ditch diggers, only the most squeamish of people worried much about streets clogged with excrement, garbage, or dead animals. Anti-contagionists, of course, had long claimed that a casual connection existed between disease and odors from putrefying filth. But, while the work in the 1840s of Edwin Chadwick and other British sanitary authorities buttressed conclusions about the supposed sinister nature of deleterious atmospheric emanations called miasmas, the solution, to most American experts, involved planting trees rather than cleaning streets. Trees would serve as "lungs" or as "ventilators" designed to absorb the pernicious exhalations floating in the air. A physician writing in 1849 explained, "If cities must exist let many and large spaces be devoted to parks, and let the streets on each side of the way be lined with trees with two or three trees to every building, so that the people may be supplied with electricity and oxygen in abundance from nature's own laboratory.[18]

In the 1890's a reform mayor attempted to correct matters by appointing as sanitation commissioner, George Waring, Jr., a nationally known reformer in the area of urban health.[19] Waring, who had a flamboyant personality and a knack of obtaining considerable publicity for his undertakings, was a self-taught sanitary engineer. An occasional scientific farmer, a former army recruiter, and an author of horse stories, he had been drawn into urban sanitation after writing a series of books telling farm girls how to avoid the pitfalls of urban life. In the 1870s he had achieved considerable fame as an expert on systems of sewerage, and he edited the volumes on urban services in the 1880 census. An "anti-contagionist," he claimed "sewer gas" caused disease, although he preached that the only way to prevent epidemics was through great urban sanitation projects.

Fortunately, in the first half of the nineteenth century few cities maintained paid personnel to clean streets. Responsibility rested with residents whose homes abutted on a street, with able-bodied men chosen for specific periods off the tax rolls, and with contracted scavengers. The household system did not work effectively. A New Yorker reminiscing about local conditions in the 1830s wrote: "There was a law requiring each household as often, we believe, as once a week to sweep before his own door; not only the sidewalks, but also half way across the street, where his opposite neighbour was to meet him. The dirt, swept in heaps, was to be carried away by the carts. The dirt, swept in heaps, was to be carried away by the carts. We well remember that the householders swept as often as they pleased; and for the matter of being carried away, the dirt often remained in heaps for several days; or rather the heaps were trodden and scattered about again; and required to be swept and collected anew.[20] In theory, scavengers should have been more effective. Working in teams of several men they watered-down a street, swept loose material into the gutters, and shoveled the refuse into horse-drawn carts. The scavengers then hauled the resulting slime and smudge to the nearest dumping ground.[21]

Most Americans considered the accumulation of manure an unavoidable consequence of urban living, but believed that pigs, by virtue of certain eating habits, served as a cheap answer to the problem of collecting garbage.......A decade later, Charles Dickens wrote perceptively a-bout the characteristics of the hogs of New York City: "They are the city scavengers, these pigs, ugly brutes they are; having for the most part scanty, brown backs, like the lids of old horse-hair trunks; spotted with unwholesome black blotches. They have long, gaunt legs, too, and such peaked snouts, that if one of them could be persuaded to sit for his profile, nobody would recognise it for a pig's likeness.... During the 1850's and 1860's pigs gradually disappeared from the nation's streets, with changing conceptions of sanitation and bad publicity provided by European travellers stimulating their removal. Even so, many people mourned their passing, arguing that streets never again were as clean as they had been.

Regrettably, the growing interest did not lead automatically to clean streets. Regular garbage collection, which in many places filled the void caused by the removal of the pigs, represented a major advance in municipal sanitation. This was especially true when coupled with a more energetic enforcement of ordinances prohibiting the dumping of garbage in streets and providing for the prompt removal of dead animals, but existing levels of technology imposed restrictions on further dramatic progress. In an age in which the nation was in the verge of the industrial revolution the main thrusts of American science and technology were in other directions. Only a few Universities offered formal courses in aspects of sanitation, and most early sanitary engineers were self-taught. Other professions attracted the best available engineers, and firms selling equipment for municipal cleansing purposes did almost no research and development. The failure to perfect adequate street-sweeping machines pointed up the frustrating results of the low level of the technological effort.[22]

(d) Japan Sanitation

The sudden increase in Japan's urban population in the century and a half from the 158os to the mid-7000s may well have had no parallel in world history prior to industrialisation. Edo, re-named Tokyo in 1868, was a cluster of fishing villages around a castle in 1590, but, during the eighteenth century, it is readily acknowledged to have been one of the largest, if not the largest, city in the world. Even by I700, Edo was certainly larger than any European city, including London at 575,000, and rivaled or exceeded in population the largest of the Chinese cities at the time, Peking.

To support a metropolitan population, food and other daily necessities must be adequately supplied, and demands for housing, water, transportation, a monetary system, and numerous other requirements must be met. Even if all other requirements are satisfied, however, if sanitation is inadequate, one would not expect the population of a city to reach a million, much less be maintained at this figure over centuries. Yet Edo, which lacked modern water supply and sewage systems, and which relied primarily on manpower or boats to carry away garbage, refuse, and other human wastes, is estimated to have had a population in the range of a million from about 1700 on.

Although Edo was strategically situated, much of it was on low, marshy ground near the sea. The potable water was originally obtained from ponds and underground springs, but wells had to be deep because of the depth of the aquifer. As early as 1590, the first system constructed, the Kanda system, drew its water from the Inokashira spring east of the city. Water was carried to the city limits mainly in exposed aqueducts, and then in underground aqueducts or wooden pipes within the city. The Kanda system was over forty-one miles in length and had 3,663 subsidiary ducts which drew water from the main source and distributed it to various parts of the city.[23]

The methods developed for disposing of various kinds of wastes in both Edo and Osaka can be documented through regulations, contracts, and records of challenges or conflicts. The number and variety of the sources indicate that from the mid-seventeenth century on, waste disposal was a major concern for urban administrations. Osaka provides the best example of how different sewage disposal was in Japan, in contrast to Western nations, whereas Edo illustrates how complex waste disposal in a pre-modern Japanese metropolis was and how the problems were managed.[24]

The most important difference between waste disposal in Japan and in the West was that human excreta were not regarded as something that one paid to have removed, but rather as a product with a positive economic value. The night soil of Japanese cities and Chinese as well - was long used as fertiliser. With the growth of Japan's population, the limitation of the amount of arable land and the increasingly intensified use of land to feed the growing population, combined with the relative scarcity of animal wastes and other fertilisers, meant that human waste had a value as fertiliser that far exceeded its value in the West. Long before Edo was even established, Osaka's night soil was used as fertiliser for the surrounding farm villages. Most of it was collected, loaded onto ships, and distributed to nearby farm areas. The huge volume brought to the wharves resulted in such an unpleasant odor that there were complaints. In the Tokugawa period, the magistrates deliberated upon these complaints but concluded that "it was unavoidable for the manure boats to come into the wharves used by the tea and other ships.[25]

In Osaka, by the mid-eighteenth century, night soil was so clearly an economic good that ownership and monopoly/monopsony rights were assigned, the formation of officially recognised associations and guilds was permitted, and the price was determined by these organisations. The price was so high that the poorer farmers had difficulty in obtaining sufficient fertiliser, and incidents of theft began to appear in the records, despite the fact that going to prison if discovered was a real risk. In Edo, judging from official records, disputes over night soil seem not to have been the problem that they were in Osaka, but the government did have to step in to handle problems of orderly waste disposal. Edo's waste, other than night soil, can be divided into four major types: (1) household waste, probably mostly kitchen garbage; (2) trash discarded along the roads and in the waste water drains; (3) junk floating in waterways-moats, rivers, and the harbour; and (4) waste from fires. In addition, Edo had the problem of disposing of its waste water since its ample water supply meant that enormous quantities of water had to be discarded somewhere.[26] Regulations regarding waste began to appear in Edo during the mid-seventeenth century. The focus at this time was not waste collection per se, but the growing problem of keeping the streets, open areas, and drainage ditches free from rubbish. This was clearly viewed as a problem within the purview of city government. At the same time, problems relating to the disposal of night soil came to the attention of the authorities. In 1648, city regulations required small huts and toilets along the banks of rivers to be torn down. The repeated issuance of this and other regulations over the next half century indicates that Edo residents must have been slow to comply with the new, more sanitary arrangements for waste disposal.

The first regulations about night soil appeared; the disposal of other forms of waste was also specified. By 1655, the people of Edo were ordered to dispose of their garbage and rubbish on the island of Eitai in Edo Bay, rather than just dump it in the rivers. During the decade from 1655 to 1665, basic disposal policies were gradually put into effect: collection points for refuse collection were established in each ward; transport was contracted to specific jobbers; and the wards were ordered to bear the costs. From the ward collection points, the rubbish was loaded onto boats and transported to Eitai Island. Although the original purpose of these measures was to keep the river channels open for commerce and traffic, they resulted in the establishment of an official dump for the city located outside city limits. These policies remained in effect for the next two centuries.

Edo and Osaka were not alone among Japanese cities in their emphasis on the proper disposal of waste material and the necessity of keeping streets and waterways clean and open. Even the main streets in most castle towns were relatively narrow, about twenty-four feet wide, but they were "extremely well maintained and immaculately clean." The regulations regarding the maintenance of public roads were detailed and infractions were reported. In Tottori, for example, streets had to be cleared and then sprayed with water (which probably reduced the incidence of respiratory disease).

Metropolitan sanitation in Japan from the mid-seventeenth through the mid-nineteenth centuries was almost certainly better than in the West in terms of quality and quantity of the water supply and in terms of waste disposal, resulting in a healthier environment for urban populations as measured by the size of the population and mortality rates. But Japanese city life was also more sanitary than that in the West because of various customs concerning hygiene, food, and drink, and because of a lack of domestic animals. Finally, the government played a major role in setting and maintaining standards of sanitation in the cities.[27]

(III) Sanitation Management—A Cross-cultural Analysis

Background

It is difficult to assess the sanitation and hygiene standards of the populace in pre-modern times, but some information exists for elites, making possible a comparative evaluation for various nations. Although the sanitary conditions and the customs regarding personal hygiene of the elite cannot be considered representative of a society as a whole, they are indicative of what one would expect the highest standard to be. For example, in seventeenth and eighteenth-century France, "the palaces of the Louvre, Vincennes or Fountainebleau in places became mere latrines." A house steward wrote: "In many places in the courtyard, in the upper passages, behind the doors and almost everywhere, one can see a thousand heaps of ordure; one can smell a thousand unbearable stenches caused by the necessities of nature which everybody discharges there daily.

By the mid-nineteenth century, conditions in France were no longer so primitive, but the problems with sewage and contamination of the water supply indicated that major sanitation problems remained. In mid-nineteenth century Britain, even royalty was not immune from the effects of inadequate sewage disposal. Prince Albert, Queen Victoria's consort, is thought to have died of typhoid fever contracted from faulty drains.

Japan from the late sixteenth into the early seventeenth century, noted that the Japanese provide their guests with very clean privies set apart in an unfrequented place far from the rooms. . . . The interior of the privies is kept extremely clean and a perfume-pan and new paper cut for use are placed there. The privy is always clean without any bad smell, for when the guests depart the man in charge cleans it out if necessary and strews clean sand so that place is left as if it had never been used. A ewer of clean water and other things needed for washing the hands are found nearby, for it is an invariable custom of both nobles and commoners to wash their hands every time after using the privy for their major and minor necessities.

In Japan in the 1870s in the privies in the "better class of private homes," an American visitor found "less annoyance and infinitely less danger . . . than are experienced in many houses of the wealthy in our great cities." His description of the privies is similar to Rodrigues' in the sixteenth century, except that attendants did not clean out the receptacle after every use, but rather it "was emptied every few days by men who have their regular routes." Morse was taken not only by the cleanliness of Japanese toilets, but also by the amount of artful carpentry work that decorated them in homes that he visited toilet facilities of the elite but those in the houses that he visited during his extensive stays in Japan.

Moreover, the Japanese had strong notions about what was dirty and clean, many of which can be traced back to the Japanese native religion of Shinto and its concepts of pollution. Much of the pollution in Shinto is ritualistic, but what is considered polluting and what is purifying are related to contamination and cleanliness. Anything to do with blood, death, and illness such as childbearing, menstruation, contact with a sick or dying person, and funerals—is considered unclean, and people used to be prohibited from participating in religious rituals, mixing with other people, and even returning home from a funeral without being purified. Salt, water, and fire were all considered purifying agents and were used both to perform religious rituals and to clean and purify. This emphasis on purification is not unique to Japan; it can be found throughout Asia, but it is particularly strong in Japan and has persisted into modern times.

Although the demographic statistics available for Japan and Europe indicate a similarity in the figures, by the nineteenth century Western European nations had available modern technology and by 1850 were well into the process of industrialisation with its concomitant rising standard of living. Japan, however, did not begin to use any modern technology until nearly the end of the century. Given the high proportion of Japanese who lived in cities, had sanitation been poor and the level of living low, this combination would have been reflected in high rates of morbidity and mortality. In fact, Japan seems to have been surprisingly free from the devastating effects of epidemics. The plague never reached Japan, and cholera came only in the nineteenth century when it spread throughout the world. Intestinal worms and enteric infections—those that enter through the mouth and are spread through contamination of food and water—tended to be localised and to appear in endemic rather than epidemic form. Based upon above facts, one does infer that the level of sanitation was higher in Japanese cities than in Western ones during the same period. Not only was Japan able to provide better water and disposal systems, but Japanese customs led to better hygiene and sanitation than did Western modes of behaviour.[28]

(a) Environmental Sanitation in the British Colonies

During the latter part of the nineteenth century, medical research established for the first time the relationship between crowded, filthy environments and ill-health stimulating the development of a powerful public health movement improving urban living conditions. The impact of this public health movement was manifest not only in Europe but also in the colonies. The motives and methods of public health measures in the colonies differed significantly from those in Europe. In Europe, massive public works significantly improved the health and life expectancy of the broad masses. In the colonies, the primary goal was to protect the health of colonial officials and troops from the alleged threat to health of native communities. Racial segregation achieved the same objective for Europeans in the colonies as public works in Europe. Meanwhile, the indigenous populations were left to live essentially as before.[29]

The model for British habitation in the tropical colonies was developed in India (King, 1976).[30] There, the health of British troops and officials was protected by constructing low-density communities on carefully-selected high, well-drained sites. European cantonments and civil stations were well-removed from indigenous settlements, from which they were separated by a building-free zone (*cordon sanitaire*). Indian troops, clerks and servants residing in these stations were housed a substantial distance from the British. This Indian model of segregation cum sanitation was used in Africa to define the form of new urban centres and to redefine the form of previously-existing cities.

In Northern Rhodesia, for example, sanitation was the official rationale for several measures to control the migration of Africans to the cities, and to ensure that Africans resident there would be a compliant, captive labour force. Africans were prevented from growing crops in the cities, ostensibly as a malaria control measure. This, together with the prohibition on health grounds of petty trading meant that urban Africans were entirely dependent on European wages. The requirement that all African workers be housed by their employers provided a further powerful check on migration to the cities, and on the location of Africans dwelling in the city.

In Cape Town and Port Elizabeth, South Africa, officials seized upon epidemics of bubonic plague at the turn of the century as a pretext for the wholesale forced relocation of Blacks and Coloureds from their inner-city homes to remote barren sites outside the city (Swanson, 1977).[31] Thus, apartheid in these formerly-integrated cities started with the labelling of non-whites as a threat to the health of whites. In Johannesburg, the 'sanitation imperative' gave the city council its expressed rationale for a protracted fight to suppress the African informal sector. Rogerson (1983) has documented this process with particular reference to the struggle of independent food sellers ('coffee cart' operators) for survival against a city council determined to eliminate them.[32]

Northern Nigeria, at the time of the colonial occupation, had several substantial cities and, for the most part, a nuclear settlement pattern. European settlements were grafted onto these existing cities, the new capital city of Kaduna being the major exception. The sanitation problem was seen to be the effective isolation of these European settlements from the allegedly unhealthy environments of African settlements. While the colonial control of sanitation in the indigenous cities was indirect and confined to the promotion of certain programmes of particular interest to Europeans, sanitation in European townships was both directly controlled and comprehensive in scope, with the Resident initiating programmes recommended by the Chief Medical Officers. Regulations for the organisation of European townships were contained in a series of ordinances, the most important of which were as follows (Mohammed, 1979): (a) The Cantonment Ordinance, 1904.[33] (b) Instruction of Political and other Officers, 1906. (c) The Township and Public Health Ordinance, 1917. (d) The Town Planning Memoranda, 1926 and 1927[34]

The complex meanings of 'environmental sanitation' encompassing both its overt and covert meanings have been labelled the 'sanitation syndrome'. Swanson (1977) has described the 'sanitation syndrome' as a powerful metaphor, since any reference to sanitation as a means of protecting people's health served to legitimate draconian measures against those deemed to be a threat to health. The seeming righteousness of the cause permitted other projects having little, if anything, to do with public health to be undertaken in the name of environmental sanitation. A related characteristic of the 'sanitation syndrome' is the central role of the bourgeoisie, acting through medical officers of health, in defining sanitary problems and solutions, and in turn reaping the benefits of sanitation initiatives.

European townships were to be separated from African settlements by a cordon sanitaire of at least 350 yards, later increased to 410 yards. No building was allowed within this zone. The *cordon sanitaire* was said to be necessary to keep out fever-carrying mosquitoes originating in the indigenous city and to minimise the risk of fires. Moreover, it was said to protect Europeans from drumming and similar disturbances emanating from African quarters! (Lugard, 1970 quoted in Mohammed, 1979). British officials, non-official expatriates and Nigerians resident within the townships were to live in separate clusters. European houses were to be situated on large lots which provided privacy but sufficient space to isolate servant's quarters and stables at the back of compounds. Separate provision was made for functional establishments such as churches, hospitals and recreational facilities for Europeans.

(b) South Asian People's Perspective on Sanitation[35]

The first South Asia Conference on Sanitation (SACOSAN) in Dhaka in 2003 gave a call for 'people-centred, community-led, gender-sensitive and demand-driven sanitation', firmly locating the people at the centre of action.[36] Understanding and creating demand and encouraging wider and sustained community participation were clearly identified as the critical route to success. Seven years and three SACOSANs later, where do the people of South Asia—especially its poor and marginalised one billion without access to sanitation stand?[37] In particular, what are the people's perspectives regarding sanitation and hygiene? What is their understanding of the concept, the urgency of their needs, their ability and capacity to access facilities, and most of all their observations about the extent and nature of the support they receive from the state and civil society?

The multi-country review is a joint initiative of Freshwater Action Network South Asia (FANSA), WaterAid and the Water Supply and Sanitation Collaborative Council (WSSCC). These institutions and networks have formed a coalition to engage with SACOSAN and collectively advocate for faster and more effective improvements in the situation across the region. This synthesis review draws its thematic messages from separate studies on people's perspectives from Bangladesh, India, Nepal, Pakistan and Sri Lanka.

The major perspective in which sanitation was understood in the South Asian countries was as follows:

(i) A Matter of Dignity : Understanding of sanitation was closely related to open defecation and the need for toilets, especially in crowded urban settlements. In fact, an open defecation-free environment and use of toilets were repeatedly identified with sanitation across all countries. Whether recalling exposure to a sanitation intervention or not, almost all women and most male respondents reported feeling acutely embarrassed in front of neighbours as well as outsiders in the absence of a private toilet. Privacy and dignity are especially important to women.

Dignity, apart from practical aspects of convenience, was also a consideration for differently-abled people. For instance, Jeevan Paudel from Ilam and Dhan Prasad Subedi from Dhading, Nepal, are differently-abled people whose lives have been dignified by sanitation interventions in their settlements. They said that sanitation is an essential component of life that affects the healthy environment of any community. Availability of safe water was seen as essential to sustain sanitation services.

The safety of men, women and children was often found to be compromised by poor sanitation. Open fields—especially in the night or during the rainy season—or railway tracks were described as unsafe and instances of people losing their limbs, or even their lives and of women being molested were frequently reported.

(ii) Impact on Health, Education and Poverty: Many people across all the countries believed that keeping one's body and environment clean, leading a healthy life and protecting oneself from disease constitute sanitation and hygiene. Those who had a clear understanding of hygiene, perceived that, living in an unhygienic environment led to all kinds of diseases. They said that following simple hygiene practices, like washing hands before meals or cooking food, keeping the drinking water covered and so on, would eliminate many of the diseases. They were clear that it would therefore also contribute towards reducing poverty.

(iii) Sanitation as a 'right': Although notions of sanitation as a 'right' were not always clear in many countries, most people thought that it was important and it meant that the government was responsible to provide adequate facilities and services to the people. By and large, communities now understand that using hygienic latrines, safe drinking water and improved hygiene practices are important components of sanitation that keep them healthy and free from disease burdens. Keeping the surrounding environment clean, disposing of solid waste safely, and disposing of household and kitchen wastewater safely through a drainage system are also seen as integral parts of sanitation.

What is a 'successful' sanitation programme?

Communities in Pakistan defined a 'successful' sanitation programme as having:

- An appropriate external catalyst for sanitation, hygiene promotion and behaviour change.
- An inclusive approach that reaches out to marginalised communities and individuals.
- Responsive local leadership that understands the advantages of sanitation for all inhabitants.
- Involvement of local people from the start—for example, a weekly meeting in the centre of the village to plan and decide future steps.
- Clear responsibilities, including maintenance.
- Community acceptance and ownership of the programme.
- Active participation of women in decision-making at all stages from design to implementation and monitoring.
- A process that is and remains accountable to communities.

- Regular follow up by the programme promoters.

(IV) Evolution of Sanitation in India

(a) Historical Background

Social scientists came to argue that colonial rule induced an unprecedented decline in mortality rates in densely populated regions of the colonial world, igniting a population boom.[38] Notestein and his Princeton colleague Kingsley Davis saw the decline of mortality as the first of two transitions in demographic history. In brief, they proposed a three-phased process of population change. In the first, pre-modern stage, people produced many children, but they also died rapidly, leading to long-term stability in population size. But with the advance of "the whole process of modernisation," as Notestein put it; a decline in mortality led to a transitional population boom. Indirect or direct Western influence in the form of colonialism enabled this decline in the death rate through improved governance and the transmission of medical and communication technologies. Fertility remained high, however, because it was rooted in a culture resistant to change. As transitional societies moved further along the path of modernisation, Notestein and Davis predicted, they would repeat the experience of Europe and its settler colonies. Demographic stability would then return under the modern stage of low fertility and low mortality.[39]

In India, from the establishment of the census in the 1870s until the 1920s, mortality was egregiously high, and population grew at only .4 per cent a year. This resulted in part from the transmission of disease linked to irrigation projects and the expansion of transport systems under colonial rule, in addition to factors like poor living standards and ineffective village sanitation. Historical demographers estimate high death rates in the period before the census as a result of recurrent famines and epidemics

The model of India has long played a central role in the shaping of demographic thought.[40] Several prominent theorists of population maintained close connections with the British colonial project there. Malthus himself taught colonial bureaucrats as a professor of political economy at the East India Company College in Haileybury. Not only a proverbial land of famine, since the early nineteenth century India was seen as a major world exporter of disease, another of Malthus' principal "positive checks."[41]

In this period, attitudes towards disease were distant from those that would reign in the era of development. In the late eighteenth and early nineteenth centuries, British writers tended to associate the colonial encounter with the spread of mortality from disease, not its amelioration. European medical observers in India and elsewhere made sense of the miserable health conditions of Europeans—and often the cultural inferiority of Indians—based on the assumption that climate was a fundamental determinant of human health and behaviour. The significance they attributed to geographic differences encouraged European medical experts to draw upon indigenous medical practices to facilitate the assimilation of Europeans to local climatic conditions.[42]

If Britain and its colonies were basically unalike, different places requiring the adoption of different medical principles, then the two could not so simply occupy succeeding moments in the same story of development. But increasingly over the course of the nineteenth century, environmentalist understandings of disease, while persisting to some degree, came into disrepute. Within institutions of sanitary improvement, administrators tended to emphasise the significance of social practices, which could be learned through instruction, in encouraging the spread or suppression of disease.[43] This revised way of thinking made it possible to imagine the sanitary states of India and England as different moments on a common continuum.

In 1859, at the instigation of Florence Nightingale, the British colonial government established the investigatory Royal Commission on the State of the Army, which created a set of foundational institutions for sanitary improvement in India. The Commission's members readily admitted that "Apart therefore from the question of humanity, the introduction of an efficient system of hygiène in India is of essential importance to the interests of the empire.[44]"

The Royal Commission insisted that the imperial quandary of army mortality could be solved, sharply challenging the attitude of climatic determinism. They drew attention to the fact that mortality rates varied highly among different social groups. Ordinary soldiers fared the worst, while European civilians were the best off, and army officers stood in between. Meanwhile, native troops experienced mortality rates nearly equal to those of English civil servants when they lived in their own homes, but suffered from disease when stationed elsewhere. They argued that only differences in social habits and living conditions—not skin colour or a lack of physical and cultural adaptation to the environment—could explain the data. "It is natural to us to seek a scape-goat for every neglect, and climate has been made to play this part ever since we set foot in India..." as Florence Nightingale put it in her praise of the report. "One most important result of the inquiry of the Royal Commission has been to destroy this bugbear...."

Practically speaking, the colonial state would not intervene aggressively in civilian sanitary practices until the end of the nineteenth century, with the severe response to the plague epidemic of 1896–1897. What the Royal Commission did do was establish a system of civilian data collection within the provinces. Recognising that poor hygiene among civilians affected the health of the soldiers who necessarily interacted with them, the Royal Commission established a system of provincial sanitary commissions. Staffed by members of the Indian Medical Service, the commissions, which held only advisory powers, conducted regular tours and collected vital statistics for the provinces[45]

The model of the army revealed that India's sanitary future did not have to diverge from that of England, as Colonel Henry Yule argued in an 1888 report to Government of India. He called for the restructuring of the country's ineffective system of public health, and as a member of the Council of India who had sat for several years on the ASC, Yule commanded the confidence of the secretary of state.

In his 1891 census report, J. A. Baines suggested that India was in a period of demographic "probation." He projected a decline in mortality, noting that medical dispensaries were "growing in popular favour against the rivalry of the herbalist and exorciser," and that advances were being made as a result of the colonial administration's efforts to vaccinate against smallpox, prevent the spread of cholera, and prohibit religious gatherings where disease frequently spread. On the other hand, Baines observed, the persistence of longstanding attitudes towards marriage suggested that fertility rates would not decline soon. "But can there be any doubt as to the result towards which all these provisions tend?" he asked rhetorically. The answer of course was massive population growth.[46]

(b) Sanitary Measures and Their Effects[47]

According to Guha (1993), Europeans in India had traditionally died in large numbers, chiefly from disease; of those in Bombay in 1672. This was not vastly exaggerated: only one in four of the East India Company's military cadets between 1770 and 1834 finally returned to England. The rank and file probably died in similar proportion: it seems to have been viewed as the inevitable cost of Empire.

A Royal Commission on the Health of the Army was then sitting, and its *Report*, presented in 1863 did much to swell the tide of sanitary reform. Disease at that time was believed to originate either in hereditary taints, or in the ingestion of various poisons that generally disseminated themselves as miasmata arising out of decaying organic matter, or unclean human bodies. Sanitation, therefore, meant the removal of filth and refuse, the purification of water, and the provision of ample ventilation in all dwelling places, so as to dilute the effects of lingering miasmata. Sexually transmitted diseases (STD) were sought to be checked by giving Cantonment Magistrates the power to regulate prostitution, as well as to maintain the sanitary state of the area under their charge.

The public-health measures of this period were measures of environmental sanitation, aimed at creating little islands of purity in the miasmatic landscape of India in order to protect the health of both soldiers and administratively important civilians. This objective had largely been achieved by the 1880s, and during the early twentieth century Ronald Ross observed that 'British officials and troops are nearly always housed in separate locations, commonly called cantonments, so that they are frequently spared infection derived from neighbouring crowded native quarters.[48]

Special attention was paid to the water supply, and great efforts were made to ensure its purity, though before the 1890s there was no sound criterion for determining potability. Faeces and urine were mixed (from the 1870s) with dry earth and then carted away and buried. During the first years of the present century incineration began to be adopted for night-soil disposal; flush latrines and sewer lines then came into use commonly discharging into a local river or any other suitable drain).

Ignorance of the exact aetiology of infectious disease thus led medical authorities into a campaign of environmental sanitation. Their curative resources were certainly limited. On the whole, then, it seems reasonable to suggest that improvements in health, down to the beginning of the twentieth century, were almost exclusively due to better prophylaxis resulting from environmental hygiene, rather than to any other cause.[49]

It is to be emphasised that the benefits of the sanitation movement had a very limited impact on the population as a whole in nineteenth century India. Whilst the colonial government did implement some of these ideas when attempting to control cholera epidemics, most of the expenditure went on military sanitation and protecting the health of government personnel. That is, "...the colonial régime built the unequal treatment of the native and colonial areas into the sanitation system itself: spatial domination was the everyday metaphor for colonial domination." Due to fiscal conservatism, municipalities were unable to provide the funds for a new sanitation system based on the construction of sewers and labour saving technologies. Instead, the colonial government intensified the use of labour in the manual scavenging of night soil and refuse removal, despite calls for the abolition of such practices.

When the obvious inefficiencies of such a system were highlighted, colonial officials blamed the work practices of the scavengers.[50] Such unequal treatment in the provision of sanitation has continued in independent India.

There are three factors that have prevented a successful sanitation movement being replicated in India. First, as in nineteenth century Britain, the political and administrative inability of local government to deal with the problems associated with unplanned and haphazard urban growth is a factor to be noted. Such inability, along with corruption and inefficiency, has in some circumstances almost reduced urban local government to a position of irrelevance. These deteriorating urban conditions have precipitated a flight of the growing middle-class to new suburbs - which often have self-contained apartments and segregated living. The outcome, to date, is that the middle-class has yet to show any real interest in, or responsibility for, pressuring governments to improve environmental conditions.

The second factor is the antithesis of the British situation—there is an absence of a "threat from below". Trade unions in India have predominantly represented only the interests of white collar professional workers and, at most, have covered only formal sector employees who comprise about 8 per cent of the workforce.

Thirdly, the very developments in modern medicine and civil engineering that contributed to the success of the sanitation/public health movement in nineteenth century Britain have enabled the middle-class to largely ignore environmental problems and the resulting diseases. The use of antibiotics and insecticides have generally contained potential epidemics in slum areas, and hence not generated a mutual awareness among the middle-class that it would be in the interests of the whole of society if the poor were provided with decent living conditions.

In 1914, important memorandum was addressed by the Government of India to local government on the subject of sanitary administration and work. At a meeting of the East India Association an interesting paper was read by Colonel W.G. King, CLE. Colonel

King's devoted and fruitful work in the promotion of scientific and practical sanitation in the Madras Presidency entitles his views to respect; and, although exception may be taken to some of his contentions, the motive and aim of his address are undoubtedly commendable and salutary. While fully acknowledging that, through the advice and agency of the Indian Medical Service, a great reduction of sickness and mortality has taken place in communities under organised sanitary control, he does not consider the position of sanitation in India to be sound or promising. He asserts that the policy of the Government of India is one of inhibition and restraint as regards to sanitation. It is also emphasised that the Indian women are very conservative of religious and social customs. Many of these are excellent, others objectionable, and as several speakers remarked and the Indian Government has laid down, sanitary reform must recognise and preserve the former and amend the latter; and the strong hold of usage on native life and, the amenability to law of the people constitute powerful aids to sanitary amelioration. In fact, sanitation demands not contraction and specialisation, but expansion and generalisation; and in any community sanitary success must always depend largely on the concurrence and assistance of its members, and sanitary effort must be applied through the organisations established for communal purposes. At the same time the employment of a specially educated and trained executive is absolutely necessary for special sanitary work.[51]

Writing on sanitation and sweepers in colonial Delhi, Vijay Prashad broadly concurs with a constructivist stance, arguing that: ... the logic of capital during colonial rule produced a municipal sanitation regime which relied upon the control over the labour of manual sweepers mediated through jobbers, overseers and contractors. Far from being the embodiment of "tradition", the sweepers since colonial India bear on their bodies the marks of capital ... demonstrating the integral relation between the logic of capital and barbaric colonial rule (Prashad[52], 1995:1).[52]

In India, the severity of sanitation problem has a long history. In 1935 British troops suffered due to sanitation related diseases (Ramasubban, 1982).[53] Bhore (1944) and Environmental Hygiene Committee (1948) recommended better sanitation services and this became a blueprint to make budgetary allocation during the First Five Year Plan (1951-56). But the sector again came into limelight 20 years later, during the emergency 1975, and latrine construction was given priority.

The Fifth Five Year Plan endorsed priority to sanitation by stating that, "the elimination of abject poverty will not be attained as a corollary to certain acceleration in the rate of growth of the economy alone, but improvements in drinking water and environmental sanitation have direct correlation with levels of living". Thus, providing public health facilities became part of poverty alleviation programme. This is, in fact an eye opener for the policies regarding sanitation services.

In 1980 rural India was said to have a sanitation coverage rate of 1 per cent. In 1986 a Technology Advisory Group (TAG) comprising representatives from the Indian Government, UNDP, UNICEF and the World Bank, recommended one standard design for rural and urban on-site sanitation, the double vault pour flush latrine. The Centrally-Sponsored Rural Sanitation Programme provided 100 per cent subsidy for this latrine for Scheduled Castes, Scheduled Tribes and landless labourers. Subsidies for other user groups were decided by the respective states. Achievements in coverage and use were low. The cost of the double vault permanent model was relatively high and the focus was on construction, with little attention given to demand creation, loan repayment where applicable, or to user participation in such matters as latrine siting, superstructure design or future maintenance needs. With this programme rural sanitation coverage increased to four per cent in 1988, not commensurate to the plan objectives.

In 1992, following a National Seminar on Rural Sanitation, the Government launched a new strategy. Subsidies for households below the poverty line were reduced to 80 per cent and the policy stressed participation of householders in the choice of four latrine options with different cost levels. It also directed implementing agencies, both government and nongovernmental organisations, to use 10 per cent of the government funds for promotion and hygiene education. Implementation remained driven by the implementing agencies. This changed in the policy guidelines of 2001 when the programme moved to a 'Total Sanitation Campaign' with an emphasis on informing and educating rural households without sanitation, about the importance of having and using sanitary latrines. Interested households could apply for a subsidy and implementing agencies could supply the required material through designated outlets such as various government departments, Non-Governmental Organisations (NGOs) and (Community Based Organisations) CBOs, district water and sanitation missions etc. Community Governments (Panchayats) can also carry out the programme in their communities, together with local committees.

The Total Sanitation Campaign is part of the Sector Reforms Project introduced in April 1999 to make rural water supply and sanitation more sustainable. It is piloted in 200 districts. Limitations on success were due to absence of guidance and training opportunities and from a lack of appropriate expertise in some implementing organisations, particularly in knowledge of current gender and poverty-sensitive promotion and participation strategies.[54]

(c) Sanitation Status in India

As per *Census* 2001, only 36 per cent of households had access to some form of sanitation; worse, for rural India the figure is as low as 22 per cent. During the World Summit on Sustainable Development, a goal had been set up to reduce the uncovered population by 50 per cent by the year 2015. India declared to achieve the goal by 2007 and the government launched the Total Sanitation Campaign (TSC) in 1999. TSC as a part of reform principles was restructured from the earlier Central Rural Sanitation Programme (CRSP), which could not make much headway.

The TSC is designed as a comprehensive programme with an aim to improve sanitation facilities in rural areas and eradicate the practice of open defecation. The programme, aimed to encourage cost effective and appropriate technology in sanitation, requires a large-scale social mobilisation in which the district is taken as a unit for implementation. Zila Panchayat or alternatively the District Water and Sanitation Mission (DWSM) are the implementing agency for TSC.

The key intervention areas are Individual Household Latrines (IHHL), School Sanitation and Hygiene Education (SSHE), Community Sanitary Complex, Anganwadi toilets supported by Rural Sanitary Marts (RSMs) and Production Centres (PCs). However, the start-up activities and IEC are equally important components that provide the base for implementing the project.

(i) Toilet Coverage

Census 2001 indicates that of the 200 million dwelling units across the country, only some 40 million dwelling units have a toilet inside the house. Only 61 per cent households in urban areas and 17 per cent households in rural areas have access to improved sanitation. While households having bathroom facility within the house is abysmally low in rural areas and urban areas in the poor performing states, the position in respect of connectivity for waste water outlet is even more alarming. While closed drainage is available in the urban areas at least in the developed states, a large per centage of bathrooms across all states in the country have no drainage system particularly in the rural areas. This per centage is as high as 73.88 in Odisha, 72.69

in Assam and 71.81 in Chhattisgarh. The non-availability of toilets within the house is high in Bihar (71.94 per cent), Chhattisgarh (76.78 per cent) and in Jharkhand (73.03 per cent). In urban areas, the per centage of households not having toilet is marked in the case of Goa (15.26), Maharashtra (17.75), Chandigarh (17.83), Delhi (19.58) and Tamil Nadu (14.84). The total sanitation campaign aims to eliminate the practice of open defecation completely by 2012.

(ii) Urban Sanitation Status

According to census 2001, 27.8 per cent of Indians, i.e., 286 million people or 55 million households live in urban areas. Projections indicate that the urban population would have grown to 368 million by 2012. 12.04 million (7.87 per cent) urban households do not have access to latrines and defecate in the open. 5.48 million (8.13 per cent) urban households use community latrines and 13.4 million households (19.49 per cent) use shared latrines. 12.47 million (18.5 per cent) households do not have access to a drainage network. 26.83 million (39.8 per cent) household are connected to open drains. The status in respect of the urban poor is even worse. The per centage of notified and non-notified slums without latrines is 17 per cent and 51 per cent respectively. In respect of septic latrines the availability is 66 per cent and 35 per cent. In respect of underground sewerage, the availability is 30 per cent and 15 per cent respectively. More than 37 per cent of the total human excreta generated in urban India, is unsafely disposed. This imposes significant public health and environmental costs to urban areas that contribute more than 60 per cent of the country's GDP.

Impacts of poor sanitation are especially significant for the urban poor (22 per cent of total urban population), women, children and the elderly. The loss due to diseases caused by poor sanitation for children under 14 years alone in urban areas amounts to Rs 500 crore at 2001 prices (Planning Commission-United Nations International Children Emergency Fund (UNICEF), 2006). Inadequate discharge of untreated domestic/municipal wastewater has resulted in contamination of 75 per cent of all surface water across India.

Millennium Development Goals (MDGs) enjoin upon the signatory nations to extend access to improved sanitation to at least half the urban population by 2015, and 100 per cent access by 2025. On the basis of information furnished by the state agencies in charge of Urban Water Supply and Sanitation Sector, about 91 per cent of the urban population has got access to water supply and 63 per cent to sewerage and sanitation facilities (47 per cent from sewer and 53 per cent from low cost sanitation) as on 31.3.2004. However, adequacy, equitable distribution and per-capita provision of these basic services may not be as per prescribed norms in most of the cities. For instance, the poor, particularly those living in slums and squatter settlements, are generally deprived of these basic facilities.

As per assessment made by the central pollution control board (CPCB) on the status of wastewater generation and treatment in Class I cities and Class-II town during 2003-04 about 26,254 MLD of wastewater is generated in 921 Class I cities and Class II town in India (housing more than 70 per cent of urban population). The waste water treatment capacity developed so far is about 7044 MLD—accounting for 27 per cent of the total wastewater generated.

The tenth five year plan (Government of India planning term 2002-2007) targeted coverage of providing sewerage and sanitation facilities to 75 per cent of the population from 57 per cent at the beginning of the plan. An investment requirement of Rs 23,157 crore was worked out for sanitation and Rs 2,322 crore for solid waste management. There was no scheme at the beginning of tenth plan to assist the states in the sanitation sector and the Tenth Plan recommended an enhanced scope for the Accelerated Urban Water Supply Programme (AUWSP) to include sanitation. With the launch of Jawaharlal Nehru National Urban Renewal Mission (JnNURM) and Urban Infrastructure Development Scheme for Small and Medium Towns (UIDSSMT), the AUWSP programme is subsumed in UIDSSMT and the scheme now includes funding for sanitation also.

The target fixed for urban sanitation in the Eleventh Five Year plan (2007-2012) is 100 per cent population coverage with 70 per cent by sewerage facility and 30 per cent by low cost sanitation. It has been estimated that the fund requirement for this programme is Rs 53,168 crore. Funds to the tune of Rs 40,000 crore would be available from the JnNURM for water supply and sanitation. Sanitation covers the whole range of activities including human waste disposal, liquid and solid wastes form household and industrial waste.

(d) Legislation in India Related to Sanitation

The Ministry of Environment and Forests is responsible for passing and executing legislation related to Indian Laws and Regulation on Water Quality Management with specific reference to sewage is framed and includes:

(i) The Water (Prevention and Control of Pollution) Act, 1974 with its amendments deals comprehensively with water issues. It empowers the Government to constitute Pollution Control Boards to maintain the wholesomeness of national water bodies. It enables Central and State Pollution Control Boards to prescribe standards and has provisions for monitoring and compliance and penal provisions against the violators of the Act. It provides the permit system i.e., "Consent" procedure to prevent and control of water pollution. The Act empowers State Boards to issue directions to the defaulters.

(ii) Environment (Protection) Act, 1986 has a broad coverage in which 'Environment' includes water, air and land and there exists an interrelationship among water, air, land, human beings and other creatures. It empowers to take measures in protecting and improving the quality of the environment through preventing, controlling and abating environmental pollution. The Government is authorised to set national standards for ambient environmental quality and controlling discharges to regulate industrial locations, to prescribe procedure for hazardous substance management and to collect and disseminate information regarding environmental pollution. The Act provides for severe penalties for those who fail to comply with or contravenes any provision of the Act.

(iii) Institutional Setup for Sanitation and Water Management in India

(a) Governance Framework

The constitutional rights and responsibilities related to water and sanitation are blurred within the federal framework as, all the three tiers, namely, the central government, state governments, local bodies at the village (panchayat) and city (nagarpalika) levels, deal with water and sanitation. The 73rd and 74th amendments act (1992) specifies that inter alia, drinking water, water management, watershed development and sanitation are subjects to be devolved to the local bodies, i.e., Panchayats (rural) and Nagarpalikas (urban).

- Nagar Nigam (Municipal Corporation) - population greater or equal to 2,00,000
- Nagar Palika (Municipality) - population less than 2,00,000
- Nagar Panchayat (City Council) - for areas in transition from rural to urban with population of 30,000 to 1,00,000

b) Classification of cities based population[55]

- Class I – more than 100000 – 423 cities
- Class II – 50000- 100000 – 498 cities

- Class III – 20000—50000 – 1386 cities
- Class IV – 10000—20000 – 1560 cities
- Class V – 5000—10000 – 1057 cities
- Class VI – less than 5000 – 227 cities

The main aim of SSP was to provide sustainable sanitation facilities in slums located on municipal lands. The SSP was to be a participatory programme involving communities in entire implementation process - right from the initial stages of forming community-based organisations (CBOs), and collecting contributions for operation and maintenance of proposed toilet blocks, then involving people from the planning stage to the completion of the work and handing over the facilities to the communities for future operation and maintenance. A significant departure from the earlier approach of 'supply-driven' to 'demand-driven' approach is thus the main feature of the scheme.

The implementation of SSP was phased out in four stages: programme publicity and selection of communities; demand assessment and preparation of plans for operation and maintenance; design and construction of sanitation facilities; and operation, maintenance and use of maintained facilities by the beneficiaries through their CBOs. Adoption of a demand driven approach, widening of technological options to include others besides centralised public toilets, contribution by communities to capital costs (around 15 per cent of the total cost as upfront contribution, including the cost of restitution wherever necessary) and community responsibility for maintenance of new and rehabilitated toilet facilities, were the other features of the scheme.

Notes

1. Alvah H. Doty, 1912. Modern Sanitation Source: The North American Review, Vol. 196, No. 684 (Nov., 1912), pp. 673-681.
2. *Ibid*.
3. Edward Bartow, 1936. Progress in Sanitation, Science, New Series, Vol. 84, No. 2180 (Oct. 9, 1936), pp. 317-322.
4. *Ibid*.
5. PK JHA (2003): Health and social benefits from improving community hygiene and sanitation: an Indian experience, International Journal of Environmental Health Research, 13:S1, S133-S140.
6. *Ibid*.
7. See Jon C. Schladweiler, Historian, Arizona Water and Pollution

Control Association.

8. *Ibid.*
9. For details see Egyptian Sanitation. The British Medical Journal, Vol. 2, No. 1722 (Dec. 30, 1893), pp. 1435-1436.
10. Szreter, Simon (1997), "Economic growth, disruption, deprivation, disease and death: on the importance of the politics of public health for development", *Population and Development Review* Vol. 23, No. 4.
11. Flinn, M.W. (editor) (1965), *Report on the Sanitary Condition of the Labouring Population of Great Britain* by Edwin Chadwick (first published in 1842), Edinburgh University Press.
12. See For details see Susan E. Chaplin, Cities, sewers and poverty: India's politics of sanitation, Environment and Urbanisation 1999 11:145.
13. de Swaan, Abram (1988), In Care of the State: Health Care, Education and Welfare in Europe and the USA in the Modern Era, Polity Press, Oxford.
14. For details see Susan E. Chaplin, Cities, sewers and poverty: India's politics of sanitation, Environment and Urbanisation 1999 11: 145.
15. Charles Baskerville, 1911, City Sanitation, Science, New Series, Vol. 33, No. 836 (Jan. 6, 1911), pp. 16-21.
16. Louis F. Westbrook and Elizabeth Reed, 1960, Airport Sanitation, Public Health Reports (1896-1970), Vol. 75, No. 9 (Sep., 1960), pp. 835-839.
17. See the excellent material on views about the causes of diseases in Charles Rosenberg, The Cholera Years (Chicago, 1962).
18. Charles N. Glaab and A. Theodore Brown, A History of Urban America (New York, 1967), and Blake McKelvey, The Urbanisation of America (New Brunswick, N. J., 1963).
19. James W. Cassedy, "The Flamboyant Colonel Waring," in Bulletin of the History of Medicine, 36: 163-176 (March-April, 1962.
20. Warren S. Tryon, (ed.), A Mirror for Ameri-cans, Life and Manners in the United States, 1790- 1870 as Recorded by American Travelers (Life in the East, Chicago, 1952), I: 168-170.
21. Lawrence H. Larsen. 1969. Nineteenth-Century Street Sanitation: A Study of Filth and Frustration. Lawrence H. Larsen, The Wisconsin Magazine of History, Vol. 52, No. 3 (Spring, 1969), pp. 239-247.

22. Lawrence H. Larsen. 1969. Nineteenth-Century Street Sanitation: A Study of Filth and Frustration. Lawrence H. Larsen, The Wisconsin Magazine of History, Vol. 52, No. 3 (Spring, 1969), pp. 245.

23. Susan B. Hanley. 1097. Urban Sanitation in Pre-industrial Japan, The Journal of Interdisciplinary History, Vol. 18, No. 1 (Summer, 1987), pp. 1-26.

24. *Ibid.*

25. Wakita Osamu and Kobayashi Shigeru, Osaka no seisan to kotsii (Osaka, 1973), 127.

26. Hayashi Reiko, "Kinsei ni okeru jinkai shori," Ryutsi keizai ronshu, VIII (I974), 72-86.

27. Susan B. Hanley. 1997. Urban Sanitation in Pre-industrial Japan, The Journal of Interdisciplinary History, Vol. 18, No. 1 (Summer, 1987), pp. 1-26.

28. See Robert Stock, Environmental Sanitation in Nigeria: Colonial and Contemporary. Review of African Political Economy, No. 42 (1988), pp. 19-31.

29. A.D. King, Colonial Urban Development, (Routledge and Kegan Paul, London, 1976).

30. M.W. Swanson, 'The Sanitation Syndrome: Bubonic Plague and Urban Native Policy in the Cape Colony, 1900-1909', Joumal of African History, 18, 1977, pp. 387-410.

31. C.M. Rogerson, The Casual Poor of Johannesburg, South Africa. The Rise and Fall of Coffee Cart Trading, Ph.D. Thesis.

32. H.E. Mohammed, The Morphology of Urban Kano, 1903-1960: A Study of Colonial Urban Planning Policy.

33. See Robert Stock, Environmental Sanitation in Nigeria: Colonial and Contemporary. Review of African Political Economy, No. 42 (1988), pp. 19-31.

34. Based on WaterAid, FANSA and WSSCC (2011) South Asian people's perspective on sanitation: Synthesis review.

35. www.wsscc.org/resources/resource-publications/dhaka-declaration-sanitation.

36. World Health Organisation/Unicef (2010).

37. For details see Samantha Iyer, Colonial Population and the Idea of Development, Comparative Studies in Society and History 2013;55(1):65–91.

38. Notestein, "Population"; Kingsley Davis, "The World Demographic Transition," Annals of the American Academy of Political and

Social Science 237 (1945): 1–11.

39. For details see Samantha Iyer, Colonial Population and the Idea of Development, Comparative Studies in Society and History 2013;55(1): 65–91.

41 See Alan Bewell, Romanticism and Colonial Disease (Baltimore: Johns Hopkins University Press, 1999), 242–76.

42 David Arnold, The Problem of Nature: Environment, Culture and European Expansion (Oxford: Blackwell, 1996).

43 Mark Harrison, Climates and Constitutions: Health, Race, Environment and British Imperialism in India, 1600–1850 (Delhi: Oxford University Press, 1999).

44 See also Florence Nightingale, "How People May Live and not Die in India," read by Dr. Scoresby Jackson at the Edinburgh meeting of the National Association for the Promotion of Social Science, Oct. 1863, in Gérard Vallée and Lynn McDonald, eds., Florence Nightingale on Health in India, (Waterloo: Wilfred Laurier University Press, 2006).

45 Report of the Commissioners Appointed to Inquire into the Sanitary State of the Army in India [hereafter Royal Sanitary Commission Report], Parliamentary Papers (Hereafter PP), vol. 1, 1863 (Cmd. 3184), lxxxii.

46 J. A. Baines, General Report on the Census of India, 1891 (London: Printed for the Indian Government by Eyre and Spottiswoode, 1893), 58–59, 64.

47 For details see Sumit Guha (1993): Nutrition, Sanitation, Hygiene, and the Likelihood of Death: The British Army in India c. 1870–1920, Population Studies: A Journal of Demography, 47:3, 385-401.

48 R. Ross, *The Conquest of Malaria* (London, 1910), p. 285.

49 Sumit Guha (1993): Nutrition, Sanitation, Hygiene, and the Likelihood of Death: The British Army in India c. 1870–1920, Population Studies: A Journal of Demography, 47:3, 385-401

50 See Prashad, Vijay. (2000). *Untouchable freedom: A social history of a dalit community*. Oxford: Oxford University Press.

51 For details see 'Indian Sanitation. The British Medical Journal, Vol. 2, No. 2802 (Sep. 12, 1914)

52 Prashad, P. (1995) Marks of Capital: Colonialism and the sweepers of Delhi, *International Review of Social History,* 40, pp. 1-30.

53 Ramasubban, Radhika (1982). Public Health and Medical Research in India. Saree Report R 4: Swedish Agency for Research

Cooperation with Developing Countries. Stockholm.

54 Based on ACCES Sanitation Accelerating City-to-City Exchange for Sustainable Sanitation, Inventory of Sanitation Policies and Programmes in India, ICLEI-Local Governments for Sustainability—South Asia, June 2010.

55 As per 2001 Census.

3

Perspectives on Sociology of Sanitation: Key Social Scientists

(a) Sociological Theory—Towards Scientific and Rational Constructionism

Social theory provides the necessary analytical and philosophical framework within which the social sciences can develop. Social theory both sustains the achievements of the past, notes the needs and limitations of the present, and points the way to future research issues and questions. In considering social theory within a broad international framework, we need to recognise that sociology is inevitably coloured by different local, national, or civilisational circumstances. Polish sociology is obviously very different from American sociology. The growth of nationalism and the nation-state had a profound effect on the early development of social theory in Europe in the nineteenth century, and World War I brought to a tragic conclusion the enormous developments in sociology in both Germany and France. In the late twentieth century, social theory has also been responding to the specific national or regional manifestations of information technology and cultural consumption in new theories of globalisation.[1]

Thomas Hobbes (1588–1697) and John Locke (1632–1704) discussed how social order is possible. While Hobbes and Locke conceived of this in political terms as a social contract, social theory properly begins only with the recognition that society is a reality in itself. The eighteenth century Enlightenment thinkers were the first to give systematic consideration to the reality of the social phenomena. Émile Durkheim regarded Rousseau and Montesquieu as the founders of sociology. J.J. Rousseau's *The Social Contract* was published in 1762. It introduced the notion of the "general will" as the symbolic basis of social subjectivity, which he linked to the importance of citizenship. Although he tended to view social institutions as corrupting the human spirit of freedom, he articulated a notion of society that was a departure from the earlier contract philosophies of the liberal thinkers. For instance, in the earlier 'Discourse on the Origin of Inequality', he argued that inequality is a product of society as opposed to being natural.[2]

The 'French Revolution' was the event that heralded the new age of social theory as an interpretation of the modern age, for no other episode encapsulated modernity more than 1789 and its aftermath, when entirely new visions of social and political order emerged. Post-revolutionary social theory was a product of the Enlightenment's quest for intellectual mastery, but it was also a response to the realisation that the state alone was incapable of establishing social order. Thus, intellectual forces played a central role in shaping sociological theory. In the real world, of course, intellectual factors cannot be separated from social forces. The many intellectual forces that shaped the development of social theories are discussed within the national context where their influence was primarily felt. It is the view of many observers that the Enlightenment constitutes a critical development in terms of the later evolution of sociology. The Enlightenment was a period of remarkable intellectual development and change in philosophical thought. A number of long-standing ideas and beliefs—many of which related to social life—were overthrown and replaced during the Enlightenment. Overall, the Enlightenment was characterised by the belief that people could comprehend and control the universe by means of reason and empirical research. The view was that because the physical world was dominated by natural laws, it was likely that the social world was also influenced. Thus it was up to the philosopher, using reason and research, to discover these social laws. Once they understood how the social world worked, the Enlightenment thinkers had a practical goal—the creation of a "better," more rational world.[3]

With an emphasis on reason, the Enlightenment philosophers were inclined to reject beliefs in traditional authority. When these thinkers examined traditional values and institutions, they often found them to be irrational—that is, contrary to human nature and inhibitive of human growth and development. The mission of the practical and change-oriented philosophers of the Enlightenment was to overcome these irrational systems. One finds that the early history of French sociology is a fairly coherent story of the progression from the Enlightenment and the French Revolution to the conservative reaction and to the increasingly important sociological ideas of Tocqueville, Saint-Simon, Comte, and Durkheim. Auguste Comte developed *social physics*, or what in 1839 he called *sociology*. He developed his scientific view, "positivism," or "positive philosophy," to combat what he considered to be the negative and destructive philosophy of the Enlightenment.

Emile Durkheim has been seen as an inheritor of the Enlightenment tradition because of his emphasis on science and social reformism. Durkheim developed a distinctive conception of the subject matter of sociology and then tested it in an empirical study. In *The Rules of Sociological Method* (1895), Durkheim argued that it is the special task of sociology to study what he called *social Facts*. In order to help sociology move away from philosophy and to give it a clear and separate identity, Durkheim (1895) proposed that the distinctive subject matter of sociology should be the study of social facts. Crucial in separating sociology from philosophy is the idea that social facts are to be treated as "things" and studied empirically. This means that we must study social facts by acquiring data from outside of our own minds through observation and experimentation. The empirical study of social facts as things sets, Durkheimian sociology apart from more philosophical approaches. Durkheim differentiated between two broad types of social facts—material and nonmaterial. *Material social facts*, such as styles of architecture, forms of technology, and legal codes, are the easier to understand of the two because they are directly observable. Clearly, such things as laws are external to individuals and coercive over them. More importantly, these material social facts often express a far larger and more powerful realm of moral forces that are at least equally external to individuals and coercive over them. These are nonmaterial social facts. The sociologist usually begins a study by focusing on material social facts, which are empirically accessible, in order to understand nonmaterial social facts, which are the real focus of his work. The most material are such things as population size and density, channels of communication, and housing arrangements.

Later, Karl Marx took a very different position, arguing that the problems of modern life can be traced to real, material sources (for example, the structures of capitalism) and that the solutions, therefore, can be found only in the overturning of those structures by the collective action of large numbers of people. Marx offered a theory of capitalist society based on his image of the basic nature of human beings. Marx believed that people are basically productive; that is, in order to survive, people need to work in, and with, nature. In so doing, they produce the food, clothing, tools, shelter, and other necessities that permit them to live. Their productivity is a perfectly natural way by which they express basic creative impulses. Furthermore, these impulses are expressed in concert with other people; in other words, people are inherently social. They need to work together to produce what they need to survive. Basically capitalism is a structure (or, more accurately, a series of structures) that erects barriers between an individual and the production process, the products of that process, and other people; ultimately, it even divides the individual himself or herself. This is the basic meaning of the concept of *alienation:* it is the breakdown of the natural interconnection among people and what they produce. Alienation occurs because capitalism has evolved into a two-class system in which a few capitalists own the production process, the products, and the labour time of those who work for them. Instead of naturally producing for themselves, people produce unnaturally in capitalist society for a small group of capitalists.

Marx also accepted the centrality of contradictions to historical change. We see this in such well-known formulations as the "contradictions of capitalism" and "class contradictions." However, unlike Hegel, Marx did not believe that these contradictions could be worked out in our understanding, that is, in our minds. Instead, for Marx these are real, existing contradictions. For Marx, such contradictions are resolved not by the philosopher sitting in an armchair but by a life-and-death struggle that changes the social world. This was a crucial transformation because it allowed Marx to move the dialectic out of the realm of philosophy and into the realm of a study of social relations grounded in the material world. The dialectic leads to an interest in the conflicts and contradictions among various levels of social reality, rather than to the more traditional sociological interest in the ways these various levels mesh neatly into a cohesive whole. According to Marx, our particular ideas of equality and freedom emerge out of capitalism. Although we take our belief in freedom and equality to be an obvious thing, any historical study will demonstrate that it is not. Most societies would have considered the idea that all people are essentially equal as absurd. For most cultures throughout history, slavery seemed quite natural. Now, under capitalism, we believe quite the opposite: inequality is absurd, and slavery is unnatural.[4]

Max Weber's work was fundamentally a theory of the process of rationalisation. Weber was interested in the general issue of why institutions in the Western world had grown progressively more rational while powerful barriers seemed to prevent a similar development in the rest of the world. Formal rationality involves, as was usually the case with Weber, a concern for the actor making choices of means and ends. However, in this case, that choice is made in reference to universally applied rules, regulations, and laws. These, in turn, are derived from various large-scale structures, especially bureaucracies and the economy. Weber saw the bureaucracy (and the historical process of bureaucratisation) as the classic example of rationalisation.

Weber believed that history is composed of an inexhaustible array of specific phenomena. To study these phenomena, it was necessary to develop a variety of concepts designed to be useful for research on the real world. As a general rule, although Weber (as we will see) did not adhere to it strictly and neither do most sociologists and historians, the task of sociology was to develop these concepts, which history was to use in causal analyses of specific historical phenomena. In this way, Weber sought to combine the specific and the general in an effort to develop a science that did justice to the complex nature of social life. Weber's special use of the term *verstehen* in his historical research is one of his best-known and most controversial contributions to the methodology of contemporary sociology. Weber's thoughts on *verstehen* were relatively common among German historians of his day and were derived from a field known as hermeneutics. Hermeneutics was a special approach to the understanding and interpretation of published writings. Its goal was to understand the thinking of the author as well as the basic structure of the text.

Weber believed it was the responsibility of sociologists to develop conceptual tools, which could be used later by historians and sociologists. The most important such conceptual tool was the ideal type: An ideal type is formed by the one-sided accentuation of one or more points of view and by the synthesis of a great many diffuse, discrete, more or less present and occasionally absent concrete individual phenomena, which are arranged according to those one-sidedly emphasised viewpoints into a unified analytical construct . . . In its conceptual purity, this mental construct . . . cannot be found empirically anywhere in reality. Weber's entire sociology, if we accept his words at face value, was based on his conception of social action. He differentiated between action and purely reactive behaviour. The concept of behaviour is reserved, then as now, for automatic behaviour that involves no thought processes. He was concerned with action that clearly involved the intervention of thought processes (and the resulting meaningful action) between the occurrence of a stimulus and the ultimate response. To put it slightly differently, action was said to occur when individuals attached subjective meanings to their action. To Weber, the task of sociological analysis involved "the interpretation of action in terms of its subjective meaning.[5]"

Emergent Social Theories in Social Sciences

The viewpoint and perspectives of various social scientists led to the emergence of divergent social theories. These had led to the understanding of social realities in scientific and specific framework. The leading theories included evolutionary, structural-functional, structuralism, conflict, symbolic interactionist, ethnomethodology, phenomenology, subaltern and postmodern theories. Let us understand these theories in brief for applying such theories in understanding the phenomenon of sanitation and allied themes.

(a) Evolutionary Theory

The first of these theories relates primarily to the increasing size of society. Society grows through both the multiplication of individuals and the union of groups (compounding). The increasing size of society brings with it larger and more differentiated social structures, as well as the increasing differentiation of the functions they perform. In addition to their growth in size, societies evolve through compounding, that is, by unifying more and more adjoining groups. Thus, Herbert Spencer talks of the evolutionary movement from simple to compound, doubly-compound, and trebly-compound societies.

(b) Structural-functionalism

Functionalists argue that society should be understood as a system of interdependent parts. The different parts of social life depend on each other and fulfill functions contributing to social order and its reproduction. Functionalists argue that society should be understood as a system of interdependent parts. The different parts of social life depend on each other and fulfill functions contributing to social order and its reproduction.

Functionalism departs from the traditional logic of causal argument where a cause should precede its consequences. Functionalists identify a causal loop or feedback linking cause and effect. When an anthropologist asks "why do the Hopi dance for rain?" a functionalist considers the consequence of the dance and notes that it maintains group solidarity.

For Parsons, there are four different interconnected systems bearing upon human action: the human organism, the individual personality, the social system, and the cultural system. The behavioural organism is concerned with the human body as the primary vehicle for engaging the physical environment; that of personality corresponds to the individual actor viewed as a system. It includes conscious and unconscious motivations (or need dispositions). Actors respond not only to positive rewards, but also to internalised feelings of guilt, anxiety, and the need for approval. The social system is a system of positions and roles organised by expectations and maintained by sanctions; the culture system refers to the symobls and meanings that are drawn upon by actors in the pursuit of their personal projects.

Parsons's primary focus is the social system. He proposed four functional imperatives necessary to its constitution and operation (the A-G-I-L scheme). Adaptation is concerned with relationships to external environments and the utilisation of resources in the pursuit of goals. Goal attainment is concerned with the direction of systems towards collective goals. Integration refers to the maintenance of coordinated relationships among the parts of the system, while latency, or pattern maintenance, describes the symbolic order in terms of mutually reinforcing meanings and typifications. Parsons found his answer to the problem of order in structural functionalism, which operates in his view with the following set of assumptions:

1. Systems have the property of order and interdependence of parts.
2. Systems tend toward self-maintaining order, or equilibrium.
3. The system may be static or involved in an ordered process of change.
4. The nature of one part of the system has an impact on the form that the other parts can take.
5. Systems maintain boundaries with their environments.
6. Allocation and integration are two fundamental processes necessary for a given state of equilibrium of a system.

To him, Socialisation and social control are the main mechanisms that allow the social system to maintain its equilibrium. Modest amounts of individuality and deviance are accommodated, but more extreme forms must be met by re-equilibrating mechanisms.

In R.K. Merton's view, early analysts tended to confuse the subjective motives of individuals with the functions of structures or institutions. The focus of the structural functionalist should be on social functions rather than on individual motives. *Functions*, according to Merton, are defined as "those observed consequences which make for the adaptation or adjustment of a given system" (1949). However, there is a clear ideological bias when one focuses only on adaptation or adjustment, for they are always positive consequences. It is important to note that one social fact can have negative consequences for another social fact. To rectify this serious omission in early structural functionalism, Merton developed the idea of a *dysfunction*. Just as structures or institutions could contribute to the maintenance of other parts of the social system, they also could have negative consequences for them. Merton's (1968) analyse the relationship between culture, structure, and anomie. Merton defines *culture* as "that organised set of *normative values* governing behaviour which is common to members of a designated society or group" and *social structure* as "that organised set of *social relationships* in which members of the society or group are variously implicated" (1968:216). Anomie occurs "when there is an acute disjunction between the cultural norms and goals and the socially structured capacities of members of the group to act in accord with them" (Merton, 1968). That is, because of their position in the social structure of society, some people are unable to act in accord with normative values. The culture calls for some type of behaviour that the social structure prevents from occurring.

(c) Structuralism

A theoretical tradition whose formation and influence can be seen as much in the fields of linguistics (Ferdinand de Saussure), literature (Roland Barthes), psychoanalysis (Jacques Lacan), history (Fernand Braudel), anthropology (Claude Levi-Strauss), and philosophy (Louis Althusser) as it can in sociology. It is associated with the search for deep and relatively abiding structures that lie beneath the flux and change of surface events and apparent contingencies. For Saussure, and for later structuralists such as Levi-Strauss and Barthes, language is a system in which each term relies on its relations with other terms. The distinction between the signifier (the written word, image, or sound) and the signified (the meaning carried by the signifier) as joint components of the sign is central, as is the fact that neither term involves the referent (the real object referred to). The signification system is markedly autonomous from the world of referents.

(d) Conflict Theory

Conflict theory can be seen as a development that took place, at least in part, in reaction to structural functionalism and as a result of many of the criticisms discussed earlier. However, it should be noted that conflict theory has various other roots, such as Marxian and Weberian theory and Simmel's work on social conflict. Like functionalists, conflict theorists are oriented toward the study of social structures and institutions. In the main, this theory is little more than a series of contentions that are often the direct opposites of functionalist positions. Conflict theorists see whatever order there is in society as stemming from the coercion of some members by those at the top. Where functionalists focus on the cohesion created by shared societal values, conflict theorists emphasise the role of power in maintaining order in society.

Ralph Dahrendorf (1959, 1968) is the major exponent of the position that society has two faces (conflict and consensus) and that sociological theory therefore should be divided into two parts, conflict theory and consensus theory. Consensus theorists should examine value integration in society, and conflict theorists should examine conflicts of interest and the coercion that holds society together in the face of these stresses. Dahrendorf recognised that society could not exist without both conflict and consensus, which are prerequisites for each other. Thus, we cannot have conflict unless there is some prior consensus. The authority attached to positions is the key element in Dahrendorf's analysis. Authority always implies both superordination and subordination. Those who occupy positions of authority are expected to control subordinates; that is, they dominate because of the expectations of those who surround them, not because of their own psychological characteristics. Like authority, these expectations are attached to positions, not people. Authority is not a generalised social phenomenon; those who are subject to control, as well as permissible spheres of control, are specified in society. Finally, because authority is legitimate, sanctions can be brought to bear against those who do not comply.

(e) Symbolic Interactionism

G.H. Mead is the most important thinker in the history of symbolic interactionism. In Mead's view, traditional social psychology began with the psychology of the individual in an effort to explain social experience; in contrast, Mead always gives priority to the social world in understanding social experience. To Mead, the social whole precedes the individual mind both logically and temporally.

A thinking, self-conscious individual is, as we will see later, logically impossible in Mead's theory without a prior social group. The social group comes first, and it leads to the development of self-conscious mental states. The act involves only one person, but the *social act* involves two or more persons. The *gesture* is in Mead's view the basic mechanism in the social act and in the social process more generally. As he defines them, "gestures are movements of the first organism which act as specific stimuli calling forth the (socially) appropriate responses of the second organism" (Mead, 1934).

The mind, which is defined by Mead as a process and not a thing, as an inner conversation with one's self, is not found within the individual; it is not intracranial but is a social phenomenon. It arises and develops within the social process and is an integral part of that process. At the most general level, Mead uses the term *society* to mean the ongoing social process that precedes both the mind and the self. Given its importance in shaping the mind and self, society is clearly of central importance to Mead. At another level, society to Mead represents the organised set of responses that are taken over by the individual in the form of the "me." Thus, in this sense individuals carry society around with them, giving them the ability, through self-criticism, to control themselves.

Some symbolic interactionists (Blumer, 1969a) have tried to enumerate the basic principles of the theory. These principles include the following:

1. Human beings, unlike lower animals, are endowed with the capacity for thought.
2. The capacity for thought is shaped by social interaction.
3. In social interaction people learn the meanings and the symbols that allow them to exercise their distinctively human capacity for thought.
4. Meanings and symbols allow people to carry on distinctively human action and interaction.
5. People are able to modify or alter the meanings and symbols that they use in action and interaction on the basis of their interpretation of the situation.
6. People are able to make these modifications and alterations because, in part, of their ability to interact with themselves, which allows them to examine possible courses of action, assess their relative advantages and disadvantages, and then choose one.
7. The intertwined patterns of action and interaction make up groups and societies.

Symbolic interactionists primary concern is with the impact of meanings and symbols on human action and interaction. Here it is useful to employ Mead's differentiation between covert and overt behaviour. *Covert behaviour* is the thinking process, involving symbols and meanings. *Overt behaviour* is the actual behaviour performed by an actor. Some overt behaviour does not involve covert behaviour (habitual behaviour or mindless responses to external stimuli). However, most human action involves both kinds. Covert behaviour is of greatest concern to symbolic interactionists, whereas overt behaviour is of greatest concern to exchange theorists or to traditional behaviourists in general.

Meanings and symbols give human social action (which involves a single actor) and social interaction (which involves two or more actors engaged in mutual social action) distinctive characteristics. Social action is that in which the individuals are acting with others in mind. In other words, in undertaking an action, people simultaneously try to gauge its impact on the other actors involved. Although they often engage in mindless, habitual behaviour, people have the capacity to engage in social action.

The most important work on the self in symbolic interactionism is *Presentation of Self in Everyday Life* (1959) by Erving Goffman. Goffman perceived the self not as a possession of the actor but rather as the product of the dramatic interaction between actor and audience. The self "is a dramatic effect arising . . . from a scene that is presented" (Goffman, 1959). Goffman assumed that when individuals interact, they want to present a certain sense of self that will be accepted by others. However, even as they present that self, actors are aware that members of the audience can disturb their performance. For that reason actors are attuned to the need to control the audience, especially those elements of it that might be disruptive. The actors hope that the sense of self that they present to the audience will be strong enough for the audience to define the actors as the actors want them to. The actors also hope that this will cause the audience to act voluntarily as the actors want them to. Goffman characterised this central interest as "impression management." It involves techniques actors use to maintain certain impressions in the face of problems they are likely to encounter and methods they use to cope with these problems.

(f) Ethnomethodology

Harold Garfinkel, in his inimitable and nearly impenetrable style, describes the focus of ethnomethodology as follows: For ethnomethodology the objective reality of social facts, in that, and just how, it is every society's locally, endogenously produced, naturally organised, reflexively accountable, ongoing, practical achievement, being everywhere, always, only, exactly and entirely, members' work, with no time out, and with no possibility of evasion, hiding out, passing, postponement, or buy-outs, is *thereby* sociology's fundamental phenomenon.

Ethnomethodologists devote a lot of attention to analysing people's accounts, as well as to the ways in which accounts are offered and accepted (or rejected) by others. This is one of the reasons that ethnomethodologists are preoccupied with analysing conversations. In breaching experiments, social reality is violated in order to shed light on the methods by which people construct social reality. The assumption behind this research is not only that the methodical production of social life occurs all the time but also that the participants are unaware that they are engaging in such actions. The objective of the breaching experiment is to disrupt normal procedures so that the process by which the everyday world is constructed or reconstructed can be observed and studied. In his work, Garfinkel (1967) offered a number of examples of breaching experiments, most of which were undertaken by his students in casual settings to illustrate the basic principles of ethnomethodology.

Breaching experiments are undertaken to illustrate the way people order their everyday lives. These experiments reveal the resilience of social reality, since the subjects (or victims) move quickly to normalise the breach—that is, to render the situation accountable in familiar terms. It is assumed that the way people handle these breaches tells us much about how they handle their everyday lives.

(g) Phenomenology

Edmund Husserl (1859–1938) was the first to use this term as the name for a systematic and distinctive philosophical position. What we know about phenomenology is a (greatly modified) version of Husserl's doctrine that comes to us through the diligent efforts of his student, Alfred Schutz, and Schutz's students, Peter Berger and Thomas Luckmann. Husserl (1965) hoped to redirect philosophy toward the "things themselves. Consciousness mediates and colours our perceptions of the world as well as our thoughts, emotions, and physical sensations." Consciousness is what matters. The things themselves, then, are "essential forms of consciousness" through which we know the world. In order to escape from this cognitive cage, Husserl envisions a phenomenology with "absolute freedom from all presupposition." One must arrive at a pre-suppositionless frame of mind before one is ready to undertake systematic description of the objects of consciousness.

As Schutz (1967) put it, "the special aim of sociology demands a special method in order to select the materials relevant to the peculiar questions it raises." With his integrationist temperament, Schutz viewed Weber's formulation of ideal types as a procedure that was not antithetical to phenomenology. Schutz rejects the notion that intersubjectivity is simply given in the nature of human consciousness. Instead, he argues that intersubjectivity is accomplished through socialisation and social interaction.

(h) Subaltern Perspective

Gramsci, theorising out of his experience of work among the people, remarks: 'The history of subaltern groups is necessarily fragmented and episodic.[6] Subaltern groups are always subject the activity of ruling groups, even when they rebel and rise up; only 'permanent' victory breaks their subordination....' Defining the objectives of subaltern studies, Guha (in Subaltern studies I) reflects: (i) the objective formation of the subaltern social groups, by the developments and transformations occurring in the sphere of economic production. (ii) their active or passive affiliation to the dominant political formations, their attempts to influence the programmes of these formations in order to press claims of their own...(iii) the birth of new parties of the dominant groups, intended to conserve the assent of the subaltern groups and to maintain control over them; (iv) the formation which the subaltern groups themselves produce, in order to press claims of a limited and partial character; (v) those new formations which assert the autonomy of the subaltern groups, but within the old framework; (vi) those formations which assert the integral autonomy... etc.

Subaltern studies aimed removing from Indian history a top-down approach and replacing it with the study of the culture of the people. At this juncture Javed Alam rightly emphasised the publication of Subaltern as an important event in the writing of the history of colonial India.[7] The presupposition is as follows: Between the world of politics on the one hand and the economic processes of capitalist transformation on the other, there is a kind of mental space within which the social forms of existence and consciousness of the people are all their own—strong and enduring in their own right and therefore free of manipulations by the dominant groups. However, much the ruling classes may control the themes and content of politics or the sources of history, the subalterns, that is, the people, will always manage to make themselves heard. In other words, this intermediate space represents the subjectivity; the active source of the political activity of the people and therefore the basis on which they act as subjects of history and not just its objects, being merely acted upon. It is the task of people's historians, always to keep their antennae directed towards the intermediate space from where comes the voice of the people.

Subaltern Studies began its impressive career in England at the end of the 1970s, when conversations on subaltern themes among a small group of English and Indian historians led to a proposal to launch a new journal in India. Oxford University Press in New Delhi agreed instead to publish three volumes of essays called *Subaltern Studies: Writings on South Asian History and Society*. Subaltern Studies became an original site for a new kind of history from below, a people's history free of national constraints, a post-nationalist re-imagining of the Indian nation on the underside, at the margins, outside nationalism. Subaltern India emerged in fragments during the eighties and nineties, and it changed form, as we will see; but from the outset, it rejected official nationalism and developed transnationally, as did its readership and its critical appreciation. It is the first international collaboration to make a sustained impact on South Asian studies, and its ideas are intricately tangled in recent world trends. The last two decades of the 20th century, some South Asian scholars of Subaltern Studies (SS) school have claimed to be writing people's histories from the vantage point of non-western societies, an approach ignored since the 1870s. They reject the state-centred national discourse that replicates colonial power/knowledge in a world of globalisation. Instead, they declare to be free of modernity's master narrative and from the linear time framework in their writing of subaltern history. Ranajit Guha, the founder of SS school announced in 1982 the project's ambition "to rectify the elitist bias" in history writing "dominated by elitism—colonialist elitism and bourgeois-nationalist elitism". (Guha, 1982). In their research SS school revealed India's cultural roots in subaltern roots in subaltern subjectivity and in 'differences'. In 1982, Ranajit Guha's assertion that the Indian nation had failed "to come into its own" evoked failed revolution, but by 1990, it had new connotations.

Ranajit Guha's succinct definition, the word 'subaltern' is 'a name for the general attribute of subordination, whether this is expressed in terms of class, caste, age, gender, and office or in any other way'.[8] The original substance of *Subaltern Studies* emerged from work-in-progress in the late seventies. Eleven authors in the first three volumes — Shahid Amin, David Arnold, Gautam Bhadra, Dipesh Chakrabarty, N. K. Chandra, Partha Chatterjee, Arvind N. Das, David Hardiman, Stephen Henningham, Gyanendra Pandey, and Sumit Sarkar — were doing close empirical work in social, economic, and political history.

The leader of the project, Ranajit Guha, was different. Guha's effort is to recover or re-present the subaltern as a subject of history from the welter of documentary and historiographic discourses that deny the subaltern that power of agency. In that sense, his project is a continuation of the insurgency it purports to represent historically. But a subaltern study is not simply a discourse *about* the subaltern. What would be the point after all of representing the subaltern *as subaltern*? Nor is it simply about peasants or the historical past. It appears and develops as an academic practice in a contemporary setting in which new relations of domination and subalternity are produced on a daily basis and old ones are reinforced. It responds to the need of dominant groups to administer increasingly multicultural populations and a culturally heterogeneous transnational working class. The project of subaltern studies exists in a tension between a project that is 'deconstructive' of the claims of the nation, nationalism, and formal politics to represent the subaltern, and a 'constructive' articulation of new forms of collective political and cultural agency.

Subaltern studies is a school that originated in India in 1982. The founding members of the group challenged Indian Marxist historians and their claims to write people's history. In doing this they responded to a genuine need for a new methodology, epistemology, and paradigm, a need felt not only in India but worldwide. Borrowing from Gramsci the concept of 'subaltern' and drawing on the prevailing Western ideas about the historiography of mass culture, Subaltern studies tried to provide new interpretations and methodologies for writing Indian working-class history. Sublaternists maintained that colonialist, nationalist, and Marxist interpretations of Indian history denied the role of the common people and their agency. Subalternists group claimed that it was trying to recover the struggles of the poor and the outcast from the grip of 'official' left intellectuals while restoring the agency of poor people in making of Indian history.[9]

Subaltern consciousness had always been a critical feature of subalternity; and in 1987, Ajit K. Chaudhury reiterated that, "The focus of *Subaltern Studies* is on the consciousness of the subaltern classes, specifically peasants. Gayatri Chakravorty Spivak's Introduction to *Selected Subaltern Studies* (from *Subaltern Studies IV*) cites "the colonial subject" as the basic concern of theorisation and says, "The Subaltern Studies Collective .....generally perceive their task as making a theory of consciousness or culture rather than specifically a theory of change."

The meaning of subalternity in Subaltern Studies shifted as the framework of study increasingly stressed the clash of unequal cultures under colonialism and the dominance of colonial modernity over India's resistant, indigenous culture. Subalterns in India became fragments of a nation; their identity and consciousness reflected India's colonial subjugation. This approach has organised an impressive collection of enduring scholarship on colonial texts, vernacular resistance, bureaucracy, police, factories, communalism, ethnography, prisons, medicine, science, and related topics. It has also enabled Subaltern Studies to speak as India's subaltern voice. Methodologically, recuperating subaltern subjectivity entails the analytical and rhetorical liberation of Indian culture from its domination by the colonial archive and by modernity. Ingenious methods for uncovering fragments of subaltern nationality became the project's particular specialty. Critical readings of colonial texts, oral histories, and ethnographic techniques are employed to reveal India's cultural roots in subaltern subjectivity. Subaltern Studies thus becomes a post-colonial critique of modern, European, and Enlightenment epistemologies. A new kind of cultural essence for India is found in iconic residues of hidden identities, expressions of difference, and misunderstood mentalities.

The originality of Subaltern Studies came to be its striving to rewrite the nation outside the state-centred national discourse that replicates colonial power/knowledge in a world of globalisation. This new kind of national history consists of dispersed moments and fragments, which subaltern historians seek in the ethnographic present of colonialism. Writing such history constitutes subversive cultural politics because it exposes forms of power/knowledge that oppress subaltern peoples and also because it provides liberating alternatives. In this project, historians and post-colonial critics stand together against colonial modernity to secure a better future for subaltern peoples, learning to hear them, allowing them to speak, talking back to powers that marginalise them, documenting their past. A liberated imagined community can only come into its own, in this view, in subaltern language and memory, which historians can strive to recuperate, however partially and tentatively.[10]

(i) Modernity and Post-modernity

To Anthony Giddens (1991), modernity in the form of a juggernaut is extremely dynamic; it is a "'runaway world' "with great increases in the pace, scope, and profoundness of change over prior systems. Giddens defines modernity in terms of four basic institutions. The first is *capitalism*, characterised, familiarly, by commodity production, private ownership of capital, propertyless wage labour, and a class system derived from these characteristics. The second is *industrialism*, which involves the use of inanimate power sources and machinery to produce goods. Industrialism is not restricted to the workplace, and it affects an array of other settings, such as "transportation, communication and domestic life". Giddens's first two characteristics of modernity are hardly novel, the third— *surveillance capacities.* As Giddens defines it, "Surveillance refers to the supervision of the activities of subject populations [mainly but not exclusively] in the political sphere" (1990:58). The final Institutional dimension of modernity is military power, or the *control of the means of violence,* including the industrialisation of war.

Modernity is given dynamism by three essential aspects of Giddens's structuration theory: distanciation, disembedding, and reflexivity. The first is *time and space separation,* or *distanciation.* As Giddens defines it, *disembedding* involves "the 'lifting out' of social relations from local contexts of interaction and their restructuring across indefinite spans of time-space" The third dynamic characteristic of modernity is its *reflexivity.* Reflexivity is a fundamental feature of Giddens's structuration theory (as well as of human existence, in his view), but it takes on special meaning in modernity, where "social practices are constantly examined and reformed in the light of incoming information about those very practices, thus constitutively altering their character". Habermas (1987b) sees modernity as an "unfinished project," implying that there is far more to be done in the modern world before we can begin thinking about the possibility of a postmodern world. Habermas makes a case not only for modernity but also against the postmodernists. Habermas offered some early criticisms in an essay, "Modernity versus Postmodernity" (1981), which has achieved wide recognition.

Charles Lemert argues that the birth of postmodernism can be traced, at least symbolically, to the death of modernist architecture at 3:32 P.M., July 15, 1972—the moment at which the Pruitt-Igoe housing project in St. Louis was destroyed. . . . This massive housing project in St. Louis represented modernist architecture's arrogant belief that by building the biggest and best public housing planners and architects could eradicate poverty and human misery. To have recognised, and destroyed the symbol of that idea was to admit the failure of modernist architecture, and by implication modernity itself. Lemert (1990) traces the beginning of poststructuralism to a 1966 speech by Jacques Derrida, one of the acknowledged leaders of this approach in which he proclaimed the dawning of a new poststructuralist age. In contrast to the structuralists, especially those who followed the linguistic turn and who saw people as being constrained by the structure of language, Derrida reduced language to "writing" that does not constrain its subjects. Furthermore, Derrida also saw social institutions as nothing but writing and therefore as unable to constrain people. In contemporary terms, Derrida deconstructed language and social institutions. Thus, Derrida offers what is ultimately a subversive, deconstructive perspective. As we will see, subversion and deconstruction become even more important with the emergence of postmodernism, and it is poststructuralism that laid the groundwork for postmodernism. The object of Derrida's hostility is the *logocentrism* (the search for a universal system of thought that reveals what is true, right, beautiful, and so on) that has dominated Western social thought. This approach has contributed to what Derrida describes as the "historical repression and suppression of writing since Plato". Logocentrism has led to the closure not only of philosophy, but also to that of the human sciences. Derrida is interested in deconstructing, or "dismantling," the sources of this closure—this repression—thereby freeing writing from the things that enslave it. An apt phrase to describe Derrida's focus is "the deconstruction of logocentrism" (1978:230).

M, Foucault's work illustrates yet another difference between poststructuralism and structuralism. The concern for "saying the truth" relates directly to Foucault's genealogy of power because, as Foucault comes to see it, knowledge and power are inextricably intertwined. In his genealogy of power, Foucault is concerned with how people govern themselves and others through the production of knowledge. Among other things, he sees knowledge generating power by constituting people as subjects and then governing the subjects with the knowledge. He is critical of the hierarchisation of knowledge. Because the highest-ranking forms of knowledge (the sciences) have the greatest power, they are singled out for the most severe critique. Foucault is interested in techniques, the technologies that are derived from knowledge (especially scientific knowledge), and how they are used by various institutions to exert power over people.

(b) Indian Sociologists: Understanding Society and Culture

(a) G.S. Ghurye (Indologist)

Ghurye"s work, *Caste and Race in India* (1932) cognitively combined historical, anthropological and sociological perspectives to understand caste and kinship system in India.[11] He tries to analyse caste system through textual evidences using ancient texts on the one hand and also from both structural and cultural perspective on the other hand.

Ghurye highlights six structural features of caste system as follows:

1. Segmental Division
2. Hierarchy
3. Pollution and Purity
4. Civil and Religious Disabilities and Privileges of Different Sections
5. Lack of Choice of Occupation
6. Restrictions on Marriage

Besides the above characteristics, Ghurye stresses *endogamy* as the most important feature of the caste system. Any effective unit of the caste hierarchy is marked by *endogamy*. Every caste had in the paste segmented into smaller sub-divisions or sub-castes. Each of these sub-castes practiced endogamy. For example, *Vaishya (Baniya or Mahajan)* castes are divided into various sub-castes such as *Agrawal, Maheshwari* etc.

Caste is also linked with kinship through caste-endogamy and also clan (*gotra*) exogamy. *Gotra* has been treated as thoroughly exogamous unit by the *Brahmins* and later by the *non-Brahmins*. The basic notion here is that all the members of a *gotra* are related to one another, through blood, i.e., they have *rish*i (sage) as their common ancestor. Therefore, marriage between two persons of the same gotra will lead to incestuous relationship. It will lead the lineage of the *gotra* to near extinction.

Ghurye's concept of cultural unity is of a new one and is not a secular in orientation. He is concerned with India of Hindu culture and uses the term 'Indian Culture' and 'Hindu Culture' synonymously. Hinduism in traditional India, he says, provided an excellent normative base for maintaining social and political unity in the country. He thinks that it is largely as a result of Brahmanical endeavour that cultural unity in India has been built up. All the major institutions of Hindu society originated among the Brahmins and gradually they were accepted by other sections of the community. Though Ghurye calls it process of acculturation it was basically a one way flow, in which the Brahmanical ideas and institutions infiltrated among the non-Brahmins.

According to Ghurye, society is not just an aggregation of isolated individuals but that group life which provides the bridge between the individual and society. An individual acquires social attributes and socialises through groups. This is the integrative functions of groups in society. When groups perform the function efficiently, integration is achieved.

Tensions in the process of this integration in India arise today because the various groups of people have failed to transient their narrow group loyalties. Religious and linguistic minorities are the most potential source of danger to Indian unity in modern India. Religion and linguistic leasions are the crucial areas causing disintegration of the country. Ghurye gives great importance to the role of language in the process of nation building in India. The regional languages ensure the unity of territory at the local level and all efforts should be made to improve that the regional languages ensure the vicinity of the territory at the local level and all efforts should be made to improve that.

(b) Louis Dumont (Indologist)

Dumont stress the role of ideology in moulding human behaviour and, therefore, to seek to bring together sociology and Indology.[12] Following Bougle, one of the masters, he chooses the Hindu notion of the fundamental opposition between the pure and the impure as his starting point for an understanding of the caste system. Dumont stresses the importance of recognising these three features, or "principles", as mutually entailed; resting on "one fundamental conception", for the atomisation into simple elements is the student's need and not a characteristic of the system itself. What we need in order to transcend the distinction we make is "a single true principle". Such a principle, Dumont maintains, is the opposition of the pure and the impure. "This opposition underlies hierarchy, which is the superiority of the pure to the impure, underlies separation because the pure and the impure must be kept separate, and underlies the division of labour because pure and impure occupations must likewise be kept separate. The whole is founded on the necessary and hierarchical co-existence of the two opposites."

Hierarchy, defined as the superiority of the pure over the impure, then, is the "keystone" in Dumont's model of the caste system. It is of the greatest importance to realise at once that, as employed by him, the notion "is quite independent of natural inequalities or the distribution of power" (p 20). It is "the principle by which the elements of a whole are ranked in relation to the whole, it being understood that in the majority of societies it is religion which provides the view of the whole, and that the ranking will thus be religious in nature" (p 66). In other words, hierarchy is the relationship between "that which encompasses and that which is encompassed" (p xii). Such a perspective helps us to obtain a holistic view of the system, to overcome the dualism of opposition.

According to Louis Dumont (1970), caste system is an ideology, that is to say, as a system of values and ideas that is both rational and intelligible (p. 36). ....In India, hierarchy is the means by which traditional societies achieve 'holism'. The caste system can therefore be regarded as a hierarchical ranking, and hierarchy as the Indian counterpart of the notion of equality. This is the principle around which the whole society is articulated (p. 66)....The opposition between pure and impure is the first and foremost of a religious nature. Maintaining a certain degree of purity is a constant concern for Indians, and the division into endogamous castes is one way of preserving the relative purity of a group. The primary source of defilement is contact with death and organic wastes, primarily those from the human body (faeces, saliva, urine, perspiration, hair, menstrual blood etc.). Every area of social life is pervaded by this dichotomy: the type of food eaten, for instance, can be ranked, and the strictly vegetarian diet associated with Brahmins and few other high castes are considered the most pure; next comes diet that allows eggs, then fish, chicken, mutton and right at the bottom, pork and beef. Similarly, certain materials are ascribed a ritual value: silk is more pure than cotton, gold more than silver, brass more than copper. So pervasive is the opposition between pure and impure that we could go on to enumerate many more applications.

In his work he narrated various forms of hierarchy as prevalent in Indian society. Dumont follows Bougle, explaining that impurity is "the eruption of the biological into social life";' Hindus suffer temporary impurity when in contact with twelve polluting secretions of the body.' Having developed Bougle's ideas by underlining the interdependence implied to exist among the hereditary specialists whom Bougle specifies, Dumont presents, as the principles of the Hindu caste system, the scheme of hierarchy, separation, and interdependence-all of which are based upon an opposition between purity and impurity. These four elements are hierarchy, separation, interdependence, and purity-impurity. With respect to the *jajmani system*, it suggests that the key to understanding it lies in customs of purity-impurity. Indeed, certain castes specialise in removing pollution-for example, the barber and the laundryman. The castes cooperate in the jajmani system, because "the execution of impure tasks by some is necessary to the maintenance of purity for others."

With respect to the regulation of marriage, Dumont agrees with Bougle that endogamy keeps castes separate from one another; but he also takes up the challenge Bougle offers by the exceptions to endogamy, of castes that prefer hypergamous marriages, either between castes or between sections of a caste.

One of Dumont's most original insights is his point that hypergamy indicates the permeation of hierarchy within castes and between castes. Hypergamous marriages illustrate the concept of hierarchy. Dumont cites, with general approval, studies of caste-ranking in which rank is expressed in terms of food transactions and other gestures of contamination between castes. Dumont suggests that the disjunction between priest and king, with the former superior, made possible the development of a purely religious hierarchy, one based on purity-impurity. Purity is connected with the priest, because he had to be pure when he had "access to the sacred."For pure hierarchy to develop without hindrance, it was also necessary that power should be absolutely inferior to status".

(c) Radhakamal Mukerjee (Value Premise)

Radhakamal Mukerjee (1889–1968) may truly be regarded as the *primus inter pares* among the founding fathers of sociology in India. It is remarkable that at quite a young age, when he was still in his twenties, he had a clear conception of the scope and method of an interdisciplinary social science, embracing economics, sociology, political science, and social philosophy. Mukerjee recalls: 'Somehow an integrated study of the social sciences, of Economics, Political Science, Social Philosophy and Sociology stimulated in me the desire and striving to envisage man, society and civilisation as wholes that defeat any compartmentalisation and its aims' (1997: 68).

Nationalism provided the framework within which holism and humanism were established as the bedrock of Mukerjee's intellectual quest. In his first book, *The Foundations of Indian Economics* (1916), Mukerjee had already called for rehabilitation of the traditional organic village (cooperative socioeconomic system, a balancing of agriculture and industry, small-scale and large-scale industrial production, production and distribution, and so on).

(i) On Social Ecology: Conceptualising the region as a dynamic 'field' or 'configuration', he stressed the interplay of naturally given environment and culture, which tends towards 'balance' or 'equilibrium', 'shifting the life-balance now in favour of man, now against him'. Further, he wrote: 'Perhaps the most important contribution of ecology is the idea of the region as an intricate network of interrelations. The region exhibits a complex pattern of adaptation between the environmental factors and the plant and animal communities including human societies' (Mukerjee 1938a: 1–2).

He clarifies by saying that social ecology, as he conceived it, had to go beyond 'human *individual* adjustments to the environment' (the field of human ecology), and embrace 'the adjustments of man's *social* structures and functions, of the processes of interaction between region, occupation and society—the sociological equivalent of environment, function and organism [Geddes's framework, see above]—out of which arise all social phenomena' (Mukerjee 1945a: viii). Unlike American pioneers in the field of ecological studies such as Robert Park, Mukerjee emphatically includes the role of culture in the making of ecological relations. 'Culture is the guardian,' Mukerjee wrote (1945a: 339), 'that assumes not merely a true balance between different parts of institutional life, but also between man's material and non-material social equipment and his region.' Just as culture is inconceivably independent of the environment, the latter too is shaped (or distorted) by the former. Mukerjee argued that 'what is position in ecological space, status is in social space' (1945a: 159). Further, he observed (1945a: 159–60):

> It is the task of sociology to determine the nature of the status system, investigate the nature of various groupings and institutions where individuals interact in the various dominant, subordinate and co-ordinate relations, and ascertain the value and symbol systems by which rank or any social position (status) is assigned by the community. Social status and social mobility thus are, respectively, the morphological (or structural) and dynamic (or organisational) dimensions of society.

(ii) Sociology of Values: Mukerjee's last two major sociological works, *The Social Structure of Values* (1949) and *The Dynamics of Morals* (1951), are products of vast scholarship, an idealistic empiricism that rejects the fact value dichotomy, and a humanism which is grounded in the biopsychic unity of humankind, but respects cultural differences. To him, 'The problem of social values is the core of social theory', and the call to sociology to 'develop a central theory of norms and values as basic units in the description and explanation of social relationships and behaviour' (Mukerjee 1949: 6). It is important to note that Mukerjee writes of 'social values', that is, not values which may be deemed to have descended from high above, but values that arise from patterns of social interaction, which themselves are guided by value judgements.

(d) M.N. Srinivas (Structural-functionalist)

He wrote on 'Social Change in Modern India'.[13] Srinivas asks the question: What are the orientations of change in India? As is generally agreed these are two: (1) Indian and (2) exogenous, in this case Western.

The Indian orientations are towards India's past or what is generally called traditional In-dian society and culture. The Western orientations are toward the contemporary and recent Western society, particularly the nineteenth-century British society. Srinivas calls them Sanskritisation and Westernisation respectively. He defines them by de-limitation of their behavioural aspects, the former rather strictly or less vaguely than the latter.

Sanskritisation according to him is the "process by which a low Hindu caste or tribal or other group changes its customs, ritual, ideology and way of life in the direction of a high and frequently twice born caste."

The structural basis of Hindu society is caste, and it is not possible to understand Sanskritisation without reference to the structural framework in which it occurs. Speaking generally, the castes occupying the top positions in the hierarchy are more Sanskritised than castes in the lower and middle regions of the hierarchy, and this has been responsible for the Sanskritisation of the lower castes as well as the outlying tribes. The lower castes always seem to have tried to take over the customs and way of life of the higher castes. The theoretical existence of a ban on their adoption of Brahmanical customs and rites was not very effective, and this is clear when we consider the fact that many non-Brahmanical castes practice many Brahmanical customs and rites. A more effective barrier to the lower castes' taking over of the customs and rites of the higher castes was the hostile attitude of the locally dominant caste, or of the king of the region. In their case there was physical force which could be used to keep the lower groups in check.[14]

No doubt, the idea of hierarchy is omnipresent in the caste system; not only do the various castes form a hierarchy, but the occupations practiced by them, the various items of their diet, and the customs they observe, all form separate hierarchies. Thus practicing an occupation like butchery, tanning, herding swine, or handling toddy, puts a caste in a low position. Eating pork or beef is more degrading than eating fish or mutton. Castes which offer blood-sacrifices to deities are lower than castes making only offerings of fruit and flowers. The entire way of life of the top castes seeps down the hierarchy. And as mentioned earlier, the language, cooking, clothing, jewelry, and way of life of the Brahmans spreads eventually to the entire society.

Sanskritisation has significant effects on conjugal relations. Among Brahmans for instance, a wife is enjoined to treat her husband as a deity. It is very unusual for a wife to take her meal before the husband has his, and in orthodox families, the wife still eats on the dining leaf on which her husband has eaten. Normally, such a leaf may not be touched as it would render impure the hand touching it. Usually the woman who removes the dining leaf purifies the spot where the leaf had rested with a solution of cowdung, after which she washes her hands. There is no pollution, however, in eating on the leaf on which the husband has eaten.

Sanskritisation means not only the adoption of new customs and habits, but also exposure to new ideas and values which have found frequent expression in the vast body of Sanskrit literature, sacred as well as secular. Karma, dharma, papa, punya, maya, samsara and moksa are examples of some of the most common Sanskritic theological ideas, and when a people becomes Sanskritised these words occur frequently in their talk. These ideas reach the common people through Sanskritic myths and stories. The institution of *harikatha* helps in spreading Sanskrit stories and ideas among the illiterate. In a harikatha the priest reads and explains a religious story to his audience. Each story takes a few weeks to complete, the audience meeting for a few hours every evening in a temple. Harikathas may be held at any time, but festivals such as Dasara, Ramanavami, Shivaratri and *Ganesh Chaturthi* are considered especially suitable for listening to harikathas. The faithful believe that such listening leads to the acquisition of spiritual merit. It is one of the traditionally approved ways of spending one's time.

By Westernisation, he means that which characterises "the changes brought about in Indian Society and culture as a result of over 150 years of British rule and the term subsumes changes occurring at different levels-technology, institutions, ideology or values."

According to him, the most important value preference in Westernisation was humanitarianism which subsumes several other values such as equalitarianism and secularism. Srinivas's position is that the Hindu "tradition of tolerance, syncretism and self-criticism" received the value of Western humanitarianism and began to embody it in the "legal, political, educational and other institutions" in India in the late nineteenth century. This was done through the agency of the Westernised Indian intellectual elite.

Westernisation and modernisation brought about a decline in religious beliefs and practices. This was termed as Secularisation. Srinivas notes that both Sanskrisation and Secularisation were gaining ground around the same time in modern India. Although Sanskritisation primarily affected only the Hindus, Secularisation was a more general process specially marked among the urban and educated groups. Hinduism was most affected by it owing to its lack of central structure and reliance on institutions such as caste, joint family and village community, which were evolving under the forces of secularisation. To him, education, high income and urbanisation result in a secularisation of the lifestyle, which includes a radical change in the technology of eating as well as in the timing of meals and dietary. A new attitude towards food begin to emerge; it is looked at more from the point of view of whether it promotes health and efficiency and less from whether it is traditionally permitted or prohibited.

The chapter on secularisation illustrates, with examples, how ways of life and prevailing beliefs were affected by its advancement. Traditional ideas of purity gave way to rules on hygiene, rituals (*namakarna, chaula, upakarma, kanyadana, saptapadi)* were significantly shortened as per feasibility and convenience, the marriageable age for girls was increased in order to reap the benefits of higher education and new cults, built around saints, came up. The educated Hindus started believing that the purpose of monasteries was promoting education and social welfare rather than punctilious allegiance to a set of religious practices.

To him, British rule brought with it a process of secularisation of Indian social life and culture, a tendency that gradually became stronger with the development of communications, growth of towns and cities, increased spatial mobility, and the spread of education. The term 'secularisation' implies that what was previously regarded as religious is now ceasing to be such, and it also implies a process of differentiation which results in the various aspects of society, economic, political, legal and moral, becoming increasing discrete in relation to each other.

Another essential element in secularisation is rationalism, a comprehensive expression applied to various theoretical and practical tendencies which aim to interpret the universe purely in terms of thought, or which aim to regulate individual and social life in accordance with the principles of reason and to eliminate as far as possible or to relegate to the background everything irrational. Rationalism involves, among other things, the replacement of traditional beliefs and ideas by modern knowledge.

It would be safe to assume that Hindus were more affected by the secularisation process than any other religious group in India as, first, the concept of pollution and purity which are central as well as pervasive in Hinduism were greatly weakened as a result of the operation of a variety of factors. Moreover, the fact that Hinduism lacks a central and nation-wide organisation with a single head, and that it is largely dependent for its perpetuation on such social institutions which are changing in important respects—renders it peculiarity vulnerable to the forces of secularisation.

He pointed out that there is increase in the secularisation of village life. It is true that the unit of endogamy has widened somewhat, but this is more true of the higher castes than the others. The widening is more along traditional line; a crude way describing the situation would be that while the barrier between sub-castes are beginning to break-down, marriage spanning wide structural or cultural gaps are rare. Inter-dining among castes is slightly more liberal than before, but only slightly. All the 'touchable' castes will unite against Harijans who want to exercise their constitutional right of entering temples and drawing water from village wells. The processes which have affected caste and the village communities have also affected the family system. This has happened at all levels and in every section of society, but more particularly among the westernised elite, that is, the upper castes living in the larger town and cities.

Srinivas concentrated on the study of some vial aspects of Hindu society and culture and his study did it explore the dimensions of interaction and interface between the Hindu and non-Hindu segments. The area that he studied did not have a large non-Hindu presence. He hoped that other sociologists would take up the study of the non-Hindu segments of Indian society and culture without which an Indian sociology; Indian in the sense of being comprehensive and authentic and hence truly representative of the plurality and complexity of India, would not emerge.

(e) R.S. Khare (Socio-culturalist)

In his work on 'The Hindu Hearth and Home', he pointed out that, it is a common place that ideas about food, and the rules governing the way it is handled and exchanged, are highly elaborated in Hindu culture.[15] Different kinds of food are held to possess different innate qualities that alter or sustain the moral and physical state of the eater. One acquires the properties of what one ingests. Methods of cooking make foods more or less permeable to pollution; the more permeable the more particular the eater is expected to be about the ritual purity of the cook and server. Given these requirements about the status of those who handle one's food, the women of the caste group may be seen as the guardians of its purity not simply in the sense that only pure women can bear pure progeny, but also in the sense that they sustain the purity of their men-folk by preparing pure food-the source of a pure body and pure seed. Cooking and eating together are a central symbol of amity-the folk definition of the joint household being the sharing of a common cooking hearth. Conversely, a refusal to eat with those not disqualified by the dictates of status may be interpreted as an open expression of enmity or even of witchcraft.

He discusses preparation, distribution, and consumption of food are part of a moral and spiritual universe for the Hindu. "Food area" is a felicitous neologism, denoting all areas where food is handled, from storage to consumption. "Kitchen" or "dining area" would indeed be too narrow. Foods are ranked by degrees of purity. The Hindu domestic geography confers rank to food as it does to people. The highest or purest food is closest to the family shrine; ritualistically less relevant nutrients are placed farther away. The most polluted areas (for drainage and defecation) are physically most distant from the shrine. The cooked-food and food-consumption area adjoin the sacred centre. He emphasised the distinction between pollution-susceptible kacha and ritualistically insulated pakka food is a regional phenomenon specific to the area analysed by the author. The former is also the staple food in that large area. Pakka food, fried in ghee (clarified butter), is the food for feasts and for wider social-culinary exchanges.

He also made a discussion of feasting and fasting, of the handling of food during periods of birth and death pollution, and of the symbolic uses of food in marriage are particularly rich and suggestive. Equally important is the clear documentation of the considerable variation which exists between orthodox and unorthodox members of the same caste and even of the same household in the observance of the rules surrounding the consumption of food–a variation which has major implications for models of caste ranking.

(f) Ranajit Guha (Subalternist)

Subaltern historiography seeks to restore a balance by highlighting the role of the politics of the people as against elite politics played in Indian history. Guha has used ideology in subaltern studies as a schema of interpretation of the past in order to change the present world and that such a change involves a radical transformation of consciousness.[16]

The subaltern studies have immense possibility of projecting, constructing and analysing the people's lives, institutions, problems, movements, values and the processes of their formation, structuration and restructuration at local and regional levels. The meanings thus need not be viewed from Marxist perspective but from Indian historigraphical and culturological perspective. In fact, at theoretical and ideological levels, it can provide the basis for explanation of social existence of Indian people and the way people managed their lives. The Indian culturological can be constructed at ideological, theoretical and empirical levels in terms of continuity and change through analysis of classical texts and folk-rural commonality of existence. The relationship between the two provides significant framework to understand the Indian social, cultural and personality systems, at local micro-level and trans-regional macro-level. It further provides a scheme to relate past with present, empirical with ideological, segmental with pluralism and mundane with transcendental.

(c) Sociological Analysis of Urban World

(a) Sociology of City

In the history of the human species, cities are a relatively recent development. The earliest cities appeared simultaneously between 3000 and 4000 BC in the Nile Valley and in Mesopotamia. Around 2000 BC cities also developed in Crete, in the Yellow River in China, Greece and the Indus Valley. Cities arose independently in the New World in Central Mexico around 300 BC. The Mayan and Aztec cities arose in the first millennium AD, but large cities are a product of the industrial revolution and the demographic transformation of the eighteenth and nineteenth centuries.

The city has been a fundamental social institution in the history of western civilisation; this intimate interaction between the city and western culture is probably fundamentally illustrated by the etymology of such terms as civilisation, civility and citizenship. The cultivated and educated citizen is the inhabitant of a city and for historical sociologists like Norbet Elias (1978) the civilising process whereby the manners of individuals are cultivated and developed into a socially acceptable etiquette of everyday behaviour, requires the cosmopolitan context of an urban environment, namely a city-state. Elias argued in *The Civilising Process* that the historical evolution of civilisation moves from the violent lives of men on horseback to the refined manners of the court and later to the puritanical code of the bourgeois household, but this social transformation ultimately required the larger context of a city environment. In common sense terms, the primary values of western society have been associated with the moral order produced by the city, namely the values of urbanity and the urbane personality. By contrast, the countryside was connected with the negative notion of the pagan (*paganus*) whose life, because it existed outside the city, was characterised by illiteracy and vulgarity. In order to understand the significance of the city in western sociological theory, we have to understand the importance of the city for debates about individual freedom and democracy, and we have to grasp the ideological importance of the city as a strategic concept in Orientalism which specified a radical difference between the oriental despotic city as a military camp and the democratic institutions of the western city. The prevalent notion that 'the city air makes a man free', namely that within an urban western environment the possibilities of independent freedom and democracy were maximised.[17]

In order to understand the debate about the city and social change, it is important to start with an examination of the conceptual problems in defining the city. Beginning with the work of archeologists on pre-history, the classification of the city as an urban context has been an important feature of the literature on cities. If we take the work of Gordon Childe, we can start by establishing a number of important criteria for the early antiquity of the city and for its sociological definition. In his article on civilisation, cities and towns in *Antiquity*, Childe (1957) identified a number of important criteria for the definition of a city. Childe was interested in the city as the location for the development of various juridical institutions and arrangements such that a city is a community 'that comprises a substantial proportion of professional rulers, officials, clergy, artisans and merchants who do not catch or grow their own food, but live on the surplus produced by farmers or fishermen who may dwell within the city or villages outside its walls' (Childe, 1957: 37). Thus a city involves a particular framework of government which comes into existence with the development of an agricultural civilisation with a surplus to support such intellectual or mental workers. This transition in history permits us to speak of an 'urban revolution' analogous to the notion of an industrial revolution or a Neolithic revolution. Thus the origins of cities are closely associated with the growth of the institution of writing as a bureaucratic process of management and surveillance. The transition of the city from its ancient origins into a modern form is closely connected with the emergence of literate culture and the role of writing as a strategy of political regulation.

(b) Urbanism as a Way of Life

The so-called Chicago School provided a strong tradition of urban research on marginal groups, on social disorganisation, on the ghetto, on marginal occupations and on urban poverty. The Chicago School was motivated by a doctrine of pragmatism, amelioration and empirical research. Against a background of urban decay, the Chicago School and its followers embraced implicitly a positive image of the early colonial environment, the autonomous city and the free and authentic citizen. Out of this mixture of pragmatism and romanticism, there emerged a variety of theories of spatial order, zoning, ethnic segregation and social ecology. The Chicago School provided one of the most detailed and significant descriptions of the modern urban city which was genuinely sociological in its direction and dimensions.

Following a positivist epistemology, they saw their scientific role in terms of developing a detailed picture of the 'facts' of urban life. These questions about origin, location and spatial characteristics gave rise to a number of influential studies, but *The City* (Park, Burgess and McKenzie, 1925) was particularly important. From this research tradition, there emerged the so-called 'ecological theory of the city'. For Robert E. Park the city was a natural environment of modern people, which followed specific laws of development. The city grew as a complex network of communities, which came to be associated over time with specific neighbourhoods and particular suburbs. These neighbourhood communities are populated by ethnic communities, organised around a definite division of labour. For Park, the city was an organisation of social communities in space, an organisation which follows its own laws of evolutionary development. The Chicago School's approach to the city was thus based on broad assumptions that the city provided a 'natural' laboratory or framework for sociological study, there was an important cultural division between city and country, which was conceptualised in terms of a rural–urban continuum, and in an urban society the city came to define the whole life of the society. The more specific theory of the city was the concentric-zone theory of urban development.

Louis Wirth's famous essay on 'Urbanism as a Way of Life' in which Wirth (1938) attempted to specify the principal features of the large modern city. In addition to population density, he noted: heterogeneity of ethnic communities, life-styles and cultures; social relations which are transitory, anonymous, and effectively neutral; occupational specialisation and the division of labour; separation of residence and work place; secularisation of thought and values, which is facilitated by a money economy; standardisation through the growth of mass markets; dependence on formal rules of conduct, which are indicated by the dominance of the clock and traffic signals; and the predominance of secondary and segmental contacts. Wirth's seminal essay has been both criticised and elaborated by subsequent research.[18]

(c) Poverty, Social Class and the City[19]

There is considerable literature on the impact of the urban environment on physical and moral deprivation. For example, was the industrial city associated with improving standards of health or was it associated, through urban poverty, with increasing infant mortality and morbidity? There is now an important amount of social science literature on the demographic transformation of western societies which has analysed the consequences of urbanisation on the health of urban populations, especially in the second half of the nineteenth century. The analyses of medical historians on the impact of rural nurses on the urban infant populations shows a pattern of increasing morbidity and mortality. Rapid urbanisation was also connected with an increase in mental illness; different types of mental illness were associated with both social class and city zones (Faris and Dunham, 1939).

Much of the early sociology of the city was concerned with the problem of poverty, the rise of an organised and politically active working class and the negative effects of urban poverty on health in terms of both morbidity and mortality. The analysis of urban poverty gave rise to a complementary literature on urban poverty alleviation and the positive programmes for restructuring and developing the urban environment. Planning was essential for a civilised existence (Howe, 1912). For example, in the work of sociologists like Karl Mannheim the importance of planning and urban development became a fundamental basis for the development of sociological writing about democratic planning in an advanced urban environment. He argued that in a mass society the individual becomes atomised and as a result an effective democracy requires planning to overcome individualism and egoism (Mannheim, 1951).

Within a similar genre one can see the sociological work of Geddes on urban planning as a response to the negative consequences of urban disorganisation and anomie. Geddes had an optimistic vision of the positive role of rational planning on the urban environment. His work was based upon a conceptual scheme which had been developed by the French sociologist Frederic Le Play in which sociology is the study of the organic relationship between place, work and family

(d) The Economics of Sanitation Initiative (ESI)[20]

The Water and Sanitation Programme (WSP) has launched a multi-country Economics of Sanitation Initiative (ESI) to study the economic impacts of poor sanitation and the costs and benefits of improved sanitation options. The overall goal of ESI is to provide decision makers at the country and regional levels with the evidence they need to advocate for increased investment in improving sanitation and to provide an improved evidence-base for efficient planning and implementation of sustainable sanitation and hygiene options and programmes.

The inter-related objectives of the ESI India Study are to:

1. Carry out an impact study to generate evidence on the economic

impacts of current sanitation arrangements and hygiene practices in relation to the management of human excreta (and related hygiene practices), in both the rural and urban areas of India, based on an analysis of secondary data.

2. Carry out an options study to collect and analyse data on the actual costs and benefits of different sanitation options or interventions in a range of programme delivery contexts.

The ESI Impact Study is highly relevant to the sanitation challenges that the people of India face today in both rural and urban areas of the country. These challenges are substantial, with large populations defecating in the open or using unimproved toilets and a very high proportion of human fecal waste being released untreated both onto land and into bodies of water (especially from urban areas). Inadequate sanitation and poor hygienic practices lead to huge public health costs (e.g., the associated costs of deaths and diseases that are *attributable to inadequate sanitation*) as well as environmental and other welfare impacts.

In this work, economic impacts of inadequate sanitation are first estimated in non-economic units and then converted to economic units using appropriate valuation methods.

(i) Health-related impacts include:

- Premature mortality, that is, lost lives, especially those of children due to diarrheal and other diseases caused by poor sanitation;
- Cost of healthcare incurred in treating diseases caused by poor sanitation, and
- Productivity losses, that is, productive time lost due to people falling ill, as well as productive time lost when care-givers need to look after the ill.

(ii) Domestic water-related impacts include:

- Household treatment of drinking water by various methods;
- Use of bottled water by households, and
- Piped water (a fraction of this use is attributed to inadequate sanitation, and the rest to factors like convenience), and Hauling cleaner water from a distance outside the household because a nearer source of water may be contaminated due to poor sanitation.

(iii) Access time impacts include:

- Cost of additional time needed for accessing shared toilets and open-defecation sites compared to using a private toilet within the household, and

- Cost of school absence time due to inadequate toilets for girls and work-absence time due to inadequate toilets for working women.

(iv) Tourism impacts include:

- Potential loss of tourism revenues, and
- The economic impacts of gastrointestinal illnesses among foreign tourists.

Notes

1. George Ritzer, 2000. Sociological Theory, McGraw-Hill Companies, New York.
2. *Ibid.*
3. *Ibid.*
4. *Ibid.*
5. *Ibid.*
6. Antonio Gramsci, 'Notes on Italian history', selection from the prison note-books (New York: International Publishers, 1971.
7. Peasantry, politics and historiography: Critique of new trend in relation to Marxism; p. 43 in 'Ludden, D. (ed.). 2001. Reading Subaltern studies, Delhi: Permanent Black.
8. See Ranajit Guha, 'Preface', in *Selected Subaltern Studies,* Ranajit Guha and Gayatri Spivak (eds.), New York and Oxford, Oxford University Press, 1988.
9. See, What went wrong with "History from Below"—Reinstating human agency as human creativity—Vinay Bahl; 2005. K.P.Bagchi and Company.
10. Based on David Ludden, 'A Brief History of Subalternity' in *Reading Subaltern Studies.*
11. G.S. Ghurye (1969), *Caste and Race in India,* Bombay: Popular Prakashan.
12. See "Homo Hierarchicus: the Caste System and Its Implications" by Louis Dumont; translated by Mark Sainsbury, Weidenfeld and Nicolson, London, 1970.
13. See M.N. Srinivas. 1966. Social change in modern India, Orient Longman pvt. Ltd. New Delhi.
14. See A Note on Sanskritisation and Westernisation, M. N. Srinivas, The Far Eastern Quarterly, Vol. 15, No. 4 (Aug., 1956), pp. 481-

496.

15. See Khare, R.S. The Hindu hearth and home. New Delhi: Vikas, 1976.
16. Guha, Ranjit (1983), *Elementary Aspects of Insurgency in Colonial India,* Delhi: Oxford University Press.
17. See Bryan Turner 1999, Classical Sociology, SAGE Publications London, Thousand Oaks, New Delhi.
18. *Ibid.*
19. *Ibid.*
20. Economic Impacts of Inadequate Sanitation in India, 2010, Water and Sanitation Programme, www.wsp.org

4

Research Methodology in Sociology of Sanitation

Background

Social science research is an art as well as a science, and the skills and knowledge needed to be a researcher can only be acquired through experience over time. There are always judgements to be made and decisions to be taken about how best to go about research. Fundamental to the achievement of high quality is the preparedness and ability of social science researchers to critique their work and reflect on how it could have been done differently, and whether that might have changed the outcomes and, if so, how. Reflexivity, not recipes, is the hallmark of the good social science researcher.

In 'The Structure of Scientific Revolutions', Thomas Kuhn (1962) suggested that mature scientific disciplines rely upon a paradigm that defines what to study (relevance of social phenomena), why to study (formulating explanatory hypotheses) and how to study (through which methods). Not all social scientists, however, share all these assumptions or even believe in the possibility of a common definition of scientific research. Some think that social science is pre-paradigmatic, still in search of a set of unifying principles and standards; others believe that it is post-paradigmatic, having shed a set of scientistic assumptions tied to a particular conception of modernity (the post-modern approach). Some social scientists are specifically concerned with this issue, specialising in the philosophy of social science and the theory of knowledge. Others take the basic issues for granted and concentrate on empirical research. We agree that not all social scientists need to be philosophers, and certainly most social science research would never get off the ground if we had first to resolve the fundamental questions about being and knowing.

One tradition in the social sciences, that of individualism, holds that only individuals really exist (ontological individualism) or that only individuals can act and, therefore, social science is the study of what individuals do (methodological individualism). Most versions of rational choice theory start from the individual and explain broader processes as the aggregation of individual acts. Other approaches, however, use larger units of analysis, including collectivities and institutions such as classes, ethnic groups or state. A recurrent debate in social science concerns theories of action: why people do as they do. Some social scientists take an individualist perspective, adding the assumption that individuals are motivated by self-interest and will do what maximises their own benefits—the logic of consequentialism. This supposition underlies most rational choice theory, although some proponents of rational choice stretch the idea of self-interest to include altruistic behaviour. An alternative explanation for behaviour is that it is the product of learned norms and socialisation. Institutions play a role here, both in setting the incentives for rational choice and for providing the socialisation mechanisms. In addition, people may act based on what they consider to be right according to ideology or ethical criteria.

Thus, the purposes of social science research are often contested. For some, the aim is explanation of social behaviour, on the assumption that it has causes that are knowable and measurable. Few people now think that social science works like Newtonian mechanics, with fixed mechanisms that are predictable. Some social scientists, however, do aim to approximate this; if they do not always succeed, it is because there is missing information which, in principle, could be supplied. Other scholars prefer the analogy of biology, with social behaviour evolving over time in response to learning and adaptation. Some of the work in historical institutionalism is informed by this idea. Yet some social scientists disclaim the idea of explanation and causation altogether, seeking rather to understand the motivations and calculations of actors who are not pre-determined in their behaviour.

Finally, there is the issue of norms and values in social sciences. One school of thought seeks rigorously value-free social science, again on the natural science model. Norms might be a subject for study in themselves, insofar as they can be operationalised and measured; but the social scientist should set his or her own values aside. Others disagree, arguing that many concepts and much of our language has a normative content—think of terms like peace, democracy or legitimacy—and cannot be understood without it. Some go further and argue that, until the twentieth century, the social sciences were concerned with the conditions for improving the human lot and that this, rather than explanation and prediction, is what the human sciences are good at, and that they should return to it.

Forms of Research

The main classifications of research that have emerged from the management tradition described above are pure, applied and action research. Pure research, which is sometimes referred to as domain driven, is intended to lead to theoretical development: there may, or may not, be any practical implications of this. Results are disseminated through academic media. Applied research is intended to lead to the solution of specific problems and usually involves working with clients who identify the problems. In these studies it is important to try to explain what is happening. Phillips and Pugh (1987) stress that genuine research must include consideration of 'why' questions as well as 'what' questions.

Action research studies start from the view that research should lead to change, and therefore that change should be incorporated into the research process itself. Classical action research starts from the idea that if you want to understand something well you should try changing it, and this is most frequently adopted in organisation development (French and Bell, 1978). The collaborative features of action research mean that participants are likely to learn a lot from the process itself, and their interest may be on what happens next rather than on any formal account of research findings.

Methodology and Methods in Social Science Research

The history of social science is not a matter of progressing to ever better theories and methods, but rather of successive efforts to capture the social world and to answer questions that themselves may be different. It is not a search for a complete set of concepts that would be inclusive, in covering the entire world, and exclusive, in the sense of not overlapping with each other. Usually, competing approaches in the social sciences are contrasted on (a) their *ontological* base, related to the existence of a real and objective world; (b) their *epistemological* base, related to the possibility of knowing this world and the forms this knowledge would take; (c) their *methodological* base, referring to the technical instruments that are used in order to acquire that knowledge (Corbetta 2003: 12–13).

The ontological question is about *what* we study, that is, the object of investigation. Disputes about the existence of a physical world go back to the ancients. This is not the point at issue here, since few people now bother to dispute the existence of physical objects. Rather, the question is how the world fits together and how we make sense of it. Epistemology is about *how* we know things. It is a branch of philosophy that addresses the question of the 'nature, sources and limits of knowledge' (Klein 2005). Knowledge here is *propositional* knowledge—distinct from 'belief' in that it requires that we give reasons for saying that something is so and can potentially convince others.

In social science methodological discourse, the traditional approach in *positivism* (as represented in the work of Comte, Spencer and, according to some, Durkheim) is that social sciences are in many ways similar to other (physical) sciences. The world exists as an objective entity, outside of the mind of the observer, and in principle it is knowable in its entirety. The task of the researcher is to describe and analyse this reality. Positivist approaches share the assumption that, in natural as in social sciences, the researcher can be separated from the object of his/her research and therefore observe it in a neutral way and without affecting the observed object. As in the natural sciences, there are systematic rules and regularities governing the object of study, which are also amenable to empirical research.

In *neo-positivism* and then *post-positivism*, these assumptions are relaxed. Reality is still considered to be objective (external to human minds), but it is only imperfectly knowable. The positivist trust in causal knowledge is modified by the admission that some phenomena are not governed by causal laws but, at best, by probabilistic ones. This does not represent a sharp break with the natural sciences but follows modern scientific developments (Delanty 1999).

Critical realist epistemology holds that there is a real material world but that our knowledge of it is often socially conditioned and subject to challenge and reinterpretation. There are mechanisms governing human affairs that may be unobserved and unobservable, but these are not therefore to be discounted. Similar ideas are present in *(social) constructionism* (sometimes called constructivism). This approach does not, as is sometimes thought, argue that the physical world itself is the product of the imagination of the social scientist; rather, it is he/she who puts order onto it. As Hacking (1999) explains: 'Social constructionists tend to maintain that classifications are not determined by how the world is but are convenient ways to represent it.'

The *humanistic* approaches shift the emphasis further towards the subjective. In this perspective, what distinguishes human science from natural sciences is that human behaviour is always filtered by the subjective understandings of external reality on the part of the people being studied and the researcher him/herself.

On contrast to methodology, methods are no more than ways of acquiring data. Questions about methods do, however, come together with epistemology and theory in discussions about *methodology*, which refers to the way in which methods are used.

Positivists will usually start with a hypothesis deductively derived from theory and previous knowledge. Typically, this will postulate some expected state of affairs or causal relationship and be empirically falsifiable. Positivists take care to operationalise their concepts and hypotheses in scientific and general terms, while interpretivists let the concepts emerge from the work itself. Positivists usually employ the language of variables. That is, they are not interested in cases as such, but in the properties of those cases that cause them to differ. Since they are concerned with general or universal laws, they want to know what factors cause which outcomes in social life.

Neo-positivist approaches have relaxed the assumption that knowledge is context-free and that the same relationships among variables will hold everywhere and at all times. Instead, there is more emphasis on the particular and the local, and on the way in which factors may combine in different circumstances. Interpretive analyses keep a holistic focus, emphasising cases (which could be an individual, a community or other social collectivity) as complex entities and stressing the importance of context. Concepts are orientative and can be improved during the research. The presentation of the data is usually in the form of thick narratives, with excerpts from texts (interviews, documents and ethnographic notes) presented as illustration.

(a) Ethnographic Approaches

The word *ethnography* literally means 'writing about people', and it is the interest in what some would regard as distinctive about people that has led to a boom in all sorts of ethnographic varieties. The distinctive features revolve around the notions of people as *meaning-makers*, around an emphasis on understanding how people *interpret* their worlds, and the need to understand the particular cultural worlds in which people live and which they both construct and utilise.

People actively collaborate in the *construction* and maintenance of the cultural meanings which inform their actions; and that researchers therefore need to find ways of engaging with those meanings and the processes through which they are constructed. It also follows that ethnographic work tends by its very ambitions and nature to focus on a limited range of cases, often only one case or social setting. A central purpose behind ethnography therefore is to get involved in this or that social world, to find out how its participants see that world, and to be able as researchers to describe how its culture ticks. The particular 'culture' could be a hospital ward, a school, or any society (or grouping within society).

Ethnography is derived from Ancient Greek words meaning 'writing on people'—although it can also take the final form of film documentaries and other audio-visuals. Ethnology is, then, the comparative synthesis of ethnographic information. Ethnography is the researcher's main mode of recording and analysing the data gathered during fieldwork. It is initially composed of field notes with a mix of quotations from informants, descriptions of events and informants' behaviour and personal impressions and questions (Sperber 1984: 13), all self-reflectively elaborated. Ethnographic notes can also take the form of a diary. When quoting informants, it is imperative that the researcher explain the context in which the informants spoke. The ethnographic notes will also contain other material the researcher may have deemed relevant while in the field, including quantitative data such as statistics, but also artifacts, photographs and films. Ethics is a crucial aspect of the discipline of ethnography. As a person entering the lives of the people under study, the researcher holds an important responsibility to them. It is fundamental that he works transparently with respect to his research and his relationship with his informants. When delving into private aspects of their lives or making public some of his findings, the researcher must always ask permission. He must also be able to explain as clearly as possible the subject of his study and his interest in spending time with the community.

Ethnography is a research strategy that allows researchers to explore and examine the cultures and societies that are a fundamental part of the human experience. Unlike many other scientific research strategies, the ethnographer as researcher is not typically a detached or uninvolved observer. The ethnographer collects data and gains insight through *firsthand* involvement with research subjects or informants. With few exceptions, the ethnographer conducts research by interacting with other human beings that are part of the study; this interaction takes many forms, from conversations and interviews to shared ritual and emotional experiences. From the standpoint of ethnography, the only plausible way to study social and cultural phenomena is to study them *in action.* The complexity of human lives and social interaction cannot be reduced to a sterile laboratory experiment with the strict control of variables characteristic of a scientific experiment. Instead, ethnography aims to study life outside of a controlled environment. As a result, the objects of study are sometimes hard to identify and always subject to change as the result of innovation, conflict, and many other factors. Ethnographers employ a number of different research techniques and methods in a complex research strategy that matches the complexity of their objects of study.

Ethnography originally developed as a research strategy in academic circles, mainly within the discipline of anthropology. Therefore, anthropology provides many of the most famous early ethnographers and much "classic" ethnography. Names like Bronislaw Malinowski, E. E. Evans—Pritchard, Margaret Mead and Ruth Benedict, along with ethnographic subjects like the Trobriand Islanders, the Nuer, the island of Samoa, and the nation of Japan are important markers of ethnography 's early history. These ethnographers and their works have given us a number of important texts and some films that are important resources for students of ethnography.[1]

It is a methodology central to the qualitative approach in the social Sciences. Its value lies in the flexible process by which it takes place, giving precedence to empirical findings over theoretical formulating. It is described as a naturalistic approach whose main data-gathering and analysing techniques consist of participant observation and open-ended interviewing. Ethnography is also a form of writing that encompasses a research philosophy central to the qualitative approach. Ethnography provides a valuable contribution to the social sciences that can be taken into account by researchers with differing quantitative and qualitative inclinations. All are used in fieldwork, which is then written up and analysed as ethnography. Aimed at acquiring a deep knowledge of the social community and the individual, fieldwork typically entails adapting to a local area and culture, carrying out open-ended interviews, and spending time with members of the community. Knowledge is considered 'deep' when a subject is examined in the context of its complex connections.

While conventionally associated with anthropologists, ethnography may be useful for social scientists of other disciplines. Just as we challenge the mutually exclusive categorisation of quantitative and qualitative approaches in the social sciences in the introduction to this book, we argue that other social and political scientists, however quantitative their research, may at some point find it useful to consider the ethnographic approach—at least as something useful to delve into at different points in their work and as a means to further elucidate or illustrate some aspects of their findings. Ethnography lies at the heart of the social sciences because of its inherently holistic and naturalistic character. By an in-depth, holistic and naturalistic study, we mean the examination of a subject in its natural context. Whether it is the study of the macro-structures and processes that organise or affect society, such as race, ethnicity, gender and class stratification; institutions of a social, religious, political or commercial nature; or micro-processes such as interpersonal interactions and the socialisation of individuals, ethnography has an important role to play. Social and political scientists are all concerned with the dynamics of interaction between people; with the multiple ways in which power is exerted, formally and informally, seen and unseen, direct and indirect; and with how these dynamics determine relations in the domains of culture, economics and politics. Ethnography provides an approach to recording and analysing data in a flexible fashion that can help in understanding the dynamics of the human social world that the researcher will encounter as she goes about her investigation (Campelli 1996).

The ethnographic approach is intrinsically sensitive to the subtlety and complexity of human social life in a way that a quantitative approach cannot be. A researcher basing her work on quantitative methods will miss many of the subtleties of human expression as she fits her findings into purpose-built categories, however well grounded they may be. Nuances, expressive silences and insinuations on the part of informants will be ignored by the quantitative researcher, judged as soft data and, therefore, dismissed as scientifically unreliable. Yet, as the study of people, their cultures and the complex constructions of meaning through which they communicate, the social sciences cannot confine themselves to quantifiable methods (Klandermans and Staggenborg 2002).

Ethnographic research in health has often had a specific focus on improving aspects of service delivery or organisation: exploring, for example, how cultural beliefs and practices might impact on concepts of health, illness and treatment, how health professionals' ethnocentricity might affect the perceptions of clients or other health workers, and what factors affect the acceptability of certain health interventions (e.g., Savage, 2000).

Ethnography as an approach: The ethnographic approach is naturalistic, in that it attempts to work with society as it is, without trying to influence or control it. The goal is to understand behaviour in its habitual context, as opposed to an abstract or laboratory setting, and to interpret how people give meaning to their experiences. While scientifically motivated, ethnographic research is carried out with a humanist emphasis, delving empathetically into the complexity of the culture and political world of people.

Ethnographic research involves an exploration of a society's cosmogony, of the way in which people make sense of the world they live in and how, acting on the basis of their beliefs, they relate to each other and to people different from themselves. Through descriptive generalisations and the development of explanatory interpretations about how societies work, in particular contexts and time spans, the researcher seeks to account for the commonalities and variations among societies and their trajectories over time. By assuming an intrinsic link between what is observed objectively and the subjective interpretation given to it, the researcher explains how people give objects and actions meaning in accordance with their beliefs and the conventions of society. Reality is thus appreciated as inseparable from human experience, with knowledge deemed as existing only in a social context. Ethnographic research is holistic in that it is founded on the idea that something can only be more fully understood when looked at as part of its 'whole' system, and by assuming that a 'whole' is more than the sum of its parts. The general idea in ethnographic research is that, by studying a phenomenon in its own dynamic context, more can be intrinsically understood about it than by simply examining it in isolation—since everything exists in relation to other things—and reducing it systematically to a list of abstract formulae.

In ethnographic work, it is crucial that the researcher reflect, before engaging in research, on her self-awareness and cultural make-up and thereby on her capacity for interpretation in environments foreign to her. She seeks to venture into the field as a *tabula rasa*, with a willingness to be open to whatever she finds and take in facts on their own terms, rather than on hers. Only after an adequate amount of time spent gaining familiarity with the social environment can the researcher decide which courses of investigation are worth pursuing and which informants merit further analysis. Equally, the researcher has to eschew preconceived ideological notions that would lead her not only to impose her own set of values but also to favour the point of view and lifestyle of a certain group of people while neglecting those of others and remaining insensitive to the power games being played out.

The ethnographic approach to research involves three fundamental steps: initial formulation of the research subject and identification of the object of research; data-gathering; and writing and analysis of empirical material. While the first leads to the next, each requires the researcher to reflect back and review his approach, thereby contributing to the final refinement of the study. In the first step, the researcher focuses on so-called 'sensibilising concepts'. These stand in contrast with 'definitive concepts'. Instead of prescribing what should be looked at, as would be the case with definitive concepts, sensibilising concepts indicate the direction in which the researcher could look.

In the data-gathering phase, the ethnographer attempts to get to know the object of study as well as possible, principally by spending a significant length of time exposed to various situations. Any preconceptions of the object that the researcher may have had are reconsidered accordingly and the processes of participant observation and interviewing adapted. The ethnographic approach also calls for continuous attention to the presence of the researcher in the data-gathering and analytical process. The researcher must be aware that, in engaging in fieldwork, he becomes, in effect, an independent variable in the study being undertaken. People are aware of the researcher's presence.

As the ethnographic approach to research is essentially naturalistic, so are its methods. Naturalistic observation involves looking at subjects in their natural habitats, as they evolve without external intervention. Participant observation and interviewing enable an understanding of the perspective of people within the context of their everyday life. Effective ethnographic research requires taking the time to gain awareness of subtle human expressions (Wolcott 1999). Thus it is also known as longitudinal research, whereby continuous long-term study of an area or group of people forms the basis of data gathering. As the researcher also asks broad questions that allow respondents to answer choosing their own words, a longitudinal approach to fieldwork allows the researcher to qualify her understanding during the research process through further probing questions.

Participant observation is the main data-collecting technique in ethnographic research. It requires involvement on the part of the researcher with the community of people she is studying, in their natural environment and over an extended period. Originally developed as a fieldwork technique by anthropologists such as Malinowski and Boas, and by researchers in urban studies from the Chicago School of Sociology, this technique is now widely used in other disciplines in the social sciences because of its ability to delve into the complex expressions of human life in a non-quantifiable fashion. The ethnographer's perspective has effectively to become that of both an 'insider' (emic) and an 'outsider' (etic). By taking this emic and etic perspective, a balance between subjectivity and objectivity is sought (Bourdieu 1977) in order to develop a holistic understanding of the object of study. The researcher must be able to understand issues from the inside and empathise with people's experiences and points of view, at the same time analysing them critically and impartially from the outside.

(b) Observation Method

Observation is one of the most important methods of data collection. It entails being present in a situation and making a record of one's impressions of what takes place. In observation the primary research instrument is the self, consciously gathering sensory data through sight, hearing, taste, smell and touch. By various means of record-keeping, traces of those impressions are stored for careful scrutiny and analysis after the event.

What is observed is ontologically determined, that is, it depends to a very great extent on how the observer conceptualises the world and his or her place within it. Observation will need to be a systematic, structured process, so that data can later be categorised for quantitative and statistical analysis.

Participant observation was developed in anthropological research at the beginning of the twentieth century. It was the great English anthropologist (of Polish origin) Bronislaw Malinowski who codified the principles of this approach in the 'Introduction to Argonauts of the Western Pacific'—defined as the book of Genesis of modern anthropology. Participant observation emerges as a natural investigative tool when the researcher intends to study a situation in which he has taken (or takes) part himself, thus giving rise to what has been called *autobiographical sociology*.

With regard to participant observation, an important distinction must be made between overt and covert observation. Indeed, the researcher may reveal or disguise his true objectives. He may openly declare at the outset that he is a researcher, that he wishes to be part of a given social group not because he agrees with its goals, but only to study it; or he may infiltrate the group by pretending to join it and to be a member just like any other. The main advantage of covert observation stems from the fact that human beings, if they know that they are being observed, are not likely to behave naturally.

This is what Labov called the *paradox of the observer*: we want to observe how people act when they are not being observed. Thus, covert observation should allow us to view their genuine behaviour. The argument is certainly valid. Moreover, it has already been stressed that the 'reactivity' of humans is one of the main factors that differentiate research in the social sciences from research in the natural sciences. There are, nonetheless, convincing arguments against covert observation. Assuming a false identity to play a role that could be likened to that of a 'spy' is, in itself, reprehensible, and can be justified only if there are compelling ethical reasons for it. It is doubtful that the objective of social research has such a high moral value as to justify deceit and taking advantage of other people's good faith.

Moreover, the awareness of his own deceit could create anxiety and unnatural behaviour in the researcher. Even the unscrupulous may find it difficult to cultivate bogus interpersonal relationships. In covert observation, there is a constant risk of being discovered, and the consequences of discovery may be unpredictable (from the abrupt interruption of the relationship to even more dire consequences when deviant groups or groups engaged in illegal activities are involved). In certain cases, concealing the researcher's role can even be an obstacle to the final objective of observation: understanding.

Participant observation developed within anthropology is a tool for studying 'other' cultures. From the study of primitive tribes, it was extended to the study of 'urban tribes', but continued to focus on those who were considered 'different'. Later it was realised that any field of human activity that had its own cultural specificity could be analysed by means of the ethnographic approach and participant observation. *Microsociology* is the study of small everyday actions; and *ethnomethodology* is the study of the methods and practices used by ordinary people to decipher the world, give it meaning and perform actions. Everyday activities are regulated by well-defined (implicit) norms governing interaction among people. *Ethnomethodology* attempts to unveil and study such norms.

C) CASE STUDY METHOD

Case study seeks to engage with and report the complexity of social activity in order to represent the meanings that individual social actors bring to those settings and manufacture in them. Case study assumes that 'social reality' is created through social interaction, albeit situated in particular contexts and histories, and seeks to identify and describe before trying to analyse and theorise. It assumes that things may not be as they seem and privileges in-depth inquiry over coverage: understanding 'the case' rather than generalising to a population at large.

The earliest applications of the case method to social research were the historians' descriptive accounts of peoples and nations, followed later by detailed studies of smaller groups, factions, and individuals. Case studies of contemporary groups and individuals were a later development. Clifford R. Shaw defines the scope of a case study as "an individual, an institution, a community, or any group considered as* a unit for study," while "to take account of all aspects of one thing or situation" is the function of the case method according to Stuart A. Rice.[2,3] Lundberg considers the case method merely a first step in scientific method and that individual cases attain scientific significance only when "classified and summarised in such form as to reveal uniformities, types, and patterns of behaviour; and that the statistical method is the best, if not the only, scientific method of classifying and summarising large numbers of cases.[4]

Since the case method implies a comprehensive and intensive study of the subject, one of the first requisites is thoroughness. Facts must be ascertained and interpreted. Facts are obtained from documents, from the individual himself, from members of the group, or from anyone who may have any knowledge relative to the study under investigation. From this it can be seen how carefully all evidence must be weighed, tested, and sifted to eliminate fictitious and false statements, and as far as possible, rationalisations. It is hardly conceivable that the case study can ever be made wholly objective, for in the very nature of it is inherent a certain subjectivity, not only on the part of those from whom the data are obtained but also in the interpretations of the research specialist. However, such subjectivity can be reduced to a minimum if the investigator approaches his problem as a scientist. Thoroughness also implies that every phase of the problem must be studied and that it must be approached from every possible angle.

The strength of case study is that it can take an example of an activity— 'an instance in action' (Walker, 1974)— and use multiple methods and data sources to explore it and interrogate it. Thus it can achieve a 'rich description' of a phenomenon in order to represent it from the participants' perspective. Case studies can be produced of new institutions, new social programmes (e.g., new welfare-to-work or urban education programmes) or new policies (using testing to drive the reform of schooling), which aspire to tell-it-like-it-is from the participants' point of view, as well as hold policy to account in terms of the complex realities of implementation and the unintended consequences of policy in action. Case study thus is particular, descriptive, inductive and ultimately heuristic—it seeks to 'illuminate' the readers' understanding of an issue (Parlett and Hamilton, 1972).

Since the pioneering work of Frédéric Le Play at the end of the nineteenth century and the Chicago school of sociology in the 1920s and 1930s, case studies have been ubiquitous. Case studies are diverse in their objectives, characteristics and results. Their contributions to social scientific knowledge, their role in theory building, their empirical added value, and the ways in which they are conducted are regularly debated. The ordinary meanings and usages and the history of the word 'case' provide a useful starting point to getting a better grasp of its social scientific meanings and their evolutions. The word 'case', derived from the Latin *casus*, means an occurrence, something that happens, usually with an unfavourable connotation: an accident, a misfortune. The word 'case' also belongs to the religious vocabulary and refers to a particular and embarrassing, moral problem which raises a difficult ethical debate. Finally, 'case' is also used in mathematics (limit case) and in medicine, where it designates the state and the history of a patient. These common meanings point us to some key characteristics of the ways in which 'case' is used in social sciences. On the one hand, the case appears as an unusual and specific challenge to established descriptions or reasoning. A case is therefore disconcerting: it provokes reflection and points to the need for an adjustment of a theoretical framework (Platt 1992: 24; Passeron and Revel 2005: 10, 16). A case is a phenomenon, or an event, chosen, conceptualised and analysed empirically as a manifestation of a broader class of phenomena or events (on definitions: Eckstein 1975: 85). A case study is a research strategy based on the in-depth empirical investigation of one, or a small number, of phenomena in order to explore the configuration of each case, and to elucidate features of a larger class of (similar) phenomena, by developing and evaluating theoretical explanations (Ragin 2000: 64–87).

Four points related to these definitions can be emphasised. First, the case is not just a unit of analysis or an observation, understood as a piece of data. It is not a data category, but a theoretical category. Second, the case is not *a priori* spatially delimited. The delimitation of the case, spatial and otherwise, is the product of the theoretical conceptualisation used by the researcher. Third, the phenomenon under study does not have to be contemporary; it can be from the past. Fourth, in case study research, data can be collected in various ways, and it can be both qualitative and quantitative.

What purpose do case studies serve? Case studies come in different shapes and forms, and they can serve a variety of purposes, often simultaneously. First, the descriptive case study (configurative-ideographic) is a systematic description of the phenomena with no explicit theoretical intention. It is common to label this kind of research as simply suggestive and to dismiss its social scientific contribution. It is true that the notion of a descriptive case study does not sit easily with our definition, which implies a theoretical framing. Still, while the work of many historians and anthropologists might lack an explicit theoretical framework, that does not mean that a theory is altogether absent. Furthermore, in any type of case study there is an unavoidable descriptive dimension. Case studies sometimes explore subjects about which little is previously known or phenomena in need of an interpretation that sheds new light on known data, and their descriptive aspect is invaluable. Second, the interpretive case study (disciplined configurative) uses theoretical frameworks to provide an explanation of particular cases, which can lead as well to an evaluation and refinement of theories. Third, the hypothesis-generating and refining case study (heuristic) seeks to generate new hypotheses inductively and/or to refine existing hypotheses.

(d) Ethnomethodology Approach

Originating about the mid-1950s, ethnomethodology represents a development in the United States. Harold Garfinkel, one of the recognised leaders in this development, coined the title of the theory. He and other ethnomethodologists have fashioned it out of aspects of a variety of intellectual traditions that include linguistic philosophy, phenomenology, linguistics, and cognitive anthropology.

It is an approach to studying the social world developed and which focuses on how social order is created, ongoingly, in and through the practices by which people make sense of what others are doing, and display that understanding through their actions. In doing so it recommends a re-specification of the focus of sociological inquiry, away from a concern with explaining the causes, development and/or effects of social processes or institutions.

First, they see ethnomethodology, concerned with how people construct meaning or "definitions of the situation," as a version of symbolic interaction. Second, because definitions of the situation emerge from how persons announce and impart sense-making perceptions and perspectives to one another, ethnomethodology is said to be individualistic. Third, ethnomethodology is understood to have emerged as a critique of traditional ways of doing sociology.

Garfinkel (1967) developed a concern for "commonsense knowledge of social structure." He followed Kaufmann (1944) in distinguishing normative rules of social life (mores, folkways) from those fundamental or "basic" rules that enable actors to identify concrete behavioural displays as specific actions. For instance, by way of the basic rules and their "constitutive accent."[5]

Substantive concern of ethnomethodology is the achieved intelligibility and organisation of everyday activities, it can be appreciated that social order does and come about because individual actors bring their own cognitive definitions of the situation into some kind of convergence or common agreement. The focus in ethnomethodology on what are called, interchangeably, "procedures," methods," and "practices" runs contrary to a cognitive-interpretive solution to the problem of order, wherein actors produce patterned courses of action because they share internalised frames of reference and value systems that enable common definitions of situations.

In ethnomethodology, meaning is linked less to communication and becomes individualistic. In this view, each mind grasps the meaning of an object uniquely; the mind directs action by anticipating order, compiling response repertoires on the basis of typifications (Schutz[6], 1970: 11 1-122). While ethnomethodologists do not deal specifically with the subjective essence of things (which phenomenology does), they analyse people's interpretative procedures for accomplishing "reality"

(e) Phenomenology Approach

Phenomenology is the study of lived, human phenomena within the everyday social contexts in which the phenomena occur from the perspective of those who experience them. Phenomena comprise any thing that human beings live/experience. Increasingly, the value of examining the phenomena of professional practice has been emphasised. Phenomena can be *directly* researched by exploring human *knowing*, through accessing consciousness and *indirectly* by investigating human *being*, through accessing the senses and shared background meanings and practices.

Edmund Husserl's investigations (e.g., 1960, 1970) have infused the expression with the philosophical meanings it manifests today. Recognising that science presents itself as a self-contained enterprise, Husserl argued that its objects and achievements rest upon a vast pre-scientific foundation of unclarified presuppositions, which Husserl termed the Lebenswelt or life-world. He further asserted that the job of philosophy is to discern and elucidate these presuppositions in a progressive way until the ultimate grounds of knowledge are reached.

German philosophers began the search for a new interpretive science. Their ideas were based on the investigation of the life and social worlds through the study of context and individuals' own constructions and meanings within that context. This work led to the development of two philosophical frameworks that influence interpretive research methodologies today. Edmund Husserl (1859–1938) founded phenomenology, premised on epistemological concerns, so the starting point of his framework is the separation of a conscious actor in a world of objects (Husserl, 1964).

(f) Narrative Analysis

Narrative inquiry is concerned with the production, interpretation and representation of storied accounts of lived experience and is increasingly popular with researchers in many fields. When this interest in narrative inquiry joins with a desire to exercise the descriptive and analytic processes of the sociological imagination (Mills, 2000) researchers find themselves engaged in dialogue with others and stories of life that lead toward the construction of life histories.[7]

Narrative texts are packed with sociological information, and a great deal of our empirical evidence is in narrative form. Labov defined narrative as one method of recapitulating past experience by matching a verbal sequence of clauses to the sequence of events which (it is inferred) actually occurred (Labov; 1972).[8] A narrative ... shares with other narratives a common structure which is open to analysis, no matter how much patience its formulation requires (Barthes; 1977).[9]

(g) Discourse Analysis

Discourse theory aims at an understanding of the social as a discursive construction whereby, in principle, all social phenomena can be analysed using discourse analytical tools. The overall idea of discourse theory is that social phenomena are never finished or total. Meaning can never be ultimately fixed and this opens up the way for constant social struggles about definitions of society and identity, with resulting social effects. The discourse analyst's task is to plot the course of these struggles to fix meaning at all levels of the society. Discourse analysis is concerned with the investigation of language and one might reasonably expect linguistics, the discipline concerned with the study of language, to be the root for 'discourse analysis.

Discourse analysis emerging from perspectives in social anthropology and indeed approaches within sociology that have embraced ethnography and an emphasis on reflexivity. So, many practitioners of discourse analysis argue that the more one understands about the socio-historical situation of a text, the more sensitive and insightful will be one's interpretation. Such an ideal has influenced much discourse analysis in educational settings, for example. In practice the boundary between discourse analysis and qualitative methodologies in general has sometimes become blurred where language data and the construction of meanings is the focus of intensive attention. In many empirical investigations centred on bounded discourse data—transcriptions of interactions, interviews and so on—software tools have been. There are, essentially, two main ways in which discourse analysis may be relevant to your research. The first concerns your examination of data. Overwhelmingly the majority of research in the social sciences is likely to collect data some of which is in the form of texts that would benefit from close analysis. Barbara Johnstone (2002: 9) suggests that you might begin to construct a plan for such analysis from considering the following heuristic:

- discourse is shaped by the world, and shapes the world;
- discourse is shaped by language, and shapes language;
- discourse is shaped by participants, and shapes participants;
- discourse is shaped by prior discourse, and shapes the possibilities for future discourse;
- discourse is shaped by its medium, and shapes the possibilities of its medium;
- discourse is shaped by purpose, and shapes possible purposes.

Laclau and Mouffe have developed their theory through the *deconstruction* of other bodies of theory. Careful reading of other theories, they contend, uncovers their unargued assumptions and internal contradictions. In this way, the ideological content of the other theories is revealed and the contradictions identified can be transformed into tools for further thinking. Laclau and Mouffe have constructed their theory by combining and modifying two major theoretical traditions, Marxism and structuralism. Marxism provides a starting point for thinking about the social, and structuralism provides a theory of meaning. Laclau and Mouffe fuse these traditions into a single poststructuralist theory in which the whole social field is understood as a web of processes in which meaning is created. A discourse is understood as the fixation of meaning within a particular domain. All signs in a discourse are *moments*. They are the knots in the fishing-net, their meaning being fixed through their differences from one another ('differential positions'). A discourse attempts to transform elements into moments by reducing their polysemy to a fully fixed meaning. In the terms of Laclau and Mouffe's discourse theory, the discourse establishes a *closure*, a temporary stop to the fluctuations in the meaning of the signs. But the closure is never definitive: 'The transition from the "elements" to the "moments" is never entirely fulfilled' (Laclau and Mouffe 1985: 110).

Discourse aims to remove ambiguities by turning the elements into moments through closure. But this aim is never completely successful as the possibilities of meaning that the discourse displaces to the field of discursivity always threaten to destabilise the fixity of meaning. Therefore, all moments stay potentially polysemic, which means that the moments are always potentially elements. Specific articulations reproduce or challenge the existing discourses by fixing meaning in particular ways. And because of the perpetual potential polysemy, every verbal or written expression (even every social action, as we will see later on) is also, to some extent, an articulation or innovation; although the expression draws on earlier fixations of meaning—that is, it draws on discourses in which the signs have become moments—the expression is never merely a repetition of something already established (Laclau and Mouffe 1985: 113f). Therefore, every expression is an active reduction of the possibilities of meaning because it positions the signs in relation to one another in only one way, thus excluding alternative forms of organisation.

Discourse, then, can be understood as a type of structure in a Saussurian sense—a fixation of signs in a relational net. But, in contrast to the Saussurian tradition whereby structure covered all signs in a *permanent* closure, discourse, for Laclau and Mouffe, can never be total in the Saussurian sense. There are always other meaning potentials which, when actualised in specific articulations, may challenge and transform the structure of the discourse. Thus the discourse is a *temporary* closure: it fixes meaning in a particular way, but it does not dictate that meaning is to be fixed exactly in that way forever. The understanding of identity in Laclau and Mouffe's discourse theory can be summarised as follows:

- The subject is fundamentally *split*, it never quite becomes 'itself'.
- It acquires its identity by being *represented* discursively.
- Identity is thus *identification* with a subject position in a discursive structure.
- Identity is discursively constituted through *chains of equivalence* where signs are sorted and linked together in chains in opposition to other chains which thus define how the subject is, and how it is not.

- Identity is always *relationally* organised; the subject is something because it is contrasted with something that it is not.
- Identity is *changeable* just as discourses are.
- The subject is *fragmented* or *decentred*; it has different identities according to those discourses of which it forms part.
- The subject is *overdetermined*; in principle, it always has the possibility to identify differently in specific situations. Therefore, a given identity is *contingent*—that is, possible but not necessary.

(h) Action Research

Action research is a type of applied social research that aims to improve social situations through change interventions involving a process of collaboration between researchers and participants. The process is seen to be both educational and empowering. Action research directly addresses the problem of the division between theory and practice. Rather than research being a linear process of producing knowledge which is later applied to practice settings, action research integrates the development of practice with the construction of research knowledge in a cyclical process. Instead of being research *on* a social setting and the people within it, it is research *from inside* that setting carried out either by the participants themselves or researchers working in collaboration with them. It has an immediate impact since it is an integral part of day-to-day work.

The earliest action research took place in the 1940s and 1950s, led by Lewin (1988), a psychologist refugee from Germany, who worked with community groups in the USA to resolve social problems such as prejudice; Trist, influenced by Lewin, worked in a similar way at the Tavistock Institute in London, focusing during the 1950s on experimental work in organisations to help them address their practical problems (see Pasmore, 2001). Lewin's theory of action research divides the work into distinct stages within a series of cycles, starting with 'reconnaissance' and moving on to the collection of data, analysis and the development of 'hypotheses' to inform action. This then leads into the second cycle in which the hypotheses are tested in practice and the changes evaluated. The cyclical process of action research does not come to a natural conclusion, although at some point it is necessary to bring it to a close and publish the outcomes in some form.

The basic precept of action research is that it '. . . should lead to change and therefore that change should be incorporated into the research process itself' (Somekh et al., 2005, p. 11).[10] Its attraction is that it bridges the 'gap' between theory and practice, is problem-focused, is grounded in the reality of practice, and is empowering. It also appears to be an ideal vehicle for service user involvement. The promotion of action research might therefore be anticipated within health and social care research.[11]

Another important strand has been the development of participatory action research (PAR) in organisational settings and the work of non-governmental organisations (Whyte, 1991). Emanating from South America, a different tradition of PAR has been influenced by the work of Paulo Freire. Starting out as a grassroots movement carrying out small-scale work in local 'popular education' settings (Torres, 1992), PAR has become a movement 'searching for a new type of scientific plus activist/emancipatory work', action research to be led by a participant who comes into the practice situation from outside and negotiates the boundaries and parameters of the study with the participants, involving them as co-researchers without expecting them to undertake substantial amounts of additional work. The 'outsider' may be a professional who has become a graduate-student or a university based researcher working on a funded project. Again, there will be imbalances of power and control so that the working relationship will need to be carefully negotiated.

There is a wide range of different approaches to action research. Noffke (1997) groups these within three dimensions: the professional, the personal and the political. The first focuses on improving what is offered to clients in professional settings, the second is concerned with social action to combat oppression. The third, the personal, not necessarily separated from either of the others, is concerned with factors such as developing 'greater self-knowledge' and 'a deeper understanding of one's own practice.' Action research is always rooted in the values of the participants. Somekh (1995) points out that its close links with the values of practice tend to mean that action research methodology adapts and develops in rather different ways within different social groups. Action research among nurses, for example, is strongly influenced by the need to establish credibility alongside the research of the medical profession so it tends to conform rather more to standards of traditional research rigour.

(i) Participatory Rural Appraisal (PRA)

Although research strategies which emphasise participation are gaining greater respectability and acceptance within mainstream practices, they continue to be a source of considerable contention. On the one hand, participatory research methods have been proclaimed as the universal panacea for the problems besetting conventional practice (Chambers 1994).[12] Participatory research was developed in the 1970's and 1980's, primarily in the South to challenge conventional economic development projects and sought to empower poor rural and urban communities

PRA is part of a growing action oriented approach to research. It has evolved from the plethora of techniques and ideas that were developed in the 1970's and 80's as an alternative to conventional sample surveys. PRA draws its strength from five main threads: activist participatory research, agro-ecosystem analysis, applied anthropology, field research on farming systems and rapid rural appraisal (RRA).

It attempts to overcome the biased nature of 'rural development tourism'* and questionnaire surveys (Chambers 1994). PRA is based on the premise that local people have the expertise, analytical skill and knowledge, which should be incorporated in the decision making process that, affects them. It uses a combination of visual (maps, matrices, diagrams, etc.) and verbal methods. The flexibility of the method has led to its broad application in many fields of social analysis (Shah 1993).[13] Chambers (1994)' describes PRA as a term that 'is being used to describe a growing family of approaches and methods to enable local people to share, enhance and analyse their knowledge of life and conditions, to plan and to act'. The methodology has evolved from a family of approaches, which sought practical research and planning that could support more decentralised planning and more democratic decision-making, as well as place value on social diversity, work towards sustainability, enhance community participation and foster empowerment.

Like other participatory methodologies, participatory mapping has emerged as one of the single most valuable tools, which sets PRA apart from other conventional research methods. Although PRA is a confluence of many methods, its direct 'ancestor' is Rapid Rural Appraisal, from which 'rapid' was changed to 'participatory'. Norton and Francis (1992) describe the change in terminology from RRA to PRA as a reflection of the shift from an extractive mode of operation, where the aim was simply to obtain information in a rapid focused and cost effective manner, to facilitating local informants active participation in the planning of the activities. There has also emerged a particular form of PRA that aims at promoting learning of the various stakeholders to promote action. Participatory Leaning and Action (PLA), the new dimension of PRA, stands out from the family of techniques embodied in PRA in that whereas ordinary PRA emphasises the trinity of behaviour attitudes, methods and sharing. PLA promotes all these as well as an explicit emphasis towards mutual learning to lead to action. Learning and unlearning is a continuous process for all the stakeholders. It promotes the logic that scientific and indigenous knowledge presents different aspects of a broader picture, and these must be integrated for better understanding of issues.[14]

(j) Longitudinal Study

It is a social or developmental research involving collection of data from the same individuals (or groups) across time. Observing change in these individuals gives a better basis for causal inference than a cross-sectional study, because of the temporal sequencing involved. In this sense the longitudinal study (without manipulation of the sample) is a form of 'quasi-experimental design'.

Longitudinal studies can range from repeated measures of a treatment group and a control group measured at two time points in an experimental design, to a large-scale long-term birth cohort study, involving follow-ups of the same sample of individuals from birth through to adult life. The distinctive feature of such work is *prospective* data collection, that is to say, information is collected about individual sample members to assess current behaviours, feelings and circumstances; though retrospective information covering the period between 'sweeps' (also called 'waves') may also be collected. Intervals between sweeps can range from daily contact with sample members to periods of several years.

The major problem with prospective longitudinal studies is attrition, that is to say exit from the study of sample members brought about by such factors as mobility, death, changing name through marriage, or refusal. However, one advantage of the longitudinal study is that in principle the distributions of key variables in the original sample can be restored by differential weighting of the sample in later sweeps. The related problem is missing data, occurring at question level, which can seriously reduce the size of the data set for analysis across different sweeps. Statistical methods of imputation are often used to estimate missing values in these instances, but none is able fully to address the possible biases brought about by this form of sample loss.

(k)) Appreciative Inquiry (AI)

AI is a management approach to encourage participation in corporations, but the method is being deployed increasingly by NGOs in the development sector. AI focuses on 'positive change', where the strengths of the collective—rather than its failures—are highlighted so as to transform and bolster the organisation. It is defined as 'the cooperative, coevolutionary search for the best in people, their organisations, and the world around them. It involves systematic discovery of what gives life to an organisation or a community when it is most effective and most capable in economic, ecological and human terms'. To unearth the 'positive', AI uses a narrative structure, or 'storytelling', which involves four steps, known as the 4-D cycle: 'Discovery', 'Dream', 'Design' and 'Destiny'.[15]

Diagrammatic Representation of the Four Steps of Appreciative Inquiry (AI)

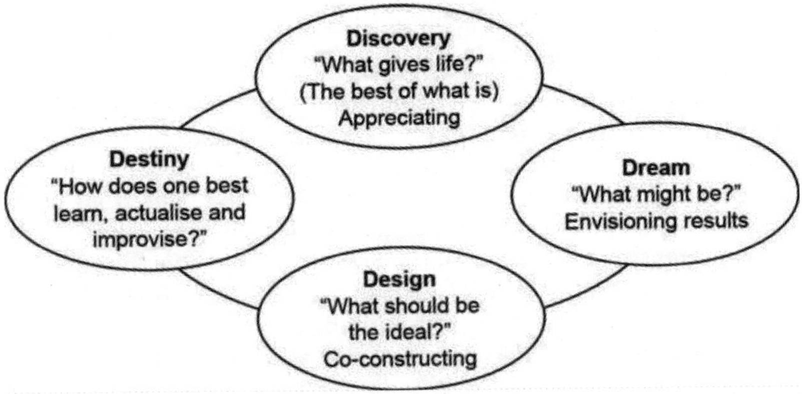

Source: Available at http://www.collectivewisdominitiative.org/papers/pioneers_dialogue/04_apprec.pdf

AI technique has potential to transform everyday problems into extraordinary opportunities for community action. AI was also attractive because it had originated in the private sector, a milieu familiar to most middle-class volunteers. Overall, AI aligned well with their notion of change as a controlled—rather than an emotional—response.

(l) Life Course Perspective

We all have stories that unfold as we progress through life. A useful way to understand this relationship between time and human behaviour is the life course perspective, which looks at how chronological age, common life transitions, and social change shape people's lives from birth to death. Of course, time is only one dimension of human behaviour; characteristics of the person and the environment in which the person lives also play a part.

Glen Elder Jr., a sociologist, was one of the early authors of a life course perspective, and continues to be one of the driving forces behind its development. In the early 1960s, he began to analyse data from three pioneering longitudinal studies of children that had been undertaken by the University of California, Berkeley. As he examined several decades of data,he was struck with the enormous impact of the Great Depression of the 1930s on individual and family pathways (Elder, 1974).[16] He began to call for developmental theory and research that looked at the influence of historical forces on family, education, and work roles.

Major Themes of the Life Course Perspective

- Interplay of human lives and historical time: Individual and family development must be understood in historical context.
- Timing of lives: Particular roles and behaviours are associated with particular age groups, based on biological age, psychological age, social age, and spiritual age.
- Linked or interdependent lives: Human lives are interdependent, and the family is the primary arena for experiencing and interpreting wider historical, cultural, and social phenomena.
- Human agency in making choices: The individual life course is constructed by the choices and actions individuals take within the opportunities and constraints of history and social circumstances.
- Diversity in life course trajectories: There is much diversity in life course pathways, due to cohort variations, social class, culture, gender, and individual agency.
- Developmental risk and protection: Experiences with one life transition have an impact on subsequent transitions and events, and may either protect the life course trajectory or put it at risk.

The life course perspective has many implications for social work practice, including the following:

- Help clients make sense of their unique life's journeys and to use that understanding to improve their current situations. Where appropriate, help them to construct a lifeline of interlocking trajectories.
- Try to understand the historical contexts of clients' lives and the ways that important historical events have influenced their behaviour.
- Where appropriate, use life event inventories to get a sense of the level of stress in a client's life.

- Be aware of the potential to develop social work interventions that can serve as turning points that help individuals, families, communities, and organisations to get back on track.
- Work with the media to keep the public informed about the impact of changing social conditions on individuals, families, communities, and formal organisations.
- Recognise the ways that the lives of family members are linked across generations and the impact of circumstances in one generation on other generations.
- Use existing research on risk, protection, and resilience to develop prevention programmes.
- When working with recent immigrant and refugee families, be aware of the age norms in their countries of origin.
- Be aware of the unique systems of support developed by members of various cultural groups, and encourage the use of those supports in times of crisis.
- Support and help to develop clients' sense of personal competence for making life choices.

Notes

1. See Murchison, Julian M., 1973. Ethnography Essentials : designing, conducting, and presenting your research, John Wiley and Sons, San Francisco.
2. See "Case Study Method," Publications of the American Sociological Society, XXI, I49.
3. Quantitative Methods in Politics, p. 35.
4. Case Work and Statisical Method," Social Forces, V, 6I-65.
5. See Garfinkel, H. 1967. Studies in Ethno-methodology. Englewood Cliffs, NJ: Prentice Hall.
6. Schutz, Alfred, 1970. On Phenomenology and Social Relations. Chicago: University of Chicago Press.
7. Mills, C.W. (2000). *The Sociological Imagination*, 40th Anniversary Edition. New York: Oxford University Press.
8. Labov W. 1972. *Language in the Inner City*. Philadelphia: Univ. Pa. Press.
9. Barthes R. 1977. (1966) Introduction to the structural analysis of narratives. In *Image Music Text. Essays Selected and Translated by Stephen Heath*, pp. 79, 124. London: Fontana.
10. Somekh, B., Burman, E., Delamont, S., Meyer, J., Payne, M., and Thorpe, R. (2005). Research communities in the social sciences. In

B. Somekh, and C. Lewin (Eds.), Research methods in the social services, part 1 (pp. 1–14). London: SAGE.

11. See Andrew McVicar, Carol Munn-Giddings and Christina Abu-Helil, Exploring the development of action research in nursing and social care in the UK: A comparative bibliometric review of action research designs in social work (2000-2010), Action Research 2012 10: 79.
12. Chambers, R. 1994. 'The origins and practice of Participatory Rural Appraisal', *World Development,* Vol. 22: No.7, 953-970.
13. Shah, M. K 1993. Using Participatory Methodologies to understand gender differences in perceptions of poverty, well-being and social change: People's Perspectives from a village in Ghana. Typescript, IDS, Sussex, June.
14. See Robert deGraft Agyarko, Influencing policy through Participatory Poverty Assessments: A theoretical and practical overview and assessment of a changing process, *Social Change* 2002 32: 81.
15. D.L. Cooperrider and Diana Whitney, Appreciative Inquiry: A Positive Revolution in Change (San Francisco: Berrett-Koehler Publishers, 2005).
16. See Elder, G. H. Jr 1974 *Children of the Great Depression,* Chicago: University of Chicago Press.

5

Forms of Sanitation

(a) Sanitation and Science

Practical sanitation is devoted to the prevention, avoidance, or destruction of the causes of disease and death, and is founded on our knowledge of these causes. This knowledge is the scientific aspect of hygiene, or what many call sanitary science. It is at present very fragmentary and imperfect. Our powers of prediction as to the effect which certain circumstances will produce on the health of an individual or a community are limited, and in many cases we cannot, with any approach to scientific precision, explain why a given locality is, or is not, unhealthy. The first step towards a scientific investigation of a phenomenon must be the verification of its existence; but in much the larger portion of this country we can obtain little positive information as to the extent to which the inhabitants of a given place are liable to special forms of disease, or even as to the death-rate to which they are subject.

Until within a comparatively recent period, the method which has been almost exclusively employed in the investigation of problems of public hygiene has been that of observation of general and special mortality rates in different communities, and of endeavouring to connect the results of such observations with the circumstances of the environment in order to discover the causal relation between the two. But in such complicated biological problems as these, in which the result observed may depend on the concurrence of many causes or circumstances, it is usually very difficult, and often impossible, to obtain precise knowledge by mere observation of results, even when such observation can be made accurately.

This experimental method is now being applied to sanitary questions, and especially to those connected with the prevention or suppression of the infective or spreading diseases, which are those of most interest in public hygiene. We can now study the causes of splenic-fever, erysipelas, infectious pneumonia, tuberculosis, glanders, and probably cholera, in the laboratory as well as in the sick-room; their causes may be cultivated, like plants, and the effects of various foods, temperatures, etc., upon them determined; and the efficacy of means proposed for eradicating them may be tested by direct experiment.[1]

It is true that as yet comparatively few diseases can be thus investigated; because for the majority we have not yet found any animals, other than man, who are susceptible to them, and we cannot use man for inoculation experiments. It is no longer a satisfactory explanation of an outbreak of diphtheria or typhoid to say that the place was filthy: if that were a sufficient cause, there are few towns that would not soon suffer from epidemics of these diseases. The apparent anomalies in the distribution of disease, which are apparent to every one who has investigated the subject, the good health of persons who work in the midst of offensive effluvia and typical filth, the progress of an epidemic along one side of a street while the other side is free from disease. Thus, for every person who is affected with typhoid, or cholera, or tubercle, there are fifty who, so far as we can see, have been exposed to the same causes, and remain unaffected.

(b) State and Sanitation

State sanitation means the efforts which State governments exert to prevent insanitary or uncleanly conditions of human environment which tend to impair the health or which are prejudicial to the comfort of the people. It is important, in the first place, to link these two terms together-the health and comfort of the people-for sanitation is concerned with them both. The two words are bound together in laws and legal decisions, as well as in common parlance. Nuisances are infringements against comfort as well as against health. Health, in its broadest sense, is something more than the absence of disease; it has a positive side. We measure health inversely in terms of sickness and death; we are beginning to attempt to measure health in terms of physical efficiency, capacity to work, and ability to enjoy life. The latter belongs on the front side of the shield; sickness and death are for the back side. Both sides of the shield should be guarded.[2]

The efforts of the sanitarian have been chiefly directed toward the keeping of man's environment in a condition so that a minimum of disease would result from it. The main problem has been to keep man's food and drink from becoming contaminated, and thus frequently infected, by direct or indirect contact with his individual or community wastes. The responsibility of the State of California toward its citizens, not only those grouped into cities, but all within its borders, was recognised by the passage in 1907 of the Sanitary Water Systems Act and the Public Health Act. The former was intended to promote the supply of pure, healthful water, and the latter was intended to promote the sanitary disposal of sewage. In 1915 the Legislature established the Bureau of Sanitary Engineering under the State Board of Health.[3]

Comfort has to do with the senses. Human discomfort is hard to measure, especially as people differ as to their sense reactions under different environments. These sense reactions are an important part of life; and the courts are sound when they decide that in-sanitary conditions are "prejudicial to health," even though the sense reaction may be, merely that of a disagreeable odor. Bad odors from faulty plumbing or from badly ventilated rooms, bad odors in water supplies, bad odors from industrial plants, excessive noise, smoke in the atmosphere, oil deposits along the banks of streams and shores, and many other sense-offending conditions may be public nuisances and are properly included within the legal scope of "health and comfort of the people."

The police power is one of the inherent powers of government, that of protecting the people from dangers from within. Under this the Government may coerce the individual, take away his liberty, his property, and even his life, if necessary, in order to safeguard the safety, health, or morals of the people. Since the time of Magna Charta the English-speaking race has been preserved from tyrannous oppression, from undue exercise of the police power, by what is called "due process of law."

In the United States the police power originates in the State. It is exercised directly by the legislature, as representing the people. It may be delegated to some State department or official, to some city or city department, or to the National Government. Fundamentally, however, authority to act under the police power must be traced back to the State government. Another function of government is that of doing for- the people those things which the Government can do better, more cheaply, or more expeditiously than the people can do for themselves. These are acts for the public benefit, acts of public service, acts for the common good. They are paid for under the taxing power of government, another of its well-established functions.

These two ideas of force and service represent the masculine and. feminine elements of government. The best government results from a proper combination of the two. State boards of health, or departments of health as they are coming to be called, are concerned with both of these parts of government-health service and police power in behalf of health.

Functions of State Health Departments

State boards of health perform several functions. One of these is quasi-legislative in character, carried on under authority delegated by the legislature. A State Board of Health may be authorised to prepare a sanitary code, plumbing regulations, rules for the protection of water supplies, rules for reporting diseases dangerous to the public health, and the like. This is done because in technical matters and in special fields where expert knowledge is needed, the legislature, composed of persons of varied attainments elected by the people, is less competent to enact such detailed legislation than a body of men selected for the special work at hand. For the best results, this delegated authority should be given to a body of men rather than to an individual. A health commissioner acting alone should not be allowed to perform functions which are legislative in character. Legislatures do well, however, to delegate authority for the preparation of rules and regulations which are essentially technical and scientific to competent boards rather than attempt to legislate directly.

A State board of health may act in a semi-judicial capacity. This authority is seen in the matter of nuisances. The board may sit as a court, hold hearings, talk testimony, and render decisions. Sometimes it sits as a court of appeal. Of course there is much work of an executive character to be done by a State department of health. Some of this is incidental to the exercise of the police power-such as laboratory work, engineering, or inspection in connection with the oversight of water supplies, stream pollution, sewage disposal, nuisances, food sanitation, sophistication of food and drugs, statistical records of sickness and death.

(c) Sanitation and Health

The aim of public health is to improve the health of people in communities and in populations (protection from environmental hazards and provision for health needs). The challenge for public health doctors is to re-establish public health leadership of communities, address social and environmental causes of ill health, and link with primary care (a) to improve the health of neighbourhoods and (b) to combine perspectives in commissioning services. Current threats derive from organisational philosophies. For example, focusing on market development does not allow for population based functions and so neglects the main influences on health. The way forward is a network model of organisation in which small teams collaborate with each other to the common good. For example, successful commissioning authorities would have the public health leadership of the director of public health and the support of the chief executive, treasurer, and representatives of primary care, including a medical adviser from the family health services authority. Public health exists to improve the health of the people, firstly, by advising on the action communities can take to improve their health; secondly, by protecting populations from environmental and biological hazards; and, thirdly, by assessing populations' needs for health services.[4]

Despite many decades of independent planning and implementation, most populations living in the developing world have yet to reach the Utopian ideal of health for all. The survival of the human body is best explained by the materialist explanation that locates the variation in health and longevity to tangible resources. The reciprocal relationship between poverty and disease had long been acknowledged by public health reformers who advocated social reform on political, economic, humanitarian and scientific grounds.

Successive governments in India have come up with many schemes for the provision of safe water, sanitation, nutrition, vaccination coverage, education and employment. Despite many attempts, millions of people do not have access to these basic needs, malnutrition is rampant in children and vaccination coverage is inadequate among the poor. Elementary education is substandard and unemployment widespread in rural areas. Despite increased budgetary support for such schemes, most states have pursued weak policies in this area and neglected the local governments, giving them a low stake in improving infra- structure. The enormity of the unfinished tasks is mind-boggling.[5]

Simultaneously, public health services, which reduce a population's exposure to disease through such measures as sanitation and vector control, are an essential part of a country's development infrastructure. In India, policies have focused largely on medical services. Public health services, and even implementation of basic public health regulations, have been neglected. Various organisational issues also militate against the rational deployment of personnel and funds for disease control. There is strong capacity for dealing with outbreaks when they occur, but not to prevent them from occurring. Impressive capacity also exists for conducting intensive campaigns, but not for sustaining these gains on a continuing basis afterwards. This is illustrated by the near-eradication of malaria through highly-organised efforts in the 1950s, and its resurgence when attention shifted to other priorities such as family planning. Public health services are conceptually distinct from medical services. They have as a key goal reducing a population's exposure to disease - for example through assuring food safety and other health regulations; vector control; monitoring waste disposal and water systems; and health education to improve personal health behaviours and build citizen demand for better public health out-comes. Thus they involve such disparate activities as improving slaughterhouse hygiene and cattle-keeping practices, cleaning irrigation canals to discourage vector breeding, and applying public health regulations.[6]

These services are largely invisible to the public—typically, the public only becomes aware of the need for them when a problem develops (e.g., an epidemic occurs). Yet unlike most medical services which focus on the needs of individual patients; these services are of high priority for assuring good health for a population as a whole. When public health systems falter people pay a high price in terms of illness, debility and death, and if full-fledged outbreaks occur the economic costs can be very large. Public health services are thus both pro-growth, as well as pro-poor in that they are self-targeted towards the poor, who face the maximum exposure to disease. Moreover, these services greatly enhance the cost-effectiveness of health services by preventing diseases.

(d) Rural Sanitation[7]

Time and again students of public health have called attention to the backward state of sanitary conditions in rural districts and to the influence of this on the health of city dwellers. When one considers the many natural advantages inherent in life in the country, it is probable that the insanitary conditions responsible for the almost stationary death rate are the results of ignorance and neglect and that they are susceptible to improvement and correction.

Several years ago, in order to ascertain more definitely what are the sanitary conditions in the rural districts of the United States, and to determine what are the most feasible methods of improving or correcting such conditions, the United States Public Health Service began a survey in 15 counties located in various parts of the United States. This study has already been so fruitful that the results obtained have been embodied in a progress report, "Rural Sanitation,"by Surg. L. L. Lumsden, under whose direction the work was conducted.[8]

The lack of knowledge concerning health matters paralleled the insanitary conditions disclosed by the survey, and very likely was largely responsible for these conditions. So far as the results thus far obtained from this survey are concerned, it is interesting to observe the course of the typhoid fever rate, for this is generally accepted as perhaps the most reliable single index of this kind of health work. With few exceptions there was a remarkable decrease in the prevalence of typhoid fever in all the 15 counties where the work was carried on.

(e) Food Sanitation

In the first annual report of the Bureau of Chemistry, Department 1 of Agriculture, after the passage of the Food and Drugs Act of 1906 (1), Dr. Harvey W. Wiley stated: "Any unfavourable conditions found in the factories inspected were subsequently discussed with the inspectors, with a view . . . of impressing upon them the necessity of sanitation in the preparation of articles of food and drugs ...." Thus, food sanitation programmes were initiated at the inception of enforcement of the first Federal food and drug law. They have continued for 50 years to occupy a prominent position in the work of the Food and Drug Administration.[9]

The Food, Drug, and Cosmetic Act of 1938, like the act of 1906, is basically a statute to protect the public health. Proper sanitation in the production and handling of foods and drugs is one of its major requirements. A sanitary food, strictly speaking, is one free from injurious substances, particularly infectious micro-organisms. But modern concepts of food control have expanded this definition to include freedom from materials that are repulsive or obnoxious regardless of their importance as agents of disease. This development is an important factor in the protection of health, since many forms of food contamination carry potential health hazards that cannot be measured, even with modern analytical techniques.

The requirements of the law and the objectives of the Food and Drug Administration with respect to food sanitation may be stated simply: that food be prepared from clean, sound, and wholesome raw materials and that sanitary conditions prevail at all stages of production and distribution. It has been the consistent policy of the Food and Drug Administration through 50 years of enforcement of the food and drug laws to seek to improve the sanitary quality of the food supply by all means and facilities at its disposal. The Food and Drugs Act of 1906 defined a food as adulterated "if it consists, in whole or in part, of a filthy, decomposed, or putrid animal or vegetable substance . . . ." This was the legal basis on which the food sanitation programmes were founded. Food sanitation, then, is the concern of State and local officials as well as national officials. The combined efforts of all are necessary to afford the degree of protection from insanitary food the consumer expects and is entitled to.[10]

(g) Household Sanitation[11]

Sanitary science is of late origin; its proposition to prevent disease by removing the conditions that provoke disease, merits the popular approval, and legislation has been quick to help sanitarians put their science to the test. Much can be done in one home to make it healthful; but the influences that affect one home are so intermixed with the influences that affect large areas, that state and national interference is demanded by sanitary science. The author has stated the sanitary conditions of healthful homes with accuracy, and with sufficient fulness to make these conditions readily comprehended. She appeals to the women of the land to familiarise themselves with the results of sanitary science, that they may be able to critically examine their own homes, and influence opinion, so that healthful conditions may be made compulsory under the law. Sanitary science includes so much, and affects all to the degree that men have no monopoly in its results. Mrs. Plunkett is right in contending that women should master these problems to aid in procuring compulsory legislation.[12]

According to the idea of home sanitation, since the home is the centre of all family life, every effort should be made to make it a healthful place to live, as well as attractive and comfortable. A number of States have enacted housing laws designed to raise the sanitary standards of housing. Health departments are also realising that home sanitation is important in the control of many diseases. Society has come to realise that it can no longer afford the consequences of poor housing and slum conditions.

Water Supply - A safe and adequate water supply is one of the primary requirements of healthful living. To be fully serviceable, it should be convenient for cleansing and bathing purposes, as well as safe for drinking. People living in large cities are usually amply protected. In rural areas, it is necessary to take extra precautions to safeguard the water supply since the danger of contamination from excreta and other sources is so much greater than in cities. The local health department should be consulted regarding the best methods of preventing pollution of the water supply.

Excreta Disposal - Indoor toilets, in addition to being a convenience, are usually much more sanitary than outdoor toilets. They should be kept clean, and there should be adequate provision for light and fresh air in the room in which they are located.

Refuse Disposal - The garbage pail should be made of metal. It should be watertight and should always be kept properly covered.

The Cellar—Dampness and low temperatures lower the normal resistance of individuals to colds and other respiratory infections. Cellars should be kept clean and frequently aired and sunned to prevent dampness. All leaky pipes should be located and immediately repaired.

Light and Fresh Air—Sunshine and fresh air are highly destructive to germ life. Every room should have at least one window, and the window area in each room should be at least 15 per cent of the floor area. In general, rooms should be 8 to 9 feet high. Not more than two persons should occupy a sleeping room at the same time.

Plumbing - All drainage pipes should be kept open and free from obstruction. The toilet bowl should not be used for the disposal of garbage, since waste materials of this type readily clog the pipes. Insanitary conditions as well as a plumber's bill are the result.

Accident Prevention—The number of accidents that occur in the home and their seriousness are not ordinarily appreciated. Improvement in heating and cooking devices and adequate lighting are aiding greatly in reducing the number of accidents.

(h) Law and Sanitation

"Great cities, when badly administered, cannot be sold or abolished; they simply become dirty, unhealthy, unsafe, disgraceful, and expensive". Achieving and maintaining a healthful community environment, however, requires, among other things, control of activities which may adversely affect that environment. Such control is achieved by laws, municipal ordinances, or regulations which inevitably run afoul of private interests. The extent to which these private interests may be required to yield to the needs of the community is determined by the constitutional scope of the governmental power, called the "police power," exercised by the State and by the community as authorised by the State. It is by the exercise of this coercive power that States and communities carry on sanitation programmes.[13]

A good starting point is the mundane and ubiquitous problem of garbage and other solid refuse, the collection and disposal of which has plagued cities for thousands of years. Although American cities spend almost $1½ billion annually for this purpose, the problem is yet unsolved.[14] The health and safety hazards of improper disposal of these solid wastes are obvious. What can be more sensible than provision by a municipality for the safe and sanitary collection and disposal of such material? But garbage and refuse are property, owned by someone, which does have value, slight though it may be. Can a city deprive a person of this property by requiring him to deliver it to a designated collector without paying him for it?

This question was considered by the Supreme Court in 1905. The case of Reduction Company *vs.* Sanitary Works involved an ordinance of the city of San Francisco, which gave an exclusive franchise to one company to collect and incinerate all garbage and solid refuse from within the city.[15] It prohibited any other person from so doing and required that all persons deliver such refuse to the incinerator at their own expense. This latter requirement could, of course, be met by paying the franchised company to collect and dispose of the refuse.

'With respect to the deprivation of the property right, the Court noted the health hazards involved in the improper disposal of such refuse, and declared that even if the material had some value, its collection and disposal as a means for the protection of the public health "cannot be properly considered, within the meaning of the Constitution, as a taking of private property for public use, without compensation simply because such garbage and house refuse may have had, at the time of its destruction, some element of value for certain purposes".

Underlying the conclusion of the Court was the basic concept that no one has a property right in a nuisance endangering the public health or welfare that is so protected that the community may not abate the nuisance without compensating the owner for the value of the property. The nuisance potential of garbage was accepted by the Court as beyond argument. This concept has long been upheld as an inherent element of the police power. Thus, in Lawton *vs.* Steele (7), the Supreme Court noted that the police power of a State ". . . is universally conceded to include everything essential to the public safety, health and morals, and to justify the destruction or abatement, by summary proceedings, of whatever may be regarded as a public nuisance. Under this power it has been held that the State may order the destruction of a house falling to decay . . . , the slaughter of diseased cattle; the destruction of decayed or unwholesome food.... '.

The above discussion emphasises the basic constitutional principles involved in sanitation programmes in order to point out that effective and vigorous enforcement activities can be developed and carried out without offending constitutional protections.

Contemporarily, the work by Thorsten Kiefer, Inga Winkler and others (2008)[16] highlights the legal resources for the right to water and sanitation in international and regional treaties and declarations as well as in national laws. At the international level, the United Nations General Assembly recognised in the 1977 Mar Del Plata Action Plan that—regardless of the level of economic development—all peoples "have the right to have access to drinking water in quantities and of a quality equal to their basic needs."

In the Programme of Action of the International Conference on Population and Development, 1994 the 178 participating States explicitly recognised that all individuals have "the right to an adequate standard of living for themselves and their families, including adequate food, clothing, housing, water and sanitation". The United Nations Committee on Economic, Social and Cultural Rights (CESCR), a body of independent experts mandated by ECOSOC to interpret and monitor the implementation of the International Covenant on Economic Social and Cultural Rights, 1966 (ICESCR), which is currently ratified by 157 States in 2002 issued General Comment No. 15: The Right to Water (General Comment No. 15). The UN Committee on Economic, Social and Cultural Rights in its General Comment on the Right to Water (General Comment No. 15), provides that States are required to ensure that each person has access to sufficient, safe, acceptable, accessible and affordable water for personal and domestic uses. These include the uses necessary to prevent death from dehydration, to reduce the risk of water-related disease and to provide for consumption, food preparation, washing, personal and domestic hygienic requirements.[17]

(A) Explicit Provisions

(i) Convention on the Rights of the Child, 1989[18]

Article 24

1. States Parties recognise the right of the child to the enjoyment of the highest attainable standard of health and to facilities for the treatment of illness and rehabilitation of health...
2. States Parties shall pursue full implementation of this right and, in particular, shall take appropriate measures: ...
   (a) to combat disease and malnutrition, including within the framework of primary health care, through, inter alia, the application of readily available technology and through the provision of adequate nutritious foods and clean

drinking-water, taking into consideration the dangers and risks of environmental pollution; ...

Article 27

1. States Parties recognise the right of every child to a standard of living adequate for the child's physical, mental, spiritual, moral and social development.

Convention on the Elimination of All Forms of Discrimination against Women, 1979.[19]

Article 14 (2)

States parties shall take all appropriate measures to eliminate discrimination against women in rural areas in order to ensure, on a basis of equality of men and women, that they participate in and benefit from rural development and, in particular, shall ensure to women the right: ...

(a) To enjoy adequate living conditions, particularly in relation to housing, sanitation, electricity and water supply, transport and communication.

(ii) International Covenant on Economic, Social and Cultural Rights, 1966[20]

Article 1(2)

All peoples may, for their own ends, freely dispose of their natural wealth and resources without prejudice to any obligations arising out of international economic co-operation, based upon the principle of mutual benefit, and international law. In no case may a people be deprived of its own means of subsistence.

Article 2

1. Each State Party to the present Covenant undertakes to take steps, individually and through international assistance and co-operation, especially economic and technical, to the maximum of its available resources, with a view to achieving progressively the full realisation of the rights recognised in the present Covenant by all appropriate means, including particularly the adoption of legislative measures.
2. The States Parties to the present Covenant undertake to guarantee that the rights enunciated in the present Covenant will be exercised without discrimination of any kind as to race, colour, sex, language, religion, political or other opinion, national or social origin, property, birth or other status.

Article 11

1. The States Parties to the present Covenant recognise the right of everyone to an adequate standard of living for himself and his family, including adequate food, clothing and housing and to the continuous improvement of living conditions. The States Parties will take appropriate steps to ensure the realisation of this right, recognising to this effect the essential importance of international cooperation based on free consent.

Article 12

1. The States Parties to the present Covenant recognise the right of everyone to the enjoyment of the highest attainable standard of physical and mental health.
2. The steps to be taken by the States Parties to the present Covenant to achieve the full realisation of this right shall include those necessary for:
   (a) The provision for the reduction of the birth rate and of infant mortality and for the healthy development of the child.
   (b) The improvement of all aspects of environmental and industrial hygiene.
   (c) The prevention, treatment and control of epidemic, endemic, occupational and other diseases.
   (d) The creation of conditions which would assure to all medical service and medical attention in the event of sickness.

(iii) International Humanitarian and Criminal Law Treaties[21]

International humanitarian law treaties, which govern the actions of States and other actors in times of war or occupation, set out obligations to respect and ensure access to water for prisoners of war, interned persons and the civilian population.

Geneva Convention (III) relative to the Treatment of Prisoners of War, 1949–

Article 20

...The Detaining Power shall supply prisoners of war who are being evacuated with sufficient food and potable water, and with the necessary clothing and medical attention....

Article 26

The basic daily food rations shall be sufficient in quantity, quality and variety to keep prisoners of war in good health and to prevent loss of weight or the development of nutritional deficiencies....

Sufficient drinking water shall be supplied to prisoners of war...

Article 29

The Detaining Power shall be bound to take all sanitary measures necessary to ensure the cleanliness and healthfulness of camps and to prevent epidemics. Prisoners of war shall have for their use, day and night, conveniences which conform to the rules of hygiene and are maintained in a constant state of cleanliness. In any camps in which women prisoners of war are accommodated, separate conveniences shall be provided for them. Also, apart from the baths and showers with which the camps shall be furnished, prisoners of war shall be provided with sufficient water and soap for their personal toilet and for washing their personal laundry; the necessary installations, facilities and time shall be granted them for that purpose.

International Declarations and Resolutions

International Declarations and Resolutions constitute political commitments made by States that can be used to assist in the interpretation of international treaties and national constitutional and other legislative provisions. They may be seen as indications of overall trends in the development of international customary law. A number of environment and development declarations, including the Mar Del Plata Declaration (1977), the Programme of Action of the International Conference on Population and Development and Agenda 21 (1994) and the Report of the UN Conference on Environment and Development (1992) explicitly mention the right to have access to drinking water.

Declarations on environment, development and sustainable development also include provisions that correspond to obligations regarding the right to water and sanitation. These declarations require States to carry out a number of actions, including:

- improving water quality;
- widely expanding access to water and sanitation;
- addressing the inequality in health status between developing and developed countries;
- ensuring access to water for older persons;
- ensuring an adequate environment for all;

- ensuring basic human needs and protection of ecosystems in water allocation, and, beyond these requirements, charging water users appropriately in order to ensure sustainability;
- for developed States, providing new and additional financial and technical resources to a variety of programmes designed to expand access to water and sanitation in developing countries.

(iv) Universal Declaration of Human Rights 1948[22]

Article 2

Everyone is entitled to all the rights and freedoms set forth in this Declaration, without distinction of any kind, such as race, colour, sex, language, religion, political or other opinion, national or social origin, property, birth or other status.

Article 7

All are equal before the law and are entitled without any discrimination to equal protection of the law. All are entitled to equal protection against any discrimination in violation of this Declaration and against any incitement to such discrimination.

Article 25

Everyone has the right to a standard of living adequate for the health and well-being of himself and his family, including food, … housing … and necessary social services…

Article 28

Everyone is entitled to a social and international order in which the rights and freedoms set forth in this Declaration can be fully realised.

Stockholm Declaration, UN Conference on the Human Environment, 1972[23]

Principle 1

Man has the fundamental right to freedom, equality and adequate conditions of life, in an environment of a quality that permits a life of dignity and well-being, and he bears a solemn responsibility to protect and improve the environment for present and future generations….

Principle 2

The natural resources of the earth including the air, water, land, flora and fauna and especially representative samples of natural ecosystems must be safeguarded for the benefit of present and future generations through careful planning or management, as appropriate.

(v) Standard Minimum Rules for the Treatment of Prisoners, 1955[24] (NEW)

Personal hygiene

15. Prisoners shall be required to keep their persons clean, and to this end they shall be provided with water and with such toilet articles as are necessary for health and cleanliness.

Food

20. (1) Every prisoner shall be provided by the administration at the usual hours with food of nutritional value adequate for health and strength, of wholesome quality and well prepared and served. (2) Drinking water shall be available to every prisoner whenever he needs it.

(vi) Rio Declaration on Environment and Development, UN Conference on Environment and Development, 1992[25]

Principle 1

Human beings are at the centre of concerns for sustainable development. They are entitled to a healthy and productive life in harmony with nature.

Principle 10

Environmental issues are best handled with the participation of all concerned citizens, at the relevant level. At the national level, each individual shall have appropriate access to information concerning the environment that is held by public authorities, including information on hazardous materials and activities in their communities, and the opportunity to participate in decision-making processes. States shall facilitate and encourage public awareness and participation by making information widely available. Effective access to judicial and administrative proceedings, including redress and remedy, shall be provided.

(vii) Habitat Agenda, UN Habitat II Conference, Istanbul, 1996[26]

Paragraph 129

Health problems related to adverse environmental conditions, including a lack of access to safe water and sanitation, inadequate waste management, poor drainage, air pollution, and exposure to excessive noise levels, as well as ineffective and inadequate health services, exact a heavy toll on the quality of life and the overall contribution to society of millions of people. They may also aggravate social tension and inequity and increase the vulnerability of people to the effects of disasters. An integrated approach to the provision of environmentally sound infrastructure in human settlements, particularly for people living in poverty in rural and urban areas, is an investment in sustainable human settlements development that can enhance the quality of life, reduce negative impacts on the environment, improve the overall health of a population, and reduce the burden of investment in curative health and poverty alleviation.

(viii) Johannesburg Plan of Implementation of the World Summit on Sustainable Development, 2002[27]

Launch a programme of actions, with financial and technical assistance, to achieve the Millennium development goal on safe drinking water. In this respect, we agree to halve, by the year 2015, the proportion of people who are unable to reach or to afford safe drinking water, as outlined in the Millennium Declaration, and the proportion of people without access to basic sanitation, which would include actions at all levels.

(i) Midwifery and Sanitation[28]

The British Medical Journal of January 25th, Dr Rentoul, in justification of his definition of "Natural Labour," quotes Leishman as follows: "Midwifery is that science and art which has for its object the management of the woman and her offspring during pregnancy, labour, and the puerperal state."

As a general practitioner, in the practice of midwifery, responsibility extends far beyond the actual birth of the child. In the light of recent advances in sanitary knowledge, I would suggest that every practitioner has now an additional duty thrust upon him, namely, that of ascertaining the sanitary condition of the premises about to be occupied by the woman during her puerperal state. Just as the surgeon ascertains that no possibility of atmospheric infection shall exist on the premises where he is about to operate, so the accoucheur should be alive to the necessity of providing for his lying-in patient wholesome surroundings.

The author emphasises that he cannot see how we dare to take the responsibility of educating the young practitioner to the idea that in midwifery sanitary conditions may be disregarded. Personally, I feel that one of the strongest objections that can be urged against the registration of midwives movement is that the opportunities for detecting disease-producing conditions may be lessened when ignorance has more control.

(j) Conservation and Sanitation[29]

Conservation is a word which, in its common use, carries always the implication of its application to renewable natural resources. Its full meaning comprehends the wise and proper use of these resources coupled with their husbanding and protection so that they may continue thus to be wisely and properly used by generations yet unborn. The concept is a logical one, the soundness of which can not be disputed by any true citizen. And yet on this continent it is a relatively new idea, one that is still appreciated in full only by the few. President Theodore Roosevelt was one of the first to stress publicly the vital need and importance of conservation in North America. Through his efforts the National Conservation Commission was set up in the United States in 1909, and correspondingly the Canadian Commission of Conservation in the same year.

In Europe, in normal times, conservation is a part of the ordinary way of life and so is not discussed as something new. There may be seen forests that have been cut, and farms that have been cultivated for many hundreds of years and which are today in as good condition as ever they were. In Japan, difficult though it may be for some to acknowledge anything in that country as good in these tragic days, soil and water conservation have been actively practiced for at least sixty years; only by such means could so small a country support so large a population.

Sanitation is, of course, concerned with far more than just this, important though water is in all sanitary work. Fundamentally, it is concerned with the safeguarding of public health. Incidental to this monumental task is the control and direction of water supplies, sewage disposal systems, swimming pools and public bathing facilities, the super vision of supplies of milk, meat and other foods, refuse collection and disposal, the control of insect and animal nuisances, and of standards of housing and housing equipment.

In its fullest sense, sanitation is concerned with the conservation of the greatest of all natural resources. Dr A.E. Berry, in a notable address delivered before the Toronto Branch of the Engineering Institute of Canada, paid eloquent tribute to this feature of sanitary work. He showed something of the great advances made in public health in recent years and of the contributions of the sanitary engineer to this achievement. Important though this subject is, it must be passed over today in favour of the more restricted connection between sanitation and the conservation of renewable natural resources. Water is clearly the resource with which the sanitary engineer is primarily concerned but some attention must also be given to the disposal of solid refuse or garbage if the responsibilities of those in sanitary work in conserving natural resources are to be adequately discussed.

All, city and country dwellers alike, are dependent ultimately upon the continued productivity of the land, its forests and its waters. The role of sanitation would therefore appear to be the attainment of the highest practicable standard of public health and sanitary services for the maximum possible number of people while ensuring that the works necessary to achieve these results do not despoil any feature of the land.

(k) Watershed Sanitation[30]

Here is the case of historical emergence of watershed sanitation. The water supply of the City of Santa Fé, New Mexico is Santa Fé Creek which is a typical mountain stream. The stream has its beginning at Santa Fé Lake, a beautiful little jewel nestled in a green forest at the foot of Lake Peak. The lake is at an elevation of something over 11,000 feet. The water in the stream is principally derived from melting snows and it is consequently very soft. The system is owned and operated by a private corporation, the New Mexico Power Company, and was formerly owned and operated by the Santa Fé Water and Light Company. The original company constructed an earth fill dam across the mouth of the canyon which impounds about 125 million gallons of water. A by-pass was built around the reservoir to take care of flood waters. The old company had its troubles in the way of supplying sufficient water.

This is now history. The city is now practically all metered and the New Mexico Power Company has constructed another earth fill dam in the canyon at a point about three miles above the original reservoir. This dam impounds about 210 million gallons, which now increases the storage to about 335 million gallons. The distribution system was put into first class shape by replacing many of the small wrought iron and galvanised pipe by larger cast iron mains. Along with these many valuable improvements it was desirable to improve and conserve the sanitary quality of the water. The water- shed is practically all covered with virgin forest.

Section 3564 of the 1915 New Mexico Code empowers the governing body of a municipal corporation to exercise control over a watershed for a distance of five miles above the point of diversion. AH of the land in question was under the control of either the Company or the Forest Service. It seemed to be understood by all parties concerned that some restrictions should be made regarding the recreational use which was to be made of the watershed, and that these restrictions should be in the form of an ordinance passed by the City Council. A group of representative business men were taken on an inspection trip up the canyon and various dangers which were in existence were pointed out in detail. The plan and the ordinance were presented before the various service clubs and their support enlisted. The ordinance was presented to the City Council and it was passed. The Forest Service and the Company employ a patrolman during the summer months who polices the canyon.

(l) Appropriate Technology and Modern Sanitation

Today modern sanitation justifies the statement that the deplorable conditions which have been referred to will never occur again where proper sanitary measures are in force. This does not imply that an outbreak of an infectious disease is promptly and easily dealt with or that its appearance in a community may not be associated with considerable concern, but it means that it is sure to be successfully controlled if proper sanitary methods are enforced.

With the facts we now possess regarding the true means by which infectious diseases are transmitted, every effort should be made to use this knowledge in the better protection of the public health. It not only enables a health official to deal more successfully with an outbreak of infectious disease, but secures more intelligent co-operation from the public in carrying out needed sanitary measures.

Heretofore the public have been apathetic and have taken but little interest in public health work, but it is largely because the people have not been properly informed regarding public sanitation in general and particularly the means by which infectious diseases are transmitted. It is the hope of sanitarians that many of the infectious diseases may be absolutely obliterated. With the co-operation of the public this may be accomplished; without it, it is impossible. Therefore, in the future, the public must be depended upon to do its share in bringing about these important results. Each home should constitute a sanitary unit. Great corporations which have in their charge large bodies of people should have some form of organisation within themselves for the improvement of sanitary methods to insure cleanliness, fresh air, pure water, proper sanitary arrangements, etc.

Appropriate technologies for environmental hygiene usually centre on the delivery of adequate and accessible water supply, and proper treatment and disposal of excreta and refuse. In the face of the International Drinking Water and Sanitation Decade of 1981-90, several research efforts are under way in the developing countries to develop technologies and approaches for improving environmental hygiene in both rural areas and urban squatter settlements. These are discussed and include the technical development and field testing of infiltration galleries, low-cost slow and fast filtration processes for water treatment, handpumps, on-site excreta disposal using aqua-privy and compost toilets, and excreta treatment and refuse through composting with refuse, biogas generation, fish culture and use of excreta as crop fertiliser. The relevant technology 'hardware' is but one of several components necessary for effective delivery of services. The dearth of qualified manpower at all levels is described as being the major constraint to the Water and Sanitation Decade. Hardware aspects of appropriate technology for water supply and sanitation has reported on research being carried out in the Third World to solve some of the problems encountered by direct technology transfer. Real health improvement implies a village level presence that incorporates an equipment maintenance programme and a continuing sanitation education activity - a capability which very few water supply agencies can muster. Major shifts in institutions and their approaches will be required if emphasis on water supply technology and improvements in health is to be transferred from the urban areas to rural communities.[31]

(m) Community Participation in Appropriate Water Supply and Sanitation Technologies

The importance of adequate drinking water supplies and sanitation (to denote excreta disposal only) as basic public health measures has been attracting increasing international attention during the 1970s. For 20 years after the Second World War these approaches were unfashionable and were eclipsed by advances in vector control, chemotherapy and immunology. However, widespread lack of progress in the control of diarrhoeal diseases, schistosomiasis, malaria and other infections, has caused interest to turn back towards environmental control strategies, and in particular to focus upon domestic water supplies and sanitation. This renewed interest in environmental health has run parallel with and is linked to, the current popularity of primary health care.

The level of international activity in the field of water supply and sanitation is increasing markedly at present in preparation for the International Drinking Water Supply and Sanitation Decade (1981-90). The Decade arises out of the resolutions passed at the U.N. Habitat Conference in Vancouver in 1976 and the U.N. Water Conference in Mar del Plata in 1977. The United Nations member states have agreed upon a target of providing the entire world's population with a safe drinking water supply and hygienic excreta disposal facilities by the year 1990. To achieve this, and generally to promote the drinking water and sanitation sectors, the International Decade has been declared.[32]

(n) Sociology Of Sanitation and Religion: A Case Study of Kumbh Mela[33]

In recent years, there has been a spectacular growth in public consciousness about the forms of environmental degradation in India. With an amazing but welcome rapidity, this awareness is being translated on the one hand into substantial media coverage, and on the other into the creation of new government departments concerned with different aspects of environment management. All over the world people from local to global level have been directly victimised by the depletion of natural resources due to the short-lived developmental activities initiated by the modern forms of state apparatuses are organised themselves to raise the voice against the over exploitation of natural resources. Although the voices were inaudible in the initial period, later on it got appreciation once the external agencies like media, civil society and social activists took this issue very seriously into the public discourse. Because of this combination of voices gave birth to institutionalisation of social movements by articulating the need for restoring our natural resources and adopting alternative views of development and modernisation. Departing from the conventional categorisation of social movements based on ethnic, class, gender differences, new social movements of this kind voyage new discourse in the public domain attracted voice of the people from different part of the world regardless of class, creed, colour or gender for a common cause called protection of our environment. Ecological modernisation theory perhaps puts forward a radical transformational phase as the way modern society grapple with the environment question. In so doing, the institutions of modern society, such as the market, the state and science and technology, need to be radically transformed in tune with the environmental crisis, but not beyond recognition.

Religion is one of the most important facets of Indian history and contemporary life. It may not be wrong to say that religion has been, and continues to be, a matter of absorbing interest for many in India still today. In former centuries no aspect of life was set apart from religion. All social relations were inevitably and legitimately suffused with religious ideas and acts. The possibility of religion in a modern world can be felt through altered functioning of religion. The marketisation of religion by religious gurus performing miracles and fascinating public, the involvement of religious organisations in the building up of hospitals and schools, working for the victims of natural disasters etc. and politicisation of religion by the outburst of fundamentalists reflect the altered character of it. Modern forces have certainly influenced folk culture and traditions in developing countries like India, but they have not as yet lost their vigour. References to modern objects, events and experiences find their way into folklore through the usual process of reworking traditional items, the composition of new pieces, and even the merger of new types. Thus in contemporary India, the impact of modernisation has led to the emergence of new religions, revivals, and reforms within the great traditions. In modern societies, with their complex fabric of social differentiations, not only among religion, but other groups and social activities, there appears a proliferation of rites (see Saxena 2009).[34] It is believed that during this auspicious astrological moment, the waters of the Ganges have the ability to wash away layer upon layer of karmic debt. Millions of Hindus have already started pouring into the northern Indian city of Allahabad for the *Kumbh Mela* festival. Such a large-scale event poses unfathomable challenges for organisers, especially when it comes to sanitation.

Those pilgrims who stay for the whole month (known as *Kalpwasis*) live in conditions that are more difficult than those they experience at home. They live in rudimentary tents without heating, often without sanitary facilities, sleeping on the ground and experiencing night-time temperatures approaching zero centigrade. The event is also very crowded, and again this contrasts with life in the villages from which the pilgrims come. The crowds make walking to the bathing areas difficult and on days that bathing is judged particularly auspicious in terms of Hindu traditions, it can take several hours to walk a kilometer or so. Another striking feature of the event is its noise level. A vast array of competing loudspeakers broadcast religious discourses, songs, announcements and other administrative information throughout the day (and into the night).

Even if enduring hardship is integral to the act of pilgrimage and even if such hardships do not deter pilgrims from attending, these various circumstances - unsanitary conditions, severe cold, dense crowding and intense noise - are all those that would be expected to be bad for well-being. But are they? We ask if, in the light of social psychological research identifying associations between involvement in social group-related activities and well-being, participation in this mass gathering could impact well-being positively. Thus against the dysfunctionality of crowd of *'Mela'* as source of nuisance, mismanagement and cheats, this work humbly tries to explore the functionality of historical 'Prayag *Kumbh*'.

It is observed that 'religious *Mela*' has a spread-effect of maintaining sanitation through collective participation. It is emphasised that socialisation of good sanitation practices to the pilgrims can be instrumental in carrying it further at far flung areas of diverse India and making clean and green India.

In Durkheimenian framework, one can observe 'sociology of sanitation' as a shift from profane to sacred elements. Locating the issue of sanitation L. Dumount rightly states that the Indian society is homo-hierarchicus resting on the religion with caste system having an element of 'pure' and 'impure'. Even M.N. Srinivas too speaks about 'purity and pollution', having bearing on caste interactions. His concept of *'sanskritisation'* has an inherent notion of sanitation for lower caste members. If one goes philosophically on the issue of sanitation of soul, one finds that 'secularisation' reflects decline in the religious intolerance and accommodation of diverse religious practices for healthy society. The doctrine of Hindu religion also focuses on sanitation with the purification of ones *'paap'* in the lifetime. Thus sanitation of body and soul as a precondition for attaining moksh after death and for once re-birth. Even, performing once duties in the holy pilgrimage is deeply embedded in religio-philosophical matrix of Indian psyche. At this juncture the pilgrimage of *'Prayag Kumbh'* becomes crucial. The paper locates issues of 'sanitation' in the pilgrimage of *'Prayag Kumbh'*. Here emphasis is on 'power of sanitation' as an ideology and an instrument of maintaining sanctity and religious purity.

Although, the first mention of a *Kumbh Mela* in British administrative reports that I have been able to find, however, is in the closing discussion of an 1868 report about pilgrimage and sanitation controls. Contemporarily, The United Provinces *Mela*s Act, 1938 is vested with the power to impose tolls, taxes and fees under section 5 in *mela* areas—tolls on any vehicle or animal entering, or person bringing goods for sale into such areas; Without prejudice the office-in-charge may allot sites for the following in particular - religious societies of persuasion, kalpbasis, market places, laterines, urinals and rubbish heaps, recreation and entertainments. Even the United Provinces *Mela*s rule miscellaneous, Oct. 16, 1940 says that a person suffering from plague smallpox or other infectious diseases shall not enter the *mela* area. The Officer-in-charge shall order any person found within *mela* area suffering from an infectious disease either to leave the *Mela* or to enter the infectious disease hospital within a fixed time.

As reflected in local and national newspapers (*Times of India*, December, 2012 and *Amar Ujala* December, 2012), recently in 2013 *kumbh mela*, the Indian government set up a special administration body that is responsible for the smooth-running of the festival. But the people who make it work are the cleaners. They're the lowest paid, and they're working around the clock. There are thousands of street cleaners, then there's a smaller group that cleans the water. There are lots of different camps of holymen, and they all want to take their dips first, because they want the water to be clear. People take dips in the water every day, but when the holymen take their dips it attracts big crowds—people want to dip at the same time as the holy men. The dips are staggered—there's always a half hour gap between each dip, so the cleaners can go into the water and clean. They don't use chemical products; they fish out any objects left behind, like the flowers people take with them to bathe.

Recently, in the run-up to the festival, around 35,000 single-seat latrines, 340 blocks of 10-seat toilets, and 4,000 urinals on-site. They're linked by a 165 kilometre network of plastic pipes which carry the waste to pits, which themselves are reinforced by brick. It'll be interesting to see how many new latrines and pits the administration will have to build; as what they've built so far may not be enough. People do not always use the toilets, particularly children—they just go in the open air. There are 9,000 sweepers, whose job it is to sweep away faeces into the pits. Waterborne diseases and a cholera outbreak are real risks. We hope to carry out research that will help the administration prevent the impact of waterborne diseases. Even, the area of the *mela* is also on the rise: from 1,495.31 hectare and 11 sectors in 2001 to 1936.56 hectare and 14 sectors in 2013 (see official website of Kumbh *mela* 2013).

According to national newspaper reports, arrangements provided 5,000 gallons of purified drinking water every minute; 8,000 buses which shuttle pilgrims in and out of the festival area that spread over 300 acres; 16,000 outlets and 6,000 poles which provided electrical facilities; 6,000 sweepers and sanitation employees who worked around the clock to maintain health standards; nine pontoon bridges which spanned the Ganges at intervals. Although, The Indian government set up a special administration body about a year ago that is responsible for the smooth-running of the festival. But the people who make it work are the cleaners. They're the lowest paid, and they're working around the clock. There are thousands of street cleaners, then there's a smaller group that cleans the water. Further, agitated over high levels of pollution and shallow water in the holy Ganga, the

Shankracharyas, seers and *Dandi swamis*, along with all the *'akaharas'*, are all set to boycott the next *'Shahi Snan'* on *Mauni Amavasya* scheduled for February 10, 2013. These saints, on Friday, threatened that if the situation remained unchanged, they will not bathe in the next *Shahi Snan*.

By going through the factors responsible for the failure of Ganga Action Plan (GAP), the parliamentary standing committee on science and technology, environment and forests has doubts if the Prime Minister's mission of cleaning Ganga by 2020 will be accomplished. Our vision is that in 12 years' time, every camp at the *Kumbh Mela* will be green, and every pilgrim will be reminded that it is the sacred duty of every Hindu to protect the environment."

It is reflected that the role of religious ideology and socio-religious leaders too have become active players towards generating environmental sanitation. In conclusion it is urged that the "size and complexity" of the *Kumbh Mela* is inspirational for inter-disciplinary research in a number of complementary fields of urban studies and design, religious and cultural studies, environmental science and public health, technology and communications. There is a need to bring the issue of 'Right to sanitation' and also *'sulabhisation'* of pilgrimage sites. Needless to mention that environmental sanitation is the growing concern of the hour.

Sanitation Issues in UNICEF Country Programme

The Executive Board ***further encourages*** the UNICEF Secretariat, in collaboration with national partners and external support agencies, selecting pertinent strategies within the framework of country programmes, to continue:

- To promote and advocate public commitment, national policy and accelerated actions for meeting the needs and rights of children and the poor in respect of water supply and environmental sanitation.
- To set, define and review national and local goals, working with government and appropriate partners and pursuing their achievement through effective monitoring systems.
- To promote and strengthen partnerships, formed and strengthened with Governments at all levels as well as with civil society, nongovernmental organisations, the private sector, external support agencies and others, ensuring cooperation and complementarity.

- To support the expansion of basic services, managed by the community, retaining strong commitment and providing catalytic support to the expansion of cost-effective services using appropriate technologies, while taking into account the potential for upgrading services by the communities themselves.
- To support emergency programmes for essential water supply and environmental sanitation needs within the framework of the United Nations system for emergency response.
- To allocate appropriate resources, as envisaged in the medium-term plan (E/ICEF/1994/3), from general resources and supplementary funds for water supply, sanitation and hygiene education, and to improve the capacity of national counterparts to effectively meet the challenge in the sector.
- To promote appropriate standardisation of technologies for water supply and sanitation services to minimise the cost of installation, operations and maintenance.

The Executive Board *urges* UNICEF to put a greater emphasis on, and allocate resources as required for:

- Environmental sanitation, hygiene and behavioural change.
- Community management of the "water environment" within the context of the Agenda 21 and primary environmental care.
- Capacity-building, adopting programme approaches that build capacity at all levels and in all segments of society, including the establishment of community resource centres, to ensure sustainable sector development.
- Community cost-sharing of capital and recurrent costs of basic levels of service, taking into account the willingness and ability to pay, and recovery of full capital and recurrent costs of higher levels of services in order to generate additional resources to extend basic services and ensure their sustainability.
- Gender-balanced approaches to meeting the objective, recognising women as key players and agents of change, and not solely as primary beneficiaries, in the context of overall efforts to empower women.
- Participatory approaches to meeting the objectives and promoting the role of the community, supported by other

stakeholders, in planning, implementing, managing and monitoring services.

- Research and development on technology and social and economic issues, including the transfer of technology, in order to promote cost-effectiveness, impact, and sustainability.
- Assistance to countries to standardise the definition of coverage and improve monitoring systems by including process and impact indicators.
- Enhanced linkages with health, education, nutrition, environment and other development programmes, exploiting synergies among all sectors that support child survival, protection and development.
- Improvement and strengthening of the capacity of UNICEF water supply and sanitation staff by, *inter alia*, increasing the proportion of women in the sector and improving staff training, including the transfer of knowledge and skills and orientation and career structure to respond effectively for meeting goals of the sector.
- Appropriate support for promotion of water supply and sanitation services in deprived, low-income urban areas

Source: As presented to the UNICEF Executive Board Annual Session in May, 1995 (Document E/ICEF/1995/17, issued 13 April 1995) and as adopted by the Executive Board with Decision 1995/22.

Notes

1. For details see Sanitation and Science, Science, Vol. 6, No. 127 (Jul. 10, 1885), pp. 21-22, Published by: American Association for the Advancement of Science
2. See George C. Whipple's work 'State Sanitation'. Public Health Reports (1896-1970), Vol. 36, No. 47 (Nov. 25, 1921), pp. 2879-2892
3. *Ibid.*
4. See Stephen J. Watkins, Public Health 2020, BMJ: British Medical Journal, Vol. 309, No. 6962 (Oct. 29, 1994), pp. 1147-1149, BMJ Publishing Group
5. See K S Jacob, Public health in India and the developing world: beyond medicine and primary healthcare, Journal of Epidemiology and Community Health (1979-), Vol. 61, No. 7 (July 2007),pp. 562-563, BMJ Publishing Group

6. See Monica Das Gupta, Public Health in India: Dangerous Neglect, Economic and Political Weekly, Vol. 40, No. 49 (Dec. 3-9, 2005), pp. 5159-5165.

7. Rural Sanitation a Present Necessity, Public Health Reports (1896-1970), Vol. 34, No. 2 (Jan. 10, 1919), pp. 36-39.

8. Rural Sanitation, A report on special studies made in 15 counties in 1914, 1915, and 191S. Public Health Bulletin 94, October, 1918. Government Printing Office, Washington, D.C.

9. Glenn G. Slocum, Food Sanitation, Public Health Reports (1896-1970), Vol. 71, No. 6 (Jun., 1956), pp. 560-565.

10. Glenn G. Slocum, Food Sanitation, Public Health Reports (1896-1970), Vol. 71, No. 6 (Jun., 1956), pp. 560-565.

11. See Household Sanitation, Science, Vol. 6, No. 128 (Jul. 17, 1885), pp. 57-58. Home sanitation is circulated by Surgeon General, U. S. Public Healtb Service, Washington, D. C. For details see, Home Sanitation, Public Health Reports (1896-1970), Vol. 55, No. 49 (Dec. 6, 1940), pp. 2282-2284.

12. H. M. Plunkett, Women plumbers, and doctors; or, household sanitation. New York, Appleton, 1885, p. 248.

13. Sidney Edelman, Legal Aspects of Sanitation Programs, Public Health Reports (1896-1970), Vol. 79, No. 8 (Aug., 1964), pp. 676-682.

14. U.S. Bureau of the Census: Summary of governmental finances. 1958, p. 30.

15. Reduction Company vs. Sanitary works, 199 U.S. 306 (1905).

16. Legal Resources for The Right to Water and Sanitation: International and National Standards—2nd edition, Centre on Housing Rights and Evictions, The Netherlands., www.cohre.org/water.

17. Sidney Edelman, Legal Aspects of Sanitation Programmes, Public Health Reports (1896-1970), Vol. 79, No. 8 (Aug., 1964), pp. 676-682.

18. At: http://www.unhchr.ch/html/menu3/b/k2crc.htm.

19. At: http://www.unhchr.ch/html/menu3/b/e1cedaw.htm.

20. http://www.unhchr.ch/html/menu3/b/a_cescr.htm

21. See http://www.icrc.org

22. At: http://www.un.org/Overview/rights.html.

23. At: http://www.unep.org/Documents/Default.asp?DocumentID=97.

24. At: http://www1.umn.edu/humanrts/instree/g1smr.htm; www.unhchr.ch/html/.
25. At: http://www.unep.org/Documents/Default.asp?DocumentID=78&ArticleID=1163.
26. http://www.unhabitat.org/unchs/english/hagenda/.
27. http://www.un.org/esa/sustdev/documents/WSSD_POI_PD/English/POIToc.htm.
28. G. Walter Steeves, Midwifery and Sanitation. The British Medical Journal, Vol. 1, No. 1837 (Mar. 14, 1896), p. 697.
29. See Robert F. Legget, Conservation and Sanitation. Sewage Works Journal, Vol. 16, No. 1 (Jan., 1944), pp. 124-131.
30. Paul S. Fox, Watershed Sanitation, Journal (American Water Works Association), Vol. 20, No. 1 (JULY, 1928), pp. 50-53
31. M. G. McGarry, Appropriate Technologies for Environmental Hygiene, Proceedings of the Royal Society of London. Series B, Biological Sciences, Vol. 209, No.1174, More Technologies for Rural Health (Jul. 28, 1980), pp. 37-46.
32. R. G. Feachem, Community Participation in Appropriate Water Supply and Sanitation Technologies: The Mythology for the Decade, Proceedings of the Royal Society of London. Series B, Biological Sciences, Vol. 209, No.1174, More Technologies for Rural Health (Jul. 28, 1980), pp. 15-29.
33. See Ashish Saxena (2013). 'Movement Towards The Green Pilgrimage: Mapping Environmental Sanitation Issues in *Kumbh Mela* At Prayag', Proceedings of Sociology of Sanitation, Sulabh International, New Delhi.
34. Saxena, Ashish. 2009. 'Religion, Caste and Community: Identity Substantiation through *'Maile'* Congregations among the *Dogras* of Jammu and Kashmir (India)' in *'Politics and Religion'* Centre for Studies of Religion and Religious Tolerance, Serbia; issue no.1/2009 Volume III.

6

Sanitation and Allied Vocabulary in Social Sciences

Introduction

Sociologically speaking, feelings of aggressiveness generated during early socialisation, admiration of force inherited from parents, lack of education, absence of information, social uprootedness, and alienation are components of the mental set of the poor. The poor are radical because they are culturally backward. The possibility of rational action, of a deliberate calculation of means and ends is seldom contemplated. Rather, popular masses are perceived as governed by impulse. Extremism permeates these groups to the extent that they are also permeated by ignorance, social isolation, and irrational aggressiveness.

Oscar Lewis notion of the 'subculture of poverty' has come to denote a situation in which people are trapped in a social environment characterised by apathy, fatalism, lack of aspirations, exclusive concern with immediate gratifications, and frequent endorsement of delinquent behaviour.[1] Not only material, but moral destitution as well, is an essential part of slum life. People who are forced to move there are lost. Regardless of their initial aspirations and willingness to work, the overwhelming social influence exercised by the new environment soon eliminates these qualities, substituting for them completely new definitions of society and life.

The subculture of poverty approach envisions behaviour in peripheral slums in terms fitting Weber's type of emotional orientation to action. Individuals are guided by the concerns of immediate gratification rather than by the expectation of future goal-attainment. Action acquires an impulsive, unpredictable quality insofar as it is directed either by shifting emotions or by complete indifference. 'Sociologically it is a way of life, a subculture with its own set of norms and values, which is reflected in poor sanitation and health practices, deviant behaviour, and characteristic attributes of apathy and social isolation.[2]

In South Asian context, social relations intersect with the management of waste in a very particular way. All over the world waste workers are stigmatised and are likely to be from marginalised groups such as ethnic or religious minorities or rural migrants. The low social status of people dealing with rubbish is compounded in South Asia by the association of this work with caste. Following Mary Douglas, Dipesh Chakrabarty argues that household dirt creates a symbolic enclosure for the purpose of protecting 'the inside' from disorder, while 'the outside', where one meets strangers, can be 'rubbished' (Chakrabarty, 1991:17).[3] Forming a bridge between the inside and outside worlds are particular categories of people who are deemed to be ritually polluted and born to work with dirt (Searle-Chatterjee, 1979).[4]

The notion of health and illness, wellness and sickness, as culturally based behaviours and belief systems has been well documented in the literature. It follows that there are broad variations in the way people perceive what constitutes the source of disease or cleanliness. Therefore, health education is a conscious intervention that is aimed at changing existing behaviour and practices.

Mainly, there are three forms of manual scavenging in which people are forced to carry out scavenging work such as removal of excreta from public streets ("open defecation") and dry latrines; removal of excreta form septic tanks and cleaning closed gutters and sewage. Especially 95 per cent women are engaged in cleaning dry toilets and public streets whereas men of scavenger community enter into manhole and septic tanks to clean it. However, Delhi Higher Court directed on 27th July, 2011 to the Indian Railways to rehabilitate sanitation workers employed into cleaning railway tracks and 1,72000 toilets. Therefore there is urgent need to re-define the term 'manual scavenger'.

In 2007, the Government of India estimated 3.42 lakhs manual scavengers still operated in the country. For rehabilitation purposes the Government established the 'Self Employment Scheme for Rehabilitation of Manual Scavengers' which was implemented from 2007 to March 2010. Through this scheme, more than 40.000 manual scavengers received livelihood training, almost 80.000 received loans for alternative forms of work, while almost 40.000 manual scavengers were not rehabilitated due to various reasons. On 17 June, 2011 however, the Prime Minister of India urged his Government to eliminate the manual scavenging practice in the next six month which further reaffirms the existence of manual scavenging practice and the difficulty of its eradication.

At the same time, the National Advisory Committee adopted a number of recommendations expediting the elimination of scavenging, while the Ministry of Labour and Employment established a Task Force on Sanitation and Leather Workers which has also been initiating a number of legislative and policy revisions to assure manual scavenging will be eradicated in India by the end of the current five year plan.

The ILO scavenging project focuses on supporting the implementation of the renewed government policy in five States, Uttar Pradesh, Bihar, Madhya Pradesh, Rajasthan and Gujarat. For this purpose, the ILO organised three consultative meetings (Lucknow, Ahmadabad and Jaipur) with representatives of the scavenger community, trade unions and civil society to gain understanding of the different forms of scavenging; rehabilitation obstacles the scavenger community is facing; and ascertain the impact and effectiveness of the available Government schemes.[5]

Thus, Sanitation and hygiene are critical to health, survival, and development. Many countries are challenged in providing adequate sanitation for their entire populations, leaving people at risk for water, sanitation, and hygiene (WASH)-related diseases. Sanitation is observed as an overall reform of any society including physical, social, psychological, economic, political and religious. It encompasses all spheres of human life which directly or indirectly affects the degree of freedom and well-being of the members of the society. It is based on the issue of justice and also removal of all forms of injustice leading to better life-chances and life-styles of human being. The discussion ahead tries to encompass the various terms having a direct or indirect bearing on the overall reform of the society i.e., sanitation of society in a holistic framework. The battery of terms and concept discussed below indicates certain issues linked to the evils or ugly aspect of human life and which needs to be sanitised for a healthy society.

(a) The Idea of Pollution

Pollution is the primary target of environmental law. During the past forty years, hundreds of federal and state statutes, administrative regulations, and international treaties have established multiple approaches to addressing pollution of the air, water, and land. Yet the law still struggles to identify precisely what constitute pollution, how much of it is tolerable, and what we should do about it. But environmental pollution is hardly the only type of pollution. Historically, the idea of pollution had two meanings: a narrow view limited to effects on the air, water, and natural environment; and a broad view that incorporated the moral connotation similar to terms such as, something changed.[6] As a result, several environmental historians are exploring the history of environmental pollution in the nineteenth and twentieth century, and how "pollution" became the term that is so familiar to us now. Professor Adam Rome wrote a comprehensive account of this development in a 1996 article.[7] According to Rome, Americans rarely used the words pollute and pollution to refer to "human degradation of the environment" until after the Civil War. 51 Instead, pollute and pollution referred to the "violation, perversion, or corruption of moral standards." What people now know as air pollution was labeled "smoke," "noxious vapours," or simply a "nuisance." Air was not polluted, but "contaminated," "tainted," "vitiated," "corrupted," or "fouled." People used "trade wastes," "industrial wastes," and other terms to describe what we now characterise as water pollution. These terms reflected the early nineteenth century understanding that cities were cleaner than the countryside, and that city air was cleaner than the air in natural environments. The prevailing "miasma" theory viewed places with abundant biological materials — swamps or forests, for example — as introducing harmful gases into the air. Some people recognised that industrial emissions were harmful, but many others saw such emissions as innocuous or even helpful, with numerous public health authorities proclaiming the chemicals released by the burning of coal cleaned biological impurities in the air.

The rapid urbanisation and industrialisation that occurred during the nineteenth century provoked increased concern about many of the problems now called pollution. Indeed, "[b]y the 1850s, a few sanitary reformers had begun to use the verb 'pollute' "to refer to emissions into the air and dischargers into the water. In 1876, the Massachusetts Board of Health published a lengthy study, 'The Pollution of Rivers'. According to Rome, river pollution is the key to the transformation of the meaning of pollution:

Though the word "pollution" originally had powerful moral connotations, the river pollution studies eventually contributed to a demoralisation of the phrase. Investigators invariably sought to discriminate between dangerous and non dangerous pollutants. Thus the word "pollution" no longer implied a judgment but instead became purely descriptive: Anything that was not naturally in a river was pollution, but only a few forms of pollution were cause for alarm.

The concept of air pollution developed later than water pollution. Justice Holmes's reference to "the pollution in the air" in the famous Georgia *vs.* Tennessee Copper Co. smelter case illustrates one of the first references to air pollution. The Oil Pollution Act of 1924, the first federal statute whose title referred to pollution, solidified the new understanding of the term. The environmental connotation of pollution became pervasive during the environmental protection movement of the 1960s and 1970s, and today it dominates popular discourse and the law.[8]

(i) Pure and Impure

Dumont specifies the nature of the opposition between pure and impure by successive approximations. On the issue of distinction applied to hereditary groups, especially the contrast between Brahmans and untouchables, it is generally agreed that the opposition is manifested in some macroscopic from in the contrast between the two extreme categories: Brahmans and Untouchables. The Brahman, being in principle priests, occupy the supreme rank with respect to the whole set of castes. The Untouchables, as very impure servants, are segregated outside the villages proper, in distinct hamlets (or at least distinct quarters). The Untouchables may not use the same wells as the others (barring recent local relaxations), access to Hindu temples was forbidden them up to the Gandhian reform, and they suffer from numerous other disabilities. The term 'Untouchable' to designate the category is English rather than indigenous: the notion is present, but in common usage these people are designated by the name of the particular caste to which they belong.

Why, it may be asked, this separation of the Untouchables?... Hygiene is often invoked to justify ideas about impurity. In reality, even though the notion may be found to contain hygienic associations, these cannot account for it, as it is a religious notion. I shall show in what follows that the immediate source of the notion is to be found in the temporary impurity which the Hindu of good caste contracts in relation to organic life. Starting from this, we shall see that it is specialisation in impure tasks, in practice or in theory, which leads to the attribution of a massive and permanent impurity to some categories of people. Ancient literature confirms that temporary and permanent impurity is identical, in nature. But one must not lose sight of the complementarily which exists between pure and impure, and also between the social groups in which these ideas are expressed. One can subsequently trace ot only the multiple derivations of the notion, but also the multiplication of the criteria of distinction and the extreme portioning out, so to speak, of hierarchical status between a large number of groups, we will end by mentioning some variants and irregularities and by sketching a semantic comparison with our own notions. Temporary impurity and permanent impurity.... In so far as the notion of impurity is present affected by this kind of event are impure for a prescribed period, and Indians themselves identify this impurity with that of the Untouchables. Thus Professor P. V. Kane, the learned jurist to whom we owe that monumental work, the History of the Dharmashastra, writes that man's nearest relatives and his best friend become untouchable for him for a certain time as a result of these events.

Historical Data: Normative literature, the dharma or religious law, has purification (*suddhi*) as one of its main themes, the impurity resulting from birth and death being specially designated *asauca*. According to Harita, the purity he calls external is of three kinds, bearing on the family (kula), objects of everyday use (artha), and the body (sarira). For the body, the main thing is the morning attention to hygiene culminating in the daily bath. According to Manu there are twelve secretions or impurities, including excrement, saliva, and the lowly fate reserved for the left hand (in Tamil the 'hand of filth'). Objects are distinguished by the greater or lesser ease of their purification (a bronze vessel is merely cleaned, an earthen ware one replaced) and their relative richness: silk is purer than cotton, gold than silver, than bronze, than copper. But above all one realises that objects are not polluted simply by contact, but by the use to which they are put, by a sort of participation by the object, in being used, with the person. Thus nowadays a new garment or vessel can be received from anybody. It is said that his own bed, his garment, his wife, his child, his water-pot are pure from pollution for the person himself, but impure for others.

Family impurity is the most important: it is that of birth (sutaka) and above all death. Birth only lastingly affects the mother and the new-born child. Death affects the relations collectively and it is a social rather than a physical matter, since the impurity essentially affects not the people in whose house someone dies, but the relations of the deceased wherever they may be. Moreover the effect varies according to the degree of kinship. The strength of these ideas can be realised in the light of the reforms proposed by Kane to counteract what he regards as being nowadays anachronistic and troublesome excesses. He suggests what he considers a sufficient maximum for mourning, namely: ten days mourning and impurity for the father, the mother, the son, the wife or the husband, the chief mourner (if he is not one of the above); three days for the other members of the joint family; for the rest it would suffice to take a bath on hearing of the death within a year.

Note some further prescriptions which are evidence to the same effect; a menstruating (or pre-pubertal) women may not mount her husband's funeral pyre, she must wait for four days and the final bath (she would have to bate in any case before burning herself alive). A marriage ceremony must be postponed if a fairly close death occurs during the preparations for it, or if the mother is menstruating. It is sometimes said that one should not come near the fire nor breathe on the fire with one's mouth if one is impure. A verse of Manu (ii, 27) clearly shows the nature of impurity: 'The pollution of semen and of the womb [that is to say, birth] is effaced for the twice-born by the sacraments of pregnancy, birth, tonsure and initiation.' (The 'twice-born' are the members of the categories who are entitled to initiation, a second birth.) It can be seen that impurity corresponds to the organic aspect of man. Religion generally speaks in the name of universal order; but in this case, though unaware in this form of what it is doing, by proscribing impurity it in fact sets up a opposition between religious and social man on the one hand and nature on the other.

How, according to the texts as well as custom, is impurity to be remedied? Through the bath, water is the great purificatory agent. Yet it must be noticed that its virtue has certain limitations: when the pollution is particularly intense, at the death of a near relative for example, one must wait for the period prescribed for the duration of mourning before taking the terminal bath. Further, not all baths are equally efficacious: most strictly a bath in running water, fully slothed, is required, and certain especially sacred waters, like the Ganges, have the maximum purificatory or in any case religious power. Mauss' statement may be verified: water acts not simply in accordance with a magical mechanism but by reason so the spiritual presences which it contains or represents. As Mauss said further, water in general 'separates' different states of purity: one sometimes bathes before encountering an impurity. Fire on the other hand has scarcely any direct purificatory value, though it has connected functions (ordeal, ritual). Shaving, especially shaving the whole head, accompanies purificatory baths, as at the end of mourning; on the other hand, the ban on shaving during mourning and in other circumstances is a mark of an ascetic performance; further, a child's head of hair is sometimes dedicated to a god. Apart from minor measures (bleeding the little finger, chewing a chilli, touching iron) and water, the main purifying agents are the five products of the cow (urine, dung, etc.). These purificatory procedures are also employed in the case of what may be called caste pollution: one bathes after the market or work, one is reintegrated into the caste by a ceremonial bat. Moreover, there is an easy transition from purification to expiation (absorption of the products of the cow, bath in the Ganga).

Thus the literature is explicit about impurity in personal life within a caste or social category particularly that of the Brahmans. From this point of view, purification already appears as a perpetual necessity. The literature also shows the transition from this occasional or temporary impurity to the permanent impurity of certain human groups. The laws of Manu say (V,85), 'When he has touched a Chandala, a menstruateing women, an outcaste, a women who has given birth, a corpse…he purifies himself by bathing.' Here the three occasional impurities are identified with that of the 'outcaste' and the Chandala, who is none other than the old prototype of the Untouchable. There is another list in the same book as (iii, 239): 'A Chandala, a domestic pig, a cock, a dog, a menstruating women and a eunuch must not look at Brahmans while they are eating', and the following verse adds that the same people likewise render certain sorts of ritual ineffective. We shall see that a man who is eating is particularly vulnerable to impurity; moreover the animals mentioned feed on refuse and fifth which they find in the village and its outskirts. Here again, functional characteristics are thus equated with individual events as sources of impurity, and different sorts of impurity are identified. (The case of the eunuch remains to be explained.) So we find that Manu said the same thing as Kane says at the present day.

If the laws of Manu are difficult to date precisely, at least it is admitted that no part of them is later than the third century AD whilst certain elements could be very much older. So it can be seen that specialisation in impurity at least, if not the caste system such as exists these days, is recorded from the beginning of our era. In the same text the Candala is relegated to cremation grounds and lives on men's refuse. In short, not only are the impurity of individual life and that of the Untouchable considered today as being of the same nature, but it was already so for the author of the laws of Manu, and the 'fatakas' (The collection of previous lives of the Buddha) show that there was a very strong feeling of impurity among certain groups and that untouchability already existed to a considerable extent.

It is clear that the impurity of the Untouchable is conceptually inseparable from the purity of the Brahman. They must have been established together, or in any case have mutually reinforced each other, and we must used to thinking of them together. In particular, untouchability will not truly disappear until the purity of the Brahman is itself radically devalued; this is not always noticed. Among Hindus, on the contrary, even the involuntary killing of a cow is a very serious crime, and one can see a relation between the transformation thus shown and the progress of ideas of non-violence. But there is also a social connection: the murder of a cow is assimilated to that of a Brahman, and we have seen that its products are powerful purificatory agents. Symmetrically, the Untouchables have the job of disposing of the dead cattle, of treating and working their skins, and this is unquestionably one of the main features of untouchability. It is noteworthy that in the Gangetic plain; for instance, by far the most numerous caste of Untouchables, which constitutes the greater part of the agricultural labour force, is that of the Camdr or 'leather' people, while in the Tamil country the typical untouchable caste is that of the paraiyar or 'those of the drum (parai)' (from which we have 'pariah'), drum skins being of course impure, and the Untouchables consequently having the monopoly of village bands.

(b) Idea of Inequality

Beteille portrayed the universal nature of inequality, though he does not support it.[9] On the one hand, the examples he has given from various societies and anthropological studies show his belief that inequality cannot be eradicated completely and its disposal in one form will reappear in some other form. On the other hand, he suggested the ways by which it can be tamed and made benevolent. According to him, "...every statement that inequalities are decreasing in some spheres of social life seems to call forward a counter statement that they are increasing in others."

According to him, the forms and elements of inequality can change with space and time for the fact that inequality is static as one or another form of it is always present in all human societies. The following idea is worth of mentioning here. According to Beteille, though we attempt to ensure equality of opportunity in a competitive society, equality can be there till the end of the competition and not after it. Thus, equality of opportunity need not always ensure equality in result. In fact, it leads to inequality of reward and reproduction of inequality in another form. This is one of the most practical and obvious observation that one can notice in the contemporary India.

Beteille has attempted to answer the question of natural inequality in a qualified way with a lot of examples from the happenings in the society. Rousseau's idea has been used by Beteille as an anchorage to develop his idea of natural inequality. Rousseau struggled to disprove the presence of natural inequality. For Rousseau, the inequalities in social institutions increased the natural inequalities of mankind. For Beteille, creation on inequality is a necessity for mankind to organise effectively. But, unlike animals, human beings seek and create reasons to fit themselves in the division of labour. Concept of natural inequality is an artificial reason created by them to justify certain forms of social inequality. The gradation of qualities depends on the scales used to assess. Rewards will be distributed in accordance with the gradation of the qualities. Therefore, for Beteille, it is not only the allocation of rewards, but the recognition of merit itself is a social process.

(c) Idea of Social Exclusion

The concept of social exclusion was originally developed in France by sociologists. In French Republican thought, it refers to a process of 'social disqualification' or 'social disaffiliation' leading to a breakdown of the relationship between society and the individual. In this sense, social exclusion is deeply rooted in the Republican tradition of solidarity in which the State plays a major role. The French notion of social exclusion is linked to this tradition where integration is achieved by key state institutions. Thus, social exclusion can be viewed as a failure of the Republican State in protecting the 'cohesion of the society'.[10] Broadly speaking, social exclusion is a set of *processes*, including within the labour market and the welfare system, by which *individuals, households, communities* or even whole social groups are pushed towards or kept to the margins of society. It encompasses not only material deprivation but also more broadly the denial of opportunities *to participate* fully in social and civil life.

Social exclusion is a complex and multi-dimensional process. It involves the lack or denial of resources, rights, goods and services, and the inability to participate in the normal relationships and activities, available to the majority of people in a society, whether in economic, social, cultural or political arenas. It affects both the quality of life of individuals and the equity and cohesion of society as a whole. Deep exclusion refers to exclusion across more than one domain or dimension of disadvantage, resulting in severe negative consequences for quality of life, well-being and future life chances. According to Amartya Sen, we define social exclusion as a process leading to a state of functioning deprivations (impossibility to reach a certain level of well-being).[11] Therefore, the "process" of social exclusion produces a "state" of exclusion that can be interpreted as a combination of some relevant deprivations. According to Walker and Walker (1997, p. 8), the dynamic process of being shut out from any of the social, economic, political and cultural systems which determine the social integration of a person in society is referred to as exclusion.[12] According to ESRC (2007) the processes by which individuals and their communities become polarised, socially differentiated and unequal is understood as exclusion.[13]

European Union commentaries identified that social exclusion has three faces:

- **Economic:** The excluded are ... the unemployed, ... those deprived of access to assets such as property or credit,
- **Social:** The loss of an individual's links to mainstream society,
- **Political:** Certain categories of the population—such as women, ethnic and religious minorities, or migrants—are deprived of part or all of their political and human rights

Percy Smith (2000:9) cites seven dimensions to social exclusion itself[14]—

- economic (for example, long-term unemployment, workless households, income poverty)
- social (for example, homelessness, crime, disaffected youth)
- political (for example, disempowerment, lack of political rights, alienation from/lack of confidence in political processes)
- neighbourhood (for example, decaying housing stock, environmental degradation)
- individual (for example, mental and physical ill-health, educational under-achievement)
- Spatial (for example, concentration/marginalisation of vulnerable groups).
- Group (concentration of the above characteristics in particular groups: elderly, disabled, ethnic minorities).

Indicators of Social Exclusion (Eurostat 2000):

1. Financial difficulties in the household
2. Unaffordability of some basic needs
3. Unaffordability of consumer durables

4. Disadvantageous housing conditions
5. Poor health: life expectancy; self-perceived health status
6. Infrequent contacts with friends and relatives
7. Dissatisfaction with work or main activity

(d) Concept of Exploitation

To exploit others is to take unfair advantage of them. Although 'exploitation' has figured prominently in Marxist theories, it is frequently invoked in ordinary moral and political discourse. This entry surveys various definitions that have appeared in the literature, attempts to identify the core elements of exploitation, and then considers its moral force.

Thus, exploitation is a complex and challenging concept. In classical Marxism this concept was elaborated in terms of a specific conceptual framework for understanding capitalist economies, the "labour theory of value." In terms of sociological theory and research, however, the labour theory of value has never figured very prominently, even among sociologists working in the Marxist tradition. And in any case, the concept of exploitation and its relevance for class analysis does not depend on the labour theory of value.

The concept of exploitation designates a particular form of interdependence of the material interests of people, namely a situation that satisfies three criteria:

(1) The inverse interdependent welfare principle: the material welfare of exploiters causally depends upon the material deprivations of the exploited.

(2) The exclusion principle: this inverse interdependence of welfares of exploiters and exploited depends upon the exclusion of the exploited from access to certain productive resources.

(3) The appropriation principle: Exclusion generates material advantage to exploiters because it enables them to appropriate the labour effort of the exploited.

Exploitation is thus a diagnosis of the process through which the inequalities in incomes are generated by inequalities in rights and powers over productive resources: the inequalities occur, in part at least, through the ways in which exploiters, by virtue of their exclusionary rights and powers over resources, are able to appropriate surplus generated by the effort of the exploited. If the first two of these principles are present, but not the third, economic oppression may exist, but not exploitation.

Marx defined the "rate of exploitation", also referred to as the rate of surplus value, as the proportion of unpaid, surplus labour a worker performs for their employer to the necessary labour workers perform, producing the value equivalent of the wage they are paid.

'. . .Marx showed how the accumulation of wealth rested on the lengthening of the working day beyond what a worker needs to work to produce their own needs [thereby demonstrating] that this constituted a form of exploitation, that is to say, that the profit a capitalist makes for themselves by means of wage labour is acquired unjustly. Marx intended the concept of exploitation to be an ethically neutral concept used in his scientic analysis of capitalism in Capital.'

At the most general level, *A* exploits *B* when *A* takes unfair advantage of *B*. One can have the following explanations for the understanding of 'exploitation'.

. "[T]o exploit a person involves the *harmful, merely instrumental utilisation* of him or his capacities, for one's own advantage or for the sake of one's own ends."[15]

- "It is the fact that the [capitalist's] income is derived through *forced, unpaid, surplus* [wage] *labour, the product of which the workers do not control*, which makes [wage *labour*] exploitive." (Holmstrom 1997, 357).[16]
- "Exploitation of persons consists in ... wrongful behaviour [that violates] the moral norm of *protecting the vulnerable*."[17]
- "There are four conditions, all of which must be present if dependencies are to be exploitable. First, the relationship must be *asymmetrical* ... Second, ... the subordinate party must *need* the resource that the superordinate supplies ... Third, ... the subordinate party must depend upon some *particular* superordinate for the supply of needed resources ... Fourth, the superordinate ... enjoys discretionary control over the resources that the subordinate needs from him..." (Goodin 1988, 37).
- "[E]xploitation is a psychological, rather than a social or an economic, concept. For an offer to be exploitative, it must serve to create or to take advantage of some recognised psychological vulnerability which, in turn, disturbs the offeree's ability to reason effectively." (Hill 1994, 637).[18]

(e) Concept of Ostracism

Acts and practices of including or excluding others as aspects of systems of stratification may be as old as much of humanity itself. Certainly, most societies display some degree of taboos and customs concerning forms of both social rejection and social acceptance (Douglas, 1966, Gruter and Masters, 1986).[19] In institutional terms, a very early form of social exclusion is evident in the scholarship of the role of ostracism in Athens, Greece, during the 5th century B.C., when the provision of an official mechanism to institutionalise ostracism was enacted.

The law of ostracism was instituted as a means to protect young democratic institutions from the resurgence of tyranny (Raubitschek, 1951).[20] Thus, ostracism was considered a democratic process in which those who were qualified to vote would "scratch onto a clay shard the name of a party leader to be banned (Rehbinder, 1986, p. 323).[21]

As institutionalised more than 25 centuries ago, ostracism was used almost exclusively as a political weapon against male generals (Raubitschek, 1951), as a means to mitigate the influence of political rivals (Kagan, 1961) and to police and control the well-being of the state.[22] Rehbinder (1986) suggested the main aim of ostracism was to "exclude the losing party leader from the state" as "early democracy could not integrate the continuous action of opposition parties into the political process" (p. 321). To address this and to solve party conflicts, a law of ostracism essentially functioned to banish the leader of the opposition.

Importantly, Athenian ostracism was levied against an already elite class who for tyrannical activities or suspicions of tyranny were considered political liabilities or dangers. These acts did not bring shame on the recipient, but rather were prestigious, even honourable—a status reflected in the convention for the ostracised individual to retain his property, and, after his return, to regain his elite personal and social status (Rehbinder, 1986).

As Aristotle wrote in *Politics*:

> Democratic states institute the rule of ostracism [because] such states are held to aim at equality above anything else; and with that aim in view they used to pass a sentence of ostracism on those whom they regarded as having too much influence owing to their wealth or the number of their connexions or any other form of political strength. (Barker, 1952).[23]

Ostracism as it came to be enacted in Attic democracy was not an event applied lightly or arbitrarily. It required careful deliberation, a large quorum, and the immunity of an ostracised person's family. In essence, ostracism acted like a safety valve that ensured a smoother, more peaceful, and less tumultuous running of the state (Kagan, 1961). For Kort (1986), ostracism can be considered as coerced or involuntary exit of an individual or individuals from the society in which they live that manifests as a range of exclusions.[24] Thus, a society demonstrating variation in ostracism practices reflects a society with solidaristic strategies for the exclusion of its members from participation and from occupying positions of respect.

(f) Stigmatism

Stigma and the act of stigmatising is a common and recognisable form of social exclusion, yet, efforts to contend with some of the prejudices and discriminations recognised as components of stigmatisation reflect forms of social inclusion. Inherent within Goffman's (1963) work: *Stigma: Notes on the Management of Spoiled Identity*, is a belief in the universality of stigma and social exclusion. Stigma as a process leads certain individuals to be "systematically excluded from particular sorts of social interactions because they possess a particular characteristic or are a member of a particular group" (Kurzban and Leary, 2001, p. 187).[25] The concept embodies the functionality of "outsiderderness"; and the utility of why humans, as "an inherently social species with a strong need for social acceptance should be so inclined to reject members of its own kind" (Kurzban and Leary, 2001, p. 187).

As a sociologist, Goffman's approach was both dramatur-gical and oriented towards a symbolic interactionist perspective. His main interest was in the structure of social interactions and the rules that governed them (Goffman, 1967). For Goffman, social structures provided the context for interactions, as it was social structure that steadied and sustained social hierarchies (Scambler, 2009).[26] Yet some have suggested that Goffman may not have sufficiently attended to political economy, or to elements considered traditionally beyond the foci of symbolic interactionists such as class, power, gender, and ethnicity (Scambler, 2009). Thus, from this biologically deterministic perspective, stigma is not so much owing to the kind of negative evaluation as theorised by Goffman and colleagues, but rather to a form of protective disassociation.

Another deterministic approach to stigmatism has considered the exclusion of stigma from the perspective of disease, and specifically as a mechanism of disease avoidance. The suggestion that stigma is not (or not only) performed and not (or not only) determined but rather is culturally produced as a social, relational, and powerful artifact is a compelling argument (Buchman and Reiner, 2009).[27]

(g) Social Inclusion

How cultures and societies stratify and divide; how they account for customs around inclusion, exclusion, belonging, and togetherness; and how the processes that include and exclude are talked about, described, understood, and experienced, all provide some clues as to the role of social integration and stratification within a given society. Indeed, how stratification is conceived and discussed can obscure the very nature of the processes by which such divisions come to be. This is precisely why the discipline of sociology is so useful. Sorokin (1998), who in considering stratification differentiated between horizontal and vertical social mobility. Sorokin suggested that horizontal mobility related to changes in occupational position or role, but not to changes within a social hierarchy, whereas vertical mobility did describe changes within the social hierarchy. Sorokin summarised his theory by reflecting that within systems of vertical and horizontal mobility, there could be individual social infiltration as well as collective social movement.

The use of inclusion and exclusion concepts has evolved to the point where within a number of contexts, they are used as a descriptor for those who represent a particular kind of threat to social harmony (Silver and Miller, 2003). In sum, the terms *social inclusion* and *social exclusion* have been used throughout the social science and humanities literature in a number of different ways—to describe acts of social stratification across human and animal societies, as a principle to reflect the ordering that occurs within societies to determine social position, and as a narrative to explain and at times justify why one or more groups merit access to the core or the periphery, to the benefit or expense of others.

Initial discourses of social inclusion are widely attributed to having first appeared in France in the 1970s when the economically disadvantaged began to be described as *the excluded* (Silver, 1995). The preliminary uses of this new parlance appeared as a means to refer to a variety of disabled and destitute groups. The government of France was among the earliest adapters of exclusion terminology, and it is there that most often the concept is suggested to have found its contemporary meaning (Silver and Miller, 2003).

(h) Idea of Marginalisation

The term "Marginalisation" generally describes the overt actions or tendencies of human societies whereby those perceived as being without desirability or function are removed or excluded (i.e., are "marginalised"...) from the prevalent systems of protection and integration, so limiting their opportunities and means for survival. Marginalisation has aspects in sociological, economic, and political debates. Marginalisation may manifest itself in forms varying from genocide/ethnic-cleansing and other xenophobic acts/activities at one end of the spectrum, to more basic economic and social hardships at the unitary (individual/family) level.

In less developed economies, women also tend to be marginalised, as also the physically and mentally challenged. In nations such as India, there is also the problem of the marginalisation of Dalits, Tribals, and other backward castes and communities. We have various forms of marginalisation—they may be blatant or subtle. Examples of subtle forms of marginalisation would be selective hiring in various industry, or discrimination against candidates for employment on the basis of religion, origin, sexuality or sexual orientation, or on medical grounds. More blatant forms would be targeting groups for violence or harsh criticism; the spreading of hatred and xenophobia and so on.

For every stage of marginalised people, there exists a hierarchy of inequality within that group, contributing to the degree of marginalisation. This hierarchy generally falls in place on the basis of two factors—Education of the group within which the marginalised fall, and that of their support structure; and the Financial situation/power for them, within their own group at a family level, and then at a (local scope) social level, and then onto the global scope. The degree also depends (internationally) on the laws and safeguards in place that aid or thwarts the upliftment of the groups.

(I) Idea of Humiliation

Humiliation means the enforced lowering of a person or group, a process of subjugation that damages or strips away their pride, honour or dignity. To be humiliated is to be placed, against your will and often in a deeply hurtful way (although in some cases with your consent) in a situation that is much worse, or much 'lower,' than what you feel you should expect. Humiliation entails demeaning treatment that transgresses established expectations. It may involve acts of force, including violent force. At its heart is the idea of pinning down, putting down or holding against the ground. Indeed, one of the defining characteristics of humiliation as a process is that the victim is forced into passivity, acted upon, and made helpless.

Margalit's concept of humiliation rests on that of self-respect.[28] He defines it as "any sort of behaviour or condition that constitutes a sound reason for a person to consider his or her self-respect injured" (p. 9). As Margalit has it, to humiliate someone is to give him a sound reason to think his self-respect injure. Margalit offers a second idea, this one in terms of rejection. He writes, "I claim that humiliation is the rejection of a human being from the Family of Man'" (p. 108). What is meant by rejection here? Clearly, it can't be expulsion; mankind forms a natural class, and the members of such a class cannot be expelled from it. Margalit speaks of rejecting people as a posture taken towards them. I take him to be saying that we reject the humanity of a person where we see him a certain way, not as a human being but as a sort of being toward whom, seen as someone of that sort, we have more freedom of action

How do people understand humiliation? Many readers will answer—together with the 52 people that were interviewed in the pilot study for the project here presented—that humiliation is the *subjugation of human beings (and of nature), and that it is illegitimate*. This sentence, if carefully dissected, can be deconstructed in three parts, namely (a) putting down (subjugation, abasement, degradation), (b) human beings (as well as material objects), and (c) lack of legitimacy (or violation of human dignity and violation of environmental sustainability).

To summarise, the core of the concept of humiliation seems to be 'putting down,' or 'pushing down,' a relational notion that invites the question of who is the actor and who is the targeted party, or who is the humiliator and who is the victim. This question leads to dyadic and relational conceptions of humiliation and to epistemological stances for explaining it, such as social constructionism as promoted.[29]

To summarise all sections, the concept of humiliation contains:

1. a core that builds on the universal idea of 'putting down,'
2. a middle layer that plays out the core in two diametrically opposing ways, namely that this 'putting down' is legitimate or not,
3. a first peripheral layer pertaining to cultural differences that affect groups of people,
4. a second peripheral layer that relates to differences in stable personality traits and the way these differences pertain to experiences of humiliation,
5. a third peripheral layer which relates to deep damage inflicted on children by humiliation altering their overall personality make-up in a deeply injurious way,
6. a fourth peripheral layer that addresses the hurt that is inflicted on adults by incidents that entail humiliation,
7. a fifth peripheral layer that concerns variations in the emotional condition of a person that influence the orientation of the person concerned towards acts and experiences of humiliation (Berkowitz, 1993).[30]

(J) Idea of Social Justice

Plato (380 BC) said that justice was achieved when each person received goods they deserved based on their prescribed position in the social order.[31] Aristotle (384-322 BC) said that justice was a principle that ensured social order by regulating the distribution of benefits.[32] However in Aristotle's view, equality and justice applied only to individuals who occupied the same stratum of the hierarchical social order. According to these ideas of social justice, unequals in the social hierarchy are to be treated unequally. These ideas did not challenge the social structures of society, but worked within them.

Utilitarians like John Stuart Mill argued that the distribution of societal goods should be for the 'greatest net balance of satisfaction' for society.[33] Mill said that utilitarianism was actually a 'standard of morality' which used happiness of the greater number of people as its ultimate goal. In principle, although utilitarianism advocates for the greatest good for the greatest number of people in a society. Rawls' concept of social justice is probably the most influential. Rawls criticised utilitarianism as being able to be used to justify concentration of goods benefiting privileged classes of society on the basis that it was for the greater good. Rawls' conception of distributive justice provided that "all social values... are to be distributed equally unless an unequal distribution of any or all of these values is to everyone's advantage".

To Amartya Sen, we might note at the outset, that we would choose to be governed by two principles of justice, the first guaranteeing fundamental individual liberties (of speech, association and worship, among others), and the second ensuring that social and economic inequalities are arranged to offer the greatest possible benefit to the worst-off in society, while upholding fair equality of opportunity.

The concept of social justice is an essential part of the broader concept of justice. In general, Greeks used the term 'justice' equivalent to 'virtue', while in modern times it is used as 'getting ones due'. The pertinent question here is how to determine what is a man's due and this brings us to the relationship between justices in general and social justice. In particular, social justice concerns the distribution of benefits and burdens throughout a society, as it results from the major social institution—property system, public organisation, etc. Thus, broadly distribution of power allocation of benefits, material as well as tangible such as wealth, prestige and self-respect have to be the most important concerns of social justice.

Historically speaking, the birth of the concept of social justice coincided with shifts in human consciousness: the "death of God", the rise of science and the rise of the ideal of the "command economy" leading to scientific socialism i.e., reasons and intellectuals were supposed to rule. The roots of social justice thus lie in the thought process of enlightenment. The development of a scientific and rational viewpoint led to corresponding changes in the social thought process, which, in turn, initiated radical changes in the political and social structure of Europe, especially during the Renaissance. Thus, social justice, both as a concept and as a socially cherished goal, came into prominence during the French Revolution (1789) as far as Europe is concerned.

Significant philosophers had propounded there own ideas of justice. John Stuart Mill gave anthropomorphic approach by stating that—'Society should treat all equally well who have deserved equally well of it, that is, who have deserved equally well absolutely. This is the highest abstract standard of social and distributive justice; towards which all virtuous citizens, should be made in the utmost degree to convergence'.

J.J. Rousseau was a dreamer of an ideal just society. He wanted to build a genuine and humane community. He argued that men are equal by nature but the institution of private property has made them unequal and further perpetuated inequalities. Therefore the perfection of man lies in the improvement of society that can be done by remaking man by cultivating natural feelings and sentiments which guarantee equality and social justice. He argued that the institution could be re-moulded in such a way as to realise a just and democratic society (Tilly 2000).

For William Frankena, the concept of just society should emphasise on the principle and practical aspect of it. Therefore he conceives social justice as part of political justice that emphasises to create just society. Charles Evans says that justice is giving every man his due and conceptualises justice as deserved treatment. For Robert Nozick historical entitlement is an important element of distributive justice where the society is aware of its wrongs and has an increased interest in compensation. Therefore, for him, backward-looking concepts are important that address the distribution of goods in society as social justice.

John Rawls conceptualise 'justice as fairness' where there is desirability of advantage for the marginalised groups in some respect. It includes the first principle that each person is to have an equal right to the most extensive total system of equal basic liberties compatible with a similar system of liberty for all; Second principle that social and economic inequalities are to be arranged so that they are both—

(a) to the greatest benefit of the least advantaged, consistent with the just savings principle, and b) attached to offices and positions open to all under conditions of fair equality of opportunity. To Rawls (Rawls; 1971), justice as fairness tries to uncover the latent ideas of freedom and equality, of ideal social cooperation, and of the person, by formulating two 'model conception', one of a 'well-ordered society and another of a 'moral person'.

There can be no single application of theory of social justice and no definite prescription of justice can be made. For Miller, therefore, a concept such as justice may possess sociological investigation awareness of cultural diversity and conceptual change (Miller, 1976).

Fundamentally, the basic premise of social justice remains to be the emancipation of the underprivileged, exploited, and oppressed section of society. Its main aim is to liberate mankind from traditional bondages of social and economic exploitation and discrimination. It postulates a social order which can guarantee freedom, mobility and equal rights to all section of society.

Social justice is a specific habit of justice that is 'social in two senses:

- The skills it requires are those of inspiring, working with, and organising others to accomplish together a work of justice. These are the elementary skills of civil society, through which free citizens exercise self-government by doing for themselves what needs to be done.
- It aims at the good of the society and not as the good of one agent only.

Here Tocqueville rightly says that—"the principle of association is the first law of democracy, and then social justice is the first virtue of democracy, for it is the habit of putting the principle of association into daily practice".

In brief, Justice in broader sense includes: principle of equality; principle of utility; principle of compensatory justice; justice as fairness; social justice.

In opposition to Rawls' theory of justice, Robert Nozick has formulated the idea of social justice as entitlement.[34] According to Nozick, individuals have a right to own property and of self-ownership, which gives them the freedom to determine what to do with what is theirs. The role of the state is that of a night-watchman, to protect individual property rights. Nozick regards any attempt by the State to (re)distribute resources, e.g., through taxation, as unjust. Miller's approach to social justice rests on the idea that the market is capable of giving individuals what they deserve. This theory treats individuals as responsible for their own actions and proportionately rewards (or punishes) them in accordance with their actions and efforts, insofar as the actions/efforts are the result of their individual choices. According to Sen, the effectiveness of government action to improve social justice is judged according to an individual's capability to do things he or she values and the freedom of individuals to choose between different ways of leading their lives.[35] Sen's approach to social justice focuses on assuring individual capacities to gain optimal wellbeing in their circumstances. He defines poverty as the deprivation of these basic 'capabilities' (such as being literate, being active in the community).

(k) Concept of Empowerment

For every stage of marginalised people, there exists a hierarchy of inequality within that group, contributing to the degree of marginalisation. This hierarchy generally falls in place on the basis of two factors—Education of the group within which the marginalised fall, and that of their support structure; and the Financial situation/ power for them, within their own group at a family level, and then at a (local scope) social level, and then onto the global scope. The degree also depends (internationally) on the laws and safeguards in place that aid or thwarts the upliftment of the groups.

Empowerment is seen by many politicians, publicists, social activists and a growing section of the intelligentsia generally as the only effective answer to oppression, exploitation, injustice and the other maladies' with which our society is beset.

Empowerment is about social transformation; it is about radical social transformation; and it is about the people .....ordinary, common people, rather than politicians, experts and other socially or culturally advantaged persons. Above all, it is about power, although the concept of power contained in it is generally left unspecified. Empowerment is both a means to an end and an end in itself. The term adapts itself differently depending on situations, and its signification is both variable and fluid.

The idea of empowerment may be invoked in virtually any context: in speaking about human rights, about basic needs, about economic security, about capacity building, about skill formation or about the conditions of a dignified social existence. It is well known that our Constitution has created many rights for all members of society, irrespective of their social or economic standing. Empowerments also invoked in the context of economic weakness and insecurity, particularly of marginalised. unorganised and other disadvantaged groups, classes and categories. It is then seen as a condition or an aspect of capacity building.

The focus on empowerment has given a new emphasis to the building of economic and social capabilities among individuals, classes and communities. As one would expect, interventions of various kinds are being considered and recommended. The supply of credit on easy terms of bullocks to impoverished farmers, of goats and poultry to tribal women - these have all been viewed at one time or another as steps towards their empowerment. Capacity building through craft training, especially for women, whether for full-time or part-time employment, is seen in a similar light. There is finally the drive towards literacy and education where much still remains to be done despite the Directive Principle of State Policy for providing universal elementary education up to the age of 14 years.

(i) Women Empowerment - A Tool for Eradicating Women Crime

The issues of empowerment is about social transformation; it is about radical social transformation; and it is about the people—ordinary, common people, rather than politicians, experts and other socially or culturally advantaged persons. Empowerment is both a means to an end and an end in itself.

The concept of 'empowerment of women' implies a mediating of the relationship between the two genders by power and thus has inbuilt within it latent conflict, one up-manship, hierarchisation and a constant glancing behind one's shoulder to make sure that the other sex is not trying to out-power or over-power one. This state of affairs, it is certain will definitely not lead to a cessation of sexual struggle for power and sexual politics but escalate it adding to its surreptitiousness, mistrust, a working against each other.

Widely used definition of women's empowerment is increased power achieved through activism and grassroots movements (Moser, 1993; Kabeer, 1994). Feminist experts have argued that women's groups are vital in enabling women to increase their control of resources and decision-making capacity (Sen and Grown, 1987). Naila Kabeer (2001) found that women's participation in micro-credit programmes in Bangladesh led to more activism in community affairs, reduction in domestic violence, and an overall sense of power (Kabeer, 2001, p. 8).

The focus on empowerment has given a new emphasis to the building of economic and social capabilities among individuals, classes and communities. As one would expect, interventions of various kinds are being considered and recommended. Capacity building through craft training, especially for women, whether for full-time or part time employment, is seen in a similar light in the idea of empowerment is ascertain theory of social change, in particular of change from a hierarchical to an egalitarian type of society (Beteille 1983).

One successful case-study of empowerment is The Self-Employed Women's Association (SEWA), formed in 1972 in Ahmedabad, which is located in the state of Gujarat in western India. EWA operates like a trade union and organises women into cooperatives. It also provides various services such as banking, child-care, legal aid, and vocational instruction. SEWA defines self-employed women to include workers who earn a living through their own small businesses or wage labour and do not receive regular salaries like formal sector workers.

Dimensions of Empowerment

- Psychological - Self-image and identity; Creating space; Acquiring knowledge
- Cultural - Redefining gender rules and norms; Recreating practices
- Social - Leadership in community action; Action for rights; Social inclusion; Literacy
- Economic - Attaining income security; Ownership of productive assets; Entrepreneurial skills
- Organisational - Collective identity; establishing representative organisation; Organisational leadership
- Political - Participation in local institutions; negotiating political power; Accessing political power

(l) Urination as Body Porous—Its Utility[36]

R. Longhurst begins with the assumption that female bodies are understood in the West to be leaky and emotional compared to bounded and rational male bodies.[37] In her analysis of white, able-bodied male use of bathrooms in New Zealand, Longhurst focuses in particular on the fear of contamination that these men express regarding coming into contact with the fluids of other men. She makes sense of this fear by arguing that these men's fear of contamination is born of their being unable to participate in the illusion that male bodies are bounded when using bathrooms, particularly shared ones.

For Mol, bodies are never closed circuits, active bodies are never isolated but constantly interact with their surroundings.[38] Enactments don't present something already made, but themselves make reality.

These conversing, urinating men are a body and have a body—yet they do the act of urinating: Adam walked to an appropriate place, positioned himself comfortably and released the pressure on his bladder, all the while talking. By starting from the position that his body—all bodies—are leaky and have permeable boundaries, we can view his going for a pee not in terms of a threatened male solidity, but as an acknowledgement that his body is not closed off. Enactments, Mol argues, make realities. Enactments make the body visible, in different ways in different settings. Yet this is more that just seen bodies, but felt, touched, heard, multi-sensory bodies experienced through different forms of knowing (see Mol, 2002). As 'dirty' substances, urine and faeces are seen as having no practical or symbolic value they are waste, substances which act as reminders of the porousness of male and female human bodies.

As discussed by Heinonen-Tanski and van Wijk-Sijbesma[39] (2005), properly managed human excremental waste is a highly valuable resource in areas with insufficient water supplies for flush toilets and for gardening without costly and environmentally damaging 'chemical' fertilisers. For these organic gardeners and farmers living in an area without plumbed water and waste removal provided by the state, with thin soil in most areas, human excrement was too valuable to be treated as 'waste'. One saw another connection enacted: that between urinator and tree, for people provided essential nutrients for the well-being of trees which consequently supported them nutritionally in return when they fruited. This symbiotic relationship had obvious utilitarian advantages. Human urine provided a free, constantly available, organic source of nutrients in an area with very shallow soil.

(m) Idea of Hygiene

Hygiene is not just about cleanliness, but also about the conditions, activities and practices which protect health and prevent diseases. Hygiene refers to a procedure or system of procedures or activities used to reduce microbial contamination on environmental sites and surfaces in order to prevent the transmission of infectious disease (IFH[40] 2001). Thus hygiene involves personal, domestic and community hygiene. In a developing country context, good hygiene practices might be particularly important in the presence of poor sanitary conditions. They include, therefore, perhaps most importantly, adequate hand washing, domestic cleaning, and removal of contamination in the outdoor environment, particularly where children are present.

The state of environmental sanitation influences both the infecting agent and any of the individuals exposed to that environment. The significance of hygiene becomes greater when environmental sanitation is poor and vice versa. Provisions, such as safe water supply, sanitary disposal of excreta and other wastes, good housing, genial climate, and pollution-free surroundings, provide effective barriers to the spread of infectious diseases. There are many human-related factors that determine whether a person is susceptible or resistant to an invading infective agent. Susceptibility to infection rests on lifestyle, behaviour and mind-set. Lifestyle factors that provide protection from infectious diseases include: positive health behaviour, healthy housing, safe occupation and work place, interest in health preservation and disease prevention, sustainable income, nutrition security, food hygiene, sanitary facilities such as for excreta disposal and safe drinking water, personal hygienic practices including washing hands before meals and after using the toilet, and good public health services. Protection has to be provided at the community, family and individual level.

On a personal level, hygiene consists of health consciousness, cleanliness, hand washing, safe drinking water, sanitary disposal of waste, freedom from addiction to tobacco and/or alcohol. Domestic and personal hygiene and the behaviour, habits and practices of its members determine the health of a household. Hygiene practice involves active efforts by every individual and family and is best instilled early on in childhood. Hygiene is largely a matter of human behaviour, which is determined by social traditions, customs and culture. Furthermore, health consciousness and awareness of factors injurious or conducive to health, and motivation and concern for taking steps to protect health and prevent disease, can change behaviour and promote a healthy lifestyle. Active efforts are possible only with the proper mind-set and if there is motivation to keep disease away. Habits such as defecation in the open are cultural. With urbanisation, modern housing, health development and national sanitation programmes, the use of sanitary latrines are on the increase. Such environmental adaptations at domestic or household situation result in variations in the degree of exposure to the risk of infection and other epidemiological factors which are locally significant and determine the state of familial and individual health or disease (Deodhar 2010).

Life and behaviour of an individual who is health conscious will be quite different from that of another person who is indifferent to health or personal hygiene. An enlightened person acquires knowledge, seeks advice, and makes an effort to improve hygiene and health behaviour, while a person or family who is apathetic does not care about what happens to them or their surroundings. Every community has these two kinds of people and the magnitude of prevalence of infectious disease in any community depends on the proportion and distribution of these two types of people. Therefore, it is not uncommon to encounter unaffected persons or families, even in an event or outbreak of infectious disease in the locality. It is important to note that a community which observes simple rules of hygiene is more healthy and free from infectious disease than one which does not. Provision of a free water supply, immunisation services, sanitary conveniences, or health education, may not necessarily benefit people, if these facilities are used indifferently or not at all.

Many traditions and customs have become ritualistic or meaningless and the hygienic principles behind these practices lost. For instance, indiscriminate spitting is largely due to the lack of aesthetic and civic sense, rather than a deliberate act to pollute the environment or promote the spread of infection. Similarly, many people do not spit simply because they regard it as unstylish or a sign of backwardness, and not because of an awareness of the risk of tuberculosis. Merely telling people that the habit is unhygienic will have little impact. On the other hand, factors such as health awareness, knowledge of health and disease, and willingness to take steps to prevent diseases, do change behaviour. A good example is the increased use of bottled mineral water for drinking while on travel or eating out. This type of behavioural change helps to prevent alimentary infections.

Health behaviour is modified by a change of mind-set. An individual may use a particular health facility or follow a hygienic practice, but this does not guarantee that they will necessarily continue to use the available facilities. Many incidences of disease or their absence are due to differences in micro-ecosystems, human behaviour and lifestyles. Improvement in public health will certainly prevent infectious diseases in some families, but unfortunately this may not be universal for everybody.

For modifying a lifestyle and making it conducive to prevention of infectious diseases, current style of living should be studied in relation to hygienic practices. According to Deodhar (2010), Elements which will have to be taken care of include:

- Regularity synchronises daily routines and habits to the body cycles and rhythms. Regularity prevents functional imbalance of various systems and enhances body defence mechanisms. Modern life has become hectic and irregular, especially in urban life, which makes people more susceptible to infectious disease.
- Moderation of food, work, recreation or rest is another golden

rule of hygiene. Avoidance of extremes has even been advocated in Indian scriptures that advise *ati sarvatra varjayet* (discard excesses universally). The stresses the body is exposed to in modern life are due to immoderation rendering it vulnerable to infection and disease.

- Housing condition and the neighbourhood influence hygiene: This includes poor ventilation and overcrowding which facilitate the spread of airborne infections. Dampness in the home predisposes the occupant to rheumatic fever, while internal air pollutants such as dry sweepings, poor ventilation, and incomplete combustion of domestic fuels like wood, coal and cow-dung can also be harmful. In India, 80 per cent of households use solid fuel and about a half million Indian children die annually from indoor air pollution, especially from acute respiratory infection (WHO 2000).[41]
- Cleanliness is a protective measure to minimise health hazards by providing an effective barrier against the risk of exposure to the disease-producing agents. Generally, the environment is full of the disease-causing germs. The hands, skin, body discharges and expired air should all be considered as potentially contaminated with harmful germs. Uncleanliness and dirty habits cause much morbidity and mortality, especially with respect to diseases of the digestive system. Washing feet or removing footwear before entering the house, washing hands thoroughly with water after using the latrine, and before cooking, handling or eating food, and cutting nails short to keep them clean, are all hygiene measures that reduce the risk of acquiring and transferring infections, particularly when used in conjunction with soap.
- Sanitation is a social and public responsibility. Faeces, animal excreta, urine and other kinds of waste often contain pathogens, necessitating proper modes of sanitary disposal. However, health authorities in India often give hygiene and sanitation a low priority. Most villagers, slum dwellers, and domestic servants, even those working in more affluent areas, have to resort to passing urine or defecation by the roadside or in open spaces. Efforts to discourage these bad habits and promote the use of sanitary latrines and urinals are worthwhile and necessary in the prevention of disease.
- Personal habits: Measures on a more personal level can be adopted. For example, regular use of proper footwear not only protects feet from injury, but also to a certain extent from diseases

such as tetanus, hookworm and snakebites. Habits such as indiscriminate spitting and littering help in spreading diseases like tuberculosis and diarrhoea. Open defecation and tolerating dirt in the environment too are examples of negative health behaviour that should be eliminated as much as possible.

- Nutrition is essential for protection against infections. The immune mechanism of the body is dependent on an adequate and balanced diet. In order to avoid the risk of infectious diseases, observance of food hygiene is essential. Secondly, if the intake of food is just adequate or marginal, once infection is introduced and caloric requirement goes up, a vicious cycle of malnutrition and infection may become established. The effects are particularly serious in children aged between six months and two years of age.
- Positive thinking, attitude and mind-set are beneficial for health and social values. Worry and anxiety are non-productive, while optimism strengthens our power to defend against infections.
- Occupation is essential for health and livelihood. However, certain occupations expose people to infective agents that may lead to diseases such as leptospirosis, brucellosis and anthrax. Sewage workers, for example, and sweepers are exposed to pathogenic germs unless they use protective clothing and proper tools.
- Social factors including working conditions, family life and friends influence domestic and personal hygiene. A high tolerance to a dirty environment is an invitation to infectious diseases and vectors like houseflies. Vegetables, food, faecal matter and any other decaying organic matter provide all the material that flies require to breed, and are readily available because people are indiscriminate in disposal of these items. Breast-feeding provides immuno-protection for the baby against diseases, while bottle-feeding on the other hand is frequently linked to contamination that causes diarrhoea in infants.
- Financial status has a significant impact on lifestyle and hygiene. Many cities and towns in India are without sewerage, and most municipal corporations discharge raw sewage without proper treatment directly into rivers thereby polluting the water. At the family level, economic status shows a direct relationship with health status (Deodhar 2010).

(i) Hygiene Promotion

Improving access to safe water and sanitation facilities leads to healthier families and communities. However, when people are also motivated to practice good hygiene—especially hand-washing with soap—health benefits are significantly increased. Because the evidence on the importance of hand-washing with soap is clear, UNICEF has made it a programme priority. It help to promote hand-washing and hygiene behavioural change by:

- advocating for increased funding for hygiene activities and the inclusion of hygiene in sectoral policies and strategies;
- supporting national and sub-national hand-washing campaigns;
- recruiting high-profile decision makers and celebrities as hand-washing advocates;
- including strong hygiene components within its own WASH programmes in the field;
- ensuring that hand-washing and hygiene are components of emergency response programmes;
- developing strategies and tools to encourage hand-washing promotion by community health and outreach workers and
- encouraging hygiene promotion in schools and the empowerment of children as agents of change within their families and communities.

Education and communication are important components of a hygiene promotion programme. All people have a right to know about the relationship between water, sanitation, hygiene and the health of themselves and their families. However, education alone does not necessarily result in improved practices. Knowing about the causes of disease may help, but new hygiene practices may be too unfamiliar, too difficult, or take too much time, especially for poor people. Promoting behavioural change is a gradual process that involves working closely with communities, studying existing beliefs, defining motivation strategies, designing appropriate communication tools and finally encouraging practical steps towards positive practices. Communities should be fully engaged in the process at all stages using participatory processes, and special attention should be given to building on local knowledge and promoting existing positive traditional practices. Behavioural change is necessary not only at the community level, but among decision makers as well. All stakeholders—from politicians and government officials to field workers and people themselves—must be encouraged to recognise the importance of hygiene.

(n) Idea of Dirt

In *Purity and Danger* Mary Douglas argued that 'dirt is essentially disorder' and 'matter out of place' (Douglas, 1991:2-35). Dirt that is tolerated in one setting is abhorred in another, while both dirt and hygiene are largely socially constructed. Beginning with a study of comparative religions and their associated rituals of purity and impurity, her analysis extended towards trying to understand what at first she referred to as moral values and social rules and later came to refer to as 'institutions' (Douglas, 1987). Her principal concern was to make sense of how ritual pollution or danger-beliefs served to maintain social categories and distinctions. These she saw as being reinforced through the strict observance of boundaries between the inside world of what is known and safe and the outside world of danger and chaos.

Mary Douglas discuss how to make sense of the interlocking 'little sub-worlds' that make up the disposal and removal of domestic waste and how these articulate with larger 'thought worlds' about the management of dirt and disorder in development (Douglas, 1987:17).

Thus, dirt, according to Douglas, is matter out of place. Things are not inherently dirty, but become so as a result of the human impulse to categorise. Applying this to Okely's findings, faeces are not inherently 'dirty' when expelled because they are outside of the ritually clean interior body, and distant from the ritually clean interior caravan. They only become dirty when out of place, such as inside the home. Composted faeces, like urine when being 'pee[d] on any tree', became matter in, not out of, place. Faeces and urine connecting people to the state rather than their immediate surroundings were not so much matter out of place as relations out of place: these technologies generated the wrong sort of relationships. Faeces became 'dirt' when disposed of in a flush toilet and into a sewer: it was matter out of place, polluting the ocean, and relations out of place, plumbing reclusive individuals into the state. Faeces and urine disposed on and in the land, however, were matter and relations in place: opposed to the state, nurturing the land and connected to a web of intimate relations (Lucy Pickering; 2010).

Notes

1. Oscar Lewis, 'The Culture of Poverty', Scientific American, 215 (October 1966), pp. 19-25
2. Marshall B. Clinard, 'Urbanisation, Urbanism, and Deviant Behavior in Puerto Rico' in Social Change and Public Policy (San Juan: Social Science Research Centre, University of Puerto Rico, 1968)
3. See Chakrabarty, D. (1991) Open Space/Public Space: Garbage, Modernity and India, *South Asia,* XIV(1), pp. 15-32.

4. See Searle-Chatterjee, M. (1979) The Polluted Identity of Work: A Study of Benares Sweepers in S. Wallman (ed.) *The Social Anthropology of Work* (London, Academic Press), pp. 269-286.
5. Manual Scavenging: stigma, discrimination and justice Safai Karmachari Andolan - New Delhi August 2012
6. See *John Copeland Nagle,* University of California, Davis, School of Law. Vol. 43, No. 1, Nov. 2009.
7. Adam W. Rome, *Coming to Terms with Pollution: The Language of Environmental Reform, 1865-1915,* 1 Envtl. Hist. 6 (1996).
8. See *John Copeland Nagle,* University of California, Davis, School of Law. Vol. 43, No. 1, Nov. 2009.
9. See Beteille, Andre, "Social Inequality", Sociological Review, XIII (3), pp. 200-201, 1970.; Beteille, Andre, "Individualism and Equality", Current Anthropology, XXVII (2), pp. 121-134, 1986.
10. See Ajit Bhalla and FreÂdeÂric Lapeyre, Social Exclusion: Towards an Analytical and Operational Framework, Development and Change Vol. 28 (1997), Institute of Social Studies 1997. Blackwell Publishers Ltd, UK.
11. Sen A., ''Social Exclusion: concept, application and scrutiny'', *Social Development Papers,* No.1, ADB, June 2000
12. See Walker, A. and Walker, C. (eds) (1997) *Britain divided: The growth of social exclusion in the 1980s and 1990s,* London: CPAG.
13. See ESRC (Economic and Social Research Council) (2004) www.esrc.ac.uk
14. Percy-Smith, J. (2000) *Policy responses to social exclusion: Towards inclusion?,* Oxford: Oxford University Press.
15. Buchanan, A., 1985, *Ethics, Efficiency, and the Market,* Totowa: N.J.: Rowman and Allanheld.
16. Holsmstrom, N., 1997, "Exploitation," *Canadian Journal of Philosophy,* 7: 353–69.
17. See Goodin, R.,1988. , *Reasons for Welfare,* Princeton: Princeton University Press.
18. Hill, J. L., 1994, "Exploitation," *Cornell Law Review,* 79: 631–99.
19. Gruter, M., and Masters, R. D. (1986). Ostracism as a social and bio-logical phenomenon: An introduction. Ethology and Sociobiology, 7, 149-158.
20. Raubitschek, A. E. (1951). The origin of ostracism. American Journal of Archaeology, 55, 221-229.

21. Rehbinder, M. (1986). Refusal of social cooperation as a legal problem: On the legal institutions of ostracism and boycott. Ethology and Sociobiology, 7, 321-327.
22. Kagan, D. (1961). The origin and purposes of ostracism. Hesperia: The Journal of the American School of Classical Studies at Athens, 30, 393-401.
23. Barker, E. (1952). Aristotle: Politics. London, England: Oxford University Press.
24. Kort, F. (1986). The politics of ostracism. Ethology and Sociobiology, 7, 367-377.
25. Kurzban, R., and Leary, M. (2001). Evolutionary origins of stigma: The functions of social exclusion. *Psychological Bulletin, 127,* 187-208.
26. Scambler, G. (2009). Health-related stigma. *Sociology of Health and Illness, 31,* 441-455.
27. Buchman, D., and Reiner, P.B. (2009). Stigma and addiction: Being and becoming. *American Journal of Bioethics,* 9(9), 18-19.
28. Margalit, Avishai, The Decent Society (Cambridge, Mass.: Harvard University Press, 1996).
29. See Lindner, Evelin Gerda (2001). The Concept of Humiliation: Its Universal Core and Culture-Dependent Periphery. Oslo: University of Oslo,
30. See Berkowitz, L. (1993). *Aggression: its causes, consequences, and control.* New York: McGraw-Hill.
31. Plato, *The Republic* (G.M.A. Grube trans, 1974).
32. Aristotle, *The Nicomachean Ethics* (D. Ross trans, J. Ackrill and J.O. Urmson revised ed, 1980).
33. John Rawls, *A Theory of Justice* (1971).
34. David Miller, *Principles of Social Justice* (1999) 149-155.
35. Amartya Sen, *The idea of justice* (2009) 7.
36. Based on Lucy Pickering, Toilets, Bodies, Selves: Enacting Composting as Counterculture in Hawai'I, *Body and Society* 2010 16:33
37. Longhurst, R. (2001) Bodies: Exploring Fluid Boundaries. London: Routledge.
38. Mol, A. (2002) The Body Multiple: Ontology in Medical Practice. Durham, NC: Duke University Press.
39. Heinonen-Tanski, H. and C. van Wijk-Sijbesma (2005) 'Human Excreta for Plant Production', Biosource Technology 96(4): 403–11.

40. IFH. (2001) Recommendations for Selection of Suitable Hygiene Procedures for the Use in the Domestic Environment. International Scientific Forum on Home Hygiene.

41. WHO (2000) Press release, No. 56, 14th September 2000.

7

Sanitation *Versus* Other Institutions

(a) Ecology and Sanitation[1]

The problems rose by the decreasing quality and quantity of fresh water resources are becoming increasingly serious. All indicators show that the world is facing a serious world water crisis which will affect all of us, but particularly the poor. The poor suffer most from this decrease in fresh water resources, and bear the brunt of water-related diseases and a damaged environment. This water crisis is in part a direct result of the failure of the current sanitation paradigm. Sewered sanitation, established in the era of European urbanisation in the 1870s, has the status of a widely accepted solution, or scientific truth. There is little discussion about its core problems, which result in health and environmental problems around the world. The fact that our current sanitary systems are, for the most part, directly connected to the water cycle requires that both the sanitation and water crises be considered, before we can begin trying to de-couple them.

A look at some of the figures of both these crises provides an insight into the scale of the problem facing us today:

- The estimated mortality rate as a result of illnesses caused by contaminated drinking water and poor sanitation and hygiene in developing countries is approximately 2.2 million people per year, most of them children under the age of five (WHO/UNICEF JMP 2000)
- An estimated 2.6 billion people, representing almost half of the

world population do not have access to adequate sanitation / wastewater treatment facilities (WHO/UNICEF JMP 2005)

- 1.1 billion people do not have access to safe drinking water (WHO/UNICEF JMP 2005)
- In the developing regions of the world between 100 per cent (Africa) and 65 per cent (Asia) of the urban wastewater are not treated appropriately (WHO/UNICEF JMP 2000)
- 80 per cent of all diseases and 25 per cent of all deaths in developing countries are caused by polluted water (UN 1992)
- World-wide, over 200 million people were infected with schistosomiasis and intestinal helminths, of which 20 million suffered serious illness, most of them children under the age of five (WHO 2003)

The United Nations Summit on Sustainable Development, held in Johannesburg, South Africa, in Autumn of 2002, returned to the targets set by the Millennium Development Goals with regard to water supply and extended it to also include the provision of sanitation. The current international target is therefore to halve the proportion of people without access to safe drinking water and to adequate sanitation by 2015.

Over the years, it became clear however that this health and hygiene driven paradigm shift was still incomplete: In practice faecal sludge management problems where often overlooked, as were negative downstream effects off effluents from sewer systems. Protection of the environment, resource conservation and waste reuse remained secondary concerns at best, or were neglected entirely, and operational problems reduced the health improvements expected of the technologies.

In the concept of ecological sanitation (ecosan) not only health issues but also conservation of water and other resources as well as the protection of aquatic ecosystems are taken into consideration. The ecosan approach places the emphasis on the hygenisation of the contaminated flow streams, and shifts the concept from waste disposal to resource conservation and safe reuse. In addition to paying particular attention to the health aspects at household level, ecosan also emphasises:

- The destruction of pathogens through flow stream separation, containment and specific treatment.
- Resource conservation through a reduced use of potable water as a transport medium for human waste and by recovering wastewater for irrigation

- The elimination or minimisation of wastewater discharges to the environment
- The need to close the resource loops through the productive use of the nutrients contained in excreta

The modern ecosan concept thus represents the culmination of the paradigm shift initiated in response to satisfying the health needs of unserved, mostly poor population groups. Education has a clear role to play, both in acknowledging the paradigm shift in sanitation and in incorporating the interdisciplinary theme of innovative sustainable sanitation systems into teaching curricula. Education on ecosan should enable the people to develop, plan and implement ecosanitation systems that are hygienically safe, socially acceptable, economically feasible, environmentally sound and technically appropriate.

Educational institutions, universities, and technical schools can contribute to the mainstreaming of the new sanitation paradigm by fully integrating the discourse and criteria for sustainability into their curricula. They should make clear that defining criteria for sustainable sanitation is a political act and influences what is the accepted, legitimate form of sanitation, including the impacts from sanitation on other sectors. Sanitation capacity building should take the stakeholders in a sanitation project not as objects, but as partners for jointly developing sustainable sanitation solutions.

The education system has to prepare students to think about urine and faeces and grey/black water as resources. Emphasis has to shift from the simple disposal to the hygienisation of contaminated flow streams, and to resource conservation and safe reuse. Teaching must make clear that health and a healthy environment is a prerequisite for human productivity, and productivity determines economic well-being.

Sanitation engineers and practitioners, policymakers, managers, and operators get their ideas and information during their education. Therefore the curricula of universities, continuing education programmes, technical schools, research institutes and training centres have to include the ecosan philosophy. Thus several objectives, such as the improvement of human health, poverty reduction in developing countries, the conservation of natural resources and sustainable water and sanitation management systems in both, industrialised and developing countries may be addressed. Those responsible for the content of curricula should be informed about the new developments in this field.

Ecological sanitation calls for participatory planning, so education should also be participatory. Ecological sanitation gives special attention to users, as active participants rather than passive recipients in a planning process. So students should also become active players rather than objects of the educational process. This change of attitudes between teacher and pupil is desirable in any case, but of particular importance in topics as complex as ecosan. This places rather challenging demands on the educational system, forcing the educational institution, in effect, to move into a new educational paradigm in order to support the new paradigm in sanitation.

The inter-disciplinary nature of ecological sanitation draws on a wide range of expertise, including:

- Integrated water management and other natural resources
- Resources protection and recycling
- Sustainable agriculture, soil conditioning and replacement of fertilisers
- Public health enhancement and reduction of children mortality
- Food security
- Job creation and unemployment reduction
- Climate change and variability
- Flood control and management

(i) Ecological Sanitation (ECOSAN): The New Sanitation Paradigm[2]

In order to reach the MDGs and achieve sustainability in the field of wastewater management and sanitation, a new paradigm is clearly needed. This was the unanimous conclusion of a group of experts from a wide range of international organisations involved in environmental sanitation that met in February 2000 in Bellagio, Italy. The group called for a radical rethinking of conventional sanitation policies and practices world-wide. This group formulated the four "Bellagio Principles" the basis for a new paradigm and approach in environmental sanitation (SANDEC/WSSCC 2000a).

The Bellagio Principles (2000)[3]:

(1) Human dignity, quality of life and environmental security at household level should be at the centre of the new approach, which should be responsive and accountable to needs and demands in the local and national setting.

   - solutions should be tailored to the full spectrum of social, economic, health and environmental concerns
   - the household and community environment should be protected

- the economic opportunities of waste recovery and use should be harnessed

(2) In line with good governance principles, decision making should involve participation of all stakeholders, especially the consumers and providers of services.

- decision making at all levels should be based on informed choices
- incentives for provision and consumption of services and facilities should be consistent with the overall goal and objective
- rights of consumer and providers should be balanced by responsibilities to the wider human community and environment

(3) Waste should be considered a resource, and its management should be holistic and form part of integrated water resources, nutrient flow and sanitation.

- inputs should be reduced so as to promote efficiency and water and environmental security
- exports of waste should be minimised to promote efficiency and reduce the spread of pollution
- wastewater should be recycled and added to the water budget

(4) The domain in which environmental sanitation problems are resolved should be kept to the minimum practical size (household, community, town, district, catchments, city) and wastes diluted as little as possible.

- waste should be managed as close as possible to the source
- water should be minimally used to transport waste
- additional technologies for waste sanitisation (sic) and reuse should be developed

The new paradigm in sanitation must be based on ecosystem approaches and the closure of material flow cycles rather than on linear, expensive and energy intensive end-of-pipe technologies. Sanitation systems are part of several cycles, of which the most important cycles are the pathogen, water, nutrient and energy cycle. In order to ensure public health, sanitation approaches primarily aim at interrupting the life cycle of pathogens. In addition, the new approach is recognising human excreta and water from households not as a waste but as a resource that could be made available for reuse, especially considering that human excreta and manure from husbandry play an essential role in building healthy soils and are providing valuable nutrients for plants. While conventional sanitation restricts health security to the in-house environment and sometimes leads to a disastrous situation in the neighbourhood or the receiving water body, the new approach is aiming at sanitising the products instead of exporting problems and apply a health oriented multi-barrier concept of treatment, crop-restriction and exposure control.

This approach, mostly addressed as "ecological sanitation" or ecosan offers an alternative to conventional sanitation. It is based on an overall view of material flows as part of an ecologically and economically sustainable sanitation system tailored to the needs of the users and to specific local conditions. It does not favour or promote a specific sanitation technology, but is rather a new philosophy in handling substances that have so far been seen merely as wastewater and water-carried waste for disposal. It carries with it a new approach to sanitation education, a new discourse, and a new way of managing knowledge. Ecosan systems restore a remarkable natural balance between the quantity of nutrients excreted by one person in one year and that required to produce their food (7.5 kg nitrate, phosphorous and potassium to produce 250 kg of grain) and therefore can greatly help in saving limited resources. This is particularly urgent with regard to fresh water and mineral resources—for example current estimates for phosphorus state that economically extractable reserves risk to be exhausted in the foreseeable future. Ecosan does not favour a particular technology but is rather a philosophy in recycling oriented resource management and offers modern, convenient, gender friendly and desirable solutions, in accordance with the Bellagio Principles as formulated by the WSSCC (Water Supply and Sanitation Collaborative Council) (SANDEC/WSSCC 2000a). The core principle of ecosan is to close the loop between sanitation and agriculture, enabling and bringing about "agricultural reuse", along with other means of closing flow cycles.

(ii) Environmental Sanitation

Environmental sanitation envisages promotion of health of the community by providing clean environment and breaking the cycle of disease. It depends on various factors that include hygiene status of the people, types of resources available, innovative and appropriate technologies according to the requirement of the community, socioeconomic development of the country, cultural factors related to environmental sanitation, political commitment, capacity building of the concerned sectors, social factors including behavioural pattern of the community, legislative measures adopted, and others. India is still lagging far behind many countries in the field of environmental sanitation.

According to Nath (2003) only 200 of more than 4,000 towns have a partially complete sewerage system.[4] There are still 400,000 scavengers and 7,210,000 dry latrines, of which 5,400,000 are in urban areas. Less than 50 per cent of the urban populations have access to sanitation, that is, safe disposal of human excreta, while in the rural population less than 20 per cent have facilities for sanitary disposal of human excreta. Open defecation is still the most popular means of toileting in rural India, while in urban areas less than 60 per cent of waste is collected and disposed of on a regular basis. The drainage infrastructure for storm water and sullage is extremely poor in urban, peri-urban and rural areas. There are other problems too. Rivers and other bodies of surface water are grossly polluted, where, for example, faecal coliform count can vary between 5,000 and 20,000 mpn 100 ml^{-1}. The holy river of the Ganges is one such river where in many parts it is unfit for bathing.

(a) Quality of water in public distribution systems

Almost all urban water supply systems in the country are prone to disruption. As a result, faecal contamination of the distribution systems is universal in most cities and towns. Ground water drawn from tube wells and dug-wells is often contaminated by chemicals, minerals, pesticides or bacteria. For example, fluoride and arsenic contamination of ground water has become a serious health risk for almost 80 million people in the country.

(b) Hazardous and toxic waste management

Monitoring and management of toxic waste from industry and biomedical waste from hospitals and other healthcare institutions is extremely poor. As a result, these have become potential sources of contamination and infection.

(c) Quality of water for domestic use

As emphasised by Nath (003), water quality for domestic use is an important determinant of personal and domestic hygiene. In a sample survey conducted in Calcutta, it was observed that most of the population in urban and rural areas use piped water or ground water (tube well) for drinking. The quality of water from these sources is variable. In rural areas, washing of utensils and clothing is often carried out in pond water, which is highly polluted (faecal coliforms>1000 mpn 100 ml^{-1}). Cloths used for wiping floors or drying utensils are mostly dirty and provide a possible source of infection and cross-infection. Utensils are cleaned with potable water and detergents in the majority of cases among the urban middle class and higher income groups of the population.

(iii) Sustainable Sanitation in India

The basic concept of collecting domestic liquid waste in water-borne sewer systems, treating the wastewater in centralised treatment plants and discharging the effluent to surface water bodies became the accepted, conventional approach to sanitation in urban areas in Europe in the last century. Although these conventional sewer systems have significantly improved the public health situation in those countries that can afford to install and operate them properly, the large number of people, particularly in fast developing countries like India, who still do not have sufficient access to adequate sanitation is a clear indication that the conventional approach to sanitation is likely to be unable to meet the needs universally.

The conventional sewer system was developed at a time, in regions, and under environmental conditions that made it in many cases an appropriate solution for removing liquid wastes from cities. Today with increased population pressure, changes in consumer habits and increasing pressure on freshwater and other resources, this human waste disposal system is no longer able to meet the pressing global needs alone.

A few decades ago it thus became a priority to—

- Identify appropriate simple, affordable decentralised sanitation systems and promote their adoption;
- Implement appropriate technologies with the participation of the communities to be served and
- Focus on health and hygiene education so that physical facilities would be properly used and maintained, and that hygienic behaviour would support the improvements brought about by the infrastructure.

Over the years, it became clear however that this health and hygiene driven paradigm shift was still incomplete: In practice faecal sludge management problems where often overlooked, as were negative downstream effects of effluents from sewer systems. Protection of the environment, resource conservation and waste reuse remained secondary concerns at best, or were neglected entirely, and operational problems reduced the health improvements expected of the technologies. The Sustainable Sanitation Alliance has therefore called for a paradigm shift from disposal towards reuse oriented sanitation systems, which take all dimensions of sustainability into account (SuSanA 2008). In addition to paying particular attention to the health aspects at household level, a holistic and re-use-oriented sanitation approach also emphasises:

- the destruction of pathogens through flow stream separation, containment and specific treatment
- Resource conservation through a reduced use of potable water as a transport medium for human waste and by recovering wastewater for irrigation
- the elimination or minimisation of wastewater discharges to the environment
- the need to close the resource loops through the productive use of the nutrients and energy (biogas) contained in excreta. Thus ideas of recycling have been developed. This modern concept represents the paradigm shift initiated in response to satisfying the health needs of unserved, mostly poor population groups.

(iv) Trajectory of Environmental Issues in Indian Cities[5]

During the colonial period, urban development, planning, sanitation policies and the evolution of municipal government were deeply influenced by the revolt of 1857 and its aftermath, the plague epidemic beginning in 1896 and the introduction of British ideas of modern town planning in the early twentieth century. When the Royal Commission into the Sanitary State of the Army in India linked health with sanitation, the colonial administration responded by physically separating the army and British officials from the indigenous city by building new cantonments and residential enclaves (known as the civil lines) where the lessons of the sanitary revolution were applied.[6] The army was provided with new, well-ventilated barracks while officials built spacious bungalows on wide streets that were serviced by piped water and underground sewers.[7] This segregation of cities into two parts—the indigenous and the European—was further enhanced by the pursuit of military security, which resulted in many cities, particularly Lucknow and Delhi, which were directly associated with the revolt, being radically restructured to reduce the threat of disease and further unrest.[8]

This need to provide new sanitary arrangements brought about the development of local government across the sub-continent during the 1870s that had the power to collect taxes to finance sanitation services and public works. In May 1882, the Viceroy, Lord Ripon, introduced his Resolution on Local Self-Government, which shaped local government until the early twentieth century. This resolution introduced a majority of elected non-official members on a limited franchise of Europeans and wealthy Indian ratepayers and was intended to create a political forum for the newly created, western-educated middle class.[9] While some Indian middle class liberals did take an interest in civic affairs, municipal authorities were generally only pushed towards reform when civic problems such as recurrent epidemics, fires and the persistent stench from unclean drains in slums threatened to impact on European or Indian middle class lifestyles.[10]

The outbreak of the plague in Bombay and Calcutta in 1896 provided just such a push for reform and was to have a long-lasting political and social impact on urban India. It brought an unprecedented level of medical and sanitary intervention into people's lives, focused attention on the insanitary conditions and overcrowding in Calcutta and Bombay and brought demands for municipal reform. The immediate response was increased spending by municipalities on sanitation, while the demands for urban reform were met by the Montagu-Chelmsford reforms of 1919, which transferred local government, along with education, public works and health, to Indian control. To address the problem of insanitary housing and congestion, improvement trusts were established in Bombay (1898) and Calcutta (1912) under the direct control of colonial authorities. The trusts had the power to demolish slums, build *chawls* for workers, create new arterial roads and develop new housing estates. But Harrison(1994) has argued that they only reflected the business interests of trust members because only one of the four schemes prepared in Bombay and in Calcutta was concerned with providing better housing for the poor and working class. Also the rental costs effectively prevented the poor from taking advantage of this new housing, which meant their only option was to move to other slum areas not targeted for demolition.

In the early twentieth century, "modern" town planning ideas that were developed in Britain changed how the environmental problems of industrial cities were addressed. Instead of using by-laws and sanitary reform, governments sought to control land use and the management of whole cities.[11] When these planning ideas were transplanted to Indian cities that were experiencing rapid urban growth and increasing concerns about public health, financially constrained local governments quickly began to use slum clearances as their method to improve living conditions and "beautify" cities.[12] After the educated Indian middle class gained control of local government, they emulated the colonial authorities in their neglect of the older parts of the city by giving preference to the newer residential areas when implementing sewage and drainage systems. Slum clearance was used extensively to modernise towns and cities and develop new residential areas. The poor were displaced and forced to seek cheaper housing in remaining overcrowded and insanitary neighbourhoods.[13]

After 1947, the Congress Party began to establish a framework for democratic political rule that was based on an interventionist development state that would guide the growth of the economy and promote the welfare of the population. The Planning Commission was established to define the goals and strategies of India's development, which have been presented in five-year plans. The first two decades were dominated by the Congress Party, as it built a coalition of interests by *"...incorporating political competition and consociation arrangements within its boundaries and yet holding it together through a delicate management of factions*[14]." This coalition included sections of the middle class, landlords, rich peasants and professional groups who were interested in preserving their position within Indian society. By accommodating their demands, Congress was able *"...to satisfy to the best of its ability the interests of all the elite groups dominant at different levels of the political system."* The outcome was a "weak state" dominated by reformism, which was unable to improve the welfare of the disadvantaged and marginalised populations. In other words, the state abandoned its role of umpire, and instead allowed this coalition of classes to make demands that excluded other groups from access to sometimes scarce resources.[15]

Contemporarily, the environmental problems confronting Indian cities today, it will be argued, are the result of the legacy of the colonial city and the nature of the post-colonial state, which includes segregated cities, marginalised local governments and a failure to manage urban growth and provide sufficient housing. This colonial legacy continued to influence the management of Indian cities, their local governments and the provision of sanitation services until the early 1990s. The nature of the post-colonial state has contributed to these environmental problems because, instead of being an instrument for socioeconomic change, it has been dominated by coalitions of interests that have been accommodated by the use of public funds to provide private goods. This has resulted in many of the decisions relating to how the state has allocated financial resources and implemented new projects and schemes being heavily influenced by political considerations rather than being based on development needs and technical considerations. Such political considerations have therefore undermined the state's capacity to address the problems that have been created by urban growth, such as the inadequate provision of sanitation services for all sections of the population.

One group in Indian society that has benefited from this accommodation of the coalitions of interests has been the middle class, who have been able to monopolise what sanitation services the state has provided because they live in neighbourhoods supplied with sewers and piped water. When combined with the benefits of modern medicine (such as antibiotics and oral rehydration therapy), accessible (largely private) health care and the use of insecticides to stop disease vectors spreading from slums, the middle class have become largely insulated from the burden of ill-health caused by insanitary living conditions. The result has been that the middle class do not place electoral pressure on governments to effectively implement public health policies—sanitation schemes in particular. And neither have the urban poor, despite their political participation, been able to force governments to effectively implement policies designed to improve their living conditions.

(v) Socio-economic Costs and Benefits of Sanitation

In India, 60 per cent of the environmental health burden is caused by the lack of access to safe drinking water and adequate sanitation. The single major cause of this burden of disease is diarrhoea, which disproportionately affects children under the age of five.[16] Each year, an estimated 180 million person-workdays are lost due to the incidence of waterborne disease. This has been estimated to cost the Indian economy Rs 12 billion.[17]

Studies that have sought to document the socioeconomic benefits of providing sanitation include a World Bank study that used available evidence from 172 demographic and health surveys in 70 countries. The authors found that the provision of adequate water and sanitation services reduced the odds of children under the age of five suffering from diarrhoea by 7.3 per cent and 12.9 per cent, respectively. Similar reductions were observed in the mortality risk for children under five. They concluded that from a "*...public health perspective... sanitation infrastructure should in our opinion receive more attention, as the private health benefits of sanitation seem to be at least equal to the benefits of water infrastructure, while the social welfare spillovers are likely substantially larger.*"[18]

(vi) Socio-cultural Aspects of Sustainable Sanitation

In recent years, there has been a growing realisation that access to sanitation does not increase unless there is demand from the user, and as most expenditure for sanitation is at the household level, where promotional efforts are most needed here. Previous attempts to market sanitation have relied on the promotion of the health benefits that sanitation and hygienic behaviour can bring. Whilst this is clearly the most important reason for promoting sanitation and hygiene from an institutional point of view, it often proves to be much less of a motivating factor for spending money on sanitation at the individual or household level. When households contemplate a shift, other factors may prove to be a greater motivation. Research by the World Bank Water and Sanitation Programme has identified several other factors that serve to motivate even very poor households to invest in sanitation (Cairncross 2004).[19] These include:

- Convenience and comfort
- Privacy and safety
- For women and girls, avoidance of sexual harassment and assault
- Less embarrassment with visitors
- Dignity and social status

Social marketing techniques are currently seen as an extremely useful tool in promoting sanitation amongst private households. They involve the application of commercial marketing techniques to advance social goals, in this case the safe use of excreta and greywater through appropriate sanitation solutions. Social marketing has been used successfully to increase sanitation coverage in rural India. The marketing side is based on the "four Ps" - Product, Price, Place, and Promotion.

Product - Toilet and sanitary system designs must respond to what people want, rather than what sanitary engineers believe they should have.

Price - Includes all costs (monetary and non-monetary) needs to be affordable, and therefore it is necessary to offer a range of products available at different prices. This is the hardest part of selling sanitation to those who lack it. The poor, who need it most, can least afford it. Hence the need to keep costs down and market a range of products with various price tags.

Place - The product must be delivered to the right place; in particular, a toilet must be installed in the customer's own home. This means that the supply chain has to reach every household.

Promotion - Promotion is communication with consumers about the product or service. This includes advertising, mass media, word of mouth, and anything in between. It can also include many other means to get customers' attention and convince them to buy the product: demonstration toilets, time-limited special offers, coupons and vouchers, competitions and prizes, door-to-door sales, credit sponsored by local traders and mutual help schemes to help the poorest with the cost and the elderly with the digging.

When designing social marketing campaigns to promote sanitation and the safe use of excreta and greywater, the possible barriers to the promotion and success of the campaign should be identified, explicitly addressed, and integrated into the campaign. With regard to sanitation Simpson-Hébert and Wood (1998) have identified 10 barriers to progress in sanitation, all of which are equally valid for the safe use of excreta and greywater:[20]

- Lack of political will;
- Low prestige, priority and recognition;
- Poor policy at all levels;
- Weak institutional framework and unclear distribution of responsibilities;
- Inadequate and poorly used resources;
- Inappropriate approaches;
- Failure to recognise defects of current excreta management systems;
- Neglect of consumer preferences;
- Ineffective promotion and low public awareness; and
- Women and children last.

Why People Want Toilets

The following responses concerning satisfaction with a new toilet were recorded in a survey of rural households conducted in the Philippines. The following reasons for having a toilet were listed in order of preference:

- Lack of flies,
- Cleaner surroundings,
- Privacy,
- Less embarrassment when friends visit, and
- Reduced gastrointestinal disease.

Similar results have been obtained from surveys conducted in other parts of the world, where health is often found to be a less important driver for obtaining sanitation for households than dignity, convenience and social status.

Source: WHO 1997 in WHO/UNICEF JMP 2000

(b) Sanitation and Education[21]

In spite of the serious problems with the conventional sanitation paradigm, educational institutions, universities, and technical schools continue to present it to new generations of students as the only legitimate form of sanitation. The problem is compounded by the fact that the training treats the sanitation system as the focus, and pure removal of faeces and urine (and the water that bears them) as the goal. The users are objectified, and their ideas and preferences are largely ignored. If the users of the sanitation system are considered at all, it is as objects of PR campaigns aimed at "changing behaviour", "enforcing" payment or use norms, or "stimulating" compliance. The potential users of the recycling products are usually completely neglected (e.g., with regard to their quality and logistical requirements how the products reach the users).

The conventional sanitation discourse as presented in engineering and technical schools simply does not accord the system users any status at all in the decision-making process, thus often leading to inappropriate expensive and/or unsustainable solutions. The current education system also fails in preparing students to think about urine and faeces and grey/black water as resources. The emphasis, as one would expect in a removal-based approach is on their negative or dangerous physical, chemical, and biological characteristics, and not on their resource value as sources of nutrients, energy, or water for irrigation or other purposes. This is the reflection of an education system influenced by the culture of the North, where societies are wealthy and still behave, as if they could afford to have a linear attitude towards resources. Sanitation engineers and practitioners, policymakers, managers, and operators get their ideas and information during the education process. And here is one key problem: Curricula of Universities, continuing education programmes, technical schools, research institutes and training centres mostly continue to present conventional sanitation as the only legitimate approach. Indeed those responsible for the content of curricula are often even unaware of the new developments in this field.

The paradigm shift in sanitation has not yet made structural inroads into the professional and university educational system. There is an urgent need for a different approach to professional and scholarly sanitation education and training, an approach that takes into consideration the need for holistic solutions, thus comprising all dimensions of sustainability, from health and socio-technical aspects to natural resources management, agriculture, micro- and macro-economics and institutional aspects.

The current educational and training infrastructure is failing the field of sanitation and development in primarily two ways:

- most institutions uncritically continue to offer curricula in the basics of centralised sewered sanitation and end-of-pipe wastewater treatment and disposal, continuing to turn out sanitation engineers and planners whose education and training has led them to believe that this is the only adequate and serious approach; and
- despite almost 20 years of practice in participatory and holistic interdisciplinary planning approaches, the basic framework of education and training in sanitation (like that in other urban environmental fields) remains narrowly focused on the technical aspects, so that neither students nor scholars are learning the basic process skills to arrive at sustainable solutions.

There are three identifiable problems in relation to sanitation and education.

1. Sanitation is failing in sustainability and in serving the world's poor. The current sanitation paradigm delivers neither equity nor sustainability. There are alternatives, but they are neither fully developed nor fully legitimatised.
2. Education is failing in adapting to the required changes in the sanitation system. While the sanitation system is in transition, the educational system remains fixed on the old paradigm, with the result that young professionals look backwards towards 20th century models, rather than forwards towards a sustainable future.
3. Knowledge management in the urban environment is outdated and obsolete. Failures to support the new sanitation paradigm can be found in abundance in the areas of research, development, documentation, and the sanitation discourse—that is, in the area of knowledge management in sanitation. These failures compound and reinforce the failures in the education system, rather than challenging and counteracting them.

(i) Advancing Knowledge Management

Research on sanitation-related socio-cultural aspects and traditions can therefore greatly contribute to the socio-cultural sustainability of sanitation systems. Generally projects and related research have to realise that:

- Defecation is a highly private and intimate topic and related habits may largely differ between regions and cultures

- In some cultures handling of excreta is subject of strong taboos and may be related to aspects of human dignity
- Knowledge and perception of the reuse of excreta largely varies between cultures and regions
- Sanitation practices differ (wet versus dry hygiene, squatting versus sitting, etc.)

Problems to be addressed by research for socio-cultural sustainable sanitation systems include:

- Household motivations to invest in sanitation
- Household expectations from the system
- Lack of awareness of hygienic risks and practices
- Traditional practices which may be wise or may pose severe hygienic risks
- The need to modify existing practices as a result of increasing urbanisation in recent years

One finds, failures in the areas of research, development, documentation, and the sanitation discourse—that is, in the area of knowledge management in sanitation—compound and reinforce the failures in the education system, rather than challenging and counteracting them. Research is still concentrated on the optimisation of centralised and unsustainable systems.

Documentation, criteria and case studies for innovative sanitation solutions are therefore urgently needed. Textbooks and scholarly articles usually are restricted to the description of centralised sanitation systems or on-site pit toilets as described above. They usually do not address the interrelation between sanitation, agriculture, food-security and job-creation - hence the inter-sectoral approach needed to address the sanitation crisis in a holistic and sustainable way.

Professional associations increasingly start addressing ecosan: The International Water Association (IWA) has since several years a specialist group on ecological sanitation and during the 4th IWA world-congress ecosan was an important topic. The Indian Water Works Association (IWWA) recently organised a larger international ecosan conference in Mumbai (Nov., 2005) and is actively engaged in a series of ecosan projects in India. The German Water Association has now put up several expert groups to focus on different aspects of ecosan, aiming at the provision of standards and reliable fact sheets for the innovative ecosan approach.

(c) Sanitation and Disease[22]

Human excreta and the lack of adequate personal and domestic hygiene have been implicated in the transmission of many infectious diseases including cholera, typhoid, hepatitis, polio, cryptosporidiosis, ascariasis, and schistosomiasis. The World Health Organisation (WHO) estimates that 2.2 million people die annually from diarrhoeal diseases and that 10 per cent of the population of the developing world are severely infected with intestinal worms related to improper waste and excreta management (Murray and Lopez 1996; WHO 2000a). Human excreta-transmitted diseases predominantly affect children and the poor. Most of the deaths due to diarrhoea occur in children and in developing countries (WHO 1999).

Proper excreta disposal and minimum levels of personal and domestic hygiene are essential for protecting public health. Safe excreta disposal and handling act as the primary barrier for preventing excreted pathogens from entering the environment. Once pathogens have been introduced into the environment they can be transmitted via either the mouth (e.g., through drinking contaminated water or eating contaminated vegetables/food) or the skin (as in the case of the hookworms and schistosomes), although in many cases adequate personal and domestic hygiene can reduce such transmission. Excreta and wastewater generally contain high concentrations of excreted pathogens, especially in countries where diarrhoeal diseases and intestinal parasites are particularly prevalent. Therefore for maximum health protection, it is important to treat and contain human excreta as close to the source as possible before it gets introduced into the environment.

Thus the proper management of excreta acts as the primary barrier to prevent the spread of pathogens in the environment. It, thus, directly impacts disease transmission through person-to person contact, water and the food chain. Human excreta may contain many types of pathogens. When these pathogens are introduced into the environment some can remain infectious for long periods of time and, under certain conditions, they may be able to replicate in the environment. The presence of pathogens presents a potential threat to human health.

Disease transmission is determined by several pathogen-related factors including:

- An organism's ability to survive or multiply in the environment (some pathogens require the presence of specific intermediate hosts to complete their lifecycles).
- Latent periods (many pathogens are immediately infectious,

others may require a period of time before they become infective).

- An organism's ability to infect the host (some pathogens can cause infections when present in small numbers e.g., *Ascaris*, others may require a million or more organisms to cause infection; Feachem *et al.* 1983).

Disease transmission is also affected by host characteristics and behaviour, including:

- immunity (natural or as a result of prior infection or vaccination)
- nutritional status
- health status
- age
- sex
- personal hygiene
- food hygiene.

Thus, sanitation is the primary barrier for preventing faecal-oral disease transmission. If excreta disposal is ineffective or non-existent (or other animals serve as sources of excreted pathogens) other measures must be taken to avoid disease transmission. Removing or destroying infectious agents by disinfecting drinking water prior to consumption or preparation of food; cleaning hands, utensils, and surfaces before food preparation and consumption; and cooking food thoroughly are interventions that will reduce disease transmission (WHO 1993). For example, the simple act of washing one's hands with soap can reduce diarrhoea by a third (WHO 2000a). Faecally contaminated water, both marine and fresh, is a frequent cause of food-borne illness. For example, some shellfish (such as mussels, oysters, and clams) obtain their food by filtering large quantities of water and are therefore particularly likely to accumulate contamination. Excreta-related human pathogens, heavy metals and other chemical contaminants are taken in with the food particles and can be concentrated in the tissues. Shellfish are also frequently eaten raw or partially cooked. Fish, and non-filter feeding shellfish (crabs, lobsters, prawns, shrimps) grown in faecally contaminated water containing high levels of human pathogens can also concentrate pathogens in their intestinal tracts and on their skin surfaces. When concentrations of faecally derived bacteria exceed a certain level they can be found in muscle tissues (WHO 1989). Infection may occur when the contaminated fish is consumed raw or lightly cooked. Food handlers may also be at risk during preparation of the contaminated product.

(i) The Health Dimension of Poor Sanitation: In the Global Burden of Disease (GBD) Study Disability Adjusted Life Years (DALYs) were ascribed to 10 selected risk factors. Water, sanitation (i.e., excreta disposal) and hygiene accounted for the second biggest per centage of DALYs behind malnutrition. Worldwide, it is estimated that there are approximately 4 billion cases of diarrhoea per year (resulting in 2.2 million deaths), 200 million people with schistosomiasis and as many as 400 million people infected with intestinal worms (UN 1998; WHO 2000a,b). All of these diseases are largely excreta-related. In less developed countries, poor nutritional status and poverty exacerbate morbidity and mortality associated with excreta-related diseases. For example, most deaths attributed to diarrhoea occur in children below the age of five (WHO 2000b).

The largest effect was seen for interventions focusing on improved excreta disposal, reflecting excreta as being the source of pathogens and the multiple routes of transmission. Moreover, it is important that all members of a community, particularly the children, make use of improved sanitation installations. Children are frequently the victims of diarrhoeal disease and other faecally/orally transmitted illnesses, and thus may act as sources of pathogens. Getting children to use sanitation facilities (or designing child-friendly toilets) and implementing school sanitation programmes are important interventions for reducing the spread of disease associated with waste and excreta (WHO 1993).

(ii) Excreta Disposal Management: The problem of excreta disposal is clearly as old as mankind itself and the need for careful disposal is highlighted in a number of religious books including Hindu, Islamic and Christian texts. There are numerous technical options for excreta management, many of which, if properly designed, constructed, operated and maintained will provide adequate and safe service as well as health benefits. It is necessary to choose technically, economically and financially feasible options for sustainable excreta management. Equally important is the involvement of all stakeholders playing a role in sanitation development, including users (or customers), community organisations, authorities and entrepreneurs. In particular, it is essential to involve women in the design and selection of domestic sanitation facilities. Research conducted in South Asia demonstrates that involving women in sanitation programmes has resulted in higher coverage, better maintenance of the facilities, increased hygiene awareness, and lower incidence of faecal-oral disease in the community (Neto and Tropp 2000). In addition, for sanitation programmes to be sustainable there must be the political will and institutional capacity to ensure adequate public services and the proper maintenance of sanitation systems. Indeed, there are numerous instances where public toilets, in particular, are poorly maintained and the latrine contents inappropriately disposed. Although, happily, this is not always the case and successful schemes (often run on a franchise basis by profit-making organisations or by social organisations) exist in a number of places including Ghana and India (Gear *et al*. 1996; National Institute of Urban Affairs 1990).

It is important to note that there is no single appropriate technology for all circumstances and all socio-economic segments of a community, town or city. The more costly or, apparently, convenient technologies may not provide the greatest health benefit or may be unsustainable from an economic or technological viewpoint. For sanitary installations to deliver health benefits they need to be able to:

- isolate the user from their own excreta
- prevent nuisance animals (e.g. flies) from contacting the excreta and subsequently transmitting disease to humans
- contain the excreta and/or inactivate the pathogens.

(d) Gender and Sanitation

(i) Global Background

Gender is a concept that refers to socially constructed roles, behaviour, activities and attributes that a particular society considers appropriate and ascribes to men and women (WHO, 2009). These distinct roles and the relations between them may give rise to gender inequalities where one group is systematically favoured and holds advantages over another. Inequality in the position of men and women can and has worked against societies' progress as a whole. Gender in Water and Sanitation highlights in brief form, approaches to redressing gender inequality in the hygiene, water and sanitation sector.

Gender is a dynamic concept, which looks at the interrelationship between men and women in the context of their society and roles in that society. Gender roles are defined as the social and cultural traits that different societies assign to males and females. Such gender roles are the patterns of behaviour, rights and obligations defined by a society as appropriate for each sex. A gender perspective is a way of looking at situations and issues taking into account the respective roles and contributions of men and women in society.

The intention behind women and gender policies has evolved over past decades. Taking a historical dimension the section below describes the philosophy underpinning various gender mainstreaming policies over the past decade. Until the early 1970s, policies addressed the needs of women entirely in the context of their role as wives and mothers. Policies shaped by this paradigm took the welfare approach, and focus was on mother and child health, childcare, and nutrition. The weakness was that policy objectives treated women as passive recipients of benefits, rather than partners.

From the 1970s and 1980s, a 'Women in Development' (WID) policy was mostly pursued, which aimed to integrate women into the existing development process by targeting them, often through women-specific activities. Although many WID initiatives improved health, income, or resources in the short term, they did not transform unequal relationships, and the structures enforcing these, which in turn negatively affected project sustainability. In spite of the weaknesses in a purely WID approach it remains useful in certain contexts, and can still be useful to incorporate within current day policy objectives.

The framework highlighted below is useful for understanding the interventions made by the state as well as in considering how and where to pitch policy goals.

(i) At the level of welfare concern is material welfare of women, relative to men and focuses on basic provision of services to enable women to fulfill their domestic role.

(ii) At the level of access focus is on access to the factors of production: land, water, labour, credit, training, and all publicly available services and benefits on an equal basis with men. Strategies related to access enable women to fulfill important reproductive roles in society.

(iii) At the level of conscientisation focus is on building understanding of the difference between sex roles and gender roles, and that the latter are cultural and can be changed.

(iv) At the level of participation focus is given to women's equal participation in the decision-making process, policymaking, planning and administration.

(v) At the level of equality of control focus is on factors of production and the distribution of benefits so that neither men nor women are in a position of dominance.

In practically all cultures, women have a lower status than men. The differences between women and men in terms of enjoyment of rights, responsibilities, decision-making and access to food and other resources needs to be understood if efforts to improve health and nutrition are to succeed. It is recognised that a gender analysis of such inequalities and their consequences can result in more effective approaches to health, nutrition, water and sanitation promotion, disease prevention, health care and services, and research.

A woman's economic, educational and health status is fundamental to human survival. Women are the main conduits for health knowledge, the main providers of health care and the primary careers of children. The consequences of woman's ill-health for her family and society are often severely underestimated. This is in part because women are statistically "invisible" in data and, as a result, priority-setting approaches can easily ignore women, in particular poor women and female children. It is increasingly recognised that development policies, including health policies, may fail or have very different outcomes than planned if gender is not considered.

Because women have so many roles in society, most of which are "hidden" from standard economic analysis, it is argued that women are often the "shock absorbers" for the neo-liberal economic policies most usually associated with globalisation. For example, it is well known that when school fees or health fees are raised as part of efforts to reduce public spending, women and girls are the first to stop receiving education or health services. In addition, the movement from hospital-based to community care is placing an increasing burden on women, who traditionally care for the ill.

There is a debate about whether globalisation has a different impact on men and women. It is argued, for example, that 90 per cent of jobs created by FDI in export processing zones are given to women. This may then mean that women are lifted out of absolute poverty, or it may mean that wages and conditions are poorer than those otherwise offered to men.

It is also argued that the health consequences of globalisation are more likely to affect poor women than poor men. For example:

- Pregnant women account for many of the deaths from malaria.
- TB is more prevalent among poor women than men as they have worse nutrition and are more likely to be confined to the home and less likely to receive treatment during their illness.
- HIV/AIDS is increasingly affecting women of the 4.2 million new HIV infections that occurred in 2002, 2 million or 48 per cent were in women and over time the incidence of HIV infections is rising faster for women than men. Women also bear the further burden of caring for sick relatives and have far less opportunity to control their own sexual health, making them more vulnerable to HIV infection.

Traditionally trade policies have been considered to be "gender neutral" However, evidence is emerging that women economic globalisation (including trade expansion) has a worse economic impact for women than for men. The effect of globalisation on women is magnified as a result of existing patterns of inequality between women and men, including:

- Distribution of the labour force by sector: In most countries, women and men are distributed differently across manufacturing sectors, between the formal and informal sectors, and within agriculture. The uneven impact of globalisation by sector therefore has gender-based effects, including increased female employment in labour-intensive manufacturing and increased male unemployment in formerly protected industrial sectors.
- Areas of comparative advantage: For many developing countries, an area of comparative advantage is low-wage, labour-intensive employment, such as garment manufacturing (in which women predominate in the workforce). An export strategy based on low-wage female labour may increase the proportion of women in the labour force but may also increase the overall wage gap between women and men and decrease the prospects for closing this gap.
- Distribution of productive assets: The ability to benefit from new opportunities is related to access to productive assets - including education, skills, property, credit - to which women traditionally have less access than men.
- Distribution of unpaid household labour between women and men: Women continue to carry out a larger share of the work necessary to maintain families than men do. This necessary but unpaid work is generally not considered in trade policy debates.

Lessons from history therefore suggests that beyond addressing access to domestic water and sanitation services, policies should target economic equality through water for productive uses, equality in decision making, and equality in the contracts, consultancy and general business around water and sanitation infrastructure development.

(ii) Gender, Sanitation and Culture

Gender refers to the culturally and socially constructed differences between males and females found in the meanings, beliefs, and practices associated with feminity and masculinity. Gender is important in defining what females and males are, what they should do, and what sorts of relations do or should exist between them. Gender organises social relations in everyday life as well as in the major social structures. Sanitation refers to the principles and practices relating to the collection, removal or disposal of human excreta, household waste water and refuse as they impact upon people and the environment. Good sanitation includes appropriate health and hygiene awareness and behaviour, and acceptable, affordable and sustainable sanitation services. A lack of adequate sanitation or inadequately maintained or inappropriately designed systems can therefore constitute a range of pollution risks to the environment, especially the contamination of surface and ground water resources.

Global water and sanitation practitioners have recognised the importance of incorporating a gender perspective based among others, the following observations:[23]

- Women and girls are most often the primary users, providers and managers of water in their households and are the guardians of household hygiene. If a water system falls into disrepair, women are the ones forced to travel long distances over many hours to meet their families' water needs.
- The water and sanitation sector can contribute to redressing inequality and can impact positively on the social, political and economic position of women. Well targeted services can improve the health and security of women and their families, and free them to engage in social, economic, and political activities, thus tackling 'time poverty' - the situation where women's time is inflexible, consumed by routine and non-productive tasks, perpetuating their absence from decision making and other profitable pursuits (World Bank, 2006).
- A gendered approach can create a framework of cooperation between men and women, so that the insights and abilities of both men and women are available to shape programmes and meet sector objectives.
- Common societal practices that determine men as property owners, heads of households and main decision makers in the public sphere often result in marginalising the views and preferences of women and girls.
- Equal involvement of men and women is positively correlated with improved sustainability of water supplies (Narayan, 1995), as well as improved transparency and governance in management. Gender analysis in water and sanitation development can ensure that projects are actually used by situating services where access is inclusive to all, and not

disadvantage women or users of different ethnic groups or castes.

- Sanitation and hygiene improvements are often low on the list of family investments, and women and girls suffer more indignity as a result. Their privacy and security are partly determined by ease of access to, and location of sanitation facilities. Children especially, have needs and concerns that should be taken into account when creating sanitation interventions to be used by them. In primary schools, toilets are often inadequate to serve the needs of girls, resulting in non-attendance during menses. Conversely, school enrolment and retention of girls, increases where there are water and sanitation services. Using a gender lens can ensure that sanitation services are given priority by decision makers and technology is tailored to meet their needs.
- Water for production relates to wealth creation, yet access to the means of production and control over resources often excludes women in some communities. A gender sensitive strategy aims to ensure that women benefit by enabling their participation as decision makers and investors.
- Gender stereotypes concerning abilities and interests of men and women, often create non-equitable and non representative decision making in the sector.[24]

Concept of gender mainstreaming is provided by the United Nations Economic and Social Council (1997), suggests that mainstreaming a gender perspective is the process of assessing the implications for women and men of any planned action, including legislation, policies or programmes, in all areas and at all levels. It is a strategy for making the concerns and experiences of women as well as men, an integral dimension of the design, implementation, monitoring and evaluation of policies and programmes in all political, economic and societal spheres, so that women and men benefit equally and inequality is not perpetuated. The ultimate goal is to achieve gender equality.

The following are the gender issues related to sanitation:

1. Women are responsible for water in the house: Women and men usually have very different roles in water and sanitation activities, these differences are particularly pronounced in rural areas. Women are most often the users, providers, and managers of water in rural households and are the guardians of household hygiene. If a water system breaks down, women, not men, will most likely be the ones most affected, for they may have to travel further for water or use other means to meet the household's water and sanitation needs. In case of drought or flood women

remain responsible for water, and have to go even further to find it, or compromise by using less and less clean water, which influences the hygienic situation of the household.

2. Women are responsible for hygiene at home. Even though the responsibility for cleanliness and hygiene should be with all, in reality it is the women of households and also of villages who are seen as the cleaners of the yard, the house, the kitchen, the bathroom and the toilet facilities. In these situations women are usually also responsible for getting water to the house, from far away, from less far, or from close by. Both the cleaning and the fetching of water take a lot of time. Women are responsible for the hygiene of themselves, their children and men folk; women have to do the work for all of them; and women suffer when they themselves have negative influence of bad hygiene, by getting ailments and diseases, but also if their children are ill, which means extra work for them. When their men folk and parents are ill that also gives them extra work, and more water to carry. So women are at the centre of hygiene for all. Either way, with or without diseases, it means a lot of work for them. Not all women are in the same position; the younger women in the household have more duties than the senior ones.
3. Women are responsible for health of family, especially of children. Women, who are aware of the connection between the dirtiness and illness of family members, will do extra effort to keep the house, the kitchen, the food and the sanitary facilities clean. This is extra daily work, but when somebody is ill, women usually have the responsibility to care for him or her and that may be even more work.
4. Women are responsible for the sick and for the elderly. Both men and women can get ill, but women are the caretakers perse. Hygiene becomes doubtly important when there are sick family members who could infect the others. Extra water is needed, and a lot of extra work needs to be done. Gender ideology prescribes that women do all this, there is no other real reason. The same is true for the elderly, with the difference that sick people in the house should be an exceptional situation, whilst to get old will happen to all who are healthy and lucky.
5. Women menstruate, get pregnant and give birth. Women in their menstruating period are generally seen as unclean. They should clean their blood themselves, and that is one of the reasons that women always have to clean everything. Not according to reason, but according to the prevailing gender ideology. During the time

of being pregnant, giving birth and breast feeding, the risk of getting infections is high. All women will try to avoid that by giving lots of attention and spending extra energy in hygiene. The direct relation with the quality and quantity of water available during that time, and the fact that she will not always be able to get it, makes her very vulnerable. Maternal mortality is directly related to hygiene, and hygiene to sanitary facilities and their cleanliness.

6. Gender issues of toilets: In both rural and urban areas, women without toilets only go out to relieve themselves in the dark, because their gender ideology tells them that they cannot take the risk to be seen. They often face risks, by snakes, scorpions, or other creatures, but also by men. There are endless stories of women getting harassed and even raped when going out in dark. For men and children this is no problem, they can go anywhere and anytime. For them urinate or to defecate has no relation to sex at all, but women who go out in the daylight are seen as light or fallen women who ask for trouble. This is again gender ideology, and even discrimination. Furthermore to wait till the dark results in constipation and adapted diet and drinking habits, which give serious health problems. In densely populated urban areas, public toilets, if available, are to be cleaned by women only. They often cannot be locked, and here again women suffer from violence.[25]

Implications of Open Defecation for Women and Girl Children's[26]

Gang rape of the young girl on her way to answer nature's call is a vivid affirmation of the harassment, molestation and indignity to which women girls and young children in urban areas are exposed. In villages almost all defecate in the open fields that surround their homes. In urban areas, especially in rapidly growing cities, all available space is devoured for housing business, etc. None is open to the poor to defecate in privacy; making them susceptible to sexual abuse.

Besides being unsafe and undignified, open defecation is a serious health threat as pathogens from excreta contaminate soil and water causing disease and death. Although difficult to isolate from other factors such as education, quality of health services etc.; absence of / poor sanitation facilities exacerbates the health burden of the poor. In poor quality settlements families lose more workdays and a higher proportion of their income to illness.

(iii) Sanitation and Gender Issues in Various Spheres[27]

Gender analysis assesses commitment to international gender targets at a national level, as articulated within policy, and the impact of this policy on livelihoods on the ground. Analysis identifies issues arising from impacts from existing programmes, gaps between men and women in participation and representation, the gaps in capacity and awareness, and identifies solutions such as institutional reform, affirmative action, training, or targeted programmes to redress inequality. Because impacts will vary from country to country and over time, gender analysis should be repeated at regular intervals and data produced analysed for decision making.

Needless to mention, that policies can play an important role in overcoming obstacles to the equal participation of men and women in decision making. Like, some policies affect not only the water sector, but also gender relations over a number of development sectors. Let us observe various spheres where gender issues need attention.

(a) Gender in the Workplace: A workplace gender policy could consider the following measures to promote a gender sensitive workplace:

- Prohibit discrimination based on sex, race, age, marital status, pregnancy, parenthood or disability in the recruitment, promotion and training of staff.
- Ensure safety in the work environment and provide for safe travel arrangements.
- Support employees in their efforts to balance work and family responsibilities e.g., include paid sick leave, flexi-time, lactation spaces, childcare, paternity or maternity leave.
- Prohibit sexual, psychological or racist language, images or harassment,
- Ensure that staff understands that they are able to directly inform the harasser that their conduct is unwelcome and must stop, irrespective of rank.
- Place staff on permanent terms where possible and review unilateral decision making on contract extension for nonpermanent staff; re-examine these procedures to ensure accountability in the process.
- Take advantage of institutional restructuring to increase capacity for gender mainstreaming and improve the ratio of men to women in a traditionally male dominated sector.

(b) Gender in Urban Sanitation—There is a need for addressing urban sanitation in a gender responsive way:

- Partnerships between local government, local women's groups and the private sector should be forged to overcome technical and financial barriers to women accessing urban sanitation.
- A sustainability plan can be introduced for the operation and maintenance of public pay-and-use facilities, allowing women to play a role in management.
- Access to and from household to public toilets should incorporate a strategy to ensure safety for women and children.
- Decisions around payment schemes should not exclude the opinion of women and consideration for the needs of children.
- Strategies should be developed to target sanitation and hygiene in primary schools, and ensure that non-access to sanitation does not hinder school attendance by girls.
- Practitioners should invest in processes that enable the inputs of men, women, and mixed groups. Different sections of society can have complementary roles in the planning, decision making and implementation of an optimal urban sanitation environment.

(c) Gender in small town and rural water operations - The rapid population growth in urban centres has resulted in the new challenge of providing services in small towns. Often services in the small growth centres are neglected and approaches to managing them exclude the role of special interest groups.

There is an urgent need for good gender mainstreaming practices in small town and rural water operations should:

- Adopt municipal level by-laws that professionalise services and incorporate a gender balanced community oversight role.
- Guarantee opportunities for women in decision making and water supply management and ensure they also enjoy the benefits.
- Provide equal opportunities to build capacity at all levels of operations.

(d) Violence Against Women Needs Sanitation of Mind

Nine major forms of violence, six being violence in the general community—physical assault, verbal abuse, sexual harassment and assault, rape, sexual exploitation, forced prostitution, kidnapping and abduction, and three being violence in the family—female foeticide and infanticide, child sexual abuse and domestic violence from natal and marital family members.

Women faced violence in the family over a range of issues, suggesting the assimilation of the larger patriarchal caste system's norms by men, with negative implications for women's personal lives and interactions in their community. Female feticide and infanticide stemmed from gender discrimination, combined with poverty or a response to the child being born of an illicit relationship.

Gender inequality and norms of female subordination formed a major category of causal factors for violence meted out by natal and marital family members to women. Examples of causal factors falling within this category include women allegedly failed to be dutiful wives. Sometimes women asserted their rights and become victim of domestic violence. Many a times, women were unable to bear children, or unable to bear sons. A second major category was economic causal factors for domestic violence, including: poverty; insufficient dowry. Women earned more income than their husbands, or their natal families had a higher economic status than their marital families.

Women asked their husbands to account for money given from their earnings to the husbands, or refused to give their earnings to fund their husbands' drinking habits, or refused to mortgage jeweler to satisfy their husbands' spendthrift habits; to deny women their share of their deceased husbands' property; a third prominent category of causal factors related to women's civil rights, which include women's insecurity is also due to their husband's unemployment or alcoholism. Sometimes, women's insecurity is a concern for widows or as destitute

Overall, much of the domestic violence arose out of a combination of factors such as internalised gender discrimination, poverty, dominant discourses of dowry, wifely fidelity and duties, and distrust of women to guard their own sexuality all leading to husbands' perceived rights over their wives, or their husbands' alcoholism.

There is a need to encourage educational institutions to adopt policies of equal opportunities coupled with affirmative action. There is a need for ensuring non-discriminatory health services and facilities with ensuring women's equitable access to adequate nutrition—including health and maternity benefits. There is a need for ensuring basic amenities for women within household dwellings and localities, especially electricity, potable water and toilet facilities, as well as decent sewage systems. There is a need to increase emphasis on vocational and skill-based education for girls and women, and equip them for job market. Also there is a need to rehabilitate all women like prostitutes, widows, manual scavengers into different occupations by linking better rehabilitation with vocational training.

Notes

1. Based on Capacity building for ecological sanitation, 2006 UNESCO/IHP. International Hydrological Programme (IHP) of the United Nations Educational, Scientific and Cultural Organisation (UNESCO).
2. Based on Capacity building for ecological sanitation, 2006 UNESCO/IHP. International Hydrological Programme (IHP) of the United Nations Educational, Scientific and Cultural Organisation (UNESCO).
3. These principles were endorsed by the members of the WSSCC during its 5th Global Forum in November 2000 in Iguacu, Brazil (SANDEC/WSSCC 2000b).
4. Nath, K.J. (2003) Home hygiene and environmental sanitation: a country situation analysis for India, International Journal of Environmental Health Research, 13:S1, S19-S28.
5. For details see Susan E. Chaplin, Indian cities, sanitation and the state: the politics of the failure to provide, 2011 23: 57 *Environment and Urbanisation.*
6. Royal Commission on the Sanitary State of the Army in India (1864), *Report of the Commissioners appointed to inquire into the Sanitary State of the Army in India,* printed under the superintendence of the HMSO, London.
7. Harrison, Mark (1994), Public Health in British India: Anglo–Indian Preventive Medicine 1859–1914, Cambridge University Press, New Delhi.
8. Oldenburg, Veena Talwar (1984), The Making of Colonial Lucknow 1856–1877, Princeton University Press, New Jersey.
9. Furedy, Christine (1976), "Contrasting models in the development of municipal administration in Calcutta", in Donald B. Rosenthal (editor), *The City in Indian Politics,* Thomson Press, Faridabad.
10. Gupta, Samita (1993), "Theory and practice of town planning in Calcutta, 1817 to 1912: an appraisal", *The Indian Economic and Social History Review* Vol 30, No 1.
11. Yeoh, Brenda (1996), *Contesting Space: Power Relations and the Urban Built Environment in Colonial Singapore,* Oxford University Press, Singapore.
12. King, Anthony D. (1990), *Urbanism, Colonialism and the World Economy: Cultural and Spatial Foundations of the World System,* Routledge, London.

13. Gooptu, Nandini (2001), *The Politics of the Urban Poor in Early Twentieth Century India*, Cambridge University Press, New York.
14. Yadav, Yogendra (1997), "Reconfigursation in Indian politics: state assembly elections in 1993–1995", in Partha Chatterjee (editor), *State and Politics in India*, Oxford University Press, Delhi.
15. Chaplin, Susan E (1999), "Cities, sewers and poverty: India's politics of sanitation", *Environment and Urbanisation* Vol. 11, No. 1, April.
16. Planning Commission (2006), *Eleventh Five-Year Plan*, Vol. 2, Chapter 5, Oxford University Press, New Delhi.
17. Bhagwat, Ishaprasad, Indira Khurana and Richard Mahapatra (2008), "Toilet trail", *InfoChange* News and Features, November, accessed 20 August, 2009 at www.infochangeindia.org.
18. Gunther, Isabel and Gunther Fink (2010), "Water, sanitation and children's health: evidence from 172 DHS surveys", Policy Research Working Paper 5275, Prospects Group, Development Economics Group, The World Bank, Washington DC.
19. See Cairncross, Sandy (2004): "The Case for Marketing Sanitation." - WSP-AF (Water and Sanitation Program for Africa) Field Notes, Nairobi, Kenya, digitally available at: http: //www.wsp.org/ publications/af_marketing.pdf
20. See Simpson-Hébert M. and Wood S. [eds] (1998): "Sanitation promotion." WHO World Health Organisation, Geneva, Switzerland (unpublished document WHO/EOS/98.5.
21. Based on Capacity building for ecological sanitation, 2006 UNESCO/IHP. International Hydrological Programme (IHP) of the United Nations Educational, Scientific and Cultural Organisation (UNESCO).
22. Based on 2001 World Health Organisation (WHO). *Water Quality: Guidelines, Standards and Health.* Edited by Lorna Fewtrell and Jamie Bartram. Published by IWA Publishing, London, UK.
23. At the international level a range of conventions and policies provide guidance to governments on the appropriate response to gender in the development process in general, and in water in particular. The Dublin principles for water resource management established in 1992 at the Earth Summit in Rio de Janeiro states that women play a central part in the provision, management and safeguarding of water, and stresses the importance of empowering women to participate at all levels of water management.
24. For details see Gender in Water and Sanitation November 2010, Water and Sanitation Programme, World Bank, Nairobi, Kenya.

25. See Shakuntala C. Shettar, Sociology of Sanitation: Incorporating Gender Issues in Sanitation, http://www.sociologyofsanitation.com/?page_id=694#sthash. qWhnjXTL. dpuf
26. See Renu Khosla, 2000, Women and sanitation: Urban reality experiences of government programmes, NGOs and CBOs, *Social Change* 2000 30: 192.
27. Based on report Gender in Water and Sanitation November 2010, Water and Sanitation Programme, World Bank, Nairobi, Kenya.

8

Social Movement and Societal Sanitation–Key Social Thinkers

Introduction

Indian society is marked by the presence of cultural diversity as well as social reforms associated at regional and national level. It is to be emphasised that no sanitation is larger than societal sanitation. The social conditioning of Indian society is the interplay between the historical events and prominent thinkers that sets the perfect example of tradition and modernity. It is to be emphasised that social movements are the outcome of societal upheavals and which gradually leads to societal transformations. Thus understanding the meaning of social movements as effective mobilisation and the role of leadership are important sources of societal sanitation.

What do we mean by social movement and what are the various types of movements are essential for gauging the social transformation? Here the social reforms initiated by the great social reformers are seen as sanitisers for the societal evils. Though it is difficult to incorporate the ideas of various leaders (social thinkers), however, the chapter ahead discusses key social thinkers whose contribution can be associated with societal sanitation in a historical framework. The non-inclusion of certain thinkers however doesn't demean their contribution towards pure and health society. Attempt has been made to concentrate only on the central philosophy and ideas of the thinkers in terms of their contribution towards sanitised Indian society.

Understanding Social Movement

Social movements are purposeful, organised groups striving to work towards a common goal. These groups might be attempting to create change, to resist change, or to provide a political voice to those otherwise disenfranchised. Social movements, along with technology, social institutions, population, and environmental changes, create social change. Social movements, then, can be thought of as organised yet informal social entities that are engaged in extra-institutional conflict that is oriented towards a goal. These goals can be either aimed at a specific and narrow policy or be more broadly aimed at cultural change.

Conventionally social movements have broadly been perceived as organised collective mobilisation to bring about changes in the thought, beliefs, values, attitudes, relationships and major institutions in society, or to resist changes in any of the above structural elements of society [Haberle 1972; Guesfield 1971].[1, 2] However in the wake of the proliferation of new social movements the dimensions of new collective identity formation and resources mobilisation have got added emphasis. Touraine emphasised that social movements are characterised by the realisation of historicity, by self-conscious awareness and collective identity. To Melucci social movements grow around relationships of new social identity that are voluntarily conceived 'to empower' members in defence of this identity. By challenging the dominant assumptions of the social order, social movements develop new ideas that are fundamental to the process of human creativity. To Allan Scott a social movement is manifested both for the articulation of common interest and a common identity (1990:6). However, the resource mobilisation theorists highlight that the participation in the social movement is not guided by the sentiments, emotions and ideologies but by the logic of cost and the benefit of the collective actions and the scope of gratification of political and material interests of the participants.

Sociologist David Aberle (1966) addresses this question, developing categories that distinguish among social movements based on what they want to change and how much change they want.[3] Reform movements seek to change something specific about the social structure. Examples include anti-nuclear groups, Mothers Against Drunk Driving (MADD), and the Human Rights Campaign's advocacy for Marriage Equality. Revolutionary movements seek to completely change every aspect of society. These would include the 1960's counter-culture movement, as well as anarchist collectives. Religious/Redemptive movements are "meaning seeking," and their goal is to provoke inner change or spiritual growth in individuals. Organisations pushing these movements might include Heaven's Gate. Alternative movements are focused on self-improvement and limited, specific changes to individual beliefs and behaviour. These include trends like transcendental meditation or a macrobiotic diet. Resistance movements seek to prevent or undo change to the social structure. Certain tribals movements fall into this category.

(a) Raja Ram Mohan Roy: Sanitation of Women and Social Evils

Raja Ram Mohan Roy was the first social reformer of Modern India and he is rightly called the 'Father of Modern India'. He had a rational and scientific approach and believed in the principle of human dignity and social equality. He was deeply devoted to the work of religious and social reform, so he founded the Brahmo Samaj in 1825. He attacked the caste system and campaigned to persuade the Government to abolish the practice of 'Sati', in which women were forced to self-immolate on the pyre of their dead husband and child marriage. He advocated equal rights for women, right of widows to remarry and right of women to property. Raja Ram Mohan Roy was a champion of women's rights in India. He laid the foundations of the women's liberation movement in this country. He revolted against the subjection of women and pleaded for the restoration of their rights. The condition of the Hindu women in those days was very pitiable. They were subjected to different kinds of injustices and deprivations. According to Roy, the root cause of the all-round deterioration of Hindu women was the complete denial of their property rights. The Hindu girl was not given the traditional right to share with her brothers the property of her deceased father. The married Hindu woman was refused the right to share with her sons the property left by her deceased husband.

Ram Mohan Roy is best known for his agitation against *sati system.* It was a funeral practice among some Hindu communities in which a recently widowed woman would either voluntarily or by use of force and coercion immolate herself on her husband's funeral pyre. Ram Mohan saw his brother's widow cruelly forced to commit *sati* in 1812, but he was unable to stop it. After that Roy set his mind to abolish the practice. Among his actions, he visited Calcutta cremation grounds to persuade widows not to die so. He also formed watch groups to do the same, and wrote and disseminated articles to show that it was never required by scripture. On 4th December, 1829, the practice was formally banned in the Bengal Presidency lands, by the then governor, Lord William Bentinck.

(b) Swami Dayanand Sarswati (Sanitation of Hinduism)[4]

Dayanand Saraswati was one of the most radical socio-religious reformers in the history of India. Swami Dayanand Saraswati was the founder of Arya Samaj and propagated egalitarian approach of the Vedas at a time when widespread casteism was prevalent in the society. He gave new interpretations to reform the stagnant Hindu thought through his book "Satyaprakash" (The Light of Truth). He profusely quoted the vedas and other religious texts to insist that salvation was not the only motto of a Hindu or Arya, as was believed. To lead a fruitful worldly life, working for a noble cause was important, and he preached that salvation was possible through social service. In the sense, Swami Dayanand meant that Hindus should stop practicing beliefs such as idol worship, caste, polytheism, pantheism, untouchability, child marriages, forced widowhood, and many other practices which he felt were wrong. Dayanand was a great supporter of the rights of women in society. He wanted to put women at par with men. He vehemently opposed child marriage.

He argued in favour of women's education as this was not denied to them in the ancient past. He however advocated *Niyoga* system and the idea according to him was neither strange nor immoral. He challenged many of the Hindu orthodoxy if they could justify their belief in these orthodoxy practices.

To summarise, Swami Dayanand condemned the evils like purdah, child marriage and illiteracy among women. Due to these evils women could not participate as equal partners with men in their social life. Swamiji advocated the complete emancipation of women through education. The network of girl's schools throughout the country organised by the Arya Samaj was an important and forceful step in that direction. Swamiji also opposed child marriages and wanted the marriage age of girls to be fixed at sixteen. The efforts of Swamiji and other social reformers later on resulted in the Sharda Act regarding fixation of marriage age of boys and girls. In order to save the position of women Dayanand also advocated inter caste marriages. For these reasons he may be considered among those humanists who take birth after centuries to arrest the downward course of human history and to uplift fallen humanity. The movement of Arya Samaj was very strong in North India especially in Punjab and there was social awakening in every sphere and attracted many prominent people.

(c) Ramaswami Naicker (Sanitation of Brahminism)[5]

Naicker was a daring non-conformist. Iconoclast, atheist, social reformer and educator, he propagated rationalist thinking. Equating poverty with race, and race with caste, he founded the Dravidian movement to fight Aryan "domination" which to him was synonymous with Brahmin domination and Brahminism. His anti-Brahmin movement had elements of Jyotiba Phule's *satyashodhak* movement in Maharashtra and also secessionist content. Even after Independence, Naicker's movement continued to represent the strong Tamil reaction to Brahminism as also the assertion of the Tamil identity *vis-a-vis* the rest of India. He became the secretary of the TNCC and incurred the wrath of its Brahmin leaders by joining the Vaikom satyagraha for Harijan temple entry in neighbouring Travancore state.

His disenchantment with Gandhi is attributed to the Cheranmahadevi incident. An ashram in Cheranmahadevi named after Gandhi practised discrimination against non-Brahmins, especially the Harijan children. Naicker's campaign took the form of a crusade against caste-ridden Hinduism, the Brahmin priest was the symbolic target. It was a revolt against the thraldom of ritualistic religion and the hierarchical structures it had built, reminiscent of Robert Ingersoll's (Naicker had rendered him into Tamil). It chose to attack casteism which Hinduism had sanctified. Naicker founded the Tamil journal *Kudiyarasu* (Republic), and later *Paguttarivu* (Commonsense or Discernment) and *Viduthalai* (Liberation). Vidu-*thalai* continues to this day. To the devoutly Hindu leadership of the Justice Party which belonged to the upper non-Brahmin castes, the attack on caste was only a propaganda lever for concessions and privileges from the British. The Justice Party leadership was not anti-religious or anti-Hindu. But Naicker's movement went further, seeking liberation of the non-Brahmin masses from the cultural domination of all upper castes including the Brahmins. The Justice Party secured for the 97 per cent non-Brahmins of the Presidency a negative identity. Naicker sought to give them a positive identity when he described them as Dravidians, on the assumption that all Brahmins were Aryans.

The break-up of the Justice Party became inevitable. At the 1944 Salem conference, it was an all-Tamil body. It split into two, Naicker reorganising the majority wing into the Dravida Kazhagam and the rump continuing to call itself the Justice Party to die later. The Kazhagam had grown during the war years. Naicker's crusade against Brahminism gained new strength. Caste-wise anti-Brahmin, communally anti-Hindu, it was by implication anti-Indian. When Independence was around the comer, Naicker made a futile attempt to get the Muslim League's support for his demand for transfer of power from the British to the Aryans and not the emancipation of the Dravidian masses.

After Independence, the Kazhagam continued to grow. Its campaigns included denigration and smashing of idols, and conduct of weddings without the officiation of the (Brahmin) priest. Such weddings were known as "reform" weddings. In 1953 the Madras High Court held them illegal. Subsequently the Special Marriages Act, 1955, validated them on condition they were registered under the Act. There was a lacuna here. While every reform wedding required registration, Hindu weddings with the officiation of the priest were free from this requirement. Not until the DMK ministry passed a law in I967 was the lacuna removed.

(d) Jotirao Phule (Sanitation of Women and Brahmanism)[6]

"The Indian Renaissance", as it is called, represents the efforts of the first generation of Indian thinkers under colonialism to come to grips with the challenge represented by the West and the seeming backwardness of their own society and culture. With ruthless self-criticism, they sought to lay the ground for a total social transformation, to weld science and rationality to Indian culture, to recreate India.

Phule's thought represented the fulfillment of the renaissance desire for social transformation along revolutionary lines. In sociological terms it makes good sense that he, not the later elite thinkers, from Ranade through Tilak should be seen as the primary renaissance figure. In terms of India, Hindu culture and the caste system rested upon Brahmanism; hence Phule, who aimed for the complete destruction of caste, superstition and inequality within Indian tradition, linked his thought with a movement of opposition to the Brahman elite. "Non-Brahmanism" in India, therefore, represents not simply communalism or a result of British divide-and-rule policies; it traces its origins to the Indian renaissance and represents the first expression of social revolution in India.

He does not reject the idea of dharma but rather attempts to establish a universalistic one. "Sarvajanik Satya Dharma" expresses this concept completely (and the introduction to this book suggests that the appropriate translation might be ("True Religion of the Community"): the moral basis of society had to be centred on truth, or rationality, and it had to be one that unified all men and women as equals rather than fragmenting and dividing them into separate social groups with separate responsibilities and rights (as the traditional idea of dharma did in separating the castes).

The basic concept is used in all Satyashodhak teachings to justify the idea of equality and the assertion that no "middleman" or priest is necessary between man and God. Because of his missionary education and the Christian influence on his thinking, Phule was accused by his orthodox opponents (until the time when it became politically suicidal for them to do so) of having become Christian. One aspect of his rationalism can be seen in the Satyashodhak Samaj with its primary emphasis on "truth-seeking". It is most significant here that the truth seeking was seen as a quest guided by the individual's own reason, and not by the dictates of any religious guru or authoritative text. This was important for the development of the Satyashodhak Samaj in that it left it, in a sense, without any centralised organisational form. This was both its strength and its weakness. The movement spread by individual propagandising efforts.

It is significant that Phule's first practical social reform efforts were involved in aiding the two social groups considered lowest in traditional Brahmanic culture - women and untouchables. He did not do so as a liberal paternalistically concerned for the "uplift" of some lower order of being, but as a radical well aware that a revolution in social relationships had to be founded on community with those most oppressed by the traditional social hierarchy. Untouchables, for example, were seen not as a group unique within India but as the most oppressed section of the masses, part of the original community of the peasants. This is related to Phule's "non-Aryan theory"; it may be noted here that while later non-Brahmans compared untouchability with Negro slavery, Phule in the book "Gulamgiri" considered peasants and untouchables together as a community of the oppressed, suffering under Brahman slavery. Indeed, it may be said to represent a failure of the Satyashodhak movement when later non-Brahmans identified as caste Hindus separate from untouchables, and untouchables under Ambedkar took their separate path to social liberation. In regard to the issue of women's liberation, Phule is one of the very few male social reformers in history who deserve a woman's respect.

(e) Mahatma Gandhi (Sanitation of Lower Caste, Social Evils and Hinduism)

The Gandhian romanticism on scavenging is retrogressive. In one of his articles in *Harijan* (Gandhi, 1934), Gandhi called scavenging 'one of the most honourable occupations'. Gandhi wanted to bring about a change in the attitudes of upper castes towards manual scavengers. He used the euphemism *Harijan*, meaning 'children of god', for manual scavengers. For him, it was not an 'unclean occupation'. The scavenger was like the Brahmin—the latter looked after 'sanitation of the soul', whereas the scavenger, the 'sanitation of the body'. A mother also handled 'dirt' (meaning faeces)—of her child—but then no one called her occupation 'unclean', Gandhi said. In his other article of 1936 (titled 'The Ideal Bhangi', published in *Harijan*), Gandhi thought that the manual scavenger was a sort of 'physician' and a 'warner'; he wrote - My ideal Bhangi [the manual scavenger] would know the quality of night-soil and urine. He would keep a close watch on these and give a timely warning to the individual concerned. Thus he will give a timely notice of the results of his examination of the excreta. That presupposes a scientific knowledge of the requirements of his profession.

Village, for Gandhi was not merely a place where people lived in small settlements working on land. For him, it reflected the essence of Indian civilisation. The Indian village had a design, a way life. He was very unhappy with the nature of changes that the Indian village life had gone through during the British colonial rule. In his views, these changes had impaired the villagers, made them less creative and more dependent on the out-side world.

While he asked for revival of the spirit of traditional village life, he also found many flaws with the actually existing villages, and not all these ills were a consequence of the western/urban influence. Two things that he commented quite frequently upon were the practice of untouchability and a general lack of cleanliness. Compared to the cities, where people were "educated and broad-minded to a little extent at least", untouchability was a more serious problem in the villages, which were "the centres of orthodoxy". While he asked for revival of the spirit of traditional village life, he also found many flaws with the actually existing villages, and not all these ills were a consequence of the western/urban influence. Two things that he commented quite frequently upon were the practice of untouchability and a general lack of cleanliness. Compared to the cities, where people were "educated and broad-minded to a little extent at least", untouchability was a more serious problem in the villages, which were "the centres of orthodoxy". and generally carry on such reforms from within as is possible" [Gandhi 1972:406].[7] The lack of hygiene and sanitation were the other things that all villagers needed to pay attention to. He was often disappointed by the disregard for cleanliness that he observed in most of the villages he visited in different parts of the subcontinent. He also wrote quite extensively on this subject.

His idea of an alternative India is perhaps best spelt-out in one of his pieces published in Harijan in 1942 where he wrote: My idea of village swaraj is that it is completely republic, independent of its neighbours for its own vital wants, and yet interdependent for many others in which dependence is a necessity. Thus every villager's first concern will be to grow its own food crops and cotton for its cloth...Then if there is more land available, it will grow useful money crops, thus excluding ganja, tobacco, opium and the like...Education will be compulsory upto the final basic course. As far as possible every activity will be conducted on the cooperative basis. There will be no castes such as we have today with their graded untouchability...The government of the village will be conducted by a panchayat of five persons annually elected by the adult villagers, male and female, possessing minimum prescribed qualifications. .. To model such a village may be the work of a lifetime. Any lover of true democracy and village life can take up a village, treat it as his world and sole work, and he will find good results... [Gandhi 1979:308-09].[8]

F) Rabindranath Tagore's (Sanitation of Agrarian Society)

Little is known, in particular in the action research world, about Rabindranath Tagore pioneering experiments to promote collective grassroots initiatives in rural West Bengal starting in the 1920s. This, one of the earliest such initiatives recorded anywhere in the world, was motivated by a philosophy of the Human Being, and of national independence and development that also anticipated later-day thinking on self-reliant, participatory development.

In 1890, at the age of thirty, Tagore was assigned by his father the responsibility of running the family estates (zamindari) in the district of Pabna, in the then East Bengal, basing himself in the town of Shilaidaha. Tagore established deep contact with the villagers and village life, and soon started developing ideas and making experiments of self-reliant village development. He advocated, in writing and through his speeches, the formation of one or more village communities (pallishamaj) to take charge of co-operative-based collective self-development. Among other tasks, the co-operatives were to take charge of literacy for all; development of local industries; community health care and recreation; safe drinking water; model farming; collective paddy stores; domestic industry-based work for women; campaigns against drinking of liquor; developing fellow-feeling and solidarity among the villagers; and the collection of demographic, economic and social statistics for every village. The experimentation with self-reliant village development was initiated in three places—Shilaidaha, Kaligram and Sriniketan.

Tagore introduced the system of loans for poor peasants who were traditionally burdened with heavy debt to the village money lenders. In perhaps the hfirst known micro-credit programme for poor peasants in the subcontinent, he introduced a system of lending to them from the estate in Kaligram at low interest rates against a mortgage of their harvests. The harvest was then deposited with the estate from which the loan was to be repaid and the peasants would take the surplus harvest home. There was a provision for writing off the interest if the harvest was poor for any debtor. Unfortunately, this pioneering action research by Tagore in Kaligram got into trouble when underground 'revolutionary' terrorism gained ground and many social activists all over Bengal came under suspicion from the authorities. But at the time, Tagore's basic idea of community self-rule and self-initiatives for village development were miles ahead of development thinking of the time which was oriented towards delivery of development by the authorities.[9]

Tagore never stopped experimenting. In 1922 he founded the Viswa-Bharati university and, as a part of this university, Sriniketan, an action research institution. The motto of Sriniketan was put in a bulletin issued by the centre, containing words like the following:

> . . . we shall do our own work ourselves, we shall not wait upon others to do things for ourselves, self-reliance and cooperative work are the two mantras of our life. We belong to the village and the village belongs to us, our good is in the good of the village. We shall develop our village; this is not the task of any one alone, this is a task for all of us. We are taking charge ourselves of advancement of our agriculture, our industries, our business, our health, our education, our joy, everything. The work included adult and child education; the clearing of jungles and turning them into farming plots and vegetable gardens; road construction; experimentation with cooperative farming; collective paddy stores; livestock production; promotion of cottage industry; malaria eradication by cleaning villages and improving drainage systems; setting up people's health care centres providing cheap medical service and medicines funded by villagers' contributions; welfare work for indigenous people; village socio-economic surveys; tree plantation; research on village economy; and many other such initiatives. The project involved villagers in exploring what they could do together for their economic and social advancement without any pre-designed development agenda. The central concepts in this paradigm of human creativity, self-reliance and collective economic and social action, were the cornerstones of Tagore's own philosophy of nationhood and national development. With this view of the mission of the human being, Tagore saw the meaning of India's independence struggle as one to fundamentally liberate the creative energies of its people. *Atmoshakti* (*atmo* = self; *shakti* = strength) as he called this energy,

was a foundational concept in Tagore's developmental thinking. He wanted to see fulfillment of people's *atmoshakti* in the realisation of their material, cultural and spiritual aspirations, and was fervently against waiting upon and demanding deliverance of any need of the people by external agencies, including the government, whether it be people's own or foreign.[10] Tagore's deep concern for universal literacy saw literacy first and foremost as a means of uniting people by giving them a means of communicating and linking with each other. As he observed:

. . . What is primary is that literacy is a road for travel of the minds of the people to each others' minds for interaction with each other, and thereby find the greater humanity within oneself and oneself within greater humanity. It is of the first importance that people see a connection between themselves. If it cannot be a big avenue it should at least be a lane. Literacy is that lane. Without this lane people are confined in their respective corners. They are unable to realise that one is not alone, one's connection with others is not merely a mystic connection, and it is a great living connection.[11]

The initiative spread in a number of villages. Adult education centres—including some night schools—grew in a number of villages where not only literacy but *baul* and *kirtan* singing (traditional folk singing styles), story telling from the mythical classics, and lectures and discussions on health care and other essential subjects were also a regular feature. In several villages a number of health cooperatives as well as general village development societies were formed. Bulletins on social education were printed and distributed as a regular feature.[12]

(g) Jawahar Lal Nehru (Sanitation of Traditionalism)

Nehru put planning on the national agenda as the only available instrument for alleviating the poverty of the Indian masses. To him, freedom for a nation and a people may be, and is, I believe, always good in the long run; but in the final analysis freedom itself is a means to an end, that end being the raising of the people in question to higher levels and hence the general advancement of humanity. The vital and most important problem that faces us in India is the appalling poverty of the people. Will political independence help us to diminish this, as well as the numerous ills that flow from it?

He pointed out that in India we still have grinding poverty, widespread illiteracy, a general absence of sanitation and medical relief—a lack, indeed, or all the good things of life. The real problems of India, as of the rest of the world, are economic, and they are so interrelated that it is hardly possible to tackle them separately. The land problem is the outstanding question of India and any final solution of it is difficult to see without revolutionary changes in our agriculture and land system. Feudal relics and the big land lord system are hindrances to development and will have to go. The tiny holdings, averaging a fraction of an acre per person, are uneconomic and wasteful and too small for the application of scientific methods of agriculture. Large-scale state and collective or cooperative farms must be established instead, and this cannot be done so long as the vested interests in land are not removed. Even when this has been done the vast urban and rural unemployment will not be reduced. For that as well as for other obvious reasons we must push forward the industrialisation of the country. This again requires the development of social services—education, sanitation, etc. And so the problem becomes a vast and many-sided one affecting land, industry and all departments of life, and we see that it can be tackled only on a nationally planned basis without vested interests to obstruct the planning. Therefore many of us think that a socialist structure is necessary, that in no other way can such planning be organised and pushed through.

The whole history of India for thousands of years past shows her essential unity and the vitality and adaptability of her culture. Behind this cultural unity, and giving strength to it, was the ceaseless attempt to find a harmony between the inner man and his outer environment. To him, this past record of Indian cultural solidarity does not necessarily help us today. It is present conditions that we have to deal with, and memories of what has been may be of little avail. But though that is perfectly true, yet an ancient people have deep roots in the past and we cannot ignore them. Both the good and the bad that we possess have sprung from those roots; they give us strength and inspiration; they also burden us and tie us down to many a harmful tradition and evil practice. What was the dynamic became more and more static. The rationalism and the scientific basis of her thought continued for a favoured few, but for others irrationalism and superstition held sway. Caste, which was a division of society by occupation, and which at the start was far from rigid, developed a fearful rigidity and became the citadel of social reaction and a basis for the exploitation of the masses.

As of old, India seeks a synthesis of the past and the present, of the old and the new. She sees the new industrial civilisation marching irresistibly on; she distrusts it and dislikes it to some extent, for it is an attack against and an upheaval of so much that is old; yet she has accepted that industrial civilisation as an inevitable development. So she seeks to synthesise it with her own fundamental conceptions, to find a harmony between the inner man and his ever-changing outer environment.[13]

To him, science has dominated the western world and everyone there pays tribute to it, and yet the west is still far from having developed the real temper of science. It has still to bring the spirit and the flesh into creative harmony. In India in many obvious ways we have a greater distance to travel. And yet there may be fewer major obstructions on our way, for the essential basis of Indian thought for ages past, though not its later manifestations, fits in with the scientific temper and approach, as well as with inter-nationalism. It is based on a fearless search for truth, on the solidarity of man, even on the divinity of everything living, and on the free and co-operative development of the individual and the species, ever to greater freedom and higher stages of human growth.

He says, we have therefore to function in line with the highest ideals of the age we live in, though we may add to them or seek to mould them in accordance with our national genius. Those ideals may be classed under two heads: humanism and the scientific spirit. Between these two there has been an apparent conflict but the great upheaval of thought today, with its questioning of all values, is removing the old boundaries between these two approaches, as well as between the external world of science and the internal world of introspection. There is a growing synthesis between humanism and the scientific spirit, resulting in a kind of scientific humanism. Science also, while holding on to fact, is on the verge of other domains, or at any rate, has ceased to deny them contemptuously.

In our individual lives also we have to discover a balance between the body and the spirit, and between man as part of nature and man as part of society. 'For our perfection,' says Tagore, 'we have to be vitally savage and mentally civilised; we should have the gift to be natural with nature and human with human society.' Perfection is beyond us for it means the end, and we are always journeying, trying to approach something that is ever receding. And in each one of us are many different human beings with their inconsistencies and contradictions, each pulling in a different direction.

At this juncture, Science does not tell us much, or for the matter of that anything about the purpose of life. It is now widening its boundaries and it may invade the so-called invisible world before long and help us to understand this purpose of life in its widest sense, or at least give us some glimpses which illumine the problem of human existence. The old controversy between science and religion takes a new form—the application of the scientific method to emotional and religious experiences.[14]

Urban life, Nehru felt, produces an "unstable society which gradually loses its vitality." "Divorce from the soil, from the good earth, is bad for the individual and the race." Later, Jawaharlal Nehru's philosophy and vision shaped—the tribal policy in the 1950s, particularly in the North-East. That they should be- "engulfed by the masses of Indian humanity" was a prospect that appalled Nehru. Gradually and towards the close of the 1950s, outlines of a policy emerged.

- People should develop along the lines of their own genius and we should avoid imposing anything on them. We should try to encourage in every way their own traditional arts and culture.
- Tribal rights in land and forests should be respected. We should not over-administer these areas or overwhelm them with a multiplicity of schemes. We should rather work through, and not in rivalry to, their own social and cultural institutions.
- We should judge results, not by statistics or the amount of money spent, but by the quality of human character that is evolved.[15]

(h) B.R. Ambedkar (Sanitation of Lower Caste and Hindu Social Order)

Dr Ambedkar's life constituted a proof and ideal for the suppressed caste in India. That is, if a person is determined to succeed, no caste or class barrier can stop him. Dr Ambedkar tackled the caste barrier and sprung forth from the dust. He rose from a family whose forefathers for generations were treated worse than animals, whose touch was taken to be polluting and whose shadow unsuspicious.

Ambedkar achieved what was virtually impossible for his people to achieve. He obtained what was beyond the dream of his community. Taking a vow of ridding untouchability and inhuman injustice, he rebelled against Manu, Ancient India's lawmaker, the supporter of the caste system, and dethroned him. Ambedkar insured by his efforts that untouchability was abolished in the Constitution of Independent India. This was a victory unparalleled in the history of India. This 'modern Manu,' by being a savior of the oppressed, made an impression on time. The vow was fulfilled; the dream was realised. Moulding the lives of eighty million people, he left a print in the history of human freedom.[16]

He was a mahar, the largest untouchable caste in Maharashtra. His actions, then, according to Zelliot, "were moulded not only by his own personal background, and achievements, and the Maharashtrian thinking of his day, but also by his status as an untouchable". This group he came from had begun social and political movements before he assumed a position of leadership. Behind this identification with a non-brahmin group laid the logic of a movement that was essentially anti-caste and not simply a movement for 'untouchability removal' or 'self-reform'. This is not to say that the Maher movement in the later 19th century was an isolated movement but only to suggest that all these influences constantly streaming in are employed by Ambedkar in a new sense and directed towards a new solution.

Ambedkar realised that the identification of Indian culture with Hinduism is incorrect. Because he believed that absorption into Hinduism meant the acceptance of Hindu leadership in the national movement, he felt it would be wiser to take chances with a religion which has many safeguards. At first, he tried to assert the path of radical autonomy, encouraged the dalits to form their own organisations and to deal independently with some basic; issues. It means that the dalits themselves, "would have to redefine and reconstitute their relations with the whole of Hindu society". But if the dalits were not Hindus, what were they? In fact, a non-Hindu choice seems to have led him finally, to identify with Buddhism. At the theoretical level, Ambedkar's language turned out to be singularly open to misconstrue. It was not easy for many to accept the Indian National Congress, social reform organisations and the Hindu Mahasabha as irreconcilable opponents of the dalits; neither was it easy to accept the praise accordled by Ambedkar to the British state for raising the status of untouchables. Even more open to misunderstanding was Ambedkar's critique of nationalism: whereas Ambedkar attacked the Congress for their failure to recognise caste issues, he was erroneously taken to reject nationalism altogether.[17]

While undertaking a study of the scheduled castes, it is necessary to throw light on the role of Ambedkar and his movement and its consequences on various aspects of the life of these people. Ambedkar appeared as the leader of the untouchables in Maharashtra by 1920. He was the first highly educated and active leader from within the community. He represented all the sufferings through his own bitter experiences of untouchability. His philosophy was such as would facilitate the social revolution in India. He was perhaps, the only leader born among the scheduled caste people, the only leader born among the scheduled caste people, who tried to unite the untouchables and created a semblance of accord. In 1924, he formed "Bahiskrit Hitkarini Sabha", an educational and cultural organisation which aimed at improving the social conditions of the untouchables. The work of this organisation continued for many years even though Ambedkar founded the "Scheduled Caste Federation" and taught this castemen to struggle for their rights. The Federation, however, could not become a powerful organisation throughout the country mainly because of lack of resources and machinery necessary for making the organisation strong and powerful. However, it is sure that the efforts of Ambedkar were necessarily responsible for this mass awakening but it was also indirectly produced by other movements directed against the British rule. The hidden social discrimination, however, which has its origin in the traditions and upbringing of the Indian people still remains and will only change when attitudes change.

Dr. Ambedkar organised a Satyagraha for the use of public lake at Mahad in Maharashtra in 1927 which was free to Muslims, Christians and 'the animals'. With his 10,000 followers, Ambedkar was finally successful in this democratic Satyagraha and won the case in the court. In the following years 1929-30, the temple entry campaign at Kalaram Mandir, Nashik and Parvati temple at Pune was launched. He could not succeed there due to strong opposition by caste Hindus. Although Gandhi objected to the use of Satyagraha (his own weapon) against fellow countrymen, he supported the aims of the temple entry campaign and asked all temples to throw open their doors to untouchables but this powerful plea of Gandhi proved to be a very damp squid since hardly anyone heeded his request. In 1928, when Simon Commission came to India to examine and report on the government system the Congress Party boycotted it but Ambedkar used the opportunity to explain the grievances of the depressed classes and suggested ways of improving their position, e.g., by having cabinet post and seats in the legislature reserved for them. In spite of Ambedkar's strong plea, the Simon Commission Report (1930) rejected this demand. It awarded separate electorates to the Sikhs, Muslims and Christians, but included the depressed classes (the term was then commonly used for scheduled castes) with the Hindus.

Ambedkar then represented the 'untouchables' cause at the Prime Minister's Round Table Conference in London in 1930. He used the conference as a platform for influencing public opinion in India. The Second Round Table Conference (1931) was very important. Ambedkar stood up to the emotional, political and spiritual pressures of Gandhi. He confronted Gandhi, who not only refused to consider a separate electorate for the depressed classes but also opposed any form of special representation involving reserved seats. After the Round Table Conference, during which period Gandhi was in jail, the British government announced a decision regarding representation of untouchables with a separate electorate which, it was hoped, would effect a compromise between the Congress and Ambedkar. Gandhi's response to this event was to enter a 'fast unto death' on September 20, 1932, which resulted in what is known as the 'Poona Pact'.

The Poona Pact in itself accomplished little more than might have emerged from an earlier compromise, but the dramatic circumstances in which it was forged gave a great deal of publicity to Gandhi's concern for the untouchables and to Ambedkar's leadership. Gandhi sought to change the heart of the caste Hindus by moral pressure within the framework of Hindu tradition. Ambedkar continued to work in the fields of education politics in and attempt to gain legal rights for the untouchables in the secular world.

In order to prepare for the elections to the provincial legislatures, under the Government of India Act of 1935, Ambedkar was preparing his people for a change in his strategy of struggle. In order to prepare for the elections to the provincial legislatures, under the Government of India Act of 1935, on all-India basis, Ambedkar formed the Independent Labour Party to guard the interests of the depressed classes. At the Yeola (Nashik district of Maharashtra) Conference on October 13, 1935, he announced his decision to leave Hinduism and join some other religion. His book *Annihilation of Caste* puts forward the various reasons why he rejected Hinduism. He believed that Hinduism was based on the caste system, and the real method of breaking up the caste system is "to destroy the religious notions on which caste system is founded'. In a speech which Ambedkar made on 18 March, 1955, he outlined three objects of his life. (1) to spread education, (2) to give more representation to the untouchables, and (3) to improve the condition of untouchables in villages.

The masses, especially in Maharashtra, were highly motivated and his leadership could make them conscious about their social and political rights. The influence of his movement could reach the villages especially through the organisation like '*Samata Sainik Dal*'. It is formed at national, state, regional and district levels. The role of the organisation was to make people aware of injustice and to prepare them to give up their traditional occupations. The organisation also played the role of propagation education and Buddhism. At the same time, Ambedkar also started Marathi newspapers like *Muknayak*, *Bahiskrit Bharat*, *Prabuddha bharat* and *Janatas*, etc., and propagated his philosophy of social and political equality.

Apart from Ambedkar's persistent and consistent efforts to improve the position of the scheduled castes in Maharashtra and other regions, several other social reformers from the high castes also took up their cause. In the 19th century, the most important social reformer before Ambedkar was Phuley. He openly came out against untouchability and propagated education for untouchables, women and the downtrodden by starting a school for these people. He carried out his movement for social equality and non-Brahmnic philosophy. He founded "Satya Shodhak Samaj" (society in search of truth) in Maharashtra in 1873. Phuley pleaded compulsory free education for untouchables before the Hunter Commission in 1884. After Phuley social reformers like Vishu Buva Brahmachari, Lokhitwadi, G.G. Agarkar, Vithal Ramji Shinde, Dhondo Keshav Karve were some outstanding social reformers.

After independence Ambedkar was the first Law Minister of free India. He was also the Chairman of the Drafting Committee of the Indian Constitution. He did his best for the betterment of the untouchables by providing a focus on their problems and thus attracting the attention of eminent political leaders and social reformers of India.

Locating Ambedkar's vision of social justice one finds that he pleaded for 'just society' and 'casteless society' having the element of liberty, equality and fraternity. His attitude towards justice was humanistic as well as nationalistic. The basic premise of social justice thus remains to be the emancipation of the underprivileged, exploited and oppressed section of the society and a guarantee for their freedom and mobility. He emphasised that the freedom of mind is the real freedom and a proof of one's existence.

One centrally pervading theme of the writings of Dr. B.R. Ambedkar was the attainment of 'social justice' and the establishment of a 'Just Society'. He not only provided a ruthless criticism of the existing social order but also came up with an alternative vision and alternative model of social order based on justice, liberty, equality, fraternity and annihilation of caste. Ambedkar was convinced that for ensuring social justice, it was essential to demolish Chaturnavarna system (See Ambedkar, 1987).

He was the architect of the present reservation policy, and can be considered a pioneer who introduced the concept of a reservation policy at the all India level in early 1930. In fact, the articulation and systematic framing of various types of remedies against discrimination including reservation/affirmative action policies for discriminated groups, internationally emerged only during the 1950's and 1960's, and since Ambedkar developed a framework for such policies and got them implemented as early as 1930's (Poona Pact). He thus could be considered a pioneer of inclusive policies in the world (Thorat and Narendra kumar: 2008; 2).

Isolation and exclusion of Untouchables is a unique feature of the Hindu social order. Denial of equal access to education is another core feature of the caste system. In Ambedkar's view, the concept of formal education in the Hindu social order was quiet narrow. Formal education was confined to the study of the Vedas. Thus, for Ambedkar, understanding the nature of the institution of caste and untouchability were essential for recognising the consequences for the excluded groups. He believed, in its classical form the caste system involved in it social, economic, cultural and political frameworks of governance of Hindu society. The caste system also draws justification from some elements of Hindu religious philosophy. It is not so much the existence of classes or segmentation, rather the idea of isolation and exclusiveness, which is inimical to a free social order.

To put it in brief, Ambedkar's interpretation of the Hindu social order as a system of governance in general, and a system of productive organisation and distribution in particular is based on three interrelated elements. These included fixed rights, unequal and hierarchical division of social and economic rights across castes, and provision of strong instruments of social and economic ostracisation to sustain the rigid system with a philosophical justification in Hindu religion. To him, the religious intervention in social and economic sphere, however, was not positive in nature such that it promoted or facilitated social and economic justice. Unfortunately, Hindu social philosophy as a form of social governance of human society, far from promoting just order, promoted the opposite. He expresses that caste cannot be abolished by inter caste dinners or stray instances of inter caste marriages. Caste is a state of mind. It is a disease of mind. The teachings of the Hindu religion are the root cause of this disease. We practice casteism and we observe untouchability because we are enjoined to so by the Hindu religion. My religious conversion is not inspired by any material motive. This is hardly anything I cannot achieve even while remaining an Untouchable. There is no other feeling than that of a spiritual feeling underlying my religious conversion. Hinduism does not appeal to my conscience. My self-respect cannot assimilate Hinduism.

Ambedkar's efforts towards sanitation of Hinduism:

- "Freedom of mind is the real freedom. A person whose mind is not free though he may not be in chains, is a slave, not a free man. One whose mind is not free, though he may not be in prison, is a prisoner and not a free man. One whose mind is not free though alive, is no better than dead. Freedom of mind is the proof of one's existence."
- "His social philosophy may be said to be enshrined in three words: liberty, equality and fraternity."
- "Democracy is not merely a form of Government. It is primarily a mode of associated living, of conjoint communicated experience. It is essentially an attitude of respect and reverence towards our fellow men."
- "Caste cannot be abolished by inter caste dinners or stray instances of inter caste marriages. Caste is a state of mind. It is a disease of mind. The teachings of the Hindu religion are the root cause of this disease. We practice casteism and we observe untouchability because we are enjoined to so by the Hindu religion. My religious conversion is not inspired by any material motive. This is hardly anything I cannot achieve even while remaining an Untouchable. There is no other feeling than that of a spiritual feeling underlying my religious conversion. Hinduism does not appeal to my conscience. My self-respect cannot assimilate Hinduism"

Ambedkar's efforts towards sanitation of women against social evils: Ambedkar's effort towards upliftment of women can be gauged through the famous statement by him as "I measure the progress of a community by the degree of progress which women have achieved". His basic idea towards subordinate group was—"Learn to live in this world with self-respect. You should always cherish some ambition of doing something in this world. But remember that the age of selflessness has ended. A new epoch is set in. All things are now possible because of your being able to participate in the politics and legislature of your country".

Dr. Ambedkar the revolutionary of 20th century has played a vital role in securing the basic human rights for the women in general and *Mulnivasi* women in particular. Dr. Ambedkar continued the pioneering work of Mahatma Jyotiba Phule and his wife. Right from the beginning of his struggle for the eradication of caste prejudices, he started involving women in the struggle. He realised that the real progress of the *mulnivasi* could not be achieved without liberating the women themselves. He started motivating the women. His first demand of adult franchise, which was met in the early 20s after resistance from the brahmins, gave voting rights to untouchables as well as to women. That was the beginning of an era of liberation for women. (Omvedt; 2011)

Dr. Ambedkar then brought women, the mulnivasi women in particular into the struggle. In December 1927 during the Mahad Tank struggle, on the first day (of the second leg) when the procession was taken out, women marched in the procession along with men. Second day, Dr. Ambedkar exclusively addressed women. He told them to participate in the struggle against the tyranny of caste system. He emphasised to them that men alone cannot fight this menace. The main theme of his speech was "Importance of participation of women in the struggle of depressed." He also wanted to prepare the women for a cultural change. He told them to change their style of dressing, to do away with unwanted ornaments, which they used to wear all the time and told them to send their girls to school, keep cleanliness etc.

The 1930s saw the organisation of independent meetings and conferences by dalit women in the Ambedkarite movement. This was an obvious consequence of Ambedkar's practice of organising a women's conference along with every general meeting and Sabha that he called. In these 'parishads' of the 1930s, dalit women delegates passed resolutions against child marriage, enforced widowhood and dowry; critiquing these practices as brahmanical. Women's participation in the Mahad Satyagraha, their support to the Independent Labour Party and the Schedule Caste Federation have been well documented [Moon and Pawar 1989: Amiihihi Itihaas Ghadtawila: Anibedakari Chalvalitil Streevancha Sahabhag, Stree, Mumbai]. Women in large numbers supported Dharmantaar as a need for a religion that would recognise their equal status. Women's participation in the Ambedkarite movement must be read in the context of the fact that in Ambedkar's theory of caste there is also a theory of the origins of sub-ordination of women and that he saw the two issues as intrinsically linked.

He argues that "the absence of intermarriage or endogamy is the one characteristic that can be called the essence of castes" (Ambedkar 1992). Thus it is the superimposition of endogamy on exogamy and the means used for the same that hold the key to the understanding of the caste system. Ambedkar then draws up a detailed analysis of how numerical equality between the marriageable units of the two sexes within the group is maintained. Thus he argues that practices of sati, enforced widowhood and child marriage come to be prescribed by brahmanism in order to regulate and control any transgression of boundaries, i.e., to say he underlines the fact that the caste system can be maintained only through the controls on women's sexuality and in this sense women are the gateways to the caste system [Ambedkar 1992:90]. In his speech at the gathering of women at the Mahad satyagraha, he draws linkages between caste exploitation and women's sub-ordination by underlining this; calls upon women to contest the claims of upper caste women's progeny to purity and the damnation of that of the lower caste to impurity.

Dr. Ambedkar was an ardent supporter of family planning. He emphasised the need of family planning way back in 1938. At that time nobody even dreamt of it. He even criticised his own parents in public speeches because he himself was the 14th child in the family. This showed his concern for the well being of the women.

Dr. Ambedkar had also been encouraging women to organise themselves. One such historic women's conference was held on 20 July, 1942 at Nagpur. Some 25,000 *mulnivasi* women participated in the conference. Dr. Babasaheb Ambedkar was highly impressed by the large gathering. In his speech he told the women to be progressive and told them to abolish traditionalism, ritualism and customary habits, which were detrimental to their progress. He also advised them not to indulge in early marriages, not to infuse inferiority complex among the children.

Efforts towards social inclusion and justice for the marginalised:

1. It was in 1919 that Ambedkar for the first time submitted a statement to the Southborough Committee, demands of the Untouchables in the political sphere in the legislative Council.
2. In 1928, he submitted a memorandum to the Simon Commission to safeguard the interest of Depressed Classes. Later, appearing at the Round Table Conference in 1930-32, he once again demanded social and political safeguards to protect the interests of excluded groups.
3. Ambedkar presented a memorandum on the safeguards of SCs to the Constituent Assembly on behalf of the All India Scheduled Castes Federation in 1946. It meant for the protection of common citizenry, and attempted to establish social democracy and state socialism.
4. On a debate of the report of the commissioner for SCs/ST 1953, Ambedkar commented comprehensively on the functioning of the safeguards for these sections in the Republican India. He maintained that as the government has not taken land into its

own hands and created land proprietors. Hence, it could not take away land and distribute equally among the masses. Therefore, the only way out was to amend the constitution and put the cultivation of wasteland within the purview of the central government so that it was utilised for the benefit of the landless.

Various interventions by Ambedkar during 1919-54 capture his understanding about the problem of deprived castes. He reiterated his position that the problems of untouchables are rooted in the historical denial of basic human rights. So the remedies against discrimination were placed with the framework of citizenship rights. He addressed the problems of 'structural inequalities' and suggested following policies for social inclusion and justice:

1. Claim for equal rights: Ambedkar demanded political representation, however, he started with a claim for equal rights to the untouchables that he called 'citizenship rights'.
2. Measures for equal opportunity and participation
3. Policies for empowerment to compensate for historical inclusion and denial of equal rights like to resources, education and employment (See Ambedkar, 1987; 1989; 1992).

To understand philosophical and liberating ideas of Dr. Ambedkar towards building an inclusive society—a society that overrides man-made differences and ensures inclusion in the restricted areas enshrining equality of opportunity as well as opportunity among the members of the society— which is essential for healthy nation and democratic principles. According to Ambedkar, democracy is not merely a form of Government. It is primarily a mode of associated living, of conjoint communicated experience. It is essentially an attitude of respect and reverence towards our fellow men."

(j) Ram Manohar Lohia (Sanitation of Social Ideology)

Lohia was an exceptionally talented person. He had mastered different schools of social and political doctrines. He was deeply influenced by thinkers of the West. Prominent among them was Karl Marx. Gandhis' concept of Satyagraha had made a strong impact on India. He advocated the realisation of socialist ideals through Satyagraha.

A woman is not considered equal to a man, such is the blind belief sustained through the ages. The law has guaranteed equality to women, but that is only on paper. Equality has not been practiced. Hence jobs must be reserved for women in all walks of life. They must be freed from the tyranny of homework. The latent talent of women should be brought to the limelight. Society does not progress as long as women remain oppressed. Society must be rid of deep-rooted beliefs and old practices. Beginning with women in villages every woman should be given justice.

Rammanohar Lohia was a fearless and dynamic freedom fighter, an outstanding socialist, an eminent parliamentarian, an exponent of new theories of Marxism and above all a leader of the masses who made immense contributions in the development of progressive thought and the spirit of nationalism during the freedom struggle. Having wholeheartedly accepted Gandhi's model of non-violent means to achieve political transition, Lohia was already heading towards further rationalisation of his socialist ideology into a renascent philosophy aimed at the humanisation of every dimension of modern knowledge, science and technology to ensure their welfarist application and thereby complete elimination of any kind of their brutal application.

Dr. Lohia summed up the essence of the great struggles in which humanity was engaged in the middle of the twentieth century, and of which he and the Socialist Party he had helped to create, were a part. The Seven Revolutions, as he called them, were: (1) for equality between man and woman; (2) against political, economic and spiritual inequality based on skin colour; (3) against inequality between backward and high groups or castes based on long tradition, and for giving special opportunities to the backwards; (4) against foreign enslavement and for freedom and world democratic rule; (5) for economic equality and planned production and against the existence of and attachment for private capital; (6) against unjust encroachments on private life and for democratic methods; (7) against weapons and for satyagrah.

Lohia used to speak about linking religion and politics. He spoke of path (way), pathik (wayfarer), dharma (the right way), adharma (the wrong way), sadhana (means), and sadhya (end). He was of the view that the crisis of the twentieth century was a cultural one. Lohia wanted to bring about a Cultural Revolution in the country". While Lohia agrees that the purpose of human endeavour is peace and happiness, his definition of happiness is not having a hoard of possessions or riches but the self-esteem of healthy values, doing hard work for oneself, family and society and living a simple but decent life. Further, the practices like individual freedom, religious faith, and choice of work or profession enhances the extent of happiness. Without these values and practices, any economic prosperity will result in a soulless joy of living and all cultural education imparted largely by the elderly people and by some social institutions will have taught nothing of significance. This is one dimension of happiness. There is another dimension viz. the social context of happiness.

)k) Kanshi Ram (Sanitation of 'Bahujan)

He was the eldest of eight siblings. He belonged to the Ramdassia (Ad Dharmi/*Mulnivasi*) community of the Scheduled Caste group, which is the largest group in Punjab. His upbringing was modest. During his education years there was nothing special about him to suggest that he would mature into great social revolutionary. It was only after he took up a government job in the western Indian state of Maharashtra that he began to be influenced by the writings and life of Baba Sahib Dr. Bhimrao Ramji Ambedkar who voiced the concerns of India's low caste community and worked hard throughout his life for their empowerment.

He devised a new strategy to regain the lost glory of the original (Adi) inhabitants of Bharat (India). He gave utmost importance to the culture of work and democratic method of struggle. He also expanded the circle of the Dalits by incorporating other Backward Classes and Minorities into it. He advocated Dalits should become rulers instead of being ruled. We must not be always at the receiving end, instead become the givers, Dalit Leader Mr. Kanshi Ram told the world dalits. Its long we have been ruled. It is long we have been taking. Now it is time we change the destiny to rule and give, he said. Mr. Kanshi Ram who is the Founder President of Bahujan Samaj Party delivered a key-note address at the opening of the 1st World Dalit Convention 'A new vision towards a casteless society' at the Kuala Lumpur Mines Resort City.[18]

According to Mr. Kanshi Ram, slum dwellers presently living in urban areas are the Dalit refugees who have migrated from the villages because of acrimony's and atrocities committed by upper case Hindus. They have not been able to influence the Planning Commission and the Government of India to allocate separate budget to provide them bread, clothes and shelter. A decent life is a matter of fundamental right of every citizen in accordance with the constitutional mandate, Mr. Kanshi Ram asserted. He advocated separate settlement for dalit people as once formulated by Dr. Babasaheb Ambedkar. He was very critical of the evil impact of caste-system in India.

Thus, from the day of launching D-S4, an agitational and awakening wing of BAMCEF, till the formation of Bahujan Samaj Party, on 14th April, 1984, Kanshi Ram conducted several experiments of social action countrywide successfully. The programmes created sufficient awareness in the Bahujan Samaj about their socio - political, economic and cultural status. Hence, D-S4 proved as a milestone preparation for the long battle of political action, social transformation and economic emancipation.

With a span of three years Kanshi Ram transformed the DS-4 into a full-fledged political party, the BSP, launched on Ambedkar's birthday with a slogan *'vote hamara, raj tumhara; nahi chalega, nahi chalega'*. The goal was based on an Ambedkarian dictum that political power was the key to all problems. The trend of fragmentation of politics through the assertion of the regional bourgeoisie in the 1970s that precipitated in the Emergency and in whose aftermath a wide coalition was ushered into power at the centre provided a congenial political climate for the BSP's strategy of exercising a lever for the balance of power. In elections, when even the mainstream parties could not muster courage to contest all the seats, the strategist in Kanshi Ram decided to do so, not to win them but to cause the defeat of and weaken the mainstream parties. This strategy resulted in rout of the Congress Party in different elections in Uttar Pradesh. The concept of a 'majboor sarkar' (dependent government) in place of everybody's claim to provide a 'majboot sarkar' (strong government) proved a stroke of genius in forcing the mainstream parties to beg support of the BSP. It is this strategy that lent it the requisite bargaining power to grab government power in UP repeatedly.

The unitary control was ensured not only in structural matters but also in all others. Kanshi Ram never promised anything or spoke of any plans, programmes or published any election manifesto. He was acutely aware that any such thing would constrict his strategic space. Purely, in terms of electoral politics, which has somehow become a major obsession with all the dalit parties, Kanshi Ram's strategy proved quite effective, albeit in only certain parts of the country. He gave a qualitative impetus to moribund dalit politics, locating itself in the wider space peopled by the downtrodden. But he identified these people in terms of their castes and communities. Notwithstanding the fact that the bahujan identity as coined by him is really a contradiction in terms, many people had believed in it but none knew how to gear it into action. Kanshi Ram seemingly succeeded in this task, at least in symbolic terms.[19]

Prevalence of Specific Social Reform Movements and Dalit Mobilisation in Contemporary Setting

Dalit Movement can be called as a collective agitation of Dalits against the exploitation both in the form of class, caste, creed, cultural and social exploitation in the society. This exploitation is due to the discrimination followed by age old caste hierarchical tradition in the Hindu Society. This hierarchy has been the cause for oppression of dalits in each and every sphere of society since centuries. It has subjected the Dalits to poverty and humiliation. Dalit movement is a struggle that tries to counter attack the socio—cultural hegemony of the upper castes. It is a movement of the masses that craves for justice through the speeches, literary works, dramas, songs, cultural organisations and all the other possible measurers. So it can be called as a movement which has been led by Dalits to seek equality with all other castes of the Hindu society.

It is indeed impossible to understand the contemporary Dalit revolt without understanding the ideas of Dr Bhimrao Ramji Ambedkar. (1891–1956). For a growing number of young Dalits across India, many born after his death in 1956, he has become a symbol of a vision that can be achieved, a vision of freedom from social and economic injustice. Ambedkar attacked two central features of the Indian order: culturally enforced inequality and economic inequality. Throughout his writings and actions there is one common thread, namely, that socio-economic transformation in India requires a cultural revolution, one that will not only destroy the culture of the past but also build something of value in its place. Ambedkar was a revolutionary who led the fight against untouchability, Hinduism and the Brahmin caste. He was convinced that the caste system was not only unjust but also immoral. He established a new dispensation, a new religion (neo-Buddhism) whose foundation is its unequivocal rejection of Hinduism.

Similarly, E.V. Ramaswamy Naicker (1879–1973), known as Periyar (great sage), too gained an intimate knowledge of the evils of popular Hinduism and also of the exploitation of the masses by Brahmin priests. Periyar became convinced that casteism and Hinduism were one and the same. He wanted Hinduism, as he saw it, to go altogether. His movement took a turn towards racial consciousness and became a 'Dravidian' movement, seeking to defend the rights of the Dravidians against Aryan domination. It blamed the Aryans for introducing an unjust and oppressive social system in the country. Naicker quit the Congress and attacked it as a tool of Brahmin domination. In 1925, he organised the 'Self-Respect Movement'.

In the history of Karnataka, it was in the first time, in 12th century Basavanna raised his voice against caste discrimination in the northern part of Karnataka state. This social reform movement led by Basvanna in 12th century A.D. gave rise to a new kind of writing in Kannada literature. It is named as "Vachana Sahitya". After this, a non- Brahmin movement took place in the old Mysore state in the year 1917. It was led by Vokkaligas and Lingayats of the then Mysore state. Its aim was to uplift the Socio-economical status of non Brahmin castes. This movement was supported by some organisations. They are—The Vokkaliga Sangha set up in 1906 and Central Muslim Association set up in 1909. After these developments among the non Brahminical castes of the then Mysore state

Untouchability in Punjab is unique, as the Brahmanical tradition of social stratification has never taken deep root in the region.[20] The word Brahmin (denoting the highest rank in the Hindu caste hierarchy) did not carry a sacerdotal connotation in Punjab. Mostly concentrated in villages, Jat-Sikhs are primarily agriculturists and landowners and are widely considered to be the backbone of the Punjab peasantry. They have diversified into transport businesses and consider employment in the armed forces highly prestigious. Although all 10 of the historic Sikh Gurus belonged to the Khatri caste, traditionally the majority of their followers have come from the Jat-Sikhs. Critically, Dalit Sikhs do not receive equal treatment in upper-caste *gurdwaras,* as reflected in a number of *gurmatas* (resolutions) adopted by the Shiromani Gurdwara Prabhandak Committee from 1926-33. Although removal of untouchability figured in the Singh Sabha movement (started in 1873 in Amritsar, Punjab, for the revitalisation of Sikhism. The movement subsequently came to be dominated by a more radical faction that emerged in Lahore in 1879), no concrete effort was made in that direction.

Ad Dharm Movement and Dalit Consciousness in Punjab: Although the abolition of untouchability was on the agenda of various social reform movements in the 1920s (Arya Samaj, Chief Khalsa Diwan, and Singh Sabha), the most virulent opposition to caste came from the Adi movements, including the Ad Dharm movement in Punjab. This effort drew inspiration from the Bhakti movement, especially from the Dalit poet-saints Ravidass, Kabir, and Namdev, and uniquely assailed the structures of social domination. The Ad Dharm movement distinguished itself from Adi movements in other parts of the country because it was reacting to the unique situation in Punjab, where untouchability related more to prejudice than pollution. Ad Dharm was the only movement in northwestern India that aimed at securing a respectable place for the SCs through cultural transformation, spiritual regeneration, and political assertion, rather than seeking patronage from above.

In the 1931 census, the Ad Dharm movement succeeded in persuading 418,789 Untouchables in Punjab to record Ad Dharm as their new religion, separate from Hinduism, Islam, and Sikhism. Since the centre of the Ad Dharm movement was in the Doaba region, nearly 80 per cent of the lower-caste population of Jalandhar and Hoshiarpur Districts reported themselves as Ad Dharmis. This was the first time in the history of the lower castes that they came forward to officially declare themselves separate and different from Hindus, Muslims, and Sikhs. This was, perhaps, the beginning of the Dalit assertion in North India. The movement gained momentum in the 1937 elections, as the Ad Dharm Mandal, a political organisation of the Ad Dharm movement with headquarters in Jalandhar city, challenged in all the reserved constituencies in the state and won all but one seat. In addition to political mobilisation, the Ad Dharm movement brought about cultural transformation in the lives of Untouchables in Punjab through its emphasis on moral principles. Through promoting a moral code of conduct, the movement tried to bring a sense of self-respect to the state's Untouchables. It also attempted to forge unity among the different Untouchable castes by bringing them into the fold of Ad Dharm, which the movement's protagonists considered to be an ancient religion indigenous to the original inhabitants of the region.

Globalisation as a Movement for Sanitation of Weaker Sections

At the outset, to address the broadly defined parameters of globalisation in its singular form, it might be useful to describe it as a historical and geographical condition. The characteristic features of this universal condition can be summarised as follows - Firstly, it means the increased political and military interdependence of a set of sovereign nation-states and the expanded and strengthened set of organisations involved. Secondly, it means the increased economic interdependence of a set of national or sub-national economies and their relevant multilaterality with international public and private organisations. Thirdly, it means an expanded flow of individual persons among societies through socio-economic migration, travel and political expulsion: here 'State' and 'individuals' is the main subject discussed. Fourthly, globalisation means the expanded interdependence of expressive culture through intensified global communication.

To be accurate, let us observe the analysis of prominent social scientist on the issue. According to Giddens (1990: 64) globalisation is the 'intensification of world wide social relations which link distant localities in such a way that local happenings are shaped by events occurring many miles away and vice versa'. However, to Robertson (1992) globalisation has been used in scholarly literature as a catch-all phrase to include an array of processes such as: time-space compression; technological commercial and cultural homogenisation; and a general intensification of the consciousnesses of the world as a whole. In his simple explanation he speaks of globalisation as a process by, which the world is becoming more and more a 'single village'. Similarly, Alberto Martinelli (2003) while defining globalisation conceptualise it as a set of related processes which interconnect individuals, groups, communities, state, market, corporation, international governmental and non-governmental organisations, in complex web of social relations.

In nutshell we may characterise globalisation as—Firstly, economic globalisation defined by both growing structural power and mobility of capital in production and financial markets is articulated with neo-liberal policies of privatisation, de-regulation and structural changes in national bureaucracies, welfare programmes and public services (Gill, 1995). Secondly, economic globalisation, defined by the liberalisation of trade and monetary policies, the growth of trans-national networks of investment, finance, advertising and consumption market as well as rise of trans national networks (Strange, 1995). Thirdly, Conventional institutions as the nation state, national military, police force, political parties, legislatives now faces new challenges posted by this interactive, mobile transnational network (Held, 1991). Fourthly, the rise of regional economic and political bodies as well as supranational bodies introduces new agents into decision- making process with which the conventional centres of political power have to negotiate and contend. Fifth, the growing influence of electronic media into everyday life has the net affect of creating multiple forms of imagined communities. (Anderson, 1992; 13).

Under such diversified ideas of the question of universal and plural manifestation of globalisation, Robertson (1995) rightly argues that the problem is not to choose one or the other, but rather to 'spell out the ways in which homogenising and hetrogenising tendencies are mutually implicative. The condition of globality facilitates the interaction between global and local forces, and it needs to be examined in concrete localities (Robertson, 1995:27). Now it may be clear from the above references that why globalisation should be taken in plural, as it involves a number of substantive social processes and more than one procedural dynamics. In brief, globalisation is multi-form, multi-facet and multi-dimensional process.

(a) 'Globalisation' *vs* 'Scheduled Castes'—The emergent possibilities

Globalisation is a complex phenomenon and is a process by which the world becomes a "global village." Globalisation affects different aspects of any country—economic, political, social, and religious. It is a concept used as a short form to convey a wide variety of process, possibilities, and positions. It is, therefore, capable of different kinds of interpretations. Hence one cannot define one's response to it until the concept is adequately specified. The challenges posed by globalisation to existing non-global forms of civic rights and collective action vary fundamentally along two axes with regard to position in the social structure and with location in the geography of globalisation i.e., context and the space. Two questions—who you are? Where you are? Make crucial differences and give very different grounds and possibilities of action. Globalisation can affect the social space of actors (here for scheduled caste) from two angles: effect from the top i.e., by directly changing their given social location in terms of consumerism, competition and development or effect from below i.e., by opening to them the new avenues from rest of the world . Thus globalisation being a central driving force behind the rapid social, political and economic changes can reshape the modern societies and world orders and no society escapes from its reach as it re-casts traditional patterns, creates new hierarchies, and most crucially reshapes the power, functioning, authority and objective of Nation-State. Regarding implications of globalisation on Scheduled Castes, Vivek Kumar (2007; 327) rightly says that Dalit Diaspora has used the internet to unite the Dalit world over. There are about 51 sites which provide information about about Scheduled Castes in India and abroad. Few important ones are www.ambedkar.org, www.dalitusa.org, www.dalistan.org, www.dalitawaj.com, www.dalitindia.com etc. Similarly Scheduled Castes also run their E-magazine like- Dalit-Internationa@yahoogroup.com,dalit@ambedkar.org, Buddhistcircle @yahoogroup. com. etc. In general, we may say that globalisation enhances democratic space for dalit population.

Keeping in mind the above discussions, let us try to analyse the possible pessimistic (here dysfunctions) and optimistic (here functions) implications of the process of globalisation on Scheduled Castes of developing countries like India.

(b) Functional Aspect of Globalisation on Scheduled Castes

In principle, the process of globalisation ultimately leads towards homogenisation of world-culture in some significant aspects. To quote Hannerz (1996:17) ' In the most general sense, globalisation is a matter of increasing long-distance interconnectedness, at least across national boundaries, preferably between continents as well.' We can say that these processes of linkages across borders include a restructuration of spaces for 'Scheduled Castes', leading to the disappearance of fixed links of them to villages, towns and national frontiers. In this regard, Waters (1995; 136) point out that process of globalisation specifies greater connectedness and de-territorialisation simultaneously. If we try to look it in positive terms then it tries to break the barriers i.e., de-capsulasation of communities and identities. At longer run this may lead to disappearance of inequalities, because it is not possible for ethnic identity to survive without a specific territory or place. This situation will have a positive impact on the people who were marginalised as against the dominating categories in specific territories. In this framework it may be perceived as a welcoming process for the Scheduled Castes, it will not only put them out of the hands of high castes but also they get a fair scope for economic empowerment and social mobility which they can't get in earlier stratified system. Further, globalisation policies will increase their free flow in the international market in terms of labour, goods, ideas and capital. Quoting Deliege (1999), one can say that "today in this global world Scheduled Castes aspire to more comfortable material circumstances and demand more dignity". This global/international mobilisation will provide them the opportunity for global solidarity and for upholding human rights.

In this regard, Jogdand (2000) has rightly argued that much cherished principle of growth with justice; social responsibilities and accountability; equity and self reliance have been rendered obsolete with the new slogan of liberalisation and globalisation. Here, Buell's (1994)) arguments stand valid that 'Tighter integration (due to globalisation) has thus paradoxically meant, and continues to mean, proliferation of asserted differences'. To add, Mendelsohn and Vicziany (1998; 1) too points out that Scheduled Castes will almost everywhere become much more assertive about their human and political rights. Evident example to support the argument is the establishment of organisation like World Social Forum (WSF) and specifically Asia Social Forum (ASF), which provide advocacy on issues regarding neo-liberal globalisation and its impact on discriminated communities. Aspects of globalisation have brought more visibility to Dalit struggles. Through the International Dalit Solidarity Network, established in 2000, NGOs have highlighted the plight of Dalits at global forums. Literate Dalit professionals have globally promoted several Dalit icons, including Buddha, Guru Ravi Das, and B.R. Ambedkar. (see Kumar, V. 2004).

According to Ram (2001: 53), the phenomenon of Ravidass deras has taken the form of a sort of a new socio-cultural Dalit movement in Punjab—what has also come to be known as the 'Ravidassia movement' or 'Ravidass Deras Dalit movement'. The Sants of Ravidass deras, again, particularly of Dera Sachkhand Ballan, have been quite successful in blending together the bani of Guru Ravidass and the philosophy of neo-Buddhism as propounded by Dr Ambedkar. Dera Sachkhand Ballan has become a paragon of the Ravidass movement in northwest India. It has also been regulating the affairs of various

Ravidass Deras overseas through its international trusts. Dera Sachkhand Ballan has established the following international charitable trusts abroad for dissemination of the *Bani* of Ravidass amongst the Dalit Diaspora: Shri Sant Sarwan Dass Charitable Trust [United Kingdom]; Shri Sant Sarwan Dass Charitable Trust [Vancouver Canada]; and Shri Sant Sarwan Dass Charitable Trust [United States]. All these trusts are managed mostly by nonresident Indian Dalits from the Doaba region of Punjab who constitute a big diasporic community (Ravidassia Samaj) of the devotees of Guru Ravidass and the followers of the Dera Sachkhand Ballan.

If we try to put the above discourse on the measuring scale, we may arrive at conclusion that globalisation is worse for Scheduled Castes but one can't negate the brighter side of the picture showing positive implications of globalisation on them. As 'critical' globalism we should welcome the mixed result of the globalisation on Scheduled Castes. Further, regarding the question of pathetic condition of Scheduled Castes in contemporary society can be supported by the fact that quantitative and politico-economic changes are observed and implemented rapidly in comparison to qualitative changes, and it takes time for assimilation and adaptation. Individually, the Indian society has to fight the problems of poverty, illiteracy, cultural oppression, ethnicity etc. that are deep rooted in the society and impedes the growth of new development. For imbibing and continuing globalisation one has to be really global in personality terms so that he/she can reap the benefits of globalisation in true sense.

Globalisation is the intensification of worldwide social relations which link distant localities in such a way that local happening are shaped by events occurring many miles away and vice-versa. To indigenous or local group, it signifies that they are suddenly catapulted from their traditional ways of life into tension and conflict, both within their own group and in their interaction with other superior groups at global level Sociologically, it may be understood as a process of "Universalisation" whereby the parochial elements has to disappear. In Utopian sense it may lead to a stage when society will be more or less homogenised and where there will be no outsiders (as the territory breaks) and everyone will share the similar norms. It may bring more transparency, de-territoralisation and homogenisation in which the concept of private or ethnic belongingness will be marginalised.

Globalisation depicts both manifest and latent functions on the society. Economic liberation is observed as the manifest consequences but it may lead to several latent consequences like decline of nation-state, threat to cultural identity, uniqueness etc. With reference to

Scheduled Castes it may show differential impact. In optimistic terms the process involves tremendous exposure of these local regional entities a new orientation. It enhances the consciousness of there identities at global level. It orients them to the forces of market and finance on one hand, and on the other side access to revolutionary means of communication and media. Thus instead of being a threat to such identities, it may become a means for their identity construction. By appropriating strategies of representation, organisations and social change through access to global system, local communities and marginal interest groups can both empower themselves and influence that global system. In this sense, the appropriation of global forms of culture may free one from local forms of dominance and oppression or at least provide the tool for a different kind of identity formation. Further we can perceive the process of global village or single village through process of globalisation in terms of an ideal village-community, where informal flow of information is very rapid. We can interpret that in the era of globalisation, information flow will be rapid and everybody will be aware of every events or happening at any corner of the world. For instance if Scheduled Castes are being oppressed at any corner, then there will be rapid flow of information and this will result into their association and coalition at the global level and the concerned interventionist may make a quick remedy to the situation, for example Asia Social Forum. Further, we can't deny the role of Dalit Diaspora, which can aid and support the native Scheduled Castes from distant. At the end we may say that Scheduled Castes in accompany with Media, NGO's and Civil society can transform their fate in the globalised world.

Notes

1. Haberle, R (1972): 'Types and Functions of Social Movement' in International Encyclopedia of Social Sciences, Macmillan Company Free Press, New York.
2. Guesfield, J R (ed) (1971): Protest, Reform and Revolt: A Reader in Social Movements, John Wiley and Sons, New York.
3. Aberle, David. 1966. *The Peyote Religion among the Navaho*. Chicago: Aldine.
4. See Ramesh Ashappa Research Link-110, Vol-XII (3), May-2013, pp. 104-105.
5. See Mohan Ram: Ramaswami Naicker and the Dravidian Movement EPW, Annual Number February 1974.

6. See Omvedt Gail. 1971, Jotirao Phule and the Ideology of Social Revolution in India. Economic and Political Weekly, Vol. 6, No. 37 (Sep. 11, 1971), pp. 1969-79.
7. See M.K.Gandhi, (1972): The Collected Works of Mahatmna Gandhi, Volume LI, Government of India, Delhi.
8. See M.K.Gandhi, (1979a): The Collected Works of Mahatlma Gandhi,Volume LXXVI, Government of India, Delhi.
9. See Anisur Rahman, Roots of action research and self-reliance thinking in Rabindranath Tagore, *Action Research* 2006 4: 231.
10. Tagore, Rabindranath (1901). Nation ki (What is a nation). *Atmoshakti. Rachanabali* (Collected Works of Tagore, henceforth CW) Part 3.
11. Tagore, Rabindranath (1914). Lokhit (People's welfare). *Kalantar*. Collected Works 24.
12. See Chakravarty, Satyodash (1998). Rabindranath: Shamakalin pallishamaj o shamobay (Rabindranath: Contemporary village society and cooperatives). Rabindrabhabonar Nanadik o Prashangikata. New Delhi: Voluntary Health Association of India.
13. See Jawaharlal Nehru, The Unity of India, Foreign Affairs, Vol. 16, No. 2 (Jan., 1938), pp. 231-243.
14. See J.L.Nehru, Discovery of India, 1985. OUP: Delhi.
15. See K.S.Singh, Transformation of Tribal Society: Integration *vs* Assimilation, K. S. Singh, Economic and Political Weekly, Vol. 17, No. 33 (Aug. 14, 1982), pp. 1318-1325.
16. See Y. Junghare. Dr. Ambedkar the Hero of the Mahars, Ex-Untouchables of India Asian Folklore Studies, Vol. 47, No. 1 (1988), pp. 93-12.
17. See Vidhu Verma Colonialism and Liberation: Ambedkar's Quest for Distributive Justice: Economic and Political Weekly, Vol. 34, No. 39 (Sep. 25 - Oct. 1, 1999), pp. 2804-2810.
18. See http://www.ambedkartimes.com/sahib_kanshi_ram.htm
19. See Anand Teltumbde, An Enigma Called Kanshi Ram, Economic and Political Weekly, Vol. 41, No. 43/44 (Nov. 4-10, 2006), pp. 4531-4532.
20. Based on the work of Ronki Ram, 2004. Untouchability in India with a Difference: Ad Dharm, Dalit Assertion, and Caste Conflicts in Punjab, Asian Survey, Vol. 44, No. 6 (November/December 2004), pp. 895-912.

9

Ramifications of Cultural Practices, Caste and Sanitation on Rural and Urban India

The Background

The practice of untouchability is found in the context of the caste system of India. If we separate the practice from its context, it loses much of its meaning. Hence, the practice of untouchability as it is found among the Hindus of India means that high caste people would regard some low castes so low that the former would avoid much contact with the latter. Caste of the priests (the Brahmins) would consider the caste of the street sweepers (the Bhangis) to be an untouchable caste. This does not mean that there is no social relationship between the two. It simply means that the relationship between the two is one of social distance, maintained and guided by the norms set by the Brahmins. Whatever social interactions take place between the Brahmins and the Bhangis will also be bound by such norms of social distance. The tension and conflict between the two usually may not be observable, because they are subdued by the normative situation. Change or disturbance in the latter is a prerequisite for conflict to come into the open. Thus, the priests may not allow street-sweepers to enter their kitchens. In turn, the street sweepers dare not address the priests by their first names. Similarly, the two castes will not dine with each other, let alone intermarry. In the case of an inadvertent breach of such norms, there are remedial actions which are followed by both castes. If the lower caste refuses to obey the upper caste, or if the former violates rules or norms which assert the authority and the power of the latter, there will be an open conflict. Where open conflict does not take place, there are conflicting interests. The interests of the upper caste lie in keeping its power, hence maintaining the *status quo*. An untouchable caste will be more interested in altering the *status quo*. When the government seeks to change the rules, or when the position of subordination is challenged by the lower caste, the upper caste may not hesitate to use violence as a weapon to "straighten out" the untouchable caste.[1]

Reference has been made to the racial exclusiveness of the Indo-Aryans of early India. Ghurye (1950:176) alludes to the origin of the caste system of India in terms of "Varna," which literally means "colour," and it seems to have been employed in contrasting the "Aryas" and the "Dasas," referring not only to their superior and inferior statuses, respectively (the former meaning "masters," the latter "slaves"), but also to their fair and dark skin colours.[2] The Indo-Europeans, who seem to have invaded India around 2,000 B.C., called themselves as "Aryas" (also called "Aryans"). These people were tall and comparatively fair-skinned. Their priests had perfected an advanced poetic technique, which they used for the composition of hymns (in Sanskrit) to be sung in praise of their gods at sacrifices. Their great collection of hymns is the Rig-Veda which, along. with the Gita, are the most sacred texts of the Hindus. The Rig-Veda, and the great body of oral religious literature which followed it in the first millennium B.C., are part of the living Hindu tradition. It is probable that most of the Rig-Veda was composed between 1500 and 1000 B.C. It is in the Rig-Vedic literature that we find references to racial distinction, as well as to the Dasas (the serfs or the slaves), the subjugated indigenous inhabitants, as "dark...bull-lipped, snub-nosed..." (Basham,1959:32).[3] In Sanskrit literature, Untouchables are known as chandala, a term that designates those who were not allowed to dwell in a town or a village but had to live in special quarters outside the village or town limits. In theory, their main task was the carrying and cremation of corpses; but they had other means of earning their livelihood as well. The law books stipulate that chandalas must eat their food from broken vessels and avoid any contact with higher castes. High-caste individuals could be reduced to the status of chandalas by mere touching the latter (A.L Basham, 1967).....Chandalas must reside outside the village limits, they may not own whole vessels, they must dress in clothes taken from the dead and must marry among themselves. They eat only table scraps and leftovers, and are not allowed to walk through the village except when on business. They should easily distinguishable from other people and not conceal their low origins. Lastly, they defile the other classes.

Based on the evidence available from scriptural literature (written in Sanskrit, the sacred language of the Aryans, and monopolised by the priests, the Brahmins, the highest caste), it is clear that during the Vedic period (which ended around 600 B.C.), Indian society was divided into four general classes, in the following rank-order: the priests (the Brahmins); the warriors (Kshtriyas); the peasant-traders (the Vaishyas); and the serfs or slaves (the Shudras). However, the ingenuity of the priestly caste of Aryans lies in using organic analogy to their advantage, by comparing the relative positions and the functions of four major castes in the Purusha-Sukta hymn of Rig-Veda. Basham (1959:144) believes that the early representatives of the people who were later called untouchables or outcastes were of a lower status than the Shudras or actually were outside the community. They were serving the Aryans in very menial and dirty tasks, and were looked on as quite outside the pale. Sometimes they were called "the fifth caste," but most (Brahmin) authorities rejected even that, insisting that they were outside the Aryan social order altogether! It is likely that all untouchables were later labeled as "Shudras," though in early Indian literature they are mentioned by such occupational names as the Chandalas (the carriers and the cremators of corpses), the leather workers, and the basket-makers. Special quarters were allocated to those out castes. They were not allowed to reside in the neighbourhood of the Aryans; they had to dwell outside the villages of the Aryans. Also, they were to be dressed in discarded garments, eat food from broken vessels, and wear only iron ornaments (Basham, 1959:145).

The colonial rule in India brought about the slow disintegration of pre-capitalist economy, and the formation of classes, especially in the modern industrial cities of India. Since India remained as a colony of the British for almost a century, the rate of change from caste to class has been noticeably slow, and there have been considerable rural-urban differences, especially in the socioeconomic position of the untouchable castes and the practice of untouchability. The economic exploitation of untouchable labourers, both in the villages and the cities of India, has been widespread. The high-caste Hindu landlords try to make village outcastes work for nothing or pay them the lowest possible wages. In cities where exchange or contractual relations have developed, the wages may be on a par with those of other castes, but untouchables, if engaged in manual work, are given the lowest possible work. So, one qualitative difference is balanced out by the other. Also, violence and terror against them means that outcastes may refuse to work only at the cost of their lives. Even where violence is absent, the poverty of landless agricultural labourers in Indian villages is proverbial, and a significantly large proportion of them are still considered to be the untouchables. Thus, the rural proletariats of India sell their labour-power as a commodity but still, unwittingly, their life is sold as a commodity; they can refuse to work only if they are ready to starve to death. The urban proletariat of India is recruited from all castes, but still the majority of them come from the lower castes, including the untouchables. In cities, they have become labourers, exchanging their wages for their labour power, but they have not yet ceased to be untouchables.

There has been a process of transition in the "pollution-purity" dimension of caste. But, the rate of change is slow, and this is manifested in slow adjustment between the two aspects of the behaviour of Indians, viz., the public and the private. The former has changed faster than the latter. This is obvious, first of all from the fact that few if any people from the lower castes are found to belong to the new elites. Secondly, the lag between the public and the private aspects of behaviour is most clearly manifested in the practice of untouchability. We have referred to occupational mobility among untouchables. This does not mean that untouchables necessarily end up changing their social status vis-a-vis other castes in the ritual rank order, despite changes in the economic position. We have also referred to the participation of the lower castes in the political processes of contemporary India. However, the ingenuity of the traditional caste elite, the Brahmins, was to bring about a closure of the castes, finally and more permanently, through the ideological elements of religion and beliefs. Hence it is natural that the changes may be slow in this sphere and the discrepancy in the public and the private aspects of behaviour of the "twice born" castes (the Dwijas or the Savarnas) may be temporarily visible in their interactions with the untouchables.

Though the idea of untouchability was first given expression in connection with the Shudras and the sacrifices performed by the Brahmins, Ghurye (1969:52-53) hypothesises that the untouchables were a degraded group of aborigines. The Brahminic literature of post-Vedic period reports a great consolidation of the Brahmin caste. It also contains the following statement: "the idea that an impure person imparts pollution by his touch and even by his near approach to the members of three castes finds definite expression in the law texts of this period, generally with reference to the persons who are outcasted" (Ghurye, 1969:79). Ideas form ideology and it in turn, supports a system of stratification. Hence, in the next section, we will examine the ideology of untouchability as related to Indian caste system.

Historicity of Caste and Untouchability

The origins of caste and of untouchability lie deep in India's ancient past and the evidence of these origins provided by the archaeological and literary sources now available is, at best, circumstantial. Consequently, scholars have been forced to engage in considerable speculation in their efforts to engage in considerable speculation in their efforts to reconstruct the past history of untouchability.

The dominant view traces the origins of caste and untouchability to the Aryans and to their ways of relating to the peoples of India with whom they came into contact. The Aryans, a set of related and highly self-conscious tribes sharing a common language and religion, began their invasion of India from the north-west in around 1500 B.C. For centuries they remained in seemingly constant conflict with the indigenous peoples, whom they looked down upon as culturally inferior and shunned as ritually unclean. Once conquered by superior military technology, some of these peoples withdrew into regions as yet unoccupied by the Aryans, while others were incorporated as separate and inferior castes within Aryans, while others were incorporated as separate and inferior castes within Aryan-dominated society. In post-Rigvedic literature there are more frequent references to primitive forest-dwellers who were kept on the fringes of Aryan society in the conquered regions. Among these were the Chandalas.

Although the Chandalas were severely stigmatised in the later Vedic age, it was only in the period between 600 B.C. and A.D. 200

that untouchability appeared as such (Webster, 1994: 2). In the Dharmasutras and in Kautilya's *Arthasastra* the Chandalas are treated as Untouchables and the 'mixed caste theory' of the origins of untouchability is enunciated. However, it is in the Manusmriti that this theory as well as the *Varna* theory and the classification of castes in a hierarchy based on occupation and degree of pollution, receives its classic statement.

According to Manu, the ancient Indian law-giver, untouchability is the punishment for miscegenation, between a number of a high caste and that of a low caste or an outcaste. The children of such an unequal pair become Untouchables, and the greater the social gap between the two parents, the lower the status of their children. The consequences are also more severe if the mother is of the superior caste. Thus the offspring of a Brahmin father and a Shudra mother is called Nishada; the child becomes a fisherman. The offspring of a Shudra father and a Brahmin mother is called Chandala; he is the most degraded of all mortals. To Manu, a degraded occupation is not the cause of untouchability; rather untouchability condemns a person to low and impure occupation. In later times, racial mixture was added as a factor of impurity. In the period after Manu, increasing numbers of the members of the lower castes belonged to different races and cultures. The practice of untouchability was intensified and applied to more groups in the years following A.D. 200, while Chandala became a label not simply for a tribe but for all whom the Aryans considered to be at the very bottom of society.

What has been described thus far relates to North India. The literature from South India suggests that the people whom the Aryans conquered were Dravidians, who subsequently moved south subjugating the indigenous people. It was only later, when Aryan influences spread to the south, that the *Varna* system and untouchability came into being there.

J.H. Hutton, eminent anthropologist and author of one of the best work on caste, *Caste in India* (1963), locates the origins of caste in the taboos and divisions of labour in the pre-Aryan tribes of India as well as in their efforts at self-preservation in the face of invasion. In his opinion untouchability is the consequence of ritual impurity. He says: 'The origin of the position of the exterior castes is partly racial, partly religious, and partly a matter of social custom. There can be little doubt but the ideal of untouchability originates in taboo' (Hutton, 1981:207). Von Fuerer-Haimendorf, another eminent anthropologist believes that untouchability is an urban development and is the result of an unclean and ritually impure occupation (Fuchs, 1950). Once untouchability had developed in urban or semi-urban settlements, its gradual spread to the villages was inevitable for it is everywhere the towns which set the standard.

Dr Stephen Fuchs proposes a new theory regarding the origin of untouchability (1981). According to him the above proposed theories as well as various others presented by a number of Indologists seem to suffer from one great defect: they do not penetrate deeply enough into the past of the dominant Indian peoples. They restrict themselves unduly to happenings in India. It is true that the caste system and untouchability developed after the arrival of the Aryans and, most probably, of the Dravidians in India that caste system, as it has grown in India is unique and not found elsewhere in the world, and that nowhere in the world are Untouchables found in such vast numbers-138 million! Yet, the roots must be sought in an age when both population groups lived on the steppes of Inner Asia. Here the animal-breeding societies developed a pronounced hierarchical structure. These animal breeders gave up cultivation completely and regarded manual work of any kind as unworthy of a shepherd and a warrior. They also developed a social structure of their own: an extended joint family system with a patriarch at its head in whom all power was vested. According to Dr. Stephen Fuchs, there is sufficient evidence to prove that the Aryans as well as the Dravidians on their arrival in India still belonged to such an animal-breeding culture. They must have brought along also their aversion to manual work and to foreign people. The Aryans, on their slow advance through northern India, and the Dravidians wandering down along the west coast into South India, encountered on their way a multitude of earlier settlers who either submitted passively to their conquest or were defeated in fierce battles. As conquerors they managed to impose many of their cultural values and prejudices on the subject peoples of India. Adding to their inherited attitude to manual work and racial purity, a new dimension, namely that of ritual purity, they gradually developed this unique Hindu caste system which is intimately connected ideologically with the concept of untouchability.

From the above explanations for the origin of untouchability are conclusively proven facts. As so often happens with human institutions, no single cause can explain untouchability. It is deeply rooted in Indian history, in the agrarian social order that dominated the Indian economy until the advent of the British, and which remains today India's largest economic sector. Though the relation of India's rural Untouchables to this social order has shifted in subtle ways in the past two centuries, there remains pervasive continuities, especially of meaning and of cultural construction, with this deeply rooted past.

Perhaps the earliest and simplest Western image of untouchability is embodied in the term 'outcaste'. In this view, to be an Untouchable is to be beyond the reach of Hindu culture and society, to be almost cultureless. The stress in the outcaste image is on the Brahmins possessing culture and the Untouchable lacking it. Thus the Abbe Dubois, a remarkable French missionary with first-hand knowledge of village India between 1792 and 1823, contrasts the Untouchable 'Pariahs' with those higher caste Hindus on whom the system has had its beneficent moral effect: 'We can picture what would become of the Hindus if they were not kept within the bounds of duty by the rules and penalties of caste, by looking at the position of the Pariahs, or outcastes of India, who, checked by no moral restraints, abandon themselves to their natural propensities' (1959: 29). (Deliege, 1997).

The Untouchables described by Dubois accept their status and believe in the legitimacy of the system so that there is no thought of equality in their mind: 'The idea that he (untouchable) was born to be in subjection to the other castes is so ingrained in his mind that it never occurs to be Pariah to think that his fate is anything but irrevocable. Nothing will ever persuade him that men are all made of the same clay' (Dubois, 1959:50; quoted in Moffatt, 1979:7).

The early outcaste image, as it is articulated by Dubois, implies a major disjunction between the higher 'caste-Hindus' and the lowermost Untouchables, or outcastes. The very terms express the disjunction. The main body of the Hindu population 'has caste', and is regulated by its social and cultural conventions, while the Untouchables are outside the system.

Another Western observer of the same period, who surveyed newly acquired territories in Mysore for the British in 1799, describes the Untouchable Madiga as follows:'(The Madiga) are divided into small tribes of ten or twelve houses, and intermarry with the daughters of these houses only, in order to be certain of the purity of their race; of which they seem to be as fond, as those castes that are esteemed infinitely superior in rank' (Buchanan, 1807:640; quoted in Moffatt, 1979:8). These two views of Untouchables and caste, the outcaste image and the simple consensus image, dominated Western thinking through the British period. This approach considered that, 'To be an Untouchable is not to be excluded from the culture of caste, but it is to possess this culture in a thinner and less convincing form' (Moffatt, 1979:8).

In recent years, social anthropologists and ethnographers of South Asia have been preoccupied with the subject of hierarchy in the Hindu social system. Definitions of the caste system have been advanced in which the authors have sought to isolate the code which differentiates Hindus into exclusive social groups and ranks them in a hierarchical relationship with one another. Two authors in particular, F. G. Bailey and Louis Dumont, have written on this subject and other social anthropologists have aligned themselves with the theories of either (Dumont, 1957; 1960; 1966; 1970; Dumont and Pocock, 1957; Bailey, 1959; 1963). India also experienced some effect of this change on its socio-economic structure along with other countries. Most of these changes were brought to India by the British. They brought with them western values of life and humanistic attitudes like liberty, equality and liberal education. All these values had important effects on the break-up of the traditional social structure of Indian society. As early as in 1830, the missionaries, for the first time in the history of India, started giving formal education to the untouchables. Apart from them the British were the first to expose the untouchables to western education on a large scale. The policy pursued by the British government in India of giving formal education to the untouchables. Apart from them the British were the first to expose the untouchables to western education on a large scale. The policy pursued by the British government in India of giving preference to the low castes for education was in accordance with its humanitarian sentiments, and it also had the effect of making lower castes look up to the British for protection.

This is significant since traditionally only the Brahmins had the right to education. The Indian society was divided into four *Varnas,* i.e., *Brahmin, Kshatriya, Vaishya and Shudra*. In the hierarchy, the Brahmins were on the top and the *Shudras* were at the bottom. *Untouchables* in Indian society were, thus, characterised by a high degree of status summation. The stratification system was less differentiated in terms of ritual, economic and political dimensions. According to *M.N. Srinivas, sanskritisation,* the most frequently employed means of mobility. Education has now come to be an important factor in social mobility (specially for the *scheduled castes). Ambedkar* foresaw this aspect and hence struggled throughout his life for the educational betterment of the depressed people of India.

Thus, for centuries, these castes were kept away from education, knowledge and culture on religious grounds. The roots of this evil are so deep that even in independent India they have to face many socio-economic disabilities. Even today, if a low caste member or an untouchable holds some property or gains some knowledge he is not easily accepted by the society. The following can be cited: "In 1917 the *Maharaja* had appointed *Dr. Ambedkar* as the Finance Adviser of Baroda State. Although he was the acknowledged expert on Indian economics, he was not acceptable to the civil servants and people of Baroda. As an untouchable, he could not be given accommodation; he could not eat or drink during the day. The civil servants thoughts it sinfull to hand over files to him, and rolled up the mats where ever he walked. Finally, a mob of angry Parsees gave him 24 hours to leave. The *Maharaja* could offer no protection, and so Dr. *Ambedkar* was forced out of Baroda, like a criminal by self appointed and vigilants."

Nandu Ram (1988) discusses four specific trends of change evolved during Pax Britannica, the period from 1857-1947. To him, the leader who helped to bring about these changes can be classified into four categories: the 'Reformist', the 'Nationalist', the 'Reformist-Nationalist' and the 'Revolutionaries'. The 'Reformist' believing in social reform had their roots in various *'Samajs'* and 'Missions'. In some regions, they adopted resolutions in favour of throwing schools and colleges open to women and lower caste children, and of abolition of sub-castes. Thus, in a broader sense, as has been argued by Ambedkar, the reformists were the true nationalists, for they tried to purify the caste and educate various segments of the population. However, they could not generate a powerful consciousness for the reorganisation and restructuring of the Hindu society or the Indian society as a whole. "These efforts left the core of the traditional beliefs practically intact and the reformist movements, therefore, remained essentially as fringe movements (Rajasekhariah, 1971)".

The second trend was generated and advanced by the 'Nationalists'; their major concern was independence from the colonial rulers. For achieving independence a powerful nationalist movement was essential. They supported those social reforms that helped the growth of a single nationalist consciousness. Tilak, Gandhi and Nehru were the pioneers of this trend of change. Ambedkar and his supporters led the third trend of Reformist- Nationalists. Bitterly criticised by the nationalists, they fought for social reform as well as for a share of the deprived people in the existing power structure first and freedom from British imperialism afterwards. The fourth trend of change was led by those 'Revolutionaries' who believed in an overall change in the structure and functioning of the Indian society to be brought about not through negotiation with but through revolt and violence against British imperialism. Its main concern was with the common problems of the exploited masses irrespective of their caste and communal background. This trend was openly opposed by the British rulers and even by those nationalists who adopted non-violent means to achieve political independence.

Untouchable castes by state in India

State	*Total no. of Untouchables*	*No. of Scheduled castes*	*Name of principal castes in the state (with No.)*
Andhra Pradesh	5,774,548	60	Adi Andhra (616,319) i.e. 10.6% Madiga (2,514,848) i.e. 43.5% Mala (2,113,393) i.e. 36.5%
Bihar	7,950,652	23	Chamar (2,382,440) i.e. 29.9% Dusadh (2,105,413) i.e. 26.4% Musahar (1,168,447) i.e. 14.6%
Gujarat	1,825,432	42	Bhambi (321,868) i.e. 17.6% Bhangi (181,601) i.e. 9.9% Mahyavanshi 510,256)i.e. 27.9% Vankhar (239,917) 13.1%
Haryana	1,895,933	37	Balmiki (374,960) i.e. 19.7% Chamar (1,004,413) i.e. 52.9% Dhanak (206,783) i.e. 10.9%
Himachal Pradesh	769,572	60	Charmar (224,574) i.e. 29.1% Koli (237,614) i.e. 30.8%
Jammu and Kashmir	381,277	13	Chamar (93,997) i.e. 24.6% Doon (78,430) i.e. 20.5% Megh (152,886) i.e. 40.0%
Kerala	1,772,168	69	Cheruman (259,966) i.e. 14.6% Kuravan (178,060) i.e. 10.0% Pulayan (586,988 (33.1%)
Madhya Pradesh	5,453,690	69	Chamarv (3,018,208) i.e. 55.3%
Maharashtra	3,025,761	69	Bhambi (439,503) i.e. 14.5% Mahar (1,071,087) i.e. 35.3% Mang (915,518) i.e. 30.2%
Mysore	3,850,034	100	Adi-Dravida (429,601) i.e. 11.1% Adi-Karnataka (1,404,946) i.e. 36.4% Holeya (374,270) i.e. 9.7%
Orissa	3,310,854	91	Bauri (303,460) i.e. 9.1% Dhoba (322,216) i.e. 9.7% Dom (370,236) i.e. 11.1% Ganda (325,053) i.e. 9.8% Pan (672,67) i.e. 20.3%
Punjab	3,348,217	37	Ad Dharmi (439,632) i.e. 13.1% Balmiki (401,960) i.e. 12.0% Chamar (981,471) i.e. 29.3% Mazhabi (962,546) i.e. 28.7%
Rajasthan	4,075,580	81	Chamarv (1580,858) i.e. 38.7% Megh (599,644) i.e. 14.7%

State	*Total no. of Untouchables*	*No. of Scheduled castes*	*Name of principal castes in the state (with No.)*
Tamil Nadu	7,315,595	75	Adi-Dravida (2,547,166) i.e. 34.8% Chakkiliyan (864,842) i.e. 11.8% Pallar (1,326,745) i.e. 18.1% Paraiyar (1,533,482) i.e. 20.9%
Uttar Pradesh	18,548,916	66	Chamar (10,121,421) i.e. 54.5% Pasi (2,572,563) i.e. 13.8%
West Bengal	8,816,028	63	Bagdi (1,291,127) i.e. 14.6% Namasudra (980,524) i.e. 11.1% Pod (975, 352) i.e. 11.0% Rajbanshi (1,35,919 (15.3%)

Source: Extracted from Robert Deliege (1999) The Untouchables of India, Berg Publication

Sociological Interpretation of Untouchability

Untouchability is not a simple matter of economic deprivation. A look at a few statistics shows this: Untouchables represent only some 15 per cent of the Indian population, whereas economists usually estimate that between 40 and 50 per cent of the population lives below the so-called 'poverty line'. However credible these figures may be, it is clear that the problem of poverty goes well beyond that of untouchability....

Nor does untouchability boil down to a problem of ritual pollution. It is true that the term 'Untouchables' designates social group that, owing to their association with death, organic waste and evil spirits, are 'permanently polluted'; but it must also be remembered that, in India, everyone is, to a greater or lesser degree, unclean. Furthermore, some group perform highly polluting task, from a ritual standpoint, without incurring the same kind of discrimination and exclusion as Untouchables; this is the case for instance, of the barbers or the washermen, but also of certain types of funeral priest. Deliege argue that the term 'Untouchables' refers to those sections of Indian society that are economically dependent and exploited, victims of many kinds of discriminations, and ritually polluted in a permanent way. It is combination of these three elements that characterise Untouchables and sets them apart from the rest of population.

Deliege[4] emphasises that events of exploitation are by no means uncommon in contemporary India. The Marathi paper carried ten stories of Harijans being burned alive in Uttar Pradesh, and one of a pregnant woman's being sacrificed to bring rain in Andhra Pradesh; there were also stories of women raped by students in Maharashtra, a girl exposed naked in a public square, human excrement dumped into an untouchable well, and so forth. Between six and nine thousand incidents of violence against Untouchables were being reported annually in the late 1970s. Untouchability can be said to be an extreme form of social oppression and economic exploitation, and it could therefore be compared to similar problems found throughout the world.

As we have seen, India's Untouchables constitutes some 15 per cent of the total population. Interestingly enough, their per centage has increased slightly over the years, from 14.67 per cent in 1961 to 15.75 per cent in the 1981 census. In this census, the Scheduled Castes, the administrative term for Untouchables, numbered some 104,754,623 individuals, a truly mind-numbering figure. Between 1971 and 1981, the population of the Scheduled Castes increased by 32.4 per cent, or 3.2 per cent per year, while the overall population of India grew by just 2.3 per cent.

Harijans are split into hundreds of castes dispersed throughout the country. No single organisation can claim to represent Untouchables as a whole, and the local associations that do exist have very little power of mobilisation. The only national leader of importance to have emerged form their ranks was not even capable, in spite of his charisma, of unifying the untouchable castes of his own There is no denying that this fragmentation is one more curse for untouchables, making it impossible for them to play on their numerical strength to win a significant role in Indian politics. Furthermore, although nearly every village has its Untouchables, they almost never constitute a majority, but tend to be divided into relatively small communities. Such fragmentation is an essential feature of Indian untouchability. Traditionally, Unotuchables even espoused the quarrels and factions of their masters, and therefore practiced vertical solidarity rather than the 'horizontal mobilisation' they had always lacked.[5] Thus, in every region, Untouchables are divided into numerous castes and subcastes that are strongly endogamous and very particular about avoiding contact with each other.

The problem of untouchability, as Oommen correctly writes, is above all one of 'cumulative deprivation', and it must be made clear that untouchables do indeed constitute a distinct group, even if the vernacular has no specific term for them and even though they are highly fragmented.[6] Beteille argues that the population of Tamil Nadu can be divided into three broad categories: Brahmins, non-Brahmins and Untouchables.[7] He argues that this division is significant from a sociological standpoint. Socio-economic dependence, material poverty, social deprivation and lack of political power combine with ritual pollution to make Untouchables a social category set apart from the rest society.

To Deliege, one of the essential features of untouchability in India is the extreme fragmentation of its constituent units...[8] They are divided into hundreds of castes and subcastes dispersed over the entire subcontinent. Some castes contain a scant few hundred individuals, while the major, best-known groups—like the Chamars, Bhangis, Paraiyars and Mahars—count hundreds of thousands and even millions of members. Some castes are highly localised, while others, like the Chamars, are dispersed over vast areas that cut across state boundaries. The larger 'castes' are no doubt more confederations than castes properly speaking, being divided into countless endogamous 'subcastes', which in turn sometimes have their own hierarchy. Within a linguistic region, the various untouchable castes are usually associated with a traditional occupation, which may also be a ritual task: in Tamil Nadu, Pallars for the most part agricultural workers, Paraiyars placed the drums for inauspicious ceremonies, and Sakkiliyars were cobblers and scavengers. In Hindi speaking regions, Chamars were tanners and cobblers, Bhangis sweeper, Koris weavers, and so on. In Maharashtra, Chambhars were leather-workers and the famous Mahars were messengers and watchmen, while their Mang rivals were rope-makers. In Andhra Pradesh, Madigas were leather-workers, and Malas 'village servants'. Many occupations were associated with untouchability in this way.[9] As a rule, however, untouchable occupations have some tie with organic waste, filth, ritual pollution, death, evil spirits or various menial tasks. For instance, the Doms of Benares are funeral attendants, while the Paraiyars of Tamil Nadu play drums at funerals to keep away evil spirits. Throughout India, the sweepers, knackers, night-soil removers and scavengers are invariably Untouchables, as are the tanners and cobblers. Basket and mat-making, too, are generally associated with untouchability. But the most frequent occupation of Untouchables is no doubt agricultural labour, together with the various menial tasks that keep the village running smoothly.

M. Moffatt distinguishes three types of approach to untouchability–outcaste model, model of diversity and model of unity.[10] The first two emphasise separation, 'disjunction', between untouchables and rest of society, while the third places the stress on 'conjunction', on the consensus that unites Untouchables with society at large.

Cultural Beliefs and Practices about Dirt and Sanitation[11]

Women who eat dirt and about this widespread habit of snacking on special clays or muds that has been reported among women in almost every part of the world—is that it's not just women who eat dirt.[12] Dirt or clay eating is more usual among women, especially pregnant women, in many parts of the world, in Nepal, Africa, India, Central America, and the American South. But in other parts of the world, and at other times in history, entire populations have been known to consume dirt. In Northern California and in Sardinia, where acorns used to be the dietary staple, the traditional bread was made by mixing acorn flour with clay and water, then baking the mixture in a slow oven. In Germany in the last century, some of the poorer workers and their families used very fine clays to "butter" their bread. In China, as in other parts of the world, clay was eaten by much of the population during times of severe want. Some clay, such as steatite, has a tendency to swell when they take up water, and these clays are present in famine food samples from China.

The list goes on and on and should make those with a peculiarly "female" explanation of dirt eating ("geophagy," as it is known in scientific circles) question their assumptions. Geophagy has often been attributed to mood swings, hormonal rushes, magical and superstitious beliefs, and/or beliefs in the fertility of the earth—causes more closely associated with the distaff population. But any cogent explanation of this behaviour, any explanation that pretends to make real and lasting sense, must also account for these examples of universal consumption.

In the United States, women make up for shortages of iron with supplements and fortified foods (or by consuming more food than they need—a subject for another discussion). Elsewhere, they might visit clay pits or termite mounds. The clays of termite mounds are rich in both calcium and iron and supply a woman who eats at least twenty grams a day with more than 100 per cent of her RDA for iron. It has never been proved that women eat these clays in order to obtain extra calcium and iron, but it is telling that, in certain parts of Africa at least, most of the pregnant population makes it a habit of visiting termite mounds.

Another problem that becomes more difficult for women during pregnancy—and one that also inclines them towards dirt eating—is the problem of plant toxins. Women who have no choice but to eat foods that are loaded with toxins; a daily dose of clay could help to minimise their effects. Small amounts of clay might also directly relieve the symptoms of pregnancy by changing the acidity of the stomach and/or by absorbing excessive amounts of saliva. Whatever the actual reasons why pregnant women eat dirt, dirt eating is an integral part of the behaviour of pregnant women in many parts of the world.

With the entire examples author given of dirt eating in humans and other animals, with all the possible benefits that dirt eating can provide, especially to pregnant women, I'm not arguing that all dirt eating in our species serves a clear nutritional purpose. Nor that all dirt eating is benign. Group and community identity, gender roles, the relative importance attached to different forms of authority and the ways in which it is exercised are all influenced by culture, i.e., all that is passed down by human society including language, laws, customs, beliefs and moral standards. Culture shapes human behaviour in many different ways including the status attached to different roles and what is deemed to be acceptable personal and social behaviour. In many cultures, for example, the elderly command traditional authority and influence within the family and community.

As regards sanitation behaviour, defecation is often a private matter which people are unwilling to discuss openly, while the burying of faeces is widely practiced to ward off evil spirits. Contact with faecal matter is unacceptable to certain individuals in societies where it is the responsibility of low-income or low-caste groups, while taboos may dictate that separate facilities should be provided for particular social groups. A particular cultural practice to be considered, which has direct technical consequences, is the method of anal cleansing used by the community. Whether water, stones, corncobs or thick pieces of paper are used will affect the design of the sanitation system.

Culture also influences how people interpret and evaluate the environment in which they live. Investments in sanitation seek to improve health by providing a clean physical environment for households. There is a logical series of technical questions that need to be asked in order that acceptable technical solutions can be found. It may be confusing, therefore, when sanitation behaviour is found to vary widely between communities within the same physical environment. Predetermined rules cannot be applied. However, the sanitation behaviour of individuals usually has a rational basis, and people are often aware of the environmental causes of ill-health. Many societies have a detailed knowledge of the physical environment as a provider of resources for curative and preventive medicine and as a cause of illness. More than this, they have an understanding of the environment, not only in its physical sense, but also in relation to social and spiritual factors. This holistic view of the environment permeates many of the cultural beliefs and customs that impinge on both water use patterns and sanitation behaviour.

Evidence of the value attached by communities to cleanliness and, by implication, environmental sanitation is found in studies of diarrhoea. People's perceptions of its causes may be divided into three categories, physical, social and spiritual. In many cases, physical causes are identified and, although the germ theory is not explicitly stated, the faecal-oral transmission routes of diarrhoea appear to be understood. Households may associate diarrhoea with a polluted environment including uncovered food, dirty water and flies. As on-site sanitation involves improving the physical environment, it may therefore be readily accepted as one means by which to reduce the incidence of disease.

Equally, social and spiritual causes are perceived to be important, and include, for example, female social indiscretions and witchcraft. But these three apparently unrelated causes of diarrhoea should not be interpreted as mutually exclusive or divergent approaches to disease. They are often closely interrelated in practice, within a holistic interpretation of the environment. Efforts should be made to determine how a community's beliefs, knowledge, and control over the environment can be harnessed in a positive way. Careful judgment is required to distinguish between those beliefs and ritual behaviour that are conducive to good sanitation practice and those that need to be changed.

Various Relevant Studies on Culture and Sanitation

A paper by May Yacoob concerns itself with ways of involving these communities with health-education projects in water and sanitation.[13] It stresses the need to scrutinise their practices—to "psych them out"—as a critical first step toward perfecting techniques that are culturally compatible with staunch Islamic traditions. In urging this, the paper attempts to show a "successful practice," an experience that has worked, an approach that at one time we might have rejected out of hand as a viable option in health education. It proposes to use religion as a vehicle for behaviour change, and it offers illustrations from projects and situations where religious values have been invoked in complementarity with development objectives. It discusses examples of health-education materials whose content derives from codes of religious behaviour, and, ultimately, from Islam as a behavioural model.

Various Moslem communities have used religious principles to organise social services relating to health, education, and basic services - including water. There are two organising principles in Islam that form the basis for a cross-cultural provision of community services: The first is the concept of *sadaka*, which is equated with alms-giving, and thus is voluntary. The second is the notion of *zakat*, whereby members of the community are obligated to contribute ten per cent of their incomes for the support and maintenance of social services.

In North Sudan, for example, some communities make both *sadaka* and *zakat* contributions for the operation of hospitals. Yet they make no similar contributions to primary health-care programmes because the ideas behind preventive health have never been explained in this region. In North Yemen, the national government has been able to introduce the traditions of *sadaka* and *zakat* into present-day development objectives. Providing water, for example, was historically a means of fulfilling a *sadaka* obligation. Wealthy men supplied water wells along the trade routes for travelers and their animals.

Islamic law stipulates that water sources that "God caused to flow"- such as springs and rivers - are shared and cannot be owned by an individual. A well, however, that requires human manipulation and investment can be considered private property if built on owned land. Similarly, while the methods for allocating and controlling irrigation water have evolved over centuries, piping domestic water into houses for the privacy of home use has introduced a new set of variables. What is established is that drinking water is something to which everyone has a right, including strangers.[14]

In a study by Nilika Mehrotra and S. M. Patnaik, the sanitation programme, Nirmal Gram Yojana, with its emphasis on a top-down approach, has failed in Bastar because it is being thrust on people in an area where water is scarce and they have few resources for maintenance.[15] Accoring ro the study, a visit to study the role of an NGO in tribal development in Bastar in Chhattisgarh in November 2006 revealed a very disappointing picture of state policy in practice. In all the six villages that were visited, Nirmal Gram Yojana was in action with prominent boards and placards. The government officials as well as NGO workers were working overtime to achieve "success". In the name of infrastructure development, *shauchalayas* were being granted to those who never asked for them. The majority of the families are still BPL households. In Bastar there is no scarcity of land. The area is arid and dusty. Villages are scattered and huge pieces of land are lying unused due to non-availability of water. Water scarcity and resultant poor agricultural production are cited as the main reasons for seasonal migration and extreme poverty. The tribal villagers have been going to the riverbanks nearby for defecation. Due to the tribal ethos, women do not feel necessarily unsafe, though they visit the riverside usually only in the early morning. The new discourse on introducing toilets and inculcating cleanliness habits through new toilet behaviour is alien to their culture.

Understanding Scavenging

In most developing countries, recuperation and recycling takes place at all levels of society. Street and dump pickers are only the most visible among many who benefit from such activities. Little of value is discarded from residences. In rich households, the servants pick over wastes; itinerant small dealers buy bottles and paper from shops and homes; offices and industrial establishments sell quantities of waste materials directly to dealers.

We do not usually class household and commercial recuperation as scavenging. The original meaning of the term to scavenge was "to scrape dirt from the streets", and a scavenger was one whose privilege or job it was to remove dirt from public places. In the nineteenth century, before the development of regular municipal waste removal services, cities licensed scavengers, who enjoyed the right to use the waste materials as they wished'. Today the legitimacy of scavenging has largely been lost with the disappearance of the recognised scavenger role. In many cities, scavenging from municipal garbage dumps is illegal, so those who engage in it are regarded as pilferers.

It would seem that we should retain at least part of the original meaning by confining scavenging to recovery of waste materials from public places. Recuperation would then refer to recovery from private spaces. Recycling refers to the transformation of recuperated waste products in some manner, rather than simple reuse of the materials. Even these simple distinctions will be difficult to maintain in the discussion of many scavenging groups, for their activities cross and recross abstract lines of definition.

In the traditional Indian society, a particular section is ordained to do scavenging work. It has been a hereditary occupation and everybody born in the sub-caste of scavenger (Bhangi), male or female, is destined to take up this sub- human profession. The members of this sub- caste were bound not only by traditional obligations and customary rules to practice this profession, by mythological sanctions also oblige them to carry night-soil physically for disposal. In the traditional social order, the Bhangis (scavengers) were required to perform their job with hands and carry the buckets containing night-soil on their heads through lanes and streets. It was about the worst kind of atrocity committed against any section of traditional Indian society.

These people are hated and shunned for this dirt job. It is clearly a denial of social justice and a manifestation of rank traditionalism. The pathetic conditions of scavengers can further be realised from the fact that there are a number of occupational groups and sub-castes which are described as depressed castes, outcastes or exterior castes. But even in this case of differences and variations from region to region, the Bhangis were labeled as exterior caste and polluted people throughout the country. The following observations made by Hutton (1981: 196) explain the situation clearly: 'For purposes, therefore, of deciding what persons are to be included in the members of the exterior castes, it has been necessary for each province to deal with the problem in its own way and to produce its own list.

It may be possible to do so in the case of certain castes, such as those of Dom and Bhangis, but it certainly is not the case that a caste which is depressed in one part of India is depressed everywhere. It is not intended that the term should have any reference to occupation as such, but to those castes which by reasons of their traditional position in the Hindu society, are denied access to temples, for instance, or have to use separate wells or are not allowed to sit inside a school but have to remain outside, or which suffered similar social disabilities. It may be stated beyond doubt that the traditional system of service latrines in urban communities (as well as rural communities) of India has been a source of insanitation and pollution of the surroundings in different ways and for different reasons. On the basis of the survey conducted by kalbermatten (1980:6) in different underdeveloped and developing areas, the investigator came to this conclusion: 'the bucket latrine is judged to be unsuitable for replication. The system is also responsible for insanitary conditions in the surrounding areas besides bad smell which causes irritation and restlessness. This system is highly injurious to health and aborts the programme of improving the hygienic conditions of the surroundings.[16]

In contemporary India, with its remarkable growth rate and corresponding investment and employment opportunities, some may find it surprising that heinous occupations like manual scavenging still persist. Manual scavenging is one of the ancient and age old occupation in India based on Caste structure. Manual Scavenging in literal terms means the manual removal and handling of human excreta; this occupation consists in the removal of human excreta with the help of brooms, tin plates and baskets in public streets, septic tanks and dry toilets. It is characterised by dramatically unhealthy and unsafe working conditions that continue to exacerbate the practice of Untouchability and marginalisation of Dalits.

How do the poor survive in poor cities? One answer is that they seek to become a part of the webs of recuperation, reuse, and recycling that link different levels of society, from rich households to small enterprises to squatters' shacks. In Africa, Asia, and Latin America we can identify many ways in which the poor attempt to share in what the cities have to offer, even if it is only the waste products of those who are better off.

Scavenging and recuperation by poor individuals and groups are so widespread in Third World countries that, apart from being condemned or suppressed by local authorities, these activities have, for the most part, been accepted without systematic study. The ubiquitous scavenger, "an object of admiration to a few, of pity or repulsion to most" (Keyes 1974), has been seen as the ultimate symbol of urban poverty.

In the last decade, a number of perspectives on urban scavengers have begun to converge. Scholars are reexamining the survival strategies of the poor (Eames and Goode 1980) and calling for a more detached, if not positive, approach to scavenging and recuperation at the lowest levels of the urban system (Keyes 1975, Mukherjee and Singh 1981). Scholars and planners investigating the informal economy see networks of reciprocity in the ways in which scavengers work and supply materials to small-scale manufacturing enterprises (Mukherjee n.d.) The desire to cope with increasing urban waste matter has led to discussion of the contribution scavengers make to reducing the bulk of urban garbage and to recovering items that cannot be mechanically retrieved (Cointreau1982). This thrust is part of a wider concern for more effective waste recovery and recycling in the developing countries (Long et al. 1983).

If we look up a dictionary the word 'scavenger' refers to an animal or bird. But in India or in any other caste affected country the word scavenger means Dalit or a human being who is considered as 'untouchable' or 'polluting' by caste persons. So for a manual scavenger, social identity and stigma is being born as a 'low caste' and as a 'scavenger'. Because of being born to a scavenger, the caste society forces her to be a scavenger for life. This is not an occupation or livelihood but really a social identity that is forced upon her. The stigma is further systematised by segregation of social location and segregated habitats of 'scavengers'. This stigma and caste discrimination has actively excluded all persons and communities engaged in manual scavenging from social and economic opportunities of equity. The greatest scourge of untouchability is felt by manual scavengers whose daily living based on cleaning faces from public and private latrines and dispose of dead animals from the village setup. Deemed to polluting and filthy occupation, this job is preformed Exclusively by Dalits, and that too, to a sub caste of Dalits who are considered even by other Dalits sub-castes to be wretched and 'untouchable.'

Manual Scavenging is not only a violation of human rights but also a disgrace to human dignity and humanity at large. This situation persists despite the fact that the Employment of Manual Scavengers and Construction of Dry Latrines (Prohibition) Act, 1993, is in enforcement, which provides for the prohibition of the employment of manual Scavengers as well as construction or continuance of dry latrines and for the regulation of construction and maintenance of water-seal latrines for assuring the dignity of the individual, as enshrined in the Preamble to the Constitution.

Manual scavenging continues to exist in India, despite being unacceptable and hazardous as a method of disposal of human waste, despite scientific and technological advancement on various fronts that saves manual labour, and despite the availability of simple and low-cost alternatives which can eradicate the twin problems of manual scavenging and safe disposal of human excreta. It passes on from generation to generation. Culture of acceptance prevailing among them is also depriving them of their basic rights.

In brief, the work of scavengers entails the clearing of waste material, including human excreta and garbage. It is they who maintain the complicated sewage disposal system of Mumbai as in other cities, which at times involves serious risks and calls for much courage. Theirs is thus a distinct and identifiable occupation/profession very essential to the city. The socio-religious and cultural situation in which they operate is such that the occupation/profession and the individuals who pursue it bear a stigma; since the work is 'dirty' those doing it are 'unclean'. Though innovations and improved equipment like the flush system, long-handle brooms and protective clothing tend to diminish direct contact of the workers with the waste matter, the stigma persists.

Practice of Scavenging in India[17]

Indians mainly live in villages. Even today more than 70 per cent of the country's population is rural. In ancient days the per centage was much higher. Being bereft of an enclosed place for defecation inside the house, people generally defecated in open fields, their women using secluded places either surrounded by trees or partly covered with crops of hidden by a raised, grassy mound. The same situation is still prevalent. The people living in towns needed specified places for defecation and hence, there was need for disposal of night- soil. In this way scavenging was not unknown even in ancient days in India. The scavenging work was done by a particular section of society constituting a caste or a sub-caste.

As discussed in Bindeshwar Pathaks (1991) work, the sacred

scriptures throw some light on the existence of a system for the disposal of night-soil. According to the content of sacred scriptures and other literature, scavenging, especially the disposal of night-soil by a particular caste or castes of Indian society has been in existence since beginning of the civilisation. One of the 15 duties for slaves enumerated in the Naradiya Samhita was to dispose of human excreta (Nagar; 1980: 9). In Vajasaneyi Samhita the Chandals and Paulkasa have been referred to as slaves for the disposal of night-soil. (Nagar; 1980:8). During the Buddhist period also, these two names have been mentioned. During the Buddist period also, these two names have been mentioned. During the Maurya period Patliputra (now known as Patna in Bihar State, India) was one of the five ancient towns where the city mayor as Nagrak was the head of the organisation entrusted with the task of looking after the civic affairs of the town. The scavengers and sweepers cleaned the city and disposed of night-soil.

During the Maurya period, the sanitary condition of towns was very much improved. Chanakya, known as Mantri (principal advisor) to the Emperor, has mentioned that every house should have a kitchen and a bathroom. He had suggested that one, who defecated in the open space, must be fined. However those defecated due to illness or any disability must be forgiven (Vachaspati; 1977). Malkani (1960) and other eminent scholars have sought to establish that the Bhangis (scavengers) of today were those people who were warriors made captives after they fall to the enemy.

The Muslims had brought with them some women who used the Burqua (veils) to cover their faces and they did not like to defecate in the open. The bucket privies were, therefore, designed and constructed for their defecation in Purdah. Those made captivies were forced to clean latrines like bucket privies and throw the night-soil at distant places. After those captives were released, they were not accepted by their castemen and, hence, they formed a separate caste of Bhangis who were re-named at Mehtar by Emperor Akbar. The people belonging to the Chandal caste requested the census officer in 1911 to accord them the status of Brahmin as they had the Brahmin origin. In that respect their customs, rituals and other sacramental roles are identical with those of Brahmins. There is no doubt that the Chandals were made to dispose of sullage. These Chandals took the initiative to enroll themselves as Brahmins only disposal of human excreta wee not at all divergent of a single caste (O' Malley, 1913).

Therefore, not only Kshatriyas, but also those who were engaged in cleaning night- soil since ancient time, such as Chandals, Paulkasa and also those who were made captive in wars either in India or in

Jurusalem or other parts of the world, are Bhangis and Mehtars of today. According to the 1931 Census, the total number of Bhangis was estimated at 19,57,460—10,38,678 males and 9, 18,782 female in India. (Hutton, 1933).

The foregoing account reveals that historical development led to the emergence of a special class of scavengers in India, known as Bhangis or Mehtars. This class became a hereditary occupational group with a fixed role and status in the Indian society. The unalterable role and status and the hereditary system made this class immobile and it developed into a caste or a sub-caste occupying the lowest stratum of society. With the allocation of hereditary occupation of scavenging and an immobile position, the caste or sub-caste of Bhangis became an integral part of the Indian social structure. This development was not possible without social sanction. The scavengers (Bhangis) were placed at the lowest rung of the caste ladder. The nature of the job or work traditionally associated with them, or imposed upon them, pushed them to the lowest, stratum of the social hierarchy of exterior castes. The task of cleaning night-soil was the most inferior job because this involved the touching of human excreta by the Bhangis. Consequently, they did not get social justice nor the humane treatment. Being economically poor and socially backward, they could not revolt against the unjust sanctions nor could they rid themselves of the scavenging work.

Mahatma Gandhi was the first to serve their cause and struggled for liberating the Bhangis from cleaning night-soil. In this way, he initiated the process leading to the liberation of scavengers and raised their status and position in society. Before Mahatma Gandhi appeared, nobody took up the cause of scavengers. When Mahatma Gandhi attended the National Congress Convention in Calcutta in 1901, he asked the volunteers not to engage scavengers. Surprisingly enough, the volunteers expressed their inability to do anything about it. Mahatma Gandhi set the pace by cleaning his own night-soil with the help of broom. But it made great impact on the minds of the volunteers and, thereafter, whenever the All-India Congress Convention was organised, the volunteers themselves had to take up the task of disposing of the night-soil.

In 1918, when Mahatma Gandhi started his Ashram at Sabarmati, he advised the inmates of the Ashram to tackle the problem of disposal of night-soil themselves and not to engage the professional Bhangis for that work. The inmates of the Ashram had arranged two buckets-one for defecation and the other for urination and ablution to water and they used to dump it in a trench and cover it with earth which was used as good manure. Mahatma Gandhi had got this idea of using night-soil as compost in 1908 while he was living at Tolstoy Farm in South Africa. In 1984 Mrs. Indira Gandhi disclosed in the Lok Sabha during the question hour that she herself had to clean night-soil while living as an inmate of the Sabarmati Ashram. It shows the concern of Mahatma Gandhi about the plight of the scavengers.

The Father of the Nation asked the volunteers to do social and constructive work simultaneously fighting for the independence of India. It is surprising that whereas in other fields of activity, programmes and other constructive works, only a very few disciples of Mahatma Gandhi engaged themselves in the programme of liberating scavengers.

Notable social organisations connected with the liberation of scavengers programme in India are:

(a) Harijan Sevak Sangh,

(b) Gandhi Smarak Nidhi,

(c) Safai Vidyalaya,

(d) Rajasthan institute of Local Self Government,

(e) Institute of Social Studies Trust, and

(f) Sulabh International (formerly known as Sulabh Shauchalaya Sansthan).

Gandhiji wanted the scavengers not to carry night-soil on head and advocated the adoption of some safer method for the disposal of night-soil, so that the manual handling of night-soil could be done away with. An attempt was made when at Sevagram (Wardha) a trench latrine was constructed, the merits and demerits of which have been discussed separately (Pathak; 1991).

With the development of human civilisation, scavengers in cities come from diverse social backgrounds. What they share in common is the low social status of their work, lack of security of employment, poor wages and health hazards. They can coalesce into a 'profession' with a common collective filtre in large cities. Sweepers and scavengers, though they perform essential tasks for city dwellers, remain an utterly neglected section of the metropolis. That they rank the lowest in the hierarchical structure of Indian society is well known. Their work is traditionally regarded as 'degrading' and 'defiled'. Society has always kept them at a distance.

The census reports do not provide information about the number and/or type of people doing this work. Apart from what may exist in the municipal corporation by way of rules that are applicable to its conservancy department, there is no separate legislation dealing with this category of workers. Again, not all of them are employed by the municipal corporation of Greater Mumbai. Many are in private employment without any rules and regulations. The work of scavengers entails the clearing of waste material, including human excreta and garbage. It is they who maintain the complicated sewage disposal system of Mumbai as in other cities, which at times involves serious risks and calls for much courage. Theirs is thus a distinct and identifiable occupation/profession very essential to the city. The socio-religious and cultural situation in which they operate is such that the occupation/profession and the individuals who pursue it bear a stigma; since the work is 'dirty' those doing it are 'unclean'. Though innovations and improved equipment like the flush system, long-handle brooms and protective clothing tend to diminish direct contact of the workers with the waste matter, the stigma persists.

We prefer the term 'safai kamgar' to 'scavenger' because it is a neutral term whereas scavenger meaning *'bhangi', mehtar', 'jamadar', 'zaduwala'*, is a valueladen and often abusive term. In Mumbai there are safai kamgars originating from various parts of India. There are Maharashtrians, Gujaratis, Haryanvis, Upiites, Punjabis, Tamilians among others. Their colonies are to be found in all parts of Mumbai city. The safai kamgars mostly live in separate congregations on the outskirts of the main slum areas in Mumbai. Some live in separate slum colonies such as *'Bhangi Pada', 'Bhangi Chawl', 'Anna Basti'* and *'Balmiki Basti'*, located at Mulund, Andheri, Malad and Sion respectively. The areas of major concentration of the safai kamgars in Mumbai are in Colaba, Matunga, Bandra, Andheri, Malad, Borivali and Bhandup.

A little more than two-thirds of the total of one lakh safai kamgars in Mumbai does not have a regular or regulated employment. Around 20,000 are employed permanently by the Municipal Corporation of Greater Mumbai in its conservancy section, and about 10,000 personnel were with the corporation irregularly on a 'daily' basis. A small number are employed in organisations like the railways, airports, state government establishments, big companies and private offices. The rest of the safai kamgar working population, which forms the majority, fall in the informal sector, they work in private co-operative housing societies, private individual bungalows or industrial estates. But this work being only of part-time nature, they have, of necessity, to take employment in a number of societies or factories.

What is common to all these informal sectors is that neither the jobs nor the terms and conditions of employment of safai kamgars are defined. Their wages and increments are not fixed. They do not have security of employment, nor any help at times of illness, incapacity due to accident or retirement. In other words, this means that two-thirds of the safai kamgars of Mumbai are outside the pale of any kind of legislative rights or protection.[18]

Mainly, there are three forms of manual scavenging in which people are forced to carry out scavenging work such as removal of excreta from public streets ("open defecation") and dry latrines; removal of excreta form septic tanks and cleaning closed gutters and sewage. Especially 95 per cent women are engaged in cleaning dry toilets and public streets whereas men of scavenger community enter into manhole and septic tanks to clean it. However, Delhi Higher Court directed on 27th July, 2011 to the Indian Railways to rehabilitate sanitation workers employed into cleaning railway tracks and 1,72000 toilets. Therefore there is urgent need to re define the term 'manual scavenger'.

In 2007, the Government of India estimated 3.42 lakhs manual scavengers still operated in the country. For rehabilitation purposes the Government established the 'Self Employment Scheme for Rehabilitation of Manual Scavengers' which was implemented from 2007 to March 2010. Through this scheme, more than 40.000 manual scavengers received livelihood training, almost 80.000 received loans for alternative forms of work, while almost 40.000 manual scavengers were not rehabilitated due to various reasons. On 17th June, 2011 however, the Prime Minister of India dated urged his Government to eliminate the manual scavenging practice in the next six month which further reaffirms the existence of manual scavenging practice and the difficulty of its eradication.

At the same time, the National Advisory Committee adopted a number of recommendations expediting the elimination of scavenging, while the Ministry of Labour and Employment established a Task Force on Sanitation and Leather Workers which has also been initiating a number of legislative and policy revisions to assure manual scavenging will be eradicated in India by the end of the current five year plan.

The ILO scavenging project focuses on supporting the implementation of the renewed government policy in five States, Uttar Pradesh, Bihar, Madhya Pradesh, Rajasthan and Gujarat. For this purpose, the ILO organised three consultative meetings (Lucknow, Ahmadabad and Jaipur) with representatives of the scavenger community, trade unions and civil society to gain understanding of the different forms of scavenging; rehabilitation obstacles the scavenger community is facing; and ascertain the impact and effectiveness of the available Government schemes.

These meeting were preceded by field visits to obtain the observations by state government officials as well to get a better impression of their awareness and activities regarding the elimination of manual scavenging, while keeping in mind their heavy workload and multiple responsibilities. Their views contributed to the development of a draft in the form of UN strategy paper (WHO, UNICEF and ILO), which is currently under construction. The paper will take into account various initiatives taken by the Government, trade unions, civil society and the scavenger's community themselves to bring out a holistic approach (health, water and sanitation, and occupational caste-based discrimination) to combat manual scavenging practice.[19]

Manual Scavenging as Social Exclusion[20]

The *safai karmi* (sewage and sanitation work) is one occupation which has been considered to be the meanest and the lowest in the hierarchy of occupations.[21] It has been the occupation of a certain caste group, which is the lowest within the category of scheduled castes (SCs).

State policy in India has had a long history of trying to abolish manual scavenging, but it continues to this day in many parts of the country (National Commission for Safai Karmcharis 2000). The Barve, Malkani and Pandya reports have been emphatic on the need for providing employment to the customary sewage and cleaning workers in relevant government departments of the municipalities, and on the improvement in their working conditions. The Basu task force report, on the other hand, argued that the employment generation capacity of the government and local bodies is limited and suggested social rehabilitation programmes that would provide alternative jobs (Ravichandran 2011).[22]

In general, manual scavenging is the removal of excreta (night soil) manually from "dry toilets", i.e., the toilets without modern flush system. The system of building public toilets and employing people to remove excreta was introduced during British rule in India, when municipalities were constituted. That time, often containers were used in such toilets that needed to be emptied daily. After the invention of flush type toilets, all other types of toilets disappeared from the western world. However, this inhumane practice continues in many developing countries including India.

Contextually, the term social exclusion encompasses a wide range of social and economic aspects. Different scholars decipher this notion in various contexts. Broadly, it indicates the relative deprivation of any person or group of persons on various predetermined criterion. Caste- based occupational groups in India, like that of manual scavengers, constitute one such socially, economically, psychologically and politically marginalised section of the society. Although manual scavenging was banned twice (in 1952 and 1993), this practice still continues in various pockets of the country under different names.

The concept of social exclusion, generally in development literature has been denned as an inability to choose or lack of capability to fully participate in the development of a society. In India, social exclusion revolves around some sections of the population, particularly, dalits, adivasis, women and minorities. They are the victims of social exclusion by caste, sex, ethnicity and by religion.

The evil of manual scavenging is directly related to the lack of availability of sanitation facilities. Like food, clothing and shelter, proper sanitation is one of the basic requirements of mankind. Poor sanitary conditions lead to water-borne diseases like diarrhoea, dysentery, etc.

While legally manual scavenging is banned, caste apartheid and poverty perpetuate this practice. In India, manual scavenging is a caste-based occupation carried out by dalits. The manual scavengers have different caste names in different parts of the country: Bhangis in Gujarat and Uttar Pradesh, Phakis in Andhra Pradesh and Sikkaliars in Tamil Nadu. These communities are invariably placed at the bottom of the caste hierarchy as well as dalit sub-caste hierarchy. Refusal to perform such manual task leads to physical abuse and a social boycott on facilities affects all individuals, children and women are particularly vulnerable. The Employment of Manual Scavengers and Construction of Dry Latrines (Prohibition) Act, 1993 punishes the employment of scavengers or construction of dry non-flushed latrines with imprisonment for up to one year and or the fine of Rs 2,000. Offenders are also liable to prosecution under the Scheduled Castes and Scheduled Tribes (Prevention of Aristocracies Act, 1989). Given the high prevalence of the illegal practice, the government of India launched a national scheme in 1992 for identifying, training and rehabilitating safai karmchari and allotted substantial funds for this purpose.

Despite the enactment of the Employment of Manual Scavengers and Construction of Dry Latrines (Prohibition) Act 1993, manual scavenging continues across the country. Apart from having to earn their livelihood by manually carrying or cleaning excreta, these workers are also discriminated against by stigmatisation and are forcibly hidden from the public sphere (EPW 2010). According to a Planning Commission study, more than six lakh people were engaged in scavenging in 1996. A nationwide awareness campaign was launched by a community organisation of former conservancy workers and manual scavengers—the Safai Karmchari Andolan—which had a significant impact and thereafter the number of manual scavengers and dry latrines have come down quickly

A random survey conducted by Action- Aid in 2002 in six states—Madhya Pradesh, Andhra Pradesh, Odisha, Uttar Pradesh, Rajasthan and Bihar—claimed that manual scavengers were found working on at least 30,000 dry toilets.[23] The survey also pointed out that, these scavengers face severe discrimination even from other dalit.

The Safai Karmi Scheme[24]

The Government of India launched a national scheme in 1992 for identifying, training and rehabilitating safai karmchari. On the same line the UP government started an innovative scheme of placing one safai karmi in each village for improving sanitation and hygiene. This scheme was also conceived as a part of the rehabilitation of the scavenger community—the Bhangis, a particular caste which has historically been forced by the caste system to clean public places, toilets and drains—by providing them government and alternative employment in place of manual scavenging.

This scheme was entrusted to the Panchayati Raj department which was expected to implement it through its administrative apparatus available at the district, block and village levels. The scheme was also expected to contribute to the eradication of manual scavenging. Under this scheme it was proposed that there would be a safai karmi in each revenue village. She/he has to be a Class VIII pass, not above the age of 40 years and should be a resident of the same community development block. However, preference is given to candidate(s) from the same village. A selection committee is constituted at the district level with the district panchayat officer as the chairperson along with three other members, nominated by the district magistrate comprising representative(s) of the SCs, Other Backward Classes (OBCs) and upper castes. Safai karmis are at the level of the Class IV employees of the state government. The number of seats in each district is reserved for different categories as per the state policy on reservation.

These safai karmis are expected to clean the lanes and by lanes of the revenue village(s) as also other public places like the school, the anganwadi centres, community toilets and also to keep the drainage system functional. Government service with clear job descriptions, duties and rights is expected to empower the safai karmis and their dependents, and thus help take them away from traditional occupations, providing them an opportunity to work their way up the social and economic ladder with dignity. This scheme is expected to pave the way for liberation and rehabilitation of manual scavengers.

Social Mobility and Weaker Section: A Background

Development involves complex processes and procedures of institutional changes and the redistribution of economic and political power for better egalitarian society. It must be broadly conceived as the expansion of opportunities and the enhancement of human capacities. The reduction of mass poverty, unemployment and inequality are the concomitant of development so conceived. In this regard, Amartya Sen (1999) rightly points that development requires the removal of major sources of unfreedom and to see the 'instrumental' perspective of freedom.

In fact, Karl Marx's favourable remarks on capitalism as against the unfreedom of precapitalist labour arrangements; related exactly to the question of viewing freedom in developmental setting. Seeing development in terms of the substantive freedoms of people has far-reaching implications for our understanding of the processes of development and also for the ways and means of promoting it. On the evaluative side, this involves the need to assess the requirements of development in terms of removing the unfreedoms from which the members of the society may suffer. The process of development, in this view, is not essentially different from the history of overcoming these unfreedoms. While this history is not by any means unrelated to the process of economic growth and accumulation of physical and human capital, its reach and coverage go much beyond these variables.

In focusing on freedom versus evaluative development, it is not being suggested that there is some unique and precise "criterion" of development in terms of which the different development experiences can always be compared and ranked. Given the heterogeneity of distinct components of freedom as well as the need to take note of different persons' versus diverse freedoms, there will often be arguments that go in contrary directions. The motivation underlying the approach of "development as freedom" is not so much to order all states or all alternative scenarios into one "complete ordering," but to draw attention to important aspects of the process of development, each of which deserves attention. Even after such attention is paid, there will no doubt remain differences in possible overall rankings, but their presence is not embarrassing to the purpose at hand.

What would be damaging would be the neglect—often to be seen in the development literature- of centrally relevant concerns because of a lack of interest in the freedoms of the people involved. An adequately broad view of development is sought in order to focus the evaluative scrutiny on things that really matter, and in particular to avoid the neglect of crucially important subjects. While it may be nice to think that considering the relevant variables will automatically take different people to exactly the same conclusions on how to rank alternative scenarios, the approach requires no such unanimity. Indeed, debates on such matters, which can lead to important political arguments, can be part of the process of democratic participation that characterises development.

It should be clear from the above discussion that the term 'freedom' here is being felt on the lines of equality and liberty to all sections of society, may it be Scheduled Castes, Scheduled Tribes or any other minority. It involves not only the processes that allow freedom of actions and decisions, but also the actual opportunities that people have, inspite of their personal and social circumstances. Unfreedom can arise either through inadequate processes (such as the violation of voting privileges or other political civil rights) or through inadequate opportunities that some people have for achieving what they minimally would like to achieve (including the absence of such elementary opportunities as the capability to escape premature mortality or preventable morbidity or involuntary starvation). It is very important to see freedom in a sufficiently broad way. It is necessary to avoid confining attention only to appropriate procedures (as so-called libertarians sometimes do, without worrying at all about whether some disadvantaged people suffer from systematic deprivation of substantive opportunities), or, alternatives that bring the opportunities about or the freedom of choice that people have). Both processes and opportunities have importance of their own, and each aspect relates to seeing development as freedom.

While presenting empirical studies; Sen (1999) discusses a number of instrumental freedoms that contribute, directly or indirectly, to the overall freedom i.e., people have to live the way they could like to live. Thus, diversities of the instruments involved are quite extensive. According to Sen (1999), the freedom can be viewed on three parameters viz:

Firstly, Political freedoms broadly conceived (including what are called civil rights), refer to the opportunities that people have to determine who should govern and on what principles, and also include the possibility to scrutinise and criticise authorities, to have freedom of political expression and an uncensored press, to enjoy the freedom to choose between different political parties, and so on. They include the political entitlements associated with democracies in the broadest sense (encompassing opportunities of political dialogue, dissent and critique as well as voting rights and participatory selection of legislators and executives).

Secondly, Economic facilities referring to the opportunities that individual respectively enjoy utilising economic resources for the purpose of consumption, or production, or exchange. The economic entitlements that a person has will depend on the resources owned or available for use as well as on conditions of exchange, such as relative prices and the working of the markets. Insofar as the process of economic development concerns increases the income and wealth of a country, as well as reflecting the corresponding enhancement of economic entitlements of the population. It should be obvious that in the relation between national income and wealth, on the one hand, and the economic entitlements of individuals (or families), on the other are to be correlated. Thus distributional considerations should go along aggregative ones.

The availability and access to finance can be a crucial influence on the economic entitlements that economic agents are practically able to secure. This applies all the way from large enterprises (in which hundreds of thousands of people may work) to tiny establishments that are run on micro credit. A credit crunch, for example, can severely affect the economic entitlements that rely on such credit.

Thirdly, social opportunities refer to the arrangements that society makes for education, health care and so on, which influence the individual's substantive freedom to live better. These facilities are important not only for the conduct of private lives (such as living a healthy life and avoiding preventable morbidity and premature mortality), but also for more effective participation in economic and political activities. For example, illiteracy can be a major barrier to participation in economic activities that require production according to specification for demand strict quality control (as globalised trade increasingly does). Similarly, political participation may be hindered by the inability to read newspapers or to communicate in writing with others involved in political activities.

Indian sociology is more than a century old, but even today Indian sociologists have not been able to evolve a politically correct language to describe the dalits. Along with other social scientists, they use the same stigmatised identities like 'lower castes', 'exterior castes', 'untouchables', 'Harijans', etc., for dalits. Against this, they use a refined language for the castes located higher in the caste hierarchy: 'upper castes', 'twice-born', etc. The language used is partisan, and it stigmatises dalits. When questioned, Indian sociologists have argued that they do it for objectivity. The objective reality, however, is different and dalits have been addressed by different nomenclatures at the grassroots: Chandalas, Hinajatians, Avarnas, Asprashya, Antyajas, Achhuts, Pariahs, Namsudras, Panchamas (the fifth class or category), etc. These social identities had sigma, segregation and contempt writ large. Is this the true social democracy we talking about?

Great change has taken place among all sections of population including the Scheduled Castes in India since its political independence. People belonging to the Scheduled Castes have availed relatively more facilities and enjoyed better social status in urban than in rural areas. During all these years, the Scheduled Castes in villages have definitely been influenced by changes occurred in their surroundings and have derived inspirations from those of their own caste fellows and others who have improved socio-economic changes positions. In such a scenario there is a great urge among the people of these castes to improve their status and achieve upward mobility in the social hierarchy in villages. In spite of the various types of socio-economic changes occurred in villages, the existing social structure in rural India has not yet changed accordingly.

The changes that have occurred are primarily in the horizontal direction and there is a greater amount of resistance to the vertical changes if there are any. Both horizontal and vertical types of changes occurred or even an urge for that among the Scheduled Castes are opposed by people of all castes and communities in villages. The concern is to have a peep into the socio-economic conditions of the Scheduled Castes and their efforts made for achieving social mobility in the villages. It is also intended to analysis the extent to which their social mobility or even their urge for that is likely to promote hostility among others leading to inter-group conflict and finally infliction of various types of atrocities on the Scheduled Castes in rural areas.

Conceptually, the term *'social mobility'* refers to the process by which individuals move from one position to another in society—positions which by general consent have been given specific hierarchical values. Thus, social mobility can be defined as "the movement of individuals, families and groups from one social position to another". Within this framework, if social mobility is to be achieved through education (the only channel available for the scheduled castes) then the contribution of higher education is crucial. It is higher education that is linked to higher occupation and income, and hence to social status. What part does education have to play in improving the social and economic status of SCs? How does social background influence one's motivation to pursue and succeed in higher education and to acquire a better job? This study assesses the role of reservation policy also after having experimented it for last 50 years. It is also worth finding out the problems the scheduled castes face after having acquired education (*Wankhede* 1999, p. 36).

Lipset and Zetterberg suggest some multiple dimensions through which a study of 'total' social mobility is possible. These dimensions are: occupational rankings, consumption rankings, social class and power rankings. Thus, social mobility of an individual or a group can be studied either through changes in one dimension (for instance, occupation) or changes in several dimensions mentioned above. There is a third explanation as well, of social mobility. There are people in the lower castes who *"are getting equipped for upward mobility in the foreseeable future"* and there are a few who have attained a marginal social status where they have improved a bit of there earlier low status and, at the psychological level, claim to be socially mobile. Such mobility may be called *'psychic'* mobility. The proofs of their mobility "can be seen, firstly, in psychological withdrawal of 'legitimation' to the stigma of pollution; secondly, in the ambivalent responses within the Scheduled Caste cluster; and finally, in the violent group confrontations with the dominant communities of the region."[25]

Distinction is usually drawn between *'social'* and *'occupational mobility'*, but the term *Social Mobility* has a very wide meaning and represents a multi- dimensional problem. As suggested by *Hall, Social Mobility* is usually approached from a number of dimensions. One such dimension is the phase of mobility. A second dimension of mobility involves it's direction. In the first dimension of mobility inter—generational mobility is included. Regarding the direction of mobility, three separate, but related directional axes can be identified. The first is vertical mobility, indicating up or down movement. The second axis is a change in social function, which does not involve change in status or horizontal mobility. The third axis is spatial mobility, change in the location of the occupation.[26]

Social mobility is such a wider term and includes within it the upward or downward changes in economic, political or occupational states of either the individual or a whole group. Modern industrial society offers increased opportunities for economic and political fluctuations through free competition and specialisation of education. Sometimes, the distinction between occupational mobility and social mobility is forgotten, but, it has to be kept in mind that occupational mobility is only a part of social mobility.

On one hand, the *social mobility* refers to the variation in the social origin of the members of a given social stratum. On the other hand it also refers to the ways in which the opportunities available to a given generation of men are distributed among them, according to their various characteristics. Consequent to the urbanisation and industrialisation, conditions of city life have broken down many of the occupational taboos imposed by caste. Traditionally caste denoted not only a rank but also a function, each caste group having a definite occupation as determined by the hereditary qualities.

The early writers on the caste system in India argued that its occupational structure was complex and rigid and possibilities for occupational change did not exist. However, there are some studies which have thrown some light on changes in the traditional occupational structure, which have occurred throughout Indian History. They have brought to light instances which were not only possible theoretically, but they have actually occurred. According to *Hazara (1940)* occupational mobility was allowed among the lower castes even during the classified Hindu period. *Brown (1959)* and *Heart (1950)* have also given the similar observations. According to *Brown,* the Phenomenon of old aristocracy in decay is probably age old. It is an aspect of the consent shifting in class composition and caste hierarchy. As far back as the Vedic period, it is possible to observe assimilation of Vaisyas and Shudras. *Hoeart* observed that this latitude is not modern, not brought about by the disturbing influence of Europe.[27]

Historical instances of upward social mobility by change of occupation from lower to higher and to respectable occupations, are cited by *Maynard (1970), Orans (1959), Pannikar (1955), Sinder (1958) and Thapper (1966). Thapper* noted that there is evidence of Jati mobility from the Gupta period as when silk weavers organised as a guild..."moved across to another region and rose to new and respectable occupations. *Stein* stated that "during the medieval period vast tracts lands were available for settlements, and enterprising families could move from one region to another and settle down as Rajas or Feudal lords and establish peasant settlements" and some of the reasons for this phenomenon are fluidity of the political system, hypergamy, legislation of Brahmina, genealogists and kings migration and availability of vast tracts of available land, the monopoly of power, wealth of dominant castes, social status, Centres of Pilgrimage, monasteries and Bhakti movements.

Macro-images of Sanitation of Indian Villages through Modernisation

After independence, the Indian Constitution, which recognised the democratic needs of a plural society, became a major source for democratic revolution and the Indian Government proceeded to promote the individual rights and equality of all. Lower-caste advancement was considered a necessary first step in the promotion of individual rights. Social justice according to this view thus requires a public policy that guarantees individual mobility by means of group allocation. In contemporary India, while there has been reformulation of caste practices in the unofficial inner domain, there has been permeation of the value of equality denying importance of caste in the outer official sphere. After independence, it was one of the foremost concerns of the government to resolve the colonial dichotomy of traditional society versus the modern state, and to integrate them in a new form of nation-state. Although the tradition of national culture was to be celebrated, any traditional features in society that were seen to be incongruent with the new 'Idea of India' based on principles of democracy and liberalism were considered suspect for the development of modern India (Khilnani; 1999). Contemporarily, the significance of the social development and empowerment of marginalised groups thus entails sincere demolition of the structure of subordination imposed on them and sharing power with the powerless lots. It raises the anxiety like—assertive castes vis-à-vis rural institutionalised structure of subordination, possible implications of declining caste hierarchy on rural India.

In the present context, Dumont's thesis on the unaffected continuity of the encompassing structure of caste hierarchy in rural India seems untenable today. Fuller (Fuller; 1996: 21) suggests instead that there is 'above all a denial, most explicitly in the public domain of the existence or continuing significance of caste in its "traditional form"'. Fundamental changes have occurred in the occupational structure of the society. A vast number of non-traditional, unbound-to-caste occupations and a new type of social relations among occupational groups have emerged. This has resulted in breaking down the nexus between hereditary? Ritual status and occupation - one of the caste-system's defining features. It is no longer necessary to justify status of one's occupation in terms of its correlation with degree of ritual purity or impurity associated with it. Situating the dynamics of 'dominant caste' phenomena, one may agree that different castes were competing over the others for showing their supremacy. Historically, this phenomenon was mainly confined to the 'twice born' castes but presently, it is applicable to lower caste groups as well.

One significant change in contemporary rural India was to transform village and caste from its restricted local and parochial confines into a national and global network. Horizontal caste solidarity was one of the important factors that made universal franchise intrinsic for any governance. The right to vote in turn gave political teeth to horizontal caste solidarity. Horizontal caste solidarity at the regional and national level qualitative changed not only the nature of the polity but also the nature of the state.

The establishment of democracy in independent India has introduced one major change in the way caste and politics interact, and that is by making all castes legally equal. It took some time for this legal equality to gain empirical momentum, but with the gradual dissolution of the closed village economy, the tempo has certainly become easily visible to the naked eye. This combination between law and economic change has allowed castes that were hitherto considered low to take the fight the traditional superior communities and even to thumb their noses at established symbolic and ritual systems (Gupta; 2005). This led to demands among many castes for special recognition by the state for receiving educational and occupational benefits as well as for political representation.

Extending the debate, it can be referred that if we compare the village studies of 1950s with the contemporary village studies, we find a shift from 'treating the village as a locale for the study of a chosen aspect of rural life' to 'treating village as an interacting community with the outside world, both at regional and national level'. Contemporary debates about the conceptual discussions on the nature of a village community have raised the issue of the transitional shift in the 'way of life' of the village. Various agents of transformation have been rightly noted by Chauhan (2005; 295), including increasing participation in the national, state levels and the fact that *Panchayati Raj* Institutions have highlighted the value of social linkages, as well as instituted a degree of local patriotism or dignity. To him, mass communication now covers the rural areas. Problem-solving mechanisms in the form of voluntary agencies—local, national and international—are at work. International organised efforts through the U.N. agencies—the World Bank, the UNCTAD, UNICEF, the FAO and donor agencies at state levels—are visible in rural areas. A new vocabulary in the identification of stakeholders, participatory planning, felt needs, and techniques of monitoring that could be centrally administered, were seen. It gave rise to new interconnections with user groups, micro-financing, self-help group, water harvesting and capacity building for repaying loans, etc.

To Atal (2005:298), studying rural India has big difference between the 1950s and now, indeed it includes the *Dalit* awakening and the shift away from governmental action towards civil society initiatives. In this regard, Shah (1992) describes the rural poor as being diverse in their composition—farmers, landlords, artisans, *Dalit*—because of which the process of change and resistance, too, had a diverse character (J Breman et al 1997; Epstein et al, 1998). This could be seen in the direction of the new farmer's movement, identity assertion, multiple identities and other social action in rural India.

As rightly emphasised by Sheth (1999), "the most important among the changes was the formation of a new, trans-local identity among 'lower castes', collectively as a people with the consciousness of being 'oppressed' by the traditional system of hierarchy". The established categories of ritual hierarchy began to be confronted with new categories like 'depressed castes' and 'oppressed classes'. Several castes occupying more or less similar locations in different local hierarchies began to organise themselves horizontally into regional and national level associations and federations, as it became increasingly necessary for them to negotiate with the state and in the process project their larger social identity and numerical strength. Secularisation of caste has detached caste from the other-worldly reasoning, ritual status hierarchy and has imparted it a character of the power-group functioning in the competitive democratic politics on the other. Changes in caste thus could be observed along these two dimensions of secularisation: de-ritualisation and politicisation. These changes have (a) pushed caste out of the traditional stratificatory system, (b) linked it to the new structure of representational power, and (c) in their cumulative impact they have made it possible for individual members of different castes to acquire new economic interest and social-political identification and own class-like as well as ethnic-type identities".

Modern villages with the rapid urbanisation and means of transport and communication weakened the rigid hierarchical order. Commercialisation of agriculture, electrification, using of canals and tube-wells for irrigation, tractors replacing plough and bullock carts, importance of cash, etc., have not only decreased the *jajmani* system but have also brought rationality in agrarian economy and exchange (Saxena: 2007). According to Rudolph and Rudolph (1967), the displacement of the large landowners by middle farmers may be accurately described as one of the most significant developments of the post-Independence period. The middle farmers today constitute the most powerful group in the countryside, economically as well as politically. Thus, India has been experiencing the emergence of new agrarianism. Millions of farmers are mobilising themselves against the State. Sharad Joshi, among other exponents of new agrarianism, advocates remunerative prices for agricultural commodities, electric supply at nominal rates, etc. This has led to a vertical mobilisation of the agrarian classes.

In the framework of the e-rural programme, ICTs are introducing new critical approaches to rurality, bringing about social and technical change, and promoting a series of services (e-governance, e-communities, e-culture, e-health, e-business, e-learning). On the one hand ICTs are shaping a much more interrelated rural scenario, on the other hand they are leading to serious challenges. Thus there is a need for reviewing the diffusion and impacts of ICTs specifically on the rural areas and focusing on their contribution in reframing a modern concept of rurality and in fostering rural development based on interdisciplinary design issues and on the involvement of local communities. Stress should be on ICT which might bring to economic development and digital equality for rural areas. The approach taken to achieve this broad objective can be a modular concept using multi-media to develop and disseminate multi-disciplinary information and knowledge from multiple-sources to multiple-users with built in user needs assessment and feedback mechanisms. This modular approach may support an evolving; pluralistic knowledge based rural extension system consisting of the following elements:

- Accelerates the transition process - recognising the importance of diverse information and knowledge user needs.
- Increasing importance of non-farm activities to supplement farm incomes especially for the emerging small private farmer.
- Evolution of diversified service providers consisting of contractual arrangements, public-private sector partnerships involving NGO's, producer organisations, association of private farmers, water user associations, etc.
- Creation of a decentralised and localised extension programme management and delivery where all forms of media - from traditional to modern will play a role.
- Creation of strong linkages between education, research, and various forms of farming systems and works in coordination with other providers of rural information and knowledge - such as health, education, micro and small enterprise credit, environment, eco-tourism, etc. (Saxena; 2014).

Sanitation of Rural India Through Various State Interventions

In the context of the growth of postcolonial studies and the indigenisation of knowledge, and with reference also to post-structural and post-modern social theory, the field of development studies has undergone a significant critique and rethinking. To quote Clark (1991), now debates were made for 'development from below'. Voluntary groups, civil societies and NGO's, were seen as having greater diversity, credibility, and creativity than official agencies in producing a 'just development' characterised by equity, democracy and social justice as well as by economic growth. Further, Participatory Action Research (PAR) as 'peoples power' came into prominence in the 1970's for the peoples of the Third World with a broader political objective to develop a more participatory, direct, and self-managed form of democracy than in the representational political systems. Extending further, Uma Kothari and Martin Minogue (2002; 101) said - beyond the participation debate, several major changes occurred in the development cooperation context throughout the 1990s, all interrelated and all relevant to the participation issue and emphasising on governance, human rights and partnership; and the ascendancy to prominence of 'civil society'.

Coming to India, we recognise that rural transformation in post-Independent India is marked by centralised development strategy to decentralised development i.e., a shift from community development to Panchayati Raj. It can be anticipated as a shift from silent revolution (top-bottom approach) to most revolutionary stage (bottom-top approach) in administration and development. Panchayati Raj is claimed to be an indigenous model of development since time immemorial and in the present context it is an innovative mechanism to bridge the gap between the policy planners/decision-makers (at the top) and the actual practitioner (at the bottom). It increases the effectiveness of the democratic system by filling up the organisational gaps between the masses and the governing national elite. Panchayanti Raj is thus projected as an apparatus dealing with democratic decentralisation and was discovered to supply the local interest and stimulate local initiative in the field of development. This apart, Panchayati Raj institutions are intended to be the agencies of socialisation for learning lessons of democratic responsibility in political education. It is to prepare the citizens for responsible living and to develop leaders who could take control of democratic institutions at state and national level.

In brief, the representative and participatory democracy for rural India signifies following agendas:

- More democracy; adequate devolution and dialogue;

- Equality of opportunity and non-discrimination in every sphere;
- Reduction of disparities, in respect of income, wealth, privileges and advantage;
- Efficient and optimum utilisation of scarce national resources;
- Elimination of extravagance and conspicuous consumption;

Coming to the issue of Panchayati Raj as facilitator of local self-government, one can say that it works on the principles of local self-government and can be analysed as:

- People centred government;
- Government run by local people;
- Peoples participation in governmental affairs;
- Involvement of government in local issues;
- Peoples representation in government machinery;
- Peoples control over government activities and
- Enabling authority, competitive council and quality services.

Though, it is true that the above projection is a transitory metamorphosis of the Indian politico-administrative scene but when we see it in the context of above global progression of development, we may realise that India's grass-root participation model, as a gauge for participatory development in federal structure, too have many flaws. Regarding the question of who participates in whose project? It is realised that at the level of practice the central challenges are marrying the participation agenda with the governance agendas. It is observed at the level of rhetoric, the participation orthodoxy no longer finds it sufficient to permit 'peripheral's' to participate in 'mainstream governing' projects, but recognises that 'mainstream governing' projects are going to change 'peripheral' lives much, and seeks to find out what 'peripheral' projects of life might be and how 'mainstream'-practitioners, academicians and official agencies might most usefully participate in them.

Emphasising on the state intervention and its implication on rural India Sathyamurthy (1996) asserts, aegis of a planned economy, modernisation, and Green revolution led a rapid growth of food production and far-reaching uneven differentiation of peasantry. Economic development in India has resulted in a number overlapping imbalance: Between the agrarian and industrial bourgeoisie; between politicians and bureaucrats; between a rapidly differentiated middle peasantry and the agrarian classes below it; between upper castes and middle/lower castes; between middle castes and Dalits; between men and women.

After the mid 60's, it is the agricultural sector, which took the lead in the growth process. The so-called Green Revolution witnessed the emergence and consolidation of powerful capitalist strata. The qualitative changes occurring in the country-side includes—a section of the old rent-receiving landlords was stimulated by the enhanced profitability of agriculture in the mid 60's to undertake productive investment in this sphere. At the same time, the rich peasantry who acquires right over land also started commercial agriculture. Through this admixture of landlord capitalism and rich peasant capitalism, a new class of agricultural bourgeoisie emerged, which consolidated its position after mid 60's.

Emerging Issues

- Agrarian reform introduced by Congress under the leadership of Nehru in 1952 brought a veritable revolution in the countryside.
- India's Community development programme has been acclaimed as reflecting the attempt to the objective of economically and socially democratic policy in the countryside since 1952. Over the last two decades, the focus on community development shifted to community participation.
- There is a need to emphasise the distinction between regular continuing relationship between village and the State. Although there is hardly any direct government intervention in the production and investment decision related to agriculture by farmers. But the government does influence the legal, material and economic environment in which farmers operate.
- After independence state not acted as neutral referee to the caste activities and launched laws relating to untouchability, reservation etc. Government intervention in the form of reservation in education and jobs in favour of OBC, has also contributed to the worsening of the relations between similar and dissimilar castes.
- The concept of citizen has provided them an equal playfield to some extent.
- Universal franchise gave motivation to horizontal caste solidarity.
- Wells, tube wells and pump set for lifting ground water are mostly in the hands of individual farmers. But they are subject to government regulation meant to serve the interest of equity and sustainability. Government provides infrastructure facilities to the rural areas.

- In order to strengthen agricultural development, the credit is flowing through institutional channel like NABARD, SIDBI, Cooperative banks, and other private banks.

Now let us systematically understand the sharp implications of state intervention on village community under following heads (See Saxena; 2005):

The process of Liberalisation, Privatisation and Globalisation and the emerging forces out of them are the most powerful and deadly to the rural community as it exposes the village globally. In some sense it seems good but it is more destructive to developing country like India. It has brought new competitors for the total village and resulting to reshape the village setting. Summarising salient issues:

- The process of liberalisation, privatisation and globalisation has restructured local and parochial configures into the national and global network.
- Liberalisation is leading to enlarging private sectors in irrigation and allied activities. Private Corporation is acquiring land for raising crops and forests.
- The current debate on globalisation focuses on the role of international trade and market as a cohesive force.
- Prior to globalisation, peasants never felt threatened, as there were no barriers to exchange, distribution or multiply seeds.
- The current debate on globalisation focuses on the role of international trade and market as a cohesive force.
- Local communities feel both unstable and unsafe in the face of global market force-bolstered up by media and too are controlled by MNC's. The media impact on local communities and culture is so shattering that the consumer culture has pushed them to the threshold of extinction. Local economies are being swallowed by the global capitalism and traditional culture is being displaced by the ever-expanding global market and consumer culture.
- Aspect of Eco-agriculture like depletion of ground water resources and land resources are emerging.

Sanitation and Disease in an Industrial Setting in India[28]

Industrialisation began in India in the middle of the nineteenth century with the building of the railways and the emergence of textile and jute mills. Until the end of the century, the major employers of the labour force were the cotton and jute mills, the railways and the coal mines. According to the Royal Commission's report, by 1929 the pattern of industry had changed somewhat. Cotton, jute and the railways remained as very large employers but plantations of tea, coffee and rubber had also become major employers. Manufacturing units had expanded into steel, general engineering, paper, cigarettes, armaments and foundries. Mining had expanded into manganese and mica, and a nascent construction sector had begun to emerge to support the industrialisation process. In addition, an 'unregulated' sector was being drawn into the market economy, a sector made up mainly of traditional activities in bidi, shellac, carpet, wool, mica, and match manufacture.

Changing pattern of industrial production and expanding work force had its own implications for the health of the workers. For example, industries like textiles, jute and mining had mechanical and dust hazards and their intrinsic dangers were combined with the insanitary conditions in which workers were forced to live. The introduction of machinery, especially high-speed machines, created higher risks of accidents while the chemical, fertiliser and petroleum industries brought in the risk of genetic diseases, chronic poisoning and ecological destruction. Thus, the total work force also expanded as industry diversified and their associated hazards increased.

Hazardous work manifests itself, in the first instance, in injuries to the human body. In the extreme case this also results in death or severe disability. Since these injuries or fatalities are required to be reported under the law and since they and their causal factors are immediately visible, considerable data exists over a large number of years on death and injury in Indian industry.

An examination of frequency rates of industrial injuries is quite revealing. It shows that the rates of fatal injuries in mines are very high as compared to the rates of fatal injuries in factories. A comparison with cases reported under the different Acts shows a marked and consistent difference between fatal injury rates as reported under the Factories Act and the Workmen's Compensation Act. According to the Workmen's Act and the rates of fatal injuries become more than double. This reveals the lacunae in the implementation of the Factories Act 1948. Despite the limitations of the data however, the rising frequency rates of injuries as recorded under the Factories Act suggest the increasingly hazardous nature of the actual working conditions in industries.

Work hazards are also responsible for occupational diseases. The official records on occupational diseases are difficult to interpret as not only do the symptoms often take long to appear, but employers are also reluctant to relate the diseases to occupational factors. Thus an extremely small number of cases come to notice, depending upon the zeal of the factory inspectors or the militancy and knowledge of the workers. According to the Labour Bureau's records, till as late as 1948 there was no way of detecting occupational diseases other than the Workmen's Compensation Act under which returns submitted by provincial governments was the main source of information.

The evidence brings out the following trends:

- There has been a significant increase in the industrial work force and a consequent increase in the population exposed to industrial work hazards both in terms of injuries, diseases, and death.
- The expansion of industries and higher growth rates has not necessarily meant better working conditions. The risk to the health of the workers has in fact increased. This is so because hazards in each industry have increased on account of higher-speed machinery, use of new and unfamiliar technology and intensification of work. The only exception to this trend is the petroleum, rubber and plastics industries, where the rates have declined over time but still remain high.
- There has been a significant diversification in industrial production. This has meant new risks for the workers. For instance, while plantation and mine workers were exposed earlier to the vagaries of the weather, dangerous working conditions and maltreatment from their employers, the emergence of heavy engineering, steel, nuclear energy and chemicals has increased exposure to heat, noise, machinery and chemical and radiation hazards.
- The traditional industries like textiles and jute, which largely suffered on account of competition and were poorly maintained, have the highest rates of accidents and injuries.

Sanitation and Health in Urban Areas[29]

The urbanisation of poverty must be understood in the context in which it occurs. The accelerated economic growth in China and India in the past two decades, although leading to rising income inequality (especially in urban areas), has lifted over half a billion people out of $1-a-day poverty between 1981 and 2004 (UN-Habitat 2008).[30]

The challenges of sanitation service delivery are exacerbated by the fact that many poor urban residents live in the unplanned and underserved informal settlements commonly known as slums or in expanding peri-urban areas. Urban administrations do not have the capacity and often are not planning for service provision in these marginalised areas. This is reflected in the most recent United Nations Joint Monitoring Programme reports that predict that the number of the world's urban population without access to a safe source of drinking water will increase from 137 million (2006) to 296 million (2015) and those without access to improved sanitation will increase from 661 million to 898 million, respectively (UN JMP 2008).[31]

In these expansive urban and peri-urban settlements, irregular water supply and 'on-site sanitation' are the norms. Yet, despite on-site low-cost sanitation being the reality for the vast majority of the developing world's urban population, much of the focus for policy-makers is still on network sewerage and centralised systems designed and implemented without consultation or participation of stakeholders and beneficiaries (Eawag 2005).[32] Many governments and international donors continue to propagate over-engineered and heavily subsidised solutions assuming that 'one size fits all' will improve access to all persons living in developing cities.

Furthermore, local authorities and utilities by-pass informal settlements and will not invest in new infrastructure because they lack formal tenure and are seen as 'illegal'. The result is an increasing gap between the 'haves' and 'have-nots' in basic services and municipalities that are locked into expensive systems without the possibilities to extend coverage to those that need it.

Despite this trend, there have been a number of recent innovative initiatives for extending the coverage of sanitation services in both rural and urban contexts. These approaches are based on demand-driven and participatory approaches that both motivate community involvement and encourage appropriate technology which better fits the realities in the field. They promote participatory processes where solutions result from the inputs of local stakeholders and not solely from 'conventional wisdom' or 'prescriptive' planning (Atkinson 2007).[33]

Some of the key challenges that make the urban area more challenging than the rural environment are given below:

Heterogeneous populations: people from different origins, ethnic backgrounds, social norms make for heterogeneous nature of urban settlements;

• *Land tenureship:* a key issue that needs to be addressed as it is much more difficult to achieve sustainable infrastructure solutions with tenants or absentee landlords in a commoditised urban land market;

• *Sanitation chain:* Urban sanitation presents great challenges in the development of integrated solutions for managing a variety of waste streams that go beyond achieving defecation-free environments (e.g. proper disposal of household wastewater; faecal sludge management)

• *Technology choice:* dense urban settlements limit the feasible technology options available

• *Institutional fragmentation:* rural institutional responsibilities are mostly straightforward while in the urban sphere a multitude of different stakeholders have a claim: local authorities, health departments, utilities, communities, etc.

The household-centred environmental sanitation approach: HCES is a multi-sector planning approach geared towards service delivery in poor urban areas: it integrates water supply, storm-water and sewage management; facilitates the incorporation of input from diverse actors and utilises the concept of urban zones for enhancing the implementation of decentralised options. The HCES guidelines (WSSCC 2000) propose a 10-step process initiated with a direct request from a community or community leader and culminating with the implementation of plans developed during the planning process.[34]

The HCES approach belongs to the family of communicative planning frameworks that focus on participatory, bottom-up methodologies where planners solicit the participation of a variety of stakeholders in a democratic planning process (Hamdi and Goethert 1997).[35]

Successful implementation of the HCES approach requires the dissemination of information on affordable and sustainable sanitation options to those responsible for improving environmental services, such as municipal officials, urban planners and community representatives or chiefs. To fulfil their new roles, process stakeholders need to be provided with information and assistance so that their capacity to make decisions, implement and manage services grows. Widening the scope of possible adapted and affordable solutions from storage to transport to treatment and disposal/re-use is a cornerstone of the household-centred approach (Lüthi *et al*. 2007).[36]

A further feature of HCES is the environmental sustainability concept based on circular resource management systems, addressing environmental sanitation problems as close as possible to their source, and emphasis is placed on resource conservation and waste reduction. This underlines recent sectoral developments that have targeted alternative approaches and solutions to the increasing environmental sanitation problem. Innovations follow the paradigm to develop a set of technologies that facilitate and allow best re-use of human waste products. Some examples are urine and faeces separation and their re-use in agriculture (Tilley *et al.* 2008) or faecal sludge collection and treatment for re-use (Koné *et al.* 2007).[37,38]

Issues on Urban Water Pollution[39]

Water is one of the most important and basic natural resources. Water is not only one of the most essential commodities of our day-to-day life, but the development of this natural resource also plays a crucial role in economic and social development processes. While the total amount of water available in the world is constant and is generally said to be adequate to meet all the demands of mankind, its quality and distribution over different regions of the world is uneven and causes problems of scarcity and suitability. It is therefore imperative that man develops, uses and manages this scarce commodity as rationally and efficiently as possible. In order to execute this task, accurate and adequate information must be available about the quality of the natural resource under constantly changing human pressures and natural forces.

Water quality management is for a great deal controlled by authorisation of discharges of dangerous substances for which monitoring of discharges, effluents and influenced surface water is essential. On national and state levels, we have several policies and regulation like Water (Prevention and Control of Pollution) Act, 1974 to regulate pollution discharges and restore water quality of our aquatic resources including the prescription of monitoring activities. Under Water Act, 1974, pollution control boards were created, which are responsible for implementation of its provisions. One of the important provisions of the Water Act, 1974 is to maintain and restore the 'wholesomeness' of our aquatic resources. To define the level of 'Wholesomeness to be maintained or restored a system of water use classification was developed. Under this system water uses are classified in five classes. If a water body or its part is used for multipurpose, then the use which demands highest quality of water is designated as 'designated best use' and accordingly water body or its part is designated. Now through regular water quality monitoring existing water quality is assessed and compared with the desired quality as identified under designated best use class and gaps are identified. Based on the identified gaps the water body or its part is identified as polluted.

Water quality monitoring is one of the first steps required in the rational development and management of water resources. In the field of water quality management, there has been a steady evolution in procedures for designing system to obtain information on the changes of water quality .The 'monitoring' comprise all activities to obtain 'information' with respect to the water system.

Water quality monitoring is a complex subject, and the scope of it is both deep and wide. Water quality monitoring has a direct relation with chemistry, biology, statistics and also economics. Its scope is also related to the types of water uses and functions which are manifold and the nature of the sources of water such as surface water (rivers and lakes), sea water groundwater.

The Central Pollution Control Board (CPCB) is an apex body in the field of water quality management in India. For rational planning of any water quality management programme, CPCB needs to know the nature and extent of water quality degradation. Therefore, a sound scientific water quality monitoring programme is prerequisite. Realising this fact, water quality monitoring was started in 1976 by CPCB with 18 stations on the Yamuna River. The programme was gradually extended. Today, there are 1032 monitoring stations in the country spread over all important water bodies.

Sanitation and Social Exclusion[40]

Titled, 'Inclusive Growth,' the Eleventh Five Year Plan of the Planning Commission, Government of India (GOI), begins its vision and strategy chapter. The central vision of the Eleventh Five Year Plan is to 'trigger a development process which ensures broad-based improvement in the quality of life of the people, especially the poor, Scheduled Castes (SCs) and Scheduled Tribes (STs), Other Backward Castes (OBCs), minorities and women' (Planning Commission [GOI] 2008a, p. 2). Moreover, the target is 'inclusive growth, that is, a growth process which yields broad-based benefits and ensures equality of opportunity for all'. On how access to services is conceived as a means to inclusive growth, the plan document argues that while in the short run access to basic facilities, such as health, education, clean drinking water, and sanitation impact welfare, in the long run they determine economic opportunity, and more importantly, equal opportunity.

Launched in 1999, the TSC is a comprehensive programme aimed at ensuring adequate sanitation facilities (toilets) in rural areas, with the specific objective of accelerating coverage to ensure access for all by 2012; to increase coverage of institutional toilets in schools and anganwadi centres (AWCs), giving preference to girls in the former;

and mobilising communities and PRIs to promote sustainable, cost-effective and ecologically safe sanitation facilities through awareness and education. It replaces the Central Rural Sanitation programme introduced in 1986 that was based on a full subsidy principle but was discontinued because of a lack of community participation and the realisation that top-down approaches to sanitation fail—simply providing a latrine to people does not ensure its use. For this reason, the TSC takes particular pride in modelling itself as a Community-Led Total Sanitation (CLTS) approach.

In order to provide added impetus for fully sanitised (100 per cent sanitation coverage for individual households and schools) and open defecation free (ODF) villages, blocks and districts, the Nirmal Gram Puraskar (NGP) was introduced by the GOI in 2003. Under this, eligible Gram Panchayats, as well as individuals and organisations that have been instrumental in the drive for full coverage, are given recognition and a monetary award. The TSC policy framework makes no attempt at articulating a cohesive plan to tackle social exclusion, with the consequence that even at the state level, there has been no conscious attempt to tackle the issue in a comprehensive manner.

It can safely be said that on design and guidelines for participation, the TSC documents are not explicitly sensitive to the problem of social exclusion. Since TSC incentives are aimed at rural BPL households, and since certain groups, that is, Scheduled Castes and Scheduled Tribes, are over-represented amongst this target group, needs of the Scheduled Castes and Scheduled Tribes are taken account of only in this tangential way. Looking at exclusion from the perspective of those who provide the service, we find that Scheduled Caste groups, such as the Bhangis, have been traditionally engaged in the offensive and ritually unclean task of manual scavenging. However, the government has banned the practice even before the TSC came into place (Planning Commission 1991–1992). The TSC has taken this further by aiming to convert all dry latrines to pour flush latrines wherever the former are in existence in rural areas.

Other excluded 'given groups', for example, women, differently-abled and the elderly, however, are overlooked by the TSC policy documents. Civil society groups seem particularly irked that women's specific needs are not articulated and written into programme guidelines, despite the fact that this group makes up 50 per cent of the target population and suffers disproportionately—owing to safety, privacy and productivity considerations—from a lack of sanitation facilities at home.

Where women have been actively enlisted as community sanitation activists, for example in Haryana, positive benefits have accrued. The TSC makes no conscious attempt to engage with Scheduled Tribes, merely assuming they will be included in the community involvement approach, which may or may not take place depending on the local context—they fare well in Chhattisgarh, in particular Sarguja district, and not so well in Tripura, for example, Dhalai district. Dalits in Vaishali and Nalanda districts of Bihar had no knowledge of the sanitation programme in the village and, consequently, never used the community toilet complex they were provided with (WaterAid 2008).

Whether implementation of the TSC has improved inclusion for Scheduled Castes who have traditionally been providers of sanitation through manual scavenging of dry latrines, the affirmative answer can be ascribed almost entirely to the awareness and activist efforts of the Safai Karamchari Andolan (SKA), a national movement spearheaded by a dynamic leader who is committed to the total eradication of the practice of manual scavenging. Using 1,400 volunteers across the country, SKA has engaged in an ongoing sample survey to document the continued existence of this practice7 and has lobbied the government incessantly to use various means to put a stop to this denigrating practice. In inclusion terms, the outcomes are nuanced in that while the SKA's efforts have gone a long way in taking Scheduled Castes out of this work, there have been variable successes in terms of getting them alternative means of livelihood and rehabilitating them.

Notes

1. See The Practice Of Untouchability: Persistence and Change Author(s): Raj S. Gandhi, Humboldt Journal of Social Relations, Vol. 10, No. 1, Race and Ethnic Relations: Cross-Cultural Perspectives (FALL/WINTER 1982/83), pp. 254-275
2. Ghurye, G.S. Caste and Race in India. Bombay: Popular Prakashan, 1969.
3. Basham, A. L. The Wonder that was India. New York: Grove Press Inc., 1959.
4. See The Untouchables of India–Robert Deliege, Berg Publishers, UK, 1999
5. L. Rudolf and S. H. Rudolf, 1967, The modernity of tradition: political development in India, Chicago: University of Chicago press, p. 84
6. T.K. Oommen, 1984, 'Sources of deprivation and Styles of protest: The case of the Dalits in India', Contribution to Indian Sociology, 18 (1984), p. 46

7. A. Beteille, Caste, Class and Power: Changing Patterns of Stratification in a Tanjore Village, Bombay: OUP, 1966, p. 3.
8. The Untouchables of India–Robert Deliege, Berg Publishers, UK, 1999.
9. S. Fuchs, 1980. At the bottom of Indian society: The Harijans and other Low Castes, Delhi: Munshiram Manoharlal.
10. See 1979, An untouchable community in South India: Structure and Consensus, Princeton: NJ: Princeton University Press.
11. See *helid.digicollection.org/en/d/Jh0210e/2.3.4.htmlý* for details.
12. See Susan Allport, 2007. Women Who Eat Dirt, Gastronomica: The Journal of Food and Culture, Vol. 2, No. 2 (Spring 2002), pp. 28-37, published by University of California Press.
13. May Yacoob, Communicating Fundamentals of Water and Sanitation in Moslem Communities, Journal of Religion and Health, Vol. 24, No. 4 (Winter, 1985), pp. 287-293.
14. May Yacoob, Communicating Fundamentals of Water and Sanitation in Moslem Communities, Journal of Religion and Health, Vol. 24, No. 4 (Winter, 1985), pp. 287-293.
15. See Culture versus Coercion: Other Side of Nirmal Gram Yojana, Economic and Political Weekly, Vol. 43, No. 43 (Oct. 25 - 31, 2008), pp. 25-27.
16. See Pathak, Bindeshwar. 1991. Road to Freedom—A Sociological study on the abolition of scavenging in India, Xtreme Office aids Pvt. Ltd. Delhi.
17. Based on Bindeshwar Pathak,. 1991. Road to Freedom—A Sociological study on the abolition of scavenging in India, Xtreme Office aids Pvt. Ltd. Delhi.
18. P. S. Vivek, Scavengers: Mumbai's Neglected Workers, Economic and Political Weekly, Vol. 35, No. 42 (Oct. 14-20, 2000), pp. 3722-3724.
19. See Manual Scavenging: stigma, discrimination and justice; Safai Karmachari Andolan, New Delhi, August 2012.
20. Rajeev Kumar Singh, Manual Scavenging as Social Exclusion: A Case Study, Economic and Political Weekly, Vol. 44, No. 26/27 (Jun. 27 - Jul. 10, 2009), pp. 521-523.
21. See Tulika Tripathi, Safai Karmi Scheme of Uttar Pradesh Caste Dominance Continues, Economic and Political Weekly, September 15, 2012 Vol XLVII no, 37.
22. Ravichandran, B (2011): "Scavenging Profession between Class and Caste?", EPW, 26 March, Vol XLVI, No 13.

23. Action Aid Report, New Delhi, 2003.

24. National Commission for Safai Karmacharis (2000): Combined Report, 1998-99 and 1999-2000, http://www.ncsk.nic.in/main1_rep3E.asp.

25. Sanjay Paswan; Paramanshi Jaideva; Encyclopedia of Dalits in India (ed.) Kalpaz Publications, 2003, p. 345, New Delhi.

26. See *Richard H., Hall, 1969, Occupational and the Social Structure, Prentice Hall, New York,* p. 306.

27. See Hazara, C.F., 1940, Studies in Puranic Records on Hindu Rites and Custom" p. 29. Quated from Laxmanna, C. "Rural Social Change, Process and Problems". Man and Life, Vol. 5, pp. 23-46.

28. Based on work by Imrana Qadeer and Dunu Roy, Work, Wealth and Health: Sociology of Workers' Health in India, Social Scientist, Vol. 17, No. 5/6 (May-Jun., 1989), pp. 45-92.

29. Based on Christoph Lthi, Jennifer McConville and Elisabeth Kvarnstrm (2010) Community-based approaches for addressing the urban sanitation challenges, International Journal of Urban Sustainable Development, 1:1-2, 49-63,

30. UN-Habitat, 2008. *State of the world's cities 2008/2009*. London, UK: Earthscan.

31. UN JMP, 2008. *Progress on drinking water and sanitation—special focus on sanitation*. Joint Monitoring Programme for Water Supply and Sanitation, Geneva.

32. Eawag, 2005. *Household-centred environmental sanitation: provisional guideline for decision makers*. Dübendorf, Switzerland: Swiss Federal Institute of Aquatic Science and Technology (Eawag).

33. See Atkinson, A., 2007. Analysis of urban trends, culture, theory, policy, action. *City*, 9 (3), 277–295.

34. WSSCC Working Group Environmental Sanitation, 2000. *The Bellagio statement* [online]. Available from: http://www.sandec.ch/sesp

35. Hamdi, N. and Goethert, R., 1997. *Action planning for cities—a guide to community practice*. New York: Wiley and Sons.

36. Lüthi, C., Schertenleib, R., and Tilley, E., 2007. HCES: a new approach to environmental sanitation planning. *Waterlines*, 12, 2–4.

37. Tilley, E., *et al.*, 2008b. *Compendium of sanitation systems and technologies*. Switzerland: Water Supply and Sanitation Collaborative Council (WSSCC) and Swiss Federal Institute of Aquatic Science and Technology (Eawag).

38. Koné, D., *et al.*, 2007. Helminth eggs inactivation efficiency by faecal sludge dewatering and cocomposting in tropical climates. *Water research*, 41 (19), 4397–4402.

39. Guidelines for Water Quality Monitoring Central Pollution Control Board Parvesh Bhawan, Delhi.

40. Based on Kaveri Gill, Promoting 'Inclusiveness': A Framework For Assessing India's Flagship Social Welfare Programmes, UNICEF India New Delhi January 2012.

10

Public and Private Interventions on Sanitation in India: An Overview

Introduction

In recent years the private sector has emerged as a major player in the development process, and the government, obsessed with achieving higher and higher economic growth targets, is trying to attract private investment in sectors as varied as power generation, manufacturing, mining, roads, airports, and housing, to name a few. SEZs for large private corporations, including multinational corporations (MNCs), are being set up to accelerate the development process. Under globalisation pressures, laws are being amended or promulgated overnight in an unseemly haste to create investor-friendly conditions, regardless of what happens to the livelihoods of farmers whose lands will be gone for a pittance. The requirement of land for such gigantic development plans is going to be enormous, and this is bound to precipitate displacement on an unprecedented scale.

Three trends become apparent when we look at the recent history of urban renewal. First, there is a manifest change in the nature of the urban economy from manufacturing to services, with more and more of the urban poor being thrown into the unprotected informal sector. In the process, all civic services are being commercialised and privatised. Second, large sections of these urban poor are being displaced from their livelihoods and shelter, and the geographical and occupational space that they occupied is being transferred to large private corporate entities or wealthier groups, such as commercial complexes and residential layouts. These are also often coupled up with labour-replacing devices ranging from automatic tellers and computer-aided machines, to vacuum cleaners and home delivery services. Third, while the driving force behind these changes is manifestly the new globalised economy, it is offered on an environmental platter of 'cleanliness' and 'beautification'. This environmental activism, in turn, is the bread and butter of those professional 'non-government organisation' that are taking up the 'public cause', as well as the judicial, legislative, administrative, and commercial apparatuses—including a very pliable media—that provide them with legitimacy and political support.[1]

As seen in any nation, human development outcomes are a function of economic growth, social policy, and poverty reduction measures at the macro-level. These, in turn, are the result of various synergies in the form of feedback loops, operating in terms of both inputs and outputs in the development process. The expansion of human functioning in terms of health and educational attainments, reduction of income poverty, and economic growth are linked in a synergistic manner through these feedback loops. These synergies lead to improved health and educational outcomes. A state-wise analysis of socially stratified Indian society reflects how different caste and religious groups fare in terms of various socio-economic indicators. It may be noted that the poorer states, namely, Bihar, Jharkhand, Madhya Pradesh, Odisha, Rajasthan, Uttar Pradesh, Chhatisgarh, and West Bengal, account for 56 per cent of the SCs and 55 per cent of STs of entire country.

The HDI for different states for 1999-2000 and 2000-08 reflects that the ranking of the states in terms of HDI has barely changed over this past decades. The generally well-performing states are Kerala, Delhi, Himachal Pradesh, Goa and Punjab, which occupy the first five places in both the years. On the other hand, Bihar, Jharkhand, Madhya Pradesh, Uttar Pradesh, Odisha, Rajasthan and Chhattisgarh appear at the bottom of the list in both the years.

The HDI has increased by 21 per cent between 1999-2000 and 2007-08. It also shows that the increase in HDI in the states that are among the poorest has been much faster than the national average, and hence there is a convergence taking place between states in terms of HDI (improvement in Income index, Education index and health index). It needs to be stated that the proportion of persons below the poverty line has fallen steadily in both rural and urban areas through the 1980s, 1990s and new millennium.

All India incidence of poverty in rural and urban areas

Year	*Rural*	*Urban*
1983	45.7	40.8
1993-4	37.3	32.4
2004-5	28.3	02.0
2007-8	14.9	14.5

Source: Eleventh Five Year Plan, Planning Commission, GOI for 1998 to 2004-5, based on uniform recall period

While it is true that the incidence of poverty has declined over time in India, the incidence of poverty among SCs and STs, however, is much higher than the national aggregate by 8.5 (SC-rural) and 19.4 (ST-rural) per centage points. Across religious groups the incidence of poverty among Muslims in rural areas is actually less than the aggregate.[2]

Status of Sanitation in India

Sanitation is important for three reasons. It helps to prevent disease, it is particularly beneficial for women and people value the advantages that it can bring. This is the rationale for promoting sanitation, and for the adoption of a sanitation target as one of the Millennium Development Goals.

Before speaking the impact of sanitation on India, it is important to assess the impact of inadequate sanitation in India.[3] The total annual economic impact of inadequate sanitation in India amounted to a loss of Rs 2.4 trillion ($53.8 billion) in 2006. This implies a per capita annual loss of Rs 2,180 ($48). In purchasing power parity (PPP) terms, the adverse economic impact of inadequate sanitation in India was $161 billion, or $144 per person.

These economic impacts were the equivalent of about 6.4 per cent of India's gross domestic product (GDP) in 2006.

The health-related economic impact of inadequate sanitation was Rs 1.75 trillion ($38.5 billion), which was 72 per cent of the total impact. Access time and water-related impacts made up the other two main losses.

Present and Future Losses

Of the Rs 2.4 trillion ($53.8 billion) lost, the loss of flow of 2006 economic value is Rs 1.1 trillion ($24.8 billion), which is 46 per cent of the total economic impact, equivalent to 3 per cent of that year's GDP. Furthermore, deaths in 2006 resulted in a loss of human capital that would have generated economic flows that year and beyond. The discounted present value of these future losses are counted in 2006, amounts to Rs 1.3 trillion ($29 billion), equivalent to 3.4 per cent of 2006 GDP.

Potential Gains from Improved Sanitation in India

The gains from improved sanitation are somewhat like the flip side of the economic costs of inadequate sanitation, although not all the adverse impacts of inadequate sanitation can be fully mitigated, due to a number of factors. Hence, the economic gains of improved sanitation are smaller than the loss due to inadequate sanitation. Nevertheless, this study estimates that a package of comprehensive sanitation and hygiene interventions, comprising greater use of toilets, improved hygiene practices, and improved access to water, could result in a potential gain of up to Rs 1.48 trillion ($32.6 billion), avoiding up to 61 per cent of the losses due to inadequate sanitation—or an equivalent of 3.9 per cent of GDP in 2006.

Potential Sanitation Market

Increasing the public investment in meeting sanitation priorities, including mobilising households to build toilets, construct and operate waste disposal systems, promote hygienic practices, combined with efforts by households to construct or upgrade to improved toilets are likely to generate a huge market for sanitary products and services in the coming years. While this is not an indication of gain in GDP, it nevertheless indicates potential economy activity that sanitation can generate. This study estimated the potential market for such activity.

Speaking on the issues of sanitation status, one finds globally, more than 1 billion people do not have access to safe drinking water and 2.6 billion do not have access to sanitation. Of this South Asia alone accounts for around 900 million people without basic sanitation. However, now things are changing as the need for proper sanitation and waste management is rapidly gaining entry into the development agenda. Although in India, water and sanitation was included as community development issue in the first five year plan in the nineteen fifties, progress was slow, rather more 'pressing' development priorities. Therefore between 1981 and 1991 the rural sanitation coverage grew from one per cent to 11 per cent - an average of mere one per cent every year.

According to Country Programme Action Plan 2013-2017, Government of India and the United Nations Children's Fund, it is found that India has reached the target on access to improved drinking water sources, yet improving sanitation and drinking water quality remains a huge challenge. Only 47 per cent of the households have access to toilet facilities and more than 600 million people, defecate in the open.[4,5] Promoting the use of toilets and quality drinking water are urgent needs.

The thrust on sanitation in India was intensified in 1999 through a policy initiative sector reforms that had the core agenda of decentralising water and sanitation management through the Panchayati Raj (PR) System or local government at the village level. The aim of the Total Sanitation Campaign (TSC) was to make the programme people-centred, demand-driven with local control over resources and funds. This concept was meant to enable and empower communities with an understanding of the sector and how best to manage the resources in a manner not detrimental to the environment. These efforts resulted in increasing access to safe water to over 90 per cent according to fixed norms; sanitation coverage measured as individual household sanitary toilets has increased to an estimated 44 per cent (rural India) in 2007. Rural sanitation coverage (toilet construction) increased from 48 per cent in 2008 to 67 per cent in 2010[6]. Advocacy led to a significant shift in the *Nirmal Bharat Abhiyan* (NBA) guidelines to focus on sustained use of sanitation facilities.[7] This, together with the *Nirmal Gram Puraskar* (clean village award), contributed to an increase of 19.7 million new toilet-users per year, of whom 12.8 million are in rural areas.

United Nations declared 2008 as the International Year of Sanitation in view of the 2.6 billion people in the world who lack even basic sanitation facilities and the deadly consequences this has for their health and human dignity. India (where 7.5 per cent of reported deaths are sanitation and water related) has been grappling with the problem of sanitation coverage, especially for the poor, for some years now. The Central Rural Sanitation Programme, started in 1986, metamorphosed into the Total Sanitation Campaign (TSC) in 1999 to ensure community participation. It aims at eradicating open defecation in rural areas by 2012, no doubt because a majority of the population lives in villages. However, slum conditions and the population density in cities ensure that lack of sanitation coverage affects the urban poor more drastically. Though the Jawaharlal Nehru National Urban Renewal Mission targets 100 per cent sanitation coverage in urban areas, it was only in October 2008 that the government came out with the National Urban Sanitation Policy (NUSP). Surprisingly, it has not received the kind of media and public attention that it merits, given the state of urban sanitation in the country. The NUSP says that 7.87 per cent of urban households defecate in the open, 8.13 per cent use community latrines, 19.49 per cent share latrines, 18.5 per cent have no access to drainage, and 39.8 per cent are connected to open drains.

It aims at community participation, raising awareness, changing behavioural attitudes, making our cities open-defecation free, and the safe disposal of solid and liquid human wastes with special emphasis on the poor and women. The states are expected to prepare their own strategies within the next two years; cities are to prepare model city sanitation plans, and a multi-stakeholder city sanitation task force will be responsible for achieving the targets set. Significantly, it directs that 20 per cent of the funds must be set aside for the urban poor. And on the lines of the TSC's Nirmal Gram Puraskar, cities with the best performance will receive awards.

National Rural Sanitation and Hygiene Strategy 2012-2022

The Ministry of Drinking Water and Sanitation administers the National Rural Drinking Water programme (NRDWP) instituted from 1/4/2009, through which support is extended to the states for implementing rural domestic water supply schemes. Powers to sanction individual projects is given to the states through their State Level Scheme Sanctioning Committees. Activities like, water quality monitoring and surveillance programme, management information system, IEC, Capacity and Communication Development Unit (CCDU) all were brought under the umbrella of NRDWP. However it requires further strengthening on various aspects in order to successfully and effectively provided at rural households with safe and adequate domestic water supply available at all times.

Drinking Water Supply Programs and Policies at a Glance

Role of (Urban Local Bodies) ULBs in Provision of Sanitation Services:[9]

Urban local bodies/municipalities play an important role in the planning and development of urban areas. An important initiative of the Government of India to strengthen municipal governance is the enactment of the Constitution (74th Amendment) Act (CAA) in 1992. The twelfth schedule of the CAA 74 has listed 18 functions and responsibilities to local bodies.

These are:

- Urban planning, including town planning;
- Regulation of land use and construction of buildings;
- Planning for economic and social development;
- Roads and bridges;
- Water supply for domestic, industrial, and commercial purposes;
- Public health, sanitation, conservancy, and solid waste management;
- Fire services;

- Urban forestry, protection of the environment, and promotion of ecological aspects;
- Safeguarding the interests of weaker sections of society, including the handicapped and mentally retarded;
- Slum improvement and up-gradation;
- Urban poverty alleviation;
- Provision of urban amenities and facilities such as parks, gardens, and playgrounds;
- Promotion of cultural, educational and aesthetic aspects;
- Burials and burial grounds; cremation grounds and electric crematoria;
- Cattle pounds, prevention of cruelty to animals;
- Vital statistics, including registration of births and deaths;
- Public amenities including street lighting, parking lots, bus-stop, and public conveniences;
- Regulation of slaughterhouses and tanneries

Inventory on Governmental Frameworks, Initiatives and Opportunities in India[10]

(i) Technical Guidelines for Sanitation in India

Items	*The Central Public Health and Environmental Engineering Organisation (CPHEEO) Guidelines*
Specific legal and regulatory aspects of it	Guidelines for implementing water supply and sanitation programmes are prescribed by CPHEEO. Technical approval for programmes sponsored by the Central Government is given by CPHEEO
Level of operation	Applicable to all levels of Governments – Provincial, regional and local governments- and their activities related to water supply and sanitation
Led by	Ministry of Urban Development, Government of India and the CPHEEO
Objectives and targets of the framework	• Policies, strategies and guidelines related to water supply and sanitation are being provided by CPHEEO to the States & Union Territories, Governments including Municipal Corporations / Committees. • CPHEEO plays a vital role in processing schemes posed for external funding agencies including World Bank / JBIC/ ADB/ and Bilateral and Multilateral funding agencies and institutional financing such as LIC. • It acts as an Advisory body at Central level to advise the concerned State agencies and Urban Local Bodies (ULBs) in implementation, operation and maintenance of urban water supply, sanitation and Solid Waste Management projects and helps to adopt latest technologies in these sub sectors. • Issues related to the Millennium Development Goal in regard to water supply and sanitation sector are being dealt with by CPHEEO.

Items	*The Central Public Health and Environmental Engineering Organisation (CPHEEO) Guidelines*
Target group of the framework	All levels of Government involved in the provision of water supply and sanitation services
Available publications and where these can be accessed	In collaboration with UNDP CPHEEO has brought out computer software for design of water supply distribution networks, sewerage networks, and economical size of pumping main and distributed them to all the States & ULBs for extensive use. To its credit, it has prepared and published the following Manuals, which are technical guide books for the help of field engineers: • Manual on Water Supply & Treatment, Third Edition, Revised-updated, May 1999. • Manual on Sewerage & Sewage Treatment, Second Edition, 1993. • Manual on Municipal Solid Waste Management, 2000. • Manual on Operation and Maintenance of Water Supply systems, 2005. These manuals are available online at: http://urbanindia.nic.in/publicinfo/manual_ws.htm http://urbanindia.nic.in/publicinfo/manual_sewage.htm http://urbanindia.nic.in/publicinfo/swm/swm_manual.htm http://www.urbanindia.nic.in/publicinfo/o_m/o_m.htm

(ii) Governance frameworks (National level)

(a) Indian National Urban Sanitation Policy

Items	*Specific Details*
Specific legal and regulatory aspects of it	State Sanitation Strategies and City Sanitation Plans
Level of operation	National, Provincial and ULB level
Led by	Ministry of Urban Development, Government of India
Date of publication and timeframe covered	November 12th, 2008 The National Urban Sanitation Policy was announced in 2008, the international year of sanitation. The Policy was formally launched through a workshop on 12th November, 2008.
Objectives and targets of the framework	It moots the idea of totally sanitised and open-defecation free cities as a target and the setting up of a multi-stakeholder City Sanitation Task Force to achieve this To transform urban India into community-driven, totally sanitized, healthy and liveable cities and towns. • Awareness generation and behaviour change • Open defecation free cities • Integrated city wise sanitation • Sanitary and safe disposal • Proper operation and maintenance of all sanitary installations • Implementation support strategy • Planning and funding through its schemes like JNNURM, UIDSSMT, 10% Lump Sum for NE States, Satellite Township Schemes, etc.

Items	*Specific Details*
Target group of the framework	National, state, city and local institutions (public, private and community) • ULBs • NGOs and Community Based Organisations (CBOs) • General Public
Available publications and where these can be accessed	National Urban Sanitation Policy as available online at: http://www.indiaurbanportal.in/data/policies/NUSP1-Released12Nov08.pdf

(b) Total Sanitation Campaign

Items	*Specific Details*
Specific legal and regulatory aspects of it	The Government of India conceived Total Sanitation Campaign (TSC) with the objective to bring about an improvement in the general quality of life in the rural areas. The strategy is to make the Programme 'community led' and 'people centered'. A "demand driven approach" is to be adopted with increased emphasis on awareness creation and demand generation for sanitary facilities in houses, schools and for cleaner environment. Alternate delivery mechanisms would be adopted to meet the community needs.
Level of operation	The TSC is being implemented with a district as unit. The States/UTs are expected to prepare TSC Projects for all the districts and submit before the Government of India for sanction. The TSC Project cycle in the Project Districts is expected to take about 4 years or less for implementation. Implementation of TSC is proposed on a project mode. A project proposal emanates from a district, is scrutinised by the State Government and transmitted to the Government of India (Department of Drinking Water Supply, Ministry of Rural Development). The strategy is to make the Programme 'community led' and 'people centered'. A "demand driven approach" is to be adopted with increased emphasis on awareness creation and demand generation for sanitary facilities in houses, schools and for cleaner environment. Alternate delivery mechanisms would be adopted to meet the community needs. Subsidy for individual household latrine units has been replaced by incentive to the poorest of the poor households. Rural School Sanitation is a major component and an entry point for wider acceptance of sanitation by the rural people. Technology improvisations to meet the customer preferences and location specific intensive IEC Campaign involving Panchayati Raj Institutions, Co-operatives, Women Groups, Self Help Groups, NGOs etc. are also important components of the Strategy. The strategy addresses all sections of rural population to bring about the relevant behavioural changes for improved sanitation and hygiene practices and meet their sanitary hardware requirements in an affordable and accessible manner by offering a wide range of technological choices.

Items	*Specific Details*
Led by	Ministry of Rural Development, Govt, of India
Date of publication and timeframe covered	1999 – Ongoing
Objectives and targets of the framework	The main objectives of the TSC are as under: • Bring about an improvement in the general quality of life in the rural areas. • Accelerate sanitation coverage in rural areas to access to toilets to all by 2012. • Motivate communities and Panchayati Raj Institutions promoting sustainable sanitation facilities through awareness creation and health education. • In rural areas, cover schools by March 2008 and Anganwadis by March 2009, with sanitation facilities and promote hygiene education and sanitary habits among students. • Encourage cost effective and appropriate technologies for ecologically safe and sustainable sanitation. • Develop community managed environmental sanitation systems focusing on solid and liquid waste management.
Target group of the framework	Rural Areas with involvement of Local Governments and NGOs
Available publications and where these can be accessed	http://indiasanitationportal.org/tsc/tscdata/TSC_Guideline_Oct07.pdf

(c) Jawaharlal Nehru National Urban Renewal Mission

Items	*Specific Details*
Specific legal and regulatory aspects of it	Centrally devised programme providing assistance to over 60 Indian cities for developing urban infrastructure and institutionalising urban sector reforms for improving management of service delivery. • Sub-Mission for Urban Infrastructure and Governance: MoUD thrust on infrastructure projects on water supply and sanitation, sewerage, SWM, road network, urban transport and redevelopment of old city areas with a view to upgrading infrastructure therein. • Sub-Mission for Basic Services to the Urban Poor: MoHUPA – Focus on integrated development of slums - providing shelter, basic services and other related civic amenities

Items	*Specific Details*
Level of operation	National
Led by	Ministry of Urban Development & Ministry of Housing and Urban Poor Alleviation
Date of publication and timeframe covered	December 2005-2012
Objectives and targets of the framework	Upgrade urban infrastructure & reform urban management • Sanitation has been accorded very high priority under JNNURM and account for approx. 20 per cent of the total number of projects • The core reforms include implementation of decentralisation measures as envisaged in the 74th Constitutional Amendment, the drawing up of publicprivate- partnership (PPP) models for development, management and financing of urban infrastructure the adoption of an accrual-based double entry system of accounting, passage of public disclosure law to facilitate quarterly performance information to all stakeholders and a community participation law to institutionalise citizen participation.
Target group of the framework	Urban Local Bodies
Available publications and where these can be accessed	Documents on Best Practises in the Ministry of Urban Development, in Cities, implementation of pilot projects, and in all sectors being addressed by JNNURM are to be found on the JnNURM website - http://jnnurm.nic.in/nurmudweb/best_prctices/bp_swm.htm

(d) Urban Infrastructure Development Scheme for Small and Medium Towns (UIDSSMT)

Items	*Specific Details*
Specific legal and regulatory aspects of it	Centrally sponsored scheme for improvement in urban infrastructure in towns and cities in a planned manner. It has integrated the existing schemes of Integrated Development of Small and Medium Towns (IDSMT) and Accelerated Urban Water Supply Programme (AUWSP).
Level of operation	Scheme for small and medium towns
Led by	Ministry of Urban Development
Date of publication and timeframe covered	2005-2006 to 2012-2013

Items	*Specific Details*
Objectives and targets of the framework	The objectives of the scheme are to: • Improve infrastructural facilities and help create durable public assets and quality oriented services in cities and towns • Enhance public-private-partnership in infrastructural development and • Promote planned integrated development of towns and cities. **The Scheme covers the following areas:** • Urban Renewal i.e. redevelopment of inner (old) city areas [this would include items like widening of narrow streets, shifting of industrial/commercial establishments from nonconforming (inner-city) to `conforming' (outer-city) areas to reduce congestion, replacement of old and worn-out water pipes by new/higher capacity ones, renewal of sewerage/drainage/solid waste disposal systems, etc. • Water Supply (including de-salination plants) and sanitation • Sewerage and Solid Waste Management • Construction and improvement of drains/storm water drains • Construction/Up gradation of roads, highways/expressways • Parking lots/spaces on Public Private Partnership basis • Development of heritage areas • Prevention & rehabilitation of soil erosion/landslides only in case of Special Category States where such problems are common and, • Preservation of water bodies.
Target group of the framework	The scheme will apply to all cities/towns as per 2001 census, excepting cities/towns covered under Jawaharlal Nehru National Urban Renewal Mission (JNNURM)
Available publications and where these can be accessed	Guidelines for preparation and submission of DPRs for sewerage/sewage treatment projects are published by the MoUD and may be found at: http://urbanindia.nic.in/programme/ud/uidssmt_pdf/UIDSSMT2.pdf

(e) Service Level Benchmarking (SLB)—Pilot Implementation

Items	*Specific Details*
Specific legal and regulatory aspects of it	The Ministry of Urban Development (MoUD), Government of India constituted a Core Group on Benchmarking under the chairmanship of Joint Secretary (UD), MoUD with the aim of developing a framework for water supply, wastewater management, storm water drainage, solid waste management services and urban transport. This group has finalised a Handbook of Service Level Benchmarks (SLB), which provides (i) a common minimum framework for monitoring and reporting on service level indicators, and (ii) guidelines on how to operationalise this framework in a phased manner.

Items	*Specific Details*
Level of operation	Central framework to be implemented by ULBs
Led by	Ministry of Urban Development
Date of publication and timeframe covered	Pilot project in 28 cities - February 2009-March 2010.(To be extended into phase II)
Objectives and targets of the framework	Standardised Indicators as per a uniform definitional framework to establish service levels to achieve stated Benchmarks (service delivery goals that should be achieved) 4 sectors- (i) Water Supply (ii) Wastewater (iii) Storm water drainage (iv) Solid Waste Management
Target group of the framework	28 Pilot cities across 14 states and 1 Union Territory.
Available publications and where these can be accessed	Handbook of Service Level Benchmarks – available online: http://www.urbanindia.nic.in/programme/uwss/slb/slb.htm SLB Data book for 2010 – available online: http://www.urbanindia.nic.in/programme/uwss/slb/slb.htm

(f) Urban School Sanitation Initiative

Items	*Specific Details*
Specific legal and regulatory aspects of it	To effectuate a quantifiable achievement in the provisions and practices of sanitation in the country.
Level of operation	Partners: Central Board for Secondary Education, Ministry of Urban Development & GTZ
Led by	Government of India
Timeframe covered	Ongoing
Objectives and targets of the framework	Addressing the water, sanitation and hygiene issues in urban schools The initiative is aimed at using "Children as agents of change" philosophy Objective of: Awareness generation and behavioural change by focusing on proper sanitation, its disposal and waste segregation in order to achieve "Open Defecation Free Life" for all the citizens.
Target group of the framework	School Students and community at large

Items	*Specific Details*
Main outputs and the potential impacts	The key deliverables are summarized as follows: **1. Hygiene Education** • Inculcation of basic and safe urban hygiene habits among school children through various educative and demonstrative means • Safe hygiene practices in the schools • Developing Waste segregation habits among school children • Capacity building and training of school teachers on sanitation and waste management issues • Schools Curriculum orientation towards safe sanitation, health and hygiene • Focus on Waste management and safe sanitation issues by "Health and Wellness Clubs" in schools • Focus on Waste management and safe sanitation issues in CBSE's "Lifestyle Management Training Programmes **2. Waste Water Management** • Waste water recycling in the schools • Spilled Water Management from wash basins and water closets • Appropriate technological interventions for Waste Water recycling • Use of Grey Waste Water • Conservation of Green spaces **3. Water Management** • Establishment of Water harvesting structures at appropriate places within the school premises • Water conservation and judicious use • Awareness regarding safe drinking water and its up keep **Institution Building through Participatory Approach** • Sustainable Sanitation : Establishment of Operation and Maintenance mechanism in a school and region specific manner • Exposure visits to appropriate places like Jungle Lodges , Eco-San centers etc for learning experiences in eco-sanitation in nature and cultural heritage, • Active and sustained participation of parents and guardians in the endeavor • Workshops and seminars for teachers, knowledge dissemination and sharing of information as well as technical know how • Sustained nationwide awareness campaign for ecological sanitation, waste and water management through print, electronic and visual media • Establishment of the National level Awards and Prizes for the performing schools **5. Technological Interventions** • Technological interventions in the improvement of the existing sanitation/toilet systems in the needy schools in the region specific manner • Waterless toilets and urinals • Separate ,and safe toilets for Girl Students • Establishment of recycling oriented wastewater management systems

Items	*Specific Details*
	• Establishment of facilities for Vermi-composting and other methods of utilising the organic kitchen wastes depending upon the specific situation • Technological interventions for recycling oriented waste water management , Waste segregation and bio-gas generation • Rain water harvesting structures • Ground water recharge methodologies Intervention towards the establishment of the Decentralised Waste water Treatment System Proper Bio-Medical Waste management in school clinics • Elaboration of strategies for nation? wide dissemination of sustainable sanitation concepts. **6. Monitoring and Evaluation** • Periodic reviews at the Central Level • Regular monitoring, reporting and assessment • Establishment of On? line Real Time monitoring systems • Health and wellness club's Quarterly reports • Designing of Road map and mile stones • Impact Assessment • Independent Monitoring and Evaluation by CBSE/ MoUD/GTZ
Available publications and where these can be accessed	http://www.schoolsanitation.com/index.php

(g) Integrated Low Cost Sanitation Scheme (ILCS)

Items	*Specific Details*
Specific legal and regulatory aspects of it	The Centrally Sponsored Scheme of Low Cost Sanitation for Liberation of Scavengers started from 1980-81 initially through the Ministry of Home Affairs and later on through the Ministry of Welfare. From 1989-90, it came to be operated through the Ministry of Urban Development and later on through Ministry of Urban Employment and Poverty Alleviation now titled Ministry of Housing and Urban Poverty Alleviation. The main objectives of the Scheme are to convert the existing dry latrines into low cost pour flush latrines and to construct new ones where none exist.
Level of operation	Local implementation
Led by	Ministry of Housing and Urban Poverty Alleviation and state governments
Date of publication and timeframe covered	Started in 1980-81. Re-deployed in 1990 – 2013. Revised guidelines issued in 2008. Scheme currently extends upto 2013.

Items	*Specific Details*
Objectives and targets of the framework	The objective of the Scheme is to convert/ construct low cost sanitation units through sanitary two pit pour flush latrines with superstructures and appropriate variations to suit local conditions (area specific latrines) and construct new latrines where Economically Weaker Sections(EWS) households have no latrines and follow the in-human practice of defecating in the open in urban areas. This would improve overall sanitation in the towns.
Target group of the framework	State Governments and Urban Local Bodies
Available publications and where these can be accessed	Guidelines of ILCS scheme: http:/mhupa.gov.in/w_new/ILCS-GUIDELINES-PLUS-DPRFORMAT. pdf

(h) Integrated Housing and Slum Development Programme under Basic Services for Urban Poor– (Valmiki Ambedkar Awas Yojana (VAMBAY) and National Slum Development Programme have been subsumed under IHSDP)

Items	*Specific Details*
Specific legal and regulatory aspects of it	The Integrated Housing & Slum Development Programme (IHSDP) aims at combining the existing schemes of VAMBAY and NSDP under the new IHSDP Scheme for having an integrated approach in ameliorating the conditions of the urban slum dweller who do not possess adequate shelter and reside in dilapidated conditions. Main Objectives of the Scheme The basic objective of the scheme is to strive for slum less cities by adopting holistic slum development with a healthy and enabling urban environment by providing adequate shelter and basic infrastructure facilities to the slum dwellers of the identified urban areas. Valmiki Ambedkar Awas Yojna (VAMBAY) was launched by Govt. Of India in 2001-02 to provide shelter or upgrade the existing shelter for people living below poverty line in urban slums which will help in making cities slum free. This scheme had an objective to provide shelter and upgrade the existing shelter for below poverty line families in urban slums.
Level of operation	Centre sponsored implementation in all non-JnNURM cities/towns.
Led by	Ministry of Housing and Urban Poverty Alleviation
Date of publication and timeframe covered	2005-2012

Items	*Specific Details*
Objectives and targets of the framework	Under this programme, Minimum Floor Area of Dwelling Unit should not be less than 25 sq.mts. and preferably two room accommodation plus kitchen and toilet should be constructed. Allocation of Funds& Funding Pattern The scheme will apply to all towns and cities excepting cities/towns covered under JNNRUM. Allocation of funds among States will be on the basis of the State's urban slum population to total urban slum population in the country Housing should not be provided free to the beneficiaries by the State Government. A minimum of 12 per cent beneficiary contribution should be stipulated, which in the case of backward/special classes (SC/ST/BC/OBC/PH) and other weaker sections shall be 10 per cent.
Target group of the framework	The target group under the scheme is slum dwellers from all sections of the community through a cluster approach.
Available publications and where these can be accessed	IHSDP scheme may be under implementation in ACCES Sanitation project cities – in such cases plans made under the ACCESS programme should duly consider the objectives and targets of already proposed programmes.

(iii) Governance Frameworks (State Level)

It is to be noted that several states have developed specific state (province) level sanitation policies. Few of the policies are briefly described below:

State Sanitation Policies: Rajasthan (2009), Bihar State Water and Sanitation Policy, Andhra Pradesh Water, Land and Tree Act, Kerala, West Bengal, Maharashtra. These policies mandate Provision of sanitation services in Urban Areas and Provision of appropriate financial resources.

Kerala Policy and Programme

- Formation of local ward committees, each representing some 500 families and with gender equity.
- Inventory of sanitation in their areas and identify households that need a subsidy for building a latrine.
- Subsidies are provided by the local government from local resources, supplemented by voluntary support from or local voluntary groups.

Central and State Governments only contribute funds for information and training.

- **Rajasthan Sanitation Policy**
  - The local bodies can utilise funds of poverty alleviation schemes for taking up sanitation projects for the benefit of the urban poor and women.
  - Municipal authorities will arrange for sanitation incorporating the policy provisions in local planning.
  - Payment of subsidy to house owners for construction of low-cost toilets as well as construction of community toilets by urban bodies.
  - Each town will have the provision of a sewerage network with which all the houses will be connected.
  - Importance given to installation of sewage treatment plants and recycling of water
- **Karnataka Water Supply and Sanitation Policy—2002**

Objective: The Government of Karnataka in partnership with urban local bodies in the State, the Karnataka Urban Water Supply and Drainage Board (KUWS&DB) and the Bangalore Water Supply and Sewerage Board (BWSSB) will continue and strengthen its efforts to provide all residents of urban areas of the State, piped water supply and sanitation services at or near their dwellings. The efforts of the Government of Karnataka and its partner agencies will be to:

- Ensure universal coverage of water and sanitation services that people want and are willing to pay for and
- To do so in a manner that preserves the sustainability of the precious water resources of the State, project and enhances the commercial ad economical sustainability of the operations at the same time
- Ensure a minimum level of service to all citizens

Institutional Arrangements: Government of Karnataka will continue to be responsible for:

- Policy formulation
- Ensuring provision of the bulk of the resources required for capacity Creation
- Regulation, monitoring and evaluation of the efficiency of operations, including prescribing reporting requirements, procurement procedures, etc
- Setting minimal service standard
- Encouraging the use of public private partnerships as well as private sector participation to achieve the sector goals
- Promotion of the economic and commercial viability of water supply systems and the exploitation of economies of scale and scope by appropriate aggregation options

- Institution of necessary incentives for urban local bodies and other service providers to implement sector reforms
- Ensuring co-ordination and collaboration among the various agencies both at the policy and operation level through the establishment of appropriate committees and agencies.

Urban Local Bodies: In accordance with the principle enshrined in Article 243 (W) of the Constitution of India read with the Twelfth Schedule. ULBs will be responsible for water supply and sewerage services form water catchments to waste water treatment. The Government of Karnataka, however, will have the responsibility to monitor that ULBs provide quality services in accordance with the standards prescribed at the State level. ULBs will have the choice of providing the services directly through public bodies or through such appropriate Private Sector Participation (PSP) arrangements. Given however, the paramount need for financial and commercial viability of the operations, the State will monitor strictly policies relating to minimal tariff operations autonomy of the municipal water operations, etc.

KUWS&DB and BWSSB: The Karnataka Urban Water Supply and Drainage Board will continue to be responsible for capacity creations and augmentation in all ULBs and O&M in selected ULBs for the present. Over the medium term, the KUWS&DB will be restructured and its role redefined. In the longer term the KUWS&DB could become a publicly owned independent provider of technical assistance and management support to ULBs who do not have adequate capacity. Similarly, the appropriate role of BWSSB will be defined in the action for the Bangalore City and surrounding areas.

(iii) Governance frameworks (Local Level)

There are several examples of local government initiatives to promote and enhance sanitation coverage. A few typical examples are briefly given below:

State of West Bengal: The Mednipore Intensive Sanitation Project (1990)

- Policy of no subsidy to any households
- A network of trained local volunteers - variety of technical options in latrine construction, with different costs to suit different abilities to pay.
- The volunteers get a small incentive. Credit is available for the poor. The Gram Panchayat is actively involved.
- Extensive network and deep roots of the principle NGO, high population density and consequent reduction of private places for defecation, high literacy rates and strong community organisation

Mumbai Slum Sanitation Programme

- Municipal Corporation of greater Mumbai (MCGM)—World Bank assisted Slum Sanitation Programme under Mumbai Sewage Disposal Project—1996-2005
- 330 community toilet blocks (CTBs) with more than 51,00 toilet seats constructed and handed over to community groups to use and maintain
- Participatory demand led approach, partnerships between MCGM, NGOs, contractors and slum communities, superior technical innovation—increased level of service provision

(iv) Non-governmental Initiatives and Programmes

(a) WES-Net India

Items	*Specific Details*
Objectives and guiding principles	To advocate for the achievement of the MDGs, with due attention to the development and implementation of policies and plans that improve the participation of the poor in effective delivery of water and sanitation services. • To strengthen and utilise the capacity of sector organisations by improving coordination, improving knowledge sharing and fostering more effective partnerships. • To enhance the exchange of knowledge and information between and within different stakeholders, working at different levels and different geographic locations across India.
Coordinator and partners	Members of WES-Net The General body of WES-Net India has two types of membership: • Institutional Members and • Individual Members Core Group: The core group of WES-Net includes members elected by the general body to guide its activities, and a limited number of special invitees. The elected members represent the governing body for all legal purposes. Special invitees, representing agencies such as the UN, facilitate WES-Net relationship with the Government and external support agencies. Functioning of WES-Net India At present, WES-Net India operates primarily at the national level and is linked to states and districts primarily through an extension of national membership. Regional activities will be initiated to reach different regions and states of the country shortly.

Items	*Specific Details*
Source of funding	WES-Net India functions with support it receives from its member organisations to maintain. Examples of the support received to date include: • **UNICEF and Plan International** jointly support the secretariat, and the production of WESNet's newsletter • **Plan International** has also provided office space, and supports the WES-Net India website • **WSP** supported a study of various institutional models for WES-Net India, and has provided specific assistance to WES-Net, such as the preparation of a draft Memorandum of Association • **UNDP** supports and manages the Solution Exchange for WES-Net, an e-mail based discussion group • **WaterAid** supports the research coordination event, in collaboration with UNDP. • **Pragmatix** and **AFPRO** are jointly supporting the preparation of a database of key sectoral documents • **SPWD, CARE India** and **FODRA** all assisted in the development of MOA and registration processes. • Apart from these, many active members across the country continue to provide support for various needs of WES-Net that arise time to time.
Timeframe	On-Going
Short description	A network of stakeholders in the Water and Environmental Sanitation sector in India;
Target group	Focus on Poverty and achievement of MDG
Website	http://www.wesnetindia.org

(b) The Country Programme, 2008-2012—UNICEF

Items	*Specific Details*
Objectives and guiding principles	The overall goal of the 2008-2012 Country Programme is to advance the fulfillment of the rights of all women and children in India to survival, development, participation and protection by reducing social inequalities based on gender, caste, ethnicity or region. UNICEF will work closely with government flagship schemes to strengthen their capacity to deliver quality services to all its citizens. UNICEF's Action on the Child's Environment • Improve the child's household hygiene and sanitation environment • Improve the child's school environment • Improve community management and sustainability of water and sanitation interventions
Coordinator and partners	Partners with and supports programmes of the Govt. of India. Works with grass root level institutions and villages, with local Governments, State Governments and the National Government

Items	*Specific Details*
Source of funding	United Nations
Timeframe	Current Programme objectives are up to 2012
Short description	UNICEF supports the national and state governments in developing and implementing a range of replicable models for sanitation, hygiene and water supply: Elements from these have influenced Government policy and programmes.
Target group	**Child Environment** improving freshwater availability, its management, conservation and equitable allocation, as well as access to sanitation and adoption of critical hygiene practices. Constitutionally, states can frame their own policy on certain issues, such as education and health, which is why state and district levels are key focuses for UNICEF action.
Website	http://www.unicef.org/india/wes_211.htm

(c) WaterAID India

Items	*Specific Details*
Objectives and guiding principles	**Mission:** WaterAid's mission is to overcome poverty by enabling the world's poorest people to gain access to safe water, sanitation and hygiene education. WaterAid India's objectives are to: enable improved access to sustainable, safe and adequate water supply and sanitation through water, sanitation and hygiene projects; • create a knowledge base for promotion and dissemination of best practice and advocacy at different levels; • Develop and foster an enabling environment for effective programme implementation, in-country funding, organisational learning and growth.
Coordinator and partners	WaterAid India works with local partners, who understand local issues, and provides them with the skills and support to help communities set up and manage practical and sustainable projects that meet their real needs. WaterAid runs campaigns to change policy and practice and ensure water and sanitation's vital role in reducing poverty is recognised. 51 Listed Local partner Organisations
Source of funding	UK based charity
Timeframe	Current Programme: 2006-2010

Items	*Specific Details*
Short description	Through programme implementation, research and advocacy, WaterAid India contributes to critical social and institutional learning. WaterAid also helps to build capacity, innovate technology options and influence policy by engaging with a range of stakeholders. WaterAid India works in both rural and urban areas, initiating community-led and integrated water, sanitation, health and hygiene projects by working with local partners. By demonstrating cost effective, practical examples using appropriate technologies that involve communities through self help groups, WaterAid India is able to influence the government's choice of methods and encourage local partner organisations to take the lead in all its work. In turn, they ensure that all members of the community, including the poorest and most marginalised, are involved in the projects.
Target group	Local Communities
Website	http://www.wateraid.org/india

(d) BORDA–South Asia (Bremen Overseas Research and Development Association)

Items	*Specific Details*
Objectives and guiding principles	To improve the livelihoods of disadvantaged groups within societies and to sustain the functioning of eco-systems through dissemination of demand oriented Basic-Needs-Services in the fields of decentralised sanitation, water- and energy supply as well as solid waste- and wastewater management.
Coordinator and partners	• BORDA-SA supports a development co-operation network that consists of 13 partner organisations employing more than 100 development experts who facilitate basic needs service projects. • BORDA-SA Project office is responsible for the co-ordination of projects, providing strategies and solutions and knowledge and quality management and act as catalysts to integrate the partner-network in a wider national sector network to ensure the anticipated dissemination and impact of supported measures.
Source of funding	For Decentralised Wastewater Treatment Systems: Commission of the European Union (CEU), German Federal Ministry for Economic Cooperation and Development (BMZ), Free Hanseatic City of Bremen (LafEZ), Australian Agency for International Development (Ausaid), Water and Sanitation Program SEA (The World Bank)
Timeframe	1. Improvement of living conditions of marginalized members of society in (peri-) urban slums in Southern India -2009-2011 2. BORDA helps 2009 – The new campaign: *School must not sicken children Support hygiene, safety and basic sanitation in schools of southern Africa and Asia,* Duration: 2009-2010

Items	*Specific Details*
Short description	• Knowledge and Quality Management • Decentralised Water Supply • Decentralised Energy Supply • Decentralised Wastewater Treatment • Community Based Sanitation • Decentralised Solid Waste Management
Target group	Peri Urban Slums, School children, Local Communities
Website	http://www.borda-sa.org

(e) GTZ and GTZ-ASEM (Advisory Services in Environmental Management)

Items	*Specific Details*
Objectives and guiding principles	The Indo-German Cooperation in the area of environmental management and sustainable development is streamlined into following Thrust Areas: • Sustainable Urban Environment • Sustainable Industrial Development • Sustainable Environmental Governance • Sustainable Consumption and Consumer Protection
Coordinator and partners	India: Ministry of Environment and Forests (MoEF), Ministry of Consumer Affairs, Food and Public Distribution (MoCA), Ministry of Urban Development (MoUD), Ministry of Housing and Urban Poverty Alleviation (MoH &UPA)
Source of funding	ASEM is a joint programme of the German Technical Cooperation (GTZ) and the Indian Ministry of Environment and Forests, with financial support from the Government of Germany
Timeframe	Up to 2012 Support to JNNURM – 2008-2010
Short description	The aim of Indo-German Cooperation during 2009 to 2012 with the focal area as Environmental Management is to make common contributions to the achievement of the MDGs and implementation of the international environmental conventions (UNFCCC, UNCCD, UNCBD) with focus on strengthening India's developmental efforts, intensifying partnerships between India and Germany, establishing linkages and partnerships between German and Indian institutions and sustainable urban and industrial development by working towards delinking economic growth from resource consumption.
Target group	Local Governments
Website	http://www.asemindia.com

(f) Ecosan Services Foundation (ESF)

Items	*Specific Details*
Objectives and guiding principles	ESF aims to transform into a sustainable key resource centre as a leading knowledge hub in sustainable sanitation and water management. Objectives: 1. Developing sustainable organizational structure and processes. 2. Strengthening their position in capacity development through training, piloting and demonstration, awareness raising, R & D and coaching in new enterprises. 3. Strengthen their networking platform with national and international experts in the sector. 4. Open dissemination of knowledge through face-to face as well as IT enabled services for institutions and individuals. 5. Quality Management and organizational learning to highlight best practices in the sector.
Coordinator and partners	GTZ support, GoI, Maharashtra pollution control Board (MPCB), TTZ Bremerhaven, SEECON Gmbh, The Network University, Kalyani University, International Ecological Engineering University, Indian Water Works Association, ENPHO, Xavier University- Philippines,
Source of funding	GTZ support, GoI, Maharashtra Pollution Control Board (MPCB), TTZ Bremerhaven, SEECON Gmbh, training and consulting activities
Timeframe	On-going
Short description	**ESF offers full Ecosan project packages including:** • Consulting • Feasibility Studies • Project Financing • Technical Designing & Project Planning • Project Implementation • Operation & Maintenance • Project Monitoring
Target group	Ecosan Services Foundation (ESF), Pune, IndiaESF is a section 25 non-profit company established in 2006, with the support of GTZ. It provides ecological sanitation services to: • Municipalities & State Governments • NGO's • Companies & Developers • Private Individuals
Website	http://www.ecosanservices.org

(g) Water and Sanitation Program (WSP)

Items	*Specific Details*
Objectives and guiding principles	The WSP works with partners in the field to seek innovative solutions to the obstacles faced by poor communities in obtaining sustained access to water supply and sanitation services, and strives to be a valued source of advice to achieve widespread adoption of these solutions. To fulfil its mission and make optimal use of its resources, the WSP: • Provides advice to help countries adopt improved policies and strategies and undertake institutional reform; • Provides advice to strengthen the investment programs and projects of its clients and partners; and • Generates, validates, and communicates innovative water supply and sanitation solutions.
Coordinator and partners	Partners are Water & Sanitation Organisations, and donor agencies. 5th World Water Forum Secretariat (World Water Council); Acacia Water; African Development Bank; Agence Française de Développement; AMCOW - African Ministerial Council on Water AquaFed (International Federation for Private Water Operators); nAsian Development Bank; Asia-Pacific Water Forum; CARE International Consortium for Dissemination of DEWATS (CDD); Deutsche Gesellschaft für Technische Zusammenarbeit (GTZ); DFID; Dutch Ministry of Foreign Affairs (DGIS); European Commission (EC); European Union; European Water Partnership; FAO; Federal Ministry for Economic Cooperation and Development (BMZ); Gender and Water Alliance (GWA); Global Handwashing Day; Global Water Systems Project; GWP - Global Water Partnership; International Center for Soil Fertility and Agricultural Development; International Water Association; International Year of Sanitation 2008; IRC Netherlands; Joint Monitoring Program - WHO/UNICEF; Netherlands Water Partnership; Nile Basin Initiative Global Public-Private Partnership for Hand washing with Soap; SIWI - Stockholm International Water Institute; Stockholm Environment Institute; Sustainable Sanitation Alliance; Swedish International Development Cooperation Agency; UN HABITAT; UN Water; UNDP; UNEP; UNICEF; UNSG's Advisory Board on Water and Sanitation (UNSGAB); USAID; USAID Environmental Health; Water Integrity Network; WaterAid; WaterNet; Wetlands International; WHO; WHO - Public Health and Environment; The World Bank; WSSCC; WTO - World Toilet Organization
Source of funding	Funds that support the WSP may come from official donors, international financial institutions and other official agencies, including developing country governments.

Items	*Specific Details*
Timeframe	Ongoing
Short description	They work directly with client governments at the local and national level in 25 countries through regional offices in Africa, East and South Asia, Latin America and the Caribbean, and in, Washington D.C. An important function of the WSP is to advance the water supply and sanitation sector agenda. To increase leverage, WSP activities will be designed and undertaken in a way that promotes cross-sectoral and donor coordination. Within the World Bank, the WSP liaises with World Bank sector operations through the World Bank's Water and Sanitation Sector Board and collaborates on work planning with World Bank country operations. Similar modes of collaboration may be established with other partners.
Target group	Poor people in developing countries
Website	http://www.wsp.org/index.cfm?page=page_disp&pid=1502

(h) Global WASH Campaigns - Water Supply and Sanitation Collaborative Council (WSSCC)

Items	*Specific Details*
Objectives and guiding principles	• WSSCC only exists to serve poor people • The people themselves are at the centre of planning and action for achieving sustainable water and sanitation • WSSCC works by enhancing collaboration among sector agencies and professionals rather than implementing its own projects • Water and sanitation are essential for social and economic development • WSSCC aims to be at the forefront of global knowledge, debate and influence in its field • The number of people without sanitation is much greater than the number without water, while the agencies working in sanitation are fewer; therefore WSSCC dedicates most of its effort to sanitation and hygiene.
Coordinator and partners	Partners: Ashoka
Source of funding	Water Supply and Sanitation Collaborative Council (WSSCC) has created the Global Sanitation Fund. The Global Sanitation Fund is a single pooled fund open to contribution from any source including governments, foundations, private sector and individuals
Timeframe	On going programme
Short description	WSSCC focuses exclusively on those people around the world who currently lack water and sanitation, with all its policies and work aimed only to serve those people. The Collaborative Council has a special interest in sanitation and hygiene and emphasises the need to view water, sanitation and hygiene (WASH) as an inseparable trinity for development.
Target group	All people
Website	http://www.wsscc.org/

(i) PLAN International

Items	*Specific Details*
Objectives and guiding principles	Plan aims to achieve lasting improvements in the quality of life of deprived children in developing countries, through a process that unites people across cultures and adds meaning and value to their lives, by: • enabling deprived children, their families and their communities to meet their basic needs and to increase their ability to participate in and benefit from their societies • building relationships to increase understanding and unity among peoples of different cultures and countries • Promoting the rights and interests of the world's children.
Coordinator and partners	Corporate Partners: CNN, Nokia, Credit Suisse, Prudential, Pepsi, Accor, Microsoft, Basware,
Source of funding	70 per cent of PLAN's income comes from child sponsorship. Grants from governments, trusts and companies help to maximise PLAN's resources and impact in developing countries.
Timeframe	Ongoing
Short description	PLAN is one of the oldest and largest children's development organisations in the world. PLAN's vision is of a world in which all children realise their full potential in societies that respect people's rights and dignity. PLAN aims to achieve lasting improvements in the quality of life of deprived children in developing countries; It works with more than 3,500,000 families and their communities each year.
Target group	Children , families and communities in Asia, Africa and America
Website	http://plan-international.org/

(j) WASTE—Advisors on urban environment and development

Items	*Specific Details*
Objectives and guiding principles	WASTE is active in four fields: • Solid waste management and resource recovery • Low-cost sanitation and liquid waste management • Community based environmental improvement • Micro- and small enterprise development
Coordinator and partners	WASTE partners with several organisations and forms regional consortia in order to carry out its projects and fulfil its objectives. Some of the partners include: ACEPESA Central American Association for Economy, Health and Environment ALPHALOG - L'Association Libre pour la Promotion de l'Habitat et du Logement BASA Bangladesh Association for Social Advancement

Items	Specific Details
Source of funding	WASTE is officially registered with a non-profit status. It has a special fund fed by the difference in the projects' income and the modest salaries paid to WASTE employees. This fund allows for own project development, small donations and occasional training to external persons. It also enables its personnel to dedicate a number or working days to voluntary community work
Timeframe	-
Short description	WASTE works towards sustainable improvement of the urban poor's living conditions and the urban environment in general. Our multi-year, multi-country programmes and projects have a focus on bottom-up development in relation to recycling, solid waste management, ecological sanitation and knowledge sharing. The focus of activities is on low-income urban areas in order to develop, together with local residents, tools and means for their own development, enabling them to improve their living conditions, the environment and to create employment as a sound economic base for their future.
Target group	Urban poor population
Website	http://www.ecosan.nl/

Review of Performance in 11th Five Year Plan[11]

Since the First Five Year Plan (1951-1956), Government of India (GoI) and State governments have till end of 2010-11 spent about Rs 1,35,000 crore on rural drinking water. Under the current Eleventh Five Year Plan (2007-2012), the total expenditure is likely to exceed Rs 90,000 crore, and it is certain that investment in rural water supply will increase even more. In the Eleventh Plan document, it was decided that the major issues which need tackling during this period are the problem of sustainability, water availability and supply, poor water quality, centralised vs. decentralised approaches and financing of O&M cost while ensuring equity in regard to gender, socially and economically weaker sections of the society, school children, socially vulnerable groups such SC, ST, Minority and people residing in LWE districts etc.

ARWSP

Under the Accelerated Rural Water Supply Programme (ARWSP) India made good progress in terms of coverage. The Uncovered habitations as of 1st April, 2005, were 55,067 (4,588 Not Covered, and 50,479 partially Covered) of which 55067 uncovered habitations were covered as on 1st April, 2011. However, out of the total number of 16, 64,186 habitations in India, the States reported that 477426 habitations,

28.69 (per cent) were partially covered and 7.2 (per cent) habitations were water quality affected as on 1st April, 2011. The reasons for this include: a) the inclusion of newly formed peri-urban habitations and small habitations with less than 100 persons in line with NRDWP guidelines. (b) Slippage of covered habitations due to poor O&M and drying up of sources. (c) Increase in population and growth of settlements. (d) Increasing contamination of sources due to natural and manmade causes (e) Increased testing of sources and improved knowledge of quality affected areas. (f) Changing norms of coverage adopted by the States due to flexibility given under NRDWP.

Swajaldhara (2002–2009)

Reforms in the rural drinking water sector were adopted in 1999 through Sector Reform Project (SRP) on a pilot basis and have been scaled up throughout the country in the form of Swajaldhara launched on 25th December 2002. The programme is a paradigm shift from supply driven to demand driven, centralised to decentralised implementation and Government's role from service provider to facilitator. It is based on empowerment of villagers to ensure their full participation in the project through a decision making role in the choice of the drinking water scheme, planning, design, implementation, control of finances, management arrangements including full ownership of drinking water assets. The community has to share partial capital cost either in cash or kind or both and 100 per cent responsibility of operation and maintenance (O&M). An integrated service delivery mechanism is also promoted which includes taking up conservation measures through rainwater harvesting and ground water recharge systems for sustained drinking water supply. The principles of Swajaldhara have been mainstreamed in NRDWP.

NRDWP (2009-2012)

In order to address the above issues flagged in the Eleventh Plan document. The Rural Water Supply Guidelines have been revised w.e.f. 1.4.2009. The revised guidelines known as National Rural Drinking Water Programme (NRDWP) focus on the following areas:

- Moving forward from achieving habitation level coverage towards household level drinking water security and coverage. Ensuring sustainability in drinking water schemes for which 20 per cent of NRDWP allocation is provided on 100 per cent Central share basis.
- Encouraging water conservation methods including revival of traditional water bodies

- Convergence of all water conservation programmes at the village level;
- Ensuring household level drinking water security through water budgeting and preparation of village water security plans, and
- Consciously moving away from high cost treatment technologies for tackling arsenic and fluoride contamination to development of alternative sources in respect of arsenic and alternate sources/ dilution of aquifers through rainwater harvesting for tackling fluoride contamination.

Bharat Nirman Phase I (2005-2009) and II (2009-2012)

Bharat Nirman, a programme to build rural infrastructure, was launched by the Government of India in 2005. Phase I of the programme was implemented in the period 2005-06 to 2008-09. Phase II is being implemented from 2009-10 to 2011-12. Rural drinking water is one of the six components of Bharat Nirman. During the Bharat Nirman

Phase—I period, 55,067 un-covered and about 3.31 lakh slippedback habitations were to be covered with provisions of drinking water facilities and 2.17 lakh quality - affected habitations were to be addressed for water quality problem.

While prioritising the addressal of the water quality problem, arsenic and fluoride affected habitations have been accorded priority followed by iron, salinity, nitrate and other contaminants. To ensure that habitations once provided with drinking water supply infrastructure do not slip back and face drinking water problem, sustainability of drinking water sources and systems has been accorded high priority. To achieve drinking water security at village/ habitation level, conjunctive use of water i.e., judicious use of rainwater, surface water and ground water is promoted.

Research and Development

Research and Development in the field of Rural Water Supply and Sanitation is one of the support activities of the Ministry of Drinking Water and Sanitation for which 100 per cent funding to research organisations is provided. A Research Advisory Committee (RAC) under the Chairpersonship of Secretary, DWS was constituted primarily to promote research and development activities in drinking water and sanitation. With the new issues and challenges emerging in the rural drinking water and sanitation sector, RAC was reconstituted and renamed as Research and Development Advisory Committee (RDAC) on December 2009. In order to promote cost-efficient, easy to maintain and innovative ideas leading to drinking water security, developing improved sanitation and hygiene habits, seven priority areas were identified in 11th Five Year Plan.

The RDAC in its first meeting in January, 2010 discussed the core areas for research and felt that R&D projects should be based on multi-centric studies. A framework needs to be developed with a vision for taking up R&D for the next 5-years. The Core areas identified for undertaking R and D Projects in the 12th Five Year Plan could be:

1. Various types of materials, structure, storage, etc. for rain-water harvesting structures;
2. Mobile instantaneous/packaged water treatment plants for calamity-affected areas;
3. Chemicals to remove choking of tube wells in drought prone areas;
4. Development of deep tube well hand pumps made up of light weight materials as a multi-centric study;
5. Focus on detergents, fertilisers, toxic elements and blue green algae contamination of drinking water sources;
6. Integrated water management using specific systems like SCADA;
7. Large scale arsenic removal through pumping oxygen into arsenic rich aquifers;
8. Use of traditional plants, seeds in water treatment;
9. Impact assessment of various water quality parameters on human health;
10. Technology development for insecticides and pesticides in drinking water;
11. Identification and protection of possible safe water zones including paleochannels;
12. Identification of core radionuclides in drinking water sources;
13. Detection of different viruses in drinking water;
14. Development of simple treatment technologies for removal of toxic metals from drinking water;
15. Identification of disinfection by-products from drinking water resources emanating from ecosystems having rich NOM;
16. In-situ dilution of geogenic contamination in drinking water aquifers in different hydro geological zones;
17. Development of economic designs for sustainability structures in hilly areas;

18. Response of shallow aquifers to water impounding and recharge structures in different agro climatic zones;
19. Research on Water resource data base, community monitoring of ground water, rainfall, Water storages, Water quality data base;
20. Impact of climate change on domestic water supply, considering the hydro geological changes over time periods; and
21. Communication needs assessment study.

Vision

The vision for rural domestic water supply should be to cover all rural households with safe piped drinking water supply @ 70lpcd. Considering the fact that the norm of 40 lpcd has been continuing from the last four decades and there is a large population that has to be provided with the higher service level, it is recommended that as an interim measure the goal be kept at 55 lpcd for the 12th FYP.

By 2017, it is targeted that at least 55 per cent of rural population in the country will have access to 55 lpcd within their household premises or at a horizontal or vertical distance of not more than 100 meters from their household without barriers of social or financial discrimination. Individual States can adopt higher quantity norms, such as 100 lpcd. By 2017, it is targeted that at least 35 per cent of rural population have individual household connections. It is recognised that States will adopt their own strategies and phased timeframes to achieve this goal. Three standards of service can be identified depending on what communities want:

- Piped water supply with all metered, household connections (designed for 70 lpcd or more) - with appropriate user charges as decided by States taking affordability and social equity into consideration.
- Basic piped water supply with a mix of household connections, public taps and handpumps (designed for 55 lpcd) -with appropriate costing as decided by States taking affordability and social equity into consideration.
- In extreme cases, handpumps (designed for 40 lpcd), protected open wells, protected ponds, etc., supplemented by other local sources—preferably free of cost.

Recommendations of Working Group on Rural Sanitation[12]

Convergence Issues

NRDWP and TSC should be administered in the State by establishing a 3-tier Governance Structure as explained below:

- Government of India level : A dedicated Monitoring Directorate should be set up.
- State level: A multi disciplinary Rural Water and Sanitation Management Organisation (RWASMO) at the State level in the shape of a Society registered under the Societies Registration Act. It should be headed by an officer from All-India Services of 12-16 years of seniority. It should have personnel with suitable academic qualifications and experience to oversee work relating to water security planning, water conservation and recharge, solid and liquid waste management, sanitation, construction of civil and engineering works, financial planning and management, social and community mobilisation, accounting, mass communication, training, etc. The organisation should be empowered to take financial and administrative decisions and should have flexibility to appoint personnel from open market on contractual basis or to take government servants on deputation.
- District level: Multi disciplinary District Water and Sanitation Mission (DWSM) for each district that would report to the RWASMO. A dedicated Group A level officer on deputation should head DWSM at District level to plan, coordinate and implement activities relating to domestic water supply and sanitation.
- Block level: Block Resource Centres with a Block Programme Officer for Sanitation that would report to the DWSM and work with the GPs/ Users Managing Committees/ VWSCs for implementing water supply and sanitation schemes. Jalsurakshak (Water) and Swachchhata Doot (sanitation) at GP level should be encouraged.

Integrated Habitat Development Scheme

- Rural housing schemes taken up under Indira Awas Yojna (IAY) will provide toilet and domestic water facilities within the houses. Provision for bathing facilities with toilets constructed should be considered under the scheme. Solid and Liquid Waste Management (SLWM) should also be an essential component of these habitats. State rural housing schemes should also be supported with NRDWP and TSC for provisioning toilets, SLWM and domestic water supply in houses to be constructed.
- Necessary funds for construction of toilets will be provided by MoDWS as a second stream under TSC and SLWM should be supported under MNREGS.

School Sanitation

- SSHE is an important component to ensure universal sanitation coverage in rural areas of the country. There should be designed capacity building of school teachers, ASHA and anganwadi workers on hygiene and sanitation. Education Departments in States and Centre should include functionality and usage of toilets and hygiene practices including handwashing with soap, in all inspection reports and reviews of programmes. Moreover, sanitation must made be a part of the school curriculum.
- Ministries in charge of School Education and Anganwadis must be exhorted to ensure functional toilets in schools and anganwadis located in private premises. On full coverage of schools and anganwadis in government buildings, Government of India must take a view on coverage of remaining such Institutions housed in private buildings and particularly Government - aided schools.

Community Toilets

- The present concept of community toilets is limited to provisions for landless and floating population apart from provisions at common places like bus stands and market places in the rural areas. Tie-ups should be made with concerned Authority like NHAI to provide public toilets, along Highways. Efforts should be made to bring out Government orders to make appropriate sanitation facilities essential for petrol pumps, restaurants and dhabas. The issue regarding operation and maintenance of such facilities should also be suitably addressed and onetime Government funding option should be included under TSC.

Role of Civil Society

- Civil Society Organisations (CSOs) should play key role in facilitating 'development planning capabilities' at the GP level. Space should be made for CSOs to be involved in policy formulation, planning and project implementation.

Sensitising Political Leadership

- The political leadership at national, state and district levels should to be sensitised on the principles of demand driven approaches to total sanitation, to enable high level political support for sanitation.
- Addressal of the sanitation issue should be ensured at the level of Chief Ministers, Ministers, and other political representatives

to convey messages of priority they attach to sanitation. Annual conference of Ministers incharge of sanitation from all States should be held to get renewed commitment from political leadership towards sanitation.

Support to the National Urban Sanitation Policy (NUSP)

The project looks at holistic improvement of urban sanitation by providing recommendations at the policy level, capacity enhancement and legal framework for mainstreaming sanitation and assisting select cities in planning, implementing, operating and maintaining sustainable sanitation. As a part of its support to the NSSI (National School Sanitation Initiative) of MoHRD, GoI, GIZ has already established a technical cell at CBSE which will act as a nodal platform for improving school sanitation and raising awareness on issues concerning sanitation and hygiene.

It aims to implement and operationalise sanitation infrastructure, and management of the sanitation sector as a whole at all levels: national, state and city with a special focus on poorer parts of the cities. The project is simultaneously working at three levels:

Central Level

- The project is currently supporting the MoUD in evaluating the City Sanitation Plans (CSP) prepared so far and documenting the best practices and lessons learnt. This document will provide suggestions to MoUD in streamlining the CSP preparation process in future. A criteria list has been prepared for the evaluation of CSPs. GIZ has so far evaluated 10 CSPs and documented their best practices.
- A national event on launching the NSSI website and the manual on school sanitation has been conducted under the presence of the MoHRD minister.
- A NSSI-cell at CBSE which currently acts as a national hub for improving school sanitation and raising awareness on sanitation and hygiene has been installed. GIZ is supporting the MoHRD and CBSE in improving school sanitation in selected schools throughout India by providing technical services for cost effective solutions. The documentation of this process will assist other schools in improving their sanitation services.

State Level

- Supporting selected states in improving/preparing their State Sanitation Strategies (SSS). It is envisaged that key issues concerning capacity enhancement, outsourcing urban services in issues such as public/community toilet complex and sewerage and legal framework will be addressed in the SSS through GIZ support which will enhance service delivery at city level.

City Level

- Four city sanitation planning documents prepared with GIZ's assistance have been approved by the elected body of the respected cities and forwarded to the state government.
- The project enables a decision process based on cost-efficient and long-term planning at city level. It supports the cities in developing bankable projects by creating sector-wise financial sustainability while strengthening service delivery. The project supports the decision-making process for outsourcing urban services.

Water, Sanitation and Hygiene (Wash)[13]

The programme will reduce WASH related disease, mortality, and morbidity, including stunting due to chronic under-nutrition in children under-two years by support to National and State Governments and partners to:

- Access data, evidence, information and knowledge to guide WASH advocacy, policy, planning, programme and budgetary action. Stimulate demand and adopt community approaches to eliminate open defecation and promote the adoption of hygiene practices, especially in the most deprived communities.
- Scale-up improved service delivery of safe and sustainable drinking water, especially in the most deprived communities.
- Improve children's learning environment by ensuring access to sustainable safe water and sanitation facilities and hygiene practices in schools.

Growing Challenges

A huge per centage of urban slums is not connected to any sewerage system. "Illegal" settlements do not have even rudimentary facilities. Sewerage and drainage facilities in most parts of unplanned and haphazardly developed urban areas are woefully inadequate. All this, plus the high population density, make urban sanitation a nightmarish challenge. Sewerage connected toilets need adequate amounts of running water and a regular supply for waste disposal; the costs of maintenance too are prohibitive.

Besides, public toilets in Indian cities and towns, run by municipal bodies, are given low official priority in terms of maintenance. Conventional sewerage systems require a prohibitive amount of continuous water supply and are costly to maintain. Mumbai had experimented with mobile toilets but, though this was a good idea, activists say that poor scheduling, poor maintenance and lack of access to sewer lines have made them ineffective. In this regard, the Sulabh Shauchalay toilet-cum-bath facilities are making a noteworthy contribution but they do not seem to be enough.

The worst victims of poor sanitation facilities are girls and women whose health, safety and quality of life are severely compromised, especially in congested urban settlements. In seven states, according to the National University of Educational Planning and Administration, 70 per cent of elementary schools are without any toilet facilities. According to educationists, lack of toilet facilities in municipal and government schools are one of the significant factors for girls dropping out around the time they are 11 or 12 years of age[14].

Sanitation, Health and Women: An Assessment

The United Nations Millennium Development Goals (MDGs) set an ambitious agenda for improving the human condition by 2015. Later, at the 2002 World Summit on Sustainable Development in Johannesburg, a similar goal for sanitation was linked to the MDG for access to clean water: to halve the number of people without sanitation. The World Health Organisation estimates that 2.4 billion people worldwide are without access to sanitation (WHO and UNICEF 2000).[15]

There is broad consensus in mainstream donor policy that women's participation is critical to the success of sanitation projects, in both the implementation and usage phases. The World Bank (2002), states that lack of gendered, community involvement is the main reason for 'poor service sustainability' in the water sector.[16] Getting women involved in water and sanitation projects can 'contribute to their satisfactory completion [of tasks] and thus to project sustainability' (Wakeman et al. 1996:7).[17] Mainstreaming gender perspectives will ensure that needs and concerns of women and men from all social groups are taken into account during water and sanitation development (UNDESA 2005:4). Women use latrines more than other household members (van Wijk-Sibesma 1998).[18] Programmes should recognise women and girls 'as primary users of water, hygiene educators and managers' (World Bank 2002). Women's participation in particular is expected to create sustainable projects by (a) including women as primary users, consumers, and managers; (b) increasing women's social capital; and (c) accessing women's knowledge.

Gender has proved a most important element in recent prescriptions for marketing latrines to potential users. The International Water and Sanitation Centre (van Wijk-Sijbesma 1998) reports that the main reasons why households will spend money on latrines are convenience, privacy and safety for women, and status. Latrines are convenient for both men and women because they are nearby and can be used day or night and in bad weather. They provide privacy and safety for women because they have doors that can be shut and locked, and their placement near the house eliminates the necessity of walking alone to a distant, private place. The status of a latrine is often tied to design and quality; they are desirable as an uncommon, luxury item.

Besides the fact that women are targeted as the primary users of latrines, their participation is often encouraged as part of an efficiency approach to sanitation. Women are viewed as having the greatest incentive to keep systems functioning: (a) access to clean water will enable women to spend their time better; (b) sanitation will lower women's risk of physical attack; and (c) family wellness and child survival will reduce women's household responsibilities (Millennium Project Task Force on Water and Sanitation 2005). Any increase in women's free time means that extra time can be spent constructing and managing water and sanitation facilities or engaging in income-generating activities.

Women are also marked as those who can best introduce behaviours that will lead to better public health. In their roles as mothers and household managers, they are best placed to improve their families' sanitation and hygiene practices (Waterkeyn and Cairncross 2005).[19] For example, 'women have accumulated an impressive store of environmental wisdom, being the ones to find water, to educate children in hygiene matters and to understand the impact of poor sanitation on health' (UNDESA 2005: 4). Taking advantage of this knowledge is cost-efficient for sanitation and hygiene projects: '[t]argeting women for training as the main role models and "teachers" within the household is [a] cost-effective way of raising awareness and skills' (UNDESA 2005:10). Women can also play an important role by mobilising demand through 'women to women' contacts (van Wijk-Sijbesma 1998: 112). The goals of water supply and sanitation projects to encourage women's participation, and their implications for women's empowerment, have been left largely unexplored. Nor do we know what an unexamined, women's participation approach to latrine marketing means for latrine usage by the target group. Water supply and sanitation projects have latrine-coverage targets that they attempt to reach through women's participation.

Although outwardly containing feminist goals, combined women's participation and latrine marketing programmes address both women's participation and latrine building as technical problems, to which the answer is the inclusion of women as 'marketers' of latrines to household and community members and 'consumers' in their own households. Sanitation programmes' proposed solutions remain largely technical: problem x can be solved by technique y. For example, simply building latrines does not mean that they will be used, but their non-use is attributed to a failure to include women, who were not involved or committed to the project (van Wijk-Sijbesma 1998). The problem: toilets are not being used. The solution: women's participation in projects. What passes largely unnoticed in these technical policy suggestions are questions of how latrines gain particular social meanings because of their linkage to women's empowerment. While policy literatures do recognise 'cultural reasons' for having latrines, more attention should be given to existing, gendered, local understandings of excretion that affect demand. Technical solutions do not go far enough in considering the role played by latrine-building programmes in the shaping of meanings about latrines, and also the shifting, gendered geographies associated with their marketing and use.

In many parts of Asia, women seem to be 'imprisoned by daylight' because they feel that they can only leave the home to defecate during periods of darkness, either in the very early morning or late at night. Thus, during the hours of daylight if the family does not have a latrine, or access to one, women are restricted, which can lead to all sorts of negative consequences. In rural and in some urban societies sexual harassment and rape are real threats when women are going to or returning from the area chosen to relieve themselves.

According to Country Programme Action Plan, the large scale of maternal and child under-nutrition poses a challenge for India in reaching the Millennium Development Goals on child nutrition, survival and development.[20] Recent government efforts in restructuring the Integrated Child Development Services (ICDS) and other initiatives exemplify national commitment to holistic child development. With a maternal mortality ratio (MMR) of 20013 deaths per 100,000 live births, India is making progress on Millennium Development Goal. One contributing factor has been the introduction of a conditional cash transfer scheme, which improved institutional delivery from 38.7 per cent in 2005-2006 to 72 per cent in 2009. However, the quality of maternal care remains a concern.

The India Country Programme 2008-2012 reflects its mandate to work for women's and children's rights and for integrating gender equality concerns into every aspect of programming. A review of ICO (India Country Office, UNICEF) programming for gender equality was completed in early 2010 to identify strategic possibilities.[21] The Review mapped the existing national policy and identified opportunities for strengthening national policy initiatives that promote gender equality. This exercise was conducted to strengthen programming interventions for gender equality.

Progress is evident in universalising primary education, and India is likely to achieve this Millennium Development Goal.[22] Enrolment and completion rates of girls in primary school have improved and are catching up with those of boys, as are elementary completion rates. In light of the Right of Children to Free and Compulsory Education Act (RTE), the challenges now are sub-optimal learning achievements and completion of upper primary education, particularly among girls, children in rural areas and those belonging to minority groups and the poorest wealth quintiles.

In child protection, issues like child marriage, child labour and gender-biased sex selection threaten the environment in which children live. Forty three per cent of women in the 20-24 age group are married before the legal age of 18 years and an estimated 28 million children in the 5-14 age group are engaged in work. Census figures show a continued decline in child sex ratios (0-6 age group), from 927 girls per 1,000 boys in 2001 to 914 girls in 2011.

The Review concluded that ongoing ICO interventions on girls' education, water and sanitation, nutrition, anemia and child protection, as well as its strategy to focus on "social inclusion", are well-designed and well-positioned to take advantage of the synergy and interconnections between women's rights and children's rights. ICO also has several interventions conceptualised from a gender equality perspective. These include:

- Campaigns against child marriage and trafficking
- Perspective-building and capacity-building on gender equality for key institutional stakeholders (such as police and teachers)
- Challenging gender stereotypes in campaign materials and teaching/learning materials
- Development and application of disaggregated databases, planning tools and monitoring tools

- Development and application of gendered strategies and tools for programme planning, budgeting and human resource management
- Evidence-based advocacy on key issues of women's and girls' rights.

Child Development and Nutrition (CDN) supported ICDS and NRHM to scale-up the adolescent anaemia control programme with state funds. By the end of 2010, the programme is being scaled-up in 11 states. A total of 16.4 million adolescent girls are reached with iron and folic acid supplements weekly, deworming prophylaxis biannually, and counselling and support to improve their diets and prevent anemia. Additionally, CDN supported MWCD in developing the framework and implementation guidelines for the Rajiv Gandhi Scheme for the Empowerment of Adolescent Girls (SABLA) and the Indira Gandhi Scheme for Maternity Protection (a conditional cash transfer scheme). These two national programmes have been developed to improve women's nutrition and opportunities throughout the life cycle.

In 2011 CDN will prioritise support to: a) implementation of National and State Plans for ICDS Universalisation with Quality, b) scale up of initiatives for improved nutrition in children 0-24 months old and their mothers through ICDS, NRHM, VHNDs and community-based programmes with a focus on equity outcomes, c) implementation of National and State Plans for the Rajiv Gandhi Scheme for the Empowerment of Adolescent Girls and the Indira Gandhi Scheme for Maternity Protection, and d) scale up state-wide programmes for the control of micronutrient deficiencies and anemia in children, adolescent girls and mothers.

MENSTRUAL HYGIENE[23]

Menstrual hygiene is a taboo subject; a topic that many women in South Asia are uncomfortable discussing in public. This is compounded by gender inequality, which excludes women and girls from decision-making processes. Low literacy levels and numeracy skills, lack of confidence and social norms were found to be critical barriers to women's involvement, and require long-term strategies to overcome.

The taboos and rituals surrounding menstruation in South Asia exclude women and girls from aspects of social and cultural life. For example, in Hinduism, notions of purity and pollution determine the basis of the caste system, and are central to Hindu culture, including gender relations. Bodily excretions are considered to be polluting, as are human bodies in the process of producing them. All women, regardless of their social caste, incur pollution through the bodily processes of menstruation and childbirth. There are two main ways to achieve purity: by avoiding contact with pollutants, or purifying oneself to remove or absorb the pollution. Water is the most common medium of purification. The protection of water sources from such pollution, particularly running water, which is the physical manifestation of Hindu deities, is, therefore, a key concern (Joshi and Fawcett 2001).

One major concern is the impact of cultural practices and lack of services for menstrual hygiene management on girls' access to education. A study in South India reported that half the girls attending school were withdrawn by their parents once they reached menarche, mostly to be married. This was either because menstruation was regarded as a sign of readiness for marriage, or because of the shame and danger associated with being an unmarried pubescent girl (Ten; 2007).

WaterAid has been working in India since 1986 supporting communities, in partnership with local organisations, to access water, sanitation and hygiene. Hygienic management of menstruation is a challenge for women in India, raising serious health concerns. However, until 2007, the hygiene promotion programme did not specifically address women's hygiene issues. Despite women and adolescent girls being a target group, the programme did not address the issues related to poor menstrual hygiene.

In order to let the women and girls to live healthy, productive and dignified lives, it is essential that they are able to manage menstrual bleeding effectively. This requires access to appropriate water, sanitation and hygiene services, including clean water for washing cloths used to absorb menstrual blood and having a place to dry them, having somewhere private to change cloths or disposable sanitary pads, facilities to dispose of used cloths and pads, and access to information to understand the menstrual cycle and how to manage menstruation hygienically. As well as addressing practical needs like this, it is also necessary to promote better awareness among women and men to overcome the embarrassment, cultural practices and taboos around menstruation that impact negatively on women's and girls' lives, and reinforce gender inequities and exclusion.

It is to be emphasised that women require access to WASH services to manage menstruation hygienically, yet this has been largely neglected by the WASH sector in development. In South Asia, the burden of this neglect is borne by millions of women and girls who are denied their rights to gender equality, education, access to water and sanitation, health and a life of dignity. As a consequence, governments' commitments to achieving national and international development goals will not be met. Lack of awareness of development practitioners, policymakers and communities about the problem, and appropriate solutions, has meant that menstrual hygiene is not prioritised in either the supply of or the demand for WASH services. This failure to priorities the issue is compounded by deeply entrenched gender inequalities and cultural perceptions and beliefs. Women's lack of meaningful participation in decision making and management of development programmes, and the cultural taboos and practices surrounding menstruation in South Asia create a critical obstacle to implementing practical solutions. This requires longer-term strategies to bring about cultural change.

Health, Sanitation and Children: An Assessment

Widespread poverty resulting in chronic and persistent hunger is one of the biggest problems of developing countries today. Poverty, in turn, is closely linked to overall standard of living and whether the population can meet its basic needs, such as access to food, housing, health care and education. The social and environmental context in which a child is raised affects his or her health and, in turn, survival chances (Sastry, 1996). This inter-sectoral and inter-related cause of under nutrition operates at many levels, from the community at large to the household and children within the household. Under-nutrition is often cited as an important factor contributing to high morbidity and mortality among children in developing countries. Under-nutrition during childhood can also affect growth potential and the risk of morbidity and mortality in later years of life. Many studies have shown that severely malnourished children are at a greater risk of dying than healthy children. According to 2001 UNICEF data (UNICEF, 2001), an estimated 150 million children under the age of five in developing countries were malnourished. Malnutrition contributes to about half of child deaths globally, because malnourished children have a low resistance to common infections locking them into the vicious cycle of recurring sickness, faltering growth and diminished learning ability. Factors like maternal age, literacy status and work outside home delay the introduction of supplementary food, even after 12 months of age. Therefore, nutrition education is essential for creating an awareness of desirable weaning practices among mothers to enhance the health status of children (Subbulakshmi and Udipi, 1990).

Though insufficient and unsafe water supplies and sanitation affect people of all ages, the well-being of young children is particularly compromised. Approximately 84 per cent of the global burden of diarrhoeal disease (still a major cause of death and illness in all age groups) affects children aged under five; 74 per cent of the burden from helminth (worm) infections affects children aged between five and fourteen.[24]

Diarrhoea and intestinal parasites, along with the poor water and sanitation provision that promotes them, have complex and reciprocal links to malnutrition in children.[25] Malnutrition weakens the body's defences and makes children more vulnerable to disease. At the same time, diarrhoea and intestinal parasites contribute to malnutrition by causing decreased food intake, impaired nutrient absorption and direct nutrient losses[26]. Even a relatively mild infestation of parasites can consume 10 per cent of a child's total energy intake as well as interfering with digestion and absorption. Unsanitary environments also contribute to malnutrition by challenging children's immune systems; nutrients that would otherwise support growth go instead towards supporting the immune response.[27]

Around half of the world's children (approximately one billion) now live in urban areas, the great majority of them in cities and towns in Africa, Asia and Latin America.[28]

In many communities, children form over 50 per cent of the population—not, in other words, a special interest group. Urban children have long been considered better off in terms of health and survival, but this urban advantage has declined in some areas and is increasingly being called into question. Those living in poor urban settlements face some of the most difficult environmental conditions, and investigations into health differentials show that child mortality and morbidity rates in these settlements equal or exceed those in rural areas.

In South Asia, although most children of primary school-going age are enrolled in school, nearly 40 million children remain out of school. A majority of the out-of-school children are girls and children from marginalised and disadvantaged groups. Investments have resulted in increased public awareness and improved coverage of Water, Sanitation and Hygiene (WASH) in schools. Despite progress in recent years, many schools in South Asia still lack quality water supply, sanitation facilities and hygiene education. Well maintained and clean school WASH infrastructure that provides safety and privacy for girls and is used by all children, still remains a challenge. Education and WASH sector policies need to reflect progressive government commitments to adequate and quality WASH in schools, in line with Millennium Development Goals and national commitments.

Guiding Principles[29]

1. WASH in Schools is an integral aspect of education and not a standalone programme, with a view to percolate in the overall learning environment and also to take advantage of systems and mechanisms available within the schools.
2. Establish national standards for WASH in Schools: Ministry of Education to lead and set standards for adequate and inclusive access to safe drinking water, sanitation and hygiene facilities in schools in collaboration with Ministries of Water Supply, Sanitation, Health, Rural Development, Women and Child Development, Local Government, etc. Highest priority must be given to provide basic safe drinking water, sanitation and hygiene to all schools, while progressively ensuring compliance with national standards. Approaches need to allow flexibility in norms, designs and costs for WASH in schools to suit diverse situations.
3. Establish menstrual hygiene management mechanisms including the safe disposal of soiled napkins in all schools and menstrual hygiene education in schools.
4. Seek increasing convergence with Health, with WASH as an integral part of comprehensive school health programme, as both depend on and reinforce each other.
5. Establish operation and maintenance mechanisms for WASH in Schools: allocate specific and adequate budgetary allocations for operation and maintenance of WASH facilities with appropriate technology (including running water, provision of soap and consumables/hygiene kits) to enable schools to keep their WASH facilities working.
6. Practice good hygiene: ensure that all students, teachers and staff members drink safe water, use clean toilets and practice basic hygiene. The Education sector will progressively build good WASH practices in school, using skills-based education, based on daily group activities using appropriate group facilities.
7. Establish EMIS as the common, reliable, database for planning and monitoring of WASH in Schools, for use by all stakeholders.
8. Monitor WASH in Schools access, functionality and use: improve WASH in Schools monitoring, (define measurable indicators and update indicators definitions as progress is made) through harmonised EMIS, and use the data for more equitable and transparent programming and resource allocations. Ensure basic hygiene behavioural practices through children participation in school and community.

9. Raise the profile of Wins and mobilise partners to create a social movement: involve community members, households, students, teachers, civil society, local and mass media, local government, parent-teacher associations, private sector, community and Ministries of Health and Social Welfare in the planning and action for WASH in schools. Ensure all children participate meaningfully in WASH in Schools and that forums are created for their voices to be heard and acted upon.

Contemporary standards, as defined by the World Health Organisation and UNICEF, describe reasonable access to an "improved" water supply as the availability of at least 20 litres per person, per day, from a safe source no more than one kilometre from the dwelling. Piped systems are considered acceptable if they operate at 50 per cent of capacity; hand pumps if they operate for 70 per cent of the time. For sanitation, "improved" provision includes connections to a public sewer or a septic system; also pour-flush latrines, ventilated improved pit latrines and simple pit latrines.[30] Public latrines are not considered to provide proper access, but shared latrines are. These standards raise the bar in terms of overall quality of provision globally. But the needs of young children and those who care for them are not adequately reflected here. It is worth looking more closely at how provision affects them in their daily lives.

The community-level variables like community education and community hygiene also play an important role in reducing the risk of child deaths under five years of age. The incidence of child mortality was found to be directly related to having no modern toilet facility in north-east India (Ladusingh and Singh, 2006). The household environment, measured by factors such as source of drinking water and toilet facilities, is an important determinant of survival for older children as well.[31]

The current Government of India-UNICEF country programme is closely aligned to Government's 11th Five Year Plan (2007-2012) and the 2008-2012 United Nations Development Action Framework (UNDAF). It contributed to the 11th Five Year Plan objectives and the following national policies and schemes through advocacy, expanded partnerships and the provision of technical assistance:

- Support to the National Rural Health Mission (NRHM) and the second phase of the Reproductive and Child Health programme resulted in increased access to institutional and community-based maternal, neonatal and child health services. This contributed to a reduction in the MMR (from 28021 to 200) and

IMR (from 58 to 44). The per centage of fully immunised children increased by 17 per centage points between 2006 and 2009;[32]

- Polio cases in India fell from 559 in 2008 to no case in 2012.24 The Government, in partnership with UNICEF, the World Health Organisation (WHO), the Bill and Melinda Gates Foundation, Rotary International and the Centres for Disease Control and Prevention contributed to almost universal awareness of the need to vaccinate all children under five against polio;
- Rates of early initiation of breastfeeding increased from 25 per cent in 2006 to 34 per cent in 2009,[33] vitamin A supplementation coverage increased from 33 per cent in 200726 to 66 per cent in 2009.27 Access to iodised salt by households increased from 54 per cent in 2006 to 71 per cent in 2009. WHO Child Growth Standards were introduced and rolled out in NRHM and ICDS. This, along with the Mother-Child Protection Card helped strengthen the continuum of care (improved access, utilisation, practices and tracking) for the delivery of essential services to mothers, newborns and children under three years of age;

According to Country Programme Action Plan, nearly 40 per cent of its estimated 1.2 billion population under the age of 18, India is home to the largest number of children in the world.[34] About half of the children from poor families belong to disadvantaged groups like Scheduled Castes and Scheduled Tribes. India contributes to more than 20 per cent of the world's child deaths, with approximately 1.73 million children dying annually before completing their fifth birthday.[35] Even, progress towards the Millennium Development Goals targets remains uneven. A 56 per cent decline in child mortality in the 1-4-year age group since 1990 notwithstanding, the overall decline in child mortality has been hindered by very limited progress in neonatal survival, especially within the first week of birth.[36] To meet the Millennium Development Goals target on child survival, the health, nutrition, educational and social status of mothers and infants needs to improve, as does early childhood feeding, care and development. Equally important is to improve access to, and use of, quality services. The infant mortality rate (IMR) declined 13 points since 2006, an average decline of slightly more than two points per year.

This section is based on UNICEF report on Child's Environment Programme.[37] According to estimates, unsafe water, lack of basic sanitation and poor hygiene claims the lives of more than 1.5 million children below five years of age every year. This is apart from other impacts like nutrition deprivation and debilitation from diarrhea and low grade infections leading to inability of children to reach their ideal growth and creating learning difficulties in many more. UNICEF's steadfast partnership with the Government of India in this sector for more than four decades has faced many challenges and witnessed contribution to the goal of child survival and development. The cooperation has grown from strength to strength starting with the International Water and Sanitation Decade of the eighties, which ushered in higher priority to the Accelerated Rural Water Supply Programme (ARWSP) followed by launching of Central Rural Sanitation Programme (CRSP) in 1986.

With UNICEF as partner the Guinea worm Eradication programme which faced monumental challenges saw success when the last bastion of this public health problem was conquered in Rajasthan and full eradication declared in India in 2000. UNICEF spearheaded the strategy to put hygiene education and behaviour change as the core of the TSC for achieving sustainable sanitation. Recognising the need to bring about a movement for generational change, UNICEF strengthened its support to the national School Sanitation and Hygiene Education (SSHE) programme making it one of UNICEF's flagship programme. Positioned as an entry point to the TSC with emphasis on hygiene education and good practices including functional toilets and safe water now reaching 357,000 schools, the programme aims to transform the learning environment and enhance the education goals.

As indicated in child information portal, the combined effects of inadequate sanitation, unsafe water supply and poor personal hygiene are responsible for 88 per cent of childhood deaths from diarrhoea.[38] Poor sanitation and unsafe drinking water cause intestinal worm infections, which lead to malnutrition, anaemia and retarded growth among children.

Of recent report by UNICEF, of December 2011, India appears to be on track in terms of interrupting the transmission of indigenous wild poliovirus (WPV), with only one child affected, as compared to 42 cases in 2010 and 741 in 2009.[39] For the first time in history, no cases of WPV have been reported in more than 12 months concurrently. According to the 2011 United Nations Inter-agency Group for Child Mortality Estimation, around 22 per cent of underfive and 30 per cent of neonatal global deaths is contributed by India, making the current rate of progress inadequate in terms of achieving MDG on child mortality. Another significant initiative contributing to improved data has been Census 2011. Provisional results show a continued decline of Child Sex Ratio (CSR) from 927 in 2001 to 914 in 2011. The phenomenon is prevalent across the country with 27 out of 35 States and Union Territories. Although the ratio is worse in urban areas

(902) than in rural areas (919), the decline in the last decade has been sharper in the latter (from 934) as compared to the former (from 906).

The Naandi Foundation released the HUNGaMA (Hunger and Malnutrition) Survey Report 2011, covering 112 districts, the choice of which was informed by UNICEFs Child Development Index. The report indicates 20 per cent reduction in the prevalence of child undernutrition with an average annual rate of reduction of 2.9 per cent. At the same time still, 42 per cent of children under the age of five are underweight and 59 per cent are stunted (half of whom are severely stunted). The Annual Status of Education Report (ASER) 2011 revealed that student enrolment increased to 96.7 per cent in rural areas in 2011, while attendance level showed a marginal decline from 73.4 per cent in 2007 to 70.9 per cent in rural primary schools. It also revealed an alarming trend of a decline in basic reading and arithmetic skills. The proportion of children in Class V who are able to read a Class II text dropped from 53.7 per cent in 2010 to 48.2 per cent in 2011. Nationally, the proportion of Class III children who are able to solve a two-digit subtraction problem with borrowing dropped from 36.3 per cent in 2010 to 29.9 per cent.

Schools as Partners in Sanitation and Hygiene; Experiences in Eco-san (Module B)—Tamilnadu and Karnataka

Of India's 1,000,000 rural primary schools, about 50 per cent have toilets of which only a third are functional; and around 60 per cent have a water source within or near the school compound. This situation deters children - especially girls - from going to schools, contributing to high drop out rates and impeding the MDG of universalisation of primary education. In India TSC implemented by the Rural Development Department and Sarva Shiksha Abhiyan (SSA) India's national programme for Education for all are encouraged to work together, mobilise human resources, pool funds and underpin in the longer term, sustainability of hygiene behaviour change with effective use of safe water and sanitation.

Learning Objectives

- To understand the goals, objectives, strategies and approaches to make SSHE sustainable;
- To look at technology and its application especially for engendering the programme;
- To understand the systems and institutional mechanisms for coordination among various departments to achieve educational outcomes;

- To gain insights in schools and community linkages;
- To observe the "Nalli Kalli" (playway learning) and UNICEF role in promoting "SWASTHH (School Water and Sanitation towards Health and Hygiene) plus" as a strategy of choice for impact on the girl child;
- To observe children's participation in promoting hygiene and sanitation through "Children's Cabinets / Health and Hygiene Clubs"
- To get a snap-shot of initiatives in rural communities exploring ecological sanitation;

Accelerating Rural Sanitation: Systems and Institutions (Module C) West Bengal and Maharashtra:

Learning Objectives

- To understand key strategies adopted for accelerating rural sanitation in India and UNICEF's role in supporting this progress
- To familiarise with components of the TSC and the operational aspects
- To get a broad understanding of decentralised management of sanitation and hygiene and the role of key players e.g. Panchayati Raj Institutions (PRI), NGOs, SHG's
- To understand the Rural Sanitary Mart (RSM) network for improving supply chain and its outreach
- To observe community mobilisation, motivational activities for demand generation and behaviour change communication
- To understand the role of 'awards' and 'incentives' in achieving the 'clean village' status
- To understand institutional mechanism for improving skills and capabilities in management and monitoring
- To see innovations in solid and liquid waste management, water and energy conservation and their application to the TSC.

Wise Water Management (Module D) Madhya Pradesh and Tamil Nadu

The Government of India is also, through its reform programme, promoting decentralised management of drinking water supply by elected representatives that form village water and sanitation committees (VWSC). These VWSCs have access to some resources and the mandate to recover user charges for maintenance.

Learning Objectives

- To have an understanding of the Water Safety Plan concept in Madhya Pradesh; observe a child focussed model which aims to make 'water safety' a popular, doable awareness building / learning tool
- Understand technological components of a wise water management system for schools and see the application of child based Water Safety Plans
- See the IEC and "learn as you play" components of wise water management
- Understand the MARS ROUNDABOUT pump technology
- Observe water reuse technology for hand washing and toilet flushing
- Familiarise with the scientific basis for effective wise water management
- Learn about Government of Madhya Pradesh's future plans for scaling up
- To have an understanding of the approaches and processes of change management in Tamil Nadu
- Initiatives relating to water governance reforms of the TWAD board
- Learn about community based water resource management systems implemented by the DHAN Foundation
- Learn about different options and technologies of harvesting rain water in Chennai, by Centre for Science and Environment (CSE) Rain Centres

The year 2010 has offered a great opportunity to present the challenges India faces in achieving equity and social inclusion, at the same time some remarkable initiatives such as the Village Health and Nutrition Day, which reaches out to women and children in villages and offers integrated services every month.

The midterm review of the 2008-2012 Government of India (GoI)-UNICEF Country Programme took place in May.[40] It was reconfirmed that interventions to ensure young child survival and development will continue to focus on accelerating reduction of undernutrition and neonatal, infant and maternal mortality; improving hygiene and sanitation; and eradicating polio. Also ensured will be protective environment for children through Education, Child Protection and HIV Programmes. Two areas of emphasis will be adolescent girls, to help break the intergenerational cycle of multiple deprivations, and equity and inclusion by design, to support the reduction of disparities and exclusion.

This year saw a remarkable achievement with the passage of the Right of Children to Free and Compulsory Education Act (RTE) enacted on 1st April, 2010 has translated the Constitutional provision under Article 21-A into a justiciable right for the children of India. This path-breaking piece of legislation provides for the right of all children to free and compulsory admission, attendance and completion of quality elementary education with the removal of all barriers. UNICEF Indias support to government in the analysis of situation of children and women has included:

- Survey of Mahadalits (the most disadvantaged of SC communities) in Bihar, undertaken at the request of government.
- Gap analysis of the issues in the tea gardens of Assam where migrant workers are legally under the protection of plantation owners and not the State, suffering from many deprivations of basic needs.
- In West Bengal, work is underway to identify indicators to assess the extent of social exclusion.
- Communication for Development Programme in cooperation with the Social Policy, Planning, Monitoring and Evaluation Programme has also undertaken a barrier analysis study in six Integrated Districts, where social and behaviour communication strategies are being implemented.

A key element of the current Country Programme is the upstream work at national and state levels in terms of policy and programme influencing, advocacy and strengthening of systems and capacity development in the flagship social sector programmes of the government leading to results for children and women. This aspiration was coined 'changing gears' to illustrate a major strategic shift from earlier focus on programme implementation through supplies, trainings, etc.

Advocacy and Partnership (A&P) Section leads ICOs advocacy efforts while all Programme sections and Field Offices engage in evidence-based advocacy and policy dialogue with decision-makers to generate consensus for enhanced policies, laws and resources to accelerate achievement of the MDGs. A&P works closely with the Parliamentary Forum on Children and various legislative fora and committees to ensure that children's rights are reflected in policies and programmes. Nationally, there were Parliamentary meets in 2010 on the Right to Education (RTE), Nutrition, Maternal and Neonatal Health and Water and Sanitation. Maximising the Executive Directors visit in December, a special session on youth was held in the Parliament entitled "Children as Agents of Change: Voices from the Field" showcasing youth leaders from around India.

Sanitation Campaign (TSC), with a focus on use of toilets: according to the GoI, the number of rural households with access to toilets further increased, up from 47 per cent of the TSC target to 57 per cent between December 9 and December 11, however usage of improved sanitation (32 per cent) is still seriously lagging behind. UNICEF packaged national and state level evidence to address the gap between access and use of toilets, as well as disparities between richest and poorest household quintiles. This resulted in the Union Minister calling for the first ever State Ministerial Sanitation Conference to review gains, growths and gaps in rural sanitation. As progress is hardly keeping up with population growth (27 million births annually). India requires, in order to achieve the MDG, 3.78 million new users of improved sanitation every month, up from the present rate of 1.82 million. Other key advocacy events included state reviews of progress against MDGs in Assam, Chhattisgarh, Odisha, Tamil Nadu (TN) and Kerala and regional consultations to draft 2012-2022 Sanitation and Water strategy papers. Evidence-based advocacy included social cost benefit analysis for sanitation in Odisha, Bihar, MP and Rajasthan. Social exclusion is being addressed through barrier analysis with specific communication and programme strategies (Andhra Pradesh, Bihar, Chhattisgarh, MP, Odisha, Jharkhand), trialling of innovative solutions for water supply in tribal areas (UP, Gujarat) and advocacy for specific strategies for excluded groups (Assam, Chhattisgarh, West Bengal). UNICEF's support to concurrent monitoring, as shown in Gujarat, Maharashtra, Jharkhand, Bihar and UP show that gaps between access and use can be effectively addressed.

In all states UNICEF advocates for convergence and integration of hygiene practices into health, polio, nutrition, education and tribal welfare programmes. Such convergence has enabled 2 million households receive messages on polio, RI, hygiene, sanitation and nutrition. Over 350,000 adolescent girls have been educated on personal hygiene. Children in 8,642 schools in high risk polio areas are drinking purified water. Hygiene practices have been integrated in training of frontline workers in Assam, Bihar, TN, UP, Maharashtra, Chhattisgarh, Rajasthan, West Bengal, Gujarat, and Jharkhand.

With UNICEF support coverage of wash facilities in schools have increased from 67 per cent in 2008-2009 to 79 per cent in 2010.[41] With joint advocacy for WASH in schools, the new RTE Act mandates water and sanitation provisions in schools. Global Hand-washing Day reached over 13 million school going children and about 5 million preschool children across 14 states.

In 2011 CE will focus on:

- Conceptualisation and preparation for implementation of a new National Communication Strategy for Sanitation
- Supporting state partners to develop and implement Community Approaches to Total Sanitation and change in social norms
- Promoting convergence to integrate hygiene promotion in the training of front line health and nutrition workers and teachers
- Capacity development for household water security and PRIs and village based committees to manage their water and sanitation infrastructure
- Development of strategies to accelerate WASH services to vulnerable communities to reduce disparities
- Integration of WASH in school concepts into child-friendly frameworks adopted by the States under the RTE.

UNICEF has been working with state governments to implement RTE through child friendly schools in teaching and learning and through improved water, sanitation, hygiene and mid-day meal scheme reaching 470,000 schools. UNICEF supported government in convening key partners, which resulted in the enactment of RTE. This has included high-level inter-department state policy forums, national and state level media advocacy including *Awaaz Do*, an on-line platform which has registered 115,000 supporters in two months, and the "Frequently Asked Questions" publication which is being widely used by policy makers, implementers and the general public.

The Child Protection programme seeks to fulfill the intentions of Chapter VI of the Millennium Declaration and contributes to all other MDGs, especially 2 and 3. The programme will directly contribute to UNDAF Outcome 1.6 on reducing gender-based violence and Outcome 1.8 on reducing the abuse, neglect and exploitation of children. The goal of the Child Protection programme is to prevent violence against children and to strengthen protection services for children in vulnerable situations. The programmes expected outcome is: "Strengthened protective environment for children with special emphasis on vulnerable and marginalised groups". For 2010, the programme focused on the following key result areas:

- **Protective environment for children**: support roll out of the Integrated Child Protection Scheme (ICPS) this includes the establishment and capacity development of statutory and non-statutory child protection structures at all levels, and specific interventions in the areas of juvenile justice, institutional care, alternative care and missing children.

- **Child marriage**: development and implementation of a national strategy on child marriage, based on the completion of ongoing studies and reviews, and on existing interventions. UNICEF will also support the design and implementation of action plans of those states and districts with highest child marriage prevalence.
- **Child labour**: increased advocacy at central level for the elimination of all forms of child labour (including child labour in agriculture) and implementation of child rights projects in 17 selected districts (including mainstreaming of child labourers into formal schools, establishment of CP structures, modification of social protection schemes).

Toilet Training Method among Children

Toilet training is an important marker of physical and psychosocial development in children and is considered to be a key developmental milestone. Methods are ever shifting and children are undergoing toilet training at a much later age than in the past: in 1980, the mean toilet trained age varied from 25 to 27 months, and in 2003, it had increased to 36.8 months.[42] Some studies suggest that this increased delay is having a negative impact: late toilet training may be more difficult for parents because the child is more likely to resist efforts to train. This can result in problems, including constipation, voiding dysfunction, and infection.[43] Although there are several strategies for toilet training developmentally normal children, the methods all generally fall into 2 broad categories: the child-oriented approaches and the parent-oriented approaches.[44] The child-oriented approaches involve waiting for the child to show signs of readiness (generally at 18 months of age or beyond) and uses praise for success while avoiding punishments. Meanwhile the parent-oriented approaches function through operant conditioning: they generally use rewards to positively reinforce proper behaviour while using punishments or withdrawal of positive reinforcement to negatively reinforce accidents.[45]

Slum Sanitation Programme in Mumbai[46]

The past experiences of urban governance and programme implementation have shattered the hopes for achieving a minimum standard of life for the poor through government policies and programmes. Local self-governments remained starved of funds and technical skills, and suffer from poor management. Several programmes that were implemented for improving quality of life in urban settlements - some of them through international funding - have had results far from satisfactory. For instance, the Department for International Development (DFID) UK made the following observations on 'poverty reduction programmes in some urban settlements'. 'Implementation of such programmes is impeded by weak local capacities and conflicting interests of political leaders, bureaucrats and other interest groups...Resources are inevitably limited. Poor management leads to inadequate services, under-investment in infrastructure and rigid adherence to rulebooks, lacking innovation. It is added to by overlapping authorities by different tiers of government and territorial fragmentation...The approach has been one of control, rather than promotion of development (DFID, undated).

According to a recent social and technical survey of all slums conducted by the Brihanmumbai Municipal Corporation (BMC) in 2001 under the Slum Sanitation Scheme (SSP), 1,959 slum settlements were counted with a total population of 62.47 lakh, this constituted 54 per cent of the city's population. Of these, 137 are non-notified slums where about 5.25 lakh people reside. According to the above survey, as many as 38.6 lakh people (62 per cent of the slum population)—residing in 1,435 slum localities are dependent exclusively on public toilets. A sizeable number of the slums (209) are devoid of public toilet facilities. Of these, households in only 18 slums have individual toilets, the rest use open fields.

World Bank Slum Sanitation Programme (SSP)

Though it may sound gratifying that in over 60 per cent slums in Mumbai city, public latrines have been constructed, a majority of them are overused and poorly serviced or maintained. Hundreds of them are badly constructed and therefore in dilapidated conditions. Conventionally, these latrines were constructed over the decades by Maharashtra Housing and Area Development Authority (MHADA) and Water Supply and Sewerage Department (WSSD) of BMC, through councillors/MLA/MLC/MP grants or ad hoc grants from the central government. These schemes to a large extent met the most basic needs of the urban poor, they were offered free of cost to the slum dwellers. It made everybody happy - the slum dwellers, the politicians, the bureaucrats and the contractors. This 'supply'-driven approach to the slum sanitation made the dwellers indifferent to their responsibility towards improving sanitation in their communities. Meanwhile, the influx of population to the city kept on burdening the existing facilities, and created growing needs in newly emerging slums.

The BMC has been implementing 'integrated water supply and sewage scheme' since 1970, with the financial assistance of World Bank/(then) ODA. One of its objectives was 'to improve health and environmental conditions in Greater Mumbai, including the slum areas'. Accordingly, a component of the Bombay Sewerage Disposal Project (BSDP) has been the construction of sanitation blocks (mainly the toilets) in slum localities. Mumbai Municipal Corporation launched the Slum Sanitation Programme (SSP) on March 3, 1997 as an integral part of the Bombay Sewerage Disposal Project (BSDP), with funding from the World Bank. The SSP had a total budget of Rs 906 millions for constructing about 18,000 toilet seats [BMC 2000].

The World Bank team prepared its mid-term appraisal of the SSP (Mid-Term Review Mission of World Bank, 2000) and decided to introduce necessary modifications due to poor out-come of the programme over the past year's efforts. Under the changed strategy, it was decided to implement the scheme under various lots which involved allocating the work of implementation of the toilet blocks (from mobilisation of the beneficiaries to constructing the toilets, training the CBOs and handing over the completed blocks to the people) to approved NGOs. The key NGOs approved for the initial pilot project were: SPARC, Sulabh Internationl and Janseva.

It happened mainly because SPARC, as a voluntary organisation, has been active in Mumbai city for over two decades. It carries high credibility within and outside India, for its work with the urban poor. The implementation of a large developmental scheme (the SSP) by a NGO (SPARC) in slum localities of Mumbai city, through a participatory approach, has emerged as an interesting case study for future lessons in 'civil society in action'. A leading local NGO - SPARC, has perhaps made history in the country in the sense that it served a contract worth Rs 480 million under the SSP for developing sanitation blocks (toilets) in various slums of Mumbai city. This has happened mainly due to the impressive record of SPARC as a NGO working for the urban poor for over two decades.

Scenario of Sanitation in India[47]

Sanitation coverage, which ought to be a way of life to safeguard health, is inadequate. The practice of open defection in India remains a major challenge for achieving the MDGs, which include reducing by half the proportion of people without access to basic sanitation by 2015.

In India, only 40 per cent of households had access to sanitation facilities in 2002, which increased to 51 per cent in 2008-9. In Bihar, Chhattisgarh, Jharkhand, Madhya Pradesh, Odisha, Rajasthan, Tamil Nadu, and Uttarakhand over 60 per cent of households were without toilets. In 2008-9, the north-eastern states were better off than most of the remaining states in terms of access to sanitation facilities. In both 2002-4 and 2008-9, the proportion of households with toilet facilities was significantly higher in urban areas than rural areas. It should be noted that in rural India as many as 65 per cent of households were without toilets. Thus, it is not surprising that in the rural areas the population has many health problems. Except for Rajasthan, Tripura, Bihar, Jharkhand, and Assam, the rural areas of all the states showed a rise in access to sanitation facilities.

National Advisory Council

Note on Recommendations for Follow-up Measures to Eradicate Manual Scavenging

The NAC in its meeting of October 23, 2010, expressed its deep anguish at the official failure to eradicate 'manual scavenging', the most degrading surviving practice of untouchability in the country. This involves mostly women, but also men and even children gathering human excreta from individual or community dry toilets with bare hands, brooms or metal scrapers into wicker baskets or buckets; and then carrying this on their heads, shoulders or against their hips into dumping sites or water bodies. Others are similarly employed to clear, carry and dispose excreta from sewers, septic tanks, drains into which excreta flows and railway lines.

The Employment of Manual Scavengers and Construction of Dry Latrines (Prohibition) Act, 1993 outlawed employing persons from manual scavenging, and government launched programmes for livelihood rehabilitation of freed manual scavengers; education of their children; and promotion of flush latrines in place of dry latrines. However, as the NAC noted in its resolution of October 23, 2010, these have not resulted in the eradication of the practice, and governments have tended to look at this as an issue of sanitation rather than human dignity as guaranteed to all citizens by the Constitution.

The chairperson of the NAC, accordingly, wrote to the Prime Minister of India on 9 November, 2010, requesting the government to take necessary steps to ensure the end of this demeaning scourge in a time-bound manner. Accordingly, the, matter was reviewed at the highest levels of Government. On April 28, 2011, the Secretaries of Social Justice and Empowerment, and of Housing and Urban Poverty, Government of India, made presentations about the efforts and plans of Government of India to deal with this practice. On May 9, 2011, some Members and officers of NAC met officials of the Government of India. The Prime Minister also wrote to NAC Chairperson Mrs. Sonia Gandhi on May 11, 2011, reiterating government's 'determination to completely eradicate this abominable practice in a very short time', including by making the employment of SC/ST persons to handle excreta an offence under the SC/ST Atrocities Act, and ensuring 'full and complete rehabilitation'.

The proportion of households without toilets is much above the national average of 49 per cent for all the three social groups—SCs, STs, and OBCs. However, OBC households were relatively better placed compared to SCs and STs with around 54 per cent of OBC households without toilet facilities as against 9 ST households and 65 per cent SC households. Among major religious communities, Hindus were worst off as 50 per cent of households lacked toilet facilities, compared to 36 per cent for Muslims. This is relatively higher access to toilet facilities among Muslims is probably explained by the fact that a higher proportion of Muslims (than Hindus) live in urban areas. Septic tanks and pit latrines have together been classified as improved sanitation by the NSS (2008-9). Going by this definition, access to improved sanitation has increased over time.

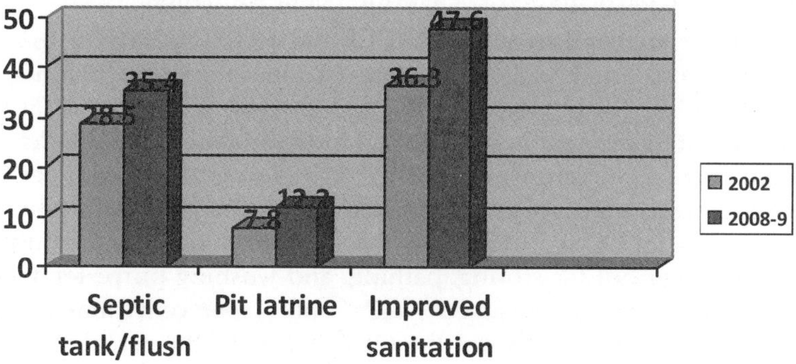

Fig. 1. Household with improved sanitation (in per cent)

Source: NSS 58th and 65th Round

Across social groups, there has been an increase in the proportion of households with improved sanitation facilities that is, septic tanks/ flush toilets and pit toilets, during the period 2002 to 2008-9, OBC households had the highest proportion of households with access to improved sanitation at 43.2. ST households were the worst with only 28 per cent households in urban areas using improved sanitation facilities. The situation is worse in the case of their rural counterparts, with only 22 per cent of rural ST households with access to improved facilities. Across religious communities, Sikhs and Christian households had the highest (over 70 per cent) access to improved sanitation facilities in 2008-9. Hindus had the least access at 45 per cent.

To address the sanitation issues faced by the country, a central government funded programme, Total Sanitation Campaign (TSC), was launched in 1999. It looks at sanitation through a holistic lens. Its objective are to improve the quality of life in rural areas, increase sanitation coverage, use awareness and health education to generate demand, provide all schools and Anganwadi centres in rural areas with sanitation facilities, and undertake efforts to prevent waterborne diseases. Under TSC, BPL families are provided subsidies to construct toilets with the objective of having ODF (Open Defection Free) villages. Open defecation free status can be ensured only if emphasis is laid on improving attitudes and knowledge about sanitation and hygiene by conducting information, education and communication (IEC) activities—a major plank of TSC. IEC seeks to create awareness among, and encourage the participation of, the entire community in a village. Given below are examples of Himachal Pradesh and Haryana where community participation is ensuring better sanitation.

In a study conducted by UNICEF and TARU in 2008, of 162 GPs which had received NGPs in six states (Andhra Pradesh, Chhattisgarh, Maharashtra, Tamil Nadu, Uttar Pradesh, and West Bengal), it was found that 81 per cent households ad individual household toilets. Of these only 64 per cent were reported to be using them and 6 per cent were using community toilets. The remaining households (30 per cent) were going for OD. Further, many toilets were not used for the purpose of defecating but for storing, bathing, and washing purposes. Of the 162 GPs which had received NGPs, only 4 per cent (mostly from Maharashtra) had sustained the ODF status. In the remaining GPs, there were households who had gone back to defecating in the open.

NGP Villages with Proportion of Peoples still Defecating in the Open, 6 States, 2008

State	*None*	*<20%*	*20-40%*	*40-60%*	*60-80%*	*>80%*	*Total*
Andhra Pradesh	-	5	4	1	-	-	10
Chhattisgarh	-	-	-	4	5	1	10
Maharashtra	6	36	4	6	7	1	60
Tamil Nadu	-	11	6	9	5	2	33
Uttar Pradesh	-	1	7	6	1	-	15
West Bengal	-	11	18	3	2	-	34
Total	6	64	39	29	20	4	162
% of Total	4	40	24	18	12	2	100

Source: The Action Research Unit (2008b)

The central government's expenditure on sanitation as a per centage of total GoI releases has increased from 48 per cent in 2005-6 to 128 per cent in 2009-10 (Department of Drinking Water and Sanitation). Three-fourth of this is spent on the construction of individual household toilets (which are often put to various other uses). Expenditure on IEC, which is an important component in generating demand for sanitation, was only 5 per cent. Himachal Pradesh and Haryana, among the best performing states in terms of ODF status spent close to 70 per cent of approved IEC funds. In contrast, in Bihar, Jharkhand, and Odisha less than 20 per cent of the approved IEC funds were spent.

Access to Improved Sources of Drinking Water

Taps and tube-wells were the two major sources of drinking water. In addition to these, protected wells and harvested rainwater are

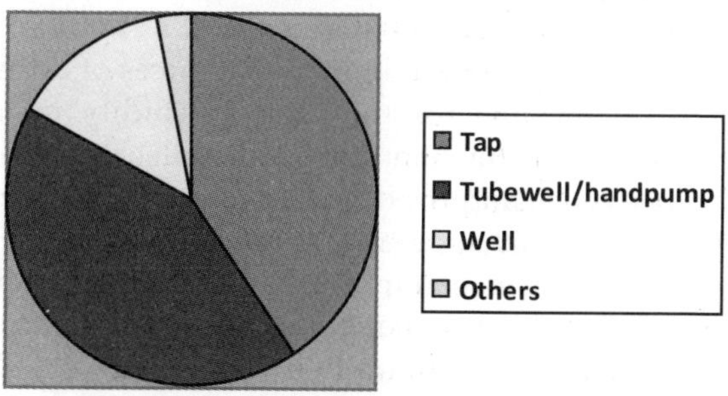

Distribution of Householdsby Source of Drinking water, 2002 (Per cent)

Source: NSSO 58th round

considered to be improved sources of drinking water. Overtime there has been a rise in the proportion of households with taps as a source of drinking water, with a corresponding fall in the proportion of households using wells as a source of drinking water.

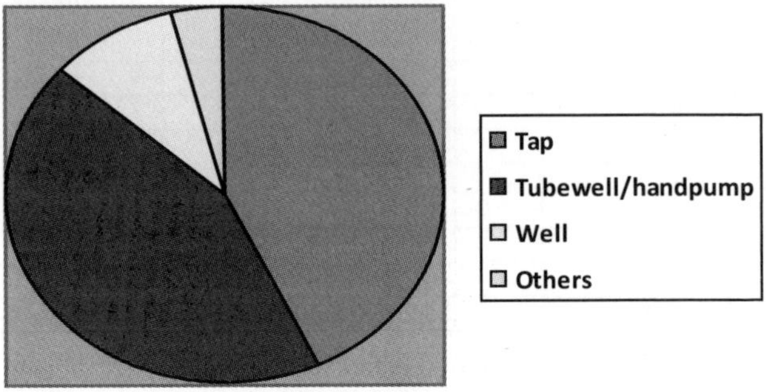

Distribution of Households by Source of Drinking water, 2008-2009 (Per cent)

Source: NSSO 65th round

The proportion of households with access to improved sources of drinking water in 2008-9 was 91 per cent. This proportion was over 90 per cent even in states like Bihar, Chhattisgarh, Madhya Pradesh, and Uttar Pradesh. This was largely because these states had over 70 per cent of their households accessing tube wells/handpumps as sources of drinking water.

The north-eastern states, except for Arunachal Pradesh, were much below the national average. So too were many other poorer states like Jharkhand, Odisha, and Rajasthan. For instance, not even 50 per cent of the households in Manipur and Mizoram had access to improved sources of drinking water, whereas only 90 per cent of households in poorer states like Bihar and Chhattisgarh did. In Kerala, only 73 per cent of households had access to improved sources of drinking water. This is partly responsible for the high morbidity on account of waterborne diseases in the state. In rural India, 90 per cent of the population had access to improved sources of drinking water. A further break-up of various sources revealed that as many as 55 per cent of households had tubewells/handpumps as sources of drinking water, the consumption of which makes the populace more vulnerable to waterborne diseases as compared to tap water. As 97 per cent households have taps, tubewells/handpumps or wells as major sources of drinking water, the analysis of social and religious communities is restricted to these categories only.

Over time, all social groups experienced a rise in the proportion of households using taps and tubewells/handpumps with corresponding fall in the proportion using wells, which are not considered safe sources of drinking water. Across social groups, OBCs have a greater proportion of households using taps compared to SCs and STs who have tubewells/handpumps as major sources of drinking water. However, SCs and STs performed much above the national average in the states of Arunachal Pradesh, Himachal Pradesh, Himachal Pradesh, Karnataka, Sikkim, Tamil Nadu, and Uttarakhand in terms of the proportion of households which had taps as a source of drinking water. Across religious communities, Sikhs have the highest proportion of household dependent on tap water (49 per cent) whereas in the case of Muslims the proportion is only 36 per cent. Over half the Muslim households were dependent on tubewells/handpumps. However, the fact that over 3/4th of the Muslims in the states of Andhra Pradesh, Arunachal Pradesh, Gujarat, Jammu and Kashmir, Karnataka, Maharashtra, Sikkim, and Tamil Nadu have taps as a source of drinking water. In the rural areas, except for Christians, all religious communities have a greater proportion of households dependent on tube wells/pumps for drinking water

Distribution of Households by Type of Toilet Facility, 2002 and 2008-2009(per cent)

Non Special Category States	*Septic Tank/Flash*		*Pit*		*Service*		*No Latrine*	
	2002	*2008-9*	*2002*	*2008-9*	*2002*	*2008-9*	*2002*	*2008-9*
Andhra Pradesh	34.8	47	1.3	3.4	1.7	0.9	61.1	47.9
Assam	16.5	26	41	48.7	1.6	2	12.7	12.1
Bihar	13.7	17.2	2.8	4.8	3.2	1.2	78.7	74.1
Chhattisgarh	17.2	21.2	0.3	3.6	0.2	0.2	82.3	72.9
Delhi	76.1	92.2	5.3	3.5	10.4	1.1	6.6	1.7
Goa	70.5	63.9	1.8	12	2.8	0.2	21.7	22.9
Gujarat	43.9	47.2	4.6	8.3	0.8	0.3	50.6	43.6
Haryana	32.8	43.3	7.6	20.7	0.7	0.7	58.8	33.7
Jharkhand	21.9	17.3	0.8	6.7	0.9	0.3	75.5	74.7
Karnataka	23.8	31.7	13.8	15.3	1.5	0.7	60.5	51.5
Kerala	28.4	29.4	61.9	65.1	0.2	0.2	8.6	4.3
Madhya Pradesh	17.8	24.2	3.1	3.6	2.5	0.6	76.6	70.2
Maharashtra	43.2	57.3	1.1	4.3	0.6	1	54.9	36.4
Odisha	13.5	15.1	1.6	2.8	4.2	1.7	79.9	78.7
Punjab	39.7	52.4	20.9	21.2	1.8	1.4	37.6	24
Rajasthan	19.4	24.7	6.7	10.5	1.5	0.6	72.1	63.6
Tamil Nadu	36	49.6	0.6	1.2	1.6	0.9	61.5	46.6
Uttar Pradesh	20.3	33.7	2.4	22.4	5	1.2	72	42.5
West Bengal	26.3	29.9	14.6	31.7	3.3	3	53.6	32.4

Special Category States

Arunanchal Pradesh	19.8 31.9	11.1 15.4	17 6.6	23.2 12.7
Himachal Pradesh	31.5 52.3	0.9 4	4.4 0.6	63.1 42.3
Jammu & Kashmir	18.6 29.5	7.4 19.9	23.3 15.5	39 29.7
Manipur	24.5 30.4	45.3 46.5	17.3 9.3	4.6 0.8
Meghalaya	16 27.2	45 57.1	2.2 4.4	27 9.3
Mizoram	33.3 54.4	56.4 43.1	6.8 0.7	2 0.7
Nagaland	48.7 43.3	37.4 43.4	7.1 2	2.5 2.6
Sikkim	53.3 73.4	35.1 24	0.2 0.1	9.4 2.1
Tripura	8.4 13.2	77.5 71.1	5 0.7	5.2 2.9
Uttarakhand	38.5 25.7	7.8 6.1	1 2.1	51.5 65

Union Territories

Andaman & Nicobar islands	45.8 62.7	4.1 8.3	0 0	50 28.8
Chandigarh	91.3 98.3	0 0	20.1 0	6.6 1.7
Dadra & Nagar Haveli	36 45.6	2.4 12.4	0.7 0	60.7 42
Daman & Diu	75.2 35.5	0 37.9	1.1 3.5	23.7 23.1
Lakshadweep	53.7 38.7	39.6 60.1	0 0.4	6.6 0.4
Puducherry	56.2 70	0.3 0.6	1.2 2.6	42.4 25.6
All india	28.2 35.4	7.8 12.2	2.6 1.4	59.8 49.2

Source: NSS 58th and 65th Rounds

Distribution of Households by Type of Toilet Facility (rural), 2002 and 2008-09(per cent)

Non Special Category States	*Septic Tank/Flash*	*Pit*	*Service*	*No Latrine*
	2002 2008-9	*2002 2008-9*	*2002 2008-9*	*2002 2008-9*
Andhra Pradesh	17.8 29.9	1.3 4.3	1.7 1	77.7 64.3
Assam	10.4 18.2	43.6 53.5	1.6 2.2	13.8 13.5
Bihar	7.5 11.8	2.7 5	3.3 1	84.9 79.8
Chhattisgarh	8.6 11.3	0 4.2	0.1 0.2	91.3 82.3
Delhi	74.9 84.5	10.8 8.1	8.7 0	55.5 7.5
Goa	63.2 40.6	2.9 22.7	1.8 0.1	27.3 36.2
Gujarat	16.5 26	5.1 6.2	0.5 0.1	78 67.3
Haryana	14.8 29.6	8.1 24.1	0.2 0.1	76.9 45.3
Jharkhand	11.5 7.3	0.5 7	0.1 0.2	86.8 84.1
Karnataka	6.6 7.4	13 16.3	0.6 0.4	79.8 75.2
Kerala	21.3 21.7	67.1 71.7	0.3 0.3	10.3 5.3
Madhya Pradesh	5.1 10.5	1.3 2.7	0.5 0.3	93.1 85.3
Maharashtra	14.2 31.6	1.3 6.3	0.1 0.6	84.1 60.7
Odisha	5.2 7.3	1.5 1.9	4.7 1.3	88.4 88.2
Punjab	21.2 32.1	27.4 29.8	0.1 0.8	51.4 36.2
Rajasthan	5.2 8.2	6.3 8.9	0.8 0.6	87.5 82.1
Tamil Nadu	14.6 23.7	0.7 1.5	1.3 0.5	83.5 73.5
Uttar Pradesh	6.9 23.2	2 21.7	3.2 1.3	87.6 53.5
West Bengal	11.7 14.8	14.5 36.9	2.5 3.4	69.4 41.7

Special Category States

Arunanchal Pradesh	12.1 23.9	10.7 16.2	16.2 5.3	28.7 16.2
Himachal Pradesh	26 47.8	0.7 4.1	2.2 0.5	71 46.5
Jammu & Kashmir	6.3 17.2	8.2 23.4	25.3 19.1	46.9 34.9
Manipur	17.1 21.8	51.6 52.7	14.1 9.4	6.3 1.1
Meghalaya	3.6 14.8	51.3 67	2.2 4.3	32.2 11.4
Mizoram	15.7 32.1	71.6 64.3	6.6 1.1	3.6 1.2
Nagaland	36.1 32.6	45.7 53.8	8.9 2.2	3.8 3.1
Sikkim	47.1 68.9	39.7 28..1	0.3 0.1	10.7 2.5
Tripura	3 5.2	82.7 76.9	4.2 0.9	5.8 3.4
Uttarakhand	30.9 12.6	5.7 5.9	0.6 1.5	61.2 79.2

Union Territories

Andaman & Nicobar islands	26.5 47.5	6.1 12.4	0 0	67.4 39.9
Chandigarh	73.6 90	0 0	3.6 0	22.8 9.6
Dadra & Nagar Haveli	25.6 32.2	2.6 14.4	0.6 0	71.1 53.2
Daman & Diu	68.5 8.4	0 57.9	0.9 2	30.6 31.9
Lakshadweep	27.4 21.7	67.8 78.3	0 0	4.7 0
Puducherry	18 34.6	0 0	0 0	82 65.4
All india	11.7 17.9	8.4 14	1.9 1.2	76.3 65.2

Source: NSS 58th and 65th Rounds

Distribution of Households by Type of Toilet Facility (Urban), 2002 and 2008-09(per cent)

Non Special Category States	*Septic Tank/Flash*	*Pit*	*Service*	*No Latrine*
	2002 2008-9	*2002 2008-9*	*2002 2008-9*	*2002 2008-9*
Andhra Pradesh	76.8 85.3	1.3 1.5	1.5 0.7	19.8 11.2
Assam	76.2 84.8	15.7 12.2	1.5 0.2	1.8 0.9
Bihar	61.3 61.9	3.8 3.3	1.9 2.1	31 27.7
Chhattisgarh	56.2 64.3	1.9 1.2	0.4 0.5	41.5 31.5
Delhi	76.4 92.8	3.6 3.2	10.9 1.2	6.9 1.2
Goa	83.1 87.6	0 1.4	4.6 0.2	12.1 9.6
Gujarat	87.5 79.5	3.9 11.5	1.4 0.7	6.8 7.3
Haryana	76.2 73.5	6.6 13.3	1.8 1.9	15 8.4
Jharkhand	62.8 70.6	2.3 3.1	3.6 0.9	30.9 24.5
Karnataka	60.2 72.8	15.8 13.6	3.6 1.1	21 11.3
Kerala	49.1 50.6	46.1 46.6	0.1 0.1	3.7 1.5
Madhya Pradesh	51.4 66.2	7.7 6.4	7.5 1.4	33.1 24.3
Maharashtra	82.7 89.4	0.7 1.9	1 1.4	15.2 5.9
Odisha	59.2 56.2	2.2 7.3	1.1 3.6	32.9 29.1
Punjab	74.5 84.1	8.6 7.8	5.2 2.3	11.6 5
Rajasthan	57.7 70.3	7.7 14.8	3.4 0.8	30.7 12.6
Tamil Nadu	74.4 79.1	0.6 0.8	2.3 1.3	21.9 16
Uttar Pradesh	- -	- -	- -	- -
West Bengal	65.4 73.4	14.9 16.5	5.4 2.2	11.2 5.6

Special Category States

Arunanchal Pradesh	51.6 61.5	13.2 12.5	20.3 11.6	0.6 0.1
Himachal Pradesh	68.6 87.5	1.9 2.7	19 1	10.3 8.8
Jammu & Kashmir	59.3 71.3	4.6 7.8	16.8 3.2	12.6 11.8
Manipur	45.6 51.6	27 31.1	26.5 9.3	0 0
Meghalaya	77.7 79.1	13.2 15.3	2.1 5.1	0.9 0.2
Mizoram	55.8 82.3	37 16.7	7.1 0.2	0 0
Nagaland	72 70.1	21.9 17.5	4.1 1.5	0 0
Sikkim	92.3 98.9	7 1.1	0 0	0.7 0
Tripura	33.1 48.6	44.5 45.7	9.8 0	0.8 0.9
Uttarakhand	65.9 72.8	15.3 6.5	2.3 4.4	16.5 14.2

Union Territories

Andaman & Nicobar islands	85.9 93.9	0 0	0 0	14 6.1
Chandigarh	92.9 99.4	0 0	2 0	5 0.6
Dadra & Nagar Haveli	92.9 87.1	1.6 6.1	1.6 0	3.8 7.1
Daman & Diu	87 986.7	0 0.7	1.4 6.3	11.7 6.4
Lakshadweep	73.7 62	18.1 32.7	0 0.9	8.2 1
Puducherry	76.2 84.8	0.4 0.9	1.8 3.7	21.7 9.1
All india	70.7 77.3	6.3 8	4.7 1.6	17.9 11.3

Source: NSS 58th and 65th Rounds

Distribution of Households by Type of Toilet Facility by Social groups (STs), 2002 and 2008-09(per cent)

Non Special Category States	*Septic Tank/Flash* *2002 2008-9*	*Pit* *2002 2008-9*	*No Latrine* *2002 2008-9*
Andhra Pradesh	0.7 26.3	0.9 1.5	74.6 70.9
Assam	0.2 15.3	0.4 53.4	16.2 16.0
Bihar	- 24.2	- 0.8	84.3 69.1
Chhattisgarh	0.9 11.7	- 5.7	91.5 81.9
Delhi	6.2 98.0	- 0.0	6.2 0.0
Goa	- 44.5	- 7.1	- 55.5
Gujarat	1.7 18.4	- 56.0	85.9 73.8
Haryana	- 19.8	- 5.9	82.7 24.2
Jharkhand	4.6 8.9	0.0 11.5	76.5 84.1
Karnataka	0.6 14.9	0.2 41.1	84.4 70.0
Kerala	- 31.0	- 1.0	9.3 27.9
Madhya Pradesh	0.1 8.1	0.2 4.1	94.3 90.2
Maharashtra	3.3 29.3	- 0.8	87.5 64.1
Odisha	2.2 5.2	1.5 0.0	86.9 91.9
Punjab	- 17.3	0.0 1.6	9.4 62.6
Rajasthan	0.0 5.2	- 0.5	94.8 92.6
Tamil Nadu	0.7 45.2	- 4.7	70.6 54.3
Uttar Pradesh	1.1 21.3	0.3 29.1	80.9 73.2
West Bengal	1.6 17.2	- -	84.7 41.4

Special Category States

Arunanchal Pradesh	2.4 27.1	2.4 10.6	27.9 15.2
Himachal Pradesh	- 29.9	1.7 3.7	57.6 65.5
Jammu & Kashmir	- 10.7	0.6 40.1	46.6 26.2
Manipur	4.2 25.0	0.9 49.4	12.6 0.8
Meghalaya	0.6 25.2	5.5 58.6	32.4 10.3
Mizoram	0.4 54.5	1.5 43.0	2.0 0.7
Nagaland	1.4 42.7	0.6 44.6	2.8 2.4
Sikkim	0.1 69.2	1.5 28.3	9.1 2.5
Tripura	0.2 7.2	- 74.5	12.0 3.8
Uttarakhand	- 33.4	- 14.0	21.5 28.1

Union Territories

Andaman & Nicobar islands	- 75.2	- 8.6	52.9 16.3
Chandigarh	36.0 100.0	- 0.0	- 0.0
Dadra & Nagar Haveli	0.1 29.1	- 13.2	82.3 57.6
Daman & Diu	36.4 2.0	- 16.1	53.3 81.8
Lakshadweep	1.0 29.9	- 68.3	5.0 0.5
Puducherry	- 100.0	- 0.0	34.6 0.0
All India	1.5 16.5	0.3 11.0	78.0 69.1

Source: NSS 58th and 65th Rounds

Distribution of Households by Type of Toilet Facility by Social Groups (SCs)

Non Special Category States	*Septic Tank/Flash*	*Pit*	*No Latrine*
	2002 2008-9	*2002 2008-9*	*2002 2008-9*
Andhra Pradesh	0.6 35.4	0.0 2.4	81.2 60.1
Assam	0.0 25.4	- 50.0	17.5 8.8
Bihar	0.9 9.9	0.0 3.3	91.4 83.9
Chhattisgarh	1.4 21.2	- 3.5	81.2 73.4
Delhi	13.2 89.8	2.4 1.5	10.9 4.2
Goa	5.3 55.3	- 2.4	4.7 38.9
Gujarat	2.5 26.9	- 4.9	53.1 67.2
Haryana	0.5 26.1	- 24.3	74.3 48.5
Jharkhand	2.8 9.1	- 17.1	90.7 71.5
Karnataka	0.9 14.3	0.8 13.5	79.9 71.5
Kerala	0.1 16.9	1.3 66.9	21.6 15.5
Madhya Pradesh	0.9 13.0	0.1 1.4	87.0 84.4
Maharashtra	13.3 53.3	0.5 3.4	66.3 40.6
Orissa	0.3 6.6	- 2.6	84.4 87.5
Punjab	0.3 36.0	0.4 22.1	55.3 39.5
Rajasthan	0.3 11.9	- 11.3	74.8 75.3
Tamil Nadu	2.2 24.8	- 0.6	83.1 72.8
Uttar Pradesh	2.1 11.5	0.1 3.3	88.3 84.1
West Bengal	3.0 22.4	0.7 32.3	66.3 39.1

Special Category States

Arunanchal Pradesh	- 63.5	- 17.3	- 0.0
Himachal Pradesh	7.0 47.8	- 2.4	75.9 49.2
Jammu & Kashmir	1.3 29.4	- 0.7	83.3 67.0
Manipur	- 15.0	- 40.5	- 0.0
Meghalaya	- 16.7	- 83.3	- 0.0
Mizoram	0.7 72.2	- 27.8	- 0.0
Nagaland	- 38.0	- 56.2	- 5.1
Sikkim	- 67.4	- 31.1	22.8 1.2
Tripura	0.1 73.8	0.1 73.8	3.0 5.3
Uttarakhand	0.5 11.7	0.5 11.7	74.3 67.8

Union Territories

Andaman & Nicobar islands	- -	- -	- -
Chandigarh	12.9 99.5	- 0.0	18.1 0.5
Dadra & Nagar Haveli	- 89.9	- 0.0	29.8 10.1
Daman & Diu	- 12.3	- 70.4	46.6 17.3
Lakshadweep	- -	- -	68.0 -
Puducherry	1.0 28.1	- 28.1	83.7 71.3
All India	2.7 22.4	2.7 22.4	74.9 65.0

Source: NSS 58th and 65th Rounds

Distribution of Households by Type of Toilet Facility by Social Groups (OBCs), 2002 and 2008-9 (per cent)

Non Special Category States	*Septic Tank/Flash* 2002 2008-9	*Pit* 2002 2008-9	*No Latrine* 2002 2008-9
Andhra Pradesh	2.2 43.0	0.0 4.2	66.5 51.4
Assam	0.4 32.9	0.0 46.2	7.3 7.9
Bihar	1.4 16.8	0.2 5.9	80.9 73.3
Chhattisgarh	1.9 20.0	0.0 1.5	85.2 75.2
Delhi	4.3 86.8	3.6 9.1	12.4 2.5
Goa	- 41.8	- 28.0	43.1 28.8
Gujarat	4.4 36.0	0.1 5.8	65.6 57.0
Haryana	0.0 42.7	- 15.0	66.1 39.9
Jharkhand	2.6 15.7	0.3 11.5	83.2 70.6
Karnataka	0.4 29.6	0.2 13.4	64.0 55.8
Kerala	0.3 26.2	1.6 69.2	8.2 3.0
Madhya Pradesh	1.5 24.8	0.2 3.9	76.5 69.0
Maharashtra	10.7 55.1	- 5.7	63.0 36.9
Odisha	1.1 15.4	- 3.2	84.5 78.4
Punjab	0.9 51.4	- 21.0	40.1 24.1
Rajasthan	0.3 20.0	0.1 11.8	79.5 67.3
Tamil Nadu	2.5 55.1	- 1.5	58.1 40.8
Uttar Pradesh	1.1 23.4	0.1 5.8	76.4 68.3
West Bengal	2.0 41.3	1.5 34.3	47.9 20.9

Special Category States

Arunanchal Pradesh	14.2	24.8	-	63.3	-	0.0
Himachal Pradesh	2.6	29.0	-	0.8	73.4	68.4
Jammu & Kashmir	0.4	8.0	14.6	38.5	22.4	26.9
Manipur	0.1	31.3	0.2	46.5	0.9	0.8
Meghalaya	-	50.2	-	39.8	4.3	0.0
Mizoram	11.2	19.0	-	81.0	-	0.0
Nagaland	-	86.5	-	13.5	-	0.0
Sikkim	0.7	73.5	-	23.2	11.9	2.3
Tripura	0.1	15.3	-	71.1	2.1	0.5
Uttarakhand	-	40.9	-	19.5	39.8	36.1

Union Territories

Andaman & Nicobar islands	-	45.3	-	29.3	-	25.3
Chandigarh	18.5	94.0	-	0.0	12.0	6.0
Dadra & Nagar Haveli	-	52.6	-	7.7	21.9	39.6
Daman & Diu	25.5	31.7	-	38.6	26.2	25.3
Lakshadweep	-	36.5	-	63.5	-	0.0
Puducherry	2.3	77.5	0.1	0.8	38.5	17.5
All India	2.3	32.9	0.2	10.3	65.9	54.2

Source: NSS 58th and 65th Rounds

Distribution of Households by Type of Toilet Facility by Major Religious Communities (Hindus), 2002 and 2008-9 (per cent)

Non Special Category States	*Septic Tank/Flash*		*Pit*		*No Latrine*	
	2002	*2008-9*	*2002*	*2008-9*	*2002*	*2008-9*
Andhra Pradesh	44.6		3.5		50.2	
Assam	32.0		45.3		8.6	
Bihar	20.2		5.4		71.0	
Chhattisgarh	20.4		3.5		73.8	
Delhi	92.3		3.5		1.7	
Goa	60.3		13.7		24.8	
Gujarat	41.2		6.8		50.6	
Haryana	43.3		21.4		32.9	
Jharkhand	17.6		19.0		60.8	
Karnataka	29.9		14.6		54.3	
Kerala	28.1		64.8		5.3	
Madhya Pradesh	22.5		3.1		72.6	
Maharashtra	59.6		4.6		34.1	
Odisha	15.0		2.9		78.8	
Punjab	63.1		15.5		19.9	
Rajasthan	23.5		9.6		65.8	
Tamil Nadu	47.2		1.2		49.3	
Uttar Pradesh	22.6		4.2		71.4	
West Bengal	38.5		30.6		25.1	

Special Category States

Arunanchal Pradesh	40.3	24.8	9.2
Himachal Pradesh	51.9	3.8	42.9
Jammu & Kashmir	32.5	1.2	63.1
Manipur	32.6	44.4	0.7
Meghalaya	40.0	55.9	0.0
Mizoram	44.4	55.4	0.0
Nagaland	61.1	27.3	4.0
Sikkim	72.7	24.4	2.5
Tripura	14.0	71.7	2.8
Uttarakhand	34.5	19.5	44.6

Union Territories

Andaman & Nicobar islands	55.1	10.0	34.7
Chandigarh	98.3	0.0	1.7
Dadra & Nagar Haveli	46.4	10.0	43.6
Daman & Diu	32.5	40.0	24.0
Lakshadweep	89.0	11.0	0.0
Puducherry	68.7	0.4	27.3
All India	34.7	10.3	52.5

Source: NSS 65th Rounds.

Distribution of Households by Type of Toilet Facility by Major Religious Communities (Muslims), 2002 and 2008-9 (per cent)

Non Special Category States	*Septic Tank/Flash*	*Pit*	*No Latrine*
	2002 2008-9	*2002 2008-9*	*2002 2008-9*
Andhra Pradesh	65.5	4.5	28.4
Assam	11.8	56.9	19.7
Bihar	23.1	9.1	57.8
Chhattisgarh	78.6	7.1	14.4
Delhi	88.8	4.3	1.9
Goa	55.3	5.7	39.0
Gujarat	48.9	15.8	34.5
Haryana	30.9	5.7	63.4
Jharkhand	12.8	20.4	63.9
Karnataka	40.1	19.9	35.4
Kerala	20.5	76.4	1.4
Madhya Pradesh	53.6	2.9	39.3
Maharashtra	74.4	3.4	18.1
Odisha	36.4	0.3	56.0
Punjab	54.2	14.5	31.3
Rajasthan	36.9	14.4	45.7
Tamil Nadu	75.7	2.5	19.7
Uttar Pradesh	35.7	10.8	46.8
West Bengal	18.2	32.5	41.0

Special Category States

Arunanchal Pradesh	33.4	11.4	10.9
Himachal Pradesh	50.8	2.2	47.0
Jammu & Kashmir	27.7	31.3	7.8
Manipur	12.7	68.6	0.8
Meghalaya	13.6	56.9	0.0
Mizoram	85.9	14.1	0.0
Nagaland	4.2	42.5	10.2
Sikkim	98.6	1.4	0.0
Tripura	6.2	71.8	3.5
Uttarakhand	27.7	49.2	21.4

Union Territories

Andaman & Nicobar islands	97.0	2.0	1.0
Chandigarh	92.9	0.0	7.1
Dadra & Nagar Haveli	38.4	61.6	0.0
Daman & Diu	85.7	2.5	4.8
Lakshadweep	29.9	68.3	0.5
Puducherry	81.9	7.0	9.4
All india	35.4	21.9	35.8

Source: NSS 65th Rounds.

Distribution of Households by Type of Toilet Facility by Major Religious communities (Christians), 2002 and 2008-9(per cent)

Non Special Category States	*Septic Tank/Flash*	*Pit*	*No Latrine*
	2002 2008-9	2002 2008-9	2002 2008-9
Andhra Pradesh	46.8	1.8	50.9
Assam	16.1	55.6	26.0
Bihar	38.9	1.0	60.2
Chhattisgarh	24.5	10.4	64.1
Delhi	100.0	0.0	0.0
Goa	74.7	10.7	13.7
Gujarat	46.0	2.8	51.3
Haryana	100.0	0.0	0.0
Jharkhand	33.2	5.1	60.4
Karnataka	59.1	30.1	10.0
Kerala	42.6	53.6	3.1
Madhya Pradesh	50.7	21.0	28.3
Maharashtra	89.4	4.3	0.8
Odisha	5.6	1.1	93.3
Punjab	47.2	0.0	52.4
Rajasthan	43.5	0.0	56.2
Tamil Nadu	69.5	0.0	23.3
Uttar Pradesh	90.9	0.0	9.1
West Bengal	32.7	25.1	36.6

Special Category States

Arunanchal Pradesh	25.7	11.9	8.2
Himachal Pradesh	90.0	0.0	10.0
Jammu & Kashmir	16.1	32.5	0.0
Manipur	25.2	49.2	0.7
Meghalaya	26.5	57.1	10.3
Mizoram	59.0	39.8	0.0
Nagaland	42.7	44.6	2.4
Sikkim	80.8	16.4	0.2
Tripura	10.4	54.9	0.0
Uttarakhand	18.5	2.4	79.1

Union Territories

Andaman & Nicobar islands	77.9	4.7	17.4
Chandigarh	100.	0.0	0.0
Dadra & Nagar Haveli	0.0	78.1	21.9
Daman & Diu	68.2	15.8	16.0
Lakshadweep	0.0	100.0	0.0
Puducherry	80.0	0.0	14.6
All india	46.9	27.4	22.1

Source: NSS 65th Rounds

Implications of Urban Development and Sanitation on Poor and Marginalised

(a) Poverty of the People: It is in this context that it is useful to investigate the Urban Poverty Removal Strategy (UPRS) spelt out by the government of India, in collaboration with the UNDP. According to the strategy document, poverty can be defined in different ways, but it is important that poverty is not only defined in terms of economic needs such as income. Poverty also has a social dimension (poor quality of housing and the living environment, i.e., lack of access to basic services like clean water, health care, education etc.). Even a definition in economic and social terms does not describe poverty adequately. Apart from not having access to the benefits of development, poverty is also lack of choice and voice, of rights and security, of participation in decision-making.

(b) Attack on Space: The attack on urban shelter began sometimes in the late 1960s when large-scale evictions took place as the first

Master Plans came into being. The climax was reached during the late 190s when the declaration of a National Emergency suspended all human rights, and the administration had a free hand to demolish and recast as they pleased. Some of the exercises in urban renewal during that period tried to bring in new technologies of transportation, construction, manufacture, and infrastructure, thus triggering off large-scale migrations from rural to urban areas, and the emergency of a working population confined to slums and resettlement colonies on the peripheries. It is also important to note that the era of 'public interest' litigation followed the Emergence, as the Supreme Court genuflected towards mass discontent and restored many of the civil liberties, particularly of the poor.

What, then are the rights that the so-called 'weaker sections' have in the city? It was in 1956 that the Slum Clearance and Improvement Act was passed to ameliorate the living conditions in the slums, although this was based on earlier legislation put in place by the colonial government. It is curious that this Act should include notions of both 'clearance' as well as 'improvement'; because it indicates that the government's understanding was that it would not be possible to remove all the slums, although this was based on earlier legislation put in place by the colonial government. It is curious that this Act should include notions of both 'clearance' as well as 'improvement', because it indicates that the government's understanding was that it would not be possible to remove all the slums by administrative fiat alone, but the dwelling conditions had to be made more liveable where the slums were located. This Act gave birth to several schemes such as the Community Development Programme, wherein there was the first attempt to include the community's social life into the technical planning process. The Environmental Improvement of Urban Slum Scheme in 1969 focused on providing water, sanitation, street, lighting, drains, and pavements at the settlement level. Still later, the Urban Basic Services and Low Cost Sanitation Schemes of 1981 attempted to provide some of these facilities at e household level. However, all these required some form of official recognition or 'notification' of the slum.

Selective variations of the same theme followed in the Slum Improvement Scheme of 1990, the Urban Basic Services for the Poor in 1991, the National Slum Development Programme in 199, and the Valmiki Ambedkar Awaas Yojana in 2001. In 1979 the government initiated the project for Urban Infrastructure Development Scheme for small and medium towns, the Integrated Housing and Slum Development programme in 1983, the Nehru Rozgar Yojana in 1989, the Twarit Nagar Jalapoorti Kartakram in 1993, the Swarna Jayanti

Shahari Rozgar Yojana in 1997 and the Infrastructure Development Project in Mega Cities in 1994. Broadly, these followed a hierarchy of strategies to deal with slums.

Lately, though, as the price of urban land has begun rising on the one hand, and on the other hand there is some concern that removing the urban working poor to distant locations may not be a wise political move, a new strategy has emerged called 'vertical in-situ upgradation'. Under this scheme a portion of the land on which the slum was originally located is given over to a property developer who can use it for commercial purposes, while on the remainder the developer as to build multi-storey flats in which the families can be resettled. The profits from the commercial development are supposed to pay for the flats. These flats were given free earlier, but now that the 'model' has been tested successfully in Mumbai, there is an increasing tendency to retrieve the cost from the family. [48]

Notes

1. See India Social Development Report 2008—Council for Social Development; OUP, New Delhi; 2008.
2. See India—Human Development Report 2011, OUP, 2011.
3. Based on Economic Impacts of Inadequate Sanitation in India, 2010, Water and Sanitation Program, www.wsp.org
4. Census 2011—Housing, Housing Amenities and Assets results 2012.
5. Joint Monitoring Programme—UNICEF and WHO, 2012.
6. Ministry of Drinking Water and Sanitation, Government of India, www.ddws.nic.in
7. Clean India Campaign. Total Sanitation Campaign has been renamed in 2012.
8. Based on Twelfth Five Year Plan—(2012-2017) Report of the Working Group on Rural Domestic Water and Sanitation, Ministry of Drinking Water and Sanitation Government of India September 2011.
9. Based on the ACCES Sanitation Accelerating City-to-City Exchange for Sustainable Sanitation, Inventory of Sanitation Policies and Programmes in India, ICLEI-Local Governments for Sustainability—South Asia, June 2010.
10. Based on the ACCES Sanitation Accelerating City-to-City Exchange for Sustainable Sanitation, Inventory of Sanitation Policies and Programmes in India, ICLEI-Local Governments for Sustainability—South Asia, June 2010; http://

indiasanitationportal.org/; http://planningcommission.nic.in/reports/genrep/wtrsani.pdf - Water Supply and Sanitation- India Assessment 2002—WHO and UNICEF Study; http://www.urbanindia.nic.in—Ministry of Urban Development, Government of India; http://www.cpheeo.nic.in—Central Public Health and Environmental Engineering Organisation, Ministry of Urban Development, Government of India; Water Aid India—Country Information; Rural Drinking Water and Sanitation in the Eleventh Plan Period (2007-2012)—Excerpts, December 2007, Planning Commission, Government of India; Sustaining the Sanitation Revolution—India Country Paper, SACOSAN, November 2008.

11. Twelfth Five Year Plan—(2012-2017) Report of the Working Group on Rural Domestic Water and Sanitation, Ministry of Drinking Water and Sanitation Government of India September 2011.
12. Twelfth Five Year Plan—(2012-2017) Report of the Working Group on Rural Domestic Water and Sanitation, Ministry of Drinking Water and Sanitation Government of India September 2011.
13. Country Programme Action Plan 2013-2017, Government of India and the United Nations Children's Fund.
14. For details see 'The Sanitation Challenge', Economic and Political Weekly, Vol. 44, No. 4 (Jan. 24-30, 2009), p. 6.
15. World Health Organisation and UNICEF (2000) Global Water Supply and Sanitation Assessment 2000 Report, World Health Organisation and UNICEF, Geneva.
16. World Bank (2002) 'Rural Water Supply and Sanitation: Topics: Hygiene and Sanitation', available at http://www.worldbank.org/html/fpd/water/ruralprinciples/hygienesan.html
17. Wakeman, W., S. Davis, C. van Wijk, and A. Naithani (1996) Sourcebook for Gender Issues at the Policy Level in the Water and Sanitation Sector. Washington, DC: World Bank.
18. van Wijk-Sijbesma, C. (1998) Gender in Water Resources Management, Water Supply and Sanitation: Roles and Realities Revisited, IRC Technical Paper Series, Delft: IRC.
19. Waterkeyn, J. and S. Cairncross (2005) 'Creating demand for sanitation and hygiene through Community Health Clubs: a cost-effective intervention in two districts in Zimbabwe', Social Science and Medicine 61 (9): 1958–70.
20. Country Programme Action Plan 2013-2017, Government of India and the United Nations Children's Fund.

21. Advancing Women's Rights and Gender Equality: Strategic Opportunities for UNICEF India (Kalyani Menon-Sen and Ranjani K. Murthy, New Delhi, UNICEF India, 2010).
22. http://unstats.un.org/unsd/mdg
23. For details see Thérèse Mahon and Maria Fernandes (2010): Menstrual hygiene in South Asia: a neglected issue for WASH (water, sanitation and hygiene) programmes, Gender and Development, 18:1, 99-113
24. WHO (1999), *World Health Report,1999 Data Base,*World Health Organisation, Geneva
25. Rice, AL, L Sacco, A Hyder and R E Black (2000), "Malnutrition as an underlying cause of childhood deaths associated with infectious diseases in developing countries", *Bulletin of the World Health Organisation* Vol 78, No 10, pp. 1207–1221
26. Stephenson, C B (1999), "Burden of infection on growth failure", *Journal of Nutrition* Vol 129 (2S Supplement), pp. 534S–538S.
27. Solomon, N W, M Mazariegos, K H Brown and K Klasing (1993), "The underprivileged developing country child: environmental contamination and growth failure revisited", *Nutrition Reviews* Vol. 51, No. 11.
28. UNICEF (2002), *"Poverty and Exclusion among Urban Children"*, Innocenti Centre, Florence, Italy.
29. See WASH IN ALL SCHOOLS: Making it a Reality, PROCEEDINGS of South Asia Regional Conference, April 2012
30. WHO/UNICEF, Joint Monitoring Programme for Water Supply and Sanitation (2000), *Global Water Supply and Sanitation Assessment, 2000 Report,*World Health Organisation, Geneva.
31. Also See Manasi Bawdekar And Laishram Ladusingh (2008). Contextual Correlates of Child Malnutrition in Rural Maharashtra. Journal Of Biosocial Science, 40, pp. 771-786.
32. NFHS 2005-2006 and the Coverage Evaluation Survey (CES) 2010.
33. NFHS 2005-2006 and CES 2009. A more recent GoI Annual Health Survey (2010); UNICEF, The State of the World's Children Report 2009: Maternal and Newborn Health.
34. Country Programme Action Plan 2013-2017, Government of India and the United Nations Children's Fund.
35. UNICEF, *The State of the World Children's Report 2012: Children in an Urban World.*
36. based on 1990 and 2008 figures, Sample Registration System, Registrar General of India, Government of India.

37. International Learning Exchange In Water, Sanitation and Hygiene Rural Communities display their water and sanitation skills 13-23 November 2006 UNICEF (India).
38. http://www.childinfo.org/sanitation.html
39. See UNICEF India Country Office Annual Report 2011.
40. For details see India Country Office Annual Report 2010, UNICEF
41. DDWS Online Monitoring *<ddws.gov.in>*
42. Blum NJ, Taubman B, Nemeth N. Why is toilet training occurring at older ages? A study of factors associated with later training. *J Pediatr*. 2004;145:107-111
43. Bakker E, Wyndaele JJ. Changes in the toilet training of children during the last 60 years: the cause of an increase in lower urinary tract dysfunction? *BJU Int*. 2000;86: 248-252.
44. Spock B, Bergen M. Parents' fear of conflict in toilet training. *Pediatrics*. 1964; 34:112-116.
45. Brazelton TB. A child-oriented approach to toilet training. *Pediatrics*. 1962;29:121-128.
46. See R. N. Sharma and Amita Bhide, World Bank Funded Slum Sanitation Programme in Mumbai: Participatory Approach and Lessons Learnt, Economic and Political Weekly, Vol. 40, No. 17 (Apr. 23-29, 2005), pp. 1784-1789.
47. Based on India—Human Development Report 2011, OUP, 2011
48. See Dunu Roy. 2008. Urban development projects and displacement of the poor in India Social Development Report 2008—Council for Social Development; OUP, New Delhi; 2008.

37. International Learning Exchange in Water, Sanitation and Hygiene [illegible] that display their water and sanitation [illegible] [illegible] The [illegible] India.

38. http:// [illegible] sanitation.[illegible]

39. See UNICEF India Country Office Annual Report 2010.

40. [illegible] India Country Office Annual Report 2010 [illegible]

41. [illegible] Online Monitoring [illegible]

42. [illegible] [illegible] What is toilet training [illegible] [illegible] [illegible] [illegible] [illegible] associated with later [illegible] [illegible] 2003, 111 [illegible]

43. [illegible] Changes in the toilet training of children [illegible] [illegible] [illegible] [illegible] lower urinary [illegible]

44. [illegible] toilet training [illegible] [illegible]

45. [illegible] [illegible] [illegible]

46. [illegible] World [illegible]

47. [illegible] [illegible] Approaches and [illegible] [illegible]

48. [illegible] 2011, 2012 [illegible]

49. [illegible] India [illegible] Development [illegible] [illegible] Development [illegible] New Delhi, [illegible]

11

Toilet as a Tool of Change: Exemplifying Sulabh International Social Service Organisation as Catalyst

Introduction

The effects of poor sanitation seep into every aspect of life—health, nutrition, development, economy, dignity and empowerment. It perpetuates an intergenerational cycle of poverty and deprivation. To meet the country's sanitation and hygiene challenge there is an urgent need to focus on triggering the *demand* to build toilets, ensuring their quality, *use* and maintenance. This is achieved by creating a culture of "social sanctions" that challenge the acceptance of open defecation once and for all. Making this happen requires substantial resource and time investment to inculcate a lasting change in behaviour and adoption of key hygiene practices at the community and household level.

Social development through sanitation is about human progress; it centres on equality between women and men, social inclusion, access to education, community cohesion and poverty eradication. At its core are human dignity and human rights. For the billion people who have to defecate behind bushes, in plastic bags or buckets, along railway tracks or in roadside ditches, human dignity is under daily assault. The humble toilet can speed social development in a number of ways. At thus juncture, it is to be emphasised that toilets are relational.[1] Toilets are no mere receptacles for waste, but a domestic feature that connects us to the world: that which exits our bodies goes somewhere, whether we choose to think about it or not. This group of people chooses to think about it. In looking at composting toilets, a popular alternative to the flush toilets connected to the county water supply largely unavailable in the area.

Toilets, it should be noted, are not at the forefront of anthropological enquiry. Defecation is one of those neglected aspects'. In some cases, analysing the toilet can be regarded with active hostility, as in the case of a 2002 special issue of Postcolonial Studies whose call for papers on toilets and defecation was met with a barrage of emails. The first sewers in Sydney were built in the 1850s and drained raw sewage straight into the now famous harbour. Since then, the use of the ocean as a site of elimination has continued: 'all drains built in Sydney have pointed seaward' (Hawkins, 2006: 61). Among the consequences of this policy decision have been sewage washed ashore, high levels of faecal coliform, sick fish and sick swimmers. What is particularly interesting about Hawkins' discussions on toilets, sewers and drainage in Sydney, however, is the construction of this problem of disposal as a specifically public issue. Numerous alternatives to the Water Board's proposition to build outfalls further out to sea were offered during the POOO (Public Opposition to Ocean Outfalls) protests of 1989, yet none addressed domestic practice: none sought to reform that most intimate sphere of domestic disposal. In fact, Hawkins describes a public outcry over the imposition of water restrictions in 2003. Despite sanitation's massively networked connections from public waste facilities to private homes it is not experienced as a state intervention. It is just the hidden linchpin of our most intimate rituals of care. Water flows in, shit flows out, where from and where to we hardly care. The thing is that the flows are maintained, that our bathroom works to protect us from encountering our waste, so that certain ethical and aesthetic sensibilities that are fundamental to the making of the purified private self will not be threatened. (Hawkins, 2006: 61)

Norbert Elias in his The Civilising Process (1994 [1939]) presents a picture of changing manners in Europe since the 16th century, highlighting increased individualism, privacy and feelings of shame relating to bodily waste. Managing that which exits the body—from faeces to farts—is central to the development of individualism in Europe, he argues. Where Elias provides a broad sweep history of changing manners in Europe, of which attitudes towards excretions form only a part, Corbin (1986) spells out an aromatic history of one nation, France, much of which focuses on urbanisation and waste management, and he too traces a simultaneous pattern of increased individualism and privacy surrounding space, health, defecation and increased intervention by the state in daily life. Individual water closets only became possible through the development of, and connection to, state-organised sewers. In his analysis, expanding notions of individualism are dependent upon increased state intrusion into the home that are indistinguishable from mechanisms of power, as state representatives imposed (upper-) class-based notions of good health on the lower classes.

Sewer systems appear inextricable from reformed selves and state power. Something similar can be read in Zizek's use of the example of toilets to demonstrate that ideology is stamped all over the material world. In a traditional German toilet, he explains, 'the hole in which shit disappears after we flush water is way in front, so that the shit is first laid out for us to sniff at and inspect' ('German reflective thoroughness'); in a French lavatory, 'the hole is in the back—that is, the shit is supposed to disappear as soon as possible' ('French revolutionary radicalism'), and the Anglo-Saxon (English or American) is a synthesis of these, 'the basin is full of water, so that the shit floats in it—visible, but not to be inspected' ('English moderate liberalism') (1997: 4–5). Through this analysis of lavatories Zizek is able to discern: three different attitudes towards excremental excess: ambiguous contemplative fascination; the hasty attempt to get rid of the unpleasant excess as fast as possible; the pragmatic approach to treat the excess as an ordinary object to be disposed of in an appropriate way. (1997: 5).

Zizek identifies toilets as a site where ideology is imprinted upon the material world, where there is no utility without ideology. The state's tendrils extend to the toilet even when analysis of the state stops short of the sewer. Toilets mediate different sorts of relations: between nation-states and national ideologies, and also between one's body and one's self. In the case of van der Geest (1998, 2002), they can also mediate interpersonal relationships.

Technology and Toilets[2]

(a) A Dry Toilet - It is a toilet that operates without water. The Dry Toilet may be a raised pedestal that the user can sit on, or a squat pan that the user squats over. In both cases, excreta (both urine and faeces) fall through a drop hole. Dry Toilets are easy for almost everyone to use. Because there is no need to separate urine and faeces, they are often the most physically comfortable and natural option.

Squatting is a natural position for many people and so a well-kept squatting slab may be the most acceptable option. Since Dry Toilets do not have a water seal, odours may be a problem depending on the Collection and Storage/Treatment technology to which it is connected. The sitting or standing surface should be kept clean and dry to prevent pathogen/disease transmission and to limit odours. There are no mechanical parts and so the Dry Toilet should not need repairs except in the event that it cracks.

(b) Urine Diverting Dry Toilet (UDDT) - A Urine Diverting Dry Toilet (UDDT) is a toilet that operates without water and has a divider so that the user, with little effort can divert the urine away from the faeces. The UDDT toilet is built such that urine is collected and drained from the front area of the toilet, while faeces fall through a large chute (hole) in the back. Depending on the Collection and Storage/Treatment technology that follows, drying material such as lime, ash or earth should be added into the same hole after defecating.

It is important that the two sections of the toilet are well separated to ensure that a) faeces do not fall into, and clog the urine collection area in the front, and that b) urine does not splash down into the dry area of the toilet. There are also 3-hole separating toilets that allow anal cleansing water to be separated from the urine and the faeces into a third, dedicated hole. It is important that the faeces remain separate and dry. When the toilet is cleaned with water, care should be taken to ensure that the faeces are not mixed with water.

The UDDT is not intuitive or immediately obvious to some users. At first, users may be hesitant about using it and mistakes (e.g., faeces in the urine bowl) may deter others from accepting this type of toilet as well. Education and demonstration projects are essential in achieving good acceptance with users. A UDDT is slightly more difficult to keep clean compared to other toilets because of both the lack of water and the need to separate the solid faeces and liquid urine. For cleaning, a damp cloth may be used to wipe down the seat and the inner bowls. Some toilets are easily removable and can be cleaned more thoroughly.

(c) Urinal - A Urinal is only used for collecting urine. Urinals are generally for men, although Urinals for women have also been developed. The Urinal can be used with or without water and the plumbing can be developed accordingly. If water is used, it is mainly used for cleaning and limiting odours (with a water-seal).

Water-based Urinals use 8 to 12 litres of flushwater, whereas low-flush models use less than four litres of flushwater. Because the Urinal is exclusively for urine it is important to also provide another toilet to be used for faeces. The Urinal is a comfortable and easily accepted User Interface. In some cases, the provision of a Urinal is useful to prevent the misuse of dry systems (e.g., UDDT). Urinals, although simple in construction and design, can have a large impact on the well-being of a community.

(d) Pour Flush Toilet - A Pour Flush Toilet is like a regular Flush Toilet except that instead of the water coming from the cistern above, it is poured in by the user. When the water supply is not continuous, any cistern Flush Toilet can become a Pour Flush Toilet. Just like a traditional Flush Toilet, there is a water seal that prevents odours and flies from coming back up the pipe.

Water is poured into the bowl to flush the toilet of excreta; approximately 2 to 3L is usually sufficient. The quantity of water and the force of the water (pouring from a height often helps) must be sufficient to move the excreta up and over the curved water seal. Both pedestals and squatting pans can be used in the pour flush mode. Due to demand, local manufacturers have become increasingly efficient at mass-producing affordable, Pour Flush Toilets and pans. The S-shape of the water seal determines how much water is needed for flushing. To reduce water requirements, it is advisable to collect toilet paper or other dry cleansing materials separately.

The water seal is effective at preventing odours and it is appropriate for those who sit or squat (pedestal or slab) as well as those who cleanse with water. It is only appropriate when there is a constant supply of water available. The Pour Flush Toilet requires (much) less water than a traditional cistern Flush Toilet. However, because a smaller amount of water is used, the Pour Flush Toilet may clog more easily and thus, require more maintenance. The Pour Flush Toilet (or squatting pan) prevents users from seeing or smelling the excreta of previous users. Thus, it is generally well accepted.

(e) Cistern Flush Toilet - The Cistern Flush Toilet is usually porcelain and is a mass-produced, factory made User Interface. The Flush Toilet consists of a water tank that supplies the water for flushing the excreta and a bowl into which the excreta are deposited. The attractive feature of the Flush Toilet is that it incorporates a sophisticated water seal to prevent odours from coming back up through the plumbing. Depending on the age and design of the toilet, approximately 3 to 20L of water may be used per flush. Water that is stored in the cistern above the toilet bowl is released by pushing or pulling a lever.

This allows the water to run into the bowl, mix with the excreta and carrying them away.

A Cistern Flush Toilet should not be considered unless all of the connections and hardware accessories are available locally. The Cistern Flush Toilet must be connected to both a constant source of water for flushing and a Collection and Storage/Treatment or Conveyance technology to receive the blackwater. Although flushwater continuously rinses the bowl, the toilet should be scrubbed clean regularly. Maintenance is required for the replacement or repair of some mechanical parts or fittings.

(f) Urine Diverting Flush Toilet (UDFT) - The Urine Diverting Flush Toilet (UDFT) is similar in appearance to a Cistern Flush Toilet except for the diversion in the bowl. The toilet bowl has two sections so that the urine can be separated from the faeces. When the user sits on the toilet, urine is collected in a drain in the front (where there is no water) and faeces are collected in the back (where there is water). The urine is collected without water, but a small amount of water is used to rinse the urine-collection bowl after the user stands up. The urine flows into a storage tank for further use or processing, while the faeces are flushed with water to be treated. The system requires dual plumbing (i.e., plumbing for the urine and for the brownwater). The toilet should be installed carefully with an understanding of how and where clogs may occur so that they can be easily removed Information cards and/or diagrams are essential for ensuring proper use and for promoting acceptance; if users understand why the urine is being separated they will be more willing to use the UDFT properly. Proper plumbing will ensure that there are no odours. As with any toilet, proper cleaning is important to keep the bowl(s) clean and prevent organic residues and stains from forming. Because urine is collected separately, calcium- and magnesium-based minerals can precipitate out and build up in the fittings and pipes.

Technologies and Methods Used to Dispose of the Output Products in a Eco-friendly Mode[3]

ARBORLOO - To decommission a pit, it can simply be filled with soil and covered. Although there is no benefit recovered, the full pit poses no immediate health risk, and with time, the contents will degrade naturally. Alternatively, the 'Arborloo' is a shallow pit that is filled with excreta and soil/ash and then covered with soil; a tree planted on top will grow vigorously in the nutrient-rich pit. Filling and covering pits is an adequate solution when emptying is not possible and when there is space to continuously re-dig and fill pits.

The Arborloo can be applied in rural, peri-urban, and denser areas if space is available. Planting a tree in the abandoned pit is a good way to reforest an area, provide a sustainable source of fresh fruit and prevent people from falling into old pit sites. There is a minimal risk of infection if the pit is properly covered and clearly marked. It may be preferable to cover the pit and plant a tree rather than have the pit emptied, especially if there is no appropriate technology available for treating the faecal sludge. Users do not come in contact with the faecal material and thus there is a very low risk of pathogen transmission. Demonstration projects that allow community members to participate are useful ways of showing both the ease of the system, its inoffensive nature, and the nutrient value of composted excreta.

(a) Application of Urine - Separately collected, stored urine is a concentrated source of nutrients that can be applied as a liquid fertiliser in agriculture to replace all or some commercial chemical fertiliser. The guidelines for urine use are based on storage time and temperature. However, it is generally accepted that if urine is stored for at least one month, it will be safe for agricultural application at the household level. If urine is used for crops that are eaten by those other than the urine producer, it should be stored for six months. Urine should not be applied to crops within one month before they are harvested. From normal, healthy people, urine is virtually free of pathogens. Urine also contains the majority of nutrients that are excreted by the body. Urine varies depending on diet, gender, climate and water intake among other facts, but roughly 80 per cent of nitrogen, 60 per cent of potassium and 55 per cent of phosphorus that is excreted from the body is excreted through urine. Because of its high pH and concentration, stored urine should not be applied directly to plants. Urine is especially beneficial where crops are lacking nitrogen. Examples of some crops that grow well with urine include: maize, rice, millet, sorghum, wheat, chard, turnip, carrots, kale, cabbage, lettuce, bananas, paw-paw, and oranges.

Urine application is ideal for rural and peri-urban areas where agricultural lands are close to the point of urine collection. Households can use their own urine on their own plot of land. Alternatively, if facilities and infrastructure exist, urine can be collected at a semi-centralised location for distribution and transport to agricultural land. There is a minimal risk of infection, especially with extended storage. Still, urine should be handled carefully and should not be applied to crops less than one month before they are harvested. Social acceptance may be difficult. Stored urine has a strong smell and some may find it offensive to work with or be near. If urine is diluted, and/or immediately tilled into the earth, the smells can be reduced. The use of urine may be less accepted in urban or peri-urban areas where household gardens are close to houses than in rural areas, where houses and crop lands are separated.

(b) Application of Dehydrated Faeces - When faeces are stored in the absence of moisture (i.e., urine) they dehydrate into a crumbly, white-beige coarse, flaky material or powder. Dehydration means that the moisture naturally present in the faeces evaporates and/or is absorbed by the addition of a drying material (e.g. ash, sawdust, lime). Dehydration is different from composting because the organic material present is not degraded or transformed; only the moisture is removed. After dehydration, faeces will reduce in volume by about 75 per cent. The shells and carcasses of worms and insects that also dehydrate will remain in the dried faeces. When the faeces are completely dry they will emerge as a crumbly, powdery substance. The material is rich in carbon and nutrients, but may still contain pathogens or oocysts (spores which can survive extreme environmental conditions and re-animate under favourable conditions). The material can be mixed into soil, either for agriculture or at another site (depending on acceptance). Faeces that are dried and stored between 2 and 20°C should be stored for between 1.5 to 2 years before they are used at the household or regional level. Dried faeces are not as well treated or as useful as a soil amendment as composted faeces. However, they are useful at replenishing poor soils and for boosting the carbon and water-storing properties of a soil with low-risk of pathogen transmission. The handing and use of dried faeces may not be acceptable to some. However, because the dried faeces should be dry, crumbly, and odour free, the use of dried faeces may be more acceptable than that of manure or sludge. Dry faeces are a hostile environment for organisms and consequently, they do not survive (for long). If water or urine mixes with the drying faeces, odours and organisms may become problematic; wet faeces allow bacteria to survive and multiply. A warm, moist environment will permit anaerobic processes to generate offensive odours.

(c) Application of Compost/EcoHumus - Composting is the term used to describe the controlled aerobic degradation of organics into a soil-like substance called compost. 'EcoHumus' is a term taken from Peter Morgan (see references) and is a more appropriate word to use for the material removed from a Fossa Alterna because it is produced passively underground and has a slightly different composition. The process of thermophilic composting generates heat (50 to 80°C) which kills the majority of pathogens present. For the composting process to occur there must be adequate carbon, nitrogen, moisture, and air. The Fossa Alterna (S5) and Arborloo (D1) are ambient temperature variations of high-temperature composting. In these technologies, there is almost no temperature rise because vegetable matter is lacking. For that reason, the material is not actually 'compost' and is therefore referred to as 'EcoHumus'.

The WHO guidelines stipulate that the compost should achieve and maintain a temperature of 50°C for at least one week before it is considered safe (although to achieve this value, a significantly longer period of composting is required). The WHO guidelines should be consulted for detailed information. For systems that generate EcoHumus in-situ (i.e., Fossa Alterna), a minimum of one year of storage is recommended to eliminate bacterial pathogens and reduce viruses and parasitic protozoa.

Compost/EcoHumus can be used beneficially to improve the quality of soils by adding nutrients and organics and improving the soil's ability to store air and water. The texture and quality of the EcoHumus depends on the materials which have been added to the excreta (especially the type of soil). A small risk of pathogen transmission exists, but if in doubt, any material removed from the pit can be composted further in a regular compost heap, or mixed with additional soil and put into a 'tree pit', i.e., a nutrient-filled pit used for planting a tree. Acceptability may be low at first, but demonstration units and hands-on experience are effective ways of demonstrating the non-offensive nature of the material.

(d) Irrigation - To reduce dependence on freshwater and maintain a constant source of irrigation water throughout the year, waste waters of varying qualities can be used in agriculture. Generally, only waters that have had secondary treatment (i.e., physical and biological treatment) should be used to limit the risk of crop contamination and the health risk to workers. There are two kinds of irrigation technologies that are appropriate for using treated wastewaters: 1)Drip irrigation where the water is dripped slowly on or near the root area; and 2)Surface water irrigation where water is routed overland in a series of dug channels or furrows. To minimise evaporation and contact with pathogens, spray irrigation should be avoided. Properly treated wastewater can significantly reduce dependence on freshwater, and/ or improve crop yields by supplying increased water and nutrients to plants. Raw sewage or untreated black water should not be used, and even well-treated water should be used with caution. Long-term use of poorly or improperly treated water may cause long-term damage to the soil structure and its ability to hold water.

Appropriate pre-treatment should precede any irrigation scheme to limit health risks to those who come in contact with the water. As well, depending on the degree of treatment that the effluent has undergone, it may be contaminated with the different chemicals that are discharged into the system. When effluent is used for irrigation, households and industries connected to the system should be made aware of the products that are and are not appropriate for discharging into the system. Drip irrigation is the only type of irrigation that should be used with edible crops, and even then, care should be taken to prevent workers and harvested crops from coming in contact with the treated effluent. Despite safety concerns, irrigation with effluent is an effective way to recycle nutrients and water.

Aquaculture Ponds - Aquaculture refers to the controlled cultivation of aquatic plants and animals; this technology sheet refers exclusively to the raising of fish while the following page on Floating Macrophytes (D9) addresses the cultivation of plants. Fish can be grown in ponds where they feed on algae and other organisms that grow in the nutrient-rich water. Through feeding, the nutrients from the wastewater are removed and the fish are eventually harvested for consumption.

Three kinds of aquaculture designs for raising fish exist:

(1) fertilisation of fish ponds with excreta/sludge;

(2) fertilisation of fish ponds with effluent; and

(3) fish grown directly in aerobic ponds.

When introducing nutrients in the form of effluent or sludge it is important to limit the additions such that aerobic conditions are maintained. BOD should not exceed $1g/m^2d$ and oxygen should be at least 4mg/L. Fish introduced to aerobic ponds can effectively reduce algae and help control mosquito populations. A fish pond is only appropriate when there is a sufficient amount of land (or preexisting pond), a source of fresh water and a suitable climate. The water that is used to dilute the waste should not be too warm, and the ammonia levels should be kept low or negligible. Only fish that are tolerant of low dissolved oxygen levels should be chosen. They should not be carnivores and they should be tolerant to diseases and adverse environmental conditions. Different varieties of carp, milkfish and tilapia have been successful, but the specific choice will depend on local preference and suitability. This technology is only appropriate for warm or tropical climates with no freezing temperatures, and preferably with high rainfall and minimal evaporation.

Floating Plant (Macrophyte) Pond

A floating plant pond is a modified maturation pond with floating (macrophyte) plants. Plants such as water hyacinths or duckweed float on the surface while the roots hang down into the water to uptake nutrients and filter the water that flows by. Water hyacinths are perennial, freshwater, aquatic macrophytes that grow especially fast in wastewater. The plants can grow large: between 0.5 to 1.2m from top to bottom. The long roots provide a fixed medium for bacteria which in turn degrade the organics in the water passing by Duckweed is a fast growing, high protein plant that can be used fresh or dried as a food for fish or poultry. It is also tolerant of a variety of conditions and can remove significant quantities of nutrients from wastewater. To provide extra oxygen to a floating plant technology, the water can be mechanically aerated but at the cost of increased power and machinery. Aerated ponds can withstand higher loads and can be built with smaller footprints. Non-aerated ponds should not be too deep otherwise there will be insufficient contact between the bacteria-harbouring roots and the wastewater. The technology can achieve high removal rates of both BOD and suspended solids, although pathogen removal is not substantial. Harvested hyacinths can be used as a source of fibre for rope, textiles, baskets, etc. Depending on the income generated, the technology can be cost neutral.

Duckweed can be used as the sole food source to some herbivorous fish. Water hyacinth has attractive, lavender flowers. A well designed and maintained system can add value and interest to otherwise barren land. Adequate signage and fencing should be used to prevent people and animals from coming in contact with the water.

Land Application of Sludge

Digested or stabilised Faecal Sludge is refered to as 'Biosolids'. Depending on the quality of the biosolids, they can be applied to public or private lands, for landscaping or for agriculture. The USEPA defines different levels of biosolids depending on the treatment and quality, and therefore the health risk. Class A biosolids (i.e., biosolids that can be sold for public use) can be used with nearly no restrictions. Please consult the guidelines for specific use criteria. Biosolids can be used in agriculture, home gardening, forestry, sod and turf growing, landscaping, parks, golf courses, mine reclamation, dump cover, or erosion control. Although biosolids have lower nutrient levels than commercial fertilisers (for nitrogen, phosphorus and potassium respectively), they can be used to replace part or all of commercial fertilisers that are used. Additionally, biosolids have been found to have properties that are superior to those of fertilisers, such as bulking properties, water retention properties and the slow, steady release of nutrients. Although bio-solids are sometimes criticised for containing potentially high levels of metals or contaminants, commercial fertilisers are also contaminated to varying degrees, most likely with cadmium or other heavy metals. Faecal sludge from pit latrines has no, if any, chemical inputs and is therefore not a high risk source of contamination. Faecal sludge that originates at large-scale wastewater treatment plants is more likely to be contaminated since it receives industrial and domestic chemicals, as well as surface water run-off which may contain hydrocarbons and metals. Depending on the sludge source, biosolids can serve as a valuable and often much-needed source of nutrients. Land application of biosolids may be less expensive than disposal. Application rates and usages for biosolids should take into account not only the presence of pathogens and contaminants, but also the quantity of nutrients such that they are spread at a sustainable and 'agronomic' rate.

Toilet as Community Organisation

The importance of adequate drinking water supplies and sanitation as basic public health measures has been attracting increasing international attention during the 1970s. widespread lack of progress in the control of diarrhoeal diseases, schistosomiasis, malaria and other infections, has caused interest to turn back towards environmental control strategies, and in particular to focus upon domestic water supplies and sanitation. This renewed interest in environmental health has run parallel with, and is linked to, the current popularity of primary health care.

The level of international activity in the field of water supply and sanitation is increasing markedly at present in preparation for the International Drinking Water Supply and Sanitation Decade (1981-90). The Decade arises out of the resolutions passed at the U.N. Habitat Conference in Vancouver in 1976 and the U.N. Water Conference in Mar del Plata in 1977. The United Nations member states have agreed upon a target of providing the entire world's population with a safe drinking water supply and hygienic excreta disposal facilities by the year 1990. To achieve this, and generally to promote the drinking water and sanitation sectors, the International Decade has been declared.

Appropriate Technology[4]

The appropriate or intermediate technology movement is now acquiring some badly needed maturity of view. A few years ago it was popular to believe that a major constraint, maybe the major constraint, to water pumping, cereal milling, furniture making, vaccine storage, etc., was the lack of the appropriate pump, mill, lathe, fridge, etc. The invention, or rediscovery, of the appropriate technical device would release the key constraint and set in motion a chain of development activity that had hitherto been impossible. This view gained considerable support among scientists in Europe and North America because of its essential appeal to the intellect of researchers. It is extremely satisfying to apply the most advanced scientific knowledge and techniques to produce something ingeniously simple.

Selecting appropriate technology has become somewhat mystified by the exponents of the cause and one sees developing country officials being exhorted by foreigners to adopt a particular technology simply because it has the magic word 'appropriate' stamped on it. Recently, economists have pointed out that selection of appropriate technology may be reduced to correctly computed social cost-benefit analysis and that, without overcoming fundamental distortions in the apparent cost of resources, there can be no long-run incentive to adopt appropriate technology.[5] Appropriate technology can be defined as 'that process or technique which provides a socially and environmentally acceptable level of service or quality of product at the least social cost'.

Further, Community participation is a 'buzz phrase'. Its virtues are extolled in numerous conferences and seminars. A continuing stream of documents, the flow of which increases as the Decade approaches, plead, state, exhort or demand that community participation must be included in all water supply and sanitation projects. But community participation is a very vague and open concept and is used to mean very different things. It often subsumes other substantial concepts and approaches (such as 'self-help', self-reliance', 'user-choice', 'community involvement' and 'participatory planning and development') which are themselves ill-defined. In connection with community participation, people will often talk of 'felt needs', 'local perceptions', 'bottom-up planning', 'motivation', 'latent development potential', 'catalytic development inputs', 'integrated development at the village level', etc. Yet these concepts are each highly complex and diffuse and their meaning in any particular context is often obscure.

Much has been written recently about the anticipated or actual benefits from investments in water supply and sanitation. The primary benefit sought is improved health, but several studies have shown that this benefit is often not achieved.[6] It is now widely believed, although on slender evidence, that the full integration of water supply and sanitation projects, coupled with vigorous and sustained hygiene education, has the best prospect of achieving a reasonable level of health benefit. Such an approach requires community participation, at least in the educational component. Indeed, it is now common to link community participation with community education under the general concept of 'software', and to claim that careful design and implementation of software are quite as crucial to project success as good 'hardware'. Substantial educational efforts are an essential part of any water or sanitation programme. These must include: (i) education concerning correct operation and maintenance of the new facilities; (ii) education concerning correct use of the new facilities; (iii) education concerning personal and domestic hygiene; (iv) education concerning other measures which may be taken against the target diseases.

It is observed that worldwide, 2.6 billion people do not have access to sanitation facilities that safely separate human excreta from human contact (WHO/UNICEF 2010). As a result, sanitation related diseases like diarrhoea kill thousands of children each day and contribute to malnutrition and poverty. Approaches for increasing sanitation coverage at scale and with sustainable results are urgently needed. Community Led Total Sanitation (CLTS) is a sanitation approach aiming for 100 per cent Open Defecation Free (ODF) communities. While several variants of CLTS exist, all attempt to work with the entire community rather than with selected individuals or households, and focus on the elimination of open defecation rather than on the construction of a particular type of latrine. Pioneered in Bangladesh in 1999, CLTS has been implemented in Asia, Latin America and sub Saharan Africa.

CLTS has shown promise in rural areas especially, but sustainability and results beyond community level pilots have met with varied success. Strides forward have certainly been achieved (WSP 2010), but, coverage and behaviour change are sometimes overestimated. Sound evidence of sustainability is lacking (Chambers 2009).

CLTS programmes don't provide toilet subsidies, but provide information on a range of technology options. Households use local materials—including low cost and locally available materials such as grass roof-thatching, bamboo or mud—to build a toilet they want and can afford. In most programmes, very poor households without the required materials, labour or minimum of cash depend on solidarity within their community to get the help that they need (Kar and Chambers 2008). External funds are used for programme costs, capacity building and sometimes also community awards for achieving ODF status. One critique of CLTS has been that some low-cost toilets do not effectively separate faeces or are not durable (Kalimuthu and Hossain 2008; Palakudiyil 2008). Building in mechanisms for helping the weaker and poorer has also been identified as an urgent area for innovation (Chambers 2009).

Many CLTS programmes do not structurally include measures to ensure that all households, including the poorest or otherwise disadvantaged are able to construct toilets. Solidarity within the community is simply expected (Kar and Chambers 2008). Inclusiveness and equity can be improved by: (1) adding the identification and mapping of the poorest households as explicit steps in the CLTS process and (2) planning, monitoring and accounting for the support to the most vulnerable or poorest households. These measures were developed in sanitation programmes by IRC and local NGOs: SEUF in South India, Pradipta Paramithi in Java, COSI in Sri Lanka and NEWAH in Nepal.

Welfare classification and mapping should happen after mapping open defecation sites in the community and calculating how much faeces is being produced and before planning community action.

It is done in three steps:

1. Welfare classification - The facilitator organises a meeting with local women and men and asks them to form three or four sub-groups representing the main local welfare groups: e.g., better off, intermediate, poor and ultra-poor. Each group gets a sheet of paper and felt-tipped pens in different colours. Each group depicts the typical characteristics of a specific welfare category by listing indicators, drawing the indicators, or a typical household in that category. The groups then present their results and note down the number households in each category in their community.

2. Stratification of community sanitation map - The whole group then chooses a colour for each welfare category and draws a stratified community sanitation map on a large sheet of paper. Each house is drawn in the agreed colour indicating 'ultra-poor', 'poor', etc. They also indicate if the house already has a toilet, by adding a dot behind the house or placing a T or a cross in the house. If cultural norms make it difficult for (young) women to participate in mixed-sex sessions, men and women each make their own maps, discuss and then jointly decide which one the community will use for action planning and monitoring.

3. Preparing a community sanitation matrix - The participants then compile the community sanitation matrix. They list the welfare categories and note the number of households with sanitary, non-sanitary and no toilet in the respective columns. The facilitator helps participants discuss how a toilet effectively separates human faeces from human contact. A toilet that drains into surface water, for example, is listed as 'unsanitary'. Households that share a toilet with relatives or neighbours may be listed separately. The map and matrix can then be used to plan, monitor and account for community support in cash and/or kind to those least able to build a toilet.

Monitoring Quality of Construction and Hygiene Behaviour

Achieving ODF status does not guarantee that all community members continue to use, maintain and upgrade toilets in the long term. The next section describes steps for improving sustainability of toilets, hygienic behaviours and CLTS outcomes.

Community-based monitoring of technical and environmental sustainability: Transparent support for poor households and community monitoring have led to lower corruption, contributed to 100 per cent coverage and an estimated 25 per cent lower latrine cost (Mathew et al. 2008) in Kerala, India. When sufficient households wish to install a toilet, they choose an Implementation Team (IT). Assisted by a technically trained person from an NGO or the local government, the IT lists the amounts of material to be purchased, such as cement, bricks and tiles. The IT then visits local suppliers and builders and comes to an agreement. The agreement could specify for example that no more than five per cent of the delivered bricks may be damaged and that the final payment will be made only after the quality has been checked and accepted by the committee and the households.

Monitoring of behavioural sustainability. Merely having a toilet or hand washing facility is not enough: use of facilities by all household members is critical for achieving hygiene and health benefits. A community monitoring plan with simple, objective quality criteria is needed. The monitoring system includes ratio scores (e.g., per cent toilet ownership by class) and ordinal scores from 0–100. In-between scores are used when the specific indicators of a scale are not fully met.

The Kerala Programme built in several monitoring moments: female members of the sanitation committee visited each household upon toilet construction, after one month and after three months. Among other things, hygienic operation, maintenance and use of the toilet by all household members, the presence of water and, if affordable, soap were observed and discussed. They inquired about help from male members in keeping toilets clean, especially when water needed to be collected from a distance.

Institutionalising support to communities to ensure ODF status and safe toilet habits are sustained. The preceding sections described activities at community level, but to be sustainable CLTS requires long-term facilitation and support from higher institutional levels. Proven measures to improve sustainability are: linking CLTS to ongoing government programmes or institutions, providing capacity building to CLTS facilitators and the private sector.[7]

Community-led Total Sanitation: Reflections On Issues and Ways Forward[8]

1. Diversity, definition and principles - Three overlapping phases can be discerned:

1. Pioneering, enthusiastic excitement, and rapid initial national and international spread, through traveling trainers. There is demand for standardisation and manuals.
2. Abuse, bad practice and problems. Polarisation between 'evangelists' and 'sceptics' (to borrow Musyoki's terms). Second and third generation problems coming to light. The originators and enthusiasts may react strongly, issue warnings and seek to assure quality.
3. Creativity, diversification, learning and changing leading to exponential uncontrolled spread, with mixed quality, but better performance based on core principles and practices, merging with other approaches, and local adaptation and ownership.

CLTS is straddling all three, and is in different phases in different countries and organisations. From PRA and Reflect we can learn the paramount need for openness, flexibility, communication and review and reflection. With CLTS, institutional forms for this will have to be improvised on the run. With both PRA and Reflect, a key aspect was continuous and intensive networking and sharing ideas, insights and practices.

Some might consider that the term 'CLTS' should only be used when six basic principles are followed:

- Community self-help action
- Hands-off triggering
- Facilitation, not teaching
- No standard designs
- Poorer and weaker people are helped by others

- No individual household hardware subsidy (IHHS).

2. Synergies with other approaches - There has been a stage when CLTS was seen by some to be competitive with other approaches, or a distraction from them. But there are often complementarities. Objectives are shared. CLTS is about behaviour change. All aspects of hygienic behaviour are implicated and can follow on from triggering. Faecal-oral transmission routes identified in participatory analysis include those through the hands. Handwashing is an integral part of triggering, for example in Zambia, with the recognition that without it people might not be eating one another's shit but still their own or their children's. The first immediate action after triggering is often digging pits. Complementary hygienic campaigns and actions may have preceded CLTS or may follow and be part of it. The question here is sequence and style of sharing information. A teaching and lecturing mode is inconsistent with a relationship of facilitating and making information available. The traditional approach of instructing people induces deference and diminishes self-help and contrasts with situations in which they come to their own conclusions. This is an area about which more needs to be known and understood. Synergies should be strong with approaches (sometimes described as ecological) in which faeces have economic value.

3. Scale, speed and quality - CLTS is now in widespread demand. Governments including those of Cambodia, Ethiopia and Indonesia are seeking to make CLTS into national programmes. Major international organisations have come to support and advocate CLTS. Early on, the Water and Sanitation Programme of the World Bank in South Asia was a champion and disseminator, leading the field. WaterAid, Plan International, and other INGOs have been changing their policies and practices to support and promote CLTS, country by country, in Asia and Africa, with support from their head offices. Most significantly, UNICEF, the largest and most influential player among the relevant aid agencies, has decisively begun the transformation of its policies and practices. In these organisations, resistance is on the wane and increasingly isolated in single country programmes and in pockets. In some countries, the demand for CLTS is escalating exponentially. Driven by its successes and its champions, and drawn by demand, CLTS has become part of the sanitation discourse and could be described now as a movement. Its spread seems to have a gathering momentum.

The problem and opportunity are to find ways to combine scale, speed and quality. The classic view is that there are trade-offs. ptimal scale and speed are difficult, even impossible, to judge with any confidence. A purist may argue for small, slow and beautiful. A policymaker may demand big and fast, unaware that it may be fatally flawed. The best for human wellbeing may lie in between, with trade-offs between scale and speed on the one hand, and quality on the other.

4. Creative diversity - With any PM, there is a temptation to codify and standardise, justifying this in the interests of quality. With Reflect, this was an own goal: a Mother Manual was produced and distributed, but soon abandoned when it was found to inhibit rather than promote good practice. Despite abuses, PRA survived and flourished with many applications, hybridisations and offshoots, including CLTS. There is a lesson from ActionAid's Accountability, Learning and Planning System (ALPS). The notes for the core of ALPS—the Participatory Review and Reflection Process—had at the head of every page 'Health Warning: Ideas and options only—innovate and learn'.

5. Sustainability: physical, social and policy—

Physical factors in sustainability include:

- collapse of the walls of a hole
- general collapse with flooding (Bangladesh) and/or a seasonally high
- water table
- damage to superstructure
- hole filling up
- smelly and unpleasant conditions especially when latrines are hurriedly constructed
- lack of water, or effort collecting it, when water is needed
- groundwater pollution
- progress up the ladder of improved forms of sanitation
- effectiveness of market supply of hardware after initial peak demand

Social factors in sustainability include:

- tensions over sharing latrines, including reluctance because of the speed of filling up
- taboos over joint use of latrines by certain family members
- reluctance to continue to help the poorest and weakest after the initial enthusiasm has passed
- unwillingness or lack of funds to empty latrines when they are

full (and when land for another hole is difficult to come by)

- weakening with time of community sanctions against those who practice OD

The environment of policies and practices affecting sustainability includes:

- individual household hardware subsidies in neighbouring areas arousing expectations, leading to demands and undermining self-help
- conflict or competition with other policies and practices
- didactic and criticising teaching styles in health extension
- All of these could undermine the spirit, energy and effectiveness of CLTS triggering and follow-up.

Innovating, Learning and Sharing in CLTS[9]

For the future, four key areas for innovating, learning and sharing, stand out: methodological development and action learning; creative innovation and critical awareness; learning alliances and networks; and seeding and strengthening CLTS as a movement.

1. *Methodological development and action learning.* All the aspects of sustainability above are potential subjects for research. For further methodological development and action learning, some priorities reinforced by findings and discussion at the December 2008 IDS conference are:

(i) *Helping the weaker and poorer.* How to facilitate analysis and action to encourage those who are stronger and better off to support and help those who are weaker and poorer. Research findings reveal both inspiring examples and serious problems.[10] Incorporating social mapping creatively into the post-triggering phase and post-ODF phases appears promising. This is a most vital and urgent area for innovation and learning.

(ii) *Minimising water contamination.* How to optimise the siting, depth and maintenance of toilets to minimise risks of contaminating water supplies; and introducing this into CLTS. This applies not just to CLTS but to all rural sanitation. Where conditions are suitable, the Arborloo is a promising winwin; its shallow pit and rapid composting reduce contamination of groundwater and at the same time contribute to agricultural and home garden production.

(iii) *Combining and sequencing.* How to combine and sequence complementary actions and approaches. Handwashing is already part of CLTS. The safe disposal of children's faeces is another priority. Throughout the challenge is to find an optimal balance of behaviour and attitudes between hands-off facilitation and providing information and advice.

(iv) *Sustained support and interventions.* How to follow up with communities that do not become ODF in a first phase, and post-ODF with those that do. This can entail, for example, participatory monitoring for sustainability, guarding against relapse, and encouraging movement up the sanitation ladder.

(v) *Initiating CLTS.* How to introduce CLTS into new countries, organisations and contexts. This includes practices and sequences for policy change, for finding and supporting champions, and for training and piloting CLTS.

2. *Creative innovation and critical awareness.* Methodological development and action learning, in the above five areas as in others, demand creative innovation and critical awareness. At the field level, identifying and embracing principles of CLTS can be the core of good practice as it spreads and develops, bearing in mind that principles themselves can evolve. At all levels, including policy influence, creative innovation includes inventing and adapting practice to overcome obstacles and shortcomings, and to suit local capacities and conditions.

Critical awareness for rapid and sensitive learning and change demands reflexivity—that is, being reflective about one's own mindset, predispositions and perceptions, embracing error, and learning from what works and what does not. The litmus test is behaviours, attitudes and processes that have good results, including being effective and equitable, optimising multiple trade-offs, and leading to dynamically sustainable outcomes.

3. *CLTS Learning Alliances and Networks.* In learning alliances actors and agencies network, share experiences and plan together. This can be through virtual communication, websites, and/or meeting together. The IDS website for CLTS www.communityledtotalsanitation.org is the principal resource at present for CLTS information and sources. In Ethiopia, for five years, and preceding the introduction of CLTS but now embracing it, there has been an annual meeting of IRC, Plan Ethiopia and others to share experiences and findings from action research. More recently in the UK, an informal CLTS Action and Learning Group has been meeting, hosted each time by a different agency, and taking turns in recording learning and action alliances can be at different levels depending on scale—whether national, regional/provincial or district or some combination—and can evolve to be optimally inclusive, for example with complementary programmes.

4. *Seeding and strengthening CLTS as a movement.* Movements are typically self-spreading. Seeking to seed CLTS to become self-spreading has been on the agenda for over five years. A few cases are reported where Natural Leaders are strongly motivated, as reported in western Kenya, or are trained and then contracted, for example by local government as intended in Pakistan and as researched in Bangladesh. Also promising is Indonesia where CLTS is government policy, there is no hardware subsidy and budgets are decentralised to districts. There 'stakeholders agree that CLTS has the potential to spread spontaneously in the densely populated Java and Bali islands'.[11] Elsewhere, existing social movements present an opportunity that has not yet been explored. Women's organisations and movements may have special promise. An example of what can happen is the spread of Non-Pesticidal Management recently in three years from 225 acres to 700,000 in Andhra Pradesh through action by the federation of women's self-help groups known as the Mandal Mahila Samakhya.[12] Could this movement, and others, go from strength to strength by adding CLTS to their activities?

Challenges and Misconceptions Regarding Toilet Sanitation[13]

Research in India over the past decade offers useful insights on factors leading to the persistence of open defecation and non-adoption of safe hygiene practices.

- Open defecation is a socially accepted traditional behaviour. Many households and Communities consider toilets unclean and the availability of open defecation fields in rural areas supports the continuation of such a belief. The major challenge is to *Change behaviours* established over centuries which have resulted in open defecation being considered socially acceptable. It is not.
- Lack of awareness of the linkages between using a toilet, the safe disposal of faces and hygiene and health. Improved sanitation is not prioritised in many households and the links between open defecation and common diseases, including diarrhea are not understood. Practicing open defecation creates an environment where disease transmission takes place and it is young children in particular who pay the highest price. Over 80 per cent of all deaths due to diarrhea among children under-

five years of age are *directly attributable* to poor sanitation, unsafe drinking water and unhygienic practices. However, most communities do not view diarrhea as life threatening.

- Acceptance of open defecation means that girls and women remain *"imprisoned by daylight."* In the absence of toilets girls and women (be they daughters, wives, mothers, aunts, grandmothers or nieces) are forced to wait for early morning or late at night to defecate. This sees them vulnerable to harassment, rape, disease and Accidents, for example, snake bite.
- Child faeces are considered to be harmless. Many fathers, mothers and caregivers do not perceive child faeces as harmful. It is common practice to throw faeces out in the open and not ensuring its proper disposal. Caregivers also fail to wash their hands with soap after handling and cleaning soiled babies and infants. According to UNICEF IYS Fact Sheet 2008 One Gram of Faces Contains - 10,000,000 viruses; 1,000,000 bacteria; 1000 parasite cysts
- A significant gap exists between knowledge and practice. Even when people are aware of the health risks related to poor sanitation—and specifically not using a toilet, and critical hygiene behaviours—they *continue* with unhealthy practices.
- Access to a toilet does not always mean it is used or maintained. Ownership of a toilet does not always lead to better adoption of sanitation and hygiene practices. Often faulty design, lack of proper maintenance, lack of knowledge about proper toilet usage and insufficient running water in the vicinity raises dissatisfaction levels, resulting in a return to open defecation. Along with highlighting the relevant benefits of constructing toilets there is an *urgent* need to provide information about the availability of improved and affordable design options and how these can easily be maintained.
- It is considered totally acceptable for some people in society not to have a toilet. Although access to improved sanitation is increasing the gains are *highly inequitable.* Households below the poverty line exhibit least access to sanitation—including use of a toilet. Extending sanitation to the poorest, second and third poorest quintile of the population must be done if India is to make progress in terms of equity and targets.

Contrastingly, more people practice open defecation in India than anywhere in the world—more than 600 million individuals. Although access to improved sanitation is steadily increasing in India since the year 2000 the pace of change is too slow. If the current trend continues,

India will miss the Millennium Development Goal (MDG) target for sanitation, and without India the world will not be able to achieve its targets. Clearly accelerating access to and use of toilets and hygiene practices have become a national priority for India.

To accelerate the process the Ministry of Drinking Water and Sanitation (MDWS) along with UNICEF and other partners have developed the National Sanitation and Hygiene Advocacy and Communication Strategy Framework for 2012-2017. The overall goal is to make sure that people have access to, *and use a toilet* and practice good hygiene, including hand washing with soap after the toilet and before food. The strategy focuses on increasing knowledge and perceived importance of sanitation and hygiene practices, with the long term objective of changing the way society thinks so that open defecation is no longer acceptable in India.

The Advocacy and Communication Strategy focuses on four critical sanitation and hygiene behaviour:[14]

1. Building *and* use of toilets,
2. The safe disposal of child feces,
3. Hand washing with soap after defecation, before food and after handling child faces, and
4. Safe storage and handling of drinking water.

The Communication Strategy is divided into three phases, each with specific communication objectives. It clearly defines,

- The audience receiving the information (the who);
- The content of the information (the what)
- The methods to be used to convey the information (the how); and
- The approaches to promote action for change (the action).

This is *achieved through advocacy,* interpersonal communication and community mobilisation with overall multi-media support including mass media, digital media and social media. A detailed implementation framework lists out the key audiences, the activities to be used with each of them and the communication tools required. A preliminary monitoring and evaluation framework with regular assessments allows for local modification and refinement of the strategy. Indicators for each of the phases are organised at three levels–outcome, output and process.

A District Communication Plan Template supports the overall framework. It outlines the steps required for the development of a

Communication Action Plan and for roll out at the district, block and village/GP level.

Using the Sanitation and Hygiene Advocacy and Communication Strategy Framework Document:

Developed through a consultative process, the Sanitation and Hygiene Advocacy and Communication Strategy 2012-2017 is a framework to guide the execution of advocacy and communication efforts related to toilet construction and use and key critical sanitation and hygiene behaviours at the national, state and district level, including:

National Level

- Increasing population-wide and mass awareness of the importance of using a toilet and practicing good hygiene, with an emphasis on the positive outcomes for health.

State Level

- Contextualising the national framework to a state-specific strategy with implementation plans to roll out the four critical sanitation and hygiene behaviours at scale.
- Using a Menu of Activities at each Phase within the Implementation Framework to reach different audience segments within the population. This will take account of different socio-cultural and geographic diversities, focus audiences, media penetration and reach.

District Level

- Using the District Communication Plan Template to develop a Communication Action Plan at district level for the roll out of this action plan. This will include identifying who will be responsible for driving the communication activities and capacity building at different levels and the communication tools required, together with the tentative cost for the communication activities and tools.
- Undertaking monitoring and evaluation based on an agreed matrix and taking corrective actions.

Successful Community-designed, Built and Managed Toilet Blocks in India[15]

The Government of India has promoted various models of household toilets for safe disposal in rural areas depending on leach pit technology (GOI 2003). In general, all the models are similar, where water and urine are usually absorbed through the pores of the pit and solid material gets decomposed into manure. This technology maintains the system under hygienic conditions, free from odour and insect nuisance. The quality and design of the pan is the important item of the toilet. There are various designs of pans available on the market. Flat types of pans are not suitable for leach pit toilets due to the low gradient. They need lots of water and the pit fills up quickly. However, experts are of the opinion that a sanitary pan with a high gradient is technologically more suited for rural areas because it has the following advantages: (i) less water consumption for immediate flushing; (ii) easy disposal of waste; and (iii) the pit does not fill up easily (GOI 2003).

The construction of a toilet block includes digging the pit and installing a squatting plate or bowl. The pour flush toilet used in villages of the study area in Gujarat is composed of a circular pit (area 25 ft) lined with a supporting honeycomb of bricks and cement. The uncemented bottom lets water seep into the ground. Since the study area is located in the drylands of western India with low rainfall, the seeping fluid reaches only a few feet radius from the septic tank. Thus it usually dries without contaminating nearby farms and water systems. The negative impact of having this type of cheaper toilet is minimal since the area is predominantly dry land with very low annual rainfall (300 to 1000 mm) and the ground water level is deep, almost 300 ft below ground. The squatting plate and toilet bowl is fixed on top. Different superstructures can be built on top, but the toilets in this study included a concrete room around the toilet. This low-cost toilet is estimated to last for 10 to 15 years, after which people have to dig up the manure and renovate the pit again or construct another pit nearby. Humans produce a cubic foot of dry waste a year, becoming manure in about two years; it can be used as organic manure in agricultural fields.

Three Indian organisations in community-designed, built and managed toilet blocks that now serve more than half a million low-income urban dwellers in eight cities in India. These three organisations are SPARC, the National Slum Dwellers Federation and Mahila Milan. SPARC is an Indian NGO established in Mumbai in 1984 that began working with women pavement dwellers. The National Slum Dwellers Federation (NSDF) links together and represents organisations and federations of slum dwellers throughout India and, by March 2002, was operating in 52 cities and nine states with over 750,000 members. The largest membership is in Mumbai where 250,000 households are members. Mahila Milan ("women together") is the name given to collectives of women slum and pavement dwellers that work closely with the National Slum Dwellers Federation. The community toilet blocks are part of a larger programme of work in which the SPARC–NSDF–Mahila Milan Alliance is involved. It includes community managed resettlement programmes, slum rehabilitation programmes (for instance, the construction of apartment blocks in Dharavi, Mumbai's largest and perhaps most dense slum, to allow housing improvements without displacing any inhabitants) and housing programmes for pavement and slum dwellers.[16]

In Indian cities, what little investment that has been made in sanitation in low-income areas has generally been through local bodies (slum boards, housing authorities, development authorities and Municipal Corporations) building public toilet blocks; these bodies are also meant to maintain them. But the number of toilet blocks built in any year does not seem to be based on an assessment of need in relation to the population or on available budgetary resources. The need is far greater than what is planned for, even though resources allocated for sanitation often remain underutilised.

For the toilet blocks that are built, the traditional method has been for the corporation to estimate the construction costs according to a government schedule of rates, and then to call for tenders from contractors. Generally, the engineering wings of local bodies deal with these matters, and there is rarely any consultation with inhabitants regarding the location, design, construction and provision for maintenance. The agencies responsible for construction and maintenance generally have little accountability to the communities in which they build, and there is no sense of ownership among the inhabitants or their organisations for the new toilet blocks. The quality of toilet construction (undertaken by contractors) is often poor and the design often inappropriate—for instance, with limited water supplies so the toilets get blocked and dirty, and with no access to drainage.

The public toilet blocks are often in serious disrepair within three months of being constructed, leaving people with little or no alternative but to defecate in the open. The space around the public toilets often becomes heavily used for open defecation which, in turn, produces a very large health burden and contributes to high infant and child death rates. Toilet blocks also become places where household wastes are dumped, since communities often have no garbage collection. Women suffer most from having no accessible and safe toilet. To protect their modesty, they often wait until nightfall to defecate in the open—but this need to wait until dark also causes widespread gastric disorders.

Various organisations such as charitable trusts, NGOs, international agencies and local business associations (such as Rotary

Clubs) have had some involvement in "toilets for the poor" projects. They often build "pay-and-use" toilets. In many cities, there are agencies that function as contractors, construct sanitation facilities and appoint caretakers to keep the facilities clean. User charges help to pay the salaries of caretakers and cleaners, provide materials and cover maintenance. These public toilets work well in large concourses such as railway stations and bus stops, but are not a workable solution in slums because of the high prices charged.

It is found that some of the earliest experiences with community toilet blocks took place in Mumbai, Kanpur and Bangalore between 1988 and 1996; community toilets were also being built during these years in Hyderabad and Lucknow. The construction of these community toilet blocks was usually preceded by community-managed slum surveys to demonstrate the need and the inadequacy of public provision.

SPARC in Mumbai

In 1985, as the women pavement dwellers in central Mumbai began to discuss their needs and priorities with SPARC, access to water and toilets was one of the most common themes. The pavement dwellers had no place to defecate and no legal access to water. Many of the women worked as servants in nearby houses, and so used their employers' toilet facilities, or they defecated in the open or into newspaper and threw it away. As noted earlier, women often waited until nightfall to defecate. Not surprisingly, good provision for water and sanitation was a high priority. These women recognised that, even if toilets in each home were preferable, the size of most homes (usually less than 100 square feet or ten square metres) made this unrealistic. The toilet would also have to be next to the "wet area", where washing, laundry and cooking took place—and the women knew that their irregular water supplies would make it difficult to keep toilets clean. They also recognised that community toilets were much cheaper per household served, and that community toilets could include large tanks to ensure regular water supplies.

When they suggested that community processes could result in better quality, better designed community toilets at a lower unit cost, they were ignored. International donors were approached for support but they lacked the mechanisms to fund such a project. The Alliance decided to build some toilet blocks, drawing funding from the UK charity Homeless Internationals.

Source: For details see Sundar Burra, Sheela Patel and Thomas Kerr, Community-designed, built and managed toilet blocks in Indian cities, Environment and Urbanisation 2003, 15:11

Community Toilets in Bangalore

The first community-built toilet block was in Doddigunte in Banglore city, with work beginning in 1994. This is a large and fairly recent settlement of 375 houses at the city limits. It is a "declared slum", and most people have identity cards from the slum clearance board. Only a few hand pumps serve the 2,000 inhabitants and, although a sewer line runs along one side of the settlement, there were no toilets. People were defecating in nearby fields but, as development in surrounding areas was intensifying, it was getting increasingly difficult to do so, especially for women as they sought private places to squat. With 20,000 rupees start-up money from SPARC, a group of residents started building a communal toilet.

The second community-built toilet was a modest four-seat toilet in Basha Compound, serving 30 houses. The four pour-flush latrines drained into a small brick-lined soakpit and then into a drain, as there were no sewers to connect to. The toilets were entirely community-built, with the enthusiastic involvement of women who dug, mixed concrete and carried bricks. The construction took ten days and cost 3,000 rupees.

Source: For details see Sundar Burra, Sheela Patel and Thomas Kerr, Community-designed, built and managed toilet blocks in Indian cities, Environment and Urbanisation 2003, 15:11

Problems and Prospects of Toilets in Rural India[17]

When the Sadguru Foundation started building toilets in villages during 2001, it gave a 90 per cent subsidy from funds raised through the European Commission and people paid 10 per cent from their savings. During the second year, the government of Gujarat provided an 80 per cent subsidy with 20 per cent contributions from people. The following year, the government reduced the subsidy to 50 per cent while the rest was covered by the people. It certainly showed the growing interest from rural people to build their own toilets. The awareness and education programs targeted at the grassroots ultimately changed the mindset of the people.

In 2007, the government of Gujarat announced the Nirmal Gram Award to honour tribal villages where all households have toilets. Subsequently, five of the 12 villages where the Sadguru Foundation had built toilets received the highest sanitation honour from the President of India. The award included a citation, certificate and cash incentive of USD 2000–8000, depending on the size of the village.

Motivated by the award, the Presidents of Village Councils declared that all households must have toilets in their villages to qualify for government grants, subsidies, children education funds, bank loans, and so on. Despite this aggressive approach by village leaders, the progress has been slow at the grassroots because poverty is rampant in tribal areas—people could no longer afford to construct toilets without adequate government subsidies. Regardless of India's middle and upper classes' prosperity in recent years due to the booming economy, poverty remains a serious stumbling block for growth in rural areas. The World Bank estimates that 450 million people live below the poverty line in India, while the country is projected to be the world's most populous nation by 2050, with 1.6 billion people.

The major downside of India's rural development strategy is the historic neglect of catchment areas in remote drylands where the tribals have lived for centuries (Jagawat 2005).[18] The area, roughly 950 miles long and 350 miles wide, stretching across central India starting from Dungarpur in the west and going to Dumka in the east, provides brilliant prospects for sustainable development work to relieve poverty (Jagawat 2005). The above region covers 70 per cent of India's tribal populations, spread across 100 districts, representing one of the largest concentrations of Asia's rural poverty. India's tribal communities are the poorest since they have less access to public services in health, education and commerce (Phansalkar and Verma 2005).[19] From the government's point of view, a single tribal settlement is too small to economically justify a school or a health centre and the poor infrastructure in villages makes other facilities elsewhere difficult to access, but now most villages have substandard schools. Furthermore, the low density of the tribal people and the lack of purchasing power make village business not at all feasible. Within the economic rankings of the traditional Indian caste system, tribes are beneath even untouchables, thus the most economically and socially downtrodden (Agoramoorthy and Hsu 2006).[20] The Indian constitution of 1950 singled them out for preferential treatment, in a kind of permanent affirmative action plan, but the government has not done enough in a half century. Most of India's 70 million tribal people are illiterate, with short life expectancy compared to other castes. So no strategy of rural development can succeed that neglects India's ignored tribal populations that are scattered throughout the harsh drylands (Agoramoorthy 2008).[21]

Toilet as Changing Agent[22]

The humble toilet can speed social development in a number of ways:

(a) By aiding progress towards gender equality: Poor women and girls are hit hardest by the absence of toilets. They care for the sick and are in greatest physical contact with human waste. Lacking toilets in overcrowded slums means going the whole day without relieving oneself and then risking exposure—or even assault—at night, a humiliating daily routine that can damage health. Menstruation adds considerably to the need for sanitary facilities.

Sexual harassment and rape are also a risk in rural areas, where women often seek privacy in the darkness, and in refugee camps, which all too often fail to provide safely located, women-only toilets. These realities absorb women's time, imperil their physical well-being, and limit their free and equal participation on in the economic and social life of their societies.

(b) By promoting social inclusion: Poverty is more than a lack of income or a shortage of material goods. Human poverty, the lack of basic capabilities for participating in the standard activities of the community, is greatly exacerbated by lack of sanitation. For urban slum dwellers, living surrounded by human waste and garbage is stigmatising and marginalising, creating embarrassment and depriving people of participation, choices and opportunities. Around 800,000 people in India still live by personally removing faeces from other people's latrines, taking it away in baskets on their heads, a livelihood that bars their inclusion in mainstream society.

(c) By increasing school attendance: Nearly RPP million school-days would be gained each year if the sanitation goal were met. In addition, most schools in the developing world are built without sanitation and hand-washing facilities. Where no toilet block is set aside for girls, parents often won't allow their daughters to attend school, especially once they have started menstruating and need somewhere discrete to change and dispose of used cloths. This fuels the discrepancy in primary school completion rates: one in four girls do not complete primary school, compared to one in seven boys. In Alwar District, India, school sanitation increased girls' enrolment by one-third, and improved academic performance for boys and girls by RU per cent.

(d) By building community pride and social cohesion: When families and influential local figures focus on ending open defecation, the condition of the whole community can be transformed. Pride in keeping paths and streets unsoiled can help build and maintain community morale. The need for sanitation and self respect from a clean environment has provided incentives for a transformation of local governance; sanitary reform has historically been the starting point for civic improvement. Recent efforts in Bangladesh and India have resulted in significant numbers of rural communities declaring themselves "open defecation- free"—meaning that the entire community have jointly committed to eliminate open defecation and use basic covered latrines. Once new standards are the norm, social attitudes change, and families may not be willing to marry their daughters into households without proper toilets. In fact, in some villages in Maharashtra, the first Indian state to pilot an approach centred on ending open defecation, residents have painted signs that read: "Daughters from our village are not married into villages where open defecation is practiced."

(e) By contributing to poverty eradication: Poor sanitation is often a symptom of poverty; in Vietnam, hardly anyone from the poorest income quintile has a toilet, but WP per cent of those in the richest quintile do. It also causes poverty by making people ill, reducing their productivity and incomes, and by forcing them to use their time unproductively, either waiting to use public toilets or, in the case of open defecation, searching for seclusion. The chief asset a poor person has is often his or her physical health and resulting ability to work; illness robs the poor of this asset while also diverting scant resources from critical areas like education.

In Indian context, the establishment of community toilet blocks was seen as a tool for social change on following parameters:

- **To bring communities together** - Toilets can bring people together; everyone uses them and has opinions about them. A toilet project is small enough to be planned and built within a small budget and time frame but big enough to start many things happening, including involving women, allowing people to work together, to tap skills in the community, to manage money and, finally, to enjoy defecating in private. If you have squatted along an open drain all your life, it is hard to imagine toilets being clean places. If they are clean and well-cared for, they become points of congregation.
- **To test new pro-poor policies** - Given the lack of provision for sanitation in cities, this was an important chance to advocate for and test new pro-poor policies.
- **To expand livelihood options** - This was the first time that many poor communities were involved on this scale. Although the poor are constantly involved in informal petty construction, there is never space and resources for their more formal

participation. The construction and management of the toilet blocks expanded their livelihood options and developed their skills.

- **Changing national policies** - The Alliance also seeks to change attitudes and policies at the level of the national government. It worked with the United Nations Human Settlements Programme to launch a good governance campaign in 2000, and the National Slum Dwellers Federation demanded that sanitation be seen as an indicator of good governance, especially women and children's access to it. Good governance is also about choices regarding investment priorities. The Indian government has now introduced a new programme—the Nirmal Bharat Abhiyan—where a 50 per cent subsidy for the construction of community toilets is available to local bodies and public authorities. This was influenced by the community toilets built in Pune and Mumbai.
- **Making room for communities to learn by experimenting and by making mistakes -** Solutions to complicated problems do not happen quickly, and generally come from trial and error. Learning for any individual generally means having to do something more than once and making mistakes before finally getting it right. This is also true for poor communities, where solutions are a lot more complicated. To those mistrustful of community involvement in urban improvement, mistakes only confirm entrenched attitudes that poor people are ignorant or lazy. Built into many community participation programmes is an "only one chance" clause, which does not allow the learning and training capital, produced by mistakes to be reinvested in new processes. Instead, it stops participation at the first sign of error. Poor communities are unable to experiment because they have no margin within their limited resources to absorb mistakes. This is one of the crises of poverty, and this is why these toilet projects make room for, and even encourage, mistakes.
- **People on the move: training others and breaking isolation -** People in communities that have built their own toilets are the best teachers for others interested in doing the same. Whether or not their project was successful, their experience can give a head start to other communities who do not have to start from scratch every time. In order for skills to be refined and spread around, it is important that as many people as possible visit the toilets, participate in their building, and return to their own settlements stocked with new ideas. In this way, the learning potential of

these experiences is maximised, and their successes and failures are discussed and digested by many others.

- **Don't waste time waiting for ideal conditions -** None of these toilet blocks are perfect. Most were built under circumstances that could be considered impossible. But every toilet block represents a vital investment in learning and human capacity. These are the building blocks of large scale change, much more than perfect designs or innovative engineering.
- A sharp city administrator would have difficulty in ignoring these features:
    - sharing costs with a community reduces the city's sanitation cost burden;
    - when communities build toilets, the city's construction burden is eliminated;
    - When communities maintain the toilets, the city's maintenance costs are eliminated and
    - community-built toilets often cost less than those the city builds, so a city's infrastructure budgets can be spread further, increasing service delivery.

Role of NGO's in Sanitation

NGOs and local governments are very different in terms of their ethos, ways of working and staffing, and are subjected to very different conditioning factors across a range of sectors. Reconciling such differences has been difficult for many NGOs that work with local government, often leading to tensions and non-productive engagement. In community-based sanitation service delivery, there are considerable potential advantages for both NGOs and local governments in working together more effectively, in terms of complementary roles

For the sanitation sector in South Asia, a limited field of the programmes of collaboration between governments and NGOs was available for research, although there were more cases in Bangladesh where NGOs are more prominent in the sector.[23]

NGOs that work in urban sanitation often focus on serving low-income and informal areas where government investments are limited. Community-based sanitation programmes have emerged in poorer communities, particularly in South Asia, in response to such a lack of investment.

Such programmes have common characteristics such as the following:

- a focus on removing the need for open defecation;
- an emphasis on promoting sanitation to generate demand;
- participatory working with community groups in project areas including joint planning of the new services and
- capacity building for sustainable management of the sanitation facilities created.

Technical Aspects

In South Asia, many people lack access to basic sanitation and resort to open defecation; 705 million people practice open defecation in rural areas and 74 million in urban areas (UN, 2009).[24] The cost of conventional sewerage and wastewater treatment is substantial. Such services have been unaffordable in most developing countries, so cheaper service options have been pursued in recent decades. Sewers are used mainly in commercial and higher income areas in urban areas, whereas septic tanks, low-cost sewerage and public/community toilet blocks are more common in low and middle income areas. In rural areas, various forms of latrine are widely used. Although more choice has been provided through these cheaper technical options, sanitation programmes that relied in the past on implementation by actors from outside the community and focused on subsidising the 'hardware' of sanitation have not been sustainable. This is because they failed to create sufficient demand for such sanitation services, particularly amongst the poor (Chambers, 2009a). The reported rate of non-use of toilets built under a subsidised national Indian sanitation programme was 50 per cent (Government of India, 2003).[25] More recently, there has been growing realisation by governments, development agencies and civil society of the importance of sanitation and the fact that a government cannot deliver against agreed targets on its own but has to work with non-state providers. This is reflected in the increased funding for sanitation and in government policies that acknowledge the importance of non-state providers such as NGOs and private sectors. The policy commitment is evident in the more recent national policy documents in each country that deal with sanitation and working with civil society.

Economic and Social Aspects

Poor sanitation causes sickness, inability to work and high healthcare expenditure that collectively undermine livelihoods. It impacts on the education of children and causes women suffering, embarrassment and inconvenience (Chambers, 2009b). Governments, therefore, have good reasons to promote sanitation and persuade households to invest in it to achieve the public good benefits. Yet local governments rarely have dedicated staff or departments that can promote sanitation on a sustained basis. This vacuum has led to NGOs filling, to some extent, the gap in government sanitation services, where capable NGOs are willing and able to take on this challenging work. Cultural and attitudinal barriers pose challenges to the adoption of modern sanitation practices, let alone to the operation and management of community-based schemes. In many parts of South Asia, open defecation is a longstanding and socially sanctioned practice. The implementation of community-based schemes is bound to suffer if the delivery of physical infrastructure is stressed without addressing the attitudes that are not conducive to its proper use (Jha, 2010). Thus, effective sanitation promotion and working with communities can enable more effective and sustainable sanitation in poorer communities. NGOs that have previously worked intensively in such communities, often on broader urban or rural development issues, are often well placed to work on community sanitation improvements if they are motivated to work in this sub-sector.

Institutional Aspects

Sanitation is usually not regarded as a service sector in its own right but as a sub-sector of water supply. It has generally been combined with water supply in terms of government responsibilities and project design, but water supply is invariably given more priority under such arrangements. To complicate matters further, it is also often regarded as part of the health sector, in terms of primary health care, but government health staff tends to focus more on curative care. Urban sanitation is also often addressed as part of wider urban development, particularly in poorer urban areas, through slum improvement programmes and the like. Consequentially, sanitation generally has no clear institutional home in government and is often addressed through programmes across several departments.

Sulabh International Social Service Organisation: An Exemplification of Toilet as a Catalyst to Change[26]

Sanitation is a basic condition for development. It is not only the problem of keeping clean; it is also an economic and social problem of raising production and promoting a good life. A concern for sanitation involves not only the waste disposal systems, water supply and sewerage networks but also our rich ecological heritage. It is interesting to note that Modern civilisation has increased rather than lessened the problem of scavenging.

Despite the importance of toilets for health, people still build houses without them, which can indicate skewed attitudinal and cultural preferences. Official agencies are also to blame since they do not give sufficient stress to sanitation, especially toilet facilities, when building community houses. There are also economic and technological difficulties for sanitation programmes, for instance, a sewage system is very costly and may not be sustainable. In India, there is neither enough water in rivers to flush out city effluents nor enough money to set up sewage treatment plants.

Low sanitation coverage in India is primarily due to insufficient motivation/awareness by people and a lack of affordable sanitation technology. Most of these people are from lower socio-economic groups and are not aware of the health and environmental benefits of sanitation. It is still not seen as a high priority, resulting in absence of people's participation. The lack of choice of toilet design, area-specific technologies, inadequate supporting delivery systems and absence of trained masons, skilled workers and technical manpower are also important for low coverage. Additionally, by tradition, Indian society and culture value personal hygiene, but give little importance to a clean and healthy community environment. Human excreta are regarded as the most hated object, and anything connected with latrines is considered so defiling because of psychological and religious taboos that a person is supposed to take a bath immediately after using a latrine and before going into a kitchen. Sanitation is regarded as a matter of individual initiative and not as a collective obligation of the community. In this socio-cultural background, environmental sanitation has been given the lowest priority.

In developed countries, the standard solution for the sanitary disposal of human waste is through sewerage systems. However, septic tanks have not been widely accepted, partly due to high costs and other limitations. Furthermore, after the tank is filled, it contains fresh and degraded excreta mixed with water. Since there is no mechanical means easily available to empty the tank, it is cleaned manually by scavengers, which is an unhygienic process. The Government of India has forbidden the practice of scavenging, but unless the technology of the septic tank is completely banned, it would be very difficult to ban the practice of scavenging. Even after the septic tank is emptied mechanically, sludge effluent has to be kept in ditches for at least two years before it becomes free from pathogens, which is a very cumbersome and time-consuming process. Generally, such untreated human waste along with water is discharged into an open drain or onto the soil surface causing nuisance, health hazards and environmental pollution.

(a) Sulabh sanitation movement

The Sulabh sanitation movement arose out of a concern for sanitation, ecology and scavengers. Sulabh is an extension of the movement which Gandhiji launched to liberate scavengers from having to carry excreta in baskets on their heads. Since then, much has been done. The founder Prof. Bindeshwar Pathak developed a low-cost, affordable, culturally appropriate technology that did not need emptying by scavengers - the Sulabh two-pit pourflush water-seal toilet system. This system has been installed in more than one million households and is used in over 3,000 community toilets.

It is now being used by about 10 million people everyday. The World Bank, UNESCO and other agencies and institutions in India and abroad have approved Sulabh technology for adoption in South Asian countries. Sulabh toilets function independently of the city sewerage system and, to that extent, the rivers are not polluted. Nor is there a need to build treatment plants or expand the sewerage network, both of which are very expensive.

The Objectives of the Sulabh sanitation movement are broadly two-fold. First, to *restore human rights and dignity to scavengers.* This includes liberating the scavengers from the unhealthy and sub-human occupation of manually handling excreta by converting bucket privies into Sulabh *shauchalayas* (pourflush toilets with two pits for on-site disposal of human waste). It also means ensuring that the former scavengers and their wards get training in other occupations, thus helping in their social upgrading and their promotion as equals in society. This requires the setting up of information and employment exchange centres and helping scavengers obtain employment either in government or non-government organisations. Scavengers have also been supported in building their houses away from slums.

Second, *to prevent environmental pollution.* Sulabh seeks to:

- educate people not to defaecate in the open, in lanes, by-lanes, parks, streets, by the sides of roads or railway tracks;
- motivate people to convert bucket privies into Sulabh *shauchalayas* and to have toilet facilities in their houses;
- provide community toilets with bathing, washing, and urinal facilities on a pay and use basis in slums, and also for pavement dwellers, rickshaw pullers, any "floating" population and for those communities in whose houses toilets cannot be constructed due to space constraints;
- persuade people to plant at least five trees per family and also plant trees around public toilets for the protection of environment;
- harness non-conventional energy sources from human waste and save fuel and forests;

- procure manure from Sulabh *shauchalayas* and use it to increase farm productivity;
- promote job oriented education and primary health care;
- form groups of people from all walks of life throughout the country and abroad to build public opinion against social evils and for the cause of the economically poor and neglected sections of society;
- create new employment avenues by training change agents for integrated rural development; and
- promote consultancy, research and development in technical and social fields. Also, promote diffusion of innovations, education, motivation and awareness through mass communication.

The Sulabh International Social Service Organisation is the leading non-profit outfit working to promote sanitation and prevent environmental pollution, both of which are critical components to a healthy and productive society. Growing urbanisation has helped to produce serious house shortages, forcing people to live in shanty colonies without toilet facilities. From its beginnings in a small town in the state of Bihar, Sulabh now works virtually all over India with the help of a large work force of nearly 50,000 committed volunteers belonging to various disciplines including administrators, financial and management experts, engineers, architects, sociologists, scientists and media persons. It is one of the largest non-government organisations (NGO) in the world.

The Sulabh human waste disposal system is a radical departure from the conventional sewage system and is eminently suitable for use in both individual and cluster houses. The advent of Sulabh International in the field of sanitation in 1970 gave new impetus to the sanitation movement by evolving a low-cost pour-flush water-seal toilet with two pits for on-site disposal of human waste as an alternative to bucket latrines. Thus, it abolished the need for the manual handling of human waste. Sulabh has also been able to improve environmental sanitation and community health and hygiene.

The Sulabh toilet system is a cost-effective and most appropriate technology option. It needs only one-fifth of the water of conventional toilets - only two litres in comparison to the ten litres used by the conventional water closets (WC) - and thus conserves water, which is scarce in most African, Asian and Latin American countries. The system is also much cheaper than using sewers and septic tanks, and the toilets built on Sulabh technology have a large variety of designs to suit different income levels, topographical terrains and local resources. The system is economically and socio-culturally acceptable to the people. It is free from foul odours and can be built using locally available materials. It is easy to build and can be maintained by the homeowners themselves and, with a high potential for upgrading, it can also be easily connected to sewers, if sewers are introduced into the area. It does not need the emptying services of scavengers and the two pits work alternately for several years. The system also makes available high quality manure which is a good soil conditioner.

(b) Sulabh Shauchalaya (twin-pit pour-flush toilet)

Sulabh Shauchalaya is a pour-flush water-seal twin-pit toilet, which is technically appropriate, socio-culturally acceptable and economically affordable. It uses indigenous technology and can easily be used to construct latrines and from local materials and using local labourers. The toilet provides all the health benefits for safe disposal of human excreta on-site, requires only 1.5-2 l of water for flushing, thus conserving water, and does not need the services of scavengers to clean the pits.

(c) Two-pit pour-flush toilet

There are two pits, the size and capacity of which vary according to the number of users. Each pit is generally used for three years, after which use it is switched to the other. If one of the pits becomes full during this time excreta are diverted into the second pit. Within a two year rest period, the sludge is digested and becomes almost dry and pathogen-free, and is thus safe for handling as manure. Digested sludge is odourless and is a good manure and soil conditioner. It can be dug out easily and used for agricultural purposes. The Sulabh Shauchalaya can also be constructed on the upper floors of buildings, and easily upgraded and connected to sewers if these are introduced into the area. To date, Sulabh has constructed more than one million individual household toilets in different parts of the country.

Two-pit pour-flush toilet

(d) Sulabh public toilet complexes

Provision of public toilet complexes in public places and in slums on a pay and use basis marked an important point for Sulabh's community health, hygiene and environmental sanitation. As far back as 1878, the then Bengal Government had passed a law to set up toilet facilities in Calcutta, but for various reasons such facilities were either not provided or poorly maintained. From 1878 to 1973, public toilets were not seen by the authorities as being practical. The concept of implementation of public toilets and their maintenance on a pay and use basis, originated in 1974 in Sulabh and was highly successful throughout the country. For some years, studies were made of the attitudes and reasons why people did not use public toilets in cities and towns. Results showed that the unsanitary and neglected state of public toilets deterred people from using them. It was felt that along with the community toilets, if facilities for bathing and washing clothes were also provided and above all kept clean, and then people would have no hesitation in using them and paying for their use.

To date, Sulabh has constructed more than 5,500 of these toilet complexes in various parts of the country, where maintenance is provided both day and night. These complexes are located in public places, including bus stands, hospitals, markets and in slum areas. For the construction, operation and maintenance of these complexes, the organisation plays the role of catalyst and partner between official agencies and the users of the toilet complexes.

(e) Sulabh public toilet

The Sulabh complexes are manned by attendants day and night, and have separate enclosures for men and women. For washing hands, soap powder is provided for users. The system of operation and maintenance of community toilets evolved by the organisation has proved a boon for local authorities in their endeavour to keep the towns clean and improve the environment. This is a unique example of partnership of local authorities, non-governmental organisations and the community. The cost of individual Sulabh toilets varies from US$10 to US$1000 making them affordable for every economic group of people.

(f) Self-sustaining Public Toilets

Sulabh's innovativeness is best demonstrated in the public toilet system operated on a pay-and-use basis which can be self-sustaining from the funding that customers generate. As well as the public toilets. Sulabh provides bathing, washing and urinal facilities with separate compartments for men and women. In some places, additional amenities such as a cloakroom, public telephone, primary health care, drinking water, schools for children in slums, etc., have also been provided. User charges are nominal, with the disabled, children and those who cannot pay allowed to use the facilities free; and the authorities do not have to provide funds for the maintenance of the public conveniences for a period of up to 30 years.

In addition, these toilet complexes have provided dignity and safety since they allow for private defaecation and bathing. This is especially important for women, who are the greatest beneficiaries. Sulabh also plays the role of catalyst between and among government, local authorities and the users of community facilities.

(g) Sulabh biogas plant linked with public toilet

Based on the Sulabh model, over one hundred biogas plants of 35—60 cu m capacity have been constructed by Sulabh in different states of the country so far. Biogas from human excreta contains 65 – 66 per cent methane, 32–34 per cent carbon dioxide and residual amounts of hydrogen sulphide and other gases. Biogas is being used in a number of ways including cooking, lighting through mantle lamps, heating and electricity generation. A public convenience used by about 2,000 people daily produces approximately 60 cu m of biogas, which can run a 10 KVA generator for eight hours day, producing 65 kWh of energy. The electricity generated from the biogas is being supplied for use in places such as in toilet complexes, bus stands and public parks.

(h) Sulabh Effluent Treatment (SET) technology

Biogas produced from human excreta is used for a variety of purposes—cooking, lighting, heating and electricity generation. As well as biogas, digested effluent can be used as fertiliser, as it contains a high per centage of nitrogen, potassium and phosphate. At the same time, though, its aesthetically bad colour, odour and presence of pathogens limit its use for agricultural and horticultural purposes.

As Sulabh maintains more than 5,500 public toilet complexes throughout the country, over one hundred of which are linked to biogas plants, the organisation deemed it necessary to make the effluent free of odour, colour and pathogens so that it could be used safely for agricultural and aquacultural purposes. After a series of experiments, the organisation developed a new and convenient technology that turned effluent of human excreta from biogas plants into colourless, odourless and pathogen-free liquid manure. The technology is based on filtration of waste water through activated charcoal followed by ultraviolet light. The water from human waste has a Biological Oxygen Demand (BOD) of about 200 mg l71 that is reduced to less than 10 mg l71 after treatment, making it safe for agriculture, aquaculture or discharge into any expanse of water. It can also be used, for example, to clean the floors of public toilets in drought-prone areas, where Sulabh had until then to purchase water for maintenance of public toilets, thereby saving a substantial amount of money.

Sulabh Effluent Treatment (SET) technology to treat waste water

(i) Duckweed based waste water treatment

A major problem of waste-water treatment methods is that none of the current technologies have a direct economic return. Technologies currently available are unaffordable due to high capital and maintenance costs, which means that local authorities are generally not interested in taking up treatment of waste water. This causes severe health hazards and environmental pollution. Throughout the country, of about 4,700 towns and cities only about 232 have sewerage system and these are only partial. Most of the untreated waste water is discharged into rivers or other bodies of water. In rural areas, it is common practice to discharge waste water and sullage without even collecting, treating or even re-using waste water or sullage, as people are generally unaware of the technology.

Sulabh has successfully developed and demonstrated projects on duckweed based cost-effective waste-water treatment in rural as well as urban areas with direct economic return from pisci-culture. Although duckweed grows widely in ponds and ditches, the near complete absence of knowledge in this area means that the potential of duckweed, including its nutritional value and economic benefits, had not been exploited earlier.

(j) Impact and Spread

Sulabh has constructed and converted over one million household toilets and 3,154 public toilets, respectively, which are being used by 10 million people every day. Over 37,500 scavengers have been liberated from the task of manual scavenging and 3,500 wards and family members of the liberated scavengers have been given vocational training. As many as 240 towns in India have been made scavenging free and there has been a dramatic change in the physical environment of the towns where the Sulabh system is used. In towns which have become scavenging free, all dry (or bucket) household privies have been converted into the new twin-pit pour flush Sulabh toilets. The houses which had no latrine have been provided with sanitary toilets. For those who could not afford toilets, or where space was a constraint, well-managed community toilets have been provided. Thus, the dumping of fresh pathogenic night-soil has stopped, leading to an improvement in the physical environment.

(k) Liberation and rehabilitation of scavengers

The inhuman practices of manual cleaning and carrying human excreta from bucket privies by 'scavengers'—a particular class of people, has been practiced in India for a very long time. The two-pit pour-flush toilet, as outlined above, does not require scavengers to clean the pits as human excreta turns into an odourless, pathogen-free, semi-solid humus-like structure after a 2-year resting period, making it suitable for use in agriculture. The beneficiaries themselves can remove such manure with ease thereby making its use economical. The scavengers, newly liberated from this practice, are re-training in various market-oriented trades, becoming shorthand-users and typists, tailors, carpenters, electricians, drivers, beauticians, clothing designers, etc., enabling them to be self-employed or to obtain a job in government or private organisations. To date, Sulabh has made 240 towns scavenger-free in India, by liberating more than 60,000 scavengers from their degrading employment. From these, 4,000 have been trained in different trades by the organisation.

(l) Sulabh Centre for Action Sociology

The Sulabh Centre for Action Sociology was established to study social problems and to find solutions. It imparts training in various vocations to scavengers and their dependents, and runs an English-speaking school in Delhi for educating the children of scavengers who are given a free modern education in a variety of subjects. The main concentration is on vocational training, including computers and office management. To help develop the personality of scavenger children, boys and girls at Sulabh institutes are given training in dance and music. Education is a great redeemer; it is only through education that the final solution can be found to any social problem, especially when it comes to abolishing attitudinal prejudices. The scavengers' children are taught in English so that they can compete as equals in the job market. Hindi is taught as the national language along with Sanskrit, the latter being a source of *Brahmin* dominance in society.

(m) Technical research and development

The Sulabh International Institute of Technical Research and Training is engaged in research and development in the fields of low-cost sanitation and biogas technology for overall environmental improvement. It has studied the performance of different types of biogas plants in various situations in Bihar at the request of the Ministry of Non- Conventional Energy Sources. At present, it is working on the optimum utilisation and techno-economic evaluation of biogas plants fuelled by human excreta and other mixed wastes to ensure effective waste disposal and harnessing of bio-energy. An Indo-German collaborative study on a low maintenance waste water treatment system is being carried out in Delhi. Study and research were carried out on optimising low-cost sanitation technology, and on the pollution of ground water and soil likely to occur from on-site sanitation near Calcutta, with radioisotope tracers in high sub-soil water level areas.

(n) Health and sanitation education

Sulabh realised that mere construction of toilets will not go far in improving sustainable sanitation—sanitation must be supported by elementary health education. Most people, particularly those from lower socio-economic groups, are not aware of health and environmental benefits of improved sanitation, or of the availability of affordable technological options or government efforts and programmes. General awareness and community involvement in social programmes enables the development of self-reliance and confidence in the community resulting in sustainable benefits. Sulabh has set up primary healthcare centres at some of the community toilets where health and hygiene education is given to slum dwellers. The organisation has also launched a programme to train women in sanitation and health. So far, it has trained more than 6,000 women from different slum areas in Delhi and 1,000 women volunteers from urban slums of the neighbouring states in various aspects of health hygiene and sanitation. The main focus has been on health check-up camps, immunisation, prenatal care, family planning services, safe food and drinking water, safe environmental sanitation and health education.

The awareness and participation programme, including health check-ups and rural sanitation, has been taken up in Budhgaon, Sangli (Maharashtra), Ranichauri, New Tehri (Uttaranchal) and 12 villages near Bhondsi (Gurgaon in Haryana State). The programme of people's participation with awareness training on health, hygiene and sanitation was also taken up under Yamuna Action Plan in collaboration with Japan Bank of International Cooperation (JBIC) and Public Health Engineering Department, Haryana Government, in Faridabad and Gurgaon, and also in collaboration with WHO in the rural areas of Punjab, Uttar Pradesh, Rajasthan and Madhya Pradesh.

Realising that the women have by far the most important influence in determining household hygiene practices and in forming the habits of their children, Sulabh ensures the participation of women at every stage of implementation of the sanitation programme. One of the thrust areas in the educational curriculum of Sulabh Public School, established specially for the children of scavengers, is to teach at a very young age the benefits of sanitation and personal hygiene.

(o) Employment opportunity

In total, there are 50,000 volunteers working with Sulabh, including technologists, managers, scientists, engineers, social scientists, doctors, architects, planners and other non-revenue staff. Sulabh has a 30-year maintenance guarantee for the toilet complexes it has constructed, and therefore provides regular employment for everybody associated with this work. Those people associated with construction are almost in full employment too.

(p) People's movement

Sulabh plays an important part in identifying ways and means of solving common social problems through people's participation on a self-sustaining basis. Sulabh has proved that people themselves, and not the government, can solve problems and NGOs should play the role of catalyst in making this happen. Women's problems are largely due to a lack of education and a skewed social structure which is set against them in gender biases, especially in low and middle income countries. Yet, women hold the key to the success of sanitation programmes; they can bring about lasting changes in the family and society. Sulabh's strategy is to ensure the full participation of women in the sanitation programme by discouraging the prejudices which emanate from the caste system, religious radicalism and untouchability, and which have also been the sources of backwardness and poverty. Sulabh seeks to combat these by organising the poor in cooperation with others for creating an equitable and just social order.

(q) Capacity-building

Community participation has been central to the Sulabh movement, which has laid special emphasis on health education and on creating an awareness of sanitation and the environment. It has set up primary health care centres at community toilets, as a result of which considerable awareness has been created of the importance of personal hygiene and sanitation. It has helped bring about a change in social values and hygiene habits of the urban poor and helped them adopt cleanliness and sanitation as part of their daily routine. In fact, Sulabh works to turn the development process into a people's movement, with the people themselves becoming agents of change. Its innovative approach provides a sustainable environmental sanitation strategy to change the habits and attitudes of the people, which approach has helped build the capacity of the community and ushers a new self-sustaining sanitation order into society. Literacy, especially for women, is the major ideological foundation of the Sulabh movement, a knowledge and technology based organisation seeking to change social norms and preferences by education, campaign, persuasion and pressure.

Gandhiji's Technique .... A potent weapon for TSC

In the fight against open defecation, 16th November, 2006 is etched as a historic day not only for Sidlipura GP, Bhadravathi Taluk but also for the entire Karnataka State. This was the day when Sri Babu, Vice President, Sidlapura GP undertook fasting Satyagraha to achieve 100 per cent toilet coverage in the village. All have heard of rotests/satyagraha for wage rise, road construction, drinking water provision etc. But Satyagraha for toilet ......unheard off but yet was a reality by this enterprising Vice President.

For the last 7-8 months, the Total Sanitation Campaign was being implemented successfully in all the five villages coming under this GP. Construction of individual household toilets was almost complete except for 28 households living in A. K. Colony. This backward community was averse to having individual toilets citing one reason or the other like the flowing river by the side, growth of thick bushes etc., being conducive for practising open defecation. To overcome the above hindrance to Sanitation and hygiene in the village, the Gram Panchayat members engaged a J C B and ensured that all the bushes, weeds etc., in the surrounding were uprooted, cleaned and levelled the ground. The members also took a conscious decision and reduced the food grain ration to those houses which did not have a toilet. Still the colony people were stoic and unmoved. Just as freedom was a passion dear to Gandhi, 100 per cent toilet coverage was dear to Sri Babu. Having exhausted all methods of persuasion, this genius Babu embarked on the Gandhiji's non—violent weapon - Satyagraha. On the morning of 16th November 2006, Babu sat in the Temple belonging to A. K. Colony and started his fasting Satyagraha without water or food.

Finally unable to withstand this non violent emotional threat for a noble cause, the A. K. Colony people in unison agreed to Babu's wish of each of them having a household toilet. Babu broke his fast and started assisting the Colony people in digging of pits, laying of pans and the super structure of the toilets. Thus 16th November became a red letter day in the history of Siddlipura GP for having achieved 100 per cent toilet promotion leading to 'Open Defecation Free' Gram Panchayat. The success in Sidlipura GP demonstrates that anything is possible with true conviction and right strategy.

Changing the face of rural hygiene: West Garo Hills

Total sanitation Campaign was launched in West Garo Hills in 2004 and is implemented by District Water and Sanitation Mission (DWSM). At the beginning of TSC programme in the district, only 5 per cent households have safe toilets. Of the rest 76 per cent had unsafe toilets and 19 per cent practiced open defecation.

To bring about a radical change in achievement of the sanitation objectives, the DWSC adopted first an improved institutional mechanism and community approach to total sanitation to effectively bring out a change in the entire community. DWSC has put a dedicated team at the district level and block level, entrusted with specific responsibilities, appropriate reporting and co-ordination. Transparency, accountability, effective monitoring and reporting mechanism were identified as the building blocks of garnering community support.

TSC is all about behaviour change which requires personal approach. It was also observed that a one-to-one and community approach yielded excellent results instead of big hoardings and other such IEC tools. It was thus decided to launch a more comprehensive community approach to bring about behavioural change. Community based approach helps to change the sanitary behaviour of the community, focusing on igniting/triggering a change in sanitation behaviour rather than on constructing toilets. It makes the people realise the link between open defecation and negative health impacts. However, this happens through a process of social awakening that is stimulated by facilitators from within or outside the community.

Transparency and accountability were identified as the building blocks of garnering community support. Follow up by the community was the main agenda to ensure community participation and usage. The tribal society has a lot of respect for commitments given and, to emphasise this fact, a Social Agreement was designed in the local language. The approach adopted gave exceptional results. It proved the faith imposed in community participation and its linkage to the success of the programme.

Source: Twelfth Five Year Plan—(2012-2017) Report of the Working Group on Rural Domestic Water and Sanitation, Ministry of Drinking Water and Sanitation Government of India September 2011.

Medinipur: An Example of Better Sanitation Principles in Action

The UNICEF-assisted Integrated Sanitation Project in Medinipur, West Bengal, India, demonstrates many elements of sound programming principles in achieving a successful sanitation grassroots movement:

The project shifts institutional responsibilities to the local level—successfully forging an action coalition between local NGOs, community-based organisations, and Panchayats (the lowest form of local government, usually covering three villages). Existing local youth groups and their cluster organisations, working together with local panchayats, are galvanised by an effective intermediary NGO, the Ramakrishna Mission Lokashiksha Parishad (RMLP). The youth clubs conduct much of the implementation in coordination with the Panchayat, and a subcommittee called the "WATSAN committee" is responsible for community-level implementation. Cluster organisations of the youth clubs, at block level, backstop with logistics and coordinate hardware inputs. They are, in turn, supported by RMLP. The role of the central and state governments and district officials has been to provide financial and technical support and to help adjust appropriate supportive policies.

UNICEF has provided technical and financial assistance for the overall effort.

The project facilitates widespread participation in all project stages supporting a demand led process. The NGO and associated youth groups help local people make considered choices regarding a range of sanitation options, based on what they want and are willing to pay for. A wide range of training, communication, and information methods are used to catalyse informed local decision making and action. Training is provided to cluster and youth leaders, panchayat and WATSAN committees, masons, and in turn other community members—on matters such as community development, construction, and organisational development. Through home visits, motivation camps, and exhibitions supported by materials kits, the community develops hygiene and sanitation awareness. Communication and motivational activities include the use of local media, e.g., wall writings, song squads, posters, videos, and slide shows. Villagers are engaged in choosing technologies, planning activities, working as paid producers and as procurers of materials and services, and also in managing their projects.

The project has involved a holistic approach to sanitation. First, the project focuses on behaviour change through integrated and intensive hygiene and sanitation education. This helps to stimulate demand and is followed-up with provision of real and affordable options, resulting in the construction and use of a wide range of waste-management measures (e.g., low-cost latrines, soakage pits, improved smokeless chulas, garbage pits, bathing platforms, and handpumps) and in the sale of oral rehydration salts (ORS) packets.

Financing arrangements focus on local resource mobilisation, without subsidies. The initial emphasis was on stimulating latent demand, and providing an initial revolving loan fund. After this had served its purpose and demand grew, the fund was phased out. Technologies are now self-financed.

The project stimulated political will for a policy change and demonstrated benefits to the poor through self-reliance. Given the success of the "no-subsidy" approach in West Bengal, the Government of India agreed to relax guidelines in that state on providing subsidies, instead providing only minimal support in-kind to the neediest cases. Over 78 per cent of the beneficiaries were below the poverty line and had successfully paid for most of the programme themselves. All these elements contributed to sustainable, dramatic gains in the last six years, with 127 villages and three Gram Panchayats attaining full latrine coverage, and many others making substantial gains in integrated hygiene and sanitation.

Source: Sanitation, the Medinipur Story, Intensive Sanitation Project, UNICEF-Calcutta, India 1994, and *Integrated Sanitation Project,Medinipur,* K.S. Ramasubban, UNDP-WB Water and Sanitation Programme, and B.B. Samanta, UNICEF, India.

Notes

1. For details see Lucy Pickering, Toilets, Bodies, Selves: Enacting Composting as Counterculture in awai'I, *Body and Society* 2010 16: 33.
2. Based on Tilley, Elizabeth et al, 2008. Compendium of Sanitation Systems and Technologies. Swiss Federal Institute of Aquatic Science and Technology (Eawag). Dübendorf, Switzerland.
3. Ibid.
4. Based on R. G. Feachem, Community Participation in Appropriate Water Supply and Sanitation Technologies: The Mythology for the Decade, Proceedings of the Royal Society of London. Series B, Biological Sciences, Vol. 209, No.1174, More Technologies for Rural Health (Jul. 28, 1980), pp. 15-29.
5. Gunnerson, C. G., Julius, D. A. and Kalbermatten, J. M. 1978 Alternative approaches to sanitation technology. Paper presented at the Workshop on Water Pollution Problems Arising from Development held by the International Association for Water Pollution Research, Stockholm, 14 June.; also Saunders, R. J. and Warford, J. J. 1978 Economic incentives and appropriate technology in village water supply. Paper presented at the American Society of Civil Engineers Annual Convention, 16-20 October, Chicago.
6. Feachem, R., Bradley, D., Garelick, H. and Mara, D. 1980 Health aspects of excreta and wastewater management. Baltimore: Johns Hopkins University Press/World Bank.
7. See Carmen da Silva Wells and Christine Sijbesma (2012): Practical innovations for strengthening Community-Led Total Sanitation: selected experience from Asia, Development in Practice, 22:3, 417-426.
8. See Robert Chambers (2009), Going to Scale with Community-Led Total Sanitation: Reflections on Experience, Issues and Ways Forward, Institute of Development Studies.

9. Ibid.
10. See Haq, Anowarul and Bode, Brigitta (2008) 'Hunger, Subsidies and Process Facilitation: The Challenges for CLTS', paper for the conference on CLTS, IDS, Sussex, December.
11. Mukherjee, Nilanjana and Shatifan, Nina (2008) 'The CLTS Story in Indonesia: Empowering Communities, Transforming Institutions, Furthering Decentralisation', paper for the conference on CLTS, IDS, Sussex, December.
12. Prasad, Shambu, C. (2008) Learning Alliances for Poverty Reduction, www.capacity.org/en/layout/set/print/content/view/full/109/(issue)/15869
13. Sanitation, Health, and Society: Sanitation And Hygiene Advocacy and Communication Strategy Framework 2012-2017.
14. Sanitation, Health, and Society: Sanitation and Hygiene Advocacy and Communication Strategy Framework 2012-2017.
15. For details see Sundar Burra, Sheela Patel and Thomas Kerr, Community-designed, built and managed toilet blocks in Indian cities, Environment and Urbanisation 2003 15: 11.
16. See Patel, Sheela, Celine d'Cruz and Sundar Burra (2002), "Beyond evictions in a global city; people managed resettlement in Mumbai", *Environment and Urbanisation* Vol 14, No 1, pages 159–172.
17. Based on work by Govindasamy Agoramoorthy and Minna J. Hsu (2009): India needs sanitation policy reform to enhance public health, Journal of Economic Policy Reform, 12:4, 333-342.
18. Jagawat, H., 2005. Transforming the dry lands. The Sadguru story of western India. Delhi: India Research Press.
19. Phansalkar, S.J. and Verma, S., 2005. *Mainstreaming the margins.* Delhi: Angus and Grapher.
20. Agoramoorthy, G. and Hsu, M.J., 2006. Do animals suffer caste prejudice in Hinduism? *Social Compass,* 53, 244–245.
21. Agoramoorthy, G., 2008. Can India meet the increasing food demand by 2020? *Futures,* 40, 503–506.
22. Clarissa Brocklehurst, Chief Water, Environment and Sanitation, UNICEF, New York, USA, cbrocklehurst@unicef.org
23. For details see Sansom, Kevin, Complementary Roles? NGO–Government Relations for Community-Based Sanitation in South Asia, Public Admin. Dev. 31, 282–293 (2011).
24. UN. 2009. The Millennium Development Goals Report, 2009, United Nations: New York.

25. See Government of India. 2003. Towards total sanitation and hygiene: a challenge for India, paper presented at the South Asia Conference on Sanitation (SACOSAN), Dhaka, Bangladesh.
26. This unit is mainly based on work by Bindeshwar Pathak, Sanitation is the key to healthy cities - a profile of Sulabh International, Environment and Urbanisation, Vol. 11, No. 1, April 1999; PK JHA (2003): Health and social benefits from improving community hygiene and sanitation: an Indian experience, International Journal of Environmental Health Research, 13:S1, S133-S140.

Bibliography

Allman, Dan. 2013. 'The Sociology of Social Inclusion', SAGE Open, January-March, 2013: 1–16.

Ambedkar, B. R. 1990. Annihilation of Caste: An Undelivered Speech. Delhi: Arnold Publisher.

Ambedkar, B.R. 1982-90. Castes in India, Speeches and Writings of Dr Bahasaheb Ambedkar, Vol I, Bombay: Government of Maharashtra.

Ambedkar, B.R. 1987. Dr. Babasaheb Ambedkar's writings and speeches (BAWS), Vol. 3, Bombay: Government of Maharashtra Publication.

Anderson,B. 1992. '*The New World Disorder*', New Left Review, No. 93, 13.

Atal, Y. 2005. "Intensive studies in Village: In Retrospect and Prospect" *The Eastern Antropologist*, Vol. 58, No. 3-4, July-Dec. Serial Publication, Delhi.

Bayly, C.A. 1975. The Local Roots of Indian Politics, Allahabad, 1880-1920. Oxford: Clarendon Press.

Beall, Jo. 2006. 'Dealing with dirt and the disorder of development: managing rubbish in urban Pakistan'. *Oxford development studies*, 34 (1). pp. 81-97.

Berman, Marshall. 1988. *All That Is Solid Melts into Air: The Experience of Modernity*, New York: Viking Penguin.

Beteille, A 1983. The Idea of Natural Inequality and Other Essays, Oxford University Press, Delhi.

Beteille, A (1999): 'Empowerment', Economic and Political Weekly, Vol. 34, No. 10/11 (Mar. 6-19, 1999), pp. 589-597.

Bhagwati, Jagdish. 1993. India in Transition. Oxford: Clarendon Press.

Bharadwaj, S. and A. Patkar. 2004. Menstrual Hygiene and Management in Developing Countries: Taking Stock, Mumbai, India.

Bourdieu, Pierre 1977. *Outline of a Theory of Practice.* Cambridge University Press.

Campelli, E. 1996. 'Metodi qualitativi e teoria sociale', in C. Cipolla and A. De Lillo (eds.), *Il sociologo e le sirene. La sfida dei metodi qualitativi.* Milan: Franco Angeli.

Census 2001. Government of India, New Delhi.

Chambers R. 2009a. Going to scale with Community Led Total Sanitation: Reflections on Experience, Issues and Ways Forward. Practice paper, volume number 1. Institute of Development Studies, Sussex University: UK.

Chambers R. 2009b. Beyond subsidies—triggering a revolution in rural sanitation. IDS in focus policy briefing, Issue 10. Institute of Development Studies, Sussex University, UK.

Chambers, R. 2009. 'Going to Scale with Community-Led Total Sanitation: Reflections on Experience, Issues and Ways Forward', IDS Practice Paper 1, University of Sussex', Brighton, UK: Institute of Development Studies, available at www.communityled totalsanitation.org/sites/community ledtotalsanitation.org/files/ Chambers_Going per cent20to percent20Scale percent20with percent20CLTS.pdf.

Chauhan, B.R 2005. "Intensive studies in Village: In Retrospect and Prospect" *The Eastern Antropologist*, Vol. 58, No. 3-4, July-Dec. Delhi: Serial Publication, 2005:298.

Childe, G. 1957. Civilisation, cities and towns., Antiquity, 13: 36.8.

Christoph Lthi, Jennifer McConville and Elisabeth Kvarnstrm. 2010. Community-based approaches for addressing the urban sanitation challenges, International Journal of Urban Sustainable Development, 1:1-2, 49-63.

Clark, J. 1991. Democratising Development: The Role of Voluntary Organisations. West Hartford, CT: Kumarian Press.

Cohen, B. S. 1955. "The Changing Status of a Depressed Caste, Village India," edited by Mckim Marriot, Asia Publication House Bombay.

Corbetta, Piergiorgio 2003. *Social Research. Theory, Methods and Techniques.* London: Sage.

Corbin, A. 1986. The Foul and the Fragrant: Odour and the French Social Imagination. Leamington Spa: Berg.

Dahrendorf, Ralf 1959 Class and Class Conflict in Industrial Society. Stanford, Calif.: Stanford University Press.

Delanty, Gerald 1999. *Social Theory in a Changing World.* Cambridge: Polity.

Deliege, R., 1994. "Caste without a System", in Marry Searle Chatterjee and Ursula Sharma eds., "Contextualising Caste", Publish, New Delhi.

Deliege, R., 1999. *The Untouchables of Hindu Organisation,* Berg Press: New York.

Deliege, Robert. 1999. The Untouchables of India, Berg Publication, UK. Democratic Politics. London: Verso.

Deodhar, N.S. (2003): Epidemiological perspective of domestic and personal hygiene in India, International Journal of Environmental Health Research, 13:S1, S47-S56.

Derrida, Jacques 1978 Writing and Difference. Chicago: University of Chicago Press

Douglas, M. 1966. Purity and danger: An analysis of concept of pollution and taboo. London, England: Routledge.

Douglas, M. 1987 *How Institutions Think.* London: Routledge and Kegan Paul.

Douglas, M. 1991. *Purity and Danger: An Analysis of the Concepts of Pollution and Taboo,* London, Routledge.

Dumont, L. 1980. *Homo Hierarchicus, The Caste System and its Implications,* Chicago and London, University of Chicago Press.

Durkheim, Emile 1982 The Rules of Sociological Method. New York: Free Press.

Durkheim, Emile 1964 The Division of Labour in Society. New York: Free Press.

Eckstein, Harry 1975. 'Case Study and Theory in Political Science', in Fred I. Greenstein and Nelson W. Polsby (eds.), *Handbook of Political Science.* Reading, Mass.: Addison-Wesley, pp. 79–138.

Elias, N. 1978. The Civilising Process. The History of Manners and State Formation and Civilisation, Oxford: Basil Blackwell.

Faris, R.E.L. and Dunham, H.W. 1939. Mental Disorders in Urban Areas. An Ecological Study of Schizophrenia and Other Psychoses. Chicago: University of Chicago Press.

Foucault, Michel 1969. The Archaeology of Knowledge and the Discourse on Language. New York: Harper Colophon.

Foucault, Michel 1966. The Order of Things: An Archaeology of the Human Sciences. New York: Vintage.

French, W.L. and Bell, C.H. 1978. Organisational Development. Englewood Cliffs, NJ: Prentice-Hall.

Fuller, C. 1996. 'Introduction', in C. Fuller (ed.), *Caste Today*. Delhi: Oxford University Press, pp. 1–31.

Fusfeld, Warren E. 1974. "The Kumbh *Mela* in Allahabad: Networks of Communication in Nineteenth Century North India." Master's thesis, University of Pennsylvania.

Gandhi, M.K. 1958. The Collected Works of Mahatama Gandhi, Publication Division: New Delhi.

Garfinkel, Harold 1967 Studies in Ethnomethodology. Englewood Cliffs, N.J.: Prentice-Hall.

Gear, S., Brown, A. and Mathys, A. 1996. *Strategic Sanitation Plan—the Kumasi Experience*. UNDP/World Bank Water Supply and Sanitation Program. Regional Water and Sanitation Group—West Africa.

Geetha, V.and S.V. Rajadurai. 1998. Towards A Non-Brahmin Millenium: From Iyothee Thass to Periyar, Samya Calcutta.

Ghurye, G.S. 1950. "Caste and Class in India", Bombay Publish, Bombay.

Giddens, A. 1990. *Consequences of Modernity*, Stanfort University Press: Stanford.

Giddens, Anthony 1991 Modernity and Self-Identity: Self and Society in the Late Modern Age. Stanford, Calif.: Stanford University Press

Gill, Kaveri. 2012. Promoting 'Inclusiveness': A Framework For Assessing India's Flagship Social Welfare Programmes, UNICEF India New Delhi January

Gill, S. 1995. 'Knowledge, Politics and Neo-liberal Economy' in R. Stubbs and G.R. Underhill (ed.) *Political Economy and the changing Global order*. Fernwood: Halifax.

Goffman, E. 1963. Stigma: Notes on the management of spoiled identity. Englewood Cliffs, NJ: Prentice Hall.

Goffman, Erving 1959 Presentation of Self in Everyday Life. Garden City, N.Y.: Anchor.

Guha, Sumit. 1993. Nutrition, Sanitation, Hygiene, and the Likelihood of Death: The British Army in India c. 1870–1920, Population Studies: A Journal of Demography, 47:3, 385-401.

Gupta, Dipankar. 2005. 'Caste and Politics: Identity over System', *Annual Review of Anthropology*, Vol. 34 (2005), pp. 409-427.

Hacking, Ian 1999. *The Social Construction of What?* Cambridge, Mass.: Harvard University Press.

Hall, S. 1990. "Cultural Identity and Diaspora", in J. Rutherfords ed., Identity: Community, Culture and Difference, Publish, London.

Hannerz, Ulf. 1996. *Transnational Connection: Cultures, People, Places*, London: Routledge.

Hardgrave, Robert. 1965. The Dravidian Movement. Bombay: Popular Prakashan.

Hawkins, G. 2006. The Ethics of Waste: How We Relate to Rubbish. Lanham, MD: Rowman and Littlefield.

Held, D.1991. 'Democracy, the Nation-state and the Global system' in D. Held (ed.) *Political Theory Today*, Polity Press : Cambridge

Howe, F.C. 1912. The city as a socialising agency., American Journal of Sociology, xvii: 590-601.

Husserl, E. 1964. *The Idea of Phenomenology*. trans. W. Aston and G. Nakhikan. The Hague: Nijhoff.

Hutton, J.H. 1933. Census of India, 1931, Volume I—India, Part II—Imperial tables, Manager of Publications, Delhi.

Hutton, J.H. 1981. Caste in India, its nature, function and origins, Bombay: Oxford University Press.

Jaffrelot, Christophe. 1993. The Hindu Nationalist Movement in India. New York: Columbia University Press.

Jha N. 2010. Barriers to community-based water supply and sanitation in India, UNDP's Poverty in Focus Number 18, August 2009. International Policy Centre for Inclusive Growth: UNDP, Brazil.

Jha, P.K. 2003. Health and social benefits from improving community hygiene and sanitation: an Indian experience, International Journal of Environmental Health Research, 13:S1, S133-S140.

Jogdand, P.G. 2000. *New Economic Policy and Scheduled Castes,*. Rawat Publications: New Delhi.

Johnstone, B. 2002. *Discourse Analysis*. Oxford: Blackwell.

Joshi, D. and B. Fawcett. 2001. 'Water, Hindu Mythology and an Unequal Social Order in India', paper presented at the Second Conference of the International Water History Association, August, Bergen, Norway, 10_/12 August

Kabeer, N. 1998. 'Money Can't Buy Me Love'? Re-evaluating Gender, Credit and Empowerment in Rural Bangladesh', *IDS Discussion Paper* No. 363, Brighton: IDS.

Kalbermatten, J.M. 1980. Sanitation convenience for a few or health for many; the report on the international seminar on low-cost techniques for disposal of human wastes in urban communities, Calcutta.

Kalimuthu, A. and Y. Hossain (2008) 'Crossfire: Community-Led Total Sanitation is the best method of achieving sustainable sanitation for all in rural areas', Waterlines 27 (3): 177–83.

Kar, K. and R. Chambers. 2008. Handbook on Community Led Total Sanitation, Brighton, UK: Institute of Development Studies and Plan UK, available at www.communityledtotalsanitation.org/resource/handbook-community-led-total-anitation.

Khilnani, S. 1999. *Idea of India* (updated paperback edition). New Delhi: Penguin Books.

Klandermans, Bert and Suzanne Staggenborg (eds.) 2002. *Methods of Social Movement*

Klein, Peter D. 2005. 'Epistemology', in *Routledge Encyclopaedia of Philosophy Online*. www.rep.routledge.com/article/P059.

Kumar, Vivek 2004. Understanding Dalit Diaspora, *Economic and Political Weekly*, Vol. 39, No. 1 (Jan. 3-9, 2004), pp. 114-116.

Kumar, Vivek. 2007. 'Governance and development in the era of Globalisation: Understanding Exclusion and Assertion of Scheduled Castes in India' in Kameshwar Choudhary (ed.) *Globalisation, Governance Reforms and Development in India*. Sage Publication: New Delhi.

Laclau, E. and Mouffe, C. 1985. Hegemony and Socialist Strategy.

Ladusingh, L. and Singh, C.H. 2006. Place, community education, gender and child mortality in North-East India. *Population Space and Place* 12, 65–76.

Lemert, Charles. 1990 "The Uses of French Structuralisms in Sociology." In George Ritzer (ed.), Frontiers of Social Theory: The New Syntheses. New York: Columbia University Press: 230–254.

Lewin, K. 1988. 'Group decision and social change', in S. Kemmis (ed.) The Action Research Reader. Victoria, Australia: Deakin University Press, pp. 47–56.

Lloyd I. Rudolph and Susanne Hoeber Rudolph. 1967. *The Modernity Of Tradition—Political Development In India*, University of Chicago Press, Chicago and London.

Lohia, Rammanohar. 1964. The Caste System. Hyderabad: Lohia Samta Vidyalaya Nyas.

Lynch, Owen M. 1969. "The Politics of Untouchability: Social Mobility and Change in a city of India, Colombia University Press, New York.

MacLean, Kama. 2003. Making the Colonial State Work for You: The Modern Beginnings of the Ancient *Kumbh Mela*in Allahabad, The Journal of Asian Studies, Vol. 62, No. 3 (Aug., 2003), pp. 873-905.

Mandelbaum, David. 1972. *Society in India: Continuity and Change*, Bombay: Popular Prakashan.

Mannheim, K. 1951. Freedom, Power and Democratic Planning. London: Routledge and Kegan Paul.

Martinelli, A. 2003. *'Market, Government, Communities and Global governance'*, in International Sociology, Vol. 18 (2).

Marx, Karl 1843. "A Contribution to the Critique of Hegel's Philosophy of Right." In Marx/Engels Collected Works, Vol. 3. New York: International Publishers: 3–129.

Marx, Karl 1847. The Poverty of Philosophy. New York: International Publishers.

Mayoux, L. 1999. 'Questioning virtuous spirals: microfinance and women's empowerment in Africa', *Journal of International Development*, November-December: 957-984.

McKenzie, R.D. 1933. The Metropolitan Community. New York and London: McGraw-Hill.

Mead, George Herbert, 1934. Mind, Self and Society: From the Standpoint of a Social Behaviorist. Chicago: University of Chicago Press.

Mendelsohn. O. and M. Vicziany. 1998. *The Untouchables: Subordinates, Poverty and the State in Modern India*, University Press: Cambridge.

Merton, Robert K. 1968 Social Theory and Social Structure. New York: Free Press.

Michael, M.S. 1999 (ed.). "Dalits in Modern India: Vision and Values," Vistaar Publications, New Delhi.

Moon, Vasant 1991. (ed). Dr. Babasaheb Ambedkar, *Writings And Speeches*, Vol. 9, Education Department, Government of Maharashtra.

Moulik SG, Sen S. 2006. The Mumbai Slum Sanitation Programme. Waterlines 25(2): 19–21.

Mukerjee, Radhakamal 1938a. *The Regional Balance of Man: An Ecological Theory of Population*. Madras: University of Madras.

Mukerjee, Radhakamal 1945a. *Social Ecology*. London: Macmillan.

Mukerjee, Radhakamal 1949.*The Social Structure of Values*. London: Macmillan.

Mukerjee, Radhakamal. 1916. *The Foundations of Indian Economics*. London: Longman, Green and Co., Ltd.

Mumford, L. 1938. The Culture of Cities. New York: Harcourt.

Nagar, Amrit Lal. 1980. Nachyo Bahut Gopal, Rajpal and sons, Kashmiri Gate, Delhi.

National Commission on Population. 2001. Report of the Sub-Group on 'Drinking Water Supply and Sanitation'. Constituted by the Planning Commission, Government of India.

Navlakha, Gautam, 1989. A Show of 'Hindu Power', Economic and Political Weekly, Vol. 24, No. 13 (Apr. 1, 1989), p. 658.

Nehru, Jawaharlal. 2001. The Discovery of India, Penguin Publication: New Delhi.

Neto, F. and Tropp, H. 2000. Water supply and sanitation services for all: global progress during the 1990s. *Natural Resources Forum* 24, 225–235.

Noffke, S. 1997. 'Professional, personal, and political dimensions of action research', Review of Research in Education, 2: 305–43.

O'Malley, L.S.S. 1913. Census of India, 1911, Volume 5, Bengal Secretariat Book Depot, Calcutta.

Omvedt, Gail . 1994. Dalits and the Democratic Revolution - Dr Ambedkar and the Dalit Movement in Colonial India. Sage Publications. London and New Delhi.

Omvedt, Gail. 2011. Understanding Caste—From Buddha to Ambedkar and beyond, New Delhi: Orient BlackSwan.

O'Reilly, Kathleen 2010: Combining sanitation and women's participation in water supply: An example from Rajasthan, Development in Practice, 20:1, 45-56.

Palakudiyil, T. 2008. 'Total—but Sustainable? An Enquiry into the Sustainability Aspects of Community Led Total Sanitation—Evidence from South Asia and West Africa', paper presented at the IDS Conference on CLTS, Sussex, (Brighton, UK: Institute of Development Studies. IDS), 16–18 December, 2008.'

Pandian, M.S.S. 1993. "Denationalising The Past: 'Nation' In E.V. Ramasamy's Political Discourse", *Economic and Political Weekly*, October 16, p. 2282.

Park, R.E., Burgess, E.W. and McKenzie, R.D. 1925. The City. Chicago: University of Chicago Press.

Parlett, M.R. and Hamilton, D. 1972. 'Evaluation and illumination', reprinted in R. Murphy and H. Torrance (eds) (1988). Evaluating Education: Issues and Methods. London: Paul Chapman Publishing, pp. 57–73.

Parsons, Talcott 1937. The Structure of Social Action. New York: McGraw-Hill.

Parsons, Talcott 1951. The Social System. Glencoe, Ill.: Free Press.

Pasmore, W. 2001. 'Action research in the workplace: the socio-technical perspective', in P. Reason and H. Bradbury (eds), Handbook of Action Research: Participative Inquiry and Practice. London and Thousand Oaks, CA: Sage, pp. 38–47.

Passeron, Jean-Claude and Jacques Revel 2005. 'Penser par cas. Raisonner à partir des singularités', in Jean-Claude Passeron and Jacques Revel (eds), *Penser par cas*. Paris: École des Hautes Études en Sciences Sociales-Enquête, pp. 9–44.

Pathak, Bindeshwar. 1991. Road to Freedom—A Sociological study on the abolition of scavenging in India, Xtreme Office Aids Pvt. Ltd. Delhi.

Pathak, Bindeshwar. 1999. Sanitation is the key to healthy cities - a profile of Sulabh International, Environment and Urbanisation, Vol. 11, No. 1, April 1999.

Phillips, E.M. and Pugh, D.S. 1987. How to Get a PhD: A Handbook for Students and Their Supervisors. Buckingham: Open University Press.

Pickering, Lucy. 2010. Toilets, Bodies, Selves: Enacting Composting as Counterculture in Hawai'I, Body and Society 2010, 16: 33.

Platt, Jennifer 1992. "Case Study" in American Methodological Thought', *Current Sociology*.

Poovey, M. 1995. Making a Social Body. Chicago, IL: University of Chicago Press.

Ragin, C. and Becker, H. (eds) 1992. What Is a Case? Cambridge: Cambridge University Press.

Ragin, Charles. 2000. *Fuzzy Set Social Science*. Chicago: University of Chicago Press.

Rajasekhariah, A.M. 1971. *B.R. Ambedkar: The Politics of Emancipation*, Bombay: Sindhu Publisher, p. 18.

Ram, Nandu. 1988. *The Mobile Scheduled Castes-Rise of a New Middle Class*, Delhi: Hindustan publisher.

Ram, Ronki. 2011. Beyond Conversion and Sanskritisation: Articulating an Alternative Dalit Agenda in East Punjab, *Modern Asian Studies, pp.* 1-64.

Ritzer, George, 2000. Sociological Theory, McGraw-Hill Companies, New York.

Robertson, R. 1992. *Globalisation: Social Theory and Global Culture,*. Sage Publication: London.

Rodrigues, Valerian (ed.) 2002. *The Essential Writings of B.R. Ambedkar*, New Delhi: Oxford University Press.

Rudolph, L.I and S.H. Rudolph. 1967. *The Modernity of tradition: Political development in India*, Chicago: University of Chicago Press.

Sachchidananda, 1977. "The Harijan Elite, Thomson Press (India) Ltd., Faridabad.

Sandec/WSSCC (Water and Sanitation in Developing Countries/ Water Supply and Sanitation Collaborative Council) (2000a): "Bellagio Statement: Clean, Healthy and Productive Living: A New Approach to Environmental Sanitation. "WSSCC (Water Supply and Sanitation Collaborative Council), Geneva, Switzerland, digitally available at: http: //www.sandec.ch/EnvironmentalSanitation/Documents/Bellagio_Statement.pdf

Sandec/WSSCC (Water and Sanitation in Developing Countries/ Water Supply and Sanitation Collaborative Council) (2000b): "Report of the Working Group on Environmental Sanitation to the 5th Global Forum of the WSSCC in Iguaçu, 24 - 29 November 2000." - WSSCC (Water Supply and Sanitation Collaborative Council), Geneva, Switzerland, digitally available at: http: //www.sandec.ch/EnvironmentalSanitation/Documents/Report_ Fifth_ Global_ Forum_Nov00.pdf

Sastry, N. 1996. Community characteristics, individual and household attributes and child survival in Brazil. *Demography* 33, 211–229.

Sathyamurthy, T.V. (ed) 1996. Class Formation and Political Transformation in Post-colonial India, Delhi: Oxford University Press.

Savage, J. 2000. 'Ethnography and Healthcare', British Medical Journal, 321: 1400–2.

Saxena, Ashish 2005. "Village Studies in India: Old and New" in S.L. Sharma, S.K. Sharma and J.R. Panda (eds), Ethnic, Rural and Gender Issues in Contemporary North-West, Delhi: Anamika Publishers.

Saxena, Ashish. 2009. *Shifting Manifestations: Scheduled Castes in Jammu and Kashmir*, Jammu: Saksham Books International.

Saxena, Ashish. 2007. 'Rethinking Indian Villages: A Sociological appraisal' in E-Bulletin *International Sociological Association*, No. 8, November 2007.

Saxena, Ashish. 2013. *Marginality, Exclusion and Social Justice*, Jaipur: Rawat Publications.

Saxena, Ashish. 2015. *Movement towards Green Pilgrimage: Managing environment sanitation issues in Kumbh Mela at Prayag* in Bindeshwar K. Pathak (ed.), Sociology of Sanitation, Kalpaz Publications, New Delhi.

Schutz, A. 1932. The Phenomenology of the Social World, trans. G. Walsh and F. Lehnert. Evanston, IL: Northwestern University Press.

Schutz, A. 1945. On Phenomenology and Social Relations, ed. H.R. Wagner. Chicago: University of Chicago Press.

Sen, Amartya, 1999. "Development as a Freedom", Oxford University Press: Mumbai.

Shah. G. 1992. "Protests by the rural poor" in A. Bhalla and P. Bumke (eds) *Images of rural India in the 20th century*, New Delhi: Sterling.

Sharma, K.L. 1994. "Social Stratification and Mobility," Rawat Publication, Jaipur.

Sheth, D.L. 1999. Secularisation of Caste and Making of New Middle Class, Economic and Political Weekly, Vol. 34, No. 34/35 (Aug. 21-Sep. 3), pp. 2502-2510.

Silver, H. 1995. Reconceptualising social disadvantage: Three paradigms of social exclusion. In G. Rodgers, C. Gore, and J.B. Figueiredo (Eds.), Social exclusion: Rhetoric, reality, responses (pp. 57-80). Geneva, Switzerland: International Institute for Labour Studies, United Nations Development Programme.

Silver, H., and Miller, S.M. 2003. Social exclusion: The European approach to social disadvantage. Indicators, 2(2), 1-17.

Somekh, B. 1995. 'The contribution of action research to development in social endeavours: a position paper on action research methodology', British Educational Research Journal, 21(3): 339–55.

Somekh, Bridget and Cathy Lewin. 2005. Research Methods in the Social Sciences, Sage Publications, London.

Sorokin, P. A. 1998. Social and cultural mobility. London, England: Routledge.

Sperber, Dan 1984. *Il sapere degli antropologi*. Milan: Feltrinelli.

Srinivas, M.N. 1966. Social Change In Modern India. Berkeley: University of California Press.

Stein, Burton. 1968. "Social Mobility and Medieval South Indian Hindu Sects", in J. Silverberg ed., Social Mobility in the Caste System in India", Publish, Hague.

Strange, S. 1995. *'The Limits and Politics'*; Government and Opposition, No. 30(3).

Subbulakshmi, G. and Udipi, S.A. 1990. Environmental factors, maternal attributes and children's age at introduction of supplementary foods in rural and urban Maharashtra and Gujrat. *Food and Nutrition Bulletin* 12(4), 318–322.

Talbot, Marion. 1896. Sanitation and Sociology, American Journal of Sociology, Vol. 2, No. 1 (Jul., 1896), pp. 74-81.

Ten, V.T.A. 2007. Menstrual Hygiene: A Neglected Condition for the Achievement of Several Millennium Development Goals, Zoetermeer, the Netherlands: Europe External Policy Advisors.

Thorat, S.K. and Narender Kumar. 2008. *B.R. Ambedkar—Perspectives on social exclusion and inclusive policies*, New Delhi: Oxford University Press.

Torres, C.A. 1992. 'Participatory action research and popular education in Latin America', Qualitative Studies in Education, 5(1): 51–62.

Turner, Bryan. 1999. Classical Sociology, SAGE Publications London · Thousand Oaks, New Delhi.

Uma Kothari and Martin Minogue 2002. Development theory and practice: Critical Perspectives, London: Palgrave.

UNDESA. 2005. Background Paper No. 2, 'A Gender Perspective on Water Resources and Sanitation', submitted by: Interagency Task Force on Gender and Water.

UNDP. 1998. *Human development report 1998*. New York: United Nations Development Programme.

UNICEF . 2001. *The State of the World's Children*. UNICEF, New York.

UNICEF 2007. 'Water, Environment and Sanitation: Gender Mainstreaming in Water and Sanitation', available at http://www.unicef.org/wes/index_main_streaming.html

United Nations Population Division. 1998. *World Population Nearing 6 Billion Projected Close to 9 Billion by 2050*. New York, United Nations Population Division, Department of Economic and Social Affairs (Internet communication of 21 September 2000 at www.popin.org/pop1998/1.htm)

Vachaspati, Sri. 1977. Artha Sashtra of Kautilya, The Chaukhamba Surabharati Prakshan, Varanasi.

Van der Geest, S. 2002. 'The Night Soil Collector: Bucket Latrines in Ghana', Postcolonial Studies 5(2): 197–206.

Van Wijk-Sijbesma, C. 1998. Gender in Water Resources Management, Water Supply and Sanitation: Roles and Realities Revisited, IRC Technical Paper Series, Delft: IRC.

Wakeman, W., S. Davis, C. van Wijk, and A. Naithani 1996. Source book for Gender Issues at the Policy Level in the Water and Sanitation Sector. Washington, DC: World Bank.

Walker R. 1974. 'The Conduct of Educational Case Studies: Ethics, Theory and Procedures', reprinted in M. Hammersley (ed.) (1993)

Controversies in Classroom Research, 2nd edn. Buckingham: Open University Press.

Wankhede, G.G., 1999. "Social Mobility and Scheduled Castes", Rawat Publications, Jaipur.

WaterAid. 2007. 'Global Cause' and Effect: How the Aid System is undermining the Millennium Development Goals, Water Aid.

Waters, Malcolm. 1995. *Globalisation*,. R&KP.: London.

Weber, M. 1958. The City. Glencoe, Ill.: Free Press.

Weber, Max. 1917. The Methodology of the Social Sciences. Ed. Edward Shils and Henry Finch.

WHO . 1989. *Health Guidelines for the Use of Wastewater in Agriculture and Aquaculture*. Report of a WHO Scientific group, Technical Report Series No. 778, World Health Organisation, Geneva.

WHO . 1993. *Improving Water and Sanitation Hygiene Behaviours for the Reduction of Diarrhoeal Disease*. Report of an Informal Consultation, WHO.CWS 90.7, 18–20 May 1992, Geneva.

WHO . 1999. *WHO Report on Infectious Diseases—Removing obstacles to healthy development*. World Health Organisation, Geneva.

WHO 2000a. *Global Water Supply and Sanitation Assessment*. World Health Organisation, Geneva.

WHO. 2000b. *The World Health Report 2000—Health systems: Improving performance*. World Health Organisation, Geneva.

WHO/UNICEF JMP (World Health Organisation and United Nations Childrens Fund Joint Monitoring Programme for Water Supply and Sanitation) (2000): "Global Water Supply and Sanitation Assessment 2000 Report."—World Health Organisation, Geneva, Switzerland, digitally available at: http: //www.who.int/docstore/water_ sanitation_ health/Globassessment/GlobalTOC.htm

WHO/UNICEF Joint Monitoring Programme for Water Supply and Sanitation (JMP) (2010) Progress on Sanitation and Drinking-water: 2010 Update. Geneva, Switzerland, World Health Organisation (WHO);, New York, USA: UNICEF.

Whyte, W.F. (ed.) 1991. Participatory Action Research. Newbury Park, CA and London: Sage.

Wirth, L. 1938. Urbanism as a way of life., American Journal of Sociology, 44 (July): 1.24.

Wolcott, Harry F. 1999. *Ethnography: A Way of Seeing*. Walnut Creek, Calif.: AltaMira.

WSP (Water and Sanitation Program) 2010. 'Global Scaling Up Sanitation Project Progress Report July 1–December 31, 2009, Washington, DC, USA: Water and Sanitation Programme, WSP, available at http://www.wsp.org/wsp/sites/wsp.org/files/ publications/WSP_ProgressReport_JulyDec09_TSSM.pdf

Zeitlin, Irving M. 1996 Ideology and the Development of Sociological Theory. 6th ed. Englewood Cliffs, N.J.: Prentice-Hall.

Zelliot, E. 1998. "From Untouchable to Dalit, Essays on the Ambedkar Movement," Manohar Publications. New Delhi.

Zizek, S. 1997. The Plague of Fantasies. London: Verso.

Index

Acknowledgement

Dr. Bindeshwar Pathak , Sociologist, Social Reformer and Founder, Sulabh Sanitation Movement , who gave the theory of "Sociology of Sanitation" to be included in the universal domain of Sociology , for teaching and research in the Universities of India , and across the globe. It will not only enlarge the scope of sociology ,but will also be helpful in solving the problems of society in relation to sanitation, social deprivation, water, public health, hygiene, poverty, gender equality, welfare of children and empowering knowledge for sustainable development. This will strengthen sociological quest for knowledge on sanitation.

Dr. Pathak has given his entire life to the cause of sanitation, and in emancipation of scavengers with dignity and mainstreaming them. He has invented "Sulabh Shauchalya " as a tool of social change, which has revolutionised the field of sanitation.

Dr. Pathak has propounded the theory of Sociology of Sanitation, which is as follows:

"Sociology of Sanitation is a scientific study to solve the problems of society in relation to sanitation, social deprivation, water, public health , hygiene , ecology , environment, poverty, gender equality, welfare of children and empowering people for sustainable development and attainment of philosophical and spiritual knowledge."

Truly, he is founder and father of Sociology of Sanitation.

Ashish Saxena